MW01517432

Persuasions
&
Prejudices

Persuasions
&
Prejudices

An Informal Compendium of
Modern Social Science
1953-1988

First paperback printing 2016

Copyright © 1989 by Transaction Publishers, New Brunswick, New Jersey.

All rights reserved under International and Pan-American Copyright Conventions. No part of this book may be reproduced or transmitted in any form or by any means, electronic or mechanical, including photocopy, recording, or any information storage and retrieval system, without prior permission in writing from the publisher. All inquiries should be addressed to Transaction Publishers, 10 Corporate Place South, Suite 102, Piscataway, New Jersey 08854. www.transactionpub.com

This book is printed on acid-free paper that meets the American National Standard for Permanence of Paper for Printed Library Materials.

Library of Congress Catalog Number: 88-28795
ISBN: 978-0-88738-261-1 (hardcover); 978-1-4128-6289-9 (paperback)
Printed in the United States of America

Library of Congress Cataloging in Publication Data

To the memory of my sister

Paula
1919–1985

Contents

Preface

At first blush the preparation of a volume based on reviews and review essays seemed like one of the less onerous tasks that I have had to face in recent years. After all, how complicated can it be to assemble a lifetime of reviews, stack up the relatively decent ones, organize them into some sort of thematically meaningful mosaic, discard the irrelevant or blatantly poor ones and offer them to the professionally interested public?

That was nine months ago. Far from being a simple chore, this turned out to be a Draconian task involving a great amount of time, a substantial intellectual challenge, and the participation at technical levels of some extraordinary colleagues and support staff. If nothing good comes easy, then this should be a well received volume indeed.

To start with, materials that appeared in many and diverse journals are proof positive that there is simply no uniform standards in matters of grammar, punctuation, spelling—the *Manual of Style* issued by the University of Chicago Press notwithstanding. To assemble these 87 items, drawn from more than 50 professional journals and public interest magazines represented a daunting challenge—one met with considerable skill by Christian Kirkpatrick, who copy edited the volume.

Then there was the problem of whether to follow unfailingly the published version, or the manuscript version. The latter, when available, tended to be longer and less tailored to the needs of the journal, and more in tune with my exact thinking at the time. On the other hand, one wants to be fair to the published version, for the sake of authors reviewed, no less than for the journals carrying such reviews. For the most part, the published version was adhered to closely. But when paragraphs or phrases had been exorcised at the hands of remorseless editors, the manuscript version became critical. In short, no effort was made to embellish or improve the text. But an effort was made to restore the statement to its full-bodied flavor, if it made a difference.

In several instances, when the published version appeared only in a foreign language journal, a different sort of problem arose: the absence of an English language version in any form. Thus I was in the position of either translating the review or review-essay back into English, or ignoring such efforts. One can become extremely selective under such trying circumstances. Speaking of English and translation: since quite a few of these texts first appeared in the United Kingdom, the gap between "American" and "British" versions of the language had to be attended. I chose to make standard "American" usage uniform throughout, despite my personal affection of the language of the Isles.

In a number of important instances, I found that I had reviewed the same author on more than one occasion. In these cases, and again some important figures were involved, I chose to place the two reviews into a single review panel—preferring the risk of being slightly different in appraisal, rather than leaving the materials in their pristine form and running the far graver risk of appearing to display a weak editorial hand. When the reviews were not separated by many years, the results are fluid, but when the reviews were distinguished by being five and sometimes as many as fifteen years apart, this technique did not work as well. Here one must simply ask for a reader's indulgence.

Not every item in the volume that follows was actually a review. In a few cases, the review portion was ensconced in a larger intellectual canvas, while in other instances, the individual under consideration was dealt with in a context of self-analysis rather than appraising the work of others. After all, the purpose, or at least a purpose, of this volume is to come to terms with those figures who shaped my own sense of the fabric of modern social science. While in most cases the review process has given me this opportunity, there were a few figures on whom I have commented, who would have been left out of the reckoning on a strict constructionist basis. Again, this is all a matter of walking the fine line—with what success I can only leave to the judgment of reviewers and critics.

But for all of the challenges and pitfalls this sort of effort entails, the actual undertaking was deeply satisfying. I am able to present in a format and to a forum those elements of my work that have been obscured by the nature of the review process itself—the limits imposed upon the assessment of the work of others, rather than the positive statement of self. This is, in short, the critical side of my work. I do not mean by "critical" negative, since I like to think of criticism as a positive act of shared dialogue and overcoming the obstacles of one-sidedness, together. I would like to think that the readers of this volume will receive a basic education in some main currents of contemporary social and political thought, and as I say in the introduction, a sense of theory construction that results from a constant examination of the practice of other theorists.

I have been blessed with the opportunity, just about from the outset of my intellectual life, of being able to discuss the major figures of our times and not a few works written by less-than-major scholars, who nonetheless performed the noble task of examining and interpreting the major figures of other times. If this sometimes leads to a remoteness in the review process, to a process of analysis twice removed from the actual realities that social science must deal with, it also affords a sense of the whole, an overview that the workers in the vineyards both need and rarely receive. Many of the people whose books I have commented upon over the years remain good friends. I like to think that the force of criticism (and sometimes response) only served to strengthen the bond of friendship.

Reviews are not fashionable in social science. They expose the reviewer to ridicule and rebuttal. They sometimes do take away from other, more constructive work. They often reflect more the biases of the reviewer than the shortcomings of the writer. Yet reviewing is a very active way of reading. The review assignment is a matching of wits and talents. It is an act of literary analysis no less than of academic synthesis. But when performed with skill and moral decency, the review, better than any other device, serves to alert a community of scholars to just what are the main issues of an age. The review provides a sense of the whole in an environment of discrete parts. It is an interactive dialogue in which the reviewer not only enters the ring with an author but compels the professional reader to consider and choose between authorial and editorial judgments. In short, the review process is a high risk process—but one well worth taking in the name of the survival of science itself.

I have already mentioned the yeoman efforts of Christian Kirkpatrick. I should also add that nearly all of these reviews, written over the thirty five year period covered, were read, criticized and improved by either or both Danielle Salti, whose friendship dates back to my years in South America; and Mary E. Curtis, my wife and love for many years. Both have sharp professional judgments, and both rendered their opinions with a strong sense of protecting me no less than making the final product better. It would be unpardonable to load on them any problems in what finally emerged, but it would also be unthinkable to pass up this opportunity to express my special thanks to them both.

This is the first time that I have worked through the magic of computer-generated composition. That means many things—above all, a very close involvement with every stage of the prepublication process. At first, this meant the careful supervision of our wonderful administrative assistant at Transaction, Marlena Davidian—who inputted every single one of these reviews and review essays and who made every correction indicated with her usual sense of craft and concern. The proofing and indexing of the work was undertaken by myself. Again, the word processing programs are now so highly refined that errors that in the past were readily overlooked or simply not picked up no matter how many times the work has been gone over, now become a matter of routine—time-consuming routine to be sure.

I have saved for last my appreciation to my colleague of two decades at Transaction, and dear personal friend, Scott B. Bramson. His work at the technical level has been nothing short of revelatory. What one can do with computer spacing and design is an indication of just how momentous cold type composition has become in the last few years. The remaining crudities and weaknesses of such computer generated script have been overcome with stunning and telling effect by Scott. In addition, by working together throughout this lengthy process, we were able to make the changes and alterations necessary that would simply have not been possible in more conventional modes of composition. But Scott's labors went far beyond the technical and to the heart of the intellectual. His understanding of what each review essay attempted, how each fitted within a section, and how these sections in turn served to unify the final text, only served to make the process of creating this book a joy unto itself—so that whatever its reception in the post publication phase, the happiness of the activity, of meeting each challenge as it arose, itself represents a special and unforgettable event that I shared with Scott.

Finally, I should like to briefly explain my dedication, although none is really needed. My sister Paula was probably the first "reviewer" I ever knew. By that I mean she read with a pencil in one hand and paper next to the book. Every important book she read became a mechanism for enlarging her vocabulary (she came to the United States from Russia as a young girl of eight), as well as enlarging her sense of the world. Reading for Paula was a very active undertaking. And in a small household where English was truly a second language, this sense of text as discovery played no small part in my own intellectual formation. So it is to the memory of her dear soul that this book is consecrated.

Irving Louis Horowitz
September 1st, 1988

Introductory Essay

Persuasions and Prejudices: An Informal Compendium of Contemporary Social and Political Theory

In one of his most probing reviews, the great literary critic William Empson notes that making a book out of old reviews and articles "might seem scraping the barrel rather". One is tempted to add for special effect: *rather*. Yet, he and his executors did go ahead and do just that in *Argufying*. This only proves that in such matters, it is whose barrel is scraped and not whose ox is gored that counts the most.

If it seems odd that I am taking comfort by comparing myself with a literary type, this in part at least reflects my own opinion that the reviewing process is a literary artifact first and foremost. Even a casual look at the review sections of professional social science periodicals clearly reveals that in reviews care is given to matters of taste, judgment, and style—elements not especially apparent in the articles published in these very same journals.

As the reader can detect from this opening remark, I am sensitive to the fact that introductions too often are essentially rationalizations, or more pointedly, preemptive strikes at potential critics. They are presented with a touching belief that self-awareness or even firm declarations of shortcomings or eccentricities may be sufficient to ward off the evil spirits of the negative appraisal. This time, I have little confidence that such a tactic may work. Those who disdain special collections should have a field day with this rag-bag collection of reviews and review essays (to paraphrase another of Empson's self-deprecatory comments). On the other hand, those who enjoy their professional reading in bits and pieces should find this collection a reasonably enjoyable experience.

These wildly different responses duly acknowledged, I still dare offer this volume for a variety of reasons that I am inclined to believe are valid although entirely without proof—outside eating the pudding, or in this case, reading the book. Over the past 35 years, I have published four collections of my work, starting with *Professing Sociology*, covering the period between 1954–1966.

This was followed by *Foundations of Political Sociology*, covering the period 1967 to 1972; which in turn was followed by *Ideology and Utopia in the United States*, covering 1972–1977. Finally, and most recently, there was *Winners and Losers*, which treats the era from 1977 through 1984. I am essentially an essayist, in contrast to writers of articles or full scale monographs. This additional presentation to the marketplace of ideas, *Persuasions and Prejudices*, is a deeply gratifying opportunity to share a genre of my work spanning the entire period of my professional life.

The initial question I had to confront in compiling these essays is clear enough: What is the public virtue served by a volume of my reviews, or at least a substantial selection thereof? The answers are partially subjective: to set the record straight. However, this volume also provides me with an opportunity equally objective: to show how, in the process of evaluating others, a reviewer works toward the creation of social theory, and does so without becoming a thoroughgoing skeptic about establishing the contours and contexts of social existence. These mixed motives are not unimportant. I have a strong commitment to theoretical issues, although I have expressed such concerns in the review pages of scattered journals and periodicals over the years, rather than developing social theory in a life-long project extrapolated from everyday affairs.

I should strongly urge the patient reader who thinks that social theory must be constructed systematically, building block by block, with so many things to do, he or she need not waste time but should proceed to other forms of reading. System building is not synonymous with social theory. The history of systems is one of broken intellectual promises and visions of utopias that lead only to heartbreak and frustration. However, for readers who view theory as something more modest, albeit still substantial—using a relatively modest cluster of concepts to make sense of a large number of events, this volume can be considered an effort to understand the world. This view of theory does not demand that one knows, or even cares to know, all the other writers and thinkers whose work contributed to such a cluster of concepts. Rather, theory is constructed through a discourse of deep meaning with the spiritual remains of those thinkers long since dead in the corporeal sense. In this way, theory provides cultural continuities for the social sciences. The review process is an essential technique for revealing the benchmarks of such continuities—and at critical junctures, breaks—in the great chain of cultural being.

Admittedly, this is hardly the dominant view of the review process. Indeed, this is an age that disparages reviews in the most subtle ways: first, by denying the necessity of this form of literary activity for senior scholars, and relatedly, by assigning reviews to younger scholars as a form of socialization into the world of scholarship. Happily not everyone shares in this pleasant fiction, which has the manifest function of reducing controversy among peers and the apparent latent function of increasing a sense of the scientific by so doing. That science is itself a world of conflict and controversy seems to have escaped the notice of those who think of reviewing as a lesser form of activity.

At one and the same time, theory is a matching of wits, a summing up, and a set of guidelines with which to navigate experience. To create or examine theory in this sense means to ransom time, to traverse time. But theory is not history. Ideas are theoretically significant precisely because they transcend time, at least ordinary time. Theory permits the gradual inculcation of cultural domains, sometimes referred to as theoretical norms, that have a certain value beyond the immediacy of a particular series of events. If theory fails this test of trans-historical meaning, it is nothing more than journalism—in either the good or bad sense of providing observations on the nature of current events as experienced or remembered.

In my view, the discourse between the reviewer and the work under consideration permits several quite special aspects of the meaning of theory to emerge. First, an author's level of consistency in substance and style, over time can itself be viewed as a form of theorizing. For the author paints a picture of expectancies as well as performances in the review process. Second, the choice and quality of texts considered itself becomes part of the intellectual profile of the title reviewed and the person reviewing. Admittedly, one is not always the master of one's own fate in this matter, but surprisingly enough, a senior reviewer does at least have a chance to define through delineation. As a result, theory is in part at least a patchwork of inherited theories about society and polity that come before, the collective representation of the review process is a good guide into the nature of one's own theoretical fabric. Third, teasing out what is important in the work of others often depends on a clear-eyed notion of what has been important to one's own work. And in this process, the reviewer avoids a dialogue of the deaf and creates the foundations of professional intercourse.

In my case, the operational propositions clearly involve the pairing of several key concepts: the relationship of political democracy to socioeconomic development, the relationship of individual rights to collective obligations, the relationship of particular social practices to abstract ideological rationalizations. Each of these relationships can readily be subsumed under an old-fashioned moral code in which each person counts as one; in which evidence should determine both personal and political behavior in a society that does not take it upon itself to punish or circumscribe the behavior of individuals for mistakes in judgment.

In reflecting upon these strands of thought, I am struck by my old-fashioned sense of the new social science. For I have put forth in review after review a sense of theory that does not rest on being right while all others are wrong, or condescendingly less than right. Rather, I think that a twentieth century sense of the theoretical must accept that theory consumers can choose what economists sometimes call a basket of goods, To this I would add the need for a basket of services, since modern theory must also be judged by its sound and solid utility in a variety of circumstances. Hence, the individual has a right to change theory with a frequency normally reserved for changing commodities or services: as needed and when needed. Parenthetically, the obligations of the scholar is to continually broaden those theoretical possibilities.

This analogy does not signify that theories are of relative worth, any more than the variety of automobiles available to a consumer signifies that a Mazda is as good as a Mercedes. Many theoretical decisions are made even in choices about automobiles: ranging from how much money one can spend; to whether one wishes to purchase outright or buy on credit, to the goods that the purchaser of the higher priced, albeit superior vehicle, might have to forego. Thinking about theory in this way, I submit ensures against intellectual rigidity. It helps us to quickly realize that the concept of a society is far larger than the concept of a social science. In a primary sense, what needs changing and examination is the society. Social science is but a tool for such alterations. The review process locates the sources of such alterations and makes some educated guesses as to whether they are well articulated or have a workable prospect for success.

Over the course of the years I have been constantly impressed by how many scholars prefer to make simpletons of themselves to preserve a pet theory or grand concept rather than come to terms with a changing reality. I take as the great virtue of the new sociology its insistence on the primacy of social reality as a measure of the worth of social theory. In this way, hopefully, the old and the new in this vision of the theoretical come to a fine meeting point.

The theory set forth in this manner is not merely of the middle range, in contrast to system building on one side and narrow empiricism on the other. Rather, the range of a theory, the magnitude of its worth, depends upon circumstances that themselves change and emerge in the crucible of everyday existence. In this special sense, theory is akin to policy, providing the deep background of choice and circumstance.

The categories of investigation, like the parameters of theory, are subject to a variety of shifts that heavily depend on what is being looked at. There is something arbitrary, even unwieldy, in the self-congratulatory concept of theories of the middle range. It seems to imply that a specific range of experience is more valid than any other or that there is something peculiarly fair minded about not looking at the very small or the very large during research or investigation.

In this sense, a defining characteristic of this volume is not the range at which the people being reviewed worked, but the interesting nature of their observations and asides on the world they look at. Such judgments extend to stylistic and personal as well as contextual considerations. One of the great joys of reviewing the efforts of top flight people—and I dare say that many of the scholars and politicians reviewed herein merit such an appellation—is that the qualities of their own writings often spill over into the review itself. In this way, looking at others is a Meadian paradox, since it also entails looking at oneself. And in the psychoanalytical tradition at least, this is the highest form of theorizing.

Creating a good review is an artisan-like task, an act of intellectual craftsmanship, a strategic presentation of responses no less than a broad outline of contents. Indeed, one reads reviews for the same reason that one writes them. Or it may be vice versa: to determine if the opinions and ideas of others are in fact in concordance with one's own vision. Testing whether the views of authors can stand scrutiny in contexts other than those they stated or thought cf is after all at the foundation of theory construction. In this sense, theory is a dialogue between the author of a book and a reviewer of that book, and is built into the interaction afforded by the review process itself.

The importance that a book is said to possess derives from what reviewers and commentators establish as important. In this, the review process is not simply a parasitical attachment to the book, some necessary evil to be tolerated by a beleaguered author, but is central to both the process of theory construction and historical confirmation alike. In the social sciences, as in the sciences generally, the reviewer shares with the author a common universe of discourse, a shared domain of relevance, that makes the review an integrated part of the production of knowledge.

A central element of reviewing others is the search by an author for him or her, in this case myself—for some set of threads that emerge and reemerge over the years in reviewing a wide range of works. For it is what we are looking for, what all of us are looking for, that determines responses to a volume, no less than the review itself. As a result, it is important to be fair. The reader, the professional reader that is, fully understands that the style of presentation bespeaks loudly of the fairness and humanity of the reviewer, no less than the greatness of the volume. Such concerns have not inhibited my reviewing style, but they have made me acutely sensitive to the ordinary reader, who is profoundly aware of any hint of bias in the review process. To this reader, being attacked in a review or by the author who has been reviewed, is far less punishment than being accused of bias in one's assessment.

These review essays also reveal a personal odyssey. They convey a sense of not only what I have read but what I have considered to be important. I have been blessed, or cursed, as the case may be, with not being an expert in a narrow band of theories or subjects. Hence, I have not been confined in my reviewing assignments to a singular area. Doubtless, those who review as specialists point have an advantage, but it is a limited watch-dog edge at best.

Let me be more precise. The review process is, over time, a bracing experience. The least important question to ask a reviewer is "which side you are on?", and the most important question is: "how good is the work?" To review the work of others primarily as an act of confirmation of self-belief is doubtless the least beneficial, not to mention least enjoyable, approach. For the reviewer must assess the quality of the author's performance within parameters defined by the author. This element tests, sometimes pits, the expertise of authors and reviewers alike.

In the world of social science, both reviewers and reviewed are essentially committed to a similar universe of discourse and realm of belief. In the world of reviewing fiction this is not necessarily the case. For while a novelist sometimes reviews another novelist, much more often a person called a critic who reviews a person called a novelist. But in the scientific realm, the significance of a review derives not simply by its estimate of a book but by the personal biographies that link reviewer and author in sometimes mortal combat. Thus, both a common core of consensus and an uncommon store of background factors fuse to make the processing of reviewing, at its ultimate point, a process of theory formation and reformation.

I am aware that over the years my reviews have changed: they have become longer, less certain, more comparative. I would like to think that they have also gotten better. But what an elusive concept is this notion of the "better"! Does it mean better than one's earlier performance, or better than others now? Another way of expressing the better is the way in which criticisms can be made with a deft touch rather than a heavy hand. In short, quality in reviewing is as much a function of literary manners as it is of social scientific methods. This cross-fertilization of fields, or rather, of content and form, is nowhere more clearly set forth than in the reviewing process.

Let me now briefly turn to the organization of the volume, since it is a sufficiently unusual genre to cause some formal difficulties, or at least necessitate some special techniques for handling a variety of different contingencies. This volume is organized in terms of the "greats", that is to say, reviews of books written by important scholars or theorists of the first rank clearly merited inclusion. Volumes that are collections or biographies of great thinkers are also included under the heading of the great—to give my work a sense of literary consistency. Books I reviewed that neither have a great author, nor are works on such authors, have for the most part been excluded from consideration—even though my reviews may well have been decent statements on important subjects, in its own right.

One other matter of organization deserves attention. I have developed a table of contents organized under subject headings. The table's five-part thematic represents the broad areas of my work. They are first, philosophical antecedents to social theory; second, social research as ideology and utopia; third, ethnicity and religiosity; fourth, development and change; and fifth, the ethical foundations of political life. Of course, these categories are somewhat artificial, since their overlaps are almost as evident as the boundaries between these themes. Still I have been fortunate to have drawn review assignments that cover the major areas of my interests. I do hope that they also reflect the reader's interests.

Rather than organize this volume by either the original date of publication or by alphabetical order, I have organized it thematically, around those subject areas that I have spent a lifetime researching and examining. To be sure, the first section does tend to cluster at the earliest end of my work, when I was exploring linkages and cross-overs between philosophy, history, and the sociology of knowledge. And the second section reveals my involvement with problems of developing areas in the 1960s, doubtless as a consequence of my Latin American experiences. The remaining three segments are far less tidy in calendric terms, and perhaps no less in intellectual terms. But they do reveal my long-standing professional interests in politics and morals as the bedrock of social research, and a few personal concerns along the way.

A special category of review that must also be mentioned, the preparation of forewords for special books. A number entries are not reviews as such, but prefaces written for a special work or a deceased colleague who merits particular appreciation. For example, tributes to my dear, departed friends Gino Germani and Cesar Graña, who are significant figures in contemporary social thought, help round out a sense of the present moment in the social sciences. While these prefaces have not been selected by a third party (a journal editor) or published in an independent forum (a scholarly or professional journal), they carry sufficient weight to merit inclusion.

I should further observe that I have included one essay that does not follow my own rules for inclusion in this volume, and that is the essay on C. Wright Mills. It is in fact a set of reflections that I have delivered a number of times and in a variety of lecture halls after publication of my book, *C. Wright Mills: An American Utopian.* I could readily have included the review I wrote of Mills's last book, *The Marxists,* written for *The American Scholar* in 1962. But I felt that the essay on Mills, a self-reflection of sorts that was previously unpublished, would be of far greater interest to the reader.

While I have made much of the uniqueness, even the eccentricity of this volume, there is one sliver of tradition to which it belongs. From Pascal's *Pensees,* to La Rochefoucauld's *Maximes,* to Voltaire's *Dictionnaire philosophique,* and finally Durkheim's contributions to *L'annee sociologique,* there is a marvelous French tradition of treading lightly on heavy subjects. Indeed, the thoroughly baseless charge that the French are less substantial than the Germans and less empirical than the English, derives in some measure from this tradition in which brevity is a virtue and sanctimony a vice.

Certain practitioners of the French style are to be found in American sociology—the most notable being from opposite sides of the political pole: Lewis A. Coser and Robert Nisbet, both of whom I am proud to call friends. But certainly the sort of effort represented by this volume is clearly not favored by those who equate methodical rigor with empirical truth. For the review process is an examination of persons no less than processes, motives no less than structures.

This introduction now having provided what must pass as a rationale for the production of this volume, I commend this book to what every author hopes for: an interested reader in search of some interesting notions. To satisfy the reader, it must still pass muster as a unified whole. Whatever the points of origins of each contribution, the work has to be valuable as a statement of integration no less than of prejudices and preferences of an author. Again discussion returns to theoretical moorings as the true source of this effort.

I do not know whether this enterprise will confirm those of my critics who believe that I lack theory, since any effort to create a theory out of the thin cloth of reviews and review essays is prima facie evidence to that fact, or whether it will convert old sparring partners into new friends who recognize that theory may come wrapped in different packets serving a variety of purposes. At least the prejudices of which I speak are not wrapped in the bunting of a disguised ideology, but are stated plainly enough. Reviews have a remarkable way of exposing the reviewer no less than expressing the contents of a book reviewed. That is a risk I must obviously and willingly accept.

Part I

Philosophical Antecedents to Social Theory

1

Sense and Structure in Social History*

Baendel, Gerardo L.

More than a century ago, in 1845 to be precise, Marx described German historiography as "a series of 'thoughts' which devour one another and are finally swallowed up in self-consciousness." This is so much the present status of the theory of history in Hispanic American letters, that while one might challenge Marx's appraisal in terms of mid-nineteenth century Germany, there can be little argument that it characterizes contemporary *historiadores*. The very imbalance of materials, the mountainous literature in the philosophy of history vis-á-vis the relative paucity of useful studies in historical subjects as such, leads one to the irritating (but accurate) conclusion that Latin *pensadores* are more concerned with blue printing than with making history.

This is admittedly a harsh reading of the intellectual climate, but one that is not intended as a blanket generalization. Indeed such a judgment could not possibly cover such excellent theorists of history as José Luis Romero of Argentina, Antonio Gomez Robledo of Mexico, Gilberto Freyre of Brazil, and Arturo Ardao of Uruguay, among others. Nonetheless, there remains a strongly dominant tendency in Hispanic American historiography to follow fashionable European currents. Philosophic novelties rapidly find their way into historical discourses. Positivism, neo-Thomism, Spiritualism, Hegelianism, were some of the earlier rages. At present there is a powerful tendency to weave French existentialism into the historical fabric. So insistent has this last-mentioned tendency become in recent years, that the Uruguayan educator-philosopher Vaz Ferreira was moved to say that there was more agony (literary at least)

---

* Gerardo Leisersohn Baendel, *Estructura Y Sentido de la Historia: Según la Literatura Apocaliptica* (Santiago de Chile: Ediciones de la Universidad de Chile, 1959), pp. 147.

León Dujovne, *La Filosofía de la Historia, de Nietzsche a Toynbee* (Buenos Aires: Ediciones Galatea Nueva Vision, 1957), pp. 204.

Carlos M. Rama, *Teoría de la Historia: Introducción a los Estudios Históricos,* (Buenos Aires: Editorial Nova, 1959), pp. 238.

over the consequences of the Second World War in South America, where not a shot was fired, than in the battle fronts of Europe.

To be sure, the idols of the *pensadores* have dramatically shifted since the conclusion of hostilities in 1945. The prewar period was dominated by an existentialism of the Right—by Spengler, Dilthey, and Heidegger. The postwar period is dominated by an existentialism of the Left—by Merleau-Ponty, Sartre, and Camus. The "victorious" French have replaced the "defeated" Germans in the affections of the *pensadores*. That the shift has been more verbal than real is indicated by the fact that the fundamental tenets of the leisurely Hispanic American *Weltanschauung* have remained fully intact.

The North American intellectual nourished on a steady diet of Panamericanism must be startled by the nearly complete absence of any serious consideration of U.S. contributions to the study of history. With the exception of Toynbee, the same statement can be made of English efforts. And given the architectonic nature of Toynbee's work, this exception very definitely proves the rule. Leaving aside the reasons for this disregard, which must necessarily include the shortcomings of historical theory in the English-speaking world, such exclusion effectively narrows the scope of Hispanic-American considerations of alternative models for the study of history. Thus, in the three books under consideration, Rama makes only a passing reference to Becker's efforts (despite the fact that Becker's work and Beard's classic texts are available in good Spanish translations) and Baendel makes only a few bibliographical references to American studies in religious history. This neglect, I should add, is not due to any linguistic failings, since each of these authors has a more than adequate command of the English language.

The disregard of American or English works is matched by an overwhelming attention to French and German materials, mainly of a late nineteenth-century vintage, which gives an archaic touch to the volumes. There is Baendel's "discovery" of the analogies between the Testaments and the philosophy of history, Rama's declaration of the Nietzschean objections to history as a destroyer of social action and human morality as the last word on the subject, and Dujovne's restatement of the crisis-in-culture theme as occasioned by the rise of modern science and technology. What complicates a judicious consideration of these studies is that, considered strictly from the perspective of recent contributions to the philosophy of history, they are prosaic and pedestrian. Yet, from a Hispanic American perspective, they symbolize the actual state of affairs motivating the *historiadores*.

The scope and content of these books differ. Carlos Rama, one of Uruguay's best-known sociologists, examines history first in its relation to other literary and scientific disciplines, and then examines such problem areas of historiography as concept formation, periodization, and the cognitive status of findings. Baendel of the University of Chile correlates eschatological doctrines and the circular and linear theories of history to which they give rise. Léon Dujovne, Professor of Philosophy at Buenos Aires University, sets for himself the more modest goal of analyzing from a humanistic standpoint the theories of history advanced by Nietzsche, Spengler, Jaspers, Bergson, and Toynbee.

Given the different thematic orientations of these works, their core of consensus is surprising, especially since they were produced in obvious independence of each other. They concentrate on essentially the same range of European writings. And each volume represents a work of commentary rather than an attempt at fresh, positive insights into the problems examined. (Dujovne and Rama seem more aware of this self-imposed limitation than does Baendel.) Each work has the discomforting feeling of starting in heaven and going upwards. From the philosophy of history, these scholars move variously into the history of the philosophy of history (Rama), the religious impulse of the philosophy of history (Baendel), and the meta-philosophic criticism of theories of history (Dujovne).

There is an absence of biographical information on the figures examined; an absence of the possible social or scientific motivations of men like Spengler, Bergson, or Croce; consideration of what these theorists of history were for or against politically and economically (i.e., concretely). Thus, even when these authors voice criticisms, they convey arid formalism. Croce's familiar objections to a scientific history are presented with the standard references to Croec's mistakes—but without an historical accounting of Croce's passionate defense of liberalism in the face of the fascist alternative of Tentile and the marxist alternative of Gramsci. Jaspers' refuge in the intuitions of humanity and self-reflection of individuals is duly noted and criticized—but without considering Jasper's acute analysis of the historical causes and consequences of German nazism, and more recently, without regard for his keen analysis of the dangers of thermonuclear war in a world of conflicting nationalisms. After all, at least some of the theoretical differences between Jaspers and his existentialist mentors must be explained by the differing responses to concrete circumstances. The posture of individual heroism in military battle might have been a suitable notion for a nineteenth-century romantic, but the disappearance of the distinction between combat and noncombat zones and military and civilian personnel necessarily changes the contents of the heroic vision—rationalist or irrationalist.

Paradoxically, the common deficit of these three volumes have is their lack of historicity. They are, to put it bluntly, static. Baendel moves from a consideration of ancient Hebraic and Christian texts to a hurried and unclear examination of philosophers of history proper. Dujovne's work makes a textual analysis of several major figures that is quite independent of their social moorings, or for that matter, of each other. Rama takes a rambling canvass of the opinions of the major figures in the theory of history, without any discernible purpose. There is a sense of irresolution and indecision in these efforts. Baendel has no clear idea of where theology leaves off and history begins; Dujovne shows a similar lack of awareness as to where the philosophy of history ceases and social theory commences, and Rama's book, which potentially has the stuff of a serious accounting, ranges so superficially over standard texts that the reader is caught in an endless chain of quotations, paraphrases, and asides.

These volumes well illustrate the dilemmas of the *historiadores*. Having established standards for living the life of ideas and eschewing the life of labor, they remain confronted by a growing demand for the products of the latter and an expanding supply of the former. Thus they attempt to capture the historical muse, in the hope that providence will provide what the *historiador* cannot—an advanced, modern form of industrial life in an intellectual climate of precapitalist techniques and postcapitalist ideologies. Unfortunately, these studies in the theory of history do little to remove the suspicion that even the most adept *pensadores* (which these men can justifiably claim to be) are ensnared by this double-bind of traditionalism and futurism. The inconclusive and indecisive nature of these works reflect the larger oscillations in Hispanic-American intellectual history—a history that can examine past and future trends in the traditional manner of grand theory, but that has yet to settle accounts with the historical present.

From *History and Theory: Studies in the Philosophy of History*, vol. 2, No. 1 (1962), pp. 85–9.

2

Science and Society in the Enlightenment*

Diderot, Denis

In his book, Aram Vartanian aims to examine concretely the huge debt the philosophers of the Enlightenment owed to the physics of Descartes, by unfolding the organic connection of Diderot's materialism to the scientific materialism of Descartes. Vartanian chose these two figures as the highest expression of French philosophy in the seventeenth and eighteenth centuries respectively. What Marx asserted in his Holy Family, Vartanian proves by referring to the literature of the Enlightenment—that by sharply differentiating the realms of nature and God Cartesian dualism opened the pathway, not simply to the metaphysical-teleological reaction of Malebranche, but more profoundly to the revolutionary materialism of LaMettrie, Buffon, Holbach, and Diderot. In Descartes, materialism and idealism, naturalism and supernaturalism coexist. The demands of the eighteenth century bourgeoisie and agrarian democratic forces revolutionized Cartesianism, making consistent with the material facts of natural and social existence. In the meantime, the ancient regime purged Descartes of his materialist physics and wrapped about itself the mantle of his metaphysics of doubt. The author contends that no such bifurcation existed in Newtonian philosophy, which had erected on its physics the metaphysics of a deus ex machina and primum mobile. Descartes' assertion that the concept of matter is in and of itself sufficient cause to explain the natural world, did not require, and in fact rejected, any supernatural interference in the functioning of nature. But the reasons why LaMettrie and Diderot responded more readily to Cartesian than to Newtonian science do not necessarily follow from Vartanian's observation. For Holbach saw similar problems in Newton as in Descartes—and feared the broad adoption of a mechanistic science without shedding the theistic shell.

---

* Aram Vartanian, *Diderot and Descartes: A Study of Scientific Naturalism in the Enlightenment*, (Princeton: Princeton University Press, 1953), pp. 336.

Vartanian's main thesis is that Descartes' natural philosophy "culminated in the ideology of Diderot and certain of his contemporaries." This view was culled from a review of both great and obscure Enlightenment philosophies. The author states in his preface: "In tracing the evolution of materialist science from its Cartesian sources to Diderot . . . a definite method has been observed. This is to give the fullest scope and weight to the testimony and other materials provided by actual eyewitnesses and participants, even when these latter are no longer remembered on their own merits." This approach, whatever its shortcoming, gives a solidity to *Diderot and Descartes* often lacking in other works on the Encyclopedic movement. In examining historically how Cartesian rationalism and mechanistic biology affect the concept of man as the most complex physical and physiological machine, Vartanian has performed a service by helping to reconstruct the forces shaping French materialism. In certain respects, Vartanian has done for Descartes what E.A. Burtt did for Newton in *The Metaphysical Foundations of Modern Science*, but without quite the same command of intellectual context that Burtt exhibits.

Nonetheless, in his anxiety to reveal the link between Cartesian physics and the Enlightenment, Vartanian tends to negate the twofold derivation of Encyclopedic naturalism. Those who had a predilection for natural philosophy were more indebted to Descartes and Gassendi than to Bacon and Newton. At the same time, those oriented to social theory, such as Rousseau, Voltaire and Helvetius, responded less to the rigors of Cartesianism than to the English empirical tradition of Bacon, Hobbes, and Locke.

Vartanian tends to overlook that the deep concern and skill of English utilitarianism in questions of social theory appealed to all philosophers who understood the barrenness of a revolution in philosophy without a revolution in social practice. For this reason, Holbach, Buffon, Condillac, and Diderot owed a great deal to the social currents derived from English constitutional theory. Nor can Vartanian justifiably claim that this sort of social analysis is outside his intent. The philosophy of the Enlightenment, and particularly of militant anticlericalism, was in Diderot's words "full of humanity." The application of philosophy to the needs of society qualitatively differentiated Diderot and his associates from Descartes and the seventeenth century evolution of mechanics. By striving to show the harmonic lineage from Descartes to Diderot, however, Vartanian creates distortions that are a disservice to the view of both Descartes and Diderot. For example, that Diderot was not only a revolutionary philosopher but a philosopher of the French Revolution apparently falls outside the purview of this study in the history of ideas. Yet it is this social fact rather than philosophical doctrine that can best explain both the identity and difference between Diderot and Descartes.

From *Science and Society*, vol. 18, no. 2 (1954), pp. 185–86.

3

The Pre-History of the Sociology of Knowledge*

Dilthey, Wilhelm

Dilthey's place in modern intellectual history is securely planted, interestingly enough, no less in Latin America than in his native Germany. Dilthey's prominence as a historian and philosopher of culture has steadily increased, despite the fact that the romantic *Weltanschauung* that gave birth to his style of work has long ceased to function. It is surprising that little interpretive literature exists on Dilthey's social theories, since the real core of Dilthey's novelty inheres in his ambitious redefinition of the character and structure of social science vis-a-vis philosophy and physics. In this aspect, Dilthey no less than Simmel or Durkheim must be viewed as a pioneer in giving sociology new vistas, albeit bottled in old solutions.

In the body of his work, Dilthey acknowledged no sociology other than the sociology of knowledge, that is, a sociology of human understanding and feeling. The human sciences, *Geisteswissenschaften*, differed from the natural sciences, *Naturwissenschaften*, precisely because all human creations involved consciousness of direction. Nature *exists*, but only man *lives*. This distinction between the human and the physical is the most basic one in Dilthey's works. Embellished, altered to meet different issues, this inheritance from his early writings on Schleiermacher never leaves the center of the stage in Dilthey's intellectual drama.

Dilthey's contribution to the sociology of knowledge proceeded from a critique of sociological method as it was originally formulated by Auguste Comte. It was essentially a repudiation of the reductionism entailed by "social physics", which erroneously translated of the *Geisteswissenschaft* into a *Naturwissenschaft*—the human sciences into a natural science. "My polemic against sociology concerned the stage in its development which was characterized by Comte, Schäffle, Lillenfeld. The conception of it which was contained in their works was that of a science of the common life of men in society, including among its objects also law, morality, and religion.

---

* Wilhelm Dilthey, *Gesammelte Schriften*, 12 volumes, (Leipzig-Berlin: B.G. Teubner, 1914–1936).

Sociology could not be a theory of the forms which psychical life assumes under the conditions of relationships between individuals. Dilthey believed this role of the psyche to be the key to the social sciences in contradistinction to the physical sciences. "My rejection of sociology applies to a science which aims at comprehending everything which happens *de facto* in human society in a *single* science. The principle underlying this synthesis would be that what happens in human society in the course of its history must be comprehended in the unity of one and the same object." But this objection to unified science has deeper roots—specifically, a rejection of the belief that human beings, no less than rocks or birds, are in nature no less than of nature. In this sense, the source of Dilthey's attitude toward sociology derive from his essentiually anti-evolutionary of nature as such.

Dilthey conceived his intellectual task to offset any attempt at mimetic reproduction of the methodology of the physical or biological sciences. The human sciences needed their own methodology; without one, they could not progress in solving human problems. Physics starts from nature; sociology must begin from its unique element, consciousness. To illumine the preconditions of this new world of study, Dilthey recalled the memory of Bacon's *Novum Organum.* The German founder of *Geisteswissenschaft* saw himself as clearing the ground of the debris that gets in the way a truly understanding of man. "Ever since the celebrated work of Bacon, treatises have been drawn up, especially by natural scientists, discussing the foundation and method of the natural science and so leading up to the study of them. . . . There seems to be a need for the same service to be performed on behalf of those who are concerned with history, political theory, jurisprudence or political economy, theology, literature, or art." The "idols" in Dilthey's case consisted in appeals to transcendental laws for establishing human knowledge and in equally false appeals to the laws of physics for social knowledge. As a consequence, Dilthey's work started out as a battle against the dual terrors of supernaturalism and reductionist physicalism. The former seeks truth in transhistorical absolutes having no rational base, while the latter seeks absolute wisdom by copying the findings and methods of physical science in disregard of the differences between atoms and minds.

Dilthey's attitude toward the weaknesses of supernaturalism derived, not from naturalistic leanings, but rather from the mystical components that were the special hallmark of the German *Aufklarung.* The idea of *weltgeist* in Goethe, Schiller, and Lessing elevated the life of reason above the lofty religious spirits of antiquity. Dilthey detected the same pantheistic position in the writings of J.G. Hamaan, who saw in "the word" what Lessing saw in "the life of reason." Likewise, Dilthey's attitude towards positivism was stimulated by the negation of the Kantian *noumenal* world it entailed. If, as Comte indicated, one cannot go beyond experience for scientific knowledge, then the entire world of the human spirit, along with the *Aufklarung,* was doomed to dismal failure. Thus,

Dilthey viewed the German Enlightenment as the key point in the evolution of the human sciences to a psychologically meaningful level—because the person as starting point alone could avoid transcendental metaphysics without collapsing the range of the human spirit into a soporific positivism.

An ontology independent of both supernaturalism and positivism was only an instrument for Dilthey, his goal being an effective synthesis of the classical philosophic heritage. His inability to arrive at this synthesis led Dilthey to move the formalism of Kantian categories and the historicism of the Hegelian dialectic. Just as Kant recognized values of Comtian positivism (the better to overcome it), Dilthey saw its main asset as taking society as a given entity and making an uncompromising stand for the individual against the systematization of life. In the main, sociological positivism offered a critique of idealism not far from Dilthey's own study, "The Three Fundamental Forms of Systems in the First Half of the Nineteenth Century." This individualist ideal, however, was precisely what the Hegelian phenomenology of metaphysics with its dialectical march to reason frustrated.

In his abbreviated work "The Young Hegel," Dilthey, like Lukács forty years later, saw that Hegel had created the historicist legacy without populating this legacy with real humans. The individual was brought into harmony with a rationalist world view he never participated in as a sensuous creature. Dilthey was in the paradoxical position of trying to preserve the individual through a compulsive appraisal of history as relative, while preserving the historical by declaring the individual as sovereign. Dilthey believed that Immanuel Kant resolved the dilemma: in a total historical connection and a total philosophy of man.

Dilthey thought like a system builder, but he realized that just as Kant at the end of the eighteenth century had destroyed teleological, cosmological, and ontological proofs for supernaturalism, so had the natural sciences cut to pieces all metaphysics by the end of the nineteenth century. This was the situation as Dilthey began to examine the role of the human sciences in the historical career of men.

The intellectual locus of Dilthey's work thus fixed, we must turn to the far more difficult task of ascertaining and examining what Dilthey stood for what he fought against. For Dilthey, sociology could not be a unique science, because the sociology of knowledge—and latterly, the knowledge of society—lend a note of contingency and an irrepressible relativism to social existence. Consciousness is the great divide between the natural and the human sciences. "Mankind, if apprehended only by perception and perceptual knowledge, would be for us a physical fact, and as such it would be accessible only to the natural sciences. It becomes an object for the human sciences only insofar as human conditions are consciously lived, insofar as they find expression in living utterances, and insofar as these expressions are understood." This view, which superficially resembles Bergson's élan vital, in fact attempts to objectivize the subjective history of the individual. However fragmented by relativism his Geist became, Dilthey could not escape the perils of Comtian positivism without falling into the pitfalls of Hegelian historicismus. What began in Dilthey as a defense of the individual against the encroachments of physics, ended as defense of the historical consciousness against the encroachments of real individuals.

Dilthey linked the critique of sociology as a positive science and the parallel effort to give the sociology of knowledge a methodology over and above the ordinary scientific method, to a need to see understanding as a special category. The principle of a unified science, of placing everything in human society as a subject to be comprehended in the unity of one and the same system of thought, is at the core of Dilthey's critique. Dilthey recognized two possible views of sociology: Simmel's, which holds that sociology is a new name for old wine. (Dilthey expanded this to mean that sociology means only the second part of the philosophy of human sciences, the first part being psychology), and the second and rejected view of Comte, which sought a unifying principle for explaining and bringing together under the general interest such things as religion, art, morality, and law. Dilthey maintained that by rejecting metaphysics as a "life position," positive sociology succeeded only in the reconstruction of the most absurd, anthropocentric metaphysic, whereas the human sciences' negation and suppression of philosophy allowed for the first time a truly philosophical posture and life position.

Dilthey assigned to philosophy the task of "locating the historical position of each one of the central theories in its own development," and attempted to assess the historical values of these theories. But such an assessment, as Dilthey well knew, is specifically a sociological undertaking. Thus he expected philosophy to become transformed into the sociology of *Lebendigkeit*. Philosophy, that welding of individuality and sociality, can better treat problems of knowledge because it alone can avoid the fallacy of reducing the individual to social statistics. However, although Dilthey spoke of maintaining the integrity of the individual, he actually promoted the integrity of a telos in which the individual, far from free, is actually predetermined. This is clearly the case when he wrote that "if we could conceive an isolated individual treading the earth, supposing him to live long enough to develop, he would evolve those functions out of himself in complete isolation."

Locking the individual into a teleological context allowed Dilthey to believe that the way out of the impasse of metaphysical systems was the transformation of philosophy into a sociology of feeling and understanding. This special variant of the sociology of knowledge would become the methodology of the human sciences in contradistinction to logic, which would remain the methodology of the inorganic and physical sciences, or psychology, which would remain the method of the comparative study of languages.

Dilthey's initial call for an end to philosophy collapsed into the much less daring position that philosophy should pay more attention to social events and that sociology, should become more philosophical. Both should receive sustenance from the historical flow, the only source of truth for human beings. "The variety of ways of thought, religious systems, moral ideas, and metaphysics corresponds to the variability of forms in human life. This is an historical fact. That which is conditioned by the historical situation is relative as to its objective worth." Philosophy in this context becomes the philosophy of philosophy, or better, the historical sociology of consciousness.

While Dilthey separated questions of philosophy from those of sociology, this nascent view became the Achilles' heel of the relativist wing (Alfred Weber, Karl Mannheim, Friedrich Meinecke) in the sociology of knowledge. It philosophizes the social question by substituting the metaphysical question: how can one attain to truth?, for the empirical question: under what conditions is truth obtained or frustrated? Put briefly, while Dilthey gave philosophy a social task, he subsumed sociology under the larger category of *leben*, that is, life as a continuing historical process without a stable structure.

The further examination of Dilthey's sociological perspective involves an appreciation of his vision of philosophy and history, for clearly he viewed sociology in just such "human" terms. Dilthey's critique of philosophy is devastating: it takes the claims of science at face value and the claims of human life as a matter to be lived rather than to be evaluated.

> Always the metaphysical urge to penetrate into the kernel of this whole is at odds with the positive demand for universal validity in its knowledge. These are the two sides which belong to the essence of philosophy and which also distinguish it from the most nearly related fields of culture. In contrast to the physical sciences it seeks the solution of the riddle of the world and life. And in contrast to art and religion it aims at giving this solution in a universally valid form.

In Dilthey's opinion, philosophy as *Weltanschauung* evens the battle against all sorts of reductionist tendencies. "The time is past" he writes, "when there can be an independent philosophy of art, religion, law, or of the State. The powerful cohesion which is thus established is the highest realization of philosophy and is destined to guide the human race. The natural sciences have transformed the outer world. In the great world epoch now evolving, the human sciences are winning an ever-increasing influence." As for Hegel, the "death" of the old philosophizing only ushered in a new era for philosophy. Philosophy in its historical context as an ally and stimulant to the sciences gives way to philosophy as a private affair, a penetration into the psychological, a discipline unique in its ability to transcend the scientific world of changing reality. Thus, far from burying the tradition of absolute German idealism, Dilthey established an impregnable fortress for it to operate independent of a relativized universe.

What is new in Dilthey's style of philosophizing? What is its social role? The development of social science clears the ground for a theory of philosophy as a personal peculiarity. "Philosophy is a personal peculiarity, a type of character which has always been credited with the capacity to set the mind free from tradition, dogma, prejudice, from the power of the instinctive affections, and even from the dominion of external limiting circumstances." It is in sum an ideal of life and a world view fulfilled in individual genius. Thus, Dilthey prepared in advance an answer to his own relativism. The individual genius, like the social scientist in Mannheim, alone is free from the ideological limitations that beset the rest of mankind. Implicit in both is the intellectualist fallacy that pure knowledge is both possible and ideologically unconditioned. According to this view, the apprehension of life is something of an incantation—protection against the storms of objective history. In Dilthey, the genius, the man of knowledge, plays the role of the *freischwebende Inteligenz*. The chronic ailment of the *Geisteswissenschaft* is that it is always discontented with its own historicity, with its rationalized irrationalism.

This becomes particularly clear in Dilthey's theories of history, in which he worked with a theory of social knowledge "that is conditioned by historical situations" and therefore "relative as to its validity." Dilthey next considered world views, *Weltaun-schauungen*, in relation to life, *Lebendigkeit*. "The views of life and of the world find themselves in contradiction to one another. None of them can really be proved. More, any one of them can be refuted by demonstrating that it is insufficient in front of reality. Thus it is shown that these basic forms express the aspects of life in relation to the world posited in that life." But this thoroughgoing application of historical relativism is what Dilthey wanted to transcend. For the great polarized concepts of history and life contain the transient and the permanent, the apparent and the real, the phenomenal and the noumenal. If Dilthey discounted empirical sociology, he did so in the way that Plato discounted physics—for its audacity to claim the empirical as the realm of truth and not simply opinion.

Dilthey's radical critique of sociology, which started as an attempt to overcome dualism, itself dissolves into a bifurcation of history and psychology:

> history does indeed know of the various assertions of something unconditional as value, norm, or good. Such assertions appear everywhere in history—now as given in the divine will, now in a rational conception of perfection, in a teleological order of the world, in a universally valid norm of our conduct which is transcendentally based. But historical experience knows only the process, so important for it, of making these assertions. On its own grounds it knows nothing of their universal validity.

Even if we overlook the obvious cognitive problem of claiming that "history knows," as if history is something other than the careers of men, Dilthey was aiming for something more than historical relativism—which after all shares the same partial knowledge as do all other sciences. He desired the idea of classical idealism once again:

> The play of [to us] soulless efficient causes is here replaced by that of ideas, feelings, and motives. And there is no limit to the singularity, the wealth in the play of interaction, which is here revealed. The waterfall is composed of homogeneous forward-thrusting particles of water; but a single sentence, which is but a breath in the mouth, shakes the whole living society of a continent through a play of motives absolutely in individual units; so different is the interaction appearing here, *i.e.,* the motive arising from the idea, from any other kind of cause.

For Dilthey, the task of human understanding is to liberate the social from the empirical. An image of the world, a *Weltbild*, determines the value of life, *Lebenserfahrung*, and consequently establishes a practical ideal. In Dilthey's terms, the world view defines the experiences of life, giving them form. It is a further form of communication. For Dilthey, one can really understand only like mentalities. Thus, the doctrine of *Verstehen* comes to define the limits of wisdom. We intuit truth; we can explore factually only opinions. Consequently, sociology can never claim a special comprehension of the nature of man.

If the scientific spirit, the rationalistic approach to problems of men and society, is not the same as the ideological spirit, the impassioned approach to problems of men—and I make the assumption ex cathedra that they are in fact different—Dilthey took his stand with ideology, with the *Weltanschauung*, in direct opposition to science. For Dilthey "it is in the region of the understanding of life, of freedom, that originate and develop the valuable and powerful world views. These world views, however, are different in terms of the laws determining their formation, in terms of their structure, and of their types, according to the religious, the artistic and the metaphysical genius." The sociological relativity of knowledge does not make ideas more susceptible of social analysis, but rather, makes a place for the ideologue untouched and untouchable by the social structure.

Liberation from historical events, rather than living in them, was Dilthey's *traum*. And if his criticisms of the social sciences are sounded in a modern motif, his resolutions recall ancient Greek philosophical themes. "What man is, only his history tells. In vain others put the past behind them in order to begin life anew. They cannot shake off the gods of the past because they become haunting ghosts. The melody of our life is conditioned by the accompanying voices of the past. Only by surrendering to the great objective forces which history has engendered can man liberate himself from the pain of the moment and from ephemeral joy."

In such sentiments, one can only recollect Dilthey's claim of having performed another *Novum Organum.* However, we find a reversal of the Baconian ideal. Whereas Bacon announced as his supreme intention a method and system for man to control nature through empirical understanding, Dilthey surrenders himself to the great gods of nature, in a quaint pandemic vision. For Dilthey, one transcends history, while for Bacon, history is made to surrender to man in the art and act of discovery. This great chasm separates not only Bacon and Dilthey, but more profoundly, science and metaphysics.

I shall attempt no general assessment of Dilthey's achievement or his indebtedness to the Neo-Kantian Baden school of sociology; something of its scope and weight have been suggested in this brief exposition. I would be presumptuous to seek to place his work in an historical or philosophical perspective in a few words. It suffices to say that Dilthey has created a genuine, albeit diffuse way of raising the question: What is sociology?

Although Dilthey disclaimed any intention of propounding a specific theory of sociology, it is clear that he did just that—intentionally or otherwise. To say that sociology is not an independent science, that sociology is part of a general frame for human understanding of the conscious life, that moreover it is that part of the *Geisteswissenschaft* dedicated to pointing out the interpersonal relations of man to man, that it is a particular form of the reductionist fallacy of conceiving of sociology as an independent social science—all this is as much a general characterization of sociology as we could ask of a philosopher who has made social theory his life's work.

What then is the adequacy of Dilthey's schema in the light of present-day knowledge about social science research? Dilthey's historicism expresses itself in the classic form. Truth is subsumed under the category of process, and process in human terms is historical. The next step, and I should say, an illegitimate one (i.e., the historicist fallacy) is to conclude that truth is therefore a property of change. Since no historical truth is absolute, truth itself becomes relativized. That Dilthey recognized the problems raised by his relativism is clear. He was enough of the Hegelian to realize that a realm of truth, sacred or profane, must exist in some form—either empirical or normative. For this reason, he set upon the theme of the genius—the poet, the philosopher, or the prophet—to reveal the permanent truths for a transient civilization.

This is no more of a resolution to the relativist dilemma than that made by other sociologists of knowledge who persist in searching for a theory of how knowledge is possible. Even from an epistemological point of view, élitism, whether of the poet or the philosopher, does not resolve the question of truth; it only systematizes rules accepting social beliefs and myths. The extension of Dilthey's relativism has been intensely criticized by Karl Popper, Raymond Aron, and Charles Frankel, and it would be superfluous to detail these criticisms in a review. What can be said is that to make truth contingent upon historical evolution is to commit the genetic fallacy all over again—to ground a theory of truth, not on empirical principles, but on suppositions from a history that offers a history of consciousness apart from social life.

As a result of such theorizing, it must be granted that the relativists in the sociology of knowledge have refused to take seriously the scientific status of the sociology of knowledge. They find particularly painful the acceptance of ordinary scientific method as the means of establishing the truth of propositions, even those propositions offered by the sociology of knowledge. Thus the battle of false options continues.

This raises the further question of whether, in Dilthey's sense, a social science can exist at all. Surely, if Dilthey's critique of nineteenth century positivist sociology is accepted unqualifiedly, no social science can. However, the fruits of contemporary research, its capacity to portray and predict social structure and movement with some accuracy, tend to indicate that quantitative analysis, employing models derived from everything from physics to anthropology, do in fact contribute to a deeper understanding of that very life process Dilthey held to be apart from social analysis.

The widespread development of mathematical scales for registering beliefs (Lazarsfeld), field theories for establishing the psychic components of social behavior (Lewin), statistical surveys registering the degree of human credulity (Cantril), analysis of propaganda impact and technique (Lasswell), and the casting of historical theories as paradigms (Merton) have gone a long way in showing that fears of social science becoming a surrogate for religion, in the sense anticipated by Comte, are groundless. Certainly, if we define sociology as what the sociologists are doing, we can lay aside permanently Dilthey's fears that sociology as a science cannot arrive at empirical truths. It is only by making truth normative that Dilthey's thinking can be considered substantive. The difficulty is that this is not properly a question for sociology, as Dilthey imagined, but a question for the philosophy of the social sciences.

Dilthey's insistence upon the integrity of the human sciences is not so much incorrect as it is incapable of providing a useful and viable option to empirical social science. Dilthey's followers must show in what way the *Geisteswissenschaft* can better lead to the creation of urban and rural planning and analysis; the redistribution of political power; and the understanding of conscious deception through propaganda and unconscious self-deception through economic interests; etc. Failing in this, historicism must admit, if not its retrogressive scientific character, at least that its real focus is ideological rather than sociological. Not that sociology lacks for ideas, but a system of philosophical history simply cannot claim for itself the right to supersede or eliminate scientific activities.

My last major objection to Dilthey is his juxtaposing of social science to the sociology of knowledge. Precisely because there is such a thing as science in general, one can speak with assurance of a sociology of knowledge. Their methods are roughly analogous, and their respective limits (that is, the analysis of the formal characteristics of human beings as social beings) cannot be separated or bifurcated. The goal of the sociology of knowledge, as a part of sociology, is the objectification of the subjective, and subsequently, the rationalization of the irrational in social behavior. To devise a special method for the sociology of knowledge over and against sociology in general, as Dilthey did, only returns the sociology of knowledge to its Hegelian womb, at a stage in scientific development that has transcended the battle of the *geist* against history.

What commences as a critique of science for preempting the field of human operations attempts not to frame a realizable alternative method for studying and changing men, but a means to insulate human relations and consciousness against the impact of the scientific revolution itself. This is no less true of Dilthey than of the romantic tradition in late nineteenth century Germany, which gave his work wide currency. Romanticism attempts to insulate the feeling man from the penetration of cold analysis. While this may have been useful during the age of Enlightenment and positivism, when the bland promises of the universe of progress were apparently guaranteed by scientific findings, the present distinction in scientific work between value-predicates and value-judgments has made romanticism methodologically obsolete.

Dilthey's option to sociology serves too many inherited doctrines not to invite suspicion. He placates the sociologist at the expense of psychology; he placates the philosophers at the expense of sociology, and he placates the metaphysician at the expense of philosophy. Far from solving the issue of the actual status of social science vis-a-vis natural science and the connection of philosophy to both, Dilthey only succeeds in widening the gulf between sociology and social philosophy, between empirical efforts and theoretic constructs. Perhaps "history" will record as Dilthey's highest achievement just this indication of how far we have still to travel to realize that much heralded phrase—the union of practice and theory.

Originally published as "Prehistoria de la Sociologia del Conocimiento: Bacon y Dilthey" in *Cuadernos de Sociologia*, vol. 13, whole no. 22 (1960), pp. 189–214.

4

Staking Present Claims on Past Icons*

Durkheim, Emile

A science in a period of primitive intellectual accumulation scarcely concerns itself with its history. Even for the admitted philosophic ancestry of sociology, this maxim holds true—particularly in the United States, where sociology strives mightily to present itself in a natural science image. If studies in the history of sociology have been spared a moribund fate by the efforts of Harry Elmer Barnes, old Howard Becker, and forever young Pitirim Sorokin, it is nonetheless true that the post-World War II atmosphere in sociology, emphasizing research at the expense of theory, has not encouraged serious self-reflection and critical summation.

A notable exception to this lethargy has been Kurt H. Wolff, whose editing, translating, and authoritative analysis of the social philosophy and sociology of Georg Simmel has placed American scholarship in his debt. It would be pleasant to record that this commemorative volume on Emile Durkheim reaches the same Olympian heights as its editor. However, such a judgment is not possible, given the uneven and often erratic quality of the contributions to this volume. This extends even of some of Durkheim's shorter statements, in which landmark contributions to the *Année sociologique* (akin to Max Weber's essay on objectivity in social science at the time he became coeditor of the *Archiv fur Sozialwissenschaft und Sozialpolitik*) are offered side by side with amateurish student notes taken from Durkheim's lectures on *Pragmatism and Sociology*. The latter can only serve to offset his reputation as a sophisticated and knowledgeable philosophic observer.

---

* Kurt H. Wolff (editor), *Emile Durkheim, 1858–1917: A Collection of Essays, with Translations and a Bibliography* (Columbus: Ohio State University Press, 1960), pp. 463.

Philippe Besnard (editor), *The Sociological Domain: The Durkheimian and The Founding of French Sociology.* (Cambridge and Paris: Cambridge University Press, and Editions de la Maison des Sciences de Homme, 1983), pp. 296.

The symposium contains workmanlike essays tracing the intellectual career of Durkheim (Henri Peyre), his impact on American sociology (Roscoe C. Hinkle, Jr.), Japanese sociology (Kazuta Kurauchi), and Anglo-American trends in cultural anthropology (Paul Bohannan). There is a perfectly charming and urbane piece on the ambience of the Durkheim School between the wars (Bougle, Mauss, Fauconnet, Granet, and Levy-Bruhl) revealing the personal and social ethics of these scholars. This kind of writing is all too rare and precious to be brushed aside. Albert Salomon, in his essay on the legacy of Durkheim, ably contends that he alone among the masters of classic European sociology created a school and a style of thought. This is seconded by Honigsheim's bibliographical study showing Durkheim's influence on nearly every major study of religion undertaken by anthropologists, historians, philosophers or sociologists, after the First World War.

The essay most critical of Durkheim's work is contributed by Lewis A. Coser. His effort to prove the now fashionable thesis of Durkheim's conservatism, though rich in suggestive criticism of the holism that prevented Durkheim from studying conflicting subgroups and subcultures, is not completely successful. Neyer and Richter, each in their own way, demonstrate that a *Dreyfusard*, a supporter of Juares, an enthusiast of both Cartesian rationalism and English political pluralism can be called conservative only if one offers a special construction of the word, apart from its historical associations from Plato to Burke. Indeed, Richter catches something of the anticonservative quality in Durkheim's work quite nicely. "His perspective is dominated by his unquestioning faith in science, freedom of thought, and the reality of prog- ress. His work, when read carefully, reveals no nostalgia for the past; he finds almost nothing commendable about the type of social cohesion characterized by traditionalism and an unquestioned religious authority." The argument for Durkheim's conservatism is further weakened by the fact that his neglect of factors of social instability and power conflict can just as easily be read, as Salomon does, as a Machiavellian view of man in which instincts and passions are channeled through the *conscience collective*, whether such a conscience dictates individualism or socialism.

My own view is that Durkheim's position on the conscience collective is derived from that line in the secular French Enlightenment, extending from Montesquieu to Helvetius, that emphasizes social responsibility for individual needs. This best accounts for Durkheim's classic liberalist convictions. It must also be noted that many conservatives have dealt primarily with problems of power and violence (Burkhardt and Acton), while many liberals have shown a distinct lack of concern for such issues. This is particularly evident in the English pluralistic tradition from Locke to Mill in which consensus is viewed as the sum total of conflicting parties and classes. Nonetheless, Coser's provoc- ative statement, when juxtaposed against the presentations of Neyer, Richter, and Salomon makes for the most stimulating reading in the symposium. For

Coser shows that one can be conservative in attitudes even while expressing liberal and even radical beliefs in politics.

The essay by Talcott Parsons on the integration of social system is less an analysis of Durkheim's position than an exposition of Parsons's own outlook. As an insight into a major source of Parsons's structuralism, this is an interesting article, but as an illustration of Durkheim's interests, it is without significance. Significantly, Parsons refers to all of his own major works (and some of his minor studies as well), while paying cursory attention to any of Durkheim's writings other than *The Division of Labor in Society*. The essay by Hugh D. Duncan, an otherwise fine scholar, unfortunately falls into the same class, with the added deficit of showing every sign of being hastily assembled. The impressionistic potpourri of ideas on comedy, tragedy, ritual, and drama show little relation to Durkheim's views on social solidarity. In marked contrast to this is Albert Pierce's article, which seeks to relate Durkheim's efforts to current sociological views on functionalism. Pierce gives us an altogether superior study, arguing that Durkheim's careful separation of function from needs distinguishes him from most contemporary theorists. Pierce suggests that such distinctions leads to a useful theory of social change and not just to a formalism of structural symmetries prevalent in modern functional sociology.

In brief, *Commemoration* at its best augments the fundamental elucidations of Durkheim's thought made earlier by Alpert in the United States, Ginsberg in England, and Gurvitch and Friedmann in France. But its value for philosophers is limited by the absence of essays on Durkheim's epistemology and moral philosophy.

* * *

In his appropriately generous preface to *The Sociological Domain*, Lewis A. Coser writes that the volume edited by Philippe Besnard on *The Durkheimians and The Founding of French Sociology* is "both a contribution to the history of the Durkheimian movement and a study of the institutionalisation of a new discipline." I would say that he is right on both scores. But oddly, it is more dubious to infer from this that "Durkheim and his co-workers are in many respects our contemporaries". Indeed, after completing this set of twelve essays, the distance between the late twentieth and late nineteenth (and even early twentieth) centuries—in sociological terms at least-never seemed greater.

To his merit Professor Besnard's tight and tough editing of these papers prevents him and his colleagues, for the most part at least, from giving way to any exaggerated claims of unity within the Durkheimian school, or sweeping serious differences under old intellectual rugs. The two sets of documents, the letters of Durkheim to his colleagues Paul Lapie and Célestin Bouglé and the letters from Henri Bergson and Léon Bernard on the "Lapie affair" (i.e., the introduction of the teaching of sociology in the French Ecole Normales Primaires), underscore two of the more important papers in this volume.

Hopefully, more primary materials of this sort will soon emerge from the Durkheim circle in Paris.

Besnard's two papers, along with the finely etched paper by John E. Craig (the only non-French contributor to this volume) on Maurice Halbwachs, provide a solid framework for considering the Durkheimian tradition a school of long standing. By focusing on the *Année Sociologique*, Besnard shows concretely how Durkheim and his followers worked over the 1896–1912 period to define an area and involve a group of roughly fifty scholars who in their thousands of reviews, short notes, and comments created a field in the absence of organizational institutionalization. In this, Durkheim was the student of Diderot and the great tradition of the French *Encyclopedie*—who a century earlier also organized the life of ideas as a life of scientific organization. How strange it is that this parallel is nowhere mentioned by any of the contributors.

Marcel summarized this linkage when, in his 1930 statement in support of his application for a position as professor in the College de France, noted that the "school" represented "working together as a team." Like Diderot before him, Durkheim was convinced "that collaborating with others is a drive against isolation and the pretentious search for originality." Mauss also gives an answer, albeit a partial one, for why the Durkheim school, though it valiantly attempted to reconstitute itself after World War I, essentially failed to do so. The sociological problems had not so much changed from 1912 to 1919, as had the professional personnel. The war snapped the essential continuities of social and institutional order. It was a Durkheimian "social fact" that sundered an "intellectual force." But let Mauss's own poignant words carry the message of disintegration:

> The greatest setback of my scientific life was not the work lost during the four-and-a-half years of war, nor from a year lost due to illness, nor even my helplessness brought about by the premature deaths of Durkheim and Hubert, it was the loss of my best students and friends during these painful years. It could be said that it was a loss for this branch of French science; for me, everything had collapsed.

In efforts to reconstruct and deconstruct the history of social science, it is perhaps wise to remember how deeply and profoundly worldly—and by that I mean items of slight theoretical discourse—events impinge upon seemingly impregnable doctrinal considerations.

The papers in the first part, on the Durkheimian group and its contexts, are superb. They confirm the importance of Durkheim's intellectual force as a political factor in French life. A sense of the *Année* emerges that is quite distinct from any individual book or essay. The Durkheimians were an organizational force for secularism and republicanism—quite apart from latter-day arguments concerning Durkheim's conservatism or radicalism. Victor Karady suggests that the collapse of the Durkheim School, like its rise, was less a matter of ideas than of the integration of sociologists after World War II into the professional training of philosophy. Sociology became theoretical, even rhetorical, and ultimately empty of significant empirical content. George Weisz's paper reinforces this theme by noting that Durkheim's influence was great because his sociological domain was drawn tightly. When this knitted fabric unraveled, so too did the Durkheimians. I confess that Weisz's attack on Terry Clark's notion of the significance of clusters in French faculties of letters leaves me unconvinced; since Clark does not deny that key institutional questions were fought through at the faculties and disciplines-only that faculties can function as clusters. Roger Geiger's paper, the final one in this section, is a model of how to write about ideas in the context of institutions. He clearly shows how Durkheim's sociological style was used in secularization of the French educational system, but used in a manner that could neither preserve nor protect Durkheim's efforts from the normal processes of erosion.

The papers in the second section seek to explore the scope of Durkheim's thought on other sociologically related fields. Clearly, the areas of ethnography and law were most significantly affected as François A. Isambert and W. Paul Vogt make plain. But from my own viewpoint, Pierre Favre's paper on the *absence* of a political sociology in Durkheim is the most fascinating. His undertaking parallels my own earlier effort on Durkheim's theory of the modern state to explain this absence. But although Favre makes it quite clear that the *Année* consigned political sociology to a bibliographical category and deprived it of a place in the natural division of sociology, he fails to answer why this should be the case.

I would suggest that Durkheim and most of his colleagues thought of society as essential to the normative character of order, whereas they viewed as a legal imposition to create artificial order in society. Admitting Machiavellian and/ or Hobbesian categories would have destroyed the possibility of sociological imperialism. And in the choice between social reality and sociological theory, the former yielded to the latter—with disastrous effects on the Durkheimian school. The final two papers by Besnard and Craig make painfully clear just how damaging is this substitution of the sociological wish for the social fact.

The post-Durkheimians like François Simiand and Maurice Halbwachs struggled mightily to preserve their master's thought. But a deteriorating series of "debates" occurred between sociology on one hand and law, geography, history, and economics on the other. Then arose a parallel, internal struggle amongst the Durkheimians for the mantle of the master (i.e. whether Durkheim's vision is specific or general, quantitative or qualitative, based on statistical regularities or laws of nature). In short, Durkheim's efforts became transformed from a sociology of events into a philosophy of society. The end was at hand.

Publishing and editing journals and annuals is hard work involving much contact with others: from gate-keeping functions with authors to marketing functions with readers. Durkheim, Hubert and Mauss had the rare energy and capacity to do the hand work as well as the vision to perform the head work. Their intellectual progeny did not have such drive. In this sense, Besnard's volume might be read with profit not simply by those for whom Durkheim and his School is a towering intellectual achievement, but no less by those who consider his work a momentous publishing feat. One hopes that Professor Besnard will continue producing work in this rich vein. As a master pupil of Durkheim, he can be counted on to do so.

From *Philosophy and Phenomenological Research*, vol. 22, no. 3 (1962), pp. 419–22; and from *History of European Ideas*, vol. 7, no. 1(1986), pp. 102–05.

5

On the Social Theories of Fascism*

Gentile, Giovanni

This brief notice is intended as review, appreciation, and plea: a review of recent Anglo-American efforts to come to grips with European social and political philosophies, an appreciation of H.S. Harris's masterful effort at filling a huge void, and a plea for more of the same by indicating the sort of work that remains undone.

Italian philosophic thought in the twentieth century has clustered about three major intellectual bastions, each having a distinctive ideological trajectory. Fortunately for the historian of ideas, each philosophic position has firm and clear political correlations—fascism, liberalism, and socialism. The liberal figure, Benedetto Croce is very well known in the Anglo-American world of letters. Scarcely a work of his has not found its way into our language, on every subject from esthetics to economics. This is clearly as it should be, since on both sides of the Atlantic the major emphasis has been on developing a meaningful liberal typology—one that would include provisions for individual liberties and societal obligations. That Croce is one of the very select few twentieth century figures (along with Russell, Dewey, and Laski) who has achieved anything approximating a synthetic form of liberalism is reason enough to explain his enduring fame.

Although this interest in Croce has created a powerful and positive image of Italian social thought in the present century, the price paid for this exclusive emphasis might, in the long run, prove more costly than the benefits derived. For what we now have is a virtual absence of work on Italian social thought.

---

* H.S. Harris, *The Social Philosophy of Giovanni Gentile* (Urbana: University of Illinois Press, 1960), pp. 387.

Giovanni Gentile, *Genesis and Structure of Society* (Urbana: University of Illinois Press, 1960), pp. 228.

Giovanni Gentile, *Le Origini della Filosofia Contemporanea in Italia.* V.A. Belleza (editor), (Firenze: Sansoni, 1957)

More than a quarter century has passed since Herbert Schneider's sourcebook, *Making the Fascist State*, and we have yet to receive a work of the same caliber. Where are the much-heralded benefits of retrospective analysis? Examining why this scarcity has occurred in a world of intellectual affluence, would take us too far afield. However, it is clear that the dogma of liberalism has tended to blunt rather than to promote an understanding of the polarized forces of Right and Left (represented in Italian philosophy by two titans, Giovanni Gentile and Antonio Gramsci) by means of a presumed consensual blanket in which bygones are bygones and all cats are grey after all.

That Gentile and Gramsci, who along with Croce formed the triumvirate of the Hegelian legacy in Italy, have been comfortably ignored on American shores. This reflects an unhealthy provincialism in our political and philosophic analysis. The cult of Croce is curiously, Anglo-American rather than Italian in origin. In Italy, where the forces of politics are still the practical expression of social philosophy, the names and works of Gentile and Gramsci are equally well known. It is thus an important milestone to record a work on Gentile by an Englishman partially trained in the United States. Gentile was the spokesman for an activist idealism (I think the word activism better expresses Gentile's intent than does the more placid word actual) that resolved itself into a "pure" fascism.

If I may anticipate my comments on Harris's work, it is only to say that Harris's interest in restoring Gentile's place as a decisive figure in modern Italian thought that causes Harris to present a one-sided picture—Right and centrist intellectual forces alone figure, while the long shadow Gramsci cast is left out because it suited Gentile's purposes to do so. With the exception of the historian H. Stuart Hughes' cavalier statement of Gramsci's views in *Consciousness and Society*, no accounting of Gramsci and the whole tradition of Italian social philosophy from Labriola to Mondolfo has yet appeared.

Cassirer, in *The Myth of the State*, shrewdly observed that the potency of Hegelianism could be symbolically gauged by the conflict between the Nazi *Wehrmacht* and the Red Army. This is true enough, but an even more potent measuring rod of the Hegelian image in the modern world was Italy during the Fascist period. Here three strands of Hegelian wisdom vied with one another for supremacy: the Hegel who saw in the state of fulfillment of human organization (Gentile), the Hegel who saw the will of the state as subservient to the "indwelling spirit" of human liberty (Croce), and the Hegel who saw the state as a self-negating moment in the historical impulse toward human emancipation (Gramsci).

But I should like to examine not the confrontation of these three visions of Hegelianism, but their essential unity. For Hegel provided each of these three figures with common ground rules—including an abiding respect for unfettered thought, a historicity in looking at problems of social structure, and a respect for all hitherto existing forms of culture. Hegel proved not so much the Archimedean lever, as the Achilles heel for all three: a suspicion that Croce's liberalism was too historical and not enough empirical; an equal suspicion that Gramsci's socialism was too humanistic and not enough bolshevik; and as Harris well shows, a view of Gentile as a fossilized Fascist, unwilling to take the leap into either irrationalism or religiosity. The struggle of Italian social philosophy to uphold the honor of free men in a free society against the forces of political and intellectual obscurantism, is with all its ambiguities and frustrations, the message common to Gentile, Croce, and Gramsci—precisely because they shared Hegelian premises.

Turning now to a consideration of the book by Harris, we must first note that it is remarkably free of dogmatic attachment or criticisms of Gentile's efforts. The author sees his work as an "essay in salvage," distinguishing Gentile's philosophic idealism from his political preferences. In large measure, the salvage operation is a success. Gentile's position was forged in the crucible of post-Hegelian controversies about the relation of phenomenology to epistemology, man to authority, experience to essence, historical change to perennial values. In short, the dichotemization of post-Hegelian philosophy rather than the March on Rome shaped Gentile's thinking. Harris persuasively argues through close textual examination that Gentile's position was crystalized by the end of World War I, including his belief in an elitist reorganization of education, the participant theory of human thought, and the idealist epistemology in which no man can stand aside from practice without abdicating moral responsibility. If anything, Gentile's views resemble those of Plato as envisioned in *The Republic*, with respect to the moral center of political gravity.

In his analysis of Gentile's early period, Harris is forthright and properly critical. In comparison, the work of Gentile during the Fascist era (1922–1944) is handled with less skill. True, relating philosophic postures to political perspectives of the times and the personality of Gentile to his obligations as Fascist minister of education, is a formidable undertaking. That it was done at all attests to the capacities of Mr. Harris—his refusal to hide behind the texts. Nonetheless, a trend towards apologetics sets in as Gentile's political involvements take priority. Harris strains to show that everything from Gentile's blackjack theory of education to his blind support of the Nazi-Fascist alliance really has a virtuous "metaphysical" explanation. After all, the author tells us, a blackjack is not as damaging an educational weapon as a mace (it can only injure and not kill the student), whereas Gentile's support of the Fascist cause to the bitter end is but a living out of the practice theory of morality. Such an approach smacks of balancing the ledger entries at the end of an accounting period. Can it not be assumed that something less ethereal than moral uplift was at stake in Gentile's strange equation of fascism with the causes of humanism and liberalism? As the Italian proverb has it: when a moth is about to expire, it flaps its wings furiously.

The paradoxical conclusion is that Harris's work, rather than rehabilitating Gentile's social philosophy, only demonstrates once again how susceptible this form of actual idealism is to totalitarian uses and abuses—to that immoral exaltation of power Gentile *sometimes* worried about. Thus, rather than a resuscitation, the book is in effect a warning that an oracular and woozy idealism uninformed by the social sciences and unresponsive to the empirical and pluralist elements in the liberal tradition, can become a philosophy of the crematorium. Mr. Harris's disingenuous urge to guard his man from criticism, which seems to grow with each chapter, has an unanticipated consequence of calling into doubt his own sincere efforts at a politic-philosophic synthesis—and perhaps worse, raising doubts as to the significance of Gentile's intellectual remains.

Although one must be grateful to Mr. Harris for making available Gentile's *Genesis and Structure of Society* (volume 9 of the *Opere Complete*), it is hard to share in his judgment of the work's fundamental importance. Indeed, it is more interesting from a historical than a sociological or philosophical perspective. It shows Gentile late in his life, tormented by the decay and disintegration of the Fascist state, returning to a position of "pure" Hegelianism to find justification, if not relief, from his own commitments. Although in theory Gentile's *Genesis* is an offspring of Hegel's *Grundlinien der Philosophie des Rechts*, in philosophic acumen it is too programmatic and dogmatic to stand with the parent work. Naive formulations abound, without the redeeming qualities of Gentile's pre-Fascist writings (e.g. "It is not nationality that creates the State, but the State which creates nationality"!) or the equally fuzzy notion that "since we can also say that the State is man, it follows that nothing human can be alien to the essential nature of the State." These and similar platitudinous commentaries make this work read like a bizarre and surrealist reworking of Pope's *Essay on Man*.

Gentile's general isolation from the Franco-Italian social science of his own age, from the work of Pareto, Mosca, Michels, and Sorel, marks him apart from both Croce and Gramsci. This work, apologies for its hasty production under difficult circumstances set aside, shows Gentile to be a thinker unable to move beyond the romanticist-historicist illusions of the early nineteenth century. His failure of nerve in the face of fascist aberrations of the *Risorgimento* takes the form of a retreat from social realities through entrapment within metaphysical theories of state authority as the sole path for human salvation. If all states were indeed perfect embodiments of moral behavior, this might be useful. Until that time, however, it would be a cruel hoax to equate statist ideologies with humanism. As Harris himself acknowledges, "the worst danger involved in this tendency to confuse the transcendental state with the actual structure of governmental authority is that it leads with inevitable logic to a kind of intellectual despotism."

The four tomes of the Gentile *Opere* to be considered are actually one study on the antecedents and character of philosophy in modern Italy—from the *Risorgimento* to the First World War. Gentile's prolific and proliferating tendencies as a writer can perhaps best be gauged by the *Opere Complete*, which shows nine books on systematic philosophic exposition; twenty-seven on the history of philosophy; eleven on miscellaneous subjects ranging from the reform of the educational system to *Culture and Fascism*; eight volumes of essays and briefer monographs concerning esthetics, literature, philosophy, and its history; and four volumes of correspondence. Thus *Le Origini della Filosofia Contemporanea in Italia* must be seen as but a fraction of Gentile's output.

Several distinctive aspects of this enterprise deserve mention. Gentile's idealism, though it reveals the inevitable march in Italian thought from neo-Platonism, positivism (including its materialist variants), neo-Kantianism, to the post-Hegelian synthesis, is of interest for the secular framework in which the priority of idealist claims is said to occur. Since Gentile, views religion as a Hegelian moment in the universal judgment of morality upon men and society, he does not deal with those philosophers who place theological values in the forefront, as part of the modern philosophical movement. Indeed, he secs the most prominent such trend, neo-Thomism, as a brief appendix between the Kantian and Hegelian trends.

Some of the personal problems Gentile encountered with the Fascist movement, particularly the intellectual wing that sought a return to Catholic orthodoxy, are anticipated in these early writings. One reason he sees modern philosophy as modern is its joining the idea of the good to the idea of nation-hood. He sees Italian philosophy as a response to the legacy of Plato, Kant, and Hegel because each of these major figures, in distinctive ways, illuminated the main problems of the new epoch: the mythic dimension of the act, the ethical dimension of the act, and the historical dimension of the act. Positivism, that trend which Gentile most criticizes nonetheless belonged to the modern world because of its central focus on action as such. These volumes therefore help to explain Gentile's own philosophy no less than the philosophies of the figures he discusses.

These four books are a treasury of information on men and movements obscured by time, place, and tradition. It is nonetheless difficult to see how any future assessments of Italian philosophic history could fail to take note of *Le Origini*. The essays on Ardigo, Vera, and especially Spaventa, show to good advantage Gentile's deep penetration and fair treatment of philosophic systems other than his own. It is also clear that the influence of the Hegelian Bertrando Spaventa on Gentile's though it is much more considerable than has hitherto been stated. Gentile notes two things in particular that marked Spaventa apart from his colleagues: first, his active political role in the *Risorgimento* and second, the national idea in his philosophic approach. These are precisely the characteristics exhibited by Gentile's actual idealism. An outstanding interlude in these volumes is Gentile's critical commentary on Cesare

Lombroso's "Criminal Anthropology" as illustrative of the consequences of taking seriously Moleschott's vulgar materialism.

In concluding, we might note several attractive features of the Harris volumes that should induce more work in this field. First, there is an excellent bibliographical index, both intelligible and useful as a checklist of themes covered in the book. Second is a very high-quality introductory essay to his translation of the *Genesis*. In this essay, Harris shows exactly what has and has not been done in Gentile studies in the English language, and further, the main points yet in contention. Finally, mention ought to be made of the physical composition of the companion Harris study and translation. From the spacing and typesetting to the paper stock and cover design, nothing but the greatest care is exhibited. Few authors can boast such care on the part of their publishers. The added inducement of reasonable pricing should earn these books the representative they deserve. There can be no doubt that for many years to come, Harris' presentation will be the standard by which other investigations in *Italian social philosophy* will be judged.

From *Philosophy and Phenomenological Research*, vol. 23, no. 2 (1962), pp. 263–68.

6

On Power and Statecraft*

Hobbes, Thomas

When we consider the ever expanding relevance of such questions as the nature of state sovereignty, the role of power in the social organism, the relation of coercion to liberty, and the possibilities for developing a science of political behavior, we are invariably drawn to consider the views of Thomas Hobbes. His *Leviathan* was a monumental construction, infused with the spirit of Plato's *Republic.* For here too was an effort to account for the total functioning of man—from the source of our knowledge to the consequences of citizenship in a commonweal. Indeed, Hobbes's work is the most cogent realist exposition in classical philosophy. For those who insist that Thrasymachus' power thesis was brushed aside too conveniently by Socrates, this work rights matters. It is sometimes overlooked that over half the *Leviathan* is taken up with metaphysical, religious and linguistic issues. For it is the relation of these matters to polity that provides Hobbes with the foundations of social science.

In contrast to the crucial place Hobbes occupies in philosophic history is the small quantity of work done on his theories. For every book that examines his theory of knowledge and reality there are at least several dozen expositions of the Kierkegaardian either/or. A similar paucity may be noted in studies of his political philosophy. Part of the reason for such neglect may be that Hobbes's views have been subsumed in and provided a more mature foundation by later political philosophers like Rousseau and Hegel. Another reason may be that Hobbes's logico-deductive method is a mechanical juxtaposition of geometric axioms and thus has an arid, archaic quality. Yet another cause of this neglect may be a reaction to Hobbes's sense of self-importance, not merely as a theorist but as a political figure. However, making allowances for these and other reasons, it must be confessed that Hobbes presents too strong a diet for most contemporary critics. Highly romanticized theories of political democracy and state sovereignty, which it might be added were no less current in the seventeenth century than they are now, can only be confounded by a tough-minded philosopher who sought to expose the inner-springs of human action with the latest instruments provided by mathematics and natural science.

---

* Richard Peters, *Hobbes* (Harmondsworth, Middlesex: Penguin Books Ltd., 1956), pp. 272.

This is by way of introducing the reader to Richard Peters's excellent book, *Hobbes*. Earlier efforts, such as Frithiof Brandt's *Thomas Hobbes' Mechanical Conception of Nature* (1928), and Leo Strauss's two works on *The Political Philosophy of Hobbes* (1936), and *Natural Right and History* (1953), may each in its own realm be superior to Mr. Peters's volume. But no single book offers a more judicious appraisal of Hobbes's total philosophic standpoint.

The author notes the manifold source of Hobbes's outlook: the Baconian concept of knowledge can manipulate nature to human goals; the Cartesian belief that a sound scientific method is the key to the secrets of man and nature; the then widespread belief in the values of the geometric approach for solving problems from epistemology to ethics (i.e., an approach that started from self-evident deductive principles and concluded in a philosophy of civilization logically proceeding from such axioms). Mr. Peters also notes that Hobbes's translation of Thucydides stemmed from an appreciation of concrete historical research in the deductions of the philosopher. In addition, the author justifiably minimizes the connection between Machiavelli and Hobbes, showing the latter to represent a step forward "from shrewd, fallible, common sense about his country's plight to the certain knowledge of the scientist." It would, I believe, have been useful had Mr. Peters made more of the connection of the *Leviathan* to *The Republic*. It is possible that the entire groundwork of Plato's work (not just the shared belief in geometric method) was foremost in Hobbes' thinking. That Hobbes seems to be reacting to Plato's classic may be worth examining. For what is the *Leviathan* if not an effort to prove that self-preservation rather than justice, power instead of ideals, is the framework of society? It may also have been worth mentioning the possible indebtedness of Hobbes to his nominalist predecessors, particularly William of Occam and to the early physicalism of men like John Dumbleton. Even pre-Baconian England had a tradition amenable to the Hobbesian philosophy.

The idea, taken as a self-evident proposition by some, that materialism implies a humane libertarianism is nowhere better refuted than in Hobbes. Materialist in his theory of knowledge, disciple of the forward motion of nature and society, a confirmed critic of established religions, Hobbes defended with equal vigor an absolutism that urged a political reconstruction based upon common law and natural rights. Hobbes was concerned with developing a theory of absolute sovereignty based on his self-evident axiom that peace is the prime condition for the survival of mankind. He who provides the peace must in turn be provided with absolute popular allegiance. Men in a condition of nature, due to their essential egoism, are in a state of conflict; they therefore yield their private sovereignty to a larger authority as the only assurance for the survival of the human species, according to this thesis, the breakdown of central authority leads, not to democracy but only to dismal anarchy. As Mr. Peters cogently notes, the apparent incongruity between Hobbes's materialism and theory of the state makes quite good sense if one remembers that "the main enemies of the sort of absolutism which he envisaged were indeed those whose belief in individual liberty assumed predominantly religious forms, or those who, because of their Catholic convictions, could never give the kind of undivided allegiance to a sovereign which he demanded of them." It is nonetheless surprising that the author did not make more of a distinction between what Hobbes deemed essential and accidental in his theory of sovereignty. For Hobbes was not so much concerned with whether Charles or Cromwell or even Lilburne achieved power. He was concerned with preserving property rights. He who best achieved this proprietary end deserved popular support. Otherwise Hobbes would have no need to issue the ultimatum: either preserve the peace or be replaced by a sovereign who can.

Peters has a keener appreciation for Hobbes's England in general, than for the specific relationships Hobbes lived through. This is conveyed in his contrasting Hobbes to other thinkers of the age with whom Hobbes had little in common or in contact. The discussion of such shrewd clerics as Bishop Bramhall and Bishop Butler to his right and the constitutional democrat, John Locke, to his left indicate the actual range of discourse in political philosophy. Bramhall raised the important issue of how a determinist theory of human motivation can be meaningful, since to speak of man as rational seems to imply the free choice of men to select between alternative modes of life. Butler criticized Hobbes for failing to make a distinction between the end towards which an activity is directed and the satisfaction such ends may bring. From a quite different position, Locke denied that hedonism implies absolutism. In a solemn warning, Locke said, "he that thinks absolute power purifies men's blood and corrects the baseness of human nature need but read the history of this or any other age to be convinced to the contrary." It would have been a welcome addition had Peters informed his readers how Hobbes reacted to such broad-ranging discussions of the state of society.

In reviewing an earlier volume in the Penguin series, I noted an apparent effort to reduce the history of philosophy to the history of linguistic muddles. This opinion happily needs to be greatly modified in Mr. Peters's effort. It is particularly evident in the author's confession that even Hobbes's errors were a great achievement because he was wrong in the right sort of way, that is, he was wrong in thinking that the geometric method could provide a universally valid philosophy, but right in seeing that solution to epistemological and political problems in science. Mr. Peters's book will undoubtedly lead more people to Hobbes, and I cannot think of a better reason for reading this finely etched appreciation.

From *Science and Society*, vol. 11, no. 3 (1957), pp. 284–86.

7

Public Affairs and Private Lives*

Hook, Sidney

The challenge of writing a review of an 84-year-old life, lived to the hilt and condensed into a 628-page book, places a considerable strain on one's resources. It is difficult to avoid falling back on old preferences and recalling prejudices. An author has certain inalienable rights, among them, the right to decide what to include or exclude in an autobiographical performance. Age and rank do have their claims. But this awareness only further complicates the challenge of summary and synthesis. For many, the life and legends of Sidney Hook are inextricably interwoven with two great academic struggles of the twentieth century: the expansion of free expression against totalitarian temptations of all persuasions and an overriding search for a theoretical architectonic to link philosophy to the practical struggles of the age. Indeed, for people involved in either or both activities, this has been a much anticipated book.

Hook's autobiography is a first-person narrative of Irving Howe's *The World of Our Fathers* no less than a personal odyssey: about first-generation immigrant families whose focus was second-generation educational vistas in New York ghettos. It is about pride and prejudice in lower and higher education, and finally, the process of professionalization in New York politics as well as in European philosophy. For all of these "objective" reasons, this book deserves to be widely read.

It is a chronicle worth telling and worth reading. For those like myself, who feel the presence of ghosts who marched in the same forays a generation or two later in the New York City public-school system, in the City College of New York philosophy department, in the academic profession as an educator

---

* Sidney Hook, *Out of Step: An Unquiet Life in the 20th Century* (New York: Harper & Row, 1987), pp. 628.

Sidney Hook, *Marxism and Beyond* (Edison, N.J.: Rowman & Littlefield, 1983), pp. 225.

Paul Kurtz, (editor), *Sidney Hook: Philosopher of Democracy and Humanism* (Buffalo, N.Y.: Prometheus, 1983), pp. 360.

and in struggles over everything from McCarthyism to student opposition to the Vietnamese adventure, a certain pain, even argumentative impulse, must be curbed. After all, these are Sidney Hook's self-reflections, not those of his reviewer or his critics.

Even in this regard, the reader must be prepared for something less than a full-fledged or conventional autobiography. By conscious design, Hook has chosen to write a public record rather than a personal statement. He wants to be read and appreciated by the young, by those filled with the idealistic zeal he himself exhibited as a young man. The book is thus essentially propaedeutic. Hook aims to serve as an example of the embattled academic who seeks to expand the prospects for human freedom. Yet, he properly tries to avoid casting himself in a falsely heroic mode or as a person for whom error was impossible, He has also, and this is more problematic, assiduously avoided discussion of his private life, seeing his public life as alone worthy of public consideration. As he notes:

> I am writing primarily a political and intellectual autobiography. My family life, my loves, my friends, and bizarre personal incidents that have befallen me are largely irrelevant to the major public themes of my life. I know it is unfashionable in the extreme to regard certain areas of one's life as private and as of no public concern until evidence arises that they are indissolubly linked.

Nonetheless, one must bemoan the absence of such personal reflections and asides, in favor of a narrative perilously close to sheer essay.

This dualism between the public and the private is (happily) not quite uniformly observed. In fact, many of the more intriguing segments of the book discuss Hook's encounters with luminaries like Bertrand Russell, Whittaker Chambers. Albert Einstein, Bertolt Brecht, Lionel Trilling, and organizations like the *Partisan Review* editorial group (Rahv, Phillips, Barrett, Macdonald) and the Congress for Cultural Freedom. Not infrequently, these personal reflections are filled with an ardor and a self-righteousness that indicate old struggles do not pass gently into the night like old soldiers. If anything, these resurrections are the most intriguing aspects of Hook's book. They are vital precisely because his personal passions and public concerns are occasionally allowed to comingle. Would that this were the case consistently throughout the book, rather than the long stretches of paraphrasing his earlier works.

For in these personal segments, questions of intellectual elites and Communist politics are joined. Hook's description of how and why intellectual elites took the American pledge of democracy-as-critique most seriously while wearing its promise of democracy-as-fulfillment most lightly, provides a key insight into his career. It is the fault line between himself and his critics, and it remains the essential battleground in higher education today.

The spillover of intellectual life into anti-Americanism, even more than pro-communism, clearly rankled Hook. For the leitmotif of the Hook autobiography is not that *he* was out of step, but rather that so many of his associates were out of sync with American values, as well as global politics. Indeed, central to Hook's bedevilment was the penchant of intellectuals to betray or ignore the very model of a free society they had come to take for granted. At the same time, they adopted the illusions of slave societies (read the Soviet Union or Nazi Germany) by transforming them into utopias. In short, Hook does not really believe that he is out of step but rather that his colleagues, or many of them, were and remain so. Hook *was* penalized—from City College political clubs in the early 1920s to the halls of New York University's Loeb Center in the late 1960s—but for being too much *in* step with his times. For this is a celebrationist text, if not of a personal sort, then of a political sort. What is good is quality education. What is bad is bully-pulpit politics in the name of education. But how the aims of mass education should be squared with elite education is dealt with perfunctorily.

The book is written in a triumphal air. We are assured that not just the struggles but the achievements of the century have been best understood by Hook and a small handful of his associates. The presumption of this perspective will no doubt be excused by those who welcome this text. Nevertheless, the very problem Hook sought to avoid—namely, a self-serving apologia—is the inevitable result, even if such a celebration is writ large on a public canvas rather than small as a private agenda.

Many of Hook's worst fears of the consequences of leftist extremism did not occur. The *Walpurgisnacht* at New York University did not result in the collapse of the university; indeed, the university has reached substantially greater heights. The USSR did not stop changing after the death of Stalin; the totalitarian mold has shown signs of straining, if not cracking. Not even *Partisan Review* ceased publication after Hook's decisive break with its editorial board. There is a certain frozen-in-time quality to the book that leads one to suspect that Hook continues to believe his positions uniformly correct, and those of his opponents most often fallacious, at least during that time when Hook was involved. With pain, one must conclude that Hook is delivering the public a message rather than the promised autobiography. In that sense, his autobiography disappoints precisely as a philosophical self-reflection.

Even the prohibitions against personal backbiting are not completely observed, as in the remembrances of Russell's "unsolicited advice" on the best strategies for taking a girl to a hotel room. Hook was "rendered speechless" on this occasion, but of course Russell might well have been jousting with his younger colleague, playing on the talmudic sensibilities underlying a pragmatist's fixed moral probity. Likewise, Hook's rather petulant anger at Lionel Trilling for not declaring publicly his (Hook's) role in developing a proper strategy to combat anti-Semitism and secure Trilling's tenure at Columbia. In all probability, Hook's account is accurate. But the rendition given is carping and little comes through of Trilling's talents or thoughts. Worse, when subjectivity is permitted, it is uniformly at the expense of others. The flaws in others are said to be personal and intellectual; the flaws in self are considered to be political and principled. Therein lies a dualism that the autobiography, far from overcoming, actually compounds. Therein too lies the book's essential weakness, making it more irritating than compelling (if largely accurate) as a piece of reportage.

One also feels philosophical disappointment. True enough, an autobiography need not degenerate into an autodidactic tract. However, Hook leaves us with some gaping intellectual holes: What is the relationship between a naturalistic pragmatism and a critique of dialectical materialism? More pointedly, how does a doctrine of reliance upon experiment and experience protect us from communism? Beyond that, why is it that some varieties of pragmatism became fascist activism and not democratic socialism? And suppose that experience were to convince us that Soviet communism was more efficient in industrial production or military safeguards, would such wisdom move the pragmatist to a more positive view of communism? In Hook's case, the answer is clearly negative. Then what normative factors, beyond the Deweyan ethic of means-ends continuities, would lead Hook to maintain the struggle against totalitarian systems, even if doing so involved the abandonment, partially or wholly, of the instrumental position of his mentor?

At the risk of incurring the wrath of a great scholar, the ultimate problem with Hook's book is not only its arbitrary distinction between public affairs and private lives but the inability or unwillingness to weave a philosophic garment out of political cloth. We are left with a scholar much more often right than wrong on political issues, but he has given us few mechanisms to replicate his track record in contemporary struggles. And this is a shame, since Hook intends his autobiography to produce precisely such a heuristic outcome. Instead, we are left with the public record of a man whose motives and sentiments may have been pure, but whose philosophical premises for specific actions remain ambiguous.

It is a genuine shame that Hook did not keep much of the epistolary documentation for the statements he made. Where it has been retained—as in the remarkable exchanges between Einstein and Hook, on the occasion of the Emergency Civil Liberties Union's honoring Einstein—we have a blow-by-blow account of postwar tensions; Cold-War distinctions, and their differential roots and hopes. It would be valuable to have such source documents for other events described, like the 10th International Congress of Philosophy held shortly after the Cold War began, but they apparently no longer exist. This leads to hearsay and recapitulations, not always as full and often not as persuasive on key confrontations as one might relish.

I offer as evidence Hook's views of Jewish thought. His defense of academic freedom takes him into a powerful denunciation of genteel anti-Semitism in the academy, especially at Columbia University. Indeed, his description of pre-World War II Columbia is devastating and beyond contest. But his attitudes toward Zionism, announced as a weakness in his preface, continue to haunt the book, not to mention the chapter on his upbringing, Secular humanism, Hook's self-professed faith, remains a tombstone rather than touchstone of his thinking, much like democratic socialism itself, which becomes increasingly more remote as the autobiography grinds to a halt. Sadly, Judaism is explored with a painful superficiality quite beneath his discussion of Marxian socialism and communism. For example, we have an impassioned defense of academic freedom as an intellectual creation, but no real explanation why Jewish students, in the past at least, have outperformed others qualitatively and are overrepresented quantitatively in the academy.

What we have then is a plea for a democratic academy but little corresponding proof of the pragmatic ground for a democratic society. Professor Hook is probably right in his instincts; for such linkages there is no substitute for hard philosophic homework. If Hook's book leads others to do such homework, then it will have proven successful. As a work unto itself, and judged on the severe terms of its own design, the autobiography falls short of its loftiest intentions. This reluctant judgment rendered. Hook's personal odyssey is nevertheless well worth reading and pondering. Its tough-minded author provides a glimpse into the operations of an exemplary academic mind, and no less, a combative personality that makes the reader forget or at least overcome stereotypes of retirement as a retreat from worldly cares.

Sidney Hook recently passed his 80th birthday. As befits an elder intellectual statesman who has survived in the academic trenches, he has been receiving various honors—among them a *Festchrift* edited by Paul Kurtz. The participants in this collective homage, those whom Hook influenced either directly or otherwise, are for the most part old-timers in their own right. That is not to denigrate the distinguished cast of characters; it is merely to note the age gap between old and new Marxists, old radicals and new revolutionists, for scarcely anyone under 50 graces the pages of this tribute. To its loss, Hook simply does not figure in the community of what currently passes as Marxist.

For his part, he makes clear in his latest collection of essays, *Marxism and Beyond*, that he views such groups as the Frankfurt School and such individuals as David Caute, John Kenneth Galbraith, Robert Heilbroner, and Michael Harrington as having betrayed the democratic essence of Marxism. Unlike his writings on pragmatism, these expositions do not walk on eggs.

The essay on the Frankfurt School alone is worth the price of this *selbstbildnis.* A few choice quotes must suffice:

> The Frankfurt School has so Hegelianized Marx that it represents a form of revisionism more radical than that of Eduard Bernstein.... Once we dismiss the causal priority of the mode of production in considering the structure of society and its changes, we eviscerate the

theory of historical materialism beyond recognition.... Undisguised paternalism is incompatible with any conception of a democratic policy. It is reminiscent of the tradition of enlightened despotism from Plato to modern totalitarianism.

Hook, the guardian of a pure Marxism purged of Leninism-Stalinism-Maoism, is contemptuous of everyone from Sartre to Horkheimer who sought to improve on the original by modernization. The only problem is that he must also dampen those elements in Marx proper that not only admit but make inevitable the sort of doctrinal mélange the theorist might indeed have scornfully disavowed. Thus throughout these pieces, Hook himself commits a fundamental dualism that Marx was for the most part careful to avoid: a confusion between anti-Communism and pro-democracy. Too many of his political statements, from his observations on postwar Germany to those on present-day Poland, reveal this chasm. His analysis of neoconservatism, for example, lacks the bite and dash of his assaults on neo-Marxism. This said, it must further be recorded that *Marxism and Beyond* provides a glimpse of Hook at his best: engaged, concerned, and very often on target.

What are the origins of the profound split among those who revere Marx? No easy answer is possible. In the case of Hook's treatment by today's Marxists, there are a range of explanations extending from his pugnacious personality to his strong opposition to Communist and Leftist intellectuals purged during the McCarthy era. By all accounts he was an academic autocrat whose ideas of democracy were benign, yet whose standards struck terror in the hearts of many young scholars. Perhaps this is one reason why academics now on the Left have chosen to ignore him. On occasion, Leftist critics—Edgar Z. Friedenberg in his 1970 review of *Academic Freedom and Academic Anarchy* or Philip Green in his 1980 review of *Philosophy and Public Policy*—have lashed out at Hook; in the main, though, they attempt to tame the lion rather than beard him. Hook is a brilliant polemicist, well capable of responding to challengers, savaging them when necessary. Polemics no less than formal philosophy was his mother's milk; in that sense, he is as much a child of the Russian Revolution as of German philosophy. His commitment to pragmatism as a practical stance has been strong, but his commitment to socialism in the struggle against totalitarianism has remained even stronger.

We come, then, to the heart of the matter. The arguments Hook inspired are not so much about the importance of Marxism in the contemporary world or the place of pragmatism as they are about the uses of Marxism to defend Soviet tyranny and attack American democracy, and conversely, the uses of pragmatism to attack Soviet tyranny and defend American democracy. If Hook's works are monochromatic, it is so because his primary issue is not and never has been the status of Marxism as a social theory or philosophic system, but its status in the fight for the minds of the masses, its deployment in the central battle of the twentieth century: between open, democratic societies and sealed, totalitarian states. Hook's friends and enemies are forged on these grounds, not on shared premises about the experience of pragmatism.

Although encomiums are very much part of honoring a colleague, the number and intensity of them in *Sidney Hook: Philosopher of Democracy and Humanism* almost embarrassingly outweigh any sort of serious analytical discussion. Irving Kristol speaks of Hook as a "great legal mind." Kristol finds it "impossible to doubt that he would have been the outstanding jurist of this century in the English-speaking world. Nor is it fanciful to think that he would have ended up as a justice of the Supreme Court, in which case his reputation would have been overshadowed only by John Marshall, if by anyone." Nicholas Capaldi notes that "there is nothing more deeply ingrained than Hook's commitment to democracy, and that is why he is so resented by radicals, lunatics, and extremists who would gladly sacrifice democracy on the altar of some utopian scheme." Too many of the papers also were prepared for other occasions, and although some are interesting in their own right, they have little to report on Hook's work.

The *Festschrift*, however, does have several thoroughly outstanding pieces. Especially notable are Daniel Bell's examination of the historicism and relativism of Hook's pragmatism, Richard Rorty's brilliant critique of Hook's scientific strategy in the study of morals and religion, and Milton R. Konvitz' close reading and critical appreciation of Hook's contributions to the legal and moral aspects of freedom. Sidney Hook's vigor is attested to by his continuous and impressive publications record, included in this tribute. He is someone for whom the life of letters is the letter of life—he has thoroughly internalized the Enlightenment belief that words and ideas count. But it must also be sadly stated that the words and ideas of others tend to matter much less in his way of thinking; criticism often spills over into raw animus.

Hook's contributions to social criticism, to a critique of totalitarianism, far exceed those he has made to positive philosophy. He is much more a child of his century than a sage for all time. That is not said to detract—very few scholars succeed on either term. Immortality is for a select few who crowd our consciousness other immortals formerly thought to be indispensable. The ability to employ theoretical constructs to illumine large vistas of contemporary reality is a rarity—and with it comes scorn from narrow professionals and free-swinging ideologists.

The task of construction has long passed from the hands of the philosophers to those of the social and physical scientists. Left to the philosopher is criticism, the negation of error. This is essentially how Hook must be appreciated. *Marxism and Beyond* provides a showcase for an elder scholar who is exceptionally gifted and knowledgeable in the fundamentals of Marxist literature. Very few younger Marxists know the literature as he does, and this collection of essays is a timely corrective to the banalities and insipidities to today's Marxism.

Sidney Hook's message is a warning to the West—properly rendered and surely appropriate. His philosophy is a blend of John Dewey and Karl Marx, largely liberated of their continental exaggerations. His politics is an uncanny blend of social democracy and economic welfarism, with rarely any thought about the costs of creating such a social order. He does not so much employ Marxism as a tool of analysis as see it as a beacon by which tyrannies are perpetuated in its name. Hook epitomizes our incomplete century. He has settled accounts with nineteenth-century doctrinal disputations—for that, after all, is what Marx is about—but has not come to grips with new empirical developments of the twentieth century.

In Hook's world, there is little outside the United States and the Soviet Union: No Asia, no Africa, no Latin America. There is little outside the revolutionary-liberal axis: the social outrages of Stalin and Hitler at one end and the social decencies of Franklin D. Roosevelt at the other. The struggle over the means of communication and the place of technology in the moral order seem extrinsic. In fact, everything from the service economy to high technology to the Third World seems alien to Hook's vision. The metaphysical vice of considering all things temporal as eternal appears to have caught up with him—and perhaps with many of his celebrators as well. How unpragmatic!

Although his *Festschrift* comes at the end of the twentieth century, Sidney Hook's singular achievement has been to close out the nineteenth. The problems he has dealt with have centered around the failure of justice and history to march lock step toward a social paradise. Twentieth century varieties of communism and socialism have not measured up to the ideals of nineteenth-century Marxism. In that contradiction Hook found his voice, and we are deeply indebted to him. But the contradiction remains unresolved. There is still intellectual work for him to do.

From *Congress Monthly*, vol. 54, no. 6 (1987), pp. 16–18; and from *The New Leader*, vol. 66, no. 10 (May, 1983), pp. 7–9.

8

History and Society in Retrospect*

Kahler, Erich

This is the least impressive of Erich Kahler's three major books published in English. This is said with sincere regret, since I consider myself an admirer of both *Man the Measure* and *The Tower and the Abyss*. However, the humanistic and literary force of these previous two books has been spent, only to be replaced by the inflated currency of a padded metaphysics. Indeed, the terminological mystification often reads like a caricature of Kahler's previous essays. He trots forth the big words as does a drunk displaying his bottles on the wife's night out. "Human forms" are juxtaposed with "hierarchy of human beings," which in turn are somehow related to a "consummate historization," which of course is based on "rigorous historical coherence." Then there is a melange of sentences that to say the very least are awkward. One illustration should suffice. "Moral awareness and responsibility has therefore necessarily decreased with the increase of collectivity and depersonalization, with the emergence of a collective consciousness."

The suspicion grows that this souped-up erudition disguises a paucity of thought, which of all things seems to be based on a lack of historical good sense, or, if you will, of good historical sense. First there is the unintelligible Kitsch-dialectics, "The human world is technically one, but at the same time in a state of wildest anarchy." For another, "the West is reminiscent of the Roman Empire at the moment of its greatest expansion, a situation which seems to suggest that the life cycle of the West is approaching its end." And the entire work is summed up in an unbelievable demographic Gotterdammerung with a statement that the "overpopulation of our globe is the most disturbing common problem of humanity and may force men to migrate and found colonies on other habitable planets." Hopefully, this will not happen too soon, since we do not yet have the vehicles for the trip Mr. Kahler deems so inevitable. In the meantime, we should all sit and hold our collective breaths for the inevitable day when our neighbor will collapse on us without invitation.

---

* Erich Kahler, *The Meaning of History* (New York: George Braziller, 1964), pp. 224.

Good things are not absent from this volume. Kahler brings to his task a deep understanding of the Greek, Hebraic, and Christian traditions, especially in their religious aspects. His appreciation of the philosophies of history that motivated these early religions is often stated with insight. However, the closer the author gets to modern intellectual history, the weaker are his remarks. His comments on Bodin, Hegel, and Marx, for instance, are utterly unconvincing, while his awareness of the Anglo-American scene is entirely absent. One would think that the British and American traditions represent some sort of accommodation to practice while remaining bereft of genuine intellectual value.

Perhaps the biggest weakness is that the author has not delivered on the promise in the title, namely, to write a study of the meaning of history, especially why actual history is not synonymous with historiography. Frankly, few philosophers of history seriously support the proposition that history and historiography are identical. Further, after reading the volume, I am sadly drawn to the conclusion that I wish scientific historiography were, at least in this particular case, a little more attached to real-world events and processes. As it is, this is a step toward metaphysics through the portals of metahistory.

Kahler's work on central Europe remains peerless. Few have equaled him, and perhaps Leo Lowenthal has rivaled him, in giving expression to the cultural formations which made possible the dominance of dictatorships in that part of the world. The celebration and not just analysis of irrationalism, the discontent with ordinariness no less than the corruption of elites, is exposed in essay after essay by Kahler. And yet, the antidote to this miasma of the irrational, was never found or understood by him. It is as if constitutionalism in politics and utilitarianism in philosophy are a lesser breed. As a result, Kahler—in these essays at least—is at war with the culture of political darkness, without understanding the light that was shining in the Anglo-American world he so happily inhabited. Sadly, in this he is more a prototype than an antidote to what ails deracinated European intellectuals who can't go home again, and yet who can't find a home in their adopted Anglo-American environment.

From *Philosophy and Phenomenological Research*, vol. 26, no. 1 (1965), pp. 131–32.

9

Rationalism and Irrationalism in History*

Lewis, John

Few areas of scholarship can boast as many introductory volumes as philosophy. This may perhaps be due to the endless search for synthesis and meaning of the continuous expansion of human knowledge. Many times, however, those entrusted with writing philosophic histories are themselves not outstanding representatives, capable of rendering genuine insight into the past and present of philosophy. This has resulted in a bland acceptance of introductory texts that are repetitious and timid.

This is said to call attention to John Lewis' *Introduction to Philosophy*. The author is a distinguished contemporary British thinker who has traversed the gamut from the rationalist movement, prominent in that country earlier in the century, to dialectical materialism. Both the man and the book are characterized by genuine wisdom and independence of thought, which, combined with Lewis's sublime respect for philosophy as an end in itself, makes for an eminently useful introduction to the mansions of philosophy. Lewis remarks on the general features of Bertrand Russell's philosophy could easily stand as a description of what the author objects to most in contemporary thought, and what Professor Lewis attempts to avoid. "Too often he becomes supercilious and sinks to trivial arguments, glaring exaggerations, and prejudiced judgments. His simplifications become slick and often sheer falsifications." He might, in fairness, have added that Russell is at least unique and interesting in his observations on others who came before him.

The unifying thread of this work emerges with the first essay on Plato and carries through to the last one on Whitehead. For Lewis, the history of philosophy is the history of the conflict between a rational, scientific method of solving human problems and the irrational turning away from worldly solutions to worldly ills. In terms of the philosophy of man, it is a conflict between sociality and egoism, between the endless effort to understand and

---

* John Lewis, *Introduction to Philosophy* (London: Watts & Co., 1954), pp. 236.

conquer the material world and a viewpoint that seeks only to gratify the private wishes and deceptions of a subjective world. By posing philosophy as such a vivid contradiction, Lewis uncovers the inner springs of the development of philosophic history.

Lewis states the positive aspects of the Platonic system along with its well recognized shortcomings. We are reminded that Plato leads not simply to the mystical intuitionism of Plotinus and Augustine, but through his championing of the organizing powers of beauty and reason, to such scientific philosophers as Spinoza and Bruno and to poets of Shelley's caliber. The very fine chapters on Aristotle, Spinoza, and Hegel tap the roots of their respective geniuses. In the hands of these philosophers, rationalism did not take flight from empirical reality but remained a search for the reason in things and processes. Dr. Lewis makes this clear. For Aristotle reason "is the framework of the concrete world and not merely an 'ideal' world." The pure rationalism of Spinoza involved a monism "in which every part implies every other part and is logically deducible from wider generalizations." In Hegel, process replaces being as the key category. This "most rationalistic of the romanticists" conceived of the universe historically, in its "unfolding and development."

Lewis considers the broad patterns of rationalism to be moving in opposite directions. Lewis does not deny that probing the innermost regions of consciousness at times uncovers the power of the human will to overcome obstacles (it is in this sense that his statement that pragmatism is a "philosophy of progress" has to be taken), but by denying law in nature and society, pragmatism finds itself justifying every form of tyranny. Whether it be the irrationalism of Plotinus and Augustine that calcified into a dogmatic hatred of observation and experiment, or that of William James, whose action philosophy became a useful tool for Italian fascists like Pareto and Gentile, the "flight from reality" became in fact a fight to keep present reality intact. Lewis notes that irrationalism as a social force strongly supports what is, as against what is becoming.

Posing issues too sharply or exclusively conflicts between reason and unreason risks making the paramount criteria the functioning of ideas in abstraction and not the functioning of ideas as part of a specific social or scientific milieu. Oversimplification is inherent in this approach, and Lewis cannot escape from it. What is a fine tool of analysis in understanding the differences between Plato and Aristotle, is a good deal less than adequate in discussing contemporary British empiricism.

The problem involves both a shift in Lewis's usage of the term rationalism, and the social role of rationalism with the advent of empirical philosophies. In modern philosophy, rationalism comes not merely to signify a belief that nature and man develop according to laws, but it comes to be a theory of knowledge, a way of understanding the world primarily through the organizing powers of the mind rather than observation of the material world. Lewis does not make this alteration in the contents of rationalist philosophy clear, which leads him to evaluate modern philosophy in terms of the commitments of ancient philosophy. When Lewis accepts a philosopher he does so by making him a rationalist, that is one who recognizes the operation of causality, necessity, and determinism in the world. But in failing to deal with modern rationalism as a theory of knowledge rather than a theory of nature, he inevitably blurs the obvious lines of conflict between empiricism and rationalism. There seems to be no other justification for calling Hume and Locke "rationalistic in spirit" or showing their rejection of rationalism to be "itself based upon a rigorous use of reason and *in that sense* empiricism is rationalistic," other than the author's unconscious equation of rationalism with the good and empiricism with the bad.

If the crack in Lewis's method first becomes noticeable with Locke and Hume, it becomes obvious in his treatment of contemporaries like Whitehead and Dewey. Now it is true that Whitehead has been treated too casually and scornfully by modern naturalists, but Lewis's attempt to vindicate Whitehead the rationalist, making of him a new Hegel, flies in the face of known facts. Lewis is correct that, Whitehead repudiated subjectivism, but is it not more important to note his wholehearted acceptance of classical idealism? Whitehead himself is candid about his commitments to systematic theology. Then too, Whitehead's philosophy of the organism is more than an attempt to bring wholeness and unity back into the world; it is primarily an attempt to provide a formidable challenge to materialism, and not just dead matter as Lewis implies.

As to Dewey, Lewis seems most anxious to absolve him of his pragmatic past, This is a task Dewey himself never thought necessary to undertake. Dewey's rejection of idealism is open to serious doubt, considering the anthropocentric direction of his thought, which places man at the center of the universe in fact as well as in value status. And Lewis's comment that "Dewey's philosophy is really a philosophy of modern science" is certainly a highly controversial point. Dewey's second-hand, almost popular-science comprehension of the physical sciences would make any such statement suspect. Indeed, Dewey's repeated rejection of a genuine historical science, a science of human development, seems to preclude any possibility of his being a "philosopher of modern science" that would extend to the social sciences at least.

The closer the author gets to contemporary philosophy, the further away is he from any meaningful statements on the social functions of a philosophy. Both Whitehead and Dewey are examined without reference to democratic conditions in twentieth century America or England. If Lewis had undertaken such social analysis, I believe that a somewhat different, and more ample, picture of the two would have emerged. The author faced the theoretical dilemma to operate within a framework of traditional rationalism instead of a twentieth-century naturalism. Since scholars like Collingwood and Dewey uphold the precepts of a rational world, Lewis in a sense had to accept their philosophies as pillars of twentieth century thought. But this method, though abstractly correct, does not account for the actual functioning of these philosophies. For example, Whitehead's call for a realm of values that is extra-scientific (i.e., supernatural) plays a certain role in a society attempting to reclaim ethics for religion. Similarly, Dewey's hostility to a historical science, on the basis of its imagined destruction of individuality and freedom, has a certain meaning in a society in which historiography has been reduced to wishful thinking or fact finding. When viewed in this light, the glitter of Whitehead's and Dewey's "rationalism" quickly fades.

A number of related criticism deserve mentioning, paramount among which is Lewis' conception of French Encyclopedic materialism as an interlude (of five pages in duration), bridging the gap between Hume and Kant. If the author is correct that this philosophy breaks completely with the ideology of feudalism and stands with science, then the interlude view of Enlightenment thought is hardly comprehensible. Unfortunately, Lewis here prefers to go along with a formalist viewpoint that casts French materialism as a minor motif in philosophic history. This preference is particularly bewildering in the light of the author's own stress on the outstanding role of rationalist philosophy. His excellent essay on Spinoza is marred somewhat by the author's failure to acknowledge his intellectual indebtedness to I.K. Luppol's work on Spinoza. This debt is particularly noticeable in the discussion of the art and science of Spinoza's Holland, which closely parallels Luppol's brilliant study, *The Historical Significance of Spinoza's Philosophy*.

It is understandable that in an introductory volume, the author does not wish to burden his readers with lengthy quotations, but where given they would profit by the inclusion of the page from which the quote was taken. More confusing, however, are pages where quotes are given without any footnote at all (such as those on pages 41 and 160). Lastly, the title of the work is too general. This actually is an introduction *to the history* of philosophy and should have been so designated.

These criticisms should not be taken as a sign of the book's mediocrity. The author has provided us with a vigorous and challenging statement of the perennial and transient issues in philosophy. It is a book to be taken seriously by those concerned with the future of philosophy in Western societies.

From *Science & Society*, vol. 19, no. 4 (1955), pp. 354–58.

10

Means and Ends in Nationalism*

Machiavelli, Niccolo

The appearance of a new modern library edition of *The Prince* and *The Discourses on the First Ten Books of Titus Livius* provides a welcome opportunity to consider the ever fascinating subject: what is Machiavellianism? There are few enough occasions when an individual merits an "ism" after his name, and fewer still when the ideology has come to stand for duplicity and secrecy while the person actually stands for morality and nationality.

In considerable measure, this popular confusion, sadly compounded by scholarly misinterpretation, rests on a rather modern, one might even say Deweyan, notion of a means-ends continuity. But Machiavelli was not a pragmatist in this quite modern sense at least. His work is better understood as an effort to work out the dynamics between strategy and principles. *The Discourses* rest on a defense of a republican form of government, social equality between citizens, and the rule of universally applicable law. These were all to be made possible by achieving the unity of the Italian nation. *The Prince* should be viewed as an effort at instruction in strategy, tactics, and even logistics (i.e., how to teach un absolute ruler to use his power to reform a corrupt cluster of quasi-feudal estates into a unified nation-state).

The human instrument for this transformation of theory into practice was to be Lorenzo de Medici. And in part, his imperfections as a political leader have been grafted onto Machiavellianism as a concept. It was a tradition of both late feudalism and early monarchism for thinkers to appeal to rulers, as it was for musicians to dedicate works to rulers. This tradition arose as much from a desire for protection against bodily harm as from any genuine belief that the sovereign would magically implement all suggestions or promote all music played for that matter. Thus, Machiavelli is best understood on his own terms, and the biography of de Medici should not be confused with the history of Florentine Italy.

---

* Niccolo Machiavelli, *The Prince and The Discourses*, Luigi Ricci and Christian Detmond (translators). (New York: Random House Publishers, 1950), pp. 256.

Machiavelli was a complicated figure standing at the gateway of modern thought. The complexity of his writings mirrored more accurately than any other sixteenth-century Italian the dilemmas of that period. Although the consolidation of Italy had begun with the development of an industrial and merchant economy, the various feudal forces remained strong enough to retard its full blossoming. Instead of a unified state, Italy was divided into a number of city-states fighting each other. In this situation, the Papal State with headquarters at Rome remained very powerful.

The people suffered all the degradation and misery of a strifetorn nation. In addition to economic convulsions and bitter class struggles, the land was prey to French, Spanish, and German domination. The combination of internal and foreign exploitation made the lot of the masses unbearable. In this situation Machiavelli, the spokesman of the most economically powerful and politically conscious section, the banking and merchant interests, came forth to show a way out of the socially diseased situation.

Further examination of Machiavelli and his times needs no better commentator than himself. He knew that he wasn't the first to raise the banner of Italian independence. Such pleas went back to Petrarch and Dante. But Machiavelli saw that pleas alone produce no concrete results, because they fail to cope with reality as it was, not how someone would like it to be. One by one, Machiavelli stripped sentimental and idyllic notions from the realm of social life, changing poetics into politics.

Machiavelli tried to find the causes preventing the unification of Italy. First there was the strength of the papacy. Too weak to unite the nation itself, it remained strong enough to prevent any other ruler from doing so. Since the power of the papacy in Italy depended on the extent of Italy's disunity, the papacy invited foreign invasions and fostered domestic intrigues.

In a famous passage in the *Discourses*, Machiavelli blames the church for keeping the country divided:

> A country can never be united and happy, except when it obeys wholly one government, whether a republic or a monarchy, as is the case in France and Spain; and the sole cause why Italy is not in the same condition, and is not governed by either one republic or one sovereign, is the Church . . . . The Church, then, not having been powerful enough to be able to master all Italy, nor having permitted any other power to do so, has been the cause why Italy has never been able to unite under one head, but has always remained under a number of princes and lords, which occasion her so many dissensions and so much weakness that she became a prey not only to the powerful barbarians, but of whoever chose to assail her. (151–52).

The second major obstacle to a united Italy was the reactionary, decadent nobility who, though having long outlived any useful social function, continued to live in splendor gotten from the toll and sweat of the peasantry. This parasite class also knew that their number would be up once Italy was united economically under the capitalist classes and politically under a strong monarch.

In his profound antagonism towards mercenary soldiers paid to fight losing battles for a dying regime, Machiavelli's understanding of the importance of the popular masses emerges. His views on this score have greatly been underestimated by those seeking to prove that Machiavelli was concerned only with fooling the people. He notes as the main obstacles in the struggle for liberation, a failure to develop a citizen-army, a people's army of Italian patriots, "The mercenaries are useless and dangerous, and if any one supports his state by the arms of mercenaries, he will never stand firm or sure, as these are disunited, ambitious, without discipline, faithless, bold among friends, cowardly amongst enemies, they have no fear of God, and keep no faith with men." Only an army of citizen-patriots, could beat back foreign invaders, keep the peace at home, and thereby secure the liberation of the Italian homeland.

The concept of a united Italy, strong, vigorous, and free was not merely an ideal Machiavelli strived for. It permeated all his views on the church, state, monarchy, armies and people. The form a united nation took in his mind was conditioned by the period he lived in and the narrow class strata he represented. To his way of thinking, a united nation could be achieved if one of the Italian city-states became powerful, enough to command the total allegiance of all other portions of Italy. Nevertheless, the concept of nationhood was at the root of what he fought to establish. He hoped that somewhere there was a man, preferably from the growing banking and merchant groups, who had vision enough to imagine a unified country and strength enough to realize it.

The task of securing nationhood belonged to a strong and fearless Prince who could command the allegiance of the people, aristocracy, and clerics alike. But unlike the Utopians of later centuries who sentimentally looked to a benevolent despot to unite the aspiration of the public by providing happiness for all, Machiavelli knew that benevolence had nothing to do with the matter. It was not benevolence but the merchants, bankers, and industrialists who held the key to a united Italy. It was they who could stand behind the Prince and the coercive power of the state he presided over. His dedication of *The Prince* to the banker Lorenzo de Medici is solid proof of his faith in the ability of the new banking-merchant alliance to lead the people forward in common action.

All struggles were to be bent on uniting the country, and the Prince would be allowed the use of any means to secure this end. The state was to be the instrument, the people the raw material, the citizen-army the legal authority. In short, not duplicity but nationality was the new element that Machiavelli brought into play in his discourses.

Although Machiavelli unqualifiedly sanctioned ruthlessness, he did not lack moral scruples. This oft-repeated charge flies in the face of the real situation in Machiavelli's time (early sixteenth-century Italy). In this decayed society, murder, intrigue, incest, sexual aberration, were widely used for political reasons. In elevating self-interest, political shrewdness, and calculation to high moral levels, Machiavelli simply appropriated the methods used by the old Italian ruling classes to maintain power. It is trivial to criticize his failure to set up sentimental, non-existent moral catechisms of righteousness and goodness. The Prince, to successfully unite Italy, would have to be indifferent to clerical and idealized moral codes—for the forces preventing the growth of Italy, in spite of their talk, were in practice just as indifferent to scholasticism in politics.

Does this mean that Machiavelli had no moral code or that his morality was no better than that of his feudal opponents? Not at all. His morality was based on a single principle—the unification and liberation of Italy. Everything and everyone in support of this principle was moral; all who worked in opposition to a united Italy were immoral. What was good for the nation was good and right; what was not was evil and wrong. Lacking the warmth and humanism in other democratic-patriotic moral codes, his theories nevertheless more perfectly mirrored the real social needs of broad popular elements allied against Feudal church and state. With other political and moral doctrines of the times, even those of a progressive nature, one had to cut through a fog of sentimentality to arrive at the class and national roots of the moral outlook. Machiavelli did this for us. He was completely honest in insisting that the highest moral duty is to the life and liberty of Italy: "Where the very safety of the country depends upon the resolution to be taken, no considerations of justice or injustice, humanity or cruelty, not of glory or of shame, should be allowed to prevail. But putting all other considerations aside, the only question should be, what course will save the life and liberty of the country." Thus, the basic proposition of Machiavelli's political position maintains that a rational morality is founded on the struggle to secure a rational society. This fusion of morals and politics, theory and practice, in the fight for Italian independence is the best lesson he taught his and subsequent generations of people.

The meaning of Machiavelli for our age has been particularly obscured by the frequent claim that he was the theoretical father of Italian fascism. This slander ignores history and flies in the face of the facts. The deep-rooted theoretical differences between Machiavelli and Mussolini make these charges appear even more ludicrous.

Machiavelli said explicitly that government is more stable when it is shared by the many, and he preferred election to heredity as a mode of choosing rulers. He spoke for a general freedom to propose measures for the public good and for liberty of discussion, in order that both sides of every question may be heard before a decision is reached. He believed that a citizenry must be independent and strong, because there is no way to make them warlike without giving them the means of rebellion. Finally, he had a high opinion both of the virtue and judgment of an uncorrupted people, as compared with the need of the Prince to engage in machinations and maneuvers.

Taken as a whole or one by one, Mussolini and the Fascists defied and defiled every one of these Machiavellian tenets. Mussolini was not a follower of Machiavelli; he was his betrayer. He ruled foolishly on behalf of the propertied interests. He deprived the Italian masses of elemental economic, political, and cultural rights. He entered alliances with what was most reactionary and corrupt. And finally, he sold Italian independence and sovereignty to Hitler for a few stale crumbs off *Der Feuhrer's* table. In short, even his machinations had no virtuous or national substance.

But this does not mean that progressive humanity can stand pat with the views of Machiavelli. Tremendous changes have occurred in the 450 years since his death. He was born in an age of the blossoming of an expanding merchant capitalism. Ideas that in Machiavelli's day were rallying points of the people, are now used in turning back the wheels of human progress. History has taught us much in understanding and evaluating Machiavelli. It shows us what is still of worth and also what is worthless in his teachings.

Machiavelli suffered many shortcomings, reflecting in no small measure the limitations of the class he represented. He didn't understand that the economic functioning and divisions in society were basic. By incorrectly judging the economic base, he turned reality upside down. Machiavelli misconceived history, not as the movement of the broad masses, but as the actions of the individual rulers. Lastly, social revolutions and national independence movements arise from the need of the masses, not the dreams of a Prince. If Machiavelli had been correct, Italy would have achieved nationhood in the sixteenth century. That it was only in the nineteenth century that Italy became a unified state attests to the power of the people and the impotence of the ruler without them.

However, if Machiavelli's failing are not slight, neither are his achievements. He examined society in terms of the concrete social practices of men, not in terms of the subjective opinions of people. He made a big step forward in examining people's class needs and aspirations. He helped liberate the study of politics from the reactionary control of the church and thereby pointed the way to political science. His conception of the state as the instrument of class rule was a monumental scientific achievement. And he originated the idea that war is a continuation of politics by other means.

Machiavelli's achievements, apart from the appellations attached to his name, are gaining currency—this despite his lack of humanist and popular democratic sentiments and his acceptance of a despotic cure-all for human problems (this aspect in his outlook has been perverted and taken over by the Fascists). We should remember him as one of the finest scientists Italy or any nation has ever produced. He was a man with vision enough to see through what politicians say, into what they do. With the courage to write what he saw and felt, he enriched our understanding of the world in which we live.

From *L'unita del popolo* (*New York*), 13, 20, 27 February 1953 [in three separate installments].

11

Marxian Myths and Pragmatic Dragons*

Marx, Karl

The recent wealth of serious evaluations attest to the continuing interest in Marx and Marxism. Of particular note are studies by Rossiter, Wetter, Cornus, and Bottomore and George Lichtheim's highly satisfactory *Marxism*. If these works do not provide a consensus, they at least offer a perspective from which to evaluate the contribution of Professor Tucker. The main theme of his dissertation is simple and provocative: Marxism is neither a social nor economic science, but rather a religious and moral world view. Beyond this, and here is where the author stakes his claim for uniqueness, Marxism is essentially mythos. The book attempts to trace the origins, genesis, and consequences of this mythic core in Marx's writings.

Unfortunately, a provocative thesis is not necessarily a satisfactory one. The widest uses of the mythic element in Marx's theory of historical change through class struggle was made as early as the fin the siècle by Sorel—whose absence from consideration is no small wonder since his inclusion could have lent support, if not corroborated, Tucker's thesis. Sorel merely viewed the doctrine of myth as an implicit clement in Marx, whereas Tucker assumes the more burdensome task of proving the Marxian mythos as the explicit essence. By placing Marx in a Christian existentialist tradition (even *Capital* a myth-narrative) and by cavalierly disregarding such intellectual sources of Marxism as English classical economy and French Encyclopaedism, Tucker finds Marx the theologian and Marxism the religion.

Works that attempt to cast the peripatetic figure of Marx into a mold of a mythmaker reveal boldness rather than sagacity. To deny, as Tucker does, pragmatic, naturalist, sociological, economic, and even philosophic strains in Marx's thought—to drown him in a sea of religious mysticism and then

---

* Robert C. Tucker, *Philosophy and Myth in Karl Marx* (New York and London: Cambridge University Press, 1961), pp. 263.

C. Wright Mills, *The Marxists* (New York: Dell Publishing Company, 1962), pp. 480.

castigate him for having a shallow and dangerous religion—does less than justice to problems Marx bequeathed to modern society. Becker's *Heavenly City* has conditioned us to a style of social metaphysics more sophistical than sophisticated. Apparently, the way to still gain recognition for religiosity is to declare in favor of atheism. Thus for Tucker, Marx's atheism proved conclusively that "his atheism was a positive religious proposition." The "religious essence of Marxism" is the transvaluation of original sin into the labor theory of value, Christian good works into revolutionary practice, etc. The same kind of quixotic reasoning holds for Marx the mythmaker. Since he strenuously argues against mystifying philosophy and celebrating market relations, he must clearly be disguising a mythic essence. Tucker's ultimate proof for this is Marx's *unawareness* of himself—which is itself mythical. He deals with "what empirically *is*". Can anyone ask for sounder evidence that Marx was a Magus?

The author commits another not-so-original sin: While he promises to treat Marx's intellectual development as a continuum, from the *Economic-Philosophic Manuscripts* to *Capital* a quarter century later, he really treats Marx as a unilinear purveyor of mysticism in the name of science. Marx is said to exhibit no intellectual growth or even change over time. His later efforts are viewed as a rationalization for the youthful enterprises, thus oddly seconding the Stalinist vision of Marx. The juxtaposition of science and myth constitutes a clever sort of scandalizing through stereotyping. The history of social theory from Plato to Pareto offers abundant evidence of contributions made to logos along with, or despite, mythos. No classic figure can be reduced to only a single level of cognition and conceptualization.

For the sociologist interested in the development of Marx's ideas on social stratification, political sociology, or the sociology of knowledge—or his influence upon men like Tonnies, Weber, and Mannheim—this work will not prove particularly satisfactory. I must concur in the author's modest conclusion that "although Marx died more than three-quarters of a century ago, adequate assessment of him probably remains a matter for the future." This book, in its tendentious onesidedness and in its failure to seriously consider sociological as well as psychological hypotheses only forestalls bringing such a future to fruition.

*　*　*

The death of C. Wright Mills in March 1962, at the age of forty-five, leaves unsettled, perhaps for eternity, the questions that raged about the most controversial figure in American social science since Veblen. The later works written and edited by Mills, in particular his blazing condemnation of "grand theory" and "abstract empiricism" in *The Sociological Imagination* and his forthright defense of the Cuban revolution in *Listen, Yankee*, began almost single-handedly an authentic dialogue in the sociological community.

The last years of Mills's life were filled with ironic paradox and a deepening personal anxiety. While economists, historians and political scientists sang his praises, sociologists of the Establishment ruled him "no longer a member of the sociological community." While the political-minded the world over hailed him as a rational voice in the American academic wilderness, policymakers in the United States found a myriad of ways (including court battles) to blunt the sharp edge of his criticisms of foreign policy.

Given this complex of events, the question inevitably arose as to the degree to which Mills had come under the influence of the dragons of Marxism. While socialists from Latin America, Asia, and Europe were claiming Mills as an authentic voice of Marxism, most radical-oriented scholars in America seemed convinced that this was anything but the case. Daniel Bell wrote that "Mills is not a Marxist, and if anything, his method and conclusions are anti-Marxist." Lewis Feuer considers Mills's theory of historical specificity not only a departure from Marxism but a thoroughly non-Marxian rubric. Donald C. Hodges also sees Mills as anything but a Marxist, since his theory of "the omnipotence of elite," derived from the great chain of Franco-Italian realists (Mosca, Michels, Pareto, and Sorel).

Along with these divergent opinions must be considered Mills's own emergence as an independent political and sociological mind. In truth, Mills was first and foremost a radical. Thus, his judgment of Marxism was profoundly influenced by what he considered the continued deradicalization of Marx's thought in each of the various socialist pivots of the twentieth century—from the Social Democracy of Bernstein to the bolshevism of Stalin. It was incumbent upon him to settle affairs with Marxism, if only to make clear to himself and to others the exact relationship between the political radicalism of a midtwentieth-century American sociologist and that portion of the "classic tradition" in social science carried on by the Marxists. This is the purpose of *The Marxists*, a volume completed just prior to Mills' death.

Diderot once noted that a sense of the future is to the philosophic man what immortality is to the religious man. Here Mills, speaking as a "political philosopher," attempts to delineate the sort of future mankind can expect. In its fourteen chapters (seven written by Mills and seven written by "the Marxists" from Marx to Mao) the history of Marxian ideas is seen in present-day terms. Mills was no pious true believer; that which does not serve to illumine the contours of present society is, from a pragmatic viewpoint, ballast—and is properly and unceremoniously treated as such.

Mills had a reverence for conflicting modes of socio-historical reality and a healthy irreverence for all else. This volume sets forth his standards for the sociological imagination: historical specificity and empirical predictability; living social doctrine presented in living language; and a meaning and impact in ideas that can at least match, if not outstrip, informed biographies and informing newspapers. This is a work all people of intelligence and critical judgment will want. And the extraordinarily low price for a work of such high value (made possible paradoxically enough by capitalist mass marketing techniques) itself reflects Mills' herculean battle for a "public sociology" similar in intent, if not in content, to Walter Lippmann's "public philosophy."

As an overview of contemporary Marxisms in light of their common intellectual antecedents, no single book now available covers the ground as well or as extensively as *The Marxists*. Mills's method of historical specificity is really empiricism with the dimension of time included for good measure. With this method, he portrays the interplay of social forces that have created Marxisms, rather than a monolithic "Marxist social science." Throughout, Mills distinguishes himself from Marxists and anti-Marxists alike. Rather than celebrate or bemoan the fracturing of Marx's works by various competing factions, he sees in this very process of revision, reevaluation, and restoration the lifeblood of a social doctrine.

The thesis of the book can be stated quite simply: the Marxists are important precisely because of their distinctive and different appraisals, whereas the liberals are unimportant precisely because of the absence of differences. Mills seems to be saying that liberalism perishes as it becomes identified with an existing social establishment, in short, as it becomes monolithic. The pluralist, the man receptive to new ideas, the man interested in the social uses of social science—in short, the classic liberal—must interest himself in Marxism, because liberalism fulfills itself within its confines. The formalist and official liberalism of new and old frontiers is captive to statist dogma—whether on questions of academic freedom or foreign policy. As such, liberalism has lost its capacity to move men. And Mills was behaviorist enough to sense that ideas that have no consequences in public action have no consequences at all. Thus Mills's volume is not an appeal to partisan passions (for example, no Marxist could possibly be content with the relativism implicit in Mills's presentation of the contemporary panorama of Marxian ideas), but a realistic assessment of contemporary political philosophy and of what ideas the liberal individual must pay attention to if he wishes to carry on in the "classic tradition" of Mill and Hobhouse. This volume is an attempt to fuse the liberal and sociological imaginations—a fusion calculated to renew the sinews of political philosophy.

This book displays the same sharp phrasing and barbed wit as *The Sociological Imagination*. Mills's hilarious characterization of the law of the "negation of the negation" deserves to he reproduced—in part at least:

> One thing grows out of another and then does battle with it. In turn, the newly grown produces in itself 'the seeds of its own destruction.' Marx's texts are full of metaphors from the reproductive cycle and the hospital delivery room. Things are pregnant; there are also false alarms; wombs and midwives abound. And finally, there is 'bloody birth.'

The outcome of this jocularity, however, is quite serious, "One should not mistake metaphors of style for a method of thinking." And throughout, this is the touchstone for the essays chosen for inclusion. Thus, the selections—from the writings of the Bolsheviks Lenin, Trotsky, and Stalin; the Social Democrats Kautsky, Bernstein, and Luxemburg; the critics of Stalinism Hilferding, Borkenau, and Deutscher; and the new revisionists Khrushchev, Mao Tse-tung, and Ernesto (Che) Guevara—make for lively and intellectually provocative reading. He offers a Marxism as free of jargon as this doctrine permits.

Mills's own method for studying Marxian writings constitutes a paradigm for the study of political thought, comparable to Robert K. Merton's paradigm for the study of the sociology of knowledge. Mills's articulate approach has four main elements: (a) analysis of Marxist political philosophy in terms of ideology; (b) analysis of Marxism as an ethic, as a body of ideas and beliefs; (c) analysis of Marxist agencies of change, the instruments of reform, restoration, revolution, etc. (d) analysis of Marxism as a social and historical theory, and of the assumptions it makes about how man in society functions.

No claim is made by Mills for the sociological purity or inclusiveness of this paradigm for studying of political thought (as distinguished from the exaggerated claims made by Parsonian sociologists). Writing as a social philosopher (a natural role for Mills since, unlike most of his colleagues in sociology, he received his early training in philosophy), Mills seeks to explain his own perspectives and beliefs as much as those of the Marxians. Mills's beliefs are woven throughout the text of the book. Involved is a commitment to social science, of which Marxism is a very important part, both historically and in the present. However, the priority he gives social science as an empirical and historical whole, prevents a dogmatic outcome in favor of any one part of this tradition. Indeed, Mills' volume closes with a set of questions for the serious investigator and reader. Although Mills does not pretend to provide the answers, the long journey from cover to cover of this text leaves us more sober and better equipped to answer questions about the nature and content of Marxisms in the present world.

Mills's evaluative criteria of Marxism are empirical and critical, but theirs is not the sole level at which he operates. For Mills is too sophisticated a thinker not to understand that the social importance of ideas may not have anything to do with how scientific or rational a system is. Hence, Mills seeks to explain the widespread acceptance of Marxism in all parts of the world, on the basis of ideological and moral fervor as much as on the basis of the truth contained in its doctrine. Marxism makes possible a lively and healthy dialogue. For that very reason the plethora of Marxisms indicates both its intellectual vigor and social importance.

Mills was a man with moral convictions, and he was quite willing to stake his professional reputation in defense of these convictions. And he was above all a man of enlightenment, a believer in the practical worth and intellectual consequences of thoughts. His affinity with the writings of the Marxists lay in his belief in the human passions; something not always shared in by its own devotees. He had no illusions about Stalinist terrorism, yet he could ask himself whether Stalinism could lead to socialism no less than could reformism. He had no illusions about the cynical uses of Marxism in the Soviet Union, yet he could ask himself to what extent Marxism is sincerely used and usable as a political policy-making device. In short, Mills himself was a contributor to, no less than a commentator on, the dialogue now raging within international socialist circles. This book fulfilled Mills's own conception of the role of the man of ideas in the world of men. Thus at the point of his death, he achieved one of his major goals. He was a rare man, and this is a rare volume.

From *The American Journal of Sociology*, vol. 67, no. 6 (1962), pp. 711–12; and from *The American Scholar*, vol. 31, no. 4 (1962), pp. 646–52.

12

Utility Theory
as Social Theory*

Mill, John Stuart

John Stuart Mill has proven an enigma to commentators. Reforming liberals view him as a prophet of the gradual emancipation of the working class. Firm conservatives and Marxists join in viewing him as an arch supporter of private property. Mill has been charged, especially by his own age, with being a free-thinking unbeliever and by others as a clever apologist for theology and teleology. In Mill's own lifetime, his utilitarian friends accused him of selling out his principles to Coleridgean idealism. Paradoxically, the men at the helm of the aristocratic, romantic reaction attacked Mill as one of those business philosophers who made a fetish of the greatest happiness doctrine. Mill demands sensitive analysis, not mechanical, apriori platitudes. He is not someone given to grandiose claims. When he does offer new theories, it is in the pastel shades of psychological individualism rather than the broad claims of economic laws.

A book that does not make clear the social and philosophic basis of Mill's outlook will necessarily break down on many problems. This unfortunately is the case with Karl Britten's erudite study. Britten outlines the elements of Mill's philosophy well, but brings us only a trifle closer to a resolution of the problems that plagued Mill's romantic utilitarianism.

It is clear that Mr. Britten has a flair for logic and ontology; the chapters dealing with these aspects of Mill's thought (chapters 4, 5 and 6) contain the keenest analysis. Particularly noteworthy is the author's account of Mill's concept of the relation of science and method to the processes of induction and deduction. His comment that "Mill hoped to do for his own age what Locke had done for the eighteenth century; to conduct a fundamental inquiry into the *sources of our knowledge*" is certainly a guide to anyone exploring the labyrinth

---

* Karl Britten, *John Stuart Mill* (London: Penguin Books, 1953), pp. 224.

Iris Wessel Mueller, *John Stuart Mill and French Thought* (Urbana-Champaign: The University of Illinois Press, 1956), pp. 275.

of Mill's *Logic*. One could wish, nonetheless, for a sharper critique of the thinly veiled atomism that made Mill's "logic of experience" an empiricist ordering of sensations rather than a method for explaining the material world of flux.

The examination of Mill's views on politics and ethics is made in a vacuum. This probably accounts for the author's readiness to accept Mill at face value, an approach calculated to digest his confusions while eradicating none. Where the author tears himself away from an academic textual approach, he makes sound observations, such as his stress on the differences between Mill, his father James, and the rest of the earlier utilitarians. Just as the aristocracy had affected a political compromise with the ambitious middle class, Mill brought about an ideological compromise between the utilitarians who pushed for bourgeois goals and the romantic movement, which was nourished by an aristocracy unwilling to recognize that titled inheritance was running a poor second to moneyed inheritance in the nineteenth century. Had Britten gone beyond a statement of this connection between Wordsworth, Coleridge, and Mill to an examination of the social motivations behind this intellectual rapprochement, his case for Mill the romantic utilitarian would have been far stronger. As it is, we can be thankful for Britten's attention to this generally neglected source of the younger Mill's philosophy of man. Still, the author would have been wise to pursue his independent conclusions instead of scurrying back to Mill's texts for security. A bolder treatment, which tapped the rich storehouse of historical and intellectual materials, would have been of far greater value to layman and scholar alike.

It is appropriate to note Professor A.J. Ayer's editorial foreword to this and all other volumes in the Penguin series on philosophic history. He casually asserts that this "series is not designed to reflect the standpoint or to advance the views of any one philosophical school." However, the fact is that every volume in this series—from Stuart Hampshire's *Spinoza*, W.B. Gallie's *Pierce and Pragmatism*, and G.J. Warnock's *Berkeley* to the present work—reflects an acute, if perhaps unconscious, positivistic bias. As a result they all fail to cast the great philosophers of past ages in any socially meaningful context. These positivist authors zealously desire to reduce the history of philosophy to a history of complex linguistic problems. Rarely do they take time out from textual analysis to provide the reader with a grasp of a thinker's contribution to the heritage of human ideas and ideals. With someone like Mill, this approach has transparent weaknesses, since he was an eminently social actor as well as thinker.

The confusion over the intellectual legacy of Mill is being steadily lessened through the efforts of persevering scholars such as Hayek, Britten, Plamenatz, and St. John Packe. They have shown beyond question that the judgment of Mill's contemporaries was sound. Mill was a truly probing and practical mind. If modern historians of ideas differ on Mill's position on capital and labor, liberalism and conservatism, democracy and autocracy, it is understandable.

Mill was both scientific in methodology and eclectic in theory, liberal in terms of nineteenth-century British needs and illiberal in terms of twentieth-century realities. However not all or necessarily most of the ambiguities reside in Mill proper. His interpreters have too often viewed his writings as a solid mass requiring only synthesis to reveal the true Mill.

Mill lived a long life. He began his career at the tail end of the Enlightenment and continued well into the late Romantic epoch. The historical requirements of Mill's early years hinged on a final settlement of accounts between the aristocracy and the bourgeoisie, whereas during latter part of the nineteenth century, energies polarized between the power of commerce and the numerical power of the industrial mass. Where Mill stood on these social contests, more than general formulas on liberty, determined the character of his social philosophy, and if it made him a contradictory figure, it no less made him an interesting one. To the select group of scholars who have recognized this must now be added the author of *John Stuart Mill and French Thought*. Iris Mueller has worked out Mill's pivotal relation to St. Simon, Auguste Comte, and Alexis de Tocqueville with great clarity, and adeptly shows the impact on Mill of French upheavals of 1830, 1848, and to a lesser extent, the Paris Commune.

The concern Mill showed for the leading men and movements of France stemmed in some measure from his personal regard for the traditions and morals of a people he had come to respect first through his youthful contact with the Benthamite movement, (of which his father was a prime mover). But the basis of this concern was ultimately an awareness "that France is the key to European politics and ideology." France was reproducing the conflict between conservatism and liberalism at a more mature stage than anywhere else. The French were the first to seriously seek solutions to problems raised by a politically disenfranchised and economically dispossessed plebeian mass. And Mill is revealed as a man who steadily looked to the future to solve the riddles of the present. Naturally, just as Mill's intellectual predecessors learned from Helvetius the credo of the greatest happiness of the greatest number, so Mill was taken with the St. Simonian idea of the religion of humanity—of the need to universalize the respect of each man for every other man for the purpose of releasing human energies to achieve freedom.

Mueller's book shows Mill to be modest in his search for a solution to the problem of ensuring human freedom without compromising the libertarian tradition. In his empirical orientation, he differed decisively from his French colleagues. While learning from French philosophy, he remembered what it frequently lost sight of—that the philosopher is a seeker of truth, not necessarily its dispenser. The mystic cultism of St. Simon, no less than the spiritualism of Comte's science of sociology, fostered a radicalism that Mill feared was contrary to the spirits of science and democracy alike. Thus, while Mill absorbed and even defended the humanitarian and socialist faith of Gustave D'Eichthal and the genetic vision of Comte, he did not fall victim to the myth of infallibility common to advanced French social theory. Mueller proves groundless the charge that Mill reacted cautiously to French thought because he denied the possibility of a scientific explanation of social events. Mill's major concern was the search for factual anchors for a clearer understanding of the body politic. This search adequately attested to by Mill's *Logic* no less than his *Political Economy*. What separates him from Comte and St. Simon is the belief that truths, once possessed should be instruments for gaining further truths—not for stifling further inquiry. Mueller somewhat obscures the great divide between Mill and French utopianism and scientism, in her desire to trace Mill's indebtedness to French social philosophy.

Mill's regard for the efforts of Alexis de Tocqueville to develop an empirical sociology is illustrative of his willingness to learn from a scholar whose aristocratic bias was alien to Mill's spirit. In no small way, de Tocqueville transformed Mill from a liberal immersed in Bentham's calculus of pleasures and pains, to one who perceived the failings of political democratic theory—its substitution of the myth of the mass for the knowledge of the specialist. That *Democracy In America* had the immediate effect of turning Mill towards elitist sentiments should not obscure the fact that it had the long-range effect of turning Mill toward the "higher democracy" of socialism. As Mueller notes, it is paradoxical true that the de Tocqueville could do what the world of Victorian radicalism could not turn Mill towards socialism as the necessary economy of the future. Although Mill's socialism was of utopian vintage, it nonetheless had the merit of recognizing the threat of political despotism in the name of economic unity, long before it became an issue in the political arena.

The author is excellent in putting to rest the myth of Mill's laissez-faire ideology. It is effectively noted that Mill confined his defense of liberty to the murky areas of conscience and speculation, while in the clearly etched realm of polity, he urged a curb on individual caprice if it contrasted with the "permanent interests of a man as a progressive being." Mill emerges in this book as a far less sentimental thinker than is sometimes imagined. It is a prime merit of Mueller's work that it shows the tough-minded foundations of Mill's attitude to popular election, women's rights, labor laws, and the orderly function of government in general.

That Mill owes much of his political realism to French sources is beyond dispute. What may perhaps be questioned is whether Mill was responding to French theory or English political practice. The evidence indicates that the latter was probably the case. Mill's interest in France waned after the political quietude that followed the failure of the 1848 revolution. The author's conclusion that French theory was second only to Benthamite utilitarianism as an influence in Mill's outlook is not born out by either Mill's correspondence or activities. That the final chapter, which covers the period from 1848 to 1873, a fabulously rich period in French social history, is the most general in content and only incidentally involves Mill's relations to French philosophers or events, indicates that in Mill's late period, the period of the classic essays on freedom and organization, the influence of St. Simon, Comte, and de Tocqueville was either elliptical or nonexistent.

Mueller does much to explain the basis of the ambiguities that pervade Mill's social theory, noting that Mill served as a watchdog for freedom and economic progress, but due to the limitations of utilitarianism, proved unable to forge an adequate or consistent theory of history. The many editions of the *Political Economy*, with its attendant shifts from private property sentiments to a socialist orientation, in this reviewer's opinion more as a result of Harriet Taylor's influence than that of either St. Simon or Comte, indicate that Mill knew more about what he opposed than what he advocated. It is the prime merit of *John Stuart Mill and French Thought* that it reveals this facet of Mill's pluralism most carefully and does not attempt to present him as a consistent or synthetic figure. In sum, Iris Mueller has provided us the first clear picture in the English language of Mill's relation to French theory and politics. No one concerned with nineteenth-century intellectual history would fail to benefit from a careful reading of this comparative study.

From *Science and Society*, vol. 18, no. 3 (1954), pp. 282–283; and from *Philosophy: The Journal of the Royal Institute of Philosophy*, vol. 35, whole no. 133 (1960), pp. 181–83.

13

Phenomenological Social Science*

Natanson, Maurice

Maurice Natanson, editor of this volume, is to be complimented for his insight and initiative. The dialectical format of this reader makes possible the juxtaposition of issues in the sharpest and least cluttered way. Particularly instructive and useful is the collection of materials on the problem of *Verstehen,* which also forms the heftiest single section of the volume. The essays of Schutz, Hempel, Lavine, Nagel, Goldstein, and Natanson himself make for an extremely illuminating examination of this often neglected theme in the relationship of objectivity to subjectivity in the social sciences. However, a worthwhile addition might have been essay by Theodore Abel on this subject. It would have provided a contemporary sociological response to the *Verstehen* doctrine.

One does not judge a book by what it fails to include, but rather by the handling of the materials that are drawn upon. However, by their nature anthologies are exceptions to this rule, since the essays themselves are judged less than the format and setting that an editor provides for their presentation.

A possible shortcoming in this reader is reflected in the title itself. It is often difficult to know whether this volume is intended for philosophers interested in the social sciences or whether it is meant to clarify philosophical problems within the social sciences. The book is more successful in the first intent than the second. Absent are recent materials on the social sciences written by social scientists concerning philosophical implications of their work. Thus, there are no papers on problems of functionalism in the social sciences, an extremely vital concern for sociologists. There are no papers on the relationship between political manipulation and political science, a matter of urgent philosophical import for those in this field. There are no papers on the proper locus of anthropological activities: whether one should study mankind in a macroscopic way or kinship in a microscopic way.

---

* Maurice Natanson (editor), *Philosophy of the Social Sciences: A Reader* (New York: Random House), 1963. pp. 560.

While this reviewer is extremely sympathetic to the presentation of materials in a clearly delineated manner, the lines of debate in this reader are often drawn differently in present-day social science literature. For example, the classic paper by Max Weber on objectivity in the social sciences is herein answered by Leo Strauss's specialized critique of Weber's nihilism. As a matter of fact, the actual level of discourse has moved a considerable degree beyond this point. I am thinking particularly of the work of Abraham Edel and Maurice Mandelbaum in philosophy and Robert K. Merton and Alvin W. Gouldner in sociology.

Another aspect of the volume I would take issue with is the restriction of the dialectical format almost exclusively to the conflict between the empiricist and phenomenalist schools. As a result, all other schools of thought are left out of account. The final section, for example, is concerned with the nature of philosophy; whether it is or is not a science unto itself. A.J. Ayer's distinctions between philosophy and science are not really addressed much less answered in the paper by Maurice Merleau-Ponty. However interesting this paper is intrinsically, it deals with a different set of questions. A bolder, if more controversial choice in this section would have been I.V. Kuznetsov's direct reply to Ayer (*Soviet Studies in Philosophy*, Vol. 1, No. 1). This would have shown that philosophies other than existentialism challenge the empiricist fortress.

A good deal of material on philosophical issues related to behaviorism, operant conditioning, historicism, and the many "isms" that inhabit social science mansions, have also not found their way into the volume. Thus, the essays in the periodical literature on the philosophy of science are not adequately represented. Similarly, the philosophical studies from the social science literature are likewise inadequately accounted for.

While these criticism reveal little more than that this reviewer would have compiled such an anthology quite differently, in a deeper sense, they reveal how provocatively Professor Natanson did his job. I would not want to leave the reader with anything but the most positive attitudes toward the enterprise that Professor Natanson has herein realized. His own commentaries are just and acute. His bibliography is a fine checklist of the important writings in the areas covered. If anything, I would say this volume displays the need for Natanson to produce volume two of this reader. It would be valuable to have a sequel volume that focuses on philosophic problems arising out of social science findings, as well a an examination of the way in which social science reproduces classical philosophic rifts. And few people are better equipped for such an undertaking than the editor of *Philosophy of the Social Sciences*.

From *Philosophy and Phenomenological Research*, vol. 24, no. 1 (1964), pp. 289–90.

14

Closed Societies
and Open Minds*

Oppenheimer, J. Robert

The two books by the distinguished physicist J. Robert Oppenheimer could fruitfully be read without reference to the current situation in science and philosophy. Indeed, they were designed with such a Broad purpose in mind. Yet for a total appraisal, the milieu in which Oppenheimer works is of importance. His *Science and the Common Understanding* is as an attempt at a philosophic estimate of modern physics. And it is as an attempt to relate the scientific life to the ethical life that his *Open Mind* can be judged in all its passion and humanist impulse. Together these books reveal Oppenheimer as a man of theoretical depth and practical insight into the limits as well as the genius of human beings. His essentially optimistic view that the scientific enterprise can demonstrably heal the deepest wounds of men and nations, leads one to feel a kinship with this brilliant yet modest man, even though one may disagree with him on the premises that permit him to arrive at such a judgment.

Science and the Common Understanding, the superior of the two works by virtue of the author's intimacy with the issues involved, exhibits a keen historical sense of the transition of science from mechanism to relativism. In tracing developments in atomic physics from Newton to Rutherford and then to Bohr, Schrodinger, and Einstein, the author reveals the character of this change. Scientifically, it was a change from an externalized and mechanical description of atomic movement, to atomic analysis in terms of its internal components on one hand, and the motion of atomic phenomena in terms of the wave-particle dualism on the other.

Philosophically, relativity in physics permitted a change from a purely causal description of the world, to a complementaristic description (i.e., a partial description of events in terms of the specific phenomena under consideration).

---

* J. Robert Oppenheimer, *The Open Mind* (New York: Simon and Schuster, 1955), pp. 146.

J. Robert Oppenheimer, *Science and the Common Understanding* (New York: Simon and Schuster, 1954), pp. 120.

The development of physics, in Oppenheimer's view, necessitates an essentially pluralistic approach to social life. An object studied in isolation for its peculiar pattern of behavior is examined one way; but this same object, taken in its total group functioning, is unanalyzable with any degree of precision, and hence statistical laws must suffice.

The appeal to Bohr's complementarily principle, which is the unifying thread in Oppenheimer's book, illustrates the quandary of modern physics. Oppenheimer does not attempt to demonstrate that complementarity actually replaces causal determinism, as a necessary ontological deduction from physics. But like Bohr, he merely assumes that it is a required philosophic standpoint. Unlike Bohr, however, Oppenheimer does not attempt to use complementarity as an instrument for bludgeoning optional approaches to philosophy. He believes that only when relativity is misunderstood can it be used as a tool for destroying a determinist universe and that it would be improper to view complementarity as lending credence to Eddington's world of physical mystery based on atomic indeterminacy.

Oppenheimer uses the concept of complementarity in an enlightened, if rather novel way. It serves to vindicate his antinomic vision of physical and human nature. In physics "there are two ways of describing a system, two sets of concepts, two centers of preoccupation." In the biological realm, there are similar schisms: between change and eternity, growth and order, spontaneity and symmetry. In the human scene, there are the antinomic relations of freedom and necessity, practice and thought, the individual and the community. The essential polarity of life is the most profound philosophic consequence of the new physics. What connects the antinomies is the unitary nature of experience. And this unity has nothing in common with the vain attempt to unite all things in a closed system of mind or nature. Oppenheimer emerges as a conscious advocate of the Enlightenment in its rigorous eighteenth-century form. He could well take as his theme Diderot's belief that when there is an absence of information with which to evaluate, men still are able to live in suspension of judgment.

The difficulty with Oppenheimer's position is that in place of the inviolable closed system, his complementarist framework compels him to set up the immutability of the open system—the pluralistic, directionless world of radical empiricism. The forward motion of life stems not from a simple acceptance of antinomies but from their steady resolution. In one place, he presents a tautology that underscores the lack of anchor points in his outlook: "The greatest of the changes that science has brought about is the acuity of change." But the direction of this change is left purposefully vague. In consequence, Oppenheimer's writings tend to use humility as a cloak for eclecticism and modesty as a disguise for bowing to the groundless canon of scientific limitation.

For Oppenheimer, antinomic relations extend to the social as well as the inner functioning of science. The polarity between science as the path to abundance and also to the obliteration of civilization plays a paramount role in his thinking. This is the controversial idea that connects the final pages of *Science and the Common Understanding* with *The Open Mind.* It also perhaps had more to do with his forced retirement from government service than did any other factor. For here was an *honnête homme* wandering about the labyrinths of power, saying that universal peace is a scientific necessity. By his very presence, he served to discomfort unsocial scientists and unscientific social theorists.

For the most part, *The Open Mind* is a series of separate lectures on the theme of science and peace. It reveals Oppenheimer to have been aware from the outset that "there is only one future of atomic explosives—that they should never be used in war." It seems to this reviewer that his views on the latent power of atomic warfare are, in the light of present knowledge, far more sober than the position taken by P.M.S. Blackett in *Fear, War and the Bomb.* Blackett tended to balance nuclear weapons against conventional armaments in a sort of facetious debit and credit arrangement. On the other hand, Blackett demonstrated that he was a more realistic political by exposing some dogmas that Oppenheimer seems to take for granted (i.e., the intransigence of the Russians and the liberality of Americans concerning the issue of control of nuclear energy). It is curious that Oppenheimer makes so little of the debates within scientific circles as to the uses and abuses of atomic weapons. Given his personal odyssey, one would have expected, and welcomed, such an exposition.

In *The Open Mind*, Oppenheimer reveals himself as a man possessed by the social import of the atomic power he helped unleash. Speaking for his segment of the community of physicists, he also reveals the moral quality of his person: "Nor can we forget that these weapons, as they were in fact used, dramatized so mercilessly the inhumanity and evil of modern war. In some sort of crude sense which no vulgarity, no humor, no overstatement can quite extinguish, the physicists have known sin; and this is a knowledge which they cannot lose." His private antinomy hinges on ways of eradicating this guilt. He must resolve the moral sense, the love of humanity and enlightenment, with the tragic sense of conflict, the decimation of civilization. He feels the alienation of the scientist from society with intensity. "To put it with great brutality, the point is that the scientist is not in society today, any more than is the artist or the philosopher."

Towards this alienation he reacts in two contradictory ways. In his essay "The Scientist in Society," he urges a return to the principles of the Enlightenment, to the battle for a scientific community connected to the needs of everyman, whereas in "The Prospects in the Arts and Sciences," he seeks to combat this alienation by insulating the intellectual from the terrors of society, by a system of "local and parochial patronage that a university can give." When Oppenheimer overcomes this private antinomy, perhaps he will be in a better position to understand that the schisms of life are not just to be gazed at in reverential awe, but must be grappled with and resolved.

From *Science and Society*, vol. 12, no. 1 (1958), pp. 83–86.

15

Science, Religion and Natural Philosophy*

Westfall, Richard S.

It is a great pleasure to report the publication of two such fine complementary volumes in the social history of science. They are of fundamental importance to the comprehension of Newton and his century, but their precise virtue is to continue the work of Herbert Butterfield, G.N. Clark, Robert Merton, and B. Hessen in focusing attention on the tangled web of intelligence and ideology in seventeenth-century England. Both the Westfall dissertation and the essays in *Newton's Papers* by I. Bernard Cohen, Thomas S. Kuhn, Marie Boas, Perry Miller, and Robert Schofield and above all Charles C. Gillispie's brilliant paper on Fontenelle's biography of Newton, each in their own way serve as healthy antidotes to the anthropomorphism that riddles much work on Newton and the science of his age.

Whether Newton was ultimately the leading figure in the struggle between science and religion or ultimately the conservative showing how belief in natural religion inspires the direction of physical research, is an interesting puzzle. However, such a perspective tells us more about twentieth-century debates about the consequences of scientific method than the context in which Newton operated. Analysts of Newton have transgressed the divide between history and metaphysics more than is either necessary or desirable. Of Newton it might well be said that the poets praised him, the scientists prized him, while the philosophers of English Anglicanism made a mystery of him.

Westfall's study of the virtuosi (those Englishmen who had both a general interest in science and a specific area of empirical pursuit) and Cohen's general introduction to *Newton's Papers* both reveal an essential dualism that existed throughout the seventeenth century between the empirical requirements of

* Bernard Cohen, *Isaac Newton's Papers and Letters on Natural Philosophy and Related Documents* (Cambridge: Harvard University Press, 1958), pp. 501.

Richard S. Westfall, *Science and Religion in Seventeenth Century England* (New Haven, Conn.: Yale University Press, 1958), pp. 235.

natural science and the social and psychological attachments for revealed religion. What distinguishes Newton from the rest of the virtuosi is the fact that, although he was son to the great dualism, he was no less father to the Enlightenment efforts to cope with and overcome this split between matter and spirit.

The worth of the Westfall volume largely resides in its examination of the constituent parts of this dualism. The virtuosi (John Ray, Thomas Sprat, Robert Boyle, Walter Charleton, Joseph Glanvill, Robert Hooke, and Isaac Newton) inherited the religious attitude of wonder toward nature and yet worked mightily to explain and thus remove wonder from nature. They shared a debt to Epicurean atomism and yet had to deny the Epicurean ethical and social teachings that made the ancient a unified theorist. They insisted that scientific reason was the surest proof of religious belief yet were reticent to allow revealed religion to stand in judgment of natural science. All believed in an omnipotent God yet assigned him to impotence by making him a mechanical force. Tradition adds a wry note: it was even whispered that God was really to be found in the propositions of Newton's *Principia*. These polarities underscore the shakiness of the union of rationalistic faith and empirical discovery.

These volumes call attention to the essentially conservative social views of the scientific innovators, the virtuosi. The more shaky the theoretical underpinnings, the more desperate were their statements of dedication to theism. This is apparent even in the titles of the virtuosi nonscientific works: Charleston's *The Darkness of Atheism Dispelled by the Light of Nature*, Boyle's *The Excellency of Theology*, and Glanvill's *A Blow at Modern Sadducism*. Even Newton gave open support to Bentley's *A Confutation of Atheism*.

Accounting for the religious bent of leading scientific figures of seventeenth-century England is the task of Westfall's book and of Perry Miller's essay. Their answers run roughly along three lines. The first is the essential social middle-ground position, which led the virtuosi to fear the revolutionary potential of the "enthusiasts" no less than that of the "atheists." The rational religion, like the rational science, was to be thoughtful and reflective; Religious pietism was to entail social quietism. The second factor is the shared Anglican upbringing that informed the ideology of the life of the scientist gentleman. The third, and perhaps the decisive, element is the foreboding that the knowing virtuoso must have felt about the consequences of mechanical science. Would the next age approach science as self-sufficient and thus ignore the teleological proofs or providential rule? As Westfall indicates, the virtuosi nourished, or better, invented, the atheists within their own thoughts. Atheism was the vague feeling of uncertainty that their studies had raised—less the uncertainty of their own convictions as uncertainty as to the ultimate conclusions that might lie hidden in the principles of natural science."

Newton's relation to this tradition was the crowning contradiction. He made it easier for the Enlightenment to exclaim and propound the scientific virtues of a natural theology: "Look, the king has no natural throne." Westfall and Miller do much to dispel the myth of Newton's mysticism by citing texts that show Newton did not join the other virtuosi in their anti-atheistic clamor. He left the all-important issue of material or immaterial agents open to individual judgment. Indeed, Newton noted that "contradictious phrases" may be due to actual paradoxes in nature and that the search for metaphysical certainty was a social rather than a scientific requirement. In this, Newton was closer to Hume than to theism.

Thus, the question of whether the world harmonies postulated by theology were or were not original sources for the general theory of gravity pales in significance next to the fact that the actual consequence of Newtonian science was materialistic—verifying the private fears of the virtuosi and the exclamations of the outright enemies of natural philosophy. Newton's extension of Christianity into natural religion was but a moment away from a frank avowal of naturalism without religion. This is the transformation brought about by Voltaire and French deism. Neither the original documents nor the critical analysis lead to any other conclusion.

The most serious shortcoming in this edition of *Newton's Papers are* inherent in the disastrous consequences of a facsimile edition. We are confronted with a mélange of types. Some of the type faces are difficult enough to read in the original, but given the natural bleeding effect of offset photography, deciphering their reproduction requires formidable effort for even a hardened bibliophile. When we have innumerable editions, as in the Shakespeare works, then a facsimile edition for collectors has meaning. But what justification can be found in this case, where the Newton papers are gathered for the first time, is beyond the reviewer's comprehension. Library sponsorship for this volume should not have necessitated fossilized attitudes.

Finally, if so many pages can be given over to selections from Bentley's *A Confutation of Atheism*, then at least one of the lesser-known drafts of Newton's own work on religion, *Irenicum*, might have been included. Nonetheless, this volume is sure to take its place beside the *Principia* and the *Optiks* as a guide to understand the scope of Newton's efforts.

The objection to the Westfall study is of a more consequential sort. It involves the difference between competence and creation. The total spectrum of religious-philosophic thought involves not only the Anglican orthodoxy and the virtuosi heresy but the atheistic perspective as well. Specifically, it must include the relation of the virtuosi to Thomas Hobbes. Westfall's statements on this score are paradoxical, and his stated reasons for not dealing with Hobbes are unconvincing. Neither the singularity of Hobbes' views nor the idea that "he would require a volume by himself" can be seriously defended, since the first objection is precisely what makes Hobbes interesting and the latter objection characterizes nearly all the virtuosi. Nor does the failure of the Royal Society to propose him for membership rule out Hobbes. For contrary to Westfall's statements on an absence of concern for the activities of the Royal Society, Hobbes did indeed display great interest in participation, as evidenced by the frequency with which he submitted scientific papers and demonstrations. The Royal Society's failure to consider him for membership was unquestionably a reason for Hobbes's disdain for a scientific society that gave little attention to the fundamental theory of motion and too much time to artifacts and contraptions. Of course, Hobbes himself did not help matters. Rather than see his philosophical and political writings as sufficiently meritorious to warrant membership, he insisted on submitting papers in areas of applied technology where he was intellectually vulnerable.

Westfall is compelled to violate his reasoning on several occasions in order to explain the heat with which many of the virtuosi attacked atheism. It was not so much their feelings of guilt as a response to the threat of the "Hobbists," whom the virtuosi assured everyone were as evil as atheists and Sadducees, although none could ever be found. The examination of Hobbes' role in relation to the scientific and religious currents of the seventeenth century remains to be done. We can, however, as a result of Westfall's study, at least see what the other operative philosophies of the age included and excluded and how Westfall's thesis about the religious consciousness of the virtuosi would have to be expanded to further investigate the naturalistic alternatives that were also a part of the attempt at a theistic-scientific synthesis.

From *Diogenes*. Whole no. 27 (1959), pp. 125–128.

Part II

Development and Change

16

Politics, Labor and Development*

Alba, Victor

According to a common canard expressed by authors and publishers alike, a book loses something in translation. While this is undoubtedly true in a great many cases, the English-speaking reader of Alba's book, *Politics and the Labor Movement in Latin America*, can take comfort in the fact that he is reading a volume that has gained a great deal in the translation. For what has been done in the English language edition is not simple translation and copy editing but a considerable overhauling and rearrangement of the text. Tabular materials and charts are now integrated into the text so that the text explains them. Some of the more irrelevant tables included in the Spanish original have been eliminated altogether. Further, the narrative itself is presented in a quieter, less strident manner. Many of the flamboyant paragraphs have been toned down, and some (but not enough) of the ideological rhetoric inherited from Spanish Civil war salad days has been similarly converted into a more reasonable, appreciative analysis of the special features of labor history in Latin America—and the part played by Leftists of all persuasions in this history.

Of course, in Mr. Alba's defense, there was a great deal of sound stuff to work with, so the utilitarian results of the translation could almost be predicted. This is not simply another book from the pen of a *pensador*. It is the first serious synthesis of labor history south of the border. Until now, we have had to literally excavate materials on Latin America labor from books on communism, entrepreneurial history, and political structure. While there are individual monographs on the social study of labor and union structures—particularly papers by Aguiar-Walker, Moises Poblete (most, but by no means all of which are properly acknowledged by Alba)—this is the first true synthetic effort.

Labor conflict in Latin America dates back to the mid-sixteenth century when the black gold miners of Venezuela organized a work stoppage against

* Victor Alba, *Politics and the Labor Movement in Latin America* (Stanford: Stanford University Press, 1969), pp. 404.

their foreign oppressors. And in 1598, Indian miners in Mexico struck to protest their work conditions. Sporadic indigenous labor movements were in evidence from then until the end of the nineteenth century, when entirely new forms of organization were introduced by European immigrants. The mixture of indigenous and immigrant styles has made Latin American union organization quite unique. Militant demands are made by loosely organized federations; general strikes are called for strictly political goals; nationalistic ideologies are expressed in localistic actions, and revolutionary demands are lodged by reformist politicians.

Yet, as Alba well appreciates, the organized labor movement still attracts only a small minority of the Latin American work force. The uneven nature of socioeconomic development has its direct counterpart in the labor movement-with feudal vestiges remaining powerful even in highly developed factory management and in the relatively weak organization of workers outside the capital cities. The blunt fact is that the working class is growing at a slower rate than the population as a whole. Thus, the anomaly of industrialization without unionization threatens to undermine the working-class urban proletariat even before it launches any major effort at political control. This comforts not only the urban and rural middle classes but also adds fuel to the revolutionary fires of guerrilla ideologists who claim that the organized union movement has neither the membership size nor program scope to treat the basic problems of Latin American underdevelopment. It is unfortunate that Alba dedicates so few pages to what has clearly emerged as a central issue in the Latin American labor movement—its capacity (or lack thereof) for promoting revolutionary change.

The first part of Alba's book constitutes an excellent primer on the major sociological factors in the study of Latin America: racial and ethnic population composition, the role of immigration in stimulating revolutionary ideas about labor equality, the function of nativism in the unions, and the general stimulus provided by industrialization. This section may be valuable for introducing Latin America to North Americans, but as an interpretation of the origins of labor history, it is too journalistic and opinionated.

The second and meaty part of the book develops an ideological account of anarcho-syndicalist, socialist, Communist, and populist types of labor organization. Alba almost guarantees the considerable repetition in this section by viewing the nation as the central organizing principles. That Alba is aware of the methodological dilemmas involved in carving Latin America into nation-states is clear from the fact that he wisely ignores this approach in discussing Communist and populist influences in labor. On the other hand, Alba chooses to preserve his scheme on the grounds that Communist penetration of labor was a special phenomenon, externally induced, and hence not subject to nation-by-nation accounting. In my opinion, however, this same internationalist argument could be made about many socialist and anarcho-syndicalist unions, albeit not with any sense of Soviet Comintern direction; and hence not with the specific distortions engendered by Stalinism.

This inconsistency notwithstanding, the third and final section of the book offers the first full-scale examination of the ideology and organization of the Apristas in Peru, Acción Democratica in Venezuela, PRI in Mexico, and MNR in Bolivia. But this examination of "populist movements" suffers from an ambiguity between populism within the labor movement and a more general political party populism. What is required, and is unfortuately not provided, is some correlational analysis, if any exists, between party populism and unionization in nations such as Peru, Venezuela, and Bolivia. Recent events in at least two out of these three nations indicate that correlations are low. Further, events suggest that populism, when it becomes more real than theoretical, is quickly subjected to military domination.

The sparse section on Cuba, buried in a limited chapter on the Caribbean region, is somewhat incomplete. It makes no attempt to revise judgments in the light of Zeitlin's *Revolutionary Politics and the Cuban Working Class* and work by O'Connor on the Cuban political economy. Alba's materials on the Cuban labor movement are nearly as controversial as the movement itself. Alba has a strong tendency to treat the clandestine and conspiratorial aspects of communism in the labor movement, at the expense of a detailed analysis of labor organization and the role of radical ideologies in the formation of mass struggles. Hence, problems of labor dependence on political machines, maintaining traditionalist norms in industrial contexts, establishing conditions of social welfare, and the absence of middle-sized cities with predictable planning indices, tend to be swallowed up in broad ideological divisions of Latin labor movements that were characteristic of an earlier epoch.

Although it has long been apparent that the crux of the developmental thrust is the industrialization process, treatment of this process has been strangely one sided. Factory management, industrial exporting, and motivational studies have tended to undervalue the pivotal role of organized labor in Latin America. Alba's book, the first full-scale treatment of labor organization and ideology, should be a welcome addition to the literature on development. It will certainly stimulate additional work on labor organization.

Here too, however, the need for deeper work is evident. No attempt is made to study the effects, if any, of overseas corporate activities in inhibiting or shaping unionism in Latin America. Alba does deal with continental labor organizations—but more in terms of the effects of U.S. union activities on their Latin American counterparts than of evaluating U.S. government policy per se. The role of large mineral trusts operating in nations such as Chile and Bolivia are simply not treated. Instead, we are told that "the miners' union, under socialist leadership, struck for three months. The profits from the copper agreement were to have been used in financing land reform; the strike cost the government 30 million dollars, for political reasons; thus the miners effectively sabotaged the changes of agrarian reform." The chapter on the Chilean working class ends on this note—without a hint of what the strike was about or how the strikers perceived the issues.

This sort of writing is hardly convincing; more important, it undermines Alba's general claims concerning working-class apathy and his personal claims of intense dedication to working-class unionism. The forms of worker participation in the political process are rich and varied, but they are not uniformly deep. In this, trade unionism may have more in common with North American than European models of worker participation.

The production of the book has been materially aided by a dedicated group of scholars for whom Latin America holds few fears and many challenges. Alba has used their findings selectively and, on the whole, intelligently. Yet, despite its length, *Politics and the Labor Movement in Latin America* can best be described as suggestive. This is the kind of work that makes possible a definitive rendition of social stratification in the future. Alba's study is a clear reminder of how far we have come, no less than how much further we must go, to arrive at a general theory of Latin American social structure.

From *Economic Development and Cultural Change*, vol. 18, no. 2 (1970), pp. 290–93.

17

Misanthropism as Conservatism*

Banfield, Edward C.

Edward C. Banfield is perhaps better at reviewing, or at least summarizing, his own book of essays, *Here The People Rule,* than are most reviewers—certainly than myself. His writing style is determined rather than elegant, and his substance is uniformly consistent rather than entirely persuasive. Indeed, considerable pugnacity characterizes most of these twenty essays. Alternative approaches are dismissed rather than considered, moral prescriptions are taken for granted rather than debated. Among these first principles are the Hobbesian belief that all agreement is based upon coercion; the Burkean belief that statesmen consider circumstances while professors only possess general views of society; the Tocquevillian belief that every extension of government authority creates new opportunities and incentives for moral corruption; and a deeply held neo-Platonic belief in the venality of ordinary people—their natural propensity to consider dishonesty as the best, because most profitable, posture. These are the four cornerstones of *Here the People Rule.*

Indeed, one is led to the conclusion that Professor Banfield's title is more than slightly tinged with mockery and mirth. For this is not a celebration of two centuries of American constitutional democracy, but a warning to those who equate the rule of law with the wishes of people. In nearly every essay, Banfield gives voice to unreconstructed elitism. Thus in "Federalism and the Dilemma of Popular Government," we are informed that "what is dismaying is the prospect that eventually, perhaps soon, the American people, having forgotten that the great principles of the revolution was limited government, will demand that government do what cannot be done and the attempting of which will destroy popular government itself." And "In Defense of the American Party System," tells us that "there is a danger that reform will chip away the foundations of power upon which the society rests."

---

* Edward C. Banfield, *Here the People Rule: Selected Essays* (New York and London: Plenum Press, 1985), pp. 348.

In a sense, Banfield is less a conservative than a restorationist. He believes in the American past with far more fervor than he does the American present. In "Party Reform in Retrospect," Banfield bemoans the undoing of the American system by those liberals who fail to understand "that man is a creature more of passions than of reason" and that government "must have limited objects: to promote the life, liberty and the pursuit of happiness of its citizens, *not* to right all wrongs." Further, since we are informed that policy science is meta-physical madness" and that policy science has the absurd task of transferring "power from the corrupt, the ignorant, and the self-serving to the virtuous, the educated and the public-spirited," no solution seems in sight—save the categorical rejection of administered reform, in favor of unsponsored drift, "I do not see how, after explaining why things are as they are, one can go on to say how they could be different."

Within this strangely courageous, if quixotic framework, Banfield has collected his fugitive essays. To the unanticipated benefit of his adversaries, the policy makers rather than to any enhancement of conservative political doctrine, Banfield insists on the foolhardiness of meliorative action. But in his dogged skepticism of reforms and policies from the 1929–1981 epoch, he gives those policy analysts and liberal reformers substantial food for thought. For example, policy makers have come forth with relatively few program innovations, whereas program evaluations have "absorbed more time and money in the last decade than all has other policy research put together." Bookkeeping functions rather than theory constructions characterize too much policy research. His outstanding comparativist paper, "The Political Implications of Metropolitan Growth" scores some telling points in showing how urban policy has not so much decreased population densities, but rather increased class polarization.

We oftentimes associate the "big picture" and the "outrageous hypothesis" with the radical wing of social research. This is clearly less the case in political science than in sociology. For in fact, the value of Banfield's book is to draw attention to the big picture and the outrageous proposition that recalls for us the first principles. Even if one heartily rejects the restorationist implications of Banfield's belief that the British system has reformed itself through traditional modes, whereas the American system has become dangerously removed from its original principles of life, liberty, and happiness—the urban crisis has hardly been resolved through expediency. Likewise, Banfield's belief that public libraries should be places for serious reading not broad-based entertainment, is not just an ideological posture but a functional alternative to an institution that has become decreasingly effective. Finally, the critique of Kenneth Arrow's social choice aggregations as explanatory rather than predictive, is a corrective to economism as an ideology. Banfield restores a world in which choice involves arbitration, struggle, and values, not just an aggregated set of interests.

However, after reading these essays, even when all due allowances are made for the author's rhetorical excesses, we are left with an empty feeling. The end of this high-level theorizing is what Banfield himself terms low-level assumptions. The use of good practical judgment; familiarity with the habits, customs, traditions, and outlooks; and concern for the particulars of issues is no special preserve of the social sciences. Indeed, Banfield leans toward the view that "the gossip of the court" is its special preserve. But then we are left with a seething antagonism for all forms of policy, reform, planning, and budgeting. This animus for the present is ultimately a disbelief in the American system as it has evolved, and worse, a denial of a democratic future.

In a telltale assault on policy as an effort to change the American system, Banfield failed to appreciate the extent to which policy, its weaknesses fully registered, serves to preserve the American system. It does this by providing mechanisms for all sorts of disenfranchised, discouraged, and disengaged to make America their own, and to do so within the broad contours of the rule of law (not the rule of people). I find it strange and worrisome that restorationists and radicals should share a belief in doing nothing—the former in the name of a golden age of founding fathers, the latter in the name of a golden age yet to come, of revolutionary perfection. Instead, I find it reassuring to argue that the task of social science is to continue on its incrementalist path of explanation and prediction (even with the "waste" factor duly acknowledged). To argue for a return to an eighteenth-century of conservative moralists strikes this reader as pretentious. It is hardly an appropriate response to the omnipresent set of nineteenth-century, revolutionary antimoralists who likewise deny the meliorist claims of planners and policymakers. For those who are interested in learning more of the differences between new and old conservatisms, this set of papers is required reading; but for those with other agendas or concerns, the volume is disappointing.

From *Contemporary Sociology*, vol. 15, no. 5 (1986), pp. 774–75.

18

Democracy and Development in a One-Party State*

Casanova, Pablo Gonzalez

This is a tour de force, a theoretically sophisticated and statistically informed study of modern Mexico. It represents the coming of age, if not of Mexican sociology, at least of one Mexican sociologist. And it can be recommended strongly for readers interested in social change and economic development.

The book is a treatise in political sociology. It moves from an examination of how the Mexican political revolution was compelled to face the social problems of overcoming local *caciques* and *caudillos* to discussing the need to absorb the military and to accommodate a small but increasingly powerful managerial estate. In other words, the political structure of Mexico is defined by this unique combination of traditionalist and new economic power, neither able to overwhelm the other, both requiring the strong single-party state. Why the same sort of political system did not arise elsewhere, for example England after its Great Compromise, would make a fascinating study in contrasts.

The book provides a frank indication of North American influence, particularly an appreciation of the functional aspects of the anti-Yankee spirit. "Mexico may be one of the best established countries in Latin America and perhaps the only one in which anti-American sentiments have become transformed into a strategy of national independence and development." In this way Casanova both accounts for and yet confronts the rhetoric of the extreme Left in a calm and dispassionate way.

Casanova contends that Mexican society, in contrast to Mexican polity, had to achieve its own resolution after the revolution. It had to resolve the relationship of church and state. It had to find the way to institutionalize the counterrevolution, and it had to develop a means for redistributing wealth that would not threaten the social system. The partial and piecemeal way Mexican society handled such issues perfectly illustrates the incomplete revolution.

---

* Pablo Gonzalez Casanova, *La Democracia en Mexico* (Mexico City: Ediciones Era, S.A., 1965), pp. 262.

With the revolution frozen in its incompleteness, the chances for any kind of socialist revolution or even a fascist counterrevolution are held to be rather remote. It would seem, therefore, that Mexico is joining those societies that Gino Germani has called modernized, (i.e., fully mobilized and integrated mass societies). Mexico is rapidly becoming a country of the nonevent, or for the more militant minded, the uneventful. Paradoxically, this uneventfulness is itself one of the most remarkable aspects of the democratization of Mexico, a nation with one of the most turbulent and violent histories in all of Spanish America. Still, Casanova sometimes confuses tranquility with liberality. My own guess is that the apathy factor is much greater than he allows.

Professor Casanova manages to make a virtue of eclecticism—a rare feat in itself. He uses Marxist and liberal ideologies to overcome "the schizophrenia of social scientific analysis." And in a brilliant pair of chapters (10 and 11) he shows that both Marxist and liberalist premises lead to quite similar conclusions concerning the future of Mexico. As is suggested by contemporary political sociology, Mexico is unlikely to undergo another revolutionary upheaval in the near future, despite the pronounced political problem of single-party democracy-or what I choose to call party charisma along a Democratic-Falangist axis. The development of a strictly middle-class understanding of the Mexican revolution has led to a situation in which the revolution is the end for the ruling classes and only the beginning for the rural classes.

The authenticity of the Mexican Revolution of 1910–1920 is as significant as its incomplete character. One finds in Mexico the unresolved dualisms of a popular revolution of the masses that ended by consecrating a benign military dictatorship of the middle classes; a very rapid growth of the industrial sector, that leaves the traditional peasant sector untouched and unabsorbed; and a national culture more vital than nearly any other in a Latin America wallowing in mimesis of mass cultures. Casanova's use of the concept of democracy in Mexico has an ironic and biting aspect because the author is clearly aware not only of how far Mexico has come but of how far it has yet to go to realize a mature concept of democracy.

A number of weaknesses in *Democracy in Mexico* cannot go unnoticed. There is a gap between text and data. The two sections of the book, 196 pages of text and the nearly 100 pages of statistics are not adequately linked (This was indeed handled far better in the English language edition that appeared in 1970). Furthermore, the two portions of the book do not always reveal the same conclusion. Quite a number of the charts are subject to other interpretations than the ones provided in the text. While there is an exceptionally good analysis of the dual society in Mexico, there is no corresponding comparative analysis of mass class-dichotomies elsewhere in Latin America. Indeed, there is no real comparative international material. The only references are to the United States, yet comparisons with Brazil might have been more fruitful.

In my opinion, Casanova fails to recognize the brittle, essentially unimaginative condition of present-day politics in Mexico. The Mexican revolution was indeed pragmatic at its outset. However, this pragmatism has hardened over the years, leading to a presidentialist dictatorship of the middle. With the thorough determination of PRI to establish a universal consensus has come an ideological liberalism that is more rhetorical than real and that excludes political participation of other parties.

Due to its inelasticity, the delicately laced system of Mexican society could be irrevocably undone. Further, any drastic asymmetry in the pillars of present-day power, any political miscalculations as to which sector of society needs what at whose expense, and Mexico could once again become a dramatically eventful nation. Casanova himself, while minimizing the possibilities of further discontinuities in political development, does hold open the possibility of either (or both) revolution or counterrevolution. He leans to the latter possibility, and on this I agree with him. Yet it might have been just as important to locate more precisely the sources for potential disequilibrium as to describe the present temporary basis for equilibrium.

Whether the analysis provided in *La Democracia En Mexico* is correct in all its details (or appropriate for a define time-frame), is hard to say. Casanova warns against conversion of intuitive guesswork into scientific truisms. Yet his own position comes perilously close to celebrating a system for democratic promises yet to be delivered to the Mexican people. But despite these admissions and premonitions, *La Democracia En Mexico* should be widely read with great profit by political sociologists and by area specialists. It would not hurt Mexican politicians to do likewise.

From *American Sociological Review*, vol. 31, no. 1 (1966), pp. 143–44.

19

Taking Lives and Developing Societies*

Davis, Shelton H.

The intentional termination of life on a large, impersonal scale has become a subject of extensive public discourse. Plagues inflicted by people on people-the family of "cides": infanticide, regicide, ecocide, ethnocide, and particularly genocide—have flourished in our epoch. The taking of life, for reasons of state power, has become an increasingly significant theme for political anthropologists and political sociologists. But as Chaim Shatan indicates in his brilliant essay "Genocide and Bereavement," in *Genocide in Paraguay:* "The pulse of writing about genocide—no matter how scholarly, no matter how literary—leaves one weary, sad, with bated breath, like the writing of epitaphs."

Unquestionably, the ceaseless human rights debate, more than any impulse of social science toward large-scale relevance, is largely responsible for the interest in the spate of recent writing on genocide. It is a melancholy truth that scholarly discourse becomes part of public discourse only when it is attuned to prominent political issues. But we should at least be grateful that, as a result, attention is drawn to books like Shelton Davis's *Victims of the Miracle* and Richard Arens's *Genocide in Paraguay*, which otherwise might be discussed only in review sections of scholarly journals.

Another factor helps to account for interest in genocide. The slow, steady liquidation of Indian populations in present-day Latin America sadly recalls the Indian liquidation in nineteenth-century North America—a sequence that proceeds from opening new lands and settler communities; to legal arrangements for the protection of Indians; to violation of legal arrangements by the new, technologically armed settlers; "pacific" military expeditions; and finally to dismemberment of the population in manhunts and roundups. This

---

* Richard Arens (editor), *Genocide in Paraguay* (Philadelphia: Temple University Press, 1977), pp. 171.

Shelton H. Davis, *Victims of the Miracle: Development and the Indians of Brazil* (New York: Cambridge University Press, 1977), pp. 205.

is a phenomenon that an earlier generation of Latin Americanists assured us was not going to be repeated in Latin America.

Earlier writers on this subject claimed that the liquidation of Indians was a consequence of the Protestant desire for familial solidarity and racial purity and that Catholic traditions combined with Conquistador invasions—while oftentimes bloody and violent—would ultimately engender harmonious relations between races and groups. This neat form of apologetics simply disintegrated when Latin America entered the industrial world order. It turned out that Indian populations in Latin America were preserved only by societal backwardness. Once a nation such as Brazil entered the modern world system, the consequences for its native populations became as genocidal and fratricidal as they were for the Indian peoples of North America a century earlier.

Genocide is the best defined and least adhered to concept in the lexicon of modern times. Traditionally, it simply means efforts to destroy a group in whole or in part. With the founding of the United Nations, the General Assembly, in response to the horrors of World War II, declared in its resolution of December 11, 1946 that genocide "is a crime under international law, contrary to the spirit and designs of the United Nations and condemned by the civilized world." It received further analysis by the United Nations Economic and Social Council, which appointed a special committee that approved the convention on the subject. This convention was discussed and finally approved in the General Assembly on December 9, 1948 by a unanimous vote of 50 to 0.

Signing declarations is not sufficient proof that genocide has been outlawed in practice. While the Soviet Union was protesting genocidal practices in the United States, it was in the midst of the most savage phase of its Stalinist repression, taking tens of millions of lives and wiping out entire economically productive sectors, in the name of political conformity. Meanwhile the United States and other countries seemed particularly indifferent to the importance of the subject. The Senate refused to ratify the genocide convention even though that body had helped eliminate the most vicious aspects of past genocidal practices against blacks, Indians, and other racial minorities within the United States.

Were the question of genocide settled by legal ratification of international treaties, we would have no need for these books. But the sad truth is that there is many a slip between the legal code and the social order. As a result, the human rights debate not only continues but has achieved a high level of intensity, its ambiguities and paradoxes notwithstanding.

The book by Shelton Davis, the guiding spirit behind the Anthropology Resource Center, is an ambitious attempt to show how the Brazilian government's efforts to develop the Amazon region has been undertaken at the expense of a profound and detrimental change in its policy toward native Indians. There are 118 clearly identified Brazilian Indian tribal and cultural clusters, most of which are found in the Amazon Basin. The argument that Davis offers is simple enough: the Indians have been made to pay the price for the Brazilian "miracle" of lopsided economic development. Although the position of the Indians has eroded as Brazil emerged as a modern power, this position worsened as a result of the military coup of 1964, which reversed earlier humane efforts of the Brazilian National Indian Foundation (FUNAI). As late as 1969, the strategy of the Brazilian government toward the Indians was uncertain: as Davis reports, one posture was to protect Indian tribes from frontier encroachments, by federal government support of closed Indian parks and reserves, and to prepare the tribes to gradually become independent ethnic groups that might be integrated into the economy of Brazil. The second strategy was that Indian groups should be rapidly integrated as a reserve labor force or as producers of marketable commodities, into the expanding regional economies and rural class structures of Brazil.

Davis's book offers some fascinating political documentary of the conflict between the efforts of Orlando, Claudio, and Leonardo Villas Boas to create a protected haven for the Indians of Brazil, and the resistance of the new president of FUNAI, Gen. Oscar Jeronimo Bandeira, who saw the creation of a reservation system (national parks) as a "false experience" that converted the Indians into "guinea pigs." This documentary provides the backdrop to the more analytic portions of the book and to the discussions of the military coup and the interests of the multinational corporations. There are two sorts of ambiguity here. The first is ethical: one is not certain just what Mr. Davis considers an appropriate settlement of the Indian question. The second is economic: there really is no evidence that these corporations took a particular position on the Indian question or for that matter influenced national decision making.

Whatever the intentions behind these policies, the essential characteristics of genocide have become increasingly apparent in the Indian regions of the Amazon: outright death; economic exploitation; physical destruction; enormous increase of the incidence of disease such as black-fly illness, leading to blindness in many people; the use of chemical fertilizers to clear lands and maintain pastures—the whole miserable natural history of genocide in which the new white pioneers see the Indians as obdurate obstacles to expansion and growth. Mr. Davis has documented this tragedy with compelling data, if rather wooden prose.

The effort by Richard Arens and his colleagues is more concentrated since it isolates one group, the Aché Indians, and shows how Paraguayan policies have led to the liquidation of these gentle forest dwellers. Mr. Arens's book fleshes out those general phenomena that Mr. Davis and his colleagues explored in Brazil. Richard Arens has represented the Aché Indians as counsel for the International League for Human Rights before the United Nations and the Inter-American Human Rights Commission. He is clearly presenting a legal brief. As a result, he calls upon the work of colleagues from moral philosophy, journalism, and anthropology to confirm his views.

The Achés have endured every possible humiliation and have suffered in international silence. With the solitary exception of an article in the September 24, 1973 issue of *The Nation,* no publicity has been given to the dismemberment of a people who were massacred by machetes in order to save bullets. The only exceptions to this slaughter were those Indians who submitted to being trained as killers of their own kin and who were then rewarded with a choice of captured Aché women. The only other survivors were young children, usually girls 10 years or older, sold as slaves, principally for sexual purposes, for $5 apiece. And if this is not enough, the impoverished Guaranis ("men of reason") were used to exterminate the Achés ("rabid rats"). Eric Wolf's description of this process is evocative of the *Judenrat,* the use of Jews to police their fellow inmates and victims.

Brief mention is made of the American government's policy of dumping massive amounts of foreign aid into Paraguay since Stroessner obtained his dictatorial power in 1954. But once more, evidence of an explicit U. S. role in these genocidal practices is inconclusive, or better, absent. Still, insofar as these nations are within the American sphere of influence, the new rhetorical emphasis on human rights has had a profound impact. At least it has raised the question of whether the United States should distance itself from the ethnocide practiced by the governments of Brazil and Paraguay.

There can be no gainsaying the documentary evidence of genocidal practices. Statistics alone can hardly convey the extent to which indigenous peoples have suffered at the hands of national regimes. But the main problem persists: What is the source of genocidal practices? Here we clearly have a problem of theory no less than a problem of reality. For Professor Davis, the impulse toward economic development is unquestionably the basis of genocidal assaults. He draws attention to everything from chemical fertilizers to cattle ranchers as the source of opposition to Indian survival. Agribusiness in Brazil requires the liquidation of the Indians. Because of the international character of Brazilian agribusiness, everyone from Hanna Brothers to Caterpillar Tractor Company can be held responsible for the practice of genocide.

On the other hand, Paraguay is participating in the economic miracle. Quite the contrary, it is in the grips of permanent economic stagnation, and as Frances R. Grant quite properly notes, "Paraguay is one of those countries where its dictators have made a virtue of the country's geography and its isolation from the rest of the world in its war against its captive citizenry." Hence, in Paraguay, genocide is practiced not in the name of development but rather in the name of preventing development. In the kind of vampirism practiced by the Stroessner regime, the use of native peoples for slavery has no underlying developmental purpose but rather is fueled by an isolationist impulse to crystallize the lines between masters and slaves.

The two books by American authors represent the two philosophies currently at odds in the human rights field. One, the so-called Western approach, sees political liberty as the cornerstone of human rights and human liberation. The other, the so-called Eastern approach, sees the essence of human rights in economic guarantees of well-being, security, and job opportunities. Davis attributes genocide to the economic rapaciousness of multinational corporations, and Arens and his colleagues attribute it to the political rapaciousness of traditionalist dictators.

Until this ambiguity is resolved, forming a policy to counteract the nightmare of genocide will be exceedingly difficult. For in one case we are told to direct our efforts to altering the multinational industrial system and, in the other, to the overthrow of state power. And while these deliberations are debated, the liquidation of these indigenous people continues.

It is no accident that both books have a somewhat inconclusive and abstract quality. For example, the volume on Paraguay offers some brilliant ethnographic analyses by anthropologists Mark Munzel, Eric R. Wolf, and Norman Lewis. In addition, several unusual psychological, moral, and legal essays against genocide in general are provided by Monroe C. Beardsley, Chaim F. Shatan, and Richard Arens. But there is little to link general Paraguayan realities with the specific policies that led to the untold suffering and degradation of the Aché tribe. With the noteworthy exception of Grant's paper, just why a state moves in this direction remains rather cloudy, despite some interesting insights by each of the contributors on the problem of genocide as a whole.

The problems in Mr. Davis's work are of a different sort. We are told how important the military coup of 1964 was in reversing the liberal approach to the Indian question. But in fact, the actual data he provides would indicate that three to five years after the military revolution, intensive efforts were still made to create a humanistic model for an Indian policy. Furthermore, even prior to 1964, during the so-called constitutional period in Brazilian history, the policy toward the Indians was hardly gentle or genteel. The Amazon Basin simply hadn't been much opened. In other words, no firm evidence is adduced that the 1964 Brazilian military revolution was particularly decisive in reorienting Brazil's Indian policy.

The constant mention of the role of the United States and other multinational firms is somewhat of a red herring since no direct information indicates that either in policy or in practice any of these firms has favored or encouraged a genocidal solution to the Indian question. Rather, there is strong evidence that American physicians, biologists, and anthropologists (like Mr. Davis himself), in making the problem of genocide an international issue, have aided native peoples in resisting the nastiest and most brutal consequences of mindless developmentalism. The silent war against native peoples of the interior is the result of a Brazilian model of development, one that is at times implemented against U. S. wishes. It is a profound mistake to overestimate U.S. controls on Brazil or Paraguay.

Genocide is an evil unto itself requiring no search for external causation. To seek international devils for our opprobrium deflects attention from the goal of the survival of all peoples in a dignified way. Otherwise, the victims of genocide run the risk of being victimized by their defenders, becoming pawns in a larger political game; Indians become part of a hidden agenda in which capitalism, multinationalism or any other related "ism" is the villain, instead of an object of relief and redemption. Genocide is no respecter of social systems. It is practiced in Cambodia, Uganda, and South Africa, no less than Brazil and Paraguay. Genocide reached its flowering in Hitler's concentration camps and in Stalin's gulag archipelago.

Researchers would be well advised to put aside vague political postures and moral animosities and to work out the concrete details for the survival of indigenous peoples. Insofar as these volumes help us move in that direction, they are beneficial. To the extent that they only satisfy economic ideologies of an abstract sort, remote from the horrors and outrages of the peoples described, these books might be less valuable primers in the study of genocide than illustrations of the problem itself: namely, the apocalyptic demand to satisfy outstanding political and economic problems at once, instead of addressing the specifics of indigenous people victimized alike by the mixed blessing of twentieth-century advances and the unmixed blessing of backward enclave nation-states.

From *The Nation*, vol. 226, no. 6 (1978), pp. 181–83.

20

The Rise and Fall of Counter Insurgency*

Eckstein, Harry

"Cuba . . . Algeria . . . Vietnam . . . One wonders where the next revolution will erupt and under what banner its leaders will fight." So begins the dust jacket announcement of *Internal War.* Yet one look at the index reveals that whatever revolutions are taking place in the world at large, few are taking place in the formal analysis of international relations. Cuba and Vietnam are never discussed in the book, while Algeria comes in for some casual mention in a political-science evaluation of external involvement in internal war. The blunt fact is that some contributors to this volume would be hard pressed to distinguish between a 6.5 millimeter bullet and a hemorrhoidal suppository. But at the same time, there are some excellent and original essays.

In a review of this kind, the reviewer is necessarily torn between considering the individual papers or the recurrent themes of the volume; in this case the former approach is used. The paper by Sidney Verba and Gabriel A. Almond is a first-rate example of comparative international analysis. Using Mexico and Italy as case studies of nations having sufficient likenesses to make their differences interesting, they conclude that attachment to the state is a function of having had a national revolution, while low levels of attachment, such as are found in Italy, represent permanent sources of instability. They also point out that the continued revolutionary potential of Mexico stems from the "promissory note" aspect of the 1910 Revolution—a debt yet to be paid off. This paper, using a good sampling technique and a sound questionnaire design, shows how susceptible national units are to social science analysis.

Alexander Gerschenkron provides a serious theoretical contribution to the volume in his "Reflections on Economic Aspects of Revolutions." His criticisms of Marx and Gramsci are refreshingly original. His conclusion is that modern revolutions, whether defined as bourgeois or proletarian, tend to have a common

---

* Harry Eckstein (editor), *Internal War: Problems and Approaches* (New York: The Free Press of Glencoe, 1964), pp. 339.

base in peasant agrarian demands. In some part, the agrarian sector acts as the "battering ram" of revolution, and both French and Russian revolutions are often declared successful to the degree that they resolved prerevolutionary peasant discontent. Interestingly, Christopher Hill anticipates Gerschenkron by several years, in "Transition from Feudalism to Capitalism," which examined a discussion in which British and Japanese Marxists were engaged a decade back. Here it is noted that the economic aspects of the "bourgeois revolution" were actually accomplished by 1715 with the ending of serfdom, but that the revolution, in Marxian terms, is defined by the assumption to state power of the newly dominant social class and not simply of economic elements that accommodate themselves to the revolutionary situation.

Karl W. Deutsch offers trenchant historical comparisons in his examination of external involvements in internal warfare. He offers a useful typology of the source, character, and legitimacy of such involvements. This paper would have been strengthened by an analysis of the role of ambiguity in external interventions—for as long as the situation is ambiguous there is a hesitation to escalate the war. In an allied paper, Thomas Perry Thornton, the editor of a useful volume on the changing Soviet attitudes toward the Third World, (*The Third World in Soviet Perspective*), offers an exercise in the natural history of insurrection. The main difficulty in his study "Terror as a Weapon" is his radically dubious assumption that "guerrilla warfare is only a variant form of conventional warfare." Indeed, the amount of terror employed either in guerrilla or conventional types of maximum conflict situations may be high or low, depending on specific circumstances, but the characteristics of the two types of conflict are different enough to compel the rise of an entirely new literature in the annals of international military relations.

The essay by Lucian W. Pye is most intimately linked to the book's title. He explains why the logistics of rebellion contrive with the ideology of developing regions to create a natural linkage between them. The peasant base of the Third World and of internal war links his ambition to the papers of Thornton and Gerschenkron on many points. But the sophistication of their approach is compromised by a journalistic anticommunism. This leads to all sorts of peculiar statements to the effect that "the demands of peasants for justice and a better economic lot can usually be satisfied by means of administrative and legal measures," which in turn are followed by the astonishing remarks that this has "little effect on a Communist-organized movement"—presumably on the grounds that Communist appeals are thoroughly emotive and without practical foundation in peasant conditions. But Pye frames the problem in terms of guerrilla initiatives versus government will. He surely realizes that guerrilla initiative itself depends on discrediting a government. The basic solidity of the governments of Argentina and Brazil is reflected in the ease with which they vanquished guerrilla activities based on the Cuban model. Even the powerful national liberation front in Venezuela has become substantially isolated by a style of terrorism that is more frightening to the citizenry than were government insipidities. Thus, his conclusion that government "genius" stems from its ability to anticipate insurgent activities, is essentially an example of circular reasoning—since federal stability is what makes guerrilla activities null and void to begin with. What often maintains government forces or for that matter guerrilla forces-in the absence of meaningful social stability-is foreign support to the government (or to the guerrillas). This was as true of Hungary in 1956 as it is of Vietnam in 1965.

The problem with "internal war" is that now that the "theory of counterinsurgency" has finally been put to the full test, in Vietnam to be exact, and it is plain that the theory does not hold. There is little possibility, short of total genocide, that Hessian troops who wear their uniforms on their skin pigmentation will defeat native, colored revolutionists who not only blend into the landscape, but who actually define that landscape. Thus paradoxically to combat guerrilla war, insurgent movements, and civil revolutionists, the counter-insurgents must establish regular military lines of combat to replace the hit-and-run tactics of guerrillas. Counterinsurgents are constrained to establish a conventional war in order to survive in alien surroundings. They must establish "battle lines" which will be observed by "two sides," to replace a battlefield defined by stealth and ambush, lacking a front or a rear. Precisely the fluidity, the impossibility of determining friend from foe, revolutionist from counter-revolutionist, is what makes counter-insurgency so difficult to implement. It is disappointing that even cogent papers in the volume dealing with paramilitary violence, such as those by Thomas Perry Thornton, Andrew C. Janos, and Lucian W. Pye, fail to address such crucial issues.

When this volume is compared to the work on internal war by scholars such as Bernard Fall, Seymour J. Deitchman, and Morton H. Halperin, the technical defects of Eckstein's reader become manifest. The great tragedy of counterinsurgency studies is that even those with great technical prowess seem to prefer "hard-line" solutions to thinking about new ways of restoring civilian control of military policy. Perhaps the source of this is the extent to which scientific questions are converted into policy questions. The world of the United States is converted into the generalized "we," while the world of the developing regions becomes the generalized "they."

Finally, I confess to a certain astonishment that scholars such as Marion J. Levy, Talcott Parsons, Seymour M. Lipset, and Arnold S. Feldman were sufficiently converted to a sociology of immediate relevance as to wonder where the next revolution will take place. It is amazing enough to have them comment on present ones. For our purposes, since the works of these well-known sociologists are easily available in many other sources, these works were eliminated from this discussion of the more exciting and exploratory problem of internal war.

The pathos and tragedy of the sociological contributions to the Eckstein volume is their collective irrelevance to the master theme. If any evidence is needed that an "old sociology" does indeed exist, whatever the status of the "new sociology," let the reader peruse the stale commentaries of the sociologists of this volume. Let him further compare and contrast them to the work being done by colleagues in economics and political science. Whatever the practical problems, the results of such comparisons will hardly prove intellectually reassuring.

From *Transaction*, vol. 2, no. 1 (1964), pp. 46–47.

21

Massification, Mobilization and Modernization*

Germani, Gino

Gino Germani is one of those figures in contemporary sociology of whom it is no exaggeration to say: understand the sociologist, understand the man. Just as truthfully, to understand the man is to understand the sociologist. The interaction between his personal life history and social analysis could hardly be more evident than it is in this reluctant cosmopolitan.

Germani traversed three continents in his life. He was born, raised, and initially educated in Italy. As a consequence of fascism, he migrated in 1934 to Argentina, where he spent his middle years. In Buenos Aires he made his reputation as a sociologist of development. In the mid-sixties he moved to Harvard University and became Monroe Gutman Professor of Latin American Affairs and Sociology. Germani was not especially content at Harvard—not because of any lack of fame, recognition, or money—but because the ethnic riches with which he had grown up were hard to come by in the Harvard atmosphere. Even those select North Americans he had become close to, like myself, Joseph Kahl, Kalman Silvert, and Seymour Martin Lipset, represented in their own way an ethnic variety with which he could identify. That is why his last years, mostly spent in Naples and Rome, were perhaps his most content, if not necessarily his most triumphal period. As Gino was quick to point out, nothing in modern-day Italy admits of triumphalism. No one easily accepts transplants. In a national as profoundly hostile to the world of ideas and learning as contemporary Italy, a scholar like Germani had to carry the burdens of his fame even more lightly than he did in exile.

Germani's informal education also took place on three continents. In each instance he was an exile, an outsider, someone for whom the world itself was a strange place. His wit, his skeptical manner, his style, all professed an air of

---

* Gino Germani, *The Sociology of Modernization: Studies on Its Historical and Theoretical Aspects with Special Regard to the Latin American Case* (New Brunswick and London: Transaction Publishers, 1981), pp. 1–8.

unconcern about external circumstances, that proved disconcerting to many. Curiously enough, rarely has anyone been more concerned with these same external forces as they impinge upon individual careers.

Sociology as a profession has never meant much in a nation like Italy, with its strong belief that political rather than social forces dominate. The entire history of Italian social theory is largely enveloped by the history of its political theory. Even its definition of class tends to derive from Vilfredo Pareto and Gaetano Mosca and is linked not so much to an economic class or a social struggle, but to political classes and the struggles of parties, factions, or forces attempting to control the political arena. Between World Wars I and II, Italian social theorists from Giovanni Gentile, through Benedetto Croce, to Antonio Gramsci—that is from Right to Left—understood that the relationship between economics and politics is not a mechanical one in which economics can be considered infrastructural and politics superstructural. Quite the contrary, twentieth-century politics tends to be substructural and economics superstructural.

Politicians allocate wealth, determine levels of production, influence rates of inflation, and define national boundaries. Germani's work evolved in this kind of world milieu. It is no accident that until the end of his life, Germani was deeply concerned with problems of authoritarianism, totalitarianism, and above all, fascism—not simply as Italian national phenomena, but as the highest expression of state power, as a problem in the integration of societies and the integration of classes, masses, and elites.

The long sojourn from Italy to Argentina resulted in a curious blend of concerns: developmental interest in backwardness, modernization, and immigration—issues that can hardly be avoided in a national like Argentina—coupled with political interest in mass society, party identification, and integrating mechanisms in a period of rapid change. Argentina was a veritable laboratory for such analyses. Not only did it exhibit problems of development, but it put on display the urban/rural, native/ethnic, and upper/lower-class dichotomies. It is hard to say whether this was a consequence of internal militarism, lack of system legitimacy, external colonialism, or the multinational imposition of a more advanced form of economy. Argentina was a part of the Third World that cried out for Germani's kind of modernization analysis, even though it was never clear whether Argentina was a model or an exception.

What Germani provided was not simply inherited from Italian political theory. He established a more intimate relationship with the works of scholars such as Weber, Simmel, and Mannheim. Even during the years of Peronism, Argentina was not simply another part of Latin America, but was very much an extension of the European migratory processes. In Buenos Aires, Germani first absorbed the complete works of Weber, Simmel, Mannheim, and other classic German social theorists. Even before they were well known in North America, relatively complete works were available to sociologists in Argentina.

In a singularly creative way, Germani united the Italian school of power with the German school of authority.

This fusion accounts for what superficially appears to be Germani's indebtedness to Talcott Parsons. This superficial connection linked Germani's work to the grand theorists of North America. To be sure, it made Germani's works intellectually meaningful to an important sector of sociological opinion at Harvard, namely Parsons himself. Parsons's estimate was reinforced by scholars such as Seymour Martin Lipset, who first knew Germani in South America. Germani developed an imposing intellectual fusion of traditions, not unlike that found in the Parsonian theory of social action. But in Germani's case, this came about not through a migration to Europe, but rather from Europe. If that fusion of traditions made Parsons the premier sociologist on his return from Germany to the New World, Germani's movement from Italy to the New World made him the foremost political sociologist who entered into exile.

His later movement to North America and to Harvard University led not so much to reorientation as crystallization of concepts that he was already widely using: modernization, mobilization, urbanization, immigration. His conceptual fusion of development and modernization characterizes Germani's work after he entered the United States. It represented not so much a philosophical change as a realization of the need to reconsider work he had suspended in earlier stages. The supreme merit of the American experience was that it allowed him time and freedom. America offered an intellectually dispassionate and humanly compassionate climate that provided him with material assets to complete his task.

By the end of his life Germani, poetically enough, did complete his life's work. His three major volumes: *Authoritarianism, Fascism, and National Populism, Marginality*, and *The Sociology of Modernization* in many ways represent the main pivots of his theory of social stratification and political class. They amplify and clarify his earlier works and essays, especially *Política y Sociedad en una Epoca de Transición* and *Sociología de la Modernización*, and provide a systematic basis on which to evaluate his work. These latter works enable us to appreciate the systematic nature of his thought rather than forcing us to infer it from his earlier writings.

From a theoretical point of view, what were the main pivots of Germani's work? Germani's "big three" were modernization, mobilization, and marginality. These key notions render Germani's world view of political psychology and political sociology.

His third and most advanced work is on modernization. Germani saw modernization as the touchstone of the twentieth century. But modernization is not reducible simply to high levels of communication and transportation, nor is it the rapidity with which messages are translated from elites to masses, nor for that matter is it a purely consuming theory of automobile production as the highest expression of economic culture. Germani's notion of modernization is much more ample—and political. It has to do with how a society can harness technology for distinctly political ends and link science to distinctly economic ends. In Germani's view, modernization is in sharp contrast to other theories that heavily emphasize factors such as internal migration of the poor from country to city, overseas migration from Europe to America, unionization of the Argentine as well as the American working class, the growth of a middle sector that is unconnected and often in opposition to the old aristocracy, and the expansion of a communication network as a form of political legitimation.

Many of Germani's concepts of modernization were developed under the crazy-quilt system of Peronism. If Marx was right that the first Napoleon represented tragedy and the second comedy or farce, it could be said with equal vigor that Italy's Mussolini represented a comic figure, followed by Argentina's Perón, who was tragic in himself and for Argentine political methodology. But whether Peronism emerged as comedy, tragedy, or neither, the notion of bureaucratic authoritarianism linking arms with modernization gave Germani a special insight into the Third World as a whole.

Modernization for Germani was a problem of political systems, not economic backwardness. Argentina had in common with Italy the mobilization of a political system for modernizing ends. Mussolini harnessed futurism as an ideology of early fascism. Perón harnessed folklorism as a belief that leadership was the destiny of Argentina in a hemisphere of backwardness. The development impulse provided Argentina with countervailing this power. That Argentina failed to develop hemispheric power does not invalidate Germani's notion of modernization. However, it does call attention to the special context of a modern society suffering stagnation, not to be confused with the kinds of modernization typical in the Middle East or typical in the 1960s of the rest of Latin America and parts of Asia and Africa.

The notion of mobilization is equally important in Germani's work. It, too, derives in large measure from conditions prevalent in Italy and Argentina, or at least highly developed there because they were modernizing as well as mobilizing societies. Large numbers of people were involved in vitalizing the political system. Unlike Brazil and Germany, mass mobilization in Italy and Argentina was and remains at a high level. How modernization feeds mobilization, and in turn, how mobilization provides stimulus to the modernizing process is the basic interaction at the core of political sociology; it is the fundamental characteristic of Germani's work.

Mobilization is such a Latin concept that it sometimes comes as a rough shock to those who live in purely authoritarian societies or in those in which representationalism without mass participation has become a norm. A European concern about mobilization became the prevalent style in nations like Argentina. This concern helps to explain the Perón phenomenon: leadership not simply as a function of elites in its classic sense, but also the role of the masses in a less classic model of leadership. There are widespread notions of the mass as part of a socialist vanguard, as well as definitions of a class conscious proletarian. But Italy and Argentina represented phenomena of a conservative mass inspiring innovative elites. Germani looked at this process carefully, indeed cautiously, because mobilization leads not simply to a theory of revolutionary socialism, but just truly helps explain reactionary fascism. Mobilization theory cuts across social formations; hence, it is an important variable in its own right. It helps to account for much of the twentieth century, the totalitarian political experience in a variety of economic guises.

The third element, marginality, is a function of the fragmentation of social classes in the modern world. Germani offered a concept widely used among Latin American scholars before and after him, but he used it in a very special way. Marginality not only has to do with the notion of being outside the primary classes; it is a main feature of the stratification system within a total society with no center. In this respect, marginality characterizes the Third World societal framework, where alienation and anomie become collectivized.

Marginality not only defines individuals who are outside the main occupational activities of industrial urban civilization, but more to the point, it is a general characteristic of many people within a social system. Germani provided a political psychology to go along with his political sociology. His lifelong fascination with the psychoanalytical movement, particularly scholars like Freud, Homey, and Fromm—each of whom were translated into Spanish—was not typical of sociologists. Nor was his fascination with Marcuse, who attempted to link Marxian and Freudian elements to a larger theory of love, death, and civilization. Concepts like eros and thanatos hardly appear in Germani's writings. He used the psychoanalytic approach to show that the structure of authority is often rooted in the parental framework and the need for shared security.

For Germani, marginality became typical of modern society, typical of the way postindustrial people survive. Mobilization became the public expression of the authoritarian syndrome and conversely, modernization becomes its personal expression. The private element in marginality is closely linked to the psychiatric condition. Marginality became the general theory of alienated social classes, the way mobilization yields its private self to public control. Privatization became the opposite of socialization, both expressed ways in which the public and private are opposite. The modernizing sensibility is not simply concerned with innovation, or new things for the sake of a novel aesthetic, but it is rather a mechanism for integrating marginal social classes on one hand, and mobilizing large social sectors for political ends on the other.

This brief intellectual biography prefaces the completion of a trilogy that includes the most ambitious of Germani's English-language writings. It is always sad to lose someone, but Germani had a full life, living to nearly seventy. He lived long enough to realize, if not his life's ambition, then at least to sec his major works completed. Like most liberal antitotalitarians who have

105

suffered dictatorships of a varied and sundry type, he was suspicious of grand theory and resistant to a metaphysical world view that reified and polarized the social world. Germani's greatest sociological curse words were reification and polarization. Intellectual reification, especially in the name of synthetic grand theory, was for him not the essence of the sociological imagination, but its metaphysical corruption. Scheler, Rickert, and Dilthey, the German metaphysical tradition in social thought, were particularly unappealing to him as he grew older. Germani became increasingly familiar with the vagaries of human affairs and the impotence of neat abstractions to explain events.

Germani was not a master methodologist. He never made such a claim. But like any good social scientist, he had great respect for data: an appreciation of the degree to which all theories are falsified by reality. He understood reality as a series of data about the world. But he also viewed data as an ultimate act of faith. The sociological experience of reality became a risk for him when it limited new observations. Perhaps this is why he turned toward anthropology and culture at the end of his life.

In a Latin American context, Gino Germani was not viewed as a radical, but in the context of North American thought, even of postwar European thought, he was indeed a man of the Left, Like other critics and crusaders in social science, Germani was a synthetic figure, attempting to link Northern and Southern European intellectual traditions and ultimately wedding them to the uniqueness of the American experience in politics and society. He contributed eloquently to the *festchrift* honoring C. Wright Mills in *The New Sociology*. He participated in a wide variety of intellectual publications, not just mainline sociological journals. He steered a broad intellectual course rather well, perhaps better than most systems builders.

This panoramic vision gave Germani's work freshness, whether or not his estimates were always correct. Indeed, he was not always right. For example, the migration movement from European to American centers was not the same in cause or consequence as that from rural to urban areas, and his general underestimation of racial and religious tensions can be considered valid only where nationalism is triumphant. But in a world in which sociology needs more figures who not only attempt middle-range but upper-range theory, using the full panoply of available data, Gino Germani made a particularly vibrant and vital contribution. His loss is tempered by an appreciation of the degree to which his professional tasks were achieved and also by the degree to which his personal aims were given institutional forms. He was able to return to his beloved Italy, where he was born and where he died.

This trilogy began in 1963 when Germani first came to the United States. He had a full professorship at Harvard, but he was keenly aware of the system of publish or perish. Nowhere has that system been cultivated with the same ferocity as in the United States. We worked out an arrangement whereby I would serve as editor of a volume of his major writings, well known in

Argentina, on the social structure of Argentina. His work in this field was undoubtedly his highest claim to fame prior to the publication of this trilogy. But it was dated, in part because the data base was limited to what was available during the Perón era and prior to the post-Perón census system. Also Germani's theories evolved; by the mid-sixties, he no longer felt that he would be well served by a translation of his basic work of the late fifties. Nonetheless, we did sign an agreement with Prentice-Hall for a translation, update, and expansion of that work. This project never came to pass. In part, Gino continually rethought his earlier work. Thus despite my cajoling, my concerns, my insistence that he would have to return the modest advance to the publisher, he decided to push ahead with a final synthesis.

Whatever the cause, the volume on Argentine social structure remained untranslated. Instead, Gino first issued a series of essays that modified this earlier work, three of which were published during my tenure as editor of *Studies in Comparative International Development*. A fourth essay, the basic framework on modernization, appeared in *The New Sociology*. It became clear to me that behind these fragments on fascism and social class, and mobilization and immigration, a large corpus of work was in the making. However, it was difficult to convince a publisher of this in the absence of a decent track record. As a result, over the years, Prentice-Hall lost interest in the translation project entirely. As is characteristic of many large publishing houses, by the time any interest could be rekindled, not one of the original Prentice-Hall editors remained with the project, which, as a result, never got off the ground. I maintained close contact with Germani over the years. In the summer of 1974, he indicated he had completed a trilogy which needed "only" several more years of polishing and editing before he would be interested in seeing it published.

The next five years were occupied with internal editing and copyediting. Also Gino began his dual academic life, sharing time between Harvard and Naples. In the interim, editor, copyeditor, and author worked hard to produce the final trilogy of manuscripts. One day in 1978, Gino asked me to see him. I stopped by his office, and he presented me with three huge (or so it seemed at the time) volumes and asked me if Transaction would be interested in publishing them. If we would be interested in publishing them as a trilogy, he in turn would be willing to make such an agreement. We contracted for all three volumes on the condition that each would be edited one additional time and that their publication would be separated by at least one year, so that the full impact of each volume could be appropriately realized. The first volume, *Authoritarianism, Fascism, and National Populism,* had already been published in Italian. It came out while he was doing the final editing on the remaining two. Transaction began publication of the trilogy, and it also assumed the publishing role of an edited volume that Germani had done earlier for Little, Brown: *Modernization, Urbanization, and the Urban Crisis.* Transaction had also published a significant volume by Joseph A. Kahl, on *Modernization, Exploitation, and Dependence in Latin America,* in which the work of Germani's middle period in Argentina figured prominently.

I am a deep admirer of Germani's work; moreover, I have been profoundly influenced by his character and say so unabashedly. His kind of political sociology, his linkages between state and society represent the best of the modem sociological era. Toward the very end, he was turning his attention to the relationship of state to individuals—an early concern rekindled by his acute awareness that whimsy in the hands of leaders may turn out to be mayhem against masses.

My indebtedness to this extraordinary man—as knowledgeable about Antonio Vivaldi and Paul Klee as he was about Pareto and Weber—can never be fully discharged. This is the inevitable relationships of novice to mentor. But with the publication of *The Sociology of Modernization* and the completion of this trilogy, the full scope of Gino Germani's powerful intellect can be revealed for all to see and for many to learn from. This trilogy will also make it painfully clear what an extraordinary scholar graced our earthly midst during this long and somber century.

From the Foreword to *The Sociology of Modernization.* (New Brunswick and London: Transaction Publishers, 1981), pp. 1–8.

22

A Naive Sophisticate*

Haig, Alexander

An airplane is a wonderful place to read, and an overseas flight is especially conducive to reading a book. It is perhaps one of the few places where distractions can be limited. What brings this aside to mind is that on a trip home from England last year, I read the second volume of Henry Kissinger's remarkable memoirs, *Years of Upheaval.* This year, also on a flight from Heathrow, I read Alexander Haig's *Caveat.* I was almost put off from doing so by virtue of the two-week serialization of Haig's work in *Time* magazine. What a mistaken impression extracts can leave! For excerpts emphasize Haig's work as a crisis manager (e.g., his failed shuttle diplomacy around the Falkland Islands dispute between England and Argentina and American efforts at mediating that dispute). The book, however, is a primer in the *forms* of power, the symbols of power. At this level, Alexander Haig is a sophisticate; at the complex level of negotiating disputes, of *exercising* power; but he is indeed, as his critics maintain, also a naif.

I found myself wishing for some sort of cross-pollination between Kissinger and Haig. The former, viewing every issue as part of a geopolitical mosaic, concentrating on structures no less than events, and seeing himself as a global actor by virtue of being a historical analyst. The latter, viewing every issue as a unique and specific task; earnestly concentrating on the distribution of power and authority even more than on the consequences of events; and seeing himself as a pragmatic, political figure with a keen, even blunt sense of national purpose and presidential power. It is ironic to listen to Haig castigate Soviet Ambassador Anatoly Dobrynin for using his "bourgeois manners" and drawing-room style to disguise Soviet ambitions. In contrast, Haig is the consummate Puritan divine: blunt of manner, certain in belief. To those who charted Haig's actions in the last days of the Nixon administration, it is evident that this man is committed to the forms and symbols of the Republic. In short, if he was no putschist in 1973, he was hardly likely to become one

---

* Alexander M. Haig Jr., *Caveat: Realism, Reagan, and Foreign Policy.* (New York: Macmillan Publishers and London: Weidenfeld & Nicholson, 1984), pp. 367.

in 1981. But Haig is so lacking a sense of history, even of his own historicity, that he fails to make the case for his own collapse in any but a perfunctory way. Political differences are transformed into "the drives of human beings," while history is converted into an "upward path."

Perhaps the most surprising aspect of *Caveat* is not Haig's frontal assault on the Reagan advisory team of Edwin Meese, Michael Deaver, and James Baker, but how thoroughly ill-prepared he was to meet such a challenge. Haig appears entirely honest in his shock that the presidential group—loyal only to Reagan—would work so hard to deprive Haig and the Department of State of the formal mandate to conduct foreign policy as represented in NSDDI (National Security Decision Document I), the presidential memorandum establishing the structure of foreign policy. Haig was the only original cabinet appointee who had an independent political power base and a strong role in a previous Republican Party administration. During his eighteen-month tenure in office, he was the only real or potential rival for power to the president himself. The public sensed this when, after the assassination attempt against President Reagan, the Secretary of State announced: "I am in control," only to introduce as a limp afterthought that he had meant to say that he was the ranking senior cabinet officer present in Washington at the time. Haig's power was less an invention of the press than it was his critics' expression of the powerlessness of the other cabinet officers. No other individual could claim such credentials as White House chief of staff in the Nixon administration or supreme allied commander of NATO forces in Europe.

The leitmotif in *Caveat* is that Reagan was a man who listened to his advisors with equal dedication, exercised good sense in arriving at a decision—whether lifting the Soviet grain embargo carefully or honoring the agreements reached with the Iranian government on the release of hostages—but who was prevented from bringing about real choices by his own administrative troika of Meese, Deaver, and Baker. Not a single word admits the obvious: Reagan's *troika*, whether they coopted decision making from Haig or buried his recommendations, were essentially responding to and working for the president. Reagan emerges as more pragmatic than Haig and far less ideologically committed than the former NATO commander. Reagan could send troops to Lebanon, then back off before defeat loomed imminent. Reagan could order the CIA to mine Nicaraguan harbors, then remove the mines before it became a major international incident. Reagan could order priorities for an end to Soviet aggression in Poland, Afghanistan, and Central America—followed by arms control negotiations in 1981—only to drop these preconditions for such talks in 1984. Reagan was an elected official desirous of re-election. Haig was an appointed official desirous of defining the boundaries of his authority, and failing that, leaving his government post. Resigning is a steady available option for a cabinet officer but not for an elected, sitting president—the Nixon exception confirms the rule.

Questions of naiveté and sophistication aside, there are two critical components to *Caveat* that make it significant reading: Haig's innermost thoughts on the role of appointed officials in government service and the course of events that Haig helped to determine.

The advice on government service could serve as an appendix to Machiavelli's *The Prince*. And Haig should be left to talk for himself on these marvelous insights:

> The question that ought to be asked of nominees for high office is this: who are you and how did you become the person you are today? I am not suggesting that the Senate go in for amateur psychoanalysis. But in the life of every human being there are events that have had an important effect on the way in which he looks upon the world and lives in it. . . . . The fact that the human race. . . chooses the upward path when it is given the choice; together with the rest of mankind, we have everything that we need to make the future. . . a celebration of the possible. . . . Statesmen and others often speak of preventing World War III. One might instead suggest that World War III may actually have begun on that winter day in 1948 when Jan Masaryk was defenestrated in Prague, and that it has been going on ever since in ceaseless testing of wills and exchange of blood. . . . There is a connection between the policy of making war unthinkable through deterrence and the absence of war. Before breaking the connection, we should think long and deep. . . . A compromise had been reached. A vital relationship had been preserved. The future with all its opportunities for the two principals and for many other nations had not been foreclosed. Emotions had been put aside and reason had prevailed. That is the purpose of diplomacy.

This last pithy saying was written in conclusion to the section on China. Haig's greatest triumph was to keep the relationship between China and the United States alive and well despite differences on the future of Taiwan. He was faced with a Goldwater on the American Right and a Deng Xiaoping on the Chinese Left, both of whom felt, for radically different reasons, that the Taiwanese question could no longer be shelved. The one time in the book that Haig criticizes Reagan, he notes that the president's reassertion at a news conference that the Taiwan Relations Act would be carried out as the law of the land played havoc with his diplomatic efforts to strengthen Sino-American relations. In the end, Haig's position prevailed: strong economic assistance to China and continued medium-level arms sales to Taiwan, but with recognition of a future reunification of Taiwan to China. Haig is no dogmatist. His concern throughout *Caveat* is not with economic systems; he could hardly care less whether China is Communist or capitalist. But he is interested in political systems—whether such regimes aim at strengthening or weakening the Soviet bloc. In this concern, Haig had ready and willing counterparts in China.

The chapters on Israel, on the Saudis and the AWAC sale, and on Poland abound in good sense. Haig fittingly emerges as an American negotiator in search of settlement with honor and a maximization of U.S. influence in Europe and the Middle East. He is not unmindful that Jewish and Polish groups represent considerable voting segments. Haig's support of the AWAC sales decision contained a modified Peter Principle, "When something starts out badly, it is likely to get worse." Yet he is quite correct in noting that while the Saudis received their AWACs (with some modifications), the Israelis walked away with increased public support and media sympathy precisely because they lost the AWAC battle. Haig's success with Poland was more modest, because U.S. leverage in that besieged nation is so much more limited than in the Middle East. The key victory, if it may be called that, was the prevention, through a series of diplomatic maneuvers, of direct Soviet military intervention. The Reagan economic sanctions against the Soviet Union created the conditions for Wojciech Jaruzelski to take command and permit military rule to replace party rule. But at least a blood bath had been averted, one which the United States could not have prevented by blustering or posturing. The recitation of events, which already read like ancient history, indicates Haig's diplomatic strengths in contexts of Soviet-American rivalries.

The same tactical flexibility became meaningless in the Falklands/Malvinas conflict. For in this dispute between two American allies, the single guideline that "what is good for the United States and what is bad for the Soviet Union should guide all action" confronted a dilemma. At stake were high American interests in both the Anglo-American union and, perhaps even more, in the Latin American-North American code. There was never any doubt that in a showdown the United States would have to back Great Britain legitimately protecting its island subjects from invasion. The task was to prevent the ultimate from happening—but Haig could not prevail. And while the chapter on the Falklands makes for fascinating reading, especially on Argentine dealings and counterdealings, one is left with the impression that even today Haig is not certain why his "mission impossible" to Buenos Aires failed. The Falklands dispute was fueled and conditioned by internal Argentine history, not world history. The nationalist character of Argentine militarism, combined with internal economic crisis, made 1982 the propitious moment for an invasion of the Falklands. Neither Galieri nor Costa Mendiz could cut off the flow of nationalist rhetoric, and no one in Argentina could convert a politicized armed force into a professional sector capable of defeating even a modest British force.

Haig's nontheoretical standpoint made him the object of ridicule; charges of favoritism and grandstanding abounded. He was also impatient, even angered by the sort of theorizing that flourished in the United Nations under the direction of Jeane J. Kirkpatrick. Haig desperately wanted the president to know what was going on around him, yet it was Haig himself who failed to detect what was going on around *him*. The Lebanon crisis that erupted into an Israeli invasion after modest and hoped-for provocations, again illustrated a dilemma and weakness in Haig's thinking: when issues were regional, subnuclear, and generally not directly part of the global struggle between East and West, the Haig strategy failed. Haig understood the Cuban dangers in the Caribbean, the Polish crisis for Comecon, the need for Chinese-U.S. cooperation—because each of these fitted the paradigms within which he was working. The other "regional" struggles often did not. It was not Meese, Deaver, and Baker who brought down the Haig regime at State, but the vagaries and ambiguities of real world *forces* that could not be reduced to strange *persons.*

The deep concerns expressed by Haig about "leaks" and "plants" is a carry-over from his days in the military and business. His frankness with the Chinese, we are told, derived from the fact that "Chinese don't leak." But Haig never quite accommodated himself to the political fish bowl of democratic societies. Information is the stuff of the open society. Those reared in an atmosphere of intelligence sometimes prefer the dark shadows to the bright lights. And there are indeed real risks in populist politics—risks that neither Haig's patrician manners nor military mode found pleasant.

The dirty little well-kept secret of *Caveat* is not the role played by Messrs. Meese, Deaver, and Baker, but how perfectly they reflect the presidential style of the Reagan era. Reaganism is a social movement from below no less than a political ideology from above. Haig well understood the latter but thoroughly failed to appreciate the former. He could have easily lived out his years at State doing what he jolly well pleased with NSDDI. But he failed to appreciate that populism breeds informality, a blurring of lines of command, and an endless willing confusion of decision making. Haig was done in by the conundrums of his own ego rather than the caveats of others.

From *Cross Currents*, vol. 34, no. 2 (1984), pp. 220–24.

23

Schisms and Chasms in International Affairs*

Hoffmann, Stanley

This book of essays proved disquieting. Not because its author's brilliant shafts lacked incisiveness, nor because it dramatically altered any available picture of the world; my discomfort stemmed rather from a nagging sensation that I had been through these arguments before. *The State of War* recalled top mind dozens of issues I had grappled with—and not always as successfully as Mr. Hoffmann—in my own book of essays, *The War Game.* Yet Mr. Hoffmann's volume differs quite markedly from mine. His work called to mind the *Symphonic Fantastique,* in the beautiful waltz scherzo of the second movement is transformed into a grotesque parody of the witches' sabbath in the fifth movement. *The State of War* has a remarkable capacity for clear initial statement which slowly declines into a sad and bitter pessimism, in the name of realism, where Rousseau, Game Theory and Dialectic all become tragic, intertwined grotesqueries.

Mr. Hoffmann and I, along with many social scientists, share a theory of programmed conflict, view with similar disdain moralistic approaches to political problems, and have the same ultimate hope that the value of survival will prove to be more compelling than the interests of nation, class or prestige. But for him all of this shared wisdom is offered in the name of a hard-nosed continuance of the cold war, while I offered my interpretation as evidence that the cold war may yet prove obsolete and counter-productive. The uncomfortable feeling therefore has to do with this: that if Mr. Hoffmann and I were in accord on the facts, then our discourse was precisely over the question of morality—which I dare say we both seem too ready to dismiss as rhetoric.

But before being driven to such a conclusion, I felt it important, to myself at any rate, to see whether we were in fundamental agreement as to matters of fact and theory. With only slender satisfaction, I can say that the difference

---

* Stanley Hoffmann, *Essays in the Theory and Practice of International Politics.* New York: Frederick A. Praeger, Publishers, 1965. pp. 276.

between *The State of War* and *The War Came* is not only a moral schism, but just as assuredly, a social science chasm.

Mr. Hoffmann's text is divided into nine chapters. Six and one-half of them are more or less linked to the title, while the other two and one-half are essays in the history of ideas—from Rousseau, Kant and Hobbes to Aron, Schelling, Kahn and Tucker. Hoffmann is at his best as a historian of ideas, but the bulk of the book and the burden of the argument rest upon the chapters directly concerned with the "state of war." Chapters two, three, and the first part of chapter eight could well form the basis of a study in the theoretical underpinnings of conflict theory in political and social science; but its critical spirit somehow does not carry over into the analysis of the main body of the text. Perhaps the problem is that this is a set of papers written over a five-year period, and reflects uneasy responses to amorphous audiences. Even in their "considerably revised" form, we have a set of essays held together by the author's sentiments rather than by a systematic accounting.

Hoffmann's sense of the dialectic is magnetic, perhaps even a trifle magical. For instance, he can break out of the number three only once in the importance chapter on International Systems and International Law. A new system in the stakes of conflict is said to emerge when there is a new answer to the questions: (1) What are the units in potential conflict? (2) What can the units do one another in the conflict? (3) What do the units want to do?

Next, the kind of alteration in the system is indicated by changes (1) that do not affect the system as such, (2) merely weaken the system, (3) ruin the system altogether.

The balance of power which brought about equilibrium in the classical period is then divided into three: (1) relative equilibrium among major states which are more than two in number; (2) common ties that cut across national lines; (3) systems in which which the state exercises only limited power over its citizens.

Conversely, the process of international deterioration is also subdivided into threes: (1) irrepressible ambitions of individual rulers; (2) the destruction of transnational ties through technological innovation; and (3) strong integrative tendencies in the nation leading to a heightened nationalism. After a brief interlude during which the number four intrudes its square head, we return to dialectical gamesmanship in describing stable international systems: (1) The law of the political framework. (2) The law of reciprocity. (3) The law of community. This dialectic of "the obsolete and the premature" goes on through the entire chapter. Indeed, even the chapter itself is divided into three parts.

What becomes clearly feeble in this approach is not so much dialectics as it is didactics. Instead of specific studies or examples of international law, Professor Hoffmann gives us yet more systems to cope with. The legal order is to said to be based on (1) common ends; (2) variations in time; and (3) variations of space. The need for concrete analysis yields to the pressure of a metaphysical catalogue of law-like propositions. The purpose of this baroque jumble of categories brutally simple: to tell us that the solidity of international law remains in serious if not inevitable doubt. Out of such dialectical mountains are such pedestrian molehills fashioned.

The world which Professor Hoffmann creates is so "realistic", it is unbelievable. There are no economic forces at work propelling nations. There are no popular classes moving to gain independence from the bureaucratic empires of both East and West. There are no sloppy or untidy problems in the world but only systems about the world. As long as real dialectic is kept out of the reckoning, the dialectic of how other participants to the game of war perceive conflict and the potentials for peace—then, of course, Mr. Hoffman can hardly be confounded. But the intellectual rigidities which motivate the author is irrepressible. In a remarkable paragraph on restraints and choices in American policy, he writes:

> One is bound by one's commitments; one is committed even by one's mistakes. The United States may be free to avoid new and mistaken entanglements in the future but it is not free to tear out of its scrapbook the political misjudgments of the past. Nor is it free to avoid entanglements altogether. (The mediocrity of SEATO as an instrument of foreign policy has led, not to a United States withdrawal from the defense of Southeast Asia, but to a downgrading of this particular alliance in favor of direct United States Involvement.) Once more, freedom of action shrinks to mitigating the bitterness of the unavoidable.

What can this result in but the carefree abandonment of political expertise in favor of policy gambling. The fate of the gambler is that the rules of the game itself drive him to desperation. Programing conflict is a marvelous phrase, but such programing relics so heavily on the equilibrium which obtained even before the game gets underway, that its utility as a root concept becomes questionable.

The actual game has its own dialectic; and as Hoffmann well appreciates, Russian Roulette is inevitably the outcome. To be committed to one's mistakes is to be committed to the *probability* of defeat. To think of every concession as a political collapse is to be committed to the *inevitability* of war. It is furthermore to confess the bankruptcy of the international "peril parity." Mr. Hoffmann's celebration of indeterminacy, ambiguity, and a patternless world may lead to its opposite, a demand for determinant, precision and manifest destiny—to a commitment to one's mistakes. What is so frightening is how accurately Hoffmann's views portray the current moment and mood in United States history.

The most significant scientific dilemma involved in Hoffmann's approach is his insistence on dividing the political world into two parts: the domestic and the international. The "domestic" ostensibly reveals a consensual pattern and is "based on the model of the integrated society." The "international", for its part, is based on a conflictual pattern, and represents a "decentralized Milieu divided into separate units." This sort of dualism enables Hoffman to rule out of consideration civil wars or wars of national liberation from a global perspective. It fosters his already concentrated elitism by allowing him to consider peoples and nations of the developing world as manipulated tools of the big powers. He speaks of revolutionary movements "as proxies for both Russia and China." Having convinced himself that the domestic is grounded in the idea of community, he can come to no other conclusion than that the absence of community is internationally inspired by the "game situation."

Such a bifurcation has serious analytical consequences. It stops one from examining the interpenetration of national and international goals. Take one recent instance: that of the Dominican Republic. The Dominican crisis can be considered an example of the trade-off policies of the Democratic Party engaged in by its Presidential leadership from Woodrow Wilson to Lyndon Johnson. The Democratic Party has a long history of bartering international self-determination schemes for national social security programs. That is to say, the classical technique has been to silence the opposition by maintaining a harder-than-thou posture toward the threat of international communism. In this way, the Party can dissociate its domestic program of "creeping socialism" from any implications that such domestic legislation will aid the Communists. The Democratic Party posture—from the belated involvement of the United States in World War One, the arms embargo on weapons for Republican Spain in the thirties, the intervention in the Greek Civil War in the forties, etc., has been to accept commitments to conservative foreign regimes in order to gain the advantage for liberal domestic programs. This pragmatic policy has been highly successful: it greased the path for the New Deal, the Fair Deal, the New Frontier, and now the Great Society. There can be little doubt that this is but one set of circumstances of how national and foreign policies can be understood as two sides of the same coin, rather than as qualitatively different entities.

The most significant philosophical dilemma involved in a dualist framework, such as Hoffmann presents, is the exaggerated sense of voluntarism in politics and policy. As if political strategies of an age uninformed by past experience express anything other than the shared illusions of that age. Hoffmann speaks of "spectacular mistakes" made by political leaders without considering the possibility that the ignominious defeat which engulfed the Wehrmacht on the Russian front is not nearly so much a matter of caprice and miscalculation as it is of the inevitable clash of world empires moving in contrary geographical and military directions.

To speak of the "mistake" of risking too much or too little as a threat to security or survival is naive. In politics one calculates mistakes by the consequences rather than the prediction of events. The purpose of Hoffmann's voluntarism is to reinforce the untested premise that modern revolutions multiply the risks of war. This may be true when revolutions are carried out by small nations that leave intact the essential balance of forces, but it is just as certain that warfare is minimized when revolution is carried out by major global players that thoroughly restructure power balances., as in Russia in 1918 or China in 1949. What Hoffmann terms "risk" is therefore little more than the strident belief of current United States policy makers that any shift in the international equilibrium is in itself untenable and unacceptable.

Mr. Hoffmann uses the word "modest" in the most immodest way possible: as a warning against doing things or saying things which go beyond the confines of his personal vision of game theory; which for him is a "modest pretension" that he can't do without. He employs a barrage of terms quite differently from ordinary usage: *strategy* is used to replace rather than augment principles; *balance of power* is considered the same as bipolarization-polarization; *commitment* is a surrogate for fanaticism; *concession* is akin to capitulation; *realism* becomes the moral equivalent to whatever the situation now is, or at least to how Mr. Hoffmann perceives it to be.; *operational* is any policy unhampered by considerations other than victory. And so it goes.

What ultimately makes the book obsolete is not Hoffmann's political vocabulary but the political motives behind his rhetoric. Still, one must take seriously the notion that one of the major consequences of nuclear weapons has been to substitute crisis for wars. But this has to be modified, since nuclear weapons make obsolete only one type of war—nuclear war. In the post-nuclear era, what has become decisive is the displacement of "crisis", at least of the higher dialectical sort practiced by the major powers, with an increase in small wars. In a sense, Raymond Aron is cor-rect, while his pupil. Stanley Hoffmann is incorrect, or at least manages to draw the least importance inferences from Aron's work—which I take to be that in a world of continuing crisis, the moral basis of conflict becomes more and not less urgent and compelling.

We are told that the best social science can do is to demonstrate the limits of our knowledge and provide tools for the analysis of concrete situations. Causal analysis, single or multiple, historical or analytical, are held to be immodest and hence invalid goals by Mr. Hoffmann. Yet, he salutes his mentor, Aron,—who was nothing if not a master of historical and causal analysis—by noting that *Peace and War is a* "monument of scholarship in the service of doubt." One can only reverse the praise in dealing with the author of *The State of War*: Professor Hoffmann has provided his readers with a monument of doubt in the service of scholarship. What is now required of such erudite scholars is not a celebration of doubt, but the removal of at least some doubt through better diplomacy and improved social research by those who presume this role in the great game of life.

From *The Nation*, vol. 202, no.7 (1966), pp. 189–91.

24

Reactionary Immortality*

Hoover, J. Edgar

Critics of "Chairman" LBJ and "Poor" Richard Milhous Nixon selected quotations that, though given in jest and jibe, have left the essential integrity of these two men strangely intact. The same cannot be said of excerpts from Chairman Mao Tse-Tung and J. Edgar Hoover, who selected their own quotes. In the latter we are struck by self-celebration and a self-selection of sacred sayings that represent a profound loss of integrity—a loss made painful for others by their sheer thirst for immortality.

Hoover's work *On Communism* is a hoary collection of homilies, polemics, and recollections. It must be judged in terms of nineteenth-century America's suspicion for anything alien, atheistic, and antagonistic to the American way. The volume is remarkably free of any serious critical analysis of the enemy system. Rather than concentrate on the theoretical extrapolations represented by this collection of aphorisms, it is perhaps more significant to examine the actual government documents that serve as the deep backdrop, organizational, and financial justification for all of these ideologically transparent assumptions. For those who are deeply concerned with what Hoover himself considers to be his most relevant passages, *On Communism* will bring ample succor. However, for those who are no less concerned with the implications of his message, this collection provides disturbing evidence of the FBI director's reluctance to come to terms with changes in the political context of American society, no less than changes in the political structure of Soviet society.

Obsolescence, intellectual as well as physical, afflicts all organizations and all men. Examining the many volumes of FBI budgetary requests before the House Appropriations Committee and Hoover's excerpts from five decades of speeches and writings makes it clear that waiting for the end is a malady that overtakes the Right as well as the Left. Apart from the standard tables on crimes and punishments, these hearings and aphorisms present a spectacle of the old Right exhausting itself in symbolic battle with the old Left. In these

---

* J. Edgar Hoover, *On Communism* (New York: Random House, 1969), pp. 170.

"works," the hero is clearly John Edgar Hoover, defender of the American faith, while his antihero is Gus Hall, the tenacious, dull-witted head of the Communist party in the United States and the incarnation of the Soviet faith. Absurdly enough, the antihero is taken with the exact amount of seriousness and endowed with all the legitimacy that is now denied to him by his critics on the American Left. It is as if Mr. Hoover depends on Mr. Hall for his own raison d'etre. The two men emerge from these volumes of testimony as the Yin and Yang of American political life. One wonders why they are taken so seriously, and by whom.

Hoover's communism emerges as the eternal oneness, given the same omnipotence and powers of evil generally reserved for the devil. This allegorical approach to the world has been winning increasing appeal as more intricate models for explaining it are concocted. Hoover tells us that

> although the names of the Soviet intelligence services differ today from what they were twenty years ago when Joseph Stalin was Premier, the objective of world conquest by communism has never wavered. The change over the years has been not a change in objective but a steady intensification of the effort to reach that objective, the destruction of a capitalist country.

By the simple substitution of the word "socialistic" for "capitalistic" in the latter sentence, we have the perfect summary statement of the goals of the F.B.I. under Hoover's tutelage; he clearly thinks of capitalism as a moral movement rather than an economic system.

Communism is more than a malodorous vapor emitted by evil men to becloud the minds of good people. It settles and concentrates in geographical locales, surrounding the dwelling place of the good, in which it diabolically awaits opportunities to do them damage. Cuba is only 90 miles from Florida. The evil work of the Mexican Communists takes place in a "concentration area that was less than 150 miles from Laredo, Texas." Meetings of the Leftists are not considered part of the internal politics of sovereign nations but rather a ring of evil enveloping the American nation.

Lenin considered imperialism to be the highest stage of capitalism. In some peculiar way, Hoover sees communism as the highest stage of deviance. Deviance comes from insidious exposure to communism. We are told that (1) peaceful co-existence is not possible "with a country that every year has intensified its intelligence and espionage operations against this county" and (2) "there are many gullible people who are against the policy in Vietnam as a result of the propaganda put out by some college professors who are naive and some students lacking in maturity and objectivity and who are constantly agitating and carrying on demonstrations in some of our largest universities." It does not occur to Mr. Hoover that the size and strength of the university may be related to the size and potency of the student protest movement it harbors. Instead, he broadly hints that were Communist speakers like the perennial Gus Hall and the inevitable Herbert Aptheker presented from keeping their lecture engagements on campuses, the innocence of American youth would be preserved.

Particularly insidious is Mr. Hoover's handling of someone like Bayard Rustin, whose links with the entire antiwar movements are said to arise from having been "convicted for sodomy" and for violation of the Selective Service Act before World War II. Hoover cannot cease linking communism and deviance. When he mentions a Crime Prevention Commission being set up in a California school, he also expresses regret that people like H. Rap Brown and Stokely Carmichael are allowed to speak to young students. The use of tax funds to support men whose positions he cannot accept is immoral. He speaks of these Negro leaders as "rabble-rousers," as men who live off of rather than in "the so-called ghettoes." Hoover is clever to relate the radical protest movement in America to the behavior of Negro militants, for it is true that militants, in contrast to most black special interest groups, oppose American foreign policy.

It has long been apparent that together with his fellow octogenarians Harry Anslinger in the Federal Bureau of Narcotics and Lewis Hershey, head of the Selective Service Commission, Hoover is obsessed by the young. Drugs, military service, and radicalism each have been loosely associated with one another by some of the younger generation. It follows for Mr. Hoover that the universities have become enclaves of young radical opposition that must be broken. He relates a traditional religious suspicion of the corrupting effects of secular education with a more contemporary awareness of the political potentials of university life.

During appropriation hearings, year in and year out, Hoover attempts to convince Congress that the "corruption" of youth may be attributed to political subversion. He does this by offering a list of public appearances made by Communist party leaders at various colleges throughout the United States. But Mr. Hoover's materials indicate that fewer than 70 appearances were made by Communist officials at American campuses during each of the three years reported in these hearings. This means that the collective position of the Communist party is probably heard less often on American campuses than the views of, say, lecturers such as Arthur Schlesinger, Jr., William F. Buckley, or any other major figures on the lecture circuit. Yet the consistency with which he presents his Communist speaker's chart makes it clear that Mr. Hoover considers it an important indicator of what is wrong with American higher education. He emphatically states that although

> we all believe in academic freedom, this does not grant license to deliberately present distortions or falsehoods. Communists are not

obligated morally or otherwise to seek for or to tell the truth. Some young people are capable of recognizing and exposing propaganda and propagandists. Others are not. This is the dangerous thing, particularly when it is recognized that the Communists in this country are conducting an energetic propaganda campaign to recruit young people to the Communist banner.

It follows that youthful corruption and radicalism may be traced to the appearance on campus of an occasional Communist party speaker.

More recently, Mr. Hoover has extended his concern for the school problem to the high school level. Employing the same rhetoric, he now lists H. Rap Brown and Stokely Carmichael among the corrupters of youth. Inviting black militants to public schools is inexcusable.

> They invite an individual of that kind to talk before a public high school composed of youth not at the age yet to properly evaluate what he has to say. He is enough of a rabble-rouser in the so-called ghettoes of the country where there are militant Negro elements that like to hear him expound but to have him spew his venom in the schoolrooms is wrong.

Evidently, Hoover considers colleges and high schools the institutional framework through which the Communist ideology makes its deepest penetration. What is particularly absurd is that Gus Hall himself substantiates Hoover's charge by indicating that his Communist party is indeed involved with the leadership of campus radical struggles. And in each year of testimony, Mr. Hoover cites Mr. Hall to this effect, without ever once questioning the validity, not to mention the blind conceit, of such reasoning. At no point does Mr. Hoover challenge the veracity of Mr. Hall who, as the leading Communist menace, presumably would not be above lying and deception. Quite the contrary. The implicit contract between them is that neither shall challenge the theoretical fantasies of the other. One can confidently expect that an examination of the collective essays of Gus Hall would bear this out in reverse.

But what enables the FBI to maintain its preeminent position as defender of American youth? What are the ideological bases of its authority and prestige? Four factors seem to be of major importance.

First, there is Hoover's legalism. In each of his pronouncements. Hoover is careful to stay within the letter of the law. Nowhere in American literature may be found a clearer expression of the agonizing gap between an advocate of justice and a supporter of law. The law-lover is omnipresent in the writings of Mr. Hoover. He always distinguishes the lines of responsibility between his offices and those of the attorney general. However, and this too is a curious fact, these divisions of authority between the attorney general and the director of the Federal Bureau of Investigation are drawn most sharply in matters of civil disorder involving the Negro-white relations and least sharply in matters of civil rights involving political radicals. Demands for economic integration into the system are acceptable (even from Negroes), but demands for political separation are unacceptable (even from middle-class whites).

From the attempts of Attorney General William D. Mitchell in 1932 to the equally courageous efforts of Attorney General Ramsey Clark in 1968 to limit the scope of the Federal Bureau of Investigation in avenues ranging from the "interstate" theft of merchandise to antiwar demonstrations, the philosophies of the attorney general and the director of the FBI have been at sharp variance. The attorney general is guided by the belief that federal jurisdiction should yield to local and state regulations whenever possible. Mr. Hoover has always taken the position that federal policing of crime is made necessary by the ineptitude, bravura, and limited expertise of local officials. Thus arises the peculiar anomaly of the principle of States' rights-one of the sacred cows of conservative doctrine-being nowhere more violated and breached than by the conservative politicians who, following Hoover, are prepared to waive all constitutional objections in the name of efficiency.

The struggle between the attorney general and the bureau director reached open ideological proportions when Ramsey Clark and J. Edgar Hoover provided the first public testimonies before the special Presidential National Commission on the Causes and Prevention of Violence. In what is now a classic presentation of different positions toward the law and order issue, the attorney general saw the problem as the absence of equity in the distribution of law, and the substitution of order for justice in processing criminal cases. Mr. Hoover, needless to say, presented the problem as a breakdown of order in the nation, and the solution as the application of law without regard to the social causes of crime. But underlying this extreme legalism is the question of House appropriations. As long as Congress continues to pass enabling legislation granting the FBI jurisdiction in wide areas of national defense, kidnapping, extortion, robbery, et al., Mr. Hoover can demand and receive annual increases of funds for his agency with only the mildest quiver of protest. This extreme concern for formal law and lack of response to social equity is one of the most characteristic features of Mr. Hoover's leadership of the Bureau.

The second point, and one closely related to the issue of legality, might be called bureaucratic competence, or adherence to executive directives. The FBI is presented as an agency disseminating large volumes of information on communism and crime, but not as a policy-making agency. Here too a significant distinction may be drawn between what is formally sanctioned and what is actually undertaken. Hoover speaks of acting under "Presidential directives requiring the F.B.I. to ascertain facts pertinent to the loyalty and security risk of employees and applications for positions in the Government service or in activities incident to which the Government has an official interest." These words enable the FBI to justify its investigation of the private lives of all citizens who are in any way involved with the work of the government. Since the directives are general in character, the manner in which they are interpreted becomes of central importance. Once again the letter of the law rather than the spirit of justice clearly motivates the Hoover style.

The same demand for bureaucratic competence underlies current calls for professionalization of police work. But Mr. Hoover, more clearly than cops before and after him, understood the shift from elective to appointive power in government, and the enlarged role of expertise in this shift. In his earlier volume *A Study on Communism* Hoover points out that there are many Communist activities "with which the average citizen cannot directly contend." But more: "nor would it be desirable for the average citizen to play a direct role in combating them." The struggle against communism must be as professional an activity as "the science of espionage" necessitates. Professionalization of the F.B.I. is an essential ingredient in Hoover's vision.

> To meet effectively the Communist subversive thrusts, it is essential to employ highly professional counterintelligence measures—measures for which the average citizen is neither equipped nor trained. Modern-day counterintelligence, with its emphasis on professional skills and training as well as its reliance on competent scientific aids, is a task of experts.

A third point, to which critics of the Bureau are reluctant to grant credence, is that the FBI in fact quite legitimately has special knowledge. But this is "private" or "classified" knowledge. Hoover is not only privy to things of which the general citizenry is unaware but is also in a position to bludgeon any feeble opposition to his budgetary demands with the superior information at his disposal. The secrecy in which special knowledge is held enables the FBI to claim confidentiality is required for its effective operation. The questions asked by Congressmen on the appropriations subcommittee concerning FBI budgetary requests seem to be presubmitted, if not prearranged.

On the caseload per agent:

Mr. Rooney   What is the present caseload per agent?
Mr. Hoover   The present caseload per agent is 28. That is entirely excessive.
Mr. Rooney   Yes, but that is low compared to years ago, is it not?
Mr. Hoover   Oh, no. It was 19 in 1961. It has gone up every year.

On the law enforcement assistance program:

Mr. Rooney Looking at pages 26–9 of the justification, why does not Mr. Evans' law enforcement assistance program continue to pay for the communication lines for the NCIC which they originally paid for?

Mr. Hoover I am advised that under the authority of the Law Enforcement Assistance Act, they can only give funds to initiate various projects and when a project is working and in operation, then its cost has to be taken over by the agency that operates it and is no longer funded by the Law Enforcement Assistance Act.

Invariably when questions arise concerning matters such as case loads per agent and vague doubts are aired about the need for an increase in the number of agents. Mr. Hoover has the facts at his fingertips and the congressmen meekly respond to the terror of his information edge. Having accepted the presumptions of the Bureau, little can be done to deny the agency budgetary increments. Thus, special knowledge serves both as a weapon or organizational terror and as an instrument of high government finance.

A fourth FBI ploy—and again one not easily recognized, much less referred to, is the notion of its impartiality. The agency is said to be equally harsh toward all enemies of the nation. But its claims to equal treatment are in fact chimerical. A huge volume of pages is offered on the "Communist conspiracy." Only passing references are made to Right-wing organizations such as the Minutemen or the John Birch Society. Hoover's only real concern with the John Birch Society is that so many ex-FBI agents openly work for the Society and make their past affiliation with the FBI a featured selling point. Even under rather obvious prompting to have the FBI go on record about Birch Society activities, Mr. Hoover can only work up enough steam to resent the Birchites' jeopardizing the FBI's presumed impartiality.

Mr. Andrews In this week's *Newsweek* there is an article in "The Periscope," saying, "New Tactics by the Birchers. The John Birch Society plans to expand its nationwide campaign to link the civil-rights movement and communism. The society already is supporting some 454 local TACT (Truth About Civil Turmoil) committees, which use booklets, films, and public speakers (usually billed as ex-FBI undercover agents) to spread their word. Current TACT strongholds: California, Arizona, New Mexico, Utah, Idaho, and Colorado." This looks like more or less a deliberate attempt to capitalize on the name of the FBI."

Mr. Hoover It is an improper attempt to capitalize on the name of the FBI.

Mr. Andrews In other words, this certainly does not indicate what it would do to the average American, that the "ex-FBI undercover agents" are so frustrated in their work in the Agency that they leave and sign up with extremist organizations in order to try to protect America.

Mr. Hoover Nor does it indicate I in any way condone the use of the name "ex-FBI undercover agent" in such endeavors.

Mr. Andrews I am glad to make that clear for the record. Thank you very much. I want to commend you for your outstanding testimony.

Another way in which Mr. Hoover inadvertently discredits the Agency's impartiality is to indicate where agents of the Bureau wind up after leaving the Service.

Mr. Smith Mr. Director, have you noticed any more difficulty in the past year in obtaining and retaining agents?

Mr. Hoover No, I have not, Mr. Congressman. As I indicated, 70 per cent of our special agent personnel have been now and then, but I do not raise any obstacle to it, with us 10 years or longer. We do have a problem of large companies and corporations asking some very capable man in the Bureau to take a position in their organization, such as that of vice president. I lost one man years ago who became vice president of the Ford Motor Co. I lost a man just a few years ago who was agent in charge of my New York office and is now a vice president of American Airlines. There are nine Congressmen and one Senator who are former special agents of the Bureau. (Discussion off the record.)

Just how service in the Bureau equips one for the vice presidency of Ford Motors or American Airlines is not explained. Although one might surmise they are used in connection with plant sabotage, record tampering, and union pressures. Interestingly, vice presidencies seem to be the upper limits of the FBI as a quasi-official placement office.

On matters of impartiality, too, civil rights and political rights are confused. Mr. Hoover continually refers to the work of the enemy with respect to the rights of Negroes in the South. The Ku Klux Klan is converted into a Right-wing counterpart of the Communist party. In point of fact, its specific modes of operation and its quasi-military character distinguish it most sharply from the debating society that the American Communist party now represents. This juxtaposition of Right and Left nonetheless provides precisely that aura of impartiality and equal treatment that permits the FBI to claim a nonideological base. It also so isolates the illegitimate Ku Klux Klan from the other, now more potent (and legitimated) forms of racist organizations, as to inhibit rather than enhance the work of FBI field investigation into violations of Negro liberties.

These four points then: legalism, bureaucratism, priestly wisdom, and political impartiality, coalesce to make possible the legitimacy of the FBI in both war and peace. We must now turn finally to the world as it is perceived by

J. Edgar Hoover and to what could be called his four fears as a public figure—
for it is clear that for Mr. Hoover the world is a perpetually frightening place.

This comes through time and again in his discourses, or better, monologues,
before the House Subcommittee on Appropriations.

First, there is his fear of not living up to the images of the FBI as presented
by the mass media. Although it is clear that Hoover sincerely believes his own
rhetoric, his notion of cleanliness and sound hygienic practices is less the
outcome of an internalized Protestant ethic than it is a response to American
hero-types generated by the mass media, particularly television. Mr. Hoover is
so concerned with what he calls good character and personal appearance that he
would "rather have vacancies than employees who do not measure up to those
qualifications." He refers to the television program on the FBI and the model
inspector as portrayed by Efrem Zimbalist, Jr. Young, well-groomed, cool under
pressure, courteous to all friends of America, the FBI agent is strikingly liberated
from inner turmoil, doubt, confusion, or sophistication. Mirror, mirror on the
wall, how would I look, feel, and act if I were fifty years younger? "Like Efrem
Zimbalist, Mr. Hoover," assured the captive mirror. Without even remotely
hinting at the accuracy of the portrayal, he points out that there is an image that
people have of the FBI, and "I want our agents to live up to that special image."

Related to this whole question of imagery and appearance is Mr. Hoover's
second bugaboo, namely, homosexuality. This theme haunts the man in every
report. Perhaps the most fascinating expression of his concern is the statement
issued in response to Congressman Joelson and Rooney.

Mr. Joelson I notice you stressed appearance with regard to the qualification
of employees.

Mr. Hoover I do.

Mr. Joelson I can understand physical requirements, but why is appearance
so important?

Mr. Hoover As regards appearance, Mr. Congressman, I certainly would not
want to have any beatniks with long sideburns and beards as
employees in the Bureau.

Mr. Rooney How about members of the Mattachine Society?

Mr. Hoover No member of the Mattachine Society or anyone else who is a
sex deviate will ever be appointed to the F.B.I. If I find one in th
F.B.I. he will be dismissed. As to appearance, our special agents
in a broad sense are really salesmen, they interview the presidents
of large banks, the chairmen of the boards of large corporations,
longshoremen, and laborers. They have to sell themselves to them
to get their confidence to obtain the information they need.

The relationship between the Bureau's requirements for an effective agent
and sexuality are perceived to be intertwined themes. What is fascinating,

even puzzling, is that it is apparently perfectly permissible for agents to "sell themselves" in the line of duty but not to "give themselves" in their private experiences. The dialogue is a sobering indication that Mr. Hoover's traditionalist view of masculine behavior will, when integrated with other agent standards, presumably provide a bulwark against sexual and criminal deviance generally. Again, the Hoover hard line seems not so much linked to Protestant beliefs, but to the simple police notion of the dangers in sexual "deviance."

The third great fear is oppressive communism, or better still, the Communist party. Strangely, Mr. Hoover possesses no ideological awareness or even concern with the structure of Communist parties throughout the world. And in the 1969 report, he reveals only the bare recognition of the pluralization of radicalism in the United States. Mr. Hoover has a typical policeman's definition of a Communist, namely, a "dues paying" member of the Communist party. When asked to supply information on Herbert Aptheker, Mr. Hoover quickly jumped up and said, "Yes, and his daughter Bettina is just as much a Communist as he is"—a "dues paying member," no doubt. This constant reference to sad people like Bettina Aptheker, Herbert Aptheker, and Gus Hall indicates Hoover's need to locate a physical embodiment for the Communist evil rather than an analysis of the Party structure. It is not the political role of these poor people (or perhaps their lack of a real political role) but rather their mere existence as "card carriers" that seems so painful and yet so fascinating for Hoover to contemplate.

The primary fear, and the one that is perhaps the most awesome, since it carries implications for everyone who dares object to the behavior of the FBI and its chief, is that of criticism. It is simply impossible for Mr. Hoover to accept the idea of being wrong, to acknowledge an improper understanding of an issue, or in any way to reveal a weakness in either his organization or his personal character. The testimony provided by Mr. Hoover stands as a veritable indictment of congressional timidity and insipidity. At no point in three years of testimony do house members give anything but the most sycophantic response. Hoover is always being congratulated, and in turn the leader drops pleasantries on the home towns of the congressmen before whom he testifies. The city of Monrovia, California, is more frequently cited than any other city or town in America, simply because Congressman Lipscomb comes from Monrovia. This ludicrous conspiracy of mutual flattery serves to deflect criticism and transform the hearings into an annual celebration.

The operative postelection gag-line concerning the F.B.I. has the president-elect in the year 2000 automatically reappointing John Edgar Hoover director of the Service and turning his attention to more problematic choices. This dismal humor points up the totalitarian essence of the organization. For whether Mr. Hoover is in fact the real leader or just front man for other more dynamic figures, is less important than an encrusted situation in which he can no more be replaced or be "permitted" to retire than can Mao Tse-Tung.

Indeed, few doubt that an organizational "crisis" would occur in the FBI were such a retirement to ensue by means other than natural death. But what must also be realized is that the precipitating cause of such a crisis lies within an organizational situation in which one man alone has been permitted to embody the structure and sentiment of the entire force.

Hoover is one of America's few remaining symbols of the pristine age of primitive anticommunism. A leftover from an age of simplicity, if not of purity. His departure would therefore probably have far less effect on the nature of the FBI than it would on a restructuring of other parts of the United States government connected with law and its enforcement. With the departure of Mr. Hoover would go the legitimacy of depression politics, of a policy based on the coping with the Bolshevik Revolution as our chief internal menace. The file checks, wiretaps, security clearances would still remain. After all, they are part of the endemic features of a genteel totalitarian agency. But without Mr. Hoover, each of these interventions into the affairs of private souls would be deprived of its patriotic telos, and seen for crude impositions. Regrettably, Mr. Nixon and his advisors also know this to be true. This is why the FBI's symbol without substance remains stubbornly entombed in his Washington office, while our political leadership hopes that nature disposes of what man, or at least some men, seemingly cannot depose.

From *Catalyst,* vol. 2, no. 1, whole number 5, (1970), pp. 64–75.

25

Middle Classes and Militarism in Latin America[*]

Johnson, John J.

John J. Johnson has written a book on an important subject: the effect of militarism upon the social structure of six nations in South America and one in Central America. If his book is not particularly revealing, or for that matter satisfying, this is due more to the ambiguous nature of the Latin American military than to any defects in the author's thought or prose. It is, after all, extremely difficult to make solid judgments about situational incongruities— some of which have the force (or perhaps dross) of history to support them.

To underscore the author's problems, we will indicate a few of the more apparent incongruities. Latin America turns much too often to its military as the court of ultimate national redemption, while recognizing that the military has crushed democratic and constitutional processes more often and more painfully than any has other social force in the hemisphere. The military has been the traditional bulwark of the anti-Communist crusades without which, as Johnson himself makes plain, nearly every republic in Latin America would stand politically to the left of where it now is. At the same time in the midst of declining Left-wing mass civilian politics, (except in Chile, Bolivia, and perhaps Venezuela), military leftism has been on the crescendo in such diversified political climates as Mexico, Guatemala, Brazil, and Cuba. Indeed, "socialism from above" is just as much a rallying cry among some military elites as "anti-Communist crusade" was in the last decade. The military establishments of Latin America are exemplars of lawlessness in their public behavior and of undemocratic processes in their political action. At the same time, they always make their *golpes* and *manifestaciones* in the name of law, legitimacy, order, and security. Finally, we might mention the fact that the military as a self-seeking and self-promoting segment has no peer in Latin America,

---

[*] John J. Johnson, *The Military and Society in Latin America* (Stanford: Stanford University Press, 1964), pp. 308.

133

yet it is equally insistent (and sometimes properly) that it alone is entitled to perform the role of guardian of the national morality and of the national treasury.

Professor Johnson etches these ambiguities in a way that certainly must elicit respect and admiration for his firm ethnographic capacity, and no less for his choice of past writers on the subject of Latin American militarism. Particularly outstanding is Johnson's ability to weave the facts of history writ large with the need for a theory of military transformation. The bulk of the book, two out of three parts in fact, displays this facile capacity to elicit and to express sonic basic theoretical truths drawn from the network of social events from the independence period to the present. The substance of Johnson's fusion of history and policy is best exemplified by his discussion of the soldier as citizen and bureaucrat and by the function and role of military ideology. By seeing the Latin military first and foremost as an agency of channelized violence and only incidentally as an example of bureaucratic behavior, Johnson spares himself the needless dilemma some students of complex organization have worked themselves into: how to distinguish the military from all other bureaucratic agencies. However limited his typology of civil-militarism may turn out to be, it deserves serious attention from students of economic development, no less than from specialists in social organization.

Johnson's discussion of the social origins and early backgrounds of professional military personnel in Latin America—while drawing heavily upon the work of Silvert, Germani, Lieuwen, Blanksten, and others—is the best synopsis yet available in English.

He points to seven fundamental factors: racial origin, educational levels, small town background of the officer corps, Roman Catholicism, nonpropertied origins, and immigration patterns. These are woven into an interesting tapestry that reveals that in Latin America, (which he regards as unlike North America), social origins and sectional backgrounds count for a great deal in a definition of military stratification. His elaborate discussion of the concept civil-militarism and why it can look forward to a long life, is likewise well reasoned. Here he alludes to three variables. First, since the military is a basic instrument for removing groups in political power, coup d'etat is a part of the democratic process. Second, since the military operates in a context of violence, the choice is not between nonviolent and violent means but between different agencies of violence (the assumption being that in such choices the military ranks better on any common chart than the police or private armies supplied by land-holders or the political parties). The third variable is that the armed forces, since they are divided into interservice and intraservice rivalries, can be exploited by domestic political machines for their own elements.

Johnson's conclusion is significant. As a Latin American nation's economy develops, the country's military decreasingly performs or even desires political roles. Part of any definition of development might very well be the degree and extent of military specialization of function. This is not to be confused with the continued rise in military operations throughout the Third World. Sometimes it is not quite clear whether Johnson realizes a distinction between the size of the armed forces and its character. Development has meant a distinct rise in military expenditures from Argentina to Zanzibar. Independence is sometimes measured by such military power. Thus, while the character of the Latin American military is subject to drastic overhaul, the size of this establishment has nowhere to go but up.

The final section of the book which is on the specific characteristics of the Brazilian military, is overdue; without such analysis the reader would tend to lump the military of Latin America together in an undifferentiated way, without taking into account some of the very special features of the Brazilian historical development that led to a peculiarly nonviolent ideology on the part of the military. Nonetheless, it must be pointed out (as Johnson does in a brief footnote), somewhat somberly in the light of political developments between 1954 and 1964, that the Brazilian military, while historically distinctive, has increasingly acted less responsibly in recent years and therefore now shapes up in a form not unlike that of other Latin American countries. The interference of the Brazilian military, and the cancellation of electoral norms, the Vargas regime of 1954, the Quadros regime of 1961, and the Goulart regime of 1964, make perfectly plain that the military behavior of the Brazilian elite is unfortunately more militaristic than it is Brazilian. As a matter of fact, the Brazilian military elite's whole concept of guardianship has become part of the *Falangist* rhetoric throughout the hemisphere. Perhaps it is because of my own greater awareness of Brazil, but I feel that Johnson's treatment of the Brazilian military, while quite extensive, lacks a certain intensively. There is scant information on the relationships between the Second and Third Armies, between military chieftains such as Assiz Brasil and Castelo Branco, and between the *tenentes* and the *regulares*. This information could have been used to illustrate various dilemmas of the military in Latin America in general and Brazil in particular.

The final section especially highlights the weaknesses of the book. Although the distinction between Hispanic and Brazilian military patterns is made sharply, distinctions between military establishments are not drawn as clearly. For example, the highly professionalized military elite of Mexico and Uruguay contrasts sharply with the highly politicized military elites of Argentina and most Central American republics. But how this distinction between professionalization and politicalization links up with problems of Latin American social structure is not established. Likewise, the function of "revolution from above" and "revolution from below," which plays so pivotal a role in the developmental process of the area, is simply left out of the reckoning. Even more seriously, the disclaimers offered by Johnson in his prefatory remarks do not satisfy the requirements of the subject he has chosen. It is simply not meaningful to say that information on the police, on state and national militia, and on private armies was excluded from consideration because such factors did not substantively affect the interpretations offered in the volume. The contrary is the case. Had Johnson dealt with the militia and these private armies, only then could he have appreciated the extent and the extensiveness of military force and violence in the area. For it is with these private armies that the full force of feudalism in the agrarian sectors is maintained. The regulars may make palace uprisings, but it is the bandits who maintain the status quo.

In a country like Brazil, especially, where a regional governor can muster a private army of 40,000 troops within a fortnight, the true nature of the guerrilla movement and its feudal land holding obligations, can be ascertained. To be sure, the weakness in the political clout of Johnson's much vaunted middle sectors derive in no small part from the persistence of police power and private armies apart from established legal authority. For example, the existence of armed paramilitary units in Bolivia, over and above the regular army, stamps Bolivia as a special national situation to be studied most carefully. Left and Right meld, and the victim are those segments of civil society who, through thick and thin, retain a sense of constitutional order.

Although Johnson disclaims having any special knowledge or special qualifications to deal with Castro's Cuba, the fact that some of his large-scale generalizations stand or fall on the Cuban experience sheds doubt on his disclaimer. For example, his statement that there is nowhere in Spanish America a situation comparable to what is found in some of the Third World nations of Africa and Asia, where officers can claim the right to direct government activities on the basis of both acquired skills and moral leadership, is challenged precisely by the Cuban experience. Castroism is exactly that manifestation of Third World ideology championed by Ben Bella, Tito, Nasser, Toure, Sukarno, and other leaders of the Afro-Asian "bloc." One might add that Cuba became a Communist dictatorship despite its large middle class. In short, social class without a corresponding political power does not necessarily prevail.

It might also be a personal idiosyncrasy, but I simply cannot get used to, nor can I accept, the language of "middle sectors" and "working groups." Middle classes should be called middle class, and working classes should be called working class. However noble the intent to broaden the language of social stratification, to use an ecological concept of sectors and a concept of groups where the language of class is established and available, is a form of obfuscation that violates the spirit and substance of Occam's razor.

There is a purely esoteric, almost secretive aspect of *The Military and Society in Latin America*. The book can be read as a refutation on the part of current Johnson (1964) of vintage Johnson (1958). His earlier book, *Political Change in Latin America*, was basically a paean of praise to the middle class. But in the new work, he points out the following: (a) the middle "sectors" have forsaken radicalism in favor of conservatism; (b) the higher the stake middle classes have in society, the lower the number of risks they are willing to take to promote social change; (c) middle class support for militarism and the growing reciprocity of that support, that is, the militaristic support of the middle sectors, invalidates claims of middle class democracy; (d) statism is defined as a bureaucratic control of economic resources, and this bureaucracy is nothing if it is not the core of the middle classes; and (e) on the very last pages—irony of ironies—Johnson promulgates the strange idea that the military will save Latin American civilization for, if not from, the middle classes. For the line folks, life in the villages and in the underdeveloped portions of their own nations is held to be repugnant and a "virtual banishment from civilization." At this point the military are to be conscripted into a gigantic domestic "military Peace Corps," or what is more likely, into an enormous Works Progress Administration, all because the middle classes have little stomach for the kind of material sacrifices that identification with a serious nationalism entails.

But this is Professor Johnson's private problem. From the point of view of the book, the argument of the middle sector is not particularly decisive. It may be a necessary condition for stability and growth. It is not a sufficient condition. Since the structure of military rule is, by Johnson's own statement, the source of the problem of Latin American development (and distortions thereof); it must also be addressed by any proffered solutions.

As a final point of criticism, one would have to say that although this is a book of scholarship, it suffers from an overdose of policy-making jabberwocky. In a work of this type, there is little excuse for self-indulgent statements on the priority (Johnson or the Defense Department) of worthwhile civilian assignments for the military in Latin America. Everyone knows that Professor Johnson has friends in the Defense Department. Nor is it only a question of personal commentary that reveals the extent of substituting policy making for common sense. The entire section entitled "Retrospect and Prospect" is an example of the kind of conceit that disguises an absence of real recommendations. To end the book with the proposal that the solution to the problem of militarism is convert it into a WPA project is simply not to take seriously the degree to which militarism in Latin America is not a viable operational tool, but a narrow political stratum, interested in its own private advancement.

Despite Johnson's disclaimer, the absence of any discussion whatsoever of the role of the United States military assistance programs to Latin America has the effect of weakening the historical sections of the book. The fact that such military assistance programs got under way only after 1953 had a tremendous effect in simultaneously professionalizing the military and in increasing their political role within each nation. Between 1933 and 1953 the basic United States position was based upon Roosevelt's Good Neighbor Policy, in which economic assistance was emphasized at the expense of military assistance. Even during World War II, United States military assistance to latin America was not especially significant, with only token military combat on the part of Latin American troops.

Without evaluating the nature and impact of various United States programs, talking about the military and society in Latin America and not once making serious or critical reference to the United States distorts the situation. For example, Professor Johnson alludes to the fact that the military budgets of each Latin American nation range from between 0.1 percent and 3.3 percent, whereas in the United States it ranks at approximately 9.8 percent. But what is left out of the reckoning is that these percentages are based on the gross national product, and the defense expenditures do not include foreign aid receipts.

Once this adjustment in the defense budget is made, we find that the total military expenditures in Latin America zoom to approximately three to five times the figures based exclusively on the GNP. For example, in Argentina, military allocation is 13.2 percent of the total national budget, while it is only 2.6 percent of the GNP. Chile earmarks 18.0 percent of its total budget for military purposes, while if the GNP is used as the base line, its expenditure is only 2.8 percent. Peru likewise allocates 18.0 percent of its budget for military purposes, of which only 3.2 percent is derived from the GNP. Similar differentials occur across the Latin American board. The statistical gap is made up almost entirely by foreign aid programs. Not to deal with this factor, not even to mention it, is not a symbol of modesty but an illustration of default.

Sad as it is to report, I had the strong impression, admittedly subjective and hence tentative, that Johnson is speaking in the same optative mood with respect to the military in the sixties, that he made with respect to the middle classes in the fifties. He is endowing a stratum or a sector with a national dimension and a capacity for self-sacrifice that is only rarely met with in reality. One must conclude that the very lessons of the book have been done an injustice, as a result. I would make bold to suggest three reasons driving Johnson to a metaphysical endowment of a single social element with curative powers beyond anyone's wildest dreams.

First, there is the author's insistence on ending his book with an instruction sheet for policy makers, whether or not such instructions flow from the nature of the evidence. The blend of scholarship and counsel bespeaks well of the author's patriotism, but it does little to alleviate the ambiguities with which he begins. Second, when Johnson says military, he really means the armed forces primarily of Argentina, Brazil, and Chile—a perfectly valid limitation, but one which necessarily poses upon the author certain restrictions and restraints concerning the vitality and dynamic possibilities of the military. Were he to use as his models or at least among his models, the Central American states plus those South American nations like Peru, the optative mood might be considerably diminished. Third, there is an over-generalization from the interaction of military performance and social structure in other areas of the world. The work of Lucien Pye and Guy Pauker might have much to offer the student of comparative military elites, but as examples or case materials for the study of Latin American militarism, they are of severely circumscribed merit.

While Professor Johnson has undertaken a king-sized chore and carried it off with a certain polish and aplomb, this is not yet the major study of Latin American militarism we had anticipated and hoped would be produced by the brilliant Stanford historian. In the main, rather than a synthesis of theory and history, *The Military and Society in Latin America* is too policy oriented to be sound general theory and too panoramic to be engrossing history.

From *Economic Development and Cultural Change,* vol. 13, no. 2 (1965), pp. 238–42.

26

Prophecy and Postindustrial Myths*

Kumar, Krishan

While sharing the title *Post-industrial Society,* these two books remain at opposite vocational, as well as geographical ends of the same subject. The volume by Krishan Kumar is a useful, comprehensive, sociological overview of modern societies, whereas the volume edited by Bo Gustafsson is a collection of advanced papers presented in 1977 on the occasion of the five-hundredth anniversary of Uppsala University that seeks to shed light on fundamental economic aspects and trends of contemporary society. However, both remain volumes in search of a theory of the postindustrial. Professor Gustafsson, in introducing these economic papers, puts the matter as plainly as possible: "We need a *theory* that can subsume the selected empirical manifestations under some unifying and explanatory concepts; a theory which, given those manifestations, helps us to interpret them in terms of some underlying, more general and necessary relations of the system." Since Professor Kumar also applauds "the search" for "the way out of the present dilemma of the industrial societies," theory is clearly a shared concern of the two volumes. Both make a serious effort to locate those variables that will help to determine the "qualitative transformation" of our system, although it is hard to know if the authors mean by "system" capitalism, welfarism, liberalism, or statism. Some brief summary of where the postindustrial paradigm stands prior to the issuance of these two books is in order, if for no other reason than to assess these books for their novelty and worth.

The major axiomatic principles of postindustrial society are as follows: Ours is a society of private property and the private control of investment

---

* Krishan Kumar, *Prophecy and Progress; The Sociology of Industrial and Post-industrial Society* (London: Allen Lane Ltd. and Harmondsworth, Middlesex, and New York: Penguin Books 1978), pp. 416.

Bo Gustafsson (Editor), *Post-Industrial Society* (London: Croom-Helm Ltd. and New York: St. Martin's Press. 1979), pp. 238.

decisions, but it also is an industrial society whose primary logic is techno-logical efficiency. Using such a division we can identify different sequences of development. Along the axis of private property we have feudalism, cap-italism, and socialism, whereas along the axis of technology we have prein-dustrial, industrial, and postindustrial. There is a built-in contradiction with the principle of equality, which is based on participation. This contradiction leads to bureaucracy segmenting people into roles. Social tensions in Western democracy have been framed by the contrary logic of bureaucratization and participation; this is undergirded by a change of scale in institutions, leading to a profound shift in functions. Postindustrial society is characterized by the codification of theoretical knowledge, specifically new technological-scientific activities oriented about electronics, telecommunications, optics, polymers, and computers. Control of the means of information augments the struggle over the means of production in such a society, and hence the character of work alters significantly. Work becomes a game or struggle between persons rather than a game or struggle against either real or fabricated nature. Finally, in a postindustrial universe, society becomes a free choice of free people, rather than a banding together against nature or an involuntary fusion of routinized relations imposed from outside.

Economic writings on postindustrialism are still in search of a theory and those selected variables that make for a qualitative transformation of the sys-tem. With Gustafsson the emphasis is on changes from a goods-producing to a service economy and the centrality of knowledge itself as a source of knowledge in policy formation. Class issues evolve when a new intellectual technology becomes central. The difficulty in both elementary and advanced texts is that what constitutes post-industrial is still exceedingly vague, although Kumar in particular is sensitive to a futurology that "has been just this attempt to close off the future." Living in a world that is still for the most part preindustrial, I feel these kinds of discussions are premature. But more, the orientation toward technology creates a confusion over the nature of the social system as such. For underneath the impulse to develop a new theory is a search to beyond the economic determinism of the nineteenth century and the political determinism of the twentieth; this search stakes a claim for a technological determinism of the former and the political determinism of the latter. Sadly, neither volume takes up the question of determinism per se; neither admits that the effort to organize a new paradigm around the concept of the industrial may itself be suspect.

Such problems notwithstanding, some reasonable discussions take place in both volumes. The Kumar text, which clearly is a product of a series of lectures given over a period of years, covers a broad array of subjects and provides a capsule listing of authors (in the English language) who at one time or another have had something to say about modern society. The key chapters from the point subject matter are sections 5 through 7 (pp. 164–300), where the issues of the climax of industrialism, the rediscovery of government future studies, and an image of a new society based on services and professionalization are taken up. For those new to this area and for those seeking a basic sociological guidance, the Kumar book is quite satisfactory. It might well serve as a primer to economic sociology, based largely on Weberian concepts with an ample supply of quotations from Durkheim and Marx to quench the thirst of their devotees. The discussion of secularization, rationalization, and bureaucratization is particularly well handled. Throughout, there is a strong sense of historical continuity.

The book suffers from its classroom origins. It is altogether too chatty; it continues to refer to famous figures as if they are breathlessly being introduced for the first time. This sounds a strange note when people like Engels are mentioned as "the co-worker of Marx" 300 pages and 100 citations into the book. There is also a tendentious character to the writing, which makes for a certain tedium. For example, platitudes like "sociologists are also people," abound, leading me to suspect that the translation of materials from the lecture podium to the book was insufficiently thought through. Another irritant is the constant invocation of authorities and long quotations that are only seldom dealt with critically, and are simply invoked as a hierarchy of authority closing off discussion just when it becomes interesting, as if the fixation of belief in major figures itself warrants the truth of what is recorded in the sacred texts.

In a lecture series this sort of approach is reasonable, but a book that constantly switches back and forth from analysis of empirical realities to an elaboration of social science texts, sounds like part of a great-books series rather than an exploration into controversial themes. Perhaps this is just as well, since when Kumar does speak on his own the results are not always gratifying. For example, to speak of the GNP as "a misleading index" and even "an insane way of calculating increments of welfare," citing as an authority for this Ivan Illich, simply does not convince. The illustration provided on the falsification of the GNP is spurious. The assumption that GNP is inflated because high-rise, high-density blocks of apartments add to the GNP and are more expensive to build than the equivalent amount of housing at lower density is pure speculation. No evidence exists to indicate that such high-rise apartments are more expensive than low-rise separate units. If there is a difference it is so marginal as to scarcely affect the GNP, and it affects GNP not as an index of progress, but in terms of the total volume of goods and services sold and bought on the market. Kumar's attack on the GNP as a measurement, without offering any alternative, is simply gratuitous. His "serious questioning" of R & D as a technological measure of development is equally idiosyncratic, assuming as it does that the Leavy R & D investment in existing and applied research somehow invalidates any claim for this as a measure of "theoretical knowledge."

What this points to is a problem that becomes even more manifest in the Gustafsson collection; namely, the search for theory goes on in a world where the line between preindustrial and postindustrial is hardly resolved. In the Gustafsson volume, it turns out that the postindustrial can mean anything from the welfare state, to the mixed economics, to state monopoly capitalism. The papers themselves range from the economics history and political economy of China to the East European economics and Scandinavian societies. How China fits any model of postindustrial is hard to fathom. Even more quixotic is the intervention by the editor, indicating that the Chinese have turned the Soviet model upside down and have expressed their determination to abolish all privileges and, in so doing, change the priorities from heavy industry to a high premium on agriculture and low premium on industry. In the last three years this is precisely what has changed as the Chinese go the way of all developmental models, that is, toward maximizing development through industrialism.

One finds it odd, but nonetheless true, that all of these emphases on postindustrial analysis, based as they are on a sense of the future, make such dramatically inappropriate predictions. Some of these predictions are keenly pointed out in the comments attached to the papers by Rolf Adamson, Francis Sejersted, Ragnar Bentzel, and Leif Johansen. Hence, in his paper on East European economics, Alex Nove assumes that although each country in Eastern Europe has different traditions, they somehow are a unified block, made so by a Soviet master. The piece is so heavily taken up with ideological considerations that scant emphasis is given to the fact that some countries in Eastern Europe have been successful and others much less so in achieving reasonable rates of growth and that much of these differences can be explained on the basis of long-run secular trends in the industrialization and urbanization processes. Indeed, most of the discussion on East European economics is a critique on Soviet planning and its relative backwardness in catching up with Western theory. But no one seems willing to say plainly that the public sector might itself be the source of the problem—especially since Sweden represents a paragon of "middle-term planning." One gets the distinct impression that only the capitalist system "is subjected to crucial, or at least deep, crisis." However, the papers on the socialist and welfare systems indicate that they too are subject to parallel crises. It turns out that postindustrial has an uncomfortably Swedish cast: "The democratization of society, together with union organization and political strength of the working class, have resulted in society placing obligations on the economic system of such a far-reaching character that they cannot be fulfilled without state intervention and direction." Hence, postindustrial becomes equated with state power—benign power to be sure.

An exceptionally fine paper is Alan Peacock's "Public Expenditure Growth in Post-industrial Society." Here the focus is that the most important problem for postindustrial societies is how to develop collections that improve the functionary of suppliers of government services. The paper makes shrewd judgments and, at the same time, is statistically sophisticated, showing well the Wilensky effect (i.e., the degree to which people are happy to consume government services but increasingly restive about paying for them). This critical review of the determinism of growth and governmental expenditures is good, but it too fails to show why the problems are postindustrial rather than characteristic of the ongoing relationship of state to economy.

Another thought-provoking paper is by Karl-Gustaf Hildebrand who, while emphasizing the Scandinavian experience, points out how modern societies have witnessed revolutionary changes in the role of functionaries and salaried employees and how these changes correspond to the diffusion of higher education and the acceptance of taxation. This transformation from a concept of education as a fine art to a practical resource is a major aspect of contemporary development in industrial life. Whether such a transformation is beneficial or not, whether it serves a *technocracy* at the expense of technology, is an argument beyond the confines of this essay.

The volume retreats from its own limits, coming to rest on a definition of postindustrial society that emphasizes service and welfare. The volume theorizes about only capitalist postindustrialism, although the presence of essays on the Soviet bloc and China remains unexplained. The motivational analysis is at the level of neither grand theory nor description, but somewhere in between. For those interested in advanced problems of industrial societies, especially welfare societies of Scandinavia, this is a useful, if ancillary, text. But those interested in answers to the larger issues posed by the title and the introduction will still have to refer to the earlier writings in this area, specifically within the sociological tradition extending from Bell and the economic tradition of Schumpeter to Wilensky.

One cannot help but conclude with a feeling that the study of postindustrial society takes place in an atmosphere of continuing confusion as to what constitutes the main motivating factors in social change. As a result, postindustrialism as a paradigm turned ideology can easily disguise rather than illuminate. It can mean anything from the role of knowledge in advanced economics to the role of coercion in developing societies. As a transitional concept, postindustrial might prove pragmatically satisfactory. But as a structural statement that integrates commerce, policy, and knowledge, it clearly is not adequate. These two works are testimonials as much to what still needs to be done to work out new paradigms as they are to the fact that old paradigms no longer work.

There is a final problem with the concept of the post-industrial that scholars like Hadley Cantril, Alex Inkeles and Daniel Bell, each in their own way, have addressed, but are scarcely mentioned in these works. In a nutshell, even if we could arrive at a structural definition of the post-industrial, the personality dimensions operate at a different and often independent axis. In one and the same person we can locate the scientist, the mystic who carries a rabbit's foot for good luck, and the political conservative whose sense of the social is

145

far more prudential than his sense of the research enterprise. And it is only when a genuine integration of the structural and personality dimensions is achieved that a unified theory of social development or post-industrial economy becomes remotely plausible.

From *Technology and Culture: The International Quarterly of the Society for the History of Technology*, vol. 20, no. 4 (1979), pp. 848–52.

27

Modernization as Abstract Expression*

Levy, Marion J.

The fate of books intended to be classics in their fields is notoriously similar: heartbreaking failures in their ultimate aim. It is no easy matter to consider a volume of at least a decade in the making and—for me at least—a three-month task in the reading. But I am compelled to state at the outset and with genuine dismay that Marion Levy's *Modernization and the Structure of Societies* is less immortal than it is irrelevant.

I want to be very clear: there are times when the book rises to lucid heights, but they are too few and too far between to merit so much rhetoric. There are times when the book develops sound critiques of the developmental literature, but they are marred by a choking anger that leads nowhere or by a neglect of literature that might confound and hence blunt the thrust of polemic. There are times when the book reaches innovative patterns that will undoubtedly serve to substantiate the author's claim to have written a "setting for international relations," but they are offset by system-building gimmicks that, at their best, are reminiscent of post-Hegelian constructions and, at their worst, are reminiscent of the prose of post-World War II textbooks.

Professor Levy is an erudite and brilliant mind without the obvious traces of intellectual vanity, but he is also insensitive to the requirements of the written word, or at least to the difference between the skills of the writer and the techniques of the classroom lecturer. Levy unnecessarily burdens the reader with the trials and tribulations of intellectual production. Such scaffolding does nothing to convince the reader of an author's profundity. Indeed, it may lead to a resentment of the book as a whole. Thus, while I must applaud his effort to construct a book of general theory, it would have been more pleasant to record the success of such construction.

---

* Marion J. Levy, Jr., *Modernization and the Structure of Societies: A Setting for International Affairs* (Princeton: Princeton University Press, 1966), 2 vols., pp. 855.

And this is a book on general theory, as Levy makes clear in many ways: by turning over huge chunks of the work to studying "the structure of relatively modernized and relatively non-modernized societies," with subsections on "aspects of any relationship," and further, "aspects of any society." Since "any society" means the same as "no society," there is a strong temptation to reject Levy's framework out of hand. The demand for evidence often goes unheeded; or, to use one of Levy's own strange phrases, often deteriorates into a "capricious particularism." Nonetheless, this aspect of Levy's work is, for me, most meaningful. So often the answer to high-powered statistical data is humble personal observation. In this competition over styles of work, it is sometimes forgotten that sociology does have a generalizing function. And it is much easier to scoff at the results obtained than to offer workable contrasts.

Far more disconcerting than the general theory within which he operates is Levy's alarming tendency to take fictions as facts. Statements about the social world that he ushers forth are oftentimes one of three varieties, (1) outrightly incorrect from an empirical point of view, (2) stated in such a way as to defy any logical meaning; or (3) platitudes devoid of real in contrast to formal significance. Each of these types of statements is linked to what can only be considered a remarkably idiosyncratic approach to footnotes.

A good illustration of the outrightly incorrect is Levy's statement that "since the turn of this century the income distribution picture in the United States, which is generally considered by its own members and others to be one of the more purely capitalistic countries in the world, has been characterized more by the extent to which the mean, median, and mode of income have approached identity than by the increase in the mean of income." Evidently the mass of directly contradicting information gathered by the United States Census Bureau has no influence on Levy's cogitations. The facts are that: (1) the income distribution gap is not narrowing, but widening ever so slowly as a general pattern; (2) particular ethnic groups such as Negroes, Puerto Ricans, and Mexicans, the gap is widening dramatically with respect to the population as a whole; (3) even if we were to assume that the gap between various measures of income has come to "approach identity" (meaning, I would surmise, that America is an egalitarian society), this would make little sense since devices for measurement do not in themselves explain the actual distribution of wealth. The footnote on this odd statement (as in many other instances) offers no information whatsoever on social stratification but only an absurd discussion of truisms about capitalism and socialism that have no perceptible relevance to the substance of Levy's claims.

Examples of statements that defy logical meaning are in such abundance that it is only a question of picking out a choice item or two. Take this methodological imperative, given as a footnote on page 161: "One of the rough rules of thumb of theory is that once one exceeds six or seven distinctions on any level (and these two aspects would give us eight) some more general less complicated level should be sought." At a somewhat more oracular level is the following approach to Marx: "The degree of economic self-sufficiency of a given society is never the sole relevant variable in understanding that society, but it is never totally irrelevant either." Nor are these exclusively problems of syntax. The problem of vagrant meaning is deeply embedded in the core of the work, in the concept of nonmodernized and modernized societies. Invariably and inevitably, nearly every central concept in the book is prefaced by the modifier "relatively." But, while we are continually reminded that distinctions about modernized and non-modernized societies are relative, Levy gives us no clue as to how relative "relatively" ever is. The following *sentence* from the section on Economic Allocation is quite typical: "Apart from relatively non-modernized societies of relatively small scale, various elements of the productivity picture of relatively modernized societies for the first time in world history not only make curves of income distribution approaching type II possible, but, historically speaking, they also make them highly probable."

Finally, there is the welter of platitudes. The requirements of a review prevent us from a full exposition. But we may choose as a good indicator Levy's discussion of role deviation. We are told, for example, that "in all known societies women, not men, are mothers." Later on the same page we are told, "There never has been a society in terms of which the sex of a member is completely irrelevant to that member's position in matters of authority and responsibility." Here we have the odd situation where the footnotes are not only irrelevant but downright bizarre. It is hard to figure out whether Professor Levy is putting his readers on or whether he is serious. The evidence for his theory of role differentiation—as those who take the patience to read this volume will confirm—derives from and revolves around one basic source, and that is the phonograph record (78 rpm), *I Am My Own Grandpa*, written by Dwight Latham and Moe Jaffe and performed by Lonzo and Oscar with the Winston County Pea Pickers. For those wishing to track down this reference further, it is RCA Victor 20-2563A. Lest the reader miss the decisive role of the reference, it is actually repeated twice again in the same section. Another example of the same kind of writing is in his discussion of the role of capital formation in international affairs, a very serious subject and one that deserves and has received better in Levy's own writings on Chinese and Asian development. Here, the issue is summed up as follows: "Without getting involved in this sort of discussion the relevance of money and the use of money for the finer things of life might well be reconsidered." Many of Levy's positions have the flavor of proverbs such as "Life is like a cup of tea." "All things are relative," or "The struggle between good and evil is enduring." But such conventional wisdom hardly requires sociological embellishment.

Now, given such quixotic excesses, one would at least expect some cordiality from Mr. Levy toward his peers. But what is offered instead is an opinionated and even bad-tempered response to the few scholars cited. He speaks of Professor Wittfogel in intimate terms and, in his critique of Wittfogel's neglect of decentralization in Chinese history, says: "He probably would not or could not have made the contribution for which we are indebted to him had he not overstated and oversimplified the case." To spice this back-handed compliment, poor Professor Wittfogel is given no first name and an incorrect first initial A. Another example is Levy's dismissal of Gabriel Almond. "I regard this particular set of neologisms as one of the more clear-cut cases of unjustifiable jargon in the social sciences." At this point one can either burst into laughter or dissolve in tears at the source of this objection to neologisms and jargon. Nor does Professor Levy allow changes in the social sciences to temper his prejudices. Thus, a worthwhile section on armed forces organizations is marred by an extensive, running polemic against the neglect of the role of the military in social organization and change. While this attack may have had currency during the fifties, it is wide of the mark for 1966 (the copyright date of the book). But in footnote 4 on page 575, we are told that an "exception" to the negative characterizations offered is a book published in 1962, which Levy points out "was published after this chapter was written." In other words, the entire polemic rests on intellectual conditions at least five years old. Given the shrill stridency of this section, it would have been incumbent upon any other author to be sure that his critique is relevant. It is in the nature of the prophetic tradition to ignore such safety measures.

There is little purpose in any lengthy exposition concerning Professor's Levy's stylistic approach. Those who know his previous work must judge for themselves, and those who might read this text as their first introduction to Levy might well wonder why methodologists alone are singled out for lack of style. More to the point is the use of language to disguise ambiguity. Because endless qualifications are introduced in discussing nearly every issue raised, it is often quite impossible to say precisely what Levy is arguing for (or against) at any given point. The demand for clarity is not a literary urging but a scientific requirement. And at this level, one is simply hard pressed to say kind things about this book. Admittedly, Levy deals with a complicated subject matter. Unfortunately, the expression of such complications does little to make the difficult more intelligible. For all its length, this is a nonbook, a series of statements showing faint traces of interconnection between chapters and ideas.

Professor Levy concludes his performance with the statement that "the great vulnerability of this work does not inhere in the fact that hypotheses about the facts, though carefully labeled as such, have been flatly asserted without any accompanying attempt at empirical demonstration." Characteristically, he does not say what he perceives to be the most vulnerable part of his work. For my own part, I must simply contest Levy's apologia and assert, just as flatly, that the utter avoidance of empirical evidence (if not ignorance of it) is indeed the most vulnerable side of his approach to modernization. He is distinctly in error even concerning the lack of "adequate empirical materials."

150

Every man has his own criteria of adequacy, but those working in the field of international development know very well that what we have in greatest abundance is precisely the evidence, and what is most lacking are theories bearing upon such evidence. I regret to say that Levy's dualism of general theory and specific data is specious. It perpetuates myths about the field of international development that have kept serious scholars at bay. The truth is we know more about macroscopic situations and events than we do about intimate details of social interaction. But the theory to meet the challenges of the data has yet to be developed, precisely because of false barriers erected between ranges of fields studied.

The theory of social life is worthy or unworthy across the board: the notion of small range, middle range, and large range to meet the need of small scale, middle scale, and large scale events is largely gratuitous. What we need is a unified theory of social science that accounts for and explain variations and consistencies in the modernization of social life. I honestly feel that Professor Levy shares such a view of sociological performance, but his methodological pretensions prevent him from realizing his own vision. To imagine that "hypotheses about the facts" may serve "as challenges to the data which may some day be collected" is to deny the empirical, inductive basis of sociology as such. But sadder still, it is to equate a general theory with an oracular vision.

From *American Sociological Review*, vol. 31, no. 6 (1966), pp. 857– 60.

28

Intellectuals and Social Change*

Molnar, Thomas

This book represents a significant contribution to the current debate concerning the vitality of inherited political ideologies of Marxism, liberalism, conservatism, and fascism. The author, although receiving his advanced training in French literature in the United States, reveals a distinctly European mode of writing. Despite his acquaintance with some of the popular American social science literature, his approach is humanistic rather than scientific, rationalist rather than empirical. For those wishing reinforcement of the "end of ideology" notion, as it emerges in the refracted mirror of a European conservative conscience, this book will prove of considerable interest. Those who envision an analysis of intellectual life in terms of the "social components" of intellectuals, rather than exclusively in terms of the ideas they produce, will perhaps be disappointed. This is a book with a "message," to which the resources and findings of social science are bent.

The thesis offered by Molnar is that the emergence of the intelligentsia as a social force has to do with its capacity to act as an agency for social change, to act on behalf of the bourgeois sectors of postfeudal society, while at the same time to promote its own universal interests in peace, truth, humanity, brotherhood, and the religion of equality. But with the success of the bourgeoisie, with its victory in Europe between 1789 and 1848, the intelligentsia was caught in a double bind between the conflicting necessities of servicing bourgeois social institutions and playing its role as an agency of change. Capitalism, which promised to establish the lost unity of man and society, only served to deepen the condition of alienation. It thus set in motion against itself the very forces of criticism that prior to the French Revolution found sustenance in the bourgeois critical spirit. But the "decline" of the intellectual has to do precisely with his casting about for some other lost paradise of the whole

---

* Thomas Molnar, *The Decline of the Intellectual* (Cleveland: Meridian Books, World Publishing Co., 1961), pp. 369.

man (in the present period, the proletariat). Instead of acting as a social force in his own right, the intellectual once more seeks moral redemption in the contest of other social classes. In this way, intellectualism becomes wedded to ideology, and this very wedding betokens the break now witnessed between intellectual production and philosophical speculation, (which for Professor Molnar is the true end of the idea-workers).

But the decline of the intellectual is profoundly rooted in changed conditions and relations. Here Molnar stakes his claim to uniqueness. He maintains that, while the postfeudal relations needed intellectuals, the post-capitalist world does not. Intellectuals are needed by political-ideological elites, while the life of technological-bureaucratic societies tends to bypass the scrutinization of ideas and ideologies. The end of ideology thus comes to signify not simply the displacement of secularized social science by an older clerical intelligentsia, but the termination of the intelligentsia as such. Molnar's conservative position is possibly more radical than the liberalism of the Seymour Martin Lipset or Daniel Bell hypothesis—since the latter simply assumes that the end of ideology is a consequence of affluence, while Molnar sees in this same development a threat to the integrity of intellect as such. The search for wholeness ceases in the modem period. The break in function between intellect and practicality becomes complete. The bureaucratic pathos becomes complete, all the while celebrated by ex-intellectuals turned technicians. This material is forcibly presented in the author's section on the European intellectuals, where Molnar is clearly on solid ground. In America, this tendency for the intellectual to be displaced by the technocrat is seen in the rise of mass education, the mechanization of selection, and the routinization of mental work.

Molnar, however, girds himself for the task of redefining the function of intellect, with scanty ammunition. After categorically dismissing communism, Marxism, liberalism (which he takes in pure form to be much like the first two), and a conservatism turned fascistic, the author is left with a critical conservatism that shows yearning and nostalgia for inherited forms of intellectual thought, but does not take seriously (*a*) that such philosophical styles of thought that existed in the medieval world are indeed behind us, (*b*) that the decline of intellectuals as a special group may be a permanent situation and not a temporary aberration, and (*c*) that intellectuals have flourished in a climate of ideologies and counter-ideologies, so that Molnar's call for an end of ideology and a return to philosophy is simply a misanthropic expression of that very decline of intellectual activity the author ostensibly bemoans the loss of.

For someone who sees Marx and his successors as villains in this drama— through science, secularism, and socialism—it is disquieting to note the occasions on which Molnar's *facts* are inaccurate. Lenin did not write a book *Rationalism and Empirio-Criticism* but rather *"Materialism and Empirio-Criticism.* The poet-author Mayakovsky is not "a prohibited author" in Soviet Russia and to a remarkable degree unlike other Soviet writers of talent who could have been mentioned, has retained his audience in Party circles throughout the shifts of the last quarter century; Marx did *not* write "his doctoral dissertation on Heraclitus, the philosopher of dynamism and continuous change," but rather on Greek atomism, that is, a comparative analysis of the philosophy of nature in Democritus and Epicurus. In any event, the relation of Marx's dissertation to the fact that "for the progressive, everything is in motion" is unfathomable.

I should also like to call Molnar's attention to his statement "that law and sociology officially do not exist in the Soviet Union. Law is taught at the Police Academy and sociology is smuggled in unofficially, in the anthropology departments of the universities." After long acquiescence in Stalinist orthodoxy, which viewed sociology as consciously antisocialist, the Soviet Union now takes a more conciliatory attitude. Sociology chairs exist at major universities, while an Institute of Sociological Research (whatever its level of research) now exists at the University of Leningrad. As for the legal profession, Molnar's statement makes no sense. Law as a discipline and profession has never ceased to exist; and to maintain that law is taught at the police academy is to confuse the formal structure of Soviet law with its latent support for repressive measures. As for sociology being smuggled through "anthropology departments," this is an impossibility since anthropology departments are nonexistent. The Soviet attitude toward anthropology continues to be that this subject, as taught and applied, is an academic extension of imperialism—an attempt to interfere in the sovereignty of underdeveloped peoples. Though chairs and well-developed institutes of archaeology and linguistics exist, to the best of my knowledge, the same cannot be said for anthropology.

It is important for Molnar to base his exhortations on evidence, as well as on intuition. Factual accuracy is important in ideological discourse. Continuous lapses at the empirical level only weaken an essentially sound approach. However, despite these lapses, the book remains a stimulating, even important, contribution to the "great debate" on the nature of the beast called the modern intellectual—a rare bird courted by many although observed by few.

From *The American Journal of Sociology* vol. 68, no. 4 (1963), pp. 495–97.

29

Personal Values and Social Change*

Moore, Wilbert E.

To examine any work by Wilbert E. Moore is to confront an honest intellectual product. And by honesty I mean a degree of self-awareness that at the same time is self-critical. Not many sociologists will admit that they have "been challenged particularly and correctly on a fundamental point of social stratification. Fewer still recognize the handicap of studying social change after having "been long subject to the discipline of thought in sociology that discouraged the study of change." Having been reared myself in a tradition of "conflict sociology," I find it equally difficult to appreciate the primacy of social structure and social order. This admission should make it clear that my differences with this text may well be due to contrasting intellectual upbringings rather than to disagreement with any of its specific facts or analytic frames.

One could treat this slim volume perfunctorily, as a useful pedagogic tool well worth the attention of first-year students of sociology, and relax with a feeling of a job well done. However, the questions in *Social Change* are much too vital for such casual commentary. I propose therefore to deal with basic questions in search of an answer.

The first section on the "normality of change" contains an acute critique of functional equilibrium models, with their assumptions of perfect integration, absence of strains and inconsistencies through time, and their foreclosure on questions of the sources of change. But whether a view of social agencies as instruments of tension management does more than introduce change as a factor of structure, remains unresolved. Insofar as Aristotle's naturalism is better than Spencer's functionalism, Moore's formulation has merit. But the golden mean implied in the settlement of questions of static-dynamic, order-and-change, chaos-predictability antinomies is itself

* Wilbert E. Moore, *Social Change*, Foundations of Modern Sociologies Series (Englewood Cliffs, NJ.: Prentice-Hall. 1963), pp. 120.

a kind of long-range faith in the middle ground that has little evidential basis; indeed, none is suggested.

The second section raises critically "qualities of change," especially the "myth" of a singular theory of change or direction of change. Here again, Moore launches a powerful critique against monistic doctrines, such as those developed by Spengler, Sorokin, and the evolutionists. But it remains unclear whether Moore's "eclectic and tolerant" acceptance of all theories of change as potentially valuable in the study of different aspects of social systems, can really escape the weaknesses of extreme historical relativism. Moore appreciates the weaknesses in holistic doctrines of change better than he does equally serious shortcomings in atomistic theories. Indeed, he has a tendency to dismiss the possibility that the past was in fact better than the present, simply because nostalgic distortion is embodied in the "noble savage" perspective. He dismisses a priori the possibility that complex multivariate analytic models may actually prove the superiority of one or another holistic model.

Various theories of change are not so much differentially warranted over space as they are over time. It might be possible to deal with change in terms of primary pivots: with the eighteenth century in terms of national struggles, and with the twentieth century in terms of race struggles. It may well be that a singular theory of change can be so cast in dialectical terms that the reductionist features most objectionable in any one theory of change are removed. The contests between individualism and socialism, logos and mythos, reason and unreason, or what have you, may offer a general theory of change no less objectionable and more practicable than a general theory of action (which strangely enough rarely seems to evoke criticism for its holistic premises). But I would agree with Moore that it is only the beginning of wisdom to identify dichotomies, and it is the pursuit of wisdom to observe that polar types do not concretely exist.

Moore's analysis of the specific factors involved in generational cycles, changes in formal organization, and intergroup conflict in preclusive groups is a model of good sense and sensible goods. Particularly noteworthy is Moore's appreciation of the fact that the ascription-achievement axis is not one of mutually exclusive alternatives but of conflicting principles present in every social system. This understanding is particularly important in the study of the developmental process, given the inundation of psychologistic theories of achievement that simply rule out the importance of ascription in even the most developed societies. However, I would suggest that the struggle is not simply between partisans of inherited tradition and upholders of rational innovation. This assumes too neat a world, one in which "irrational" processes are simply ruled out on the grounds that they entail unstructured or spontaneous behavior. Yet, is it not the case that collective dynamics is the ground of change, structured or otherwise, neatly packaged or clumsily lumped together into temporary alliances? In this sense, Moore's lack of consideration of the work of Blumer, Lang and Lang, Smelser, and others is a serious defect.

Moore's study of changes in societies raises extremely important questions about the functional autonomy of certain features within the social system. His discussion of how this partial autonomy works out in relation to art, science, and technology offers very suggestive lines for further study. Strangely enough, given Moore's rejection of Marxist formulations, his description of autonomous change squares very well with the independent role assigned to the superstructural elements by men like Lukacs, Hauser, and Ossowski.

The typology of revolutions offered could have been considerably enhanced up, especially the analysis of types of revolutions. Moore's denial of the role of ideals and utopias in the actual conduct of social change is informed by an extreme rationalism. It would seem that he could have paid a good deal more attention to explaining how it comes about that revolutionary changes and mass demands for the amelioration of inequality are responses not simply to material exigencies but also to a vision of a more perfect future. It may sound trite, but Moore sometimes sounds as if he actually believes that men live by bread alone.

That this basic chapter on the developmental process is called modernization is itself highly revealing since, as a matter of fact, the basic choice in the newly emerging nations is precisely one between modernism and structural innovation. The process of modernization is not synonymous with economic development. Modernization is related to a special form of economic change that emphasizes material acquisition, entrepreneurial innovation and a host of mending processes such as education, communication, and juridical reform. In contrast, the structuralist school of development holds that the process of development requires smashing even more than mending, that is, requires an overhaul in social relations no less than in the level of industrial productivity.

Moore's failure to grapple seriously with this problem leads him to describe and completely reject as "radically inappropriate" structuralist options to modernization. On the other hand, since he recognizes that continuous growth involves the direct intervention of the state at those points where voluntary choice breaks down, he is hard put to explain how developing regions can respond to the necessity of continuous growth, short of calling upon mechanisms of persuasion and coercion such as are lodged in the state. Moore tends to speak of modernization as an autonomous social process, and hence he avoids the political problems of planned development.

That Moore concludes his book with an examination of the doctrine of "social evolution" is something like beating a dead horse. His generous sentiments toward the Spencerian philosophy of history do not address the point. And the point is the discordant processes of political revolution coincident with social development. What is the relation between social revolution and human survival? What is the distinction between mechanisms of consensus, command, and terrorism in the promotion and planning of change? What leads a specific person to adventure and change in a community setting that discourages worldly participation? What is the connection of state planning to corporate conduct? Perhaps it is unfair to burden an admittedly basic text with such profundities. Nonetheless, if pages can be spent on how to cultivate an optimistic reading of man's past and future, it seems not unwarranted to insist upon some study of the tougher problems that make historical optimism something less than sociological realism. As I mentioned at the outset, this is more a quarrel with Moore's style than with his performance. To the publisher and editor who commissioned this work, it is only fair to say that they chose well. This volume will eminently serve its purpose of introducing students to problems of development and social change. Its uses beyond the pedagogic remain problematic.

From *The American Journal of Sociology*, vol. 70, no. 2 (1964), pp. 231–32.

30

Martyrdom and Vietnam*

Muste, A.J.

Returning from an idyllic week at the East-West Center in Honolulu, Hawaii, where Vietnam never seemed more remote despite its relative geographic proximity, I received news that brought an overwhelming sense of personal loss. Not one but two friends had passed away: A.J. Muste—pacifist, radical, and believer in mass action; and Bernard B. Fall—*real*politician, conservative, and advocate of elite solutions. Muste was twice the age of Fall, and it must be frankly said, Fall was twice the theorist of Muste. But together each represented the best of his generation; each represented an authentic voice against the present American military intervention in Vietnam. Fall, painfully and slowly, came to be the intellectual backbone of resistance to the War, whereas Muste, proudly, unhesitatingly, from the very outset it seems, was the spiritual backbone to resistance. For once the cliche-ridden phrase—who will replace them?—is not only a meaningful question, but temporarily unanswerable.

The loss of these men will be felt across the board: from Fall's coolly reasoned arguments in *Foreign Affairs* for negotiating a peace settlement, to the impassioned, but no less rational, arguments in *Liberation* for an early solution. Both men left a final intellectual testament, as it were: Fall with his keen book on the collapse of the French Army at Dien Bien Phu, *Hell in a Very Small Place*, a work filled with the sight, sound, and smell of Vietnam and the foreboding of what may await the American Army; while Muste left us his collected essays edited by Nat Hentoff, under the blunt but unassuming title, *The Essays of A.J. Muste.* Fall was an intellectual who believed in the life of action and died in battle for this fusion of scholarship and journalism. Muste was a man of action who died in a struggle to bring intellect to bear on the Vietnam conflict. It is hard to believe that his already seriously impaired

---

* A.J. Muste, *The Essays of A.J. Muste*, Nat Hentoff (Editor) (Indianapolis and New York: The Bobbs-Merrill Co., 1967), pp. 515

Bernard B. Fall, *The Two Vietnams: A Political and Military Analysis* (New York: Schocken Books, 1966), pp. 596.

health was not considerably aggravated by his recent trip to Hanoi this year and by his harassed tour of Saigon last year.

Despite a world of ideology separating Muste from Fall, there were profound similarities between the two that occasioned my respect for both. Perhaps this is not quite an accurate way of stating my sentiments, since Muste was one of the few men I encountered in my adult life for whom I felt real devotion, while Fall, even when respect was compelled on the basis of his erudition, had a psychological makeup that made manifest all possible latent antagonisms. I had the distinct impression that a failure to engage in decisive intellectual combat with Fall led either to mistrust or to inattention. Muste, for his part, was also a no-nonsense person, who despite his ability to place one at case, never substituted the genteel for the vital. The close proximity of each, in my imagination at least, was their shared sense of the importance of life, the necessity of using time rather than marking time, of pulling things of value into the world and not sucking the valuable from the worldly teat.

Death is the great leveler. It justifies the linkage of Fall and Muste no less than makes possible an accounting of the lives they led. If it might appear to some pacifists that this linkage is no better than an artificial fusion of the profane with the sacred, or to some *real*politicians an equally unhappy combination of the toughminded with the tenderhearted, let each meditate on a commentary Muste made (in criticizing my own views on morality and public policy, made some years ago in the pages of the late and lamented *Council for Correspondence Newsletter*). "I freely admit that radical pacifists have not gotten very far with study of how revolutionary transition (from a war system to a peace system) might be made." In the meantime, there are moral problems, such as the relation between ends and means or the relation between power structures and moral imperatives, which cannot be evaded. Nor can the moral and political realms be separated. In real life they are in constant tension, and trying to relate them creatively is the permanent task, about which Martin Buber has said "it is difficult, terribly difficult, to drive the plowshare of the normative principle into the hard soil of political reality." And if Fall saw things differently, if he saw life in terms of driving the plowshare of political reality into the soft underbelly of the normative principle, then at least, like Muste, he saw the problem of political morality and moral politics as part of the same universe of discourse.

The advantage of meeting a person is that one gets to know him emotionally. A fascinating game that I imagine all men of the academy play is guessing the degree to which the man measures up to the word. And from my own experience, there is a far less frequent fit than might be imagined or hoped for. But in the case of Fall and Muste, the men exceeded the word. The personal charisma of each rested on his ability to transform a room full of noise into one filled with viable ideas.

Where this was most plainly evidenced in the case of Fall was at a 1962 round-table meeting in Washington. D.C., sponsored by the American Friends Service Committee on Crisis and Revolution East-West, North-South. Interestingly, Fall, whatever his intellectual disagreement with the pacifist position, maintained a deep and abiding personal respect for the AFSC and its personnel. Fall was the last speaker on the East-West side of the ledger, as I was on the North-South side. And from the outset it was clear that his address was to be radically different from those of the previous speakers. Somehow all distinctions based on ideology seemed to fade, as the main differential became one of clarity versus cloudiness. Fall's words tumbled out, all starting from the concrete experience in Vietnam—the specific mistakes of French policy and United States policy, the exact character of guerrilla warfare in Vietnam as it differed from that in China and Cuba, the time and place where the Sino-Soviet position foiled settlement, the nature of the Viet Cong, and the relationship between nationalism of the North and sectionalism of the South.

Dark historical foreboding informed Fall's every sentence. Further, it was as if Fall's words could be pinpointed on a map. He seemed to combine history and cartography as the essence of political analysis, not as a staged backdrop that could be eliminated from consideration like a cardboard prop. The core of his analysis that day can be summed up thus: The Viet Cong are not being defeated, will not be defeated, and cannot be defeated by military means—even if the military resources the American Army in Vietnam were enlarged ten times.

Yet, this was by no means the same as a victory of universal communism or a catastrophe for the West. Communist nations were divided by Fall between those that are independent and those that are satellitic. The satellite ones, such as some of those countries in Eastern Europe, are indeed part of a bloc that is lost to the West. But nations such as Yugoslavia and China—whatever their ideological disputations with each other and whatever their solid commitment to a socialist economy—represent an independent communism based on a long and bloody civil war and on genuine adhesion of the masses. In each instance, these countries, far from being allies of the Soviet Union, are copartners in a polyglot set of political experiments in collective ownership and in so being, represent the liberalization of communism. Political fragmentation of the Soviet "bloc" means its opening up, not its closing down, and certainly not the collapse of the Socialist ideal.

Fall strongly believed that a settlement with the Viet Cong would produce roughly the same situation. First, there would be a period of restoration within civil society, followed by a schism with the hard-line North Vietnamese, which in turn could well lead to the normalization of trade and diplomatic relations with the rest of the world—along lines not dissimilar to what has taken place in Poland, Hungary, Czechoslovakia, as well as Yugoslavia. Fall spoke feelingly and intelligently. It was the first time I was persuaded of the centrality of the

Vietnam War (at that time I feared much more an outbreak in Cuba or even Laos) and also its futility.

Fall was coming to suffer (and endure) what was long the fate of Muste: hostility from both Left and Right. The Soviet cartoon magazine *Krokodil* had pictured him (the week prior to that particular AFSC conference) as a writer whose pen was dipped in the blood of the Vietnamese people, while the United States Department of Defense had already begun a studied campaign not to take Fall's warnings of catastrophe and commitment at all seriously and instead to write him off as a Frenchman-turned-American, but still a Gaullist apologist. Like many intellectuals in such circumstances, Fall wore this double criticism as a badge of honor, as a proof of his correctness. In fact, these criticisms served to disguise from himself certain honorific and self-righteous properties in his thinking and writing. But five years more of the war made a tremendous impact on his conception of the Vietnam situation and on his self-conception of the role of the scholar in bringing the war to an end.

In private conversations and correspondence following that initial meeting, we had a number of discussions and debates. It was Fall's belief that one essential reason for the seriousness of the Vietnamese war, in contrast to my own emphasis on the importance of Latin America, is the different spheres of influence blanketed by each and the different thresholds of the will to fight in each area. Vietnam presented the United States with an involvement; Latin America presented the United States with an investment. From Fall's point of view, the real solution to Vietnam would come when the distinction between politics and property was formally recognized and acted upon. Fall was upset by the *lack* of economic determinism in United States thinking about Vietnam and by the substitution of a political predeterminism (the domino theory for instance) in its place. This is not the time or place to carry the debate further; indeed, the deep shock for me is that the debate, however it may continue at a transcendental level, is over, insofar as it affects two people.

As in the case of Fall, there are undoubtedly many people who knew Muste far better and more intimately, longer than I did. But in my own scale of intimacies, A.J. ranked high. He was my friend and not just an intellectual acquaintance. Things were said in a way that intimates alone can afford. It never took long before the age differential dissolved. His sense of humor was young—and this counted for much. He could exchange barbs in a way common to the young and foreign to the old. He could make demands upon your time and energies in a way also common to the young and foreign to the old. He was a wonderful model for young people because he never disparaged ideas in the cause of action and never insisted on intellectual requisites for membership in the struggle for what was just and peaceful. He walked about his weird and dilapidated office on Beckman Street not like a royalist but rather as a citizen. He commanded a respect from colleagues and secretaries, born of love, not of fear. One of his earlier secretaries said to me that he converted everyone to his beliefs by compelling the novice to face moral dilemmas in everything, but to act out those dilemmas in politics rather than psychoanalysis.

It is hard to resist the use of banal words to express pure human relations. Like everything else, a vocabulary can be cheapened through excessive use. The behavior of a man cannot be well expressed because the words available have been used too often. Perhaps one way of summing up Muste's person is that he never tried too hard. Everything he did had a sound fit; it was right and natural. He never played the sentimental old man role; he never played the crusty old man bit. He *was*; he did not *play*. He confronted you with essence. This was expressed by him politically as well as personally. His appeal to each person was measured. He never demanded of me that I be something other than I was, only that I do *better* what I believed right. Yes, he never missed an opportunity of enlisting me in the good cause at a level he knew would interest me, if not always convince me. Projects for studying the history of pacifism, grants for evaluating nonviolent responses in stress situations by social psychologists, petitions for opposing student entrance into the armed forces—all these he brought to my attention for simple universalistic ends, enlisting my support in the cause of the just.

What perhaps made Muste the incomparable figure he was in relation to the Vietnam War was his capacity to absorb the conflict in a theory of history and to not allow himself to be consumed by the uniqueness of the war. Indeed, he earned the scorn of ultrarevolutionists no less than the wrath of the reactionaries precisely because he refused to distinguish between good wars and bad wars. He thus found himself in a permanent minoritarian position throughout most of his life. Muste was, however, probably the most flexible dogmatist I have ever known. He knew the difference between a Hitler and a Roosevelt, between Axis powers and Allied powers. But he refused to sanctify these differences on moral grounds. Indeed, my chief argument with him was that while he was intent on seeing morals and politics as interrelated, and in contrasting his position with my own urgings for the primacy of politics on pragmatic grounds, his own view really amounted to asserting the practically, the utility of morality in politics. But such theoretical inconsistencies made him seem more, rather than less, like Gandhi and the pacifists of the East.

The resistance to the Vietnam War, while hardly massive in the United States, nonetheless represented the pinnacle of Muste's achievement at rallying a consensus to his pacifist's framework. If he did not live long enough to see victory for the pacifist's conscience, he at least outlived his critics who saw in World War I a war to end all wars or World War II a war for the salvation of democracy. Because of American participation in the Vietnam War, he was able to unite in his person all those forces had become exhausted and state in the attempt to unite the opposites of war and peace, tyranny and democracy. Muste also knew that peace was a small thing, a procedure, a way of conducting human relations, no less than an object, a way of attaining universal partnership. This was a real source of intellectual strength in Muste's position. He appreciated the intimate ironies in the peace movement (the issuance by the New York City Police Force of a permit for space so that young men might perform the illegal act of burning their draft cards) without losing sight of the larger grotesqueries the war brought about. He also understood the worth of a society that could permit such anomalies to take place. This may be a big reason why he incurred the displeasure of superpatriots, without inviting the scorn of real patriots. He did not confuse resistance to the war in Vietnam with acquiescence to totalitarian systems elsewhere in the world. The dualism of "bad" imperialist wars and "good" proletarian wars, which Christians from the time of Saint Thomas to Communists from the time of Lenin have tried to inculcate in the name of realism, simply has broken down on the shoals of atomic power.

Nuclear arsenals were the ultimate weapons of war, the atomic power that could destroy total populations. This sense of the totality of destruction provided the intellectual iron that made Muste's pacifism politically viable no less than morally defensible. In our personal conversations, Muste more than once admitted that the thermonuclear era really transformed the potentialities of pacifism by changing the very nature of the war system. Since victory through total nuclear output had become a contradiction and an absurdity, the very raison d'etre of warfare had been effectively collapsed by the technological rush to military judgment. This change in reality was effectively recorded in Muste's writings. His essays became less strident, less defensive in the postnuclear era. It might well be that these last years were Muste's happiest—at least he saw a meshing of his practical political concerns with his intellectual moorings in a way denied to him in previous prenuclear epoch.

The war in Vietnam was doomed from the outset to remain a conventional war in terms of weapons. The ultimate absurdity was that the arsenal of hardware belonging to the latest technologically sophisticated achievement was less viable than primitive weapons and hand-to-hand combat. As long as the war in Vietnam remained at such a level, victory was impossible. Yet, victory was equally implausible through the use of nuclear weapons, since the company of nuclear powers has become large enough and efficient enough to cancel any advantages to the use of such weapons. Thus, whatever the specific localized absurdities of the Vietnam war, the larger absurdities were plain to plain men. And in this, Muste linked intellectual arms with Fall. Both knew fully well that this was the era of debauchery, at least with respect to the Vietnam War. It was also their shared knowledge that if men are not holy, then neither are their national policies. It was finally their shared hope that debauchery would be followed by redemption—and the redeemer would come the second time as the first, as a prince of peace.

This personal memoir has strayed too far from ordinary reviewing procedures. It is already too long—moving about from the two men to the two worlds in mortal combat. All things are interrelated after all. How terrible it is that it takes death to bring this home to us. Vietnam has cost America, has cost me, a good colleague in Fall and a dear friend in Muste. Let the statistics on casualties show two more fallen heroes—without posthumous medals, without pomp and ceremony, without photos of bereaved teen-aged widows. These are hard times. War is a bad thing. It takes those we love, and it leaves us scarcer in numbers and fewer in answers. But when all is said and done, the world belongs to the living, and obituaries must be written to provide aid and comfort to those of us who are left.

From *Focus*, vol. 5, no. 36 (1967), pp. 24–27.

31

Isolation, Intervention and World Power*

Pauker, Guy J.

At the risk of oversimplification, the difference between the Democratic Johnson administration and the Republican Nixon administration can be characterized as follows: From 1963 to 1968 the United States had a leadership with considerable talent in the field of domestic affairs—achievements seriously, if not thoroughly, impaired by the colossal failure of its foreign policy. The Johnson years were marked by sharp escalation of warfare in Southeast Asia, hardening of the Cold War with the Soviet Union (thus reversing the Kennedy-Khrushchev thaw) and a frozen vision of Chinese communism inherited from the Truman-Eisenhower years. The Nixon administration, from 1969 to 1974 at least, has exhibited a diametrically opposite set of priorities and achievements. Not since President Ulysses S. Grant has an administration been so impotent in domestic affairs and so corrupt in its internal administrative apparatus. Yet in the field of foreign policy, the Nixon administration can claim to have cooled out, if not wound down, the war in Vietnam, reached a modus vivendi with the Soviet Union that includes a wide set of military and diplomatic accords, and opened up a new policy toward the People's Republic of China that only a few short years ago would have been deemed inconceivable—certainly by President Nixon's conservative admirers.

In a sense, this new RAND Report aims at extending this Nixon approach to foreign affairs to the Third World. In so doing, the worthy aim of Messrs. Pauker, Canby, Johnson, and Quandt is to move beyond the awful truths of dependency of these nations upon the United States. Indeed, a Latin American diplomat I know once told me, "Mr. Johnson acts as if my country were not so much a sovereign nation as a Southern state in the United States—a place whose ills can be cured, or at least treated, with a slap on the back and a

---

* Guy J. Pauker, Steven Canby, A. Ross Johnson, and William B. Quandt. *In Search of Self-Reliance: U.S. Security Assistance to the Third World under the Nixon Doctrine* (Santa Monica, California: The RAND Corporation, 1973).

little bit of largesse off the top." Whatever else might be said of the Nixon era, such low-level condescension has certainly passed away, perhaps never again to be resurrected. Gunboat diplomacy has finally given way to a considered estimate of American limitations and Third World possibilities that surely was unthinkable, or at least unrealizable, under previous administrations. The recent cautionary behavior of the United States in the Middle East round four conflicts is indicative of this new-found sense of diplomatic and military maturity.

One can only assay as a curious piece of rhetoric the Report's fallback position based on the Emersonian doctrine of self-reliance. The New England transcendentalists had in mind individual achievement as well as the buoyant optimism of free people to accomplish that which tyrannies disallow: the unfettered expression of mind and body. In the hands of the RAND transcendentalists, this faith in the future seems to reduce itself to a realpolitik that disguises a failure of nerve no less than a collapse of policy. Ultimately, this statement of the Nixon Doctrine, as it was first enunciated in the President's Guam speech of July 1969, is a linguistic conversion from the politics of despair into a rhetoric of self-reliance. One might say that the Nixon foreign policy doctrine as detailed in this report, is that God helps those who help themselves, and the devil take the hindmost. But whether Providence will adjudicate disputes between powerful and weak nations or between large and small nations (often an overlapping issue), tends to be dampened by the RAND formula of self-reliance.

The singling out of the Yugoslav experience is all to the good. But surely the authors of this study must realize that the circumstances surrounding the Stalin-Tito break in the late 1940s were so special that attempts to replicate the experience of national communism in Hungary, Poland, and Czechoslovakia all came to disastrous conclusions. The very effort of Eastern European leaders like Nagy, Gomulka, and Dubcek to incorporate the Yugoslav experiences of total national defense based upon a popular militia, were savagely overwhelmed by superior Soviet numbers and a passive West. The essence of the Nixon doctrine, therefore, is not so much self-reliance as spheres of influence. Similarly, Indonesia's unbroken record of success in counterinsurgency operations was made possible by a sudden, total, and uniquely successful assault on millions of rebels and guerrillas. This well coordinated effort broke the back of resistance with an alacrity unmatched elsewhere in Southeast Asia. The case of Israel is likewise so unique that even the authors acknowledge that it is unlikely to be a model for other Third World nations. What we are left with, then, is a formula for military dominion rather than political autonomy.

If the solutions worked in Greece, Turkey, and South Korea are the only means to resist a Soviet attack, that is by use of "the forward deployment of specialized defensive forces," then one must inevitably ask whether the game is worth the effort—that is to say, whether the social and political systems serviced by American hardware are all that morally superior to the sort of government that would displace such reactionary and overt military regimes. Here one gets the distinct impression that this RAND report is less convinced by the Nixon doctrine of detente than by the older Johnson doctrine of continuing the cold war by other, less costly means.

The format of this RAND report is succinct and compact. It is divided into four sections: "The Conceptual Basis of the Nixon Doctrine," inviting Third World initiatives; "Doctrines of Self-Reliance," in which the uniquely successful cases of Yugoslavia, Indonesia, and Israel are examined; "Revising Third World Defense," in which a continuous army presence, combined with police units, is recommended; and "Toward A New Operational Approach to Military Assistance," in which a shift is urged from steady long-term aid to crisis assistance of late-model hardware when and if urgently needed. The report is rich in common-sense recommendations and empirics: that because only the United States has the air power necessary to counter Soviet air power, doling or parceling out air defense units gives little military advantage to a nation under siege; that crisis assistance, in addition to its low-cost features, permits the United States to maintain control of sophisticated arms prior to their use; and finally, that military flexibility requires closer coordination with local regimes and a more open approach to the character of such regimes.

But there are micro-level problems with the report. The RAND report predicates the Nixon doctrine on increased militarization in the Third World. While this is clearly a realistic appraisal, the report seriously undervalues the extent to which such militarized countries will develop a shared hostility to the United States, rather than simply keep the lid on their national revolutionary cadres. Indeed, as such militarization emerges in the Third World, the national bourgeoisie, rather than any international alliances, becomes stronger. The new military of Latin America, Asia, and Africa share a taste for Keynesian economics to be sure, but equally they share a distaste or an open parliamentary system. In consequence, the rise of Third World militarism may shrink rather than enhance United States dominion in the Third World. One might say that a parallel reduction in influence may take place in the Third World vis-a-vis the Soviet Union as well. But one can hardly call this a Nixon or a Brezhnev doctrine of self-reliance. To be sure, the intensity of such militarization has led to an actual Nixon-Brezhnev Doctrine, in which the fate of the Third World is related to the degree that nations seek to escape dependence and enter a spirit of partnership. This is a characteristic problem from Nigeria to Peru to Thailand. The impulse to sovereignty through militarization, rather than any presumed doctrine of self-reliance in the advanced nations, is at the heart of present Third World efforts at self—determination.

While the writing in the report is terse and clear, it does suffer somewhat from its collective style. For example on page 13, Egypt (among other nations) is referred to as a "Soviet client," while on page 62, recognition is made of the fact that "in mid-1972 Egypt expelled Soviet military personnel" and that "such switching is likely to become more frequent" in a multipolar world. What this does to a concept of the Nixon doctrine is not explained. Even at the strategic level, the RAND report is not always consistent. In the penultimate paragraph of the report, we read, "The future training of U.S. military specialists and of foreign military officers in American service schools will play an important role in implementing Nixon doctrine military assistance programs in the Third World," but only two pages earlier, we are told, "But as for enhancing the defense potentials of Third World countries, results of such training programs for military officers have been at best ambiguous.... American training may also have led some to demand weapon systems and force postures that meet U.S. standards but are not necessarily best suited to the resources of their countries."

Such serious ambiguities in the report are not due to a lack of talent on the part of the authors, each of whom is an able social scientists. Rather, it reflects the special peculiarities of agency-sponsored research—what Herbert Blumer has called "a general readiness in advance to tailor research projects to fit the over-all design of a project irrespective of the premises undergirding the design." For example, one looks in vain for some sort of symmetry between the threat of possible attacks by the Soviet Union and the People's Republic of China on Third World nations, (which is discussed at considerable length), with less problematic and quite real attacks by the United States on the sovereign rights of such nations as the Dominican Republic or Cambodia in the 1960s. In the absence of social science evenhandedness, the reader is entitled to severe doubts about the social scientific status of such a scenario, whatever its efficacy may be in alerting the United States military to its essential tasks in the defense of the freedom of Third World countries under potential attack.

This kind of RAND report raises a familiar issue in a new form: whether or not any sort of policy analysis that presents only an optimizing scenario for the United States (or any other major power) can really stand the light of social science, much less the heat of the Third World nations ostensibly serviced by such a position. Indeed, one must conclude on a somewhat pessimistic note, for the RAND Report confirms, even consecrates, the fact that there is no such entity as the Nixon doctrine for the Third World and its security. Such rhetoric simply confirms an outstanding fact of the moment: the character of a Third World nation is uniquely determined from below by its class interests and racial composition, and from above by its military power and political structure. But these combinations and permutations are largely impervious to American foreign policy and are not responsible to a Nixon doctrine, but to the same interests that have always possessed those who rule.

In consecrating the realities of foreign affairs into a vision of foreign policy, the RAND report does not fudge very real shifts in the external conditions of the United States. There is no exaggeration of U.S. power. One senses a real concern with the need to carry the Nixon doctrine one step further, into the area of social equity as well as conflict resolution among nations. The difficulty goes right back to that ubiquitous notion of the Nixon doctrine. If such a doctrine does exist and has been articulated, it relates not to the Third World directly, but rather to the sorts of stability required in a big power relationships, especially American-Soviet affairs, that would add a note of tranquility to foreign affairs by reducing the margin of adventurism open to smaller, militant national liberation movements. Hence, the unreported aspect of the Nixon Doctrine is its essence: namely, multinational diplomacy in an era of transnational corporations. And this omission deprives the RAND report of an essential focus, not on the military potencies of the Third World so much as political and diplomatic potencies of the First World with respect to the Second World. In this sense, the RAND report's emphasis on military self-reliance is a throwback to an isolationist position within a cold-war rhetoric. And precisely the opposite has taken place: a sharp decline of the cold-war era despite an ever lingering presence on both sides of rhetoric inherited from the past.

From *Armed Forces and Society*, vol. 1, no. 1 (1974), pp. 133–38.

32

Multinational Parochialism*

Perlmutter, Howard V.

Multinational corporations have not escaped the general polarization of social research or of the social world as a whole. Rhetoric in the area of multinational studies is as bloated as anywhere in the literature. For some, the word multinational suggests uneven distribution of world wealth, disequilibrium between the powerful and powerless, and the spreading growth of a rapacious capitalism minimizing opportunities for autonomous development in new nations. Such familiar themes extend from the pages of *Marxist Perspectives* to the *New Yorker.*

On the other hand, an equally peculiar literature on multinationals exists in which overseas industries involve no politics, no economic rivalries, and ultimately no problem except that of organizing work loads and designing total human resources for predetermined, predisposed ends. One might say that the characteristic stomping ground for this kind of policy-oriented research is located at the graduate business schools of Harvard, MIT, Pennsylvania, and Stanford. The benign, benevolent image of multinationalism is a direct outgrowth of the rise of the business school approach to problems of multinationalism.

Organizational development, in the world of Heenan and Perlmutter, is conveniently referred to as OD, which I presume can mean overdose in case organization development theory fails. The book provides a good opportunity to show how dominant business perspectives—emphasizing as they do diagnosis, planning, and intervention—can be applied to the world arena of multinational corporate structures. Whether the relationship between multinationalism and organizational development is organic or a mechanical grafting of two quite discrete phenomena, remains a problem.

Multinational Organization Development is basically intended as a text. Carefully divided into brief chapters, it serves admirably as a handbook for students interested in, or perhaps concerned about, the rise of multinational

---

* David A. Heenan and Howard V. Perlmutter, *Multinational Organization Development: A Social Architectural Perspective* (Reading: Addison-Wesley, 1979), pp. 194.

corporations in a global context. The work is further divided into two basic parts. The first section takes up problems and prospects of building multinational corporations that are both viable and legitimate. The chapters consist of a series of scenarios that suggest that multinational corporations will remain a key factor for the balance of the twentieth century. This is followed by a taxonomy explaining the meaning of multinationals and a typology providing critical decisions and specific actions in corporate multinationalization. The fourth chapter deals with the role of the chief executive officer in the integrative process. The fifth and final chapter in the first section discusses regional organizational development in the formation of private corporations.

The second section further analyzes multinational organizational development by means of the case history method, and by using a social architectural approach. This approach seems to be the offspring, if not the shadow, of earlier social engineering approaches. It is hard to see how the tripartite examination of diagnosis, planning, and intervention moves beyond the older engineering model. Invoking the case study method only reinforces this belief. The use of the approach in four cites, Paris, Coral Gables, Philadelphia, and Honolulu strikes me as capricious, to put it mildly. Paris is a world-class city. Honolulu is a regional city of some special prominence because of its centrality to Hawaii. Philadelphia is a city that has typically local problems rather than global or national problems. Presumably, Coral Gables, Florida is where the authors, being residents of Honolulu and Philadelphia, went to do their work in a leisurely suburban environment. The case study method is used again in the seventh chapter, where the remote Leyte province of the Philippines is cited as an example of how private investment in the developmental process can be stimulated. This case deals with problems of legitimacy, but painfully avoids the nature of Philippine society, both as a political dictatorship and as an economic free market paradise. Finally, the eighth chapter deals with difficulties in building worldwide universities. Precisely what this has to do with the issue of multinational organizational development is hard to fathom. It is even more difficult to understand why the University of Hawaii is typical of this sort of issue. As throughout the book, convenience seems to be the mother of invention.

The third part is basically a final chapter. It is a brief, forward-looking vision of what might be expected by the end of the century. The authors argue that a multiple national approach to multiorganizational problems is required to enhance the legitimacy of existing and new institutions. I find such stuff platitudinous in the extreme. Such generalities escape analysis, but no less, manage to avoid criticism.

Heenan and Perlmutter are clearly well-intentioned, interested in promoting a democratic vision of doing business abroad and in developing what they refer to as the EPRG profile. They distinguish between ethnocentric and polycentric behavior, and between regioncentric and geocentric behavior showing how the vectors formed provide linkages to more favorable ways of expressing the relationships to organizations in an overseas context. The authors also identify procedures that might lessen ethnocentric and regioncentric, and urban polycentric and geocentric, courses of action. Such procedures will permit one to reach the ultimate point where nationality makes no difference in key subsidiary positions, where competence and not passports counts. Yet they do not quite explain why they refer to key subsidiary positions rather than key management positions.

Ultimately, even Professors Perlmutter and Heenan submit to the iron law of national dominion, by the back door, as it were. There are some excellent charts, graphs, and tabular material that illustrate multinational organizational themes: democratizing decision making: developing more adequate forms of manpower management in an overseas context; developing organizational tasks that enhance non-American participation in head offices and overseas offices; developing worldwide compensation and management policies and training programs; creating higher equity frameworks; and, ultimately, developing world headquarter concepts that are mediated by local, national, and regional factors. One cannot fault the authors of this work for their intent, since clearly their impulses are egalitarian. Instead, the problem is their inability to get beyond the ideology of multinationalism as necessarily and invariably promoting democratic horizons, and their consequent inability to see the potential for disequilibrium and even disruption on this global scale.

Perlmutter's social architectural approach to building the international city of Philadelphia (which he refers to as "a planning process for grassroots internationalism") illustrates the dangers of such exported democracy. In outlining how the city of Philadelphia is going to become international and in indicating who the primary clients might be, how Philadelphia might serve as a crossroads city with geocentric competence, how all of this is to be brought about in the year 2000, and why other cities may not be able to perform such a global role, Perlmutter draws a strange parallel between Paris and Philadelphia that is more fantastic than futuristic. To speak of Philadelphia as viable, as an international city, while drawing attention to the deteriorating quality of life in Paris, is to exhibit a misunderstanding of both Paris and the greater Philadelphia area that need not be labored.

The partnership concept is even more off base, for actual data do not indicate a special kind of role for Philadelphia like that presently assigned to Paris, either in economic or political or social terms. Quite the contrary, the scholarly literature supports Jean Gottman's model of megalopolis, in which Philadelphia performs subsidiary roles, feeding into the New York and Washington corridors. Philadelphia becomes something like Baltimore: a regional center of some worth and note but not necessarily an international city or center.

As other potential centers for multinational corporations, Coral Gables and Honolulu have very little in common. It might well be that tax incentives, easy access to air transportation or telecommunications, and political stability are significant in any city attempting to become headquarters for multinationals. But to argue that such profoundly different places as Honolulu and Coral Gables can function in the same way (i.e., as area centers for Asia and Latin America, respectively), is to make of globalization an extremely rarefied phenomenon that has little bearing on the main subject of the volume: multinational organizational development. It is interesting, of course, to speculate on any given city becoming a center for multinational activity. It is also interesting to consider what would happen if Tampa Bay, rather than Coral Gables, had sponsored the research in which Heenan and Perlmutter and their colleagues were involved.

There is throughout a feeling that the work is more accidental than systematic. As a result, the social architectural approach has the quality of sponsored accident rather than scientific necessity. One can hardly argue with the authors' contention that political stability is important in the development of regional centers or global centers in the new world of multinational organizational development. On the other hand, they cite as an example Beirut, Lebanon, a city which has been shattered by continual civil war between Christians and Moslems. The loss of many lives (estimated at 40,000) and the loss of 3 billion dollars in damages have led to a relocation of major industrial firms. I would further add that in cities like Montreal, where language and ethnic strife abound, the volatility is not so much political as sociological. There, too, a certain loss of business, unaccounted for by models and formulas, has been evident. The question is whether such losses are temporary or permanent and whether they can in fact be made up by the infusion of new kinds of activities. It might well be that the losses Montreal sustains when its insurance firms move to Toronto are serious. Becoming the capital of a new Quebec nation, however, might more than compensate Montreal for such a loss. Beirut has for hundreds of years suffered from extreme volatility and yet has remained a center of commerce and industry, in part precisely because of its pluralistic nature and its multi-religious population.

It is somewhat risky and naïve of Heenan and Perlmutter to view political stability as the same as political stasis, or to think that business will always and everywhere flock to a stable environment, unless that stable environment can provide new forms of growth and stability. The wisdom of the authors is in recognizing accident rather than design. Ultimately, they must admit that the growth of Coral Gables is a result of its being within ten minutes of the Miami International Airport. Without this accident, Coral Gables would not have achieved its current level of economic success. This indicates that regional centers (like Miami) are decisive in the development of multinationally satisfactory forms of organizational development and that cities in the more restricted sense (like Coral Gables) are less decisive.

Since the book makes much of its global context and global orientation, it strikes me as an anomaly that three of the four cities used as examples-Honolulu, Philadelphia, and a Miami suburb-are basically American; and the fourth, Paris, is not so much studied as revered. The authors have not taken seriously their own ethnocentricism; hence, the very model they provide to get beyond our limits is what ensnares them, and finally does in the premise of the book.

For all of its good intentions and efforts to democratize organizational development theory in a multinational context, the volume essentially fails. Its glow of Panglossian apologetics indicates a smug self-satisfaction, that is inappropriate, in light of present destabilization in world markets and world politics. To speak of multinationalization as a humanization process, without once addressing the problems of disequilibrium brought about by the relative strengths and weaknesses of the national structures that underwrite and underlie these multinationals, is a profound weakness. One might argue that regional associations like OPEC are examples of a multinationalization process that leads to anything but humanization.

Ultimately, the social architectural approach, unlike the political-sociological one, does not really deal with international organizational development in the light of states and authorities. If the states of the world were exceptionally weak, such as the Netherlands, where multinationals encounter few legal, organizational, or fiscal restrictions, then the kind of multinational organizational programs outlined by Perlmutter and Heenan would make real sense. However, in a context such as the United States, in which national structures determine multinational inputs, or at least are a profound inhibiting force, national systems become more decisive. In Japan, where the national structure determines the character and velocity of multinational expansion and growth, one still has to deal with the question of state power. All of the so-called tangible and intangible benefits that derive from the democratization of multinational organizations proceed through state power. The jump in this work from the study of the urbanization process to the study of regional, transnational, and finally multinational association on a hemispheric or global basis shows an extraordinary insensitivity to political hegemony. The leap of faith and imagination necessary to go from world headquarters to European headquarters directly to cities, bypasses the role of the state and state authority in the determination of planning coalition strategies. It is a disservice to the financial underwriters of this effort—GE, IBM, and Xerox-not to make the role of state authority clear.

It is perhaps asking too much in a volume dedicated to making multinational organizational development more humane and more responsive to the needs of nationals of all countries to take into account the structure of state authority in developing contexts. But not to have done so, to think of the political process as a problem of stability and instability rather than one of power and domination, is to falsify the terms in which multinational organizations are evolving at the end of the twentieth century. The authors make the question of organizational development rather more pleasant and painless than the current situation warrants.

Quite apart from scholarly problems, there is a faint him of boosterism in this volume, which must be viewed as an uncomfortable and disquieting element. To speak of Honolulu as capturing the benefits of the global city without its costs is to understate the limits of Honolulu because of its relative isolation from the mainland. The finite limits to its growth, not to mention the inability of the Honolulu area to provide enough physical resources, are simply not discussed. To speak of Coral Gables and not Miami as the regional center because its city planners went after multinational corporate business while Miami's did not, and to say that Coral Gables has never looked back at its past, again fails to consider that Coral Gables is part of the greater Miami area. One has a feeling that the research project and funds were not irrelevant to the iconoclastic conclusions drawn by the authors. How transferable or universal such newer centers are remains moot. Little evidence about the transferability of the virtues of Coral Gables or Honolulu as possible regional centers is provided.

Finally, the foreword provided by Edgar H. Schein is less a foreword than a self-promotional piece. Only one paragraph even mentions the book under consideration, and that particular paragraph is entirely noncommittal. Problems of organization, design, and development in a multinational context, what this book is ostensibly about, are entirely ignored! The Anderson-Leslie series on organizational development is certainly worthwhile. Yet, to be quite frank, the foreword is written as if the book itself had not been read, much less approved, by the general editor of this series. This is in itself a statement on the need to take more seriously the contents of a book on organization, if we are going to reorganize the international community.

From *Administrative Science Quarterly*, vol. 25, no. 4 (1980), pp. 695–700.

33

Power and Change in an Industrial Context*

Porter, John

Only the informal prohibition on adjectival excess prevents me from beginning this review of Porter's book with raves. Suffice it to say, this is *the* sociological study of present-day Canada, and it will doubtless remain a basic reference work on Canadian social structure for some time to come. While the book makes few attempts at theoretical innovation, its use of established theory in political sociology is virtually unparalleled. Mr. Porter takes his theory where he can find it* from Marx, Weber, Mills, Warner, Parsons. Still, he is by no means random or eclectic in selecting relevant theory, and the main purpose of the book is never forgotten: to present an accurate and factual account of class, power, status, and ethnicity as they interpenetrate in Canada. Indeed, what makes the book so astonishing is Porter's ability to use the strengths of classical sociological theories without being used by their weaknesses. He examines the concentration of economic power, with a precision and concreteness unmatched by Western Marxian economists. He discusses the Canadian political elite in Millsian terms, without falling prey to the dubious assumptions of coordinated policy making found in *The Power Elite*. His examination of the Canadian federal bureaucracy is made in Weberian terms, but without the reifications and polarizations often found in Weber. In short, the body of the literature in political sociology is heuristically employed rather than abstractly hashed over.

Mr. Porter, who is professor of sociology at Carleton University in Canada and was trained at the London School of Economics and Political Science, divides his book into two parts: the structure of class and the structure of power. But underlying this formal division are a series of propositions that reveal Canada as a mosaic rather than a finished painting. The book can be read as a set of interrelated propositions as to why Canada does not explode, despite the combustible and ill-digested elements abundantly present. Instead

---

* John Porter, *The Vertical Mosaic* (Toronto: University of Toronto Press, 1965), pp. 589.

of celebrating stability, Porter goes deeper and asks why, given the presence of utterly contradictory forces, open conflict has not taken place.

Among Porter's more significant findings, the following deserve special attention. They indicate the marked contrasts between Canada and the United States in structural rather than cultural terms. Indirectly, they also illustrate the latent comparative and developmental method used in this book.

First, Canada solves its need for skilled manpower cheaply, by importing such skills rather than evolving an educational system that would promote rapid internal social mobility. There is more closure in the Canadian mobility system than in the American. And yet, there is remarkably high satisfaction of skilled personnel needs. Second, emigration to the United States is a safety valve effect for the nonprofessonal working classes. In this way, Canada alleviates considerable marginal discontent without requiring internal structural innovation. Third, Canada displays a reciprocal relationships between ethnicity and class absent in the United States developmental process. Low status groups tend to accept their inferior economic position, and groups ranging from the Italian to the Irish tend to preserve their entrance status rather than seek to trade it in for something higher (or at least different). This is reflected in the political structure, where representatives of ethnic minority groups are only now beginning to make even a slight dent on the political system. Fourth, the absence of ethnic integration in the socioeconomic system indicates a permanent stagnation in Canadian life. The English and French charter groups retain distinctive domains in geography, language, education, and religion. The different paths taken by the charter groups provided Canada with its large bureaucracy, its educated middle sectors, and its industrial proletariat. But the class and status differentiation never added up to an integrated society, only a dual society that fulfilled functional requirements for continued survival rather than developmental requirements for national integration.

It is not that unification lacks supporters, but, as Porter shrewdly makes plain, advocates of such unity are uniformly linked to the English political tradition—to a Toryism that would create unification at the expense of democratization. Hence, the fragmentation of Canadian society is less likely to create violent revolutionary politics than would pressing demands for integration. Although the title of Porter's book relates to vertical class and power relationships, he also sees fragmentation in horizontal, latitudinal relationships (i.e., among elite groupings themselves). Corporate, bureaucratic, political, ideological and labor elites carve up the Canadian pie, but they do so in a way which minimizes elite coalitions. Here too, fragmentation is a surrogate form of democratization; any push towards integration would probably be one or another elite formation. Porter's many examples of competition and conflict among elite sectors reveal an openness in the Canadian system that is probably less evident in more advanced nations. White establishments and power elites exist; confraternity of power, reinforced by establishments of kinship and class, remains embedded in a separatist and particularist world that traditionally limits any one group from gaining an uncontested command post.

Professor Porter deals with the phenomenon of imperialism in terms of a Mosca-Pareto theory of external elites. Although he makes clear that capitalism is not restricted by national boundaries, nor conversely, do nationals necessarily delimit capitalist development, the actual role of foreign power in deciding the internal affairs of Canada seems to be unduly minimized. I say unduly because, given Porter's statement of the facts, United States stock ownership of 24 percent of Canadian firms, and an additional 8 percent by other foreign groups, one would expect much greater attention to this variable than is actually apparent in the book. The colonialist phenomenon tends simply to drop out of the profile of economic elites as the analysis develops.

Porter's brilliant discussion of the Canadian political system indicates that, unlike either the United States or Great Britain, polarization is not based on Left and Right sectors. In Canada, both Conservative and Liberal parties are closely linked with corporate enterprise. The dominant clusterings are on the Right. The forms of advancement, based as they are on what Porter terms "the practice of avocational politics," where politics is considered "an interstitial stage in a career devoted to something else," leads to a political system responsive the sectionalism, regionalism, ethnicity, and to discounting national roles. Porter's analysis, while clearly accurate, might well be supplemented by Peter Worsley's observations on Canadian polity as one dominated above all by a sensitivity to and a reflection of foreign colonial pressures and as not exclusively the arena for parochial internal pressures.

Evidently, Porter is motivated by a strong socialist consciousness as well as a sociological imagination. Consequently, he perhaps overestimates the degree of latent discontent present in Canadian society and the extent to which class membership becomes translated into class behavior. On the other hand, Porter's profile of Canadian contentment raises basic questions that are clearly outside the purview of the book. The question of moment may not be whether Canada "has a long way to go to become in any sense a thoroughgoing democracy," but whether the various bottlenecks to democracy described so fully are not themselves held as positive values, in that they are also bottlenecks to extreme authoritarianism.

A further issue is whether the vertical mosaic must not be extended to include colonialist attitudes of English Canada toward French Canada and in turn a similar attitude of the United States toward all Canada. Porter's constant reference to an emergence of a Canadian identity of a new breed in a new nation fails to specify whether such a force would be willing to aid the development of an independent French Canada, as a possible cost of minimizing an American Canada. In this sense, perhaps Professor Porter is as much a reflection of as a commentator on present dilemmas that confront Canadian society. Yet, I cannot conclude this review without mentioning the possibility that the development of mature social scientists such as James Eayrs, John Meisel, S.D. Clark, and Porter himself represents an emerging social scientific consciousness that may help transform a vertical mosaic into a unified social system after all.

From *American Sociological Review,* vol. 31, no. 4 (1966), pp. 862–863.

34

The Politics of Urban Research*

Portes, Alejandro

These two volumes combine the efforts of outstanding representatives of our younger sociologists writing on Latin America and those of Latin Americanists knowledgeable about comparative sociology. Before turning to the contents of these works, I should like to report a simple fact: this generation has proved superior in methodological techniques and sensitivity to theoretical problems of Latin American urban research to any previous professional cohort. The reasons for this are manifold, ranging from sound professional training to a greater sense of organic linkage to the region studied. As a group, these younger scholars display a clear-eyed knowledge of both research limits and the needs of the people being studied. At a time when much emphasis is placed on the crisis of sociology, it is easy to overlook (if not entirely negate) contributions to the discipline that offer the prospect of correcting past mistakes. Neither volume attempts to achieve a grand synthesis or to construct a model of models. Still, each deserves to be evaluated in a larger context of comparative sociology rather than a narrower one of urban change in Latin America. The absence of grand theory notwithstanding, these works are intellectually satisfying precisely because the pretentious scaffolding of inherited systems has largely been discarded.

The sociological linchpin of this collective effort is John Walton and Alejandro Portes's notion of a vertical unit of analysis by which significant social, economic, and political processes may be identified and related to their international and national origins, to the urban hierarchy, and to the rural hinterland. This vertically integrated analytic framework has what Walton calls four nodes: international, national, urban/regional, and hinterland. Whatever

* Alejandro Portes and Harley L. Browning (editors), *Current Perspectives in Latin American Urban Research* (Austin: Institute of Latin American Studies, University of Texas at Austin, 1977), pp. 179.

Alejandro Portes and John Walton, *Urban Latin America: The Political Condition from Above and Below.* (Texas and London: University of Texas Press, 1976), pp. 217.

its operational problems, this kind of paradigm has the great merit of breaking away from unicausal models that have so inhibited the progress of urban studies. Oscar Yujonovsky, in his workmanlike outline of ecological, spatial, and locational configurations, indicates how each of these four nodes can be integrated into a general system of resource allocation that is isomorphic to the vertically integrated analytic framework used by Walton and Portes.

There remain, however, two serious stumbling blocks in the application of this vertically integrated framework. First, the fourfold mosaic is not adequately tested in the essays in either volume. There is a strong impulse on the part of even the editors to look beyond rather than at the urban confines, and to raise questions about dependency capitalism and multinational corporations that lead away from the fourfold unit, right back to a unicausal external analysis which lodges responsibility for development, or the lack thereof, in imperial domains.

Yet, when the editors remember their own model, the results are intellectually beneficial. The relative strength of the four-factors model in contrast with a unicausal one in explaining urban networks thus becomes a central issue for further research. Second, having carefully the vertical patterns, none of the authors takes the trouble to examine the characteristics of the horizontal pattern. Is it the classic division between locational, geographical, and industrial networks? Is it an occupational framework demonstrating the advantages and disadvantages of different sectors in urban living? Or is it linked to the push/push issues all over again? In order to present an entirely satisfactory analysis, Portes, Walton, Browning, and their colleagues would have had to expand the horizontal matrix and to indicate points of intersection with the vertical matrix, thereby offering some criteria for evaluating the advantages and disadvantages in urban living. One paper that comes to grips with these issues is Michael E. Conroy's effort to determine how to achieve a policy-oriented theory of the economy of cities in Latin America. But this paper only suggests possible empirical and mathematical specifications of a model that is not included in the essay itself.

The core papers by Portes and Walton in *Urban Latin America* provide an intensive course in how far theories of urban growth have evolved since an earlier stage dealing with center and periphery only in the geographic terms of factory and residential areas within given cities. The authors appreciate the extent to which the Latin American city provides meaningful and rich possibilities for discussing fundamental issues of modernism versus industrialism in the development process and hierarchical versus democratic forms of political integration, and how cities serve elitist goals by making politics itself a game of power, in contrast to the game of economic survival played by masses in rural areas.

There is a curious problem in area research as a whole. The study of economic flows in urban settings, racial and ethnic discrimination patterns, and class composition of interest groups is hardly related to only one area. In Latin America, as in the United States a few decades ago, urban boundary maintenance problems remain (What is a city; where does it begin and end?). But these problems are yielding to new issues: In what way does social stratification affect patterns of production and consumption? How does the character of political regimes affect patterns of urban concentration? The emergence of a policy-oriented theory of urban life, in which the size and structure of city life is determined by the city's general goals of development, has provided an explanation for the location and relocation of individuals within a city. While moving a good distance beyond what has gone before, this framework still leaves unanswered more basic questions. For example, who makes relocation and allocation decisions—policy experts, political prophets, revolutionary elites, or traditional entrepreneurs? The fact that these two volumes have placed policymaking issues on the agenda of urban analysis indicates that urban phenomena are scarcely considered matters of rigid determinism and inexorable patterns explained by universal history. If the shift from determinism to voluntarism or from history to policy is in fact the essence of a new theoretical perspective, then the older forms of classical reasoning that assumed an unfolding dramaturgy and an unyielding demonology must also be reexamined.

Like Portes and Walton, I am uncomfortable with the notion of urbanism as a regional category. Although in theory, one speaks of Latin America as an ample area of analysis, in practice one is led either to study specific communities under special circumstances, as in the work of Bryan Roberts, Larissa Lomnitz, and Jorge Balán, or to lean toward more general characterizations, as in the work of the present editors. The data indicate that trends toward urbanism are inexorable and universal. Patterns characteristic of Latin American urbanism, at least in percentile terms, are not very different from those of the urban population in OECD (Organization for Economic Cooperation and Development) countries, that is, in the most industrialized nations of the West or in COMECON (Council for Mutual Economic Assistance) nations where urban concentration in certain areas is even more pronounced than in Western Europe or Latin America. United Nations urban/rural projections for the next 25 years indicate that nations such as Algeria, Egypt, Korea, and Nigeria are moving rapidly toward similar patterns of urban concentration. If this is true, then a great deal of theorizing about the impact of dependency capitalism or multinationalism must be seriously reconsidered. To achieve a comparative urban sociology, analysts may have to develop a more concrete and less regional orientation.

There is a growing demand for the study of such urban factors as types of accommodation, case of transportation, levels of communication, and forms of entertainment, factors that impose their own international logic on urban growth. These, no less than the well-known advantages for the internal population, such as health-delivery services, social welfare, and mass education, deserve careful scrutiny. In this sense, squatter takeovers and unauthorized expropriations might prove so profoundly dysfunctional in terms of servicing a world network that will be viewed as intolerable, whatever the nature of the political regime. The Mexican government is only the latest to find this out. At the same time, the Lebanese civil war indicates how resilient urban centers are. Despite years of strife and the reduction of the city and nation to ashes and rubble, Beirut remains a world economic capital remarkably aloof from Middle East military struggles. Urban needs may reconfigure certain elites and masses within cities. The condition of being urban may itself be an explanatory variable, over and against that of being dependent. For example, tendencies toward political conservatism of trade unions in Latin America, as in North America, indicate that being urban is not reducible to other variables. Urbanism may itself be an organizing framework of human experience. And this, rather than any presumed intellectual sloth, may account for the paucity of empirical studies based on what Walton refers to as the new paradigm of the dependency perspective. On this issue one detects that Portes and Browning may not be entirely in accord with their coeditor.

It might be argued that the city is a blurred category only when seen in the straight-jacketed context of class struggles or interest groups. But as an organizing premise, especially in capital-intensive economies exhibiting low proletarianization and high marginality, the city remains a safety valve, siphoning off revolutionary potential. If in Marxist terms the city is the locus of bitter strife between classes, in Weberian terms the city provides those opportunity networks that have made upward mobility possible. Perhaps, again following Weber, the city is the organizing fulcrum of contemporary experience in the same way the factory was for nineteenth-century Western Europe. This might better account for differing outcomes in social struggles than the presumed diabolical power of the cosmopolitan center and the multinational empire. Such fashionable theorizing is the weakest part of these texts.

A considerable amount of reverse labeling theory takes place in these volumes. While it is useful, following González Casanova and Stavenhagen, to continue to study problems of internal colonialism and to pursue the work of others on the special effects of dependency on Latin American urban growth, it is also time for vigorous criticism of these formulations. Not every regional imbalance has to do with internal colonialism. A central intellectual chore is to distinguish between what is imposed from without and what is generated within. All those who remain in rural areas are not necessarily lacking in innovation or simply traditionalist. Some may actually have an alternative view of the good life.

An exchange theory is required, one based on the best and latest techniques of survey research, that can give researchers and decision makers alike a better handle on problems of choice and decisions. As the work of Jorge Balán, Larissa

Lomnitz, and Bryan Roberts clearly indicates, people who remain rural are not simply caught in a deterministic web of impoverishment and exploitation. But these researchers quite proper fear of returning to an earlier state of the sociological art, in which survey research is abstracted from social conditions, prevents a full consideration of the differences between voluntary choice and involuntary constraint. There is a noticeable gap in these volumes between ethnographic and modular approaches and a tendency to substitute labeling devices for empirical examination at crucial points in the vertical analysis.

This brings me to a final problem that these volumes do not quite overcome: a sense of distance from the phenomenon of urban living. So much is left to formulization procedures that the sights, sounds, smells, feelings, and tastes that characterize urban living in Latin America fail to emerge. Debates over general models of dependency and colonialization or the need for modification of this or that variety of neo-Marxism or neofunctionalism, are clearly things these scholars want to move beyond. The next step, one already being taken by students of even this younger generation at many Latin American institutions, offers a hope of a deeper ethnography linked to sociological theory. Research in the area of multinational impact on urban communication networks; studies of the effect of world news agencies on local coverage; studies of graft, speculation, and real-estate bribery; and examinations of new class infrastructures in city living indicate a strong move to more intimately link sociological frameworks with social realities than even the scholars represented in these volumes have arrived at. Sociological research in the 1980s, it seems clear, will move considerably beyond the present critical standpoint of the new urbanologists seeking to link empirical and historical analysis.

Being far removed, I cannot rightly declare what the relationship is between the University of Texas Press at Austin and the Institute of Latin American Studies at the University of Texas at Austin. I presume that this is but one special variety of what is now common to many campuses: a cautious university press and an ambitious research agency wanting to get its findings published quickly. Guesses and conjectures apart, it might have been propitious had these two books appeared as one, despite their different origins. The editorial chores might more readily have been apportioned among Portes, Walton, and Browning, while the professional community would have benefited from a full-scale, enriched statement of urban studies in Latin America equal in impact in the present decade to that of the late Glenn Beyer's *Urban Explosion in Latin America* in the mid-1960s.

There is a certain amount of inevitable repetition and overlapping between the two volumes, while other issues, such as deviance in Latin American cities, communications between these Latin American cities, and different strategies of each nation in coping with urban sprawl, are touched upon all too briefly. Hence, each volume lacks the rich texture that a combined effort would surely have made possible, even probable, given the unusual skills of the editors and contributors alike. Again, I want to emphasize that, being outside the network of these two University of Texas publishing programs, I am not presuming that this literary fusion was ever a strong possibility. Whatever the technical case may be, these two volumes provide a rich source of ideas presented by concerned and thoughtful researchers thoroughly intimate with their subject, ideas deserving the serious attention of comparative sociologists, urbanologists, and, of course, Latin Americanists.

From *American Journal of Sociology*, vol. 83, no. 3 (1977), pp. 761–765.

35

Anthropological Sociology*

Redfield, Robert

One of the major ironies of the present period in the social sciences is that the sociologist, that professional charged with the study of society is probably further removed from the sources and object of his study than any comparable group of scholars. Marshall B. Clinard has put the matter directly when he said that "the sociologist has probably had less first hand experience with the actual data of his science than any other. Not really knowing about human beings, social institutions, and communities at firsthand he obviously feels ill-equipped to devise action programs that may have considerable immediate consequences."

Whatever the deformities and deficiencies exhibited by anthropologists, the discipline as a whole has the merit of encouraging and establishing contact with the peoples and cultures its practitioners seek to understand. The anthropologist, in comparison to the sociologist, tends to be empirical rather than empiricist, concerned rather than detached, and full-blooded in his reportage rather than vaguely rationalistic. The anthropologist tends to point out things that need doing, while the sociologist too often ends with a plea for more research of more data. And if I may be permitted a personal observation, the anthropologist seems to *enjoy* his work, whereas the sociologist often acts as if he is *enduring* his work.

There is another side to the matter, one not so pleasant to anthropological sensitivities. In comparison to sociology, anthropology is still in a stage of

* Robert Redfield, *Human Nature and the Study of Society: The Papers of Robert Redfield,* edited by Margaret Park Redfield (Chicago: The University of Chicago Press, 1962).

Ernest Becker, *The Birth and Death of Meaning: A Perspective in Psychiatry and Anthropology* (New York: The Free Press of Glencoe, 1962).

Oscar Lewis, *The Children of Sanchez: Autobiography of a Mexican Family* (New York: Random House, 1961).

Ruth Benedict, *An Anthropologist at Work: Writings of Ruth Benedict,* edited by Margaret Mead (Boston: Houghton Mifflin Co., 1959).

Abraham Edel and May Edel, *Anthropology and Ethics* (Springfield, III.: Charles C. Thomas Publishers, 1959).

theoretical confusion and methodological underdevelopment. The "science of culture" makes only the vaguest distinction between objective facts and subjective opinions, and rarely does the anthropologist take the trouble to distinguish between what is and what informants say something is. But perhaps the greatest difficulty for the anthropologist is getting over an ingrained professional provincialism. He or she too often worries about and busies himself with the archaic and not the actual. It is not potterymaking but the policymaking that is foremost in the minds of Africans and Brazilians. It is not cultural continuity (or social structure) but cultural discontinuity (or collective dynamics) that needs more attention. The reverential search for continuous cultural elements too frequently disguises an unconcern with dramatic forms of social change and, sometimes worse, a fear that attention to the tradition of the new would upset the professional anthropologist's applecart.

But any discipline operating at its maximum capacity transcends the pettiness and parochialism that infiltrates the rank and file. And anthropology performing at its maximum efficiency is a thing of brilliance and an illumination that sociologists can ill afford to ignore. Sociologists have done more talking about interdisciplinary research, but it has been the anthropologists who have taken the lead in concrete measures. Since sociologists must also meet the challenges of a new social science age of interrelation and cross-cultural exchange, the books under consideration here must be considered as more than a plea to read on a wider front. It is simple common sense to examine what has been done by our sister science on a wide variety of fronts before venturing forth ourselves. At the least such a procedure guarantees that we will avoid a senseless repetition, and at the most it may provide sociologists with the necessary initial thrust to get them into interdisciplinary orbit.

Talk about interdisciplinary research is commonplace. It forms the essential rhetoric of the grand theorists and empiricists alike. Unfortunately, too many sociologists have conceived of interdisciplinary research in terms of superordination and subordination. Thus, for the Parsonian School, nearly everything under the sun is conceived of as a subsystem of society. Economy is part of the social system. We ought not confuse sociological imperialism, however benevolent, with interdisciplinary work. And as a matter of deeper significance, the phrase interdisciplinary studies ought not to be viewed opportunistically, enabling an arbitrary linkage to a field with a good image such as medicine or physics. In this connection, the sharp words of Ernest Becker are most instructive. Arguing the case for a transcultural psychiatry, he points out that the arbitrary linkage of psychiatry to medical physiology has had destructive consequences. "In the first place, psychiatrists have a prestige contingent on their medical bona fides that they do not deserve; only a small portion of behavioral malfunction can be traced to underlying physiology. In the second place, a medical education does not provide a broad view of human behavior.

It is precisely this broad view that is necessary to understand the vast majority of behavioral malfunctions that have nothing to do with physiology. This is a vicious circle of a kind, and we should not wonder that psychiatrists are claiming larger and larger sums of Federal grant money for research into the physio-chemical bases of behavior malfunction." In short, interdisciplinary effort is neither image making nor a simple mechanical (and verbal) relation of distant fields. Such false alternatives can only result in poor social science, (e.g., the use of psychoanalytic categories of the normal and the pathological in testing the behavior of other cultures).

Arbitrary graftings may result in monstrosities. That is why interdisciplinary research needs a general theory of human behavior, as a base. This must be a theory from which all social scientists and humanists (the latter are usually the rub, for who wants to connect up with the inhabitants of the academic poorhouse!) can derive benefits. The work of the late Robert Redfield was consistently outstanding in this sphere, not only because he insisted upon a connection between anthropology and the humanities, but, more profoundly, because he forged the tools of a humanized anthropology. A review of the titles of Redfield's major papers offers a clue to how interdisciplinary work can be done: "Social Science among the Humanities," "Social Science as an Art," "Social Science as Morality," "The Peasant's View of the Good Life," "Art and Icon." If Redfield were a young instructor today, he would probably be called aside by his department chairman and gently informed that he was spreading himself too thin and that he ought to get himself a technical specialty before it is too late.

Perhaps the most illustrious paper of Redfield on the subject of interdisciplinary effort first appeared in a 1953 compendium *Anthropology Today* and is reprinted in the first volume of his collected papers. It is titled "Relation of Anthropology to the Social Sciences and the Humanities"—and the contents match the title. The point of Redfield's policy paper is not the convenience of social science linkage, but its necessity for social scientific survival. In advising men of action, in participating in social change, in performing as agents of change, the anthropologist must face the problem of the "good" and the "beautiful" as part of his work. In treating the human person as a modifier and a creator of his culture, the social scientist necessarily moves over into the study of the humanities, the study of the producers and creative products of man.

Redfield's theoretical explorations have already borne fruit in the recent work of Oscar Lewis on a transitional Mexican family. For in such an undertaking the writer must fuse the art of biography, the insight of history and the facts of society. The extension of anthropology to include civilized peoples as well as preliterates, places the researcher in the historical stream. As long as the anthropologist dealt with preliterate peoples, a case could be made out for the "historyless" nature of anthropology. But this condition no longer obtains. To deal seriously with developing societies and transitional culture entails an explicit commitment to the historical muse. Similarly, the intimate study of group life entails an equal commitment to biography. There is no doubt that viewed in cross-disciplinary terms, the demands on the social scientist, no less than the problem areas as such, mount considerably. But this is a comparatively small price to pay for the boundless enrichment of the study of man in society. Just imagine the kinds of problems that could be treated if there was a true social science cross-fertilization: Does reference group theory exist in a comparatively static society? Does the preliterate operate with our sense of time and space? Does the fact that all past societies exhibit a religious factor signify that all future societies must also contain such a factor? Do Indians have the same notion of overpopulation as do Western sociologists? One can multiply these kinds of important questions indefinitely. The point is that the present sterilities in research reflect the impotence of a bloodless methodology, and not the disappearance of what Robert Park called the Big News.

How fascinating it is to read how a brilliant anthropologist (and magnificent person) like Ruth Benedict approaches sociological problems with fresh insight. It has become so fashionable to criticize Benedict's cultural relativism that we sometimes tend to slight her concrete work. It is no exaggeration that Benedict said more on the subject of race prejudice in three pages than most sociologists have squeezed out in three hundred pages. In this connection, it should also be noted that Redfield's essay "The Cultural Role of the Cities" is the basic essay on comparative urban sociology, yet I have not seen it mentioned in a single text on urbanization! Pitifully few sociologists have dared say the obvious with any where near the clarity of Miss Benedict. "Race prejudice is deeply entrenched in American routine life and probably, measured by any objective standard, only South Africa goes further in segregation, discrimination, and humiliation."

Our sociologists too often assume that the present condition is a permanent condition. This is one reason why the field of race relations has fallen into a kind of torpor. In fact so barren has the area become, that it is being rapidly subsumed into the "high status" field of small group research—at a time in American history when the racial problem has reached a peak of critical importance. Why is it that the most significant sociological statements on the racial question comes from James Baldwin writing in the *New Yorker* and from Norman Podhoretz writing in *Commentary?* Is it not possible that the humanities may teach sociologists, no less than the other way about? Similarly, on questions of conflict and conflict resolution, the sociologist needs to know the comparative data that the anthropologist makes available for public distribution. How can such notions as the biological and instinctual impulse toward war be put to deserved rest without reference to evidence derived from the preliterate societies?

Benedict's theory of lethal and nonlethal types of conflict squares very well with present researches into safety-valves for the prevention of total conflict through programmed and controlled conflict. But perhaps what we need above all is the sagacity of a Benedict. "We wage the lethal variety of the genus War and the poisonousness of it comes not from what man is but from what society is." What a herculean challenge! If the problem is social and not rooted in man's nature, how can sociologists continue to shirk their responsibilities for studying conflict?

Each of the books under consideration calls attention to the relation between anthropology and the humanities. It would take a lengthy search to find any series of books by sociologists that reveal the same set of concerns. Perhaps the chief reason lies in the fact that anthropologists show an intimate concern for problems of mind, while the behavior-actionist emphasis in sociology tends to view man as mind-less. Only that which is translatable into forms of action tends to be included in the sociological purview. Is this realistic? Can it actually be the case that sociologists believe that all acts exhaust the contents of mind? The world of artifacts and symbols, myths, ideologies, and slogans has been relegated to a subordinate position in a desperate and futile effort to rid society of culture. The sociologist has become so alienated from cultural life that the assumption that he can then in turn study the cultural forms of social life as a subsystem has transformed from an assumption into a presumption.

The work by Abraham Edel and May Edel is a happy family fusion of cross-disciplinary interests. Abraham Edel is a philosopher, his wife a skilled anthropologist. The pivotal value of this book is its synthesis of materials on ethical beliefs in preliterate cultures. There is so much prattle in sociological quarters concerning the separation of facts and values. Utilizing the work of Benedict, Redfield, and Kluckhohn in anthropology and the naturalist tradition in American philosophy, the authors have fashioned a first-class volume. The Edels' work at many levels: they offer an accounting of ethical systems, wide and narrow, primitive and civilized; they present an inventory of what different cultures conceive of as the valuable, the good and the useful; and above all, they offer a typology for the scientific study of ethical systems. The important social science element in their work is a transcultural analysis of different ethical systems and how they relate to an overall valuational base (i.e., how a moral premise serves basic needs and meets fundamental aspirations).

The Edels' ask of a moral system no less and no more than we ask of a scientific system, that it satisfy needs and fulfill aspirations. This does not mean that science and ethics are identical in orientation or methodology. Science reflects the human need to solve the immediate and the commonplace, while ethics reflects the needs of men for transcendence, adventure, emergence, creativity, etc. The Edels' insist that a scientific study of ethics would resist foreclosure of further evaluations. The trans-cultural approach of the Edels' dovetails with Becker's similar contention that a continuing look at such psychiatric phenomena as schizophrenia and depression in the light of changing circumstances and a wider social science perspective would also have profoundly practical benefits in the fashioning of a useful ethic for modern man—a humanistic credo without the necessity of oracular misrepresentations. Supplementing the theory of a common humanities and diverse cultures, the Edels' and Becker seem to be insisting on the need for a common ethos and diverse moralities.

The monograph written by Becker goes further along an interdisciplinary path than most books attempting to correlate anthropological with psychiatric information. Becker's book is unique in its steadfast refusal to take either the going shibboleths of Freudianism as divine law, or legalistic definitions of mental illness as sociologically meaningful. The work of Becker, along with that of Szasz in psychiatry and Goffman in sociology, is leading the way toward a truly synthetic social-scientific account of mental strain in the industrial world and physical stress in the total institutional setup of insane asylums and prisons. The attempt to transfer psychiatric analysis from instinctual grounds to a cognitive base can have the most revolutionary effects on future discussions of mental health and mental deterioration. Becker's use of the naturalistic tradition in American philosophy is as worthwhile and meaningful as Edel's use of the same tradition to revise our stereotypes about moral beliefs. These books leave no doubt that interdisciplinary research is intrinsically radicalizing. Everything from academic departmentalization to hospital bureaucratization must be subject to scrutiny and change. Those who doubt this need only recollect how recent and tenuous departmental separation and professional bureaucratization are, to understand what the future has in store for technical ostriches.

Extensive commentary on the papers contained in the Benedict and Redfield volumes is not possible here. Nonetheless, it is instructive to compare the editorials for each. The Redfield volume, edited by Margaret Park Redfield, is beautifully realized. Mrs. Redfield supplies brief sketches to most of the essays, while Raymond Firth's introductory note is both to the point and in excellent taste. Ruth Benedict was not quite so successful. Her papers, subtitled *Writings of Ruth Benedict*, are edited by Margaret Mead. Unfortunately, one gets the distinct impression that Miss Mead is running in competition with her erstwhile and deceased colleague. Each section is prefaced by an essay by Miss Mead, oftentimes far more indicative of the editor's biases than Benedict's position. The editorializing is a trifle too cloying and pretentious for the occasion and seems singularly inappropriate to the nature of the book. Mead's remarks sound like a prepared brief urging Benedict's canonization but offer little illumination of Benedict as an anthropologist.

The plea of the previous generation of anthropologists for interdisciplinary effort has been turned into the practice of the present generation. And with this has come new strategies for the social sciences as a whole. The uses of this kind of anthropological research for sociologists are such that, with even a modicum of redirected energies, it is possible to forecast a large-scale improvement in the quality of the sociology and ethnography of the sixties.

From *Social Problems*, vol. 22, no. 2 (1963), pp. 201–206.

36

Militarism and Development[*]

Schmitter, Philippe C.

Not very long ago, serious work in military sociology was nonexistent. Under the impact of classical and guerrilla wars, the field blossomed. Studies ranging from the social-psychological mores of enlisted men and officer corps to second-generation analyses of the place of the military in the stratification systems of nations proliferated. Now a third generation of scholarship unites military analysis with development and political sociology; the work of Schmitter belongs to this latest, most sophisticated level of research. Schmitter's work seems to be a long way from the study of informal norms within a formal military bureaucracy. But his analysis of the military as part of a tight intertwining network of economy, sociology, polity, and military at least symbolizes the rapid march from the pleasant world of civilian sociology with its analyses of class, status, and power—to the apocalypse of the four horsemen in which the military becomes not simply a factor in the study of power or status, but a ruling class, or better, sector, unto itself and for itself. Or was this the situation all along, acknowledged only by those who took von Clausewitz on the right and Engels on the left seriously? I rather suspect it is a mixture of both. The weakness in our sociological tradition is that it has tended to suppress factors of raw power in favor of factors emphasizing order, law, and legitimacy. Beyond that, sociology has been slow to realize that classical warfare has yielded to nuclear holocaust, that the role of technological hardware rather than heroic men is now decisive. But whatever the final judgment of scholars of the evolution of sociological ideas, we are in a new epoch, one perhaps best described by Marx, when early in his career he noted that what had become decisive was not the weapon of criticism, but the criticism of weapons.

There is no need to summarize the five chapters in this reader since Philippe Schmitter has done an excellent job in this regard. Indeed, it is too bad that the contributors to this volume were unable to generate a conclusion that might have better tied the findings together, especially since it was a product of the

---

[*] Philippe C. Schmitter, *Military Rule in Latin America: Function, Consequences, and Perspectives* (Beverly Hills: Sage Publications, 1973), pp. 322.

InterUniversity Seminar on Armed Forces and Society, held at the Center for Policy Study at the University of Chicago.

The volume is divided into three parts. The first is on the changing functions of military rule. Alain Rouquié contributes an excellent essay showing that what first appears in Latin American militarism in defense of national revolution emerges finally as revolutionary nationalism. The analysis of the 1968–71 period and specifically of changes in the Peruvian, Bolivian (and by extension Brazilian) systems is of exceptional importance, although one might have hoped for deeper insight into how the military in these countries arrived at their new nationalist perspectives despite, rather than because of, United States intervention. One would also have hoped for a complementary essay on how this same process occurs in the Mexican, Chilean, Argentine military context, and similarly in a Cuban context. But, alas, these comparisons are not made, although there are untapped writings on these specific topics.

The second part, on the consequences of military rule and military aid contains two sound essays. The first is Jerry L. Weaver's summary of various theories of the armed forces in relation to national reform, middle-class hegemony and overseas imperialism. I find myself in agreement with his belief that the military is much more and much less than the guardian of the middle class. On the other hand, even if we assume that the military function is a national and not simply a class phenomenon, it does seem that economic capitalism and political traditionalism are (except in Cuba) the invariant outcomes of military dominion. Nonetheless, this useful and provocative essay generally avoids the clichés and banalities prevalent in this area of research.

The essay by Schmitter, essentially on the economics of the armed forces, is both original and thoroughly provocative. His work suggests the dangers of assuming any direct correlation between the size of the military budget or the amount of foreign military aid, and the character of the political system in each Latin American country. While not denying the impact of military intervention, he appropriately notes that the direction of changes resulting from intervention is extremely hard to predict, and military intervention may in fact lead to contradictory outcomes. His various conclusions indicate basically that wealthy countries spend more money for defense purposes than do poor countries. Military expenditures are more a part of an overall domestic resource capacity than of any foreign aid system. Foreign military assistance is considered more in terms of overall defense budgets than of anticipated political advantage from the receipt of such foreign aid. As with the Weaver essay, such conclusions tell us what the military does not accomplish in relation to its social and economic sectors, but perhaps they tell us too little about what militarism does mean to a nation. For example, the drainage effect, the cost factor in high military expenditure-low productivity nations, remains essentially unexamined by Schmitter.

The last two essays, by Geoffrey Kemp and James Kurth, deal with the prospects for arms control and military rule. The Kemp paper is especially provocative in that it shows that the military is involved in the business of arms, force, and violence. There are real conflicts and contradictions within Latin America, making the military overseas or sovereignty factor significant and demonstrating that the police role is not the military's only role, as is so often claimed in the conventional literature. I am not entirely sure I can accept the logic of Kemp's argument that to minimize the defense burden of the recipient nation, the donor nation might send the most sophisticated rather than less sophisticated weapons. In terms of sheer fiscal costs, that may be the case, but in terms of preventing military imbalance in the hemisphere and beyond, an imbalance in the relationship between the military and civilian centers supplying the most advanced defense systems, can be hazardous to the health and welfare of these nations. To deal simply with the transfer of prestige in relation to advanced military equipment but not with the transfer of terror, misses much of the point of the problems of the poor in the Third World with respect to their own leadership and to the overseas donors of sophisticated weaponry.

The final contribution on United States foreign policy and Latin American military rule is again a sophisticated piece of work showing that economic aid, direct investments, overseas trade, and military hardware do not uniquely determine the character of Latin American regimes. One weakness in the conservative argument that the role of the U.S. military aid program in Latin American politics is like the role of the one soldier out of the several who form a firing squad, is that such United States aid distorts the normal advantages and disadvantages of guerrilla insurgency operations in the area. To carry the analog further, if one soldier out of the several carries a hand SAM-7 missile, while the other troops have bows and arrows, it is not hard to determine that one particular soldier will have a quite distinct role in the determination and makeup of an execution squad. It must also be noted that what may be viewed as badly aged hardware in a NATO context, may be quite sophisticated in a Latin American context—certainly sophisticated enough to stay the hand of guerrilla movements.

Military Rule in Latin America is basically a debunking of the new orthodoxy of dependency theory, a task that very much needed doing. The book points out the complexities involved in this area of research, although it does not, ironically enough, address itself to the consequences of military rule in Latin America. One gets the feeling that many of these American and European scholars have drawn wide inferences from a data bank that improperly assesses the intimacies of life. This is an odd truth about much writing in the developing areas: there is a sociological paucity in the face of a political richness, a sense of distance rather than involvement with the societies being analyzed. Perhaps

199

this explains a reticence to employ the Cuban model as a *leitmotiv* with which to study the Brazilian, Peruvian, and Bolivian "models" of military rule.

The book as a physical entity calls forth a veritable catalog of now standard complaints about quickie scholarly anthologies. (1) The reader is not provided with either a name or a subject index. (2) There is no glossary of terms in a work filled with specialized terms and neologisms of all sorts. (3) Charts and tables are often offered without sources. (4) Contributors are not identified beyond their names. Even POWs provide their captors with rank and serial number, as well as names. In short, either the editor or the publisher must begin to develop a more responsible attitude toward the readers. In this age of exorbitant printing, composition, and binding costs, it is useless to insist on deluxe editions (although the $7.50 price tag on this paperback book makes such an insistence not entirely improper); yet there are minimum standards that deserve to be met for the sake of editor and author no less than reader. If a decision has been made to simply photograph typewritten manuscript pages, as was the case here, at the least one might expect the use of the same typewriter. This can be easily achieved an IBM Selectric, using the same type element throughout, since carbon ribbons, despite their costs, do provide uniform intensity. Instead, the publishers simply published manuscripts as submitted—meaning different typefaces for each article, and inking intensities varying by article, by page, and with style variations that would bring the editors of the *Chicago Manual of Style* to their knees in despair. I have rarely seen a book that better serves the argument that all contracts between authors and publishers should have a clause guaranteeing minimum production standards. I fear that even the bravest, battle-scarred military sociologist will be unable to read this collection from cover to cover or even chapter by chapter, and this is sad, given the significance of this volume for the field of military studies and social science alike.

From *Contemporary Sociology,* vol. 3, no. 4 (1974), pp. 307–309.

37

Class, Race and Pluralism*
Smith, M.G.

Let me start with a visceral reaction that required no vitiating revisions even after two readings: this is a first-rate book, a fine blend of ethnographic and theoretical writing. The tradition of English social anthropology embodied in Professor Smith's text causes one to wonder about the nearly complete separation of sociology from anthropology in the United States. For all of its wealth of data, the book remains uncluttered by excess baggage. The author appreciates the distinction between complexity of statement and profundity of insight. One knows what to agree with or disagree with, without wallowing about in communication problems.

The first part of this volume represents a series of studies in search of an understanding of the British West Indies. Without disregarding or minimizing the impact of external social forces—from the United States to Brazil and from other Caribbean Islands to Africa—Smith provides a strong case for certain structural linkages that define the British West Indies. He does not make assumptions about consensus or common values or actors in search of particular ends—indeed, he is highly articulate in rejecting the implicit banality in the sort of functionalism that can neither explain nor weight factors. Instead, he views the matter of cultural identity in terms of structural disparities: differences between subordinate and superordinate, pivotal and peripheral economic classes, racial strains, and educational status pockets. In this way, he not only builds up a grid of social relations in the British West Indies but also shows what these relations have been and will be. For all of this ambitious theorizing, Smith manages to retain a genuine modesty of the limits as well as the worth of his efforts.

Smith uses "pluralism" distinctively, not as an illustration of cultural democracy, but rather as a characteristic feature of dependence and decadence. That is to say, pluralism is not a philosophic statement about diversity in the marketplace of ideas, but a sociological statement of the seedbed of political

---

* M.G. Smith, *The Plural Society in the British West Indies*, (Berkeley: University of California Press, 1965), pp. 359.

dominance. Pluralism is meant to include both economic and ethnic contradictions without being reduced to either component. Beyond this, pluralism serves as a synthetic tool for the study of the British West Indies. Indeed, pluralism is one side of the intellectual apparatus; the other is a powerful comparative basis embodied in each of the essays.

The second part of the book (chapters 4–8) contains the most pellucid writing. In comparing slavery and emancipation in Jamaica and Nigeria, more specifically, the peoples of Zaria and Hausa, Smith realizes the high possibilities in the comparative-historical model over other available models. In his hands, the structural approach is shown of the metaphysics of functionalism and thus serves to make racial and economic determinisms appear futile. Smith shows the different structural features distinguishing a homogeneous-autonomous society from a heterogeneous-dependent society.

This distinction between autonomy and dependency has vital field research implications. It helps to explain why slavery has left its mark in the British Caribbean but not upon the Zaria of Africa. It reclaims for social research, subject matter that is often prematurely surrendered to those starting from a pool (a cesspool) of human nature and instinctual drives. The further dissection of the plural framework of Jamaican society in terms of such rarely operationalized variables as law, trade, and credit systems, along with the more customary distinctions of class, race, and ethnic origins, is of great significance for investigators of other areas showing similar pluralist formations. And for those laboring under the Schumpeterian myth of the beneficent character of British colonial rule, these chapters will prove of special value.

The final portion of the book (chapters 9–12) presents materials of a more technical level. Yet Smith has the rare capacity to infuse even dense material with insight and literary grace. First, he shows the strains within Jamaica society in terms of urban preferences and educational achievements among a sample of Jamaican children and adolescents. In his sample, where expectations and aspirations differ, so too do motivations and performances. Smith then goes on to indicate the enormous role played by ascribed status plays when customary tenure of land displaces legally valid land transfers. His remarkable knowledge of law, no less than of custom, transforms a prosaic topic into something of wide relevance: the tenacity of custom in the developmental process. The penultimate chapter is a fascinating study of Grenada and its little-known mass leader E. N. Gairy. Beyond that, it is a study of how political enfranchisement enables the colored masses to cope with a Western-oriented white elite. The author, by using the historical method, shows how gains in economic levels cannot guarantee status gains and status equality. The final chapter shows how tensions in the bifurcated plural society take place. Parallel increases in social mobility and education are required to reduce strain, and this is rarely the case. Even if it were, the results would be problematic, since for Smith meaningful changes in the economic system or in the status hierarchy proceed by political action. Thus, the doubts and uncertainties attendant on political action, rather than the selection of the main parameters, make prediction difficult.

I have one major and one minor criticism. For the first, Smith's multi-determinate framework sometimes obscures the total situation. In several instances the assertion of economic primacy is made, only to be obscured by secondary factors. For instance, we are told that "influence and power rest with those who control economic resources and employment opportunities in the local community." Yet an informal leadership based on age and distinct from economic power is unconvincingly introduced to explain the character of voluntary organizations. And earlier in the book the reader is informed that a genuine division of labor based on racial distinctions is maintained, yet in the same paragraph the author suggests that "cultural performance and skill is decisive rather than racial status." Had he said that racial definitions are made in terms of cultural levels of achievement, the situation might have been saved. In general, Smith is troubled by the assignment of weight to class and racial factors. The structural approach serves to disguise rather than remove the troublesome business of what factors are basic and what factors are derivatives in the process of social development.

At a much lesser level, I am curious as to why Smith has not considered the work of Wendell Bell on the political leaders of Jamaica, particularly since this has a major bearing on the thesis of Smith's work, that is, the critical role of political action in changing the economy and the society. Also, it would be interesting to see how Smith would evaluate the impact of culture shock on the overseas Jamaican, such as is provided in the analysis of Ruth Glass's work. But this is admittedly a query rather than a criticism. I have no doubt Smith could field it without much trouble.

This is an important book for social scientists concerned with developmental theory. It would be a mistake to assume that the specialized nature of the subject matter or the technical nature of the title, is a warrant for ignoring either this volume or this unique area of the world.

From *The American Journal of Sociology*, vol. 71, no. 4 (1966), pp. 451–53.

Part III

Ethnicity and Religiosity

38

Manners, Civility and Civilization*

Cuddihy, John Murray

In reviewing these two books in tandem, we are confronted with a classic case of form versus content. John Cuddihy's book, *The Ordeal of Civility*, is brilliantly written, shimmering with aphorisms, overflowing with extrapolations and so imaginative that one feels that the weight of Marx and Freud, not to mention the Jews, limit the author's flights of literary imagination. Imagine a clever young Jewish scholar engaged in a verbal joust with Irish writers like Yeats, Shaw, and O'Casey. Place these Irish masters in an exilic struggle against civility and against the norms of the dominant society. In this way, one can appreciate the heights Cuddihy reaches for in his study of Jewish writers such as Marx, Freud and, a lesser lumière, Lévi-Strauss. They are presumed to share a Diaspora struggle against false manners and decadent ideologies: in short, theirs is a collective *crie de coeur* against civility.

In the interchangeability of hypothetical Jewish scholar in search of Irish wisdom, and the very real Irish-American scholar in search of Jewish wisdom, we can immediately perceive some of the structural weaknesses of this text. For what is presented as uniquely Jewish; the revolt against civility is, in fact, the general posture of all writers, scholars, and publics in search of liberation. This, of course, does not automatically disqualify the book or its thesis from careful consideration, but it does take away that note of exoticism he pins to the Jewish intellectual tradition, which fitfully aborts a sociological attempt to understand the Jewish condition in the twentieth century and how Marx and Freud exemplify that condition.

In contrast, the book by Bruce Brown, *Marx, Freud, and the Critique of Everyday Life*, is clumsy beyond belief, with cloudy phrases, pedestrian

---

* Bruce Brown, *Marx, Freud, and the Critique of Everyday Life: Toward a Permanent Cultural Revolution* (New York: Monthly Review Press, 1973), pp. 202.

John Murray Cuddihy, *The Ordeal of Civility: Freud, Marx, Lévi-Strauss, and the Jewish Struggle with Modernity* (New York: Basic Books, 1974), pp. 272.

pedantry, and so unimaginative a style that one feels like hiding out from Marx, Freud, and their European imitators and running, not walking, to the nearest empiricist. The following *one* sentence illustrates the fact that obscurantism is by no means a monopoly of grand theory.

> Freud was able at least implicitly to outline a method for psycho-analytic investigation which is simultaneously scientific and critical inasmuch as it establishes a dialectic between theory and practice at the very core of the therapeutic experience (e.g., the theoretical total-ization of anthropological knowledge at the disposal of the analyst as reflected in the therapeutic practice) which, by unlocking the reified structures of the patient's consciousness, elicits feedback in the form of new data regarding the patient's consciousness, elicits feedback in the form of new data regarding the patient's experience which must be decoded with the analyst's help in such a way as to unmask the patient's increasingly artful rationalizations and, finally, assimilated within the anthropological theory in order to facilitate the patient's ultimate totalization of his or her own experience.

I do believe that Mr. Brown is simply arguing that psychoanalysis, because it necessarily involves a relationship between analyst and patient, thereby permits a unity of theory and practice in the effort to understand the patient's experience. But to say so involves a surrender of empty profundities; and this the author is unwilling to do.

Yet, if a choice must be made between these two books, (which thank God, it does not), I find myself opting for the clumsy effort of Brown over the sophistical effort of Cuddihy. For whatever else, Brown takes the ideas of Marx and Freud with genuine seriousness.

He sees in both socialism and psychoanalysis an effort to transcend the human problem of internal repression and external oppression. Yet, in the Cuddihy volume, one feels that Marx and Freud are simply springboards to a rather stretched-out thesis about self-imposed Jewish marginality, that asserts the primacy of underlying motivations. In point of fact, in a moment of self-celebration, we are informed that Marx, Freud, and Lévi-Strauss are only the first leg of a second triumvirate yet to come, dealing with Kafka, Wittgenstein, and Arendt. Cuddihy is simply no Edmund Wilson, and *The Ordeal of Civility is not To the Finland Station*. He frustrates rather than elaborates the sweep of history, reducing it to theological wanderings.

Both books reveal the ubiquitous character of greatness. A scholar's interpre-tation becomes a litmus test of his own ideological predilections. Freud, Marx, and the cast of twentieth century characters known as neo-Freudians and neo-Marxians tell us more about the demands of our times than about the famous figures chosen for extended commentary. In the case of Brown, it is the New Left. Both Jews and leftists will undoubtedly survive these critiques and apologies.

It is curious that the marginality of a religious group probably increasingly intersects with the marginality of a political group. The Jew as subversive and the radical as subversive are two streams that seem to move inexorably into the same river of politics and culture. Brown manages his subjects without any real concern with the Jewish question, and equally remarkably, Cuddihy manages his subjects without much reference to the political question. Both illustrate that one can draw upon great thinkers in such an endless variety of ways that what emerges is not so much biography as mosaic, not so much scientific historiography as new forms of irrational life legitimated by great thinkers. This too, is a disquieting aspect of both books, since the greatness of both Marx and Freud is much affected by their religiosity or at least their sense of the role of belief in both objective history and phylogenetic memory. Memory is to Freud what history is to Marx: the source of consciousness that precedes human rationality. This entire area is subject to considerable speculation for both these giants. However much both illustrate the search for a unified science of liberation, what seems to get sponged out is the elemental fact that Freud, Marx, and certainly people like Lévi-Strauss and Wilhelm Reich were social scientists. To be sure, the range of their practice extended from economics to psychoanalysis to anthropology. But the reputation of these figures endures because they built theories that can be confirmed or disconfirmed by evidence drawn from different contexts and changing circumstances. This must be said, or that which makes Marx or Freud giants of social thought, is ultimately reduced to ideological and theological caricature.

The Cuddihy book is divided into four parts. The first part contains thirteen chapters centering upon Freud and the neo-Freudian Wilhelm Reich. The second part has four chapters on Karl Marx and one on Claude Lévi-Strauss. A separate word on the famed French anthropologist is in order given his prominence in the book's title. He appears as remote from the thesis of this volume as any non-Jewish anthropologist living in France. Only by the most extraordinary stretch of Cuddihy's imagination could *Tristes tropiques, La Pensée sauvage*, and *L'Homme nu* be considered a direct consequence of the Jewish imagination. The author would have been better advised to choose Emile Durkheim as the third member of his Jewish triad. The problem here would be that Durkheim argues in favor of civil society (as does Lévi-Strauss, for that matter). *The Division of Labor*, Durkheim's great work upon which Lévi-Strauss built his own efforts, is constructed on the demand, no less than the need, for social structure and economic organization. The argument for the contract society as the essence of civilization and civility as the cement of social order is central to both. Durkheim and Lévi-Strauss (despite their differences on inferior and superior religions) point in the opposite direction from the thesis of Cuddihy's book, namely, that the Jewish assault on civility is a consequence of the tribal rather than the civil nature of Jewish culture.

(How the Jewish intellectual could then turn around and behave as a prophet of modernization against tribal backwardness remains unexplained.)

The third part of Cuddihy's book, entitled "The Demeaned Jewish Intellectuals: Ideologists of Delayed Modernization," is comprised of two chapters. Here the author had a perfect opportunity to link Jewish emancipation and the search for Third World emancipation. Israel has become the pariah nation within the Third World, just as Jews have been in classical terms a pariah people within Western culture. Unfortunately, there is an underlying tone of animosity toward Jewish efforts at modernization. We are told in one stroke that Hebraicism is the ideology that gave meaning to social inferiority and moral superiority. Marx's underclass of society and Freud's underside of personality were both investments in a subversive theory based on a moral critique of the superior civilization of the West. The Jews are thus reduced to special pleaders, soft-in-the-head, sentimental liberals. But once again, they turn out to be the victims rather than the heroes of this section of the book, they are punished for being nasty and twice pilloried for being nice.

The final section is comprised of two chapters, which reduce essentially to several book reviews and newspaper aphorisms. Abbie Hoffman vs. Judge Hoffman, Jewish tenants against black tenants (even though both are assessed through the literary efforts of assimilationist Bernard Malamud). As the book moves along, the essays grow less eloquent and crisp. Cuddihy as literary critic, becomes downright vulgar. Name-dropping that would indicate to the densest reader that the author has traveled among the intelligent, gratuitous advice to the famous to expand and update their works, vague attacks on various and sundry writers, and generally just plain argumentativeness with Jews the author does not especially like, seriously imperil the book's chances of being taken as seriously as he wishes. The final chapter, "Modernity, Jewry, Christianity," by far the most ambitious and far ranging, is also the least candid. For no matter how clever and however favorable Cuddihy is to the efforts of Marx, Freud, and their best followers, he ends nonetheless with a bow to assimilation tendencies which presumably have been less significant in the Jewish tradition than orthodoxy. The exemplars of Christian democracy, such as Weber and the radical Protestant tradition, which presumably gave its inner assent to the modernization process (in contrast to tribalistic Judaism which gave only its outer assent), the Church which sees no differences between Christianity and heathens, the faith ultimately in the hidden Christ to be inconspicuous yet fruitful, the invisible but tasteful God of Protestant culture who lies beyond the vulgarities of press or power—these turn out to be the saviors of the Jews, not Marx or Freud. It is on this God that ultimately not only the book ends, but Judaism itself apparently comes to a screeching halt. Precisely such a posture, however shrewdly rendered, underwrites *The Ordeal of Civility*.

By denying the anti-Semitic factor, by blaming the intellectual victor, as it were, Cuddihy liquidates the culture of revolution that the Jewish tradition is all about. The assault on manners and civility is simply a psychological reflex of that larger cultural drive. Jews can be quite civil without suffering it as an ordeal, given a modicum of equity in their treatment, as the Dutch Jews and Italian Jews demonstrate. The ordeal that the Jews have suffered is not of civility but of inequality, especially in the Germanic context Marx and Freud inhabited. The civility that they oppose is merely a patina, a gloss that would condemn them and the entire human race, to accept inequality as a social norm and the holocaust as a social fact. And it is in this area that Professor Cuddihy's work displays the least awareness.

The very formulation of the *Judenfrage* in terms of civility places the burden of responsibility entirely on the shoulders of the Jews, as if the Jew were the actor and Christians and Socialists the reactors. Because of this misplaced concreteness, the author can liquidate the problem of anti-Semitism with ease, replacing it with the strategy and tactics of manners and mores.

Yet one cannot deny the intriguing aspects of the book and the seriousness with which the argument is presented. It represents a robust Christian framework informed by Reformation values, and were it presented in those frank terms, the book might be seen as a powerful critique of Jewish emancipation. The tragedy is that Cuddihy's obvious theological biases are presented in a furtive, surreptitious manner. The author expresses "gratitude" to his parents "for their bringing me into the world and for their having brought me up a Catholic," although he hastens to add, "I am no longer a Catholic." I tend to agree, especially since a hoary Protestant theology rather than Catholicism informs much of the critique of the Jewish faith.

The purpose of the Brown book is exactly the search for a new synthesis, one that would take into account subjective as well as objective standpoints: liberation as seen by Freud and Reich, no less than emancipation as seen by Marx and perhaps Marcuse. The tragedy is that this is already an outdated book. It rests on an entity entitled the New Left, which seems to be as extinct in Europe as in the United States and which has been reduced to a series of elite debates among European academicians, rather than a mass effort in liberation of the type presumably interesting to Brown. The New Left has vanished to be replaced, not by a Socialist higher ground, but by a politics of desperation in which neither personal liberation nor political emancipation are realized. As a result, the New Left has become a movement without members and an ideology without a policy: the sort of outcome to movement politics that Wilhelm Reich cautioned about in *The Mass Psychology of Fascism* (a work absolutely central to Wilhelm Reich, but which is strangely marginal to Brown's theorizing about the relationships between socialism and psychoanalysis).

Brown himself, forced to give an alternative to the decadence of capitalism and the corruption of Bolshevism, can only come up with the capabilities of small groups which he claims have more potential for struggle than they had since Proudhon's day. Aside from the fact that collectivities, microsocieties,

and other extended family groups have by no means been uniformly successful, the more serious problem with this argument is that these Gemeinschaft
movements have outlived the New Left, albeit in a nonpolitical context. Thus,
Brown's book comes to a crashing halt on the fact that his Marx-Freud synthesis
to the problem of repression and oppression, has been unable to survive the
past decade. In short, the thinnest part of this effort, the search for forming
and multiplying spontaneous groupings of people (which often do not exist)
recalls the stringent warnings of Lenin that revolutions are organized events
stretched over time, not spontaneous occurrences announced by opium eaters.
I am suggesting that Marx on Proudhon and Lenin on Plekhanov are closer
to the marrow of reality than Proudhon on Marx or Plekhanov on Lenin. The
orthodox Left better claims to be the more serious part of the socialist tradition than does the New Left. At the level of critiquing everyday life, the New
Left seems to be most expendable, even as its valuational formulas continue
to inform new searches for appropriate lifestyles.

Nonetheless, it must be said in Brown's defense that the trend toward Freud
and Reich enables him, as it has others like David Cooper and Richard Sennett,
to commence a fundamental critique of modern civilization across national
boundaries. The critique of industrial capitalism is essentially a disguised
assault on the postindustrial world as such. Whether that assault is accurate
in its details or reflects a nostalgia for things long since past, the intellectual
attempt to synthesize Freudian psychoanalysis with Marxian sociology in the
search for a new social order continues to provide a critique of existing culture.
There are many astute comments made by Brown on weaknesses within the
socialist as well as capitalist systems within this framework. If his answers seem
tepid and weak in relation to the general level of criticism of industrial societies,
one can at least say that his work is very much in keeping with a critique of
civility that disguises oppression and repression, while permitting the kind
of critical standpoint that typifies both radicalism and Judaism at their best.

We have here, in short, two books that are more illustrative of the problems
they treat than either would care to admit. The problem of oppression remains
because the existence of oppression continues. The problem of repression
remains because the existence of repression remains. Nonetheless, both of
these volumes represent and reflect the curious continuation of marginality
as part of the social scientific imagination and the use of that marginality as a
critical perspective on the search for constructive alternatives.

I am going to continue a policy established in my previous reviews for
Contemporary Sociology of concluding with a commentary on physical
appearance and stylistic worth, since a book is a physical entity that is bought
and sold, no less than an intellectual entity that is read and digested. *The
Ordeal of Civility* is a well tailored book. The cover design and text design are
in good taste. The editing and copyediting are well-nigh perfect. The paper
stock is sturdy and the typeface is thoroughly legible. The index is generally

satisfactory, although as is often the case nowadays, the subject portion of the index is far weaker than the name portion. Running heads and folio numbers are perfectly aligned, and real care is given to production details—something generally true of Basic Books.

Marx, Freud, and the Critique of Everyday Life is much less appealing. The paper stock is brittle, breaking off at the edges, and already appears badly aged. Chemically treated book paper should not look so bad after forty years, much less one year. The editing and copyediting of the text is competent. But the same cannot be said of the notes section. Here the treatment is quite cavalier: information on publishers is missing, author's names are edited randomly, works are cited in foreign languages when English-language editions are available, references are made to opere rather than specific book titles. The book has no subject index, only a name index—and that is not complete. Simply moving the dedication (*pour la liberté*) over onto the opposite side of the bastard title page could have saved the cost of an eight-page signature. As it is, the book ends with blank pages. Indeed, Monthly Review Press could have invested the savings from that signature (actually a 16 page cost since the book was manufactured 32 pages up) into tighter editing controls. To end on a pleasant note, the jacket design is quite professional. But who did the woodcuts?

From *Contemporary Sociology*, vol. 5, no. 2 (1976), pp. 111–115.

39

Liquidation or Liberation?*

Deutscher, Isaac

When the persecution of the Jew ends, there won't be any need for writers to make portentous inquiries into what it means to be a Jew. Until that long awaited, but probably never to be realized, in our lifetimes at least, Day of Judgment, self-definition and redefinition will continue, if only as a survival mechanism for the Jewish people.

One of the high ironies of fate is that the perfect anti-Semite, the Nazi, has a thoroughly cosmic view of what defines a Jew—extending from any one whose first cousin is Jewish to anyone who identifies himself as a Jew. On the other hand, the perfect Jew, the ultra-Orthodox, Talmud-citing Jew, sees the size of Jewry shrunken to like-minded Orthodox adherents (and even some of those cannot really be trusted). However, this only means that the nastiest of oppressor and the noisiest of oppressed play the game of Jew and anti-Jew unambiguously. Everyone else—and that includes the overwhelming portion of the non-Jewish world, no less than an equally large majority of the Jewish tribes—must live in a world of paradox tinged with purpose, doubt lined with duty. The books of Isaac Deutscher and Albert Memmi are addressed to this vast majority.

Let it be said at the outset that both volumes display an intensity of feeling and a sincerity of purpose that characterizes the works of Deutscher and Memmi in general. They are, after all, not ordinary Jewish propagandists of the word. They both live with their left-wing ideology in far greater comfort than they can with their wingless and truncated theology. Deutscher was, until his recent death, one of the ablest Marxists in Europe. A prolific writer, he is best known for his biographies of Stalin and Trotsky; at the time of his death he was working on Lenin. (When we met in 1962, while I was Visiting Lecturer at the London School of Economics, he even suggested a work on Plekhanov

---

*Isaac Deutscher, *The Non-Jewish Jew*, Tamara Deutscher (editor), (New York: Oxford University Press, 1968), pp. 164.

Albert Memmi, *The Liberation of the Jew*, Translated by Judy Hyun, (New York: The Orion Press, 1968), pp. 303.

if his health and life held out long enough.) In addition, Deutscher wrote a brilliant series of essays on political themes, which, during the cold war period, served as a beacon of good sense and political decency in the face of half-crazed critics on both the Left and the Right. Deutscher's political activities reached a high point in the twenty's and thirty's, when he was involved in the affairs of the Polish Communist Party. After his self-imposed exile to England, he continued to serve as informal advisor to various left-wing Laborite causes.

The case of Memmi is somewhat distinct. Cosmopolitan in a different way, Memmi spent his entire youth in Tunisia. During World War II, as a young man he was arrested and sent to a forced labor camp (from which he escaped). After the war, he returned for a brief period to Algiers, and then went to the Sorbonne, where he studied philosophy and stayed on to teach. His book *The Colonizer and the Colonized* ranks with Fanon's *The Damned of the Earth* as a masterpiece in the social psychology of oppression and its special forms in the Third World. Indeed, I found Memmi's book superior to Fanon's precisely to the degree that the philosophical tradition is a richer field to harvest than the narrowly focused psychoanalytic intellectual constraints within which Fanon operated.

The backgrounds of these two men are important, not so much to announce their respective bona fides—they hardly need such pronunciamentos. Rather, they show the special left-wing proclivities that dominate their respective works, and the deep seriousness with which they approach the tragedy of the Jew as left-wing partisans. That they come up with different diagnoses and hence different conclusions is important, but perhaps less important than the simple fact that two such sterling figures of the European Left dared attempt to reconcile political ideology and national identity.

It would be a profound mistake to draw the conclusion that Memmi and Deutscher represent the same point of view on the Jewish question as a consequence of their shared faith in the ultimate worth of socialism. Nothing could be further from the truth. On all the big political questions of current moment, they stand at opposite poles. Memmi has become increasingly convinced of the necessity for a solution, indeed a liberation, of the Jew on the basis of Israel, while Deutscher grew increasingly hostile to Israel, until he reached a near complete condemnation of Israel's Six-Day War against the Arab states.

Before getting into specific contrasts, one must appreciate the source of these differences. They clearly are to be found in the difference between Marx and the materialist tradition represented by Deutscher, on the one hand, and Hegel and the dialectical tradition represented by Memmi, on the other. It requires no great acumen to appreciate the degree to which dialectical materialism was always an uncomfortable and at times disquieting resolution of nineteenth-century German romanticism. Like its Sturm and Drang predecessors, it neatly resolved in theory all the problems that remained to be solved in practice. Perhaps for this reason, Marx abandoned any intimate interest in expanding the philosophic horizons of his thought and left such mundane matters to his coworker Engels, who proceeded to botch things, albeit brilliantly, by going off into the deep murky waters of a "dialectics of nature."

Like all resolutions that leave the problems intact, the doctrine of dialectical materialism had a stormy career, particularly in the Soviet Union during the late twenty's and early thirty's, where first the mechanists and then the dialectical idealists were made to pay the price for their improper emphasis. But perhaps the Russians perceived politically what they were unable to respond to philosophically, namely, the untenable nature of the theoretical synthesis to begin with. This is certainly apparent if we contrast the work of Deutscher and Memmi, who in their own ways exhibit the strains within the system of thought in which they worked. Deutscher the mechanist can hardly accept the ideal of historically unsanctioned events, while Memmi the dialectician must structure his book in triads, his chapters in three parts, and even his paragraphs in three sentences.

Deutscher's book is that of "an unrepentant Marxist, an atheist, an internationalist." His vision of Judaism is shaped by a theory of marginality called the negative community. In this universe, anti-Semitism is an unspent force. Since the Jew is historically the enemy of racialism, nationalism, xenophobia and since he is the incarnation of the alien man from within, he becomes for Deutscher a prototype of radicalism, whether the Jew wills it or not. But precisely such a definition of Judaism causes Deutscher great grief in response to the current Israeli-Arab situation. He sees the Israelis "in the role of the Prussians of the Middle East"—a definition not far removed from the Soviet denunciation of Israel as the neo-Nazis of the Middle East. So far removed are the Israelis from Deutscher's prototype of the marginal Jew that they "now appear in the Middle East once again in the invidious role of agents not so much of their own, relatively feeble capitalism, but of powerful Western vested interests and as protégés of neo-colonialism. This is how the Arab world sees them, not without reason. Once again they arouse bitter emotions and hatred in their neighbors, in all those who have ever been or still are victims of imperialism." Thus it is that Deutscher's Marxism triumphs over his Judaism. But it is an empty triumph. For what is important to him is not victory but purity, not the social system but the correct values.

This neo-orthodox Marxism does more than shape Deutscher's vision of the Jews; it also distorts his statements on actual political history. In the conclusion to his essay on the "non-Jewish Jew," he notes that "the decay of bourgeois Europe has compelled the Jew to embrace the nation-state. This is the paradoxical consummation of the Jewish tragedy. It is paradoxical because we live in an age when the nation-state is fast becoming an anachronism, an archaism." This must surely represent the ultimate triumph of Deutscher's purified Marxism over common sense. For the simple question is—where are signs of anachronism to be found? Where is the nation-state crumbling? Certainly not in Africa, the Middle East, Southeast Asia, South America. Obviously the nation-state is the very alpha and omega of modern developmentalism—even revolutions made in the name of Marxism must assert the full authority of nationalism to achieve even a modest degree of mass mobilization. Deutscher's further comment that the nation-state is an anachronism even in the United States, Great Britain, France, Germany, and Russia also rates a raised eyebrow. Here, too, is the substitution of internationalist rhetoric for nationalist reality. Has Deutscher forgotten that in two world wars—with the votes and then ultimately the blood of the working classes of all of these nations—"the people" demonstrated an overriding faith in their nations and a complete lack of faith in class solidarity across national lines? In short, the Marxism of Deutscher serves to falsify the historical epoch itself and thus makes a caricature of Jewish demands for a state called Israel.

In a sense, Memmi picks up where Deutscher leaves off: To whom does Deutscher's concerns with "blame" speak? Is this what Marxism comes down to—a statement of moral perfections and imperfections? Memmi poses the question in such a way as to leave no doubt as to his antipathies for such hothouse theorizing.

In what could well stand as a Third World rebuke to the orthodox European Communist, Memmi writes in a particularly impressive passage that, for him:

> The dignity of the oppressed begins, first, the moment he becomes conscious of his burden, second, when he denies himself all camouflage and all consolation for his misery; third, and above all, when he makes an effective decision to put an end to it. May all the victims of history forgive me. I know only too well how a victim becomes a victim. I understand the subterfuges which enable him to survive. I pity his inner ruin, but I do not admire his grimaces of pain or his scars. I do not find his suffering face the most beautiful in the world nor do I consider the plight of the victim to be very admirable. Memmi recalls the Eichmann trial, particularly the irritated and slightly scornful astonishment of the young Israelis at the Jews of the Diaspora who allowed themselves to be slaughtered, too often without the slightest gesture-even of despair. I must admit that whatever the naiveté, the ignorance, the insolent thoughtlessness of these young men so freshly minted, I am in the end more on their side than on that of these perpetual victims, complaisant towards their pitiable fate, which the immense majority of us were.

And, indeed, in Deutscher there is the spectacle of the left-wing advocate celebrating precisely the sort of alienation that led the oppressed Jews of European charnel houses to defend their own misfortunes.

And for the Left, as for the Right, the issue all comes down to Israel. That nation, which has become the fulcrum of the Middle East crisis, has just as assuredly become the core of the Jewish identity crisis. For just as Deutscher sees in Israel the Middle East phalanx of imperialism, Memmi sees Israel as the vanguard of Jewish liberation, a "specific liberation" in which the "oppressed person must take his destiny into his own hands." The life of the Jew "must no longer depend on any treaty, often signed with other ends in mind, by anyone with anyone." If the Jewish condition revels a "total misfortune," so, too, for Memmi, the Jewish destiny must find a "total solution."

Following Hegel's *Philosophy of Law* rather than Kant's *Essay on Perpetual Peace*, Memmi rests his case for the Jews on nationalism, not on internationalism of either a pacifist or Marxist variety. "In short, the specific liberation of the Jews is a national liberation and for the last years this national liberation has been the state of Israel." It is not that Memmi fails to see the nationalist excesses that Deutscher speaks of, only that he fails to understand what options exist. For Memmi, "the national solution is not one of several; it is the only definitive solution, because it is the specific solution to the Jewish problem. Israel is not a supplementary contribution, a possible insurance in case of difficulties in the Diaspora; it must be the frame of reference for the Diaspora which must in the future redefine itself in relation to it." Ultimately, the question for Memmi is how to be a Jewish non-Jew—the very reverse of Deutscher's question of how to be a non-Jewish Jew. For Memmi all answers are wrapped up in the national question: "the Jew must be liberated from oppression, and Jewish culture must be liberated from religion. This double liberation can be found in the same course of action—the fight for Israel." Clearly, for Deutscher the same survival—needs dictate a reverse answer: the fight against Israel, or at least, against the imperialist forces Israel has come to represent.

I do not wish to reduce the writings of either Deutscher or Memmi to this crux issue. Indeed, some of the most incisive and interesting writings are on subjects unrelated to ultimate issues. Deutscher's best writing, for example, is on the kibbutzim and its limitations in Israeli political life, while his text on the Russian Revolution and the Jewish Problem is certainly a corrective to the often exaggerated assertions concerning Soviet anti-Semitism and the equally outrageous statements that Jews never had it so good as under Soviet rule. It is a masterful and balanced statement. Memmi's volume contains sparkling chapters on everything from mixed marriages to the art and culture of the Jew. He is both knowing and generous in his appraisals, and if the polarities drawn are sometimes caricatures, they nonetheless draw sharp attention to the major and minor irritants of secular Jews trying to reconcile their leftism and their Judaism.

Both volumes exhibit a personal touch that borders on self-congratulations. Memmi sometimes writes as if he had invented the Jewish question rather than serving as its commentator. And Deutscher had the profound misfortune of having his thoroughly delightful and charming widow prepare both the foreword and the introduction, on "The Education of a Jewish Child." The less spoken of this essay, the better for all concerned—living as well as deceased.

The uncontaminated egotism of both authors, however, is stifling—since both write as if being a marginal Jew is equivalent to knowing everything of value about all Jews, past and present. In contrast, the writings of even a generalist historian such as Arnold Toynbee are refreshingly free of such self-advertisement and personal promotion in the name of "total peoples" and "total solutions." (What an eerie phrase Memmi uses to describe the Jewish fate, in the light of Hitlerism and the Holocaust!)

These are books in the European manner: the historian writing as philosopher, and the philosopher writing as a Guide for the Perplexed. Qualifications are few, possible admissions of analytic shortcomings non-existent, and polemics against unmentioned enemies in abundance. Under such circumstances, to ask for references to other European works of scholarship, not to mention works by social scientists on the Jews, would be somehow unclean. The brilliance of the dialogue is unmatched by a level of competence most analysts in the United States have come to expect or at least desire. In this sense, Hegel and Marx are reproduced by Memmi and Deutscher, rather than transcended. How strange it is that scholars who can be quite fastidious—indeed, the Trotsky trilogy is breathtakingly rooted in all available archives data, and Memmi's, *Colonizer and Colonized* is quite free of empty assumptions—become so freewheeling on the Jewish question. One may take this as a measure of the personal and internalized nature of their respective visions of Judaism, or simply as a measure of their unstated conviction that certain things require no evidence, only insight.

Both works set for themselves the same task: to place Judaism in the mainstream of the radical movement, and the corollary, to place radicalism within the Jewish tradition. Curiously, both works devote relatively little time to this latter tough nut, preferring a rhetoric that will please either the Zionists (as in the case of Memmi) or the Marxists (as in the of Deutscher). Just what the interrelationship is, or should be, remains curiously unanswered. And it becomes apparent that the question posed in this way may not admit of any ready answer. The choice of Israel may be in fact a choice against Middle East socialism, whereas a choice in favor of Middle Eastern development may entail nothing less than the destruction of the Israeli nation—a formulation that Deutscher comes perilously close to accepting. Under such circumstances, these books will perhaps leave the reader with at least as much anxiety at the conclusion as at the beginning. I would suggest that the reason for this stems from a misanthropic view of the Jewish question—a view that shapes a Procrustean bed in which no Jew could seriously be comfortable for a single instant, and one that no radical would spend time fashioning to start with.

I cannot help wondering whether this essentially nineteenth-century dialogue between Deutscher and the ghost of Marx, and Memmi and the ghost of Hegel, is not itself largely the reason for my essential dissatisfaction with both books. For the ideological view of the Jews translates itself into a Jewish ideological view of the world. Both men present a totalistic picture of the Jewish condition, and both present an essentially totalistic response. In the case of Deutscher it is marginality, while in the case of Memmi it is nationality. But for both the European experience-rather than the two major forces in twentieth-century Jewry, the rise of a powerful American Jewry and the postwar maturation of an Israeli Jewry-remains dominant. They are men who reflect upon, respond to, and ruminate about these new factors, but always as outsiders. Deutscher's marginality is only the pale afterglow of a first-generation liberated Jew, while Memmi's powerful support of Israel as the ultimate resting home for liberated Jews comes upon the hard fact of the dust-jacket cover announcement that he and his family live in a Parisian suburb. The fact is that neither London nor Paris ranks with New York or Tel Aviv as center of Jewish activity.

Not that either man should necessarily have migrated elsewhere. Indeed, what they say derives a great deal from the spiritual richness of their cosmopolitan contexts. But these contexts are themselves limiting—a recognition that I fail to detect in their writings. It is true, as Deutscher points ut, that many Jews, in the United States particularly, have joined the celebration of a decadent system. But it is equally true that the Jews continue to form the vanguard of the critics of that system. And this has proven a neat trick, since Jews must become radicals despite the vicious prejudices against them by their friends and allies among the blacks and the Third Worlders. To support the Cuban Revolution means to do so despite Fidel's critiques of the Israeli Six-Day War. To support Egyptian Socialism is to do so despite the woeful inadequacies of the Nasserist military vision of social change. To support the black student movement is to do so despite some of the crudest and cruelest assaults on Jews ever heard in the United States.

In short, it is not that some Jews have become part of the Establishment, politically as well as economically, that is interesting, but rather how few have done so. Many Jews, especially the young, have remained loyal to the principles of radicalism despite incongruities and anomalies. Jews have always lived well with paradox. That is because, in the main, they are neither Hegelians nor Marxians, but rather the original Jamesians. They live well in a partial world, because a total world spells their doom. They function well in the marginal interstices of society because a society that fails to provide such margins spells disaster for the Jews—socialist or capitalist. To be a Jew means to operate within a framework of survival codes, principles of life as they are sometimes called, rather than Christian principles of love, capitalist principles of wealth, or socialist principles of harmony. And to accept survival as an operational codebook means to absorb the Deutschers and the Memmis into a larger liberal-democratic frame of reference that they themselves might refuse to acknowledge but that nonetheless, does exist for Jews *sui generis*.

Some years ago, when my oldest son was attending Hebrew Sunday school, his skills in reading and reciting Hebrew were brought to the attention of the local rabbi. He, in turn, contacted me, informing me of the Sunday School teacher's appraisal. He then said, "Your son should become a rabbi." At which point I simply scoffed and replied, "His interests are in pure science, not theology." The unexpected, but I-should-have-known-inevitable, retort shot back, "So what! He can become a scientific rabbi." I wonder whether this weird sense of accommodation, this poor man's pragmatism, does not operate as an unwritten handbook for keeping Jews in the fold. Dialogue is a fanciful word, behind which lurks the constant demands, rigorous demands at that, that compel Jewish atheists to speak to Jewish theists, Jewish Zionists to deal seriously with Jewish Communists, Jewish bakers to demand equality with Jewish bankers. For, however unequal the struggle between Jew and Gentile, between Jew and Jew the struggle is always between equals—between men who recognize no superior claims but wisdom.

For secretly we know that books like those of Deutscher and Memmi are going to be read, if at all, by Jews and discussed by Jews, and accepted or rejected by Jews. The non-Jewish Jew is of little concern and slender consequence to the Christian and of probably less concern to capitalists and Communists. The Jew is an intimate community of readers of Jewish books, no less than an overt community of parishioners or nation-builders. Pluralism of the heart and pragmatism of the head are the sources of strength in both of these books. Their weakness is that neither is willing to recognize that the Diaspora of men has created a pragmatism of mind.

If Jewishness is to be defeated, it will be done precisely by the same forces of fanaticism assaulting liberalism. For Judaism has become, perhaps against its own theological predilections, a cardinal expression of liberalism. And for the open societies of the West, the attitude toward Jews has become a test case of whether liberalism is possible, Insofar as nazism, communism, or any totalist system is unqualifiedly victorious, Judaism will be finished. For Jews live not only in an adoptive context of Christians, capitalists, and Communists, but in a context of other Jews. And it is precisely this double life that modern industrialism has provided, precisely because it has made possible the separation of economic and political power and has placed limits upon each aspect within the industrial system. Lurking behind Deutscher is not so much Marx as Sombart: the Jew as capitalist. The fact is that Jews as capitalists have been few in number, the Jew as petit-bourgeois is more the point. The world of middlemen, intermediaries, the unconvinced, and those who view self-reliance as a form of group survival is more easily compatible with the liberalist spirit found under capitalist democracy than under other system. It might even be that socialism, the mild anti-capitalist bias found in Israel, does more to explain the differences in character traits between Diaspora Jews and Sabras than does nationalism as such.

In short, the liberal society and the entrepreneurial economy has historically been best for Jewish subculture, whether in medieval Spain, Reformation Holland, Enlightened Germany, or industrial United States. And it is always the illiberal turn of these societies that has been worst for the Jews, these same countries in the post-halcyon days of their growth have been holy hell for Jews and liberals alike. Thus, in an attempt to my own question "what is the Jew?" I should note the following: He is the man who provides the global society with an operational set of liberal values and who in turn fares best in a global society that has a vested, legitimate interest in precisely fostering open-ended values for its own thoroughly non-Jewish reasons. And if Israel seems so hopelessly out of favor with the Third World or with the developing nations, it may well be because it uniquely combines a political framework of liberalism and a Jewish culture that accentuates and reinforces an open industrial system and developmental ideology.

We may not like literalism; we may consider it a profound anachronism. We may claim that the costs of liberalism are too great and affect too few people; we may claim that it cannot produce an accelerated developmental pattern in backwoods areas, but we cannot deny the historic and contemporary connection between Judaism and liberalism. I think we cannot either deny that whither goes liberalism, so goes the destiny of the Jewish people. For this reason, Deutscher's non-Jewish Jew and Memmi's Jewish non-Jew must both remain locked into the larger struggles for democracy—both its mass and bourgeois forms—in the twentieth century.

From *Judaism,* vol. 18, no. 3 (1969), pp. 361–67.

40

First Amendment Blues*

Downs, Donald Alexander

The *New York Times* in its editorial page of Wednesday, September 11, 1985, published the following comment on the decision of Newark's mayor to disallow a rally permit for the Ku Klux Klan:

> Mayor Kenneth Gibson of Newark has rejected a request for a rally permit by a man who purports to lead the New Jersey chapter of the Ku Klux Klan. The Klan is a terrorist organization intent only on sowing hatred, Mr. Gibson said, and it will never be allowed in Newark as long as he is Mayor. He'll find no argument here against the malign character and motives of the Klan. Staging a rally in Newark seems designed to provoke anger and anguish. Nevertheless, Mr. Gibson does his city and the law a disservice, and the Klan a favor, by denying the permit. The law is clear and it stands firmly on the side of the permit seeker, Richard Bondira, the presumed leader of the New Jersey K.K.K. Unless his meeting poses an imminent threat of uncontrollable violence, the rights to assemble and speak free are, and should be, inviolate. Mayor Gibson fears violence if other groups hold a counter-demonstration. But the Mayor has a police force to deal with such risks. Mr. Gibson also notes the Klan's indisputable history of violence and terror. That is not, however, a proper ground for abridging a constitutional right. By denying a permit, Mr. Gibson only makes white-sheeted thugs and misfits appear as victims. Far better that he grant the permit and deploy as many police officers as necessary to prevent trouble. That would send a message more powerful than white sheets and hoods. So strong is justice in Newark that even groups as loathsome as the Klan enjoy equal protection of the law.

If we substitute the Village of Trustees for the mayor of Newark, and Frank Collin, the leader of the National Socialist Party of America (NSPA–American Nazi Party) for Richard Bondira, the purported leader of the New Jersey Ku

* Donald Alexander Downs, *Nazis in Skokie: Freedom, Community, and the First Amendment*, Notre Dame Studies in Law and Contemporary Issues, vol. 1 (Notre Dame, Ind.: University of Notre Dame Press, 1985), pp. 227.

Klux Klan, we have perfect symmetry with Skokie. Further, if we invoke the logic implicit in the *New York Times* editorial, as did U.S. District Court Judge Bernard Decker, we also have the identical rationale for granting a permit for the Nazis to march in Skokie.

> The long list of cases reviewed in this opinion agrees that when a choice must be made, it is better to allow those who preach racial hate to expend their venom in rhetoric rather than to be panicked into embarking on the dangerous course of permitting the government to decide what its citizens may say and hear. As Mr. Justice Harlan reminded us in *Cohen*, where a similar choice was made, "That the air may at times seem filled with verbal cacophony is . . . not a sign a weakness but of strength." The ability of American society to tolerate the advocacy even of the hateful doctrines . . . without abandoning its commitment to freedom of speech . . . is perhaps the best protection we have against the establishment of any Nazi-type regime in this country.

It is the burden of Donald A. Downs's excellent volume on *Nazis in Skokie* to show that Judge Decker's position is hardly self-evident. Contrary to the views of those self-righteous "civil libertarians" who in 1977–78 controlled the ACLU, issues of civility, virtue, and safety do have a place in First Amendment doctrine. Downs has not given us a conservative tract (though that, indeed, is his bias). Rather he has made an effort to construct a vision of First Amendment safeguards that is compatible with Federalist concerns for the survival of the American commonwealth.

At the outset, the obvious must be stated: there is no particular uniqueness about Skokie or even about the events in the late 1970s that led to the symbolic confrontation of Nazis and Jews in that suburb of Chicago. Nor (and here I will declare a more heretical position) does it appear to me that there is any particular fascination with First Amendment legal history and its declared protection of free speech. The sheer volume of legal and extra-legal literature on the First Amendment might belie what may seem to be a personal and quixotic judgment, though I think not. What does fascinate, what remains controversial in the extreme, is the dialectic of rights and obligations at work in the First Amendment, one that gets played out on different canvasses at different points in American history. Indeed, Mr. Downs shrewdly observes that "it is *possible* that in conferring the First Amendment right upon the NSPA, the courts simultaneously conferred a subtle, hidden measure of legitimacy upon the group and its ilk. If so, the *general long-range effect* of such constitutional protection could be to confer legitimacy upon such groups."

What, then, is the content of this dialectic of rights and obligations? I would hold that it is the limits of law itself as actual events come upon the extra-legal, or social, requirement that a democratic society, no less than any other society, seek its own survival. Rights and obligations have as their political cloak the issue of sovereignty. And therefore jurisdictional or turf questions are issues of power. Hobbes well understood sovereignty to be an element that law justifies, rationalizes, and explicates—but the force of sovereignty itself is quite beyond the law. It can be and is often asked, "What would happen if the sovereign were toppled? Or, in its pure anarchist form, Why shouldn't citizens work for the destruction of the sovereign? It is no accident that *Leviathan* juxtaposes the Behemoth and the Anarch. The essential nature of the polity is encapsulated in that dialectic. The First Amendment is that set of principles which guarantees the perennial character of the struggle with the constitution in its original pristine form. The genius of the Bill of Rights is hence not to guarantee outcomes but ensure further struggles.

As a consequence, having the American Civil Liberties Union (ACLU) on one side of a struggle and the American Legal Foundation on the other helps maintain the dialectic—keeps a creative balance within democratic institutions between the rights of freedom of speech and (yes) actions and the rights of a society and its citizens to protect and maintain the political fabric. Were either contestant, or group of contestants, to permanently hold sway, the polity itself would either dissolve or ossify. Needless to say, convincing interest groups of the reality of such an undulating model is something else again, since the business of PACS is precisely to deny legitimacy to their opposite ideological number.

The Skokie affair highlights a strange turn of events in the philosophical foundations of the ACLU: What was in the past a well-modulated effort to protect First Amendment claims of citizens from all walks of life was transformed into an absolute prohibition on preventive juridical constraints. (Even the ACLU's own left has been concerned about such an absolutist position.) As a result of ideological posturing, from an operational viewpoint, the ACLU holds that one can take measures only against explicitly illegal acts but not against thoughts expressed. But take this position one magical step further and it is rendered as the converse: it is illegal for a local governing body or police power to take measures to guard the social order from a dispirited descent into social chaos, no matter how malignant the political faction working against order. While one might argue that preventive law is not analogous to preventive medicine, there are nonetheless some serious consequences to this position that were revealed in the Skokie episode, and they are nicely dealt with in Downs's book.

The most important is that as I see it, the ACLU, the advocate of civil liberties, was transformed into the advocate of civil disorder. Under this view, since every act is permissible as long as it carries a political or ideological label, society can retaliate but can never anticipate disaster. As a result, what began as a pure theory of consensus ends as the pure practice of conflict. For since no society can possibly be a passive witness to its dismemberment, and given the ACLU premise that no constraints should be placed on free speech or even free acts (if not violent), organized resistance must constantly be defensive and must as well as quick, clever, and adroit enough to respond before the society itself collapses. If, as in Weimar Germany, the response is too late, the answer is a gigantic and retrospective "tough luck!". In the absence of any doctrine of balance between citizen rights and personal responsibilities, few other options exist. This concern, rather than ethnicity, underwrote the great outpouring of resentment toward the ACLU after Skokie.

Skokie, a Chicago suburb, has a population of roughly 70,000 people. Slightly more than 40,000 residents are Jewish, and of these, 7,000 were World War II inmates of Nazi concentration camps. In 1977, Frank Collin, leader of a small bank of Nazis, decided to hold a march in this special setting. The community response was swift. The mayor of Skokie invoked three local ordinances: (1) requiring that demonstrators advance insurance against potential physical damages, set at $350,000; (2) permitting the Skokie town council to prohibit any speech or demonstration by members of political parties wearing "military-style" uniforms; and (3) preventing the public display of the swastika as a symbol that intentionally promotes and incites hatred against persons by reason of their race, national origin, or religion.

Skokie authorities contended that the activities planned by the Nazi party were so offensive to its residents that they would become violent and disrupt the Nazi assembly, initially planned to take place on the steps of city hall on May 1, 1977. Therefore, they sought an injunction against any assembly at which military-style uniforms, swastikas, or Nazi literature were present. Frank Collin appealed to the ACLU to represent the marchers' right to free speech and assembly. The president of the Chicago ACLU chapter said, "We have no choice but to take the case." In their brief, ACLU attorneys claimed that so long as the demonstrators were peaceable, no injunction could be issued against their activities; furthermore, they felt that such an injunction would constitute a prior restraint forbidden by the First Amendment. The ACLU relied on First Amendment doctrines articulated consistently over the past 50 years by the Supreme Court and more recently by Chief Justice Warren Burger, who said, "The thread running through all of these cases is that prior restraints on speech and publication are the most serious and the least tolerable infringement on First Amendment rights."

After a hearing by the town council, the Village of Skokie successfully sought an injunction and the ACLU appealed. The response of the Illinois courts did not satisfy the ACLU, so an emergency appeal was taken to the U.S. Supreme Court, which ordered the Illinois courts to expedite a ruling or grant a stay of the injunction. A short time later, the Illinois appellate court reversed portions of the injunction pertaining to the uniforms and literature but affirmed against exhibition of the swastika. It did so in part by invoking the "fighting words" doctrine that excludes from First Amendment protection words which "by their very utterance inflict injury or tend to incite an immediate breach of the peace." (This doctrine was utilized by the U.S. Supreme Court as recently as 1973). The Illinois Court held that the swastika was so offensive that its display could be enjoined anywhere in Skokie.

The ACLU immediately appealed to the Illinois Supreme Court. In its view, this use of the fighting words doctrine set a very dangerous precedent. The ACLU claimed that such a doctrine could be extended easily to blacks marching in hostile white communities or to others with unpopular ideas who choose to assemble in areas where there are deeply antagonistic listeners. Thus, it was argued, the black power symbol of the clenched fist could have been prohibited in Selma when these communities were racially tense. On January 27, 1987 the Illinois Supreme Court upheld the ACLU position, including the right of Nazis to wear swastika armbands. In addition to upholding Judge Decker's ruling, the Seventh Circuit of the United States Court of Appeals went beyond this ruling and, on April 6, 1978, voted 6-2 to reverse even the 45-day stay of his order because of its negative impact on free speech.

Downs tells of the anticlimactic outcome:

> [On April 11] Collin mailed a renewed permit application to Skokie by registered mail; he asked for a permit to demonstrate on June 25, 1978. On April 15, Skokie officials announced Collin's request to hold the demonstration on June 25. This proved to be the final date set for the demonstration, as no subsequent court action would affect the NSPA's to demonstrate on that date. On May 22, 1978, the court of appeals upheld Judge Decker's ruling, with only one partial dissent. Because the twenty-three page decision agreed with Decker in virtually every respect, it is unnecessary to examine its content here. It suffices to report that the decision, which was expected, virtually guaranteed that Collin could appear in Skokie in June, in full uniform. Skokie appealed the decision to the United States Supreme Court. Skokie also asked the appeals court and then the Supreme Court for a stay of the appeals court's ruling. On June 5, 1978, the court of appeals denied the stay request, followed by the Supreme Court's denial on June 12. Finally, on October 16, 1978 the Supreme court refused to grant certiorari to review the substance of the court of appeals' decision. But by this time the controversy had ended. Collin had decided not to come to Skokie, choosing instead to demonstrate at the Federal Plaza in Chicago on June 25. He chose not to exercise the First Amendment right he had won at such great effort to himself and others. Let us now turn to the events that led to this anticlimactic conclusion.

Shortly after the Illinois Supreme Court rendered that opinion, the ordinances were ruled unconstitutional by the federal district court for the Northern District of Illinois. The court of appeals affirmed, with one judge dissenting in part. Certiorari was denied with Justice Blackmun, with whom Justice White joined, dissenting. The Illinois Supreme Court's ruling was that the American Nazi party can display swastikas, since its showing "is symbolic political speech intended to convey to the public the beliefs of those who display it." In substance, the court allowed the Collin group to march through Skokie as originally planned. A permit was issued to the Nazis for a demonstration on June 25, 1978. The issue raised by the Skokie controversy is not, however, moot. For, as noted by Justice Blackmun in his dissent from the Court's denial of certiorari in this case: "When citizens assert, not casually but with deep conviction, that the proposed demonstration is scheduled at a place and in a manner that is taunting and overwhelmingly offensive to the citizens of that place, that assertion, uncomfortable though it may be for judges, deserves to be examined. It just might fall into the same category as one's 'right' to cry 'fire' in a crowded theater, for 'the character of every act depends upon the circumstances in which it is done.'"

The board of directors of the ACLU national office fully supported the position of the Illinois chapter, including its apparent decision to coach the American Nazi party on proper responses. For example, the main thrust has been to equate the White Power slogan with the Black Power slogan, at least in terms of legal standing, and to avoid any mention of the social and historical antecedents of national socialism. This is clearly the implication of the position taken by David Goldberger, then legal director of the Illinois ACLU, who argued that defending unpopular causes is always ethically mandated and serves to renew the legal system and the Bill of Rights.

The ACLU, as a result of its support of Nazi rights, suffered angry criticism and a loss of members of close to 25%. Goldberger noted that "nearly 2,000 of the 8,000 members of the Illinois ACLU have resigned in the year following Skokie." The Anti-Defamation League of B'nai B'rith argued that free speech could be restrained in this case because of the "psychic trauma" that would result if the Nazis marched and displayed their swastikas. Several branches of the ACLU, for example, those in St. Louis, Houston, and Jackson (Mississippi), voted not to aid the American Nazi party, although one voted so because of the direct inflammatory offering by the Nazis of a $5,000 bounty "for every nonwhite person arrested or convicted for an attack on a white person." Clearly, in this instance, Jews were classified with the nonwhite population.

The ACLU position is based on First Amendment guarantees of unimpeded free speech for all Americans. The ACLU was careful to distinguish between support for free speech and support for the ideology of the National Socialist Party of America. Rather than push this distinction or, for that matter, obliterate it as a mere legal artifact, it might be worthwhile to outline first the legal precedents, second the extralegal implication, and third the issues raised by Skokie.

The discussions between Abba P. Lerner and Aryeh Neier in the editorial pages of the *New York Times* presented the issue of Nazis marching in Skokie as a conflict between two absolute principles: (1) the maintenance of a democratic order against its avowed enemies and (2) the maintenance of freedom of speech for everyone by resisting incursions on the right to speak. Downs poses a third alternative: Is it not possible to distinguish instances in which free speech has no discernible and authentic political goal but only the goal of public disorder and riots? And hence, should we not, in these instances, invoke an operational guideline such as Oliver Wendell Holmes' injunction against falsely shouting "fire" in a crowded theater? Without wishing to stretch the analogy, Downs builds a strong case that Skokie, with its large Jewish population, is a theater in which a small bank of self-declared Nazis sought, in effect, to incite a riot rather than to hold a peaceful march and hence to induce the same sort of panic and potential physical harm in the population that would occur if one cried "fire" in a crowded theater. Arguments over stratagems elevated to a level of principles have grave organization risks; hence the First Amendment literature must be addressed directly and carefully.

The great merit of *Nazis in Skokie* is the author's sensitivity to all parties involved. The tapestry and texture of events is unfolded with great attention to events in the trenches. The work starts with a broad statement on the meaning of free speech, followed by a chapter on the ACLU titled the "Exploitation of Liberty." The great merit here is the use of statements by local ACLU officials, rather than an appeal to broad legal guidelines. This in turn is followed by the best chapter in the work, "Bearing Witness," in which the attitudes of the primarily Jewish community are stated, not so much with elegance as with bluntness. Downs has a keen sense of how this community, with its large number of Holocaust survivors, had a double-edged obligation: to prevent the spread of Nazism in its community and to educate the Jewish, and later the non-Jewish, members of the community. The notion of a community of obligation and the need to repay a historic debt informs this chapter with quiet majesty.

The burden of the book, nonetheless, is its contribution to First Amendment doctrine, to legal theory and practice. Hence, the earlier chapters, for all of their fairness, provide a foundation for presentation of the main theme: How did the Skokie legal maneuvers function to alter our notions of civil rights? Downs's analysis reviews a variety of cases that bear on *Village of Skokie v. National Socialist Party of America.* A parade of cases in unfolded: Organization for a Better Austin v. Keefe, 402 U.S. 415 (1971); Chaplinsky v. New Hampshire, 310 U.S. 88 (1940); Thornhill v. Alabama, 315 U.S. 568 (1964); and Beauharnais v. Illinois, 343 U.S. 250 (1952). It would be unfair to the book to summarize the arguments in each case. Rather, it is Downs's view—one that strikes this reviewer as eminently rational—that the issue of free speech is really no longer in contention. In a wide series of cases, ranging far and wide across the century, the principle of free speech has been established as essentially impregnable. What is at stake now is the problem of political stability in a democratic society.

What is contestable is the implication of action. Downs repeatedly and convincingly argues that abridgement of First Amendment rights should be permissible only when evidence is adduced showing the afflicting of a harm to specific individuals or definite groups. Generalized attacks on race, religion, and ethnicity, however repugnant, are protected by the First Amendment in the same fashion that majoritarian appeals to changes in public policy are protected. But when the issue spills over into targeted assaults on people because of their *ascribed*, rather than their *achieved*, characteristics, then constraints are warranted. Downs's carefully worded conclusion on abridgeable speech emphasizes the assaultive, intimidating speech content, the targeting of such expression, and the unprovoked intent to commit harm. His conclusions deserve full expression:

Speech in the public forum involving race or ethnicity may be abridged:

(1) when such expression is accompanied by the advocacy of death or violence perpetrated against that group as determined by a reasonable person; *or*, when such expression explicitly demeans or vilifies through reference to race or ethnicity as determined by a reasonable person; *or*, when such expression so vilifies or demeans in a symbolic or implicit manner as determined by a reasonable person; *and*

(2) such expression and harm are intended by the speaker and are unjustifiable due to the lack of significant provocation; *and*

(3) such expression is directed at an individual, home, neighborhood, or community in such a way as to single out an individual or specified group as the definite target of the expression.

Downs's volume could have been considerably strengthened if he had taken into account a variety of court challenges on First Amendment cases that for some strange reason he deals with peripherally or only through the secondary literature rather than through the court rulings themselves. For example, Schenck v. United States, 249 U.S. 47 (1919), in which Justice Holmes invoked the now famous and, as the century wears on, terribly ambiguous doctrine that "to falsely shout fire in a theater is akin to creating a clear and present danger to life and limb" is not dealt with. Further, Gitlow v. New York, 268 U.S. 652 (1925), in which Holmes entered a powerful dissent in arguing that political opposition is by no means the same as the manufacture of revolution, is treated by Downs only in terms of Meiklejohn's summary, with no reference to the text or context of Holmes's remarks. Brandenburg v. Ohio, 395 U.S. 444 (1969), in which the Court ruled that limits against speech are valid when advocacy is directed to producing or inciting imminent lawless action, is mentioned rather casually, although the case neatly, if somewhat primitively, embraces Downs's own conclusions. The same is true for *United States v. O'Brien* (a famed draft-card-burning incident), in which Chief Justice Earl Warren, speaking for the Court, noted that when speech and nonspeech elements are fused, the government interest in regulating nonspeech (i.e., action) can justify limitation of First Amendment freedoms. But such supportive materials are not introduced into the narrative. And while Alexander Meiklejohn's work on *Political Freedom* is cited and dealt with, the equally important efforts of Thomas I. Emerson on *Toward a General Theory of the First Amendment* is ignored. Emerson possessed a far greater sensitivity to extra-legal (economic and sociological) realities that alter constitutional law than did Meiklejohn and, again, for such reasons deserved to be dealt with by Downs, who well appreciates that Holocaust survivors are, the infelicitous phrase used notwithstanding, a "special breed of animal."

This is not said to chastise or minimize Downs's considerable achievement but rather to indicate that the wealth of materials could have been used to strengthen his concluding opinions, even at the expense of his sense of proportion. This is not said in a carping way; I find his text entirely fair minded, correct as to the facts, and moreover intellectually compatible with my own position. But in a work such as this, one does anticipate that a full review of the relevant literature will be undertaken.

Since the Skokie incident is part of Jewish life in America, one would have hoped for a much wider acquaintance with Jewish literature in America than Downs shows. There is, for instance, no awareness shown of Elazar's work on organizational life of Jews, writings on Jewish religious and legal issues as they reflect on the Holocaust, Helmreich's work on synagogue life, or even broad surveys by Whitfield, and Glazer of Jewish social patterns. That Downs's work is nonetheless scrupulously fair to the Jewish community of Skokie is a tribute to his ethnographic skills, but the same cannot be said, alas, of his awareness of Jewish life in the Midwest or in America as a whole. As a result, certain crude formulations of Jewish beliefs are allowed unencumbered by a sifting and winnowing to see the extent to which passing remarks actually reflect larger Jewish ethos.

The book jacket proudly reveals that Donald A. Downs was awarded the American Political Science Association's 1984 Edward S. Corwin Award in Public Law. Now the reasoning behind such awards for dissertations is both laudable and multiple: to honor excellence, to bring qualified degree recipients to the attention of universities considering new appointments, and to alert publishers to the availability of fine, "pre-refereed" manuscripts. However, such aims notwithstanding, the awards system may well have had the effect of deflecting and muting critical analysis prior to publication and in so doing weakening the final product. As published Downs's volume remains a very good dissertation but not quite an outstanding book. (The uninitiated may well be unaware of this distinction between dissertation and monograph, but I suspect that professional readers will easily be put off.) We have such a surfeit of awards and rewards—that the line between competence and excellence is increasingly blurred. I certainly do not wish to burden this particular author with the need to append a large-scale history of American culture; yet I cannot help feeling that more dedicated editing and prodding and less presumption as to the meaning of a professional award would have resulted in a stronger, more richly textured text. As it is, Downs, has given as a thoughtful, solid work that is informed by a sense of constitutional law, by a feeling for the people involved, and by an appreciation of history as living conscience. This is a much needed corrective to earlier partisan work, and as such, should be read by legal scholars. But it should be improved upon by other efforts to understand how, as is often the case in American constitutional history, one event helped to illumine an entire body of law.

From *American Bar Foundation Research Journal*, vol. 1986, no. 3 Summer (1986), pp. 535–46.

41

Community and Polity*

Elazar, Daniel J.

Community and Polity is a thorough account of the organizational dynamics of
American Jewry. The book helps to explain the factors in Jewish organizational
life that give it internal coherence as well as national impact. As a result, this
book deserves and should receive the attention of all social scientists concerned
with ethnic, racial, and sexual politics. The ability of Jews to articulate their
goals has led to a powerful literature delineating ideological and theological
aspects of Jewish life. But precious little of the more mundane aspects have
been dealt with, such as fundraising mechanisms, social welfare networks,
religious structures, or institutional impacts through cultural instruments
such as the Young Men's and Women's Hebrew Associations or the Council of
Jewish Federations. In this work, Daniel J. Elazar joins the ranks of people who
have made major contributions in this area, such as David Sidorsky, Marshall
Sklare, and Nathan Glazer. On the other hand, this is no *World of Our Fathers*.
Elazar has neither the literary flair nor the concern with the strictly secular
exhibited by Irving Howe in his recent masterpiece. But this comparison does
not in any way deprive this work of its own integrity and worth.

In framing the problem of the American Jewish community in terms of
assimilation versus authenticity, Elazar displays genuine appreciation for the
special circumstances of Jewish life in America, which in organizational terms
is probably better cast as local organization versus cosmopolitan ideology.
The treatment of American Jewry as a state serves as a vehicle to understand
the dialectic between political assimilation and personal authenticity. At the
very least, this formulation allows the author to account for the emergence of
federalism, or what might better be called federationism. But whether or not
there really has been a move from congregationalism to federalism in religious
terms is not made entirely clear, since the synagogue's importance, rather
than being diminished by the rise of suburbia, has actually been enhanced.
In spite of the fact that the neighborhood settlements and federations of

---

* Daniel J. Elazar, *Community and Polity: The Organizational Dynamics of American Jewry*
(Philadelphia: The Jewish Publication Society of America, 1976), pp. 421.

relatively nonreligious activities are very extensive, Elazar claims the organic links provided by the synagogue, rather than the functional ties provided by the federations, remain very much intact.

The great strength of the book is its emphasis on organizational forms and community contexts. The various tables outlining American Jewish occupational patterns, stages of acculturation and assimilation, the Jewish population as a percentage of state and city populations, and in general, the state-by-state analyses, are of great value to the researcher and a model to others interested in placing ethnic and racial patterns within a larger national framework. The tabular material on distribution of federation allocations, the data on the finances of national Jewish agencies in domestic and overseas programs, and the simple review of Jewish community studies, all illustrate the great value of the book as a statistical source of information, pulling together in one place what not even the *American Jewish Yearbook* offers in this regard. The tables, for example, are integrated into the narrative rather than simply left as a series of appendices that have little relationship to the empirical questions under consideration.

Another strength of Elazar's approach is his keen historical sense. Many of the chapters, such as "Jewish Adaptations to American Life," provide excellent historical summaries of Jewish participation and the impact of such factors as sectionalism, regionalism, and American individualism on patterns of Jewish participation in the New World. The successful adaptation pattern leads Elazar to conclude that organizationally, the American Jewish community has never been in better condition and that Jews may well have developed a pattern that can provide for communal governance within a free society. But as he well appreciates, organizational advances by themselves do not come to terms with the question of who is or who is not "seriously Jewish." Elazar understands that institutions facilitate decisions but do not exactly account for the quality of that organizational activity. Indeed, one gets the distinct impression that the pattern of adaptation he describes is not unlike that of many Protestant sects, from Congregationalism to Unitarianism, that have emphasized communal bases of religious life. The trouble is that Jews have special problems of a universal, international, and national sort that do not permit the same set of outcomes to occur, despite similar organizational devices.

A final strength of the book is the careful operational definitions given to Jewish leadership types and how these dialectical divisions between religious and secular, public and private, cosmopolitan and local, professionals and volunteers, all calibrate in various ways, particularly in Jewish communities. Here, too, the book is realistic as well as provocative, outlining the strengths and weaknesses of Jewish ethnicity in New York, its fragmentation in places like Washington and New Jersey, and segmentation in metropolitan environments such as Boston, Philadelphia, Chicago, and Miami. It makes those sections of the book "The Major Communities" and "Institutions and Decision Makers" particularly worthwhile. There is careful concern for smaller communities and how they fit the larger patterns through a series of organizational linkages, all of which underscore the author's belief in a Jewish mosaic that seems to afford maximum autonomy, while at the same time insuring large-scale interpenetration in terms of leadership, decision making, and cultural unity.

This said, I find myself not quite satisfied with the treatment on various levels. Elazar provides no real analysis of Jewish organizational life as part of a larger political network. The notion of a Jewish community exists as a closed monad without any window on the larger world of the American political system. Perhaps the author took too seriously his fronticepiece in which Richard Hooker declared, "Nor is it possible that any form of politie, much less politie ecclesiastical should be good, unless God himself be the author of it" and not seriously enough the distinction between that which belongs to Providence and those secular obligations due to the state. The manner in which Jewish administrative affairs feeds into the larger political networks clearly helps make sense of Jewish organizational life in general. As a result, in his fine appendix on the American Jewish community's response to the Yom Kippur War, Elazar is driven to introduce, albeit peripherally, some of these larger political networks, from the federal apparatus at one level to organized labor at the other.

Elazar has mandated his organizational analysis in strict terms, without much sense of ideology. As a result, there is a flattening out instead of an enrichment of a sense of Jewish life. For example, he sees the Jewish press in terms of four components: weekly newspapers, monthly house organs of Jewish organizations, independent publications, and quality magazines. Yet his concept of the Jewish press has nothing to do with the *Jewish* press, but rather with that portion of American society that writes about Jewish topics in the *English* press. So there is absolutely no discussion of such major vehicles as the *Forward, Morning Journal, The Day*, and the *Morning Freiheit*. While only the *Forward* remains as a general Jewish newspaper, the real organizational messages for nearly forty years were carried by these papers. Here, as in many other parts of the book, Elazar betrays a strong bias toward third generation Jews, who are removed from the world of their fathers by language, culture, and tradition. He also displays a peculiar second-echelon sense of organizational linkages. It is not only that the author is at Temple University, but also that he is clearly a Philadelphian in his choice of examples and illustrations. The disadvantage is that in Philadelphia, the secular sense of Judaism is perhaps weaker than it is in many other cities of comparable size, and certainly far less so than in New York.

This leads to a penultimate problem: the book offers a welter of historical and geographical organizational forms, but its portrait of communal life is curiously a world without people. Elazar's communities lack individuals—the linkages are not fleshed out, and we are left with a variety of carefully tabulated organizational forms but not much sense of the spirited, innovating framework of American Jewish life.

Toward the conclusion, Elazar indicates that contemporary Jewish life is beginning to overcome the fragmentation produced by socialism on one hand and Protestantism on the other. The difficulty with this formulation is that socialism was ingrained in and intrinsic to Jewish experience in America. Protestantism was something quite extrinsic and alien to that life. Here, the dialectic of assimilation and authenticity fails Elazar entirely, since the equation of socialism and Protestantism as fragmenting devices betrays an ideological standpoint, not so much a failure of nerve as a lack of insight into the Jewish mosaic.

Elazar's concept of Jews living in a modern and post-modern environment is cloudy and, for this reader at least, confusing. It is hard to decide from the text itself whether local federations, public and community relations organizations, organized Zionism, or community synagogue life are all on the ascent or descent, and which, if any, represents the modern or postmodern eras. Nor am I entirely certain that discussing the issue in terms of an increase in the commitment to different kinds of local organizations rather than to global aspects of Jewish existence, is anything other than a mystification of the problem posed by modernism. To speak of a new pluralism in Jewish life that "leads to federalism" does not quite address the question of Jewish survival in America. In short, this is a book whose parts remain significantly greater than the whole. As a clustering of data, information, and insight into Jewish community life in America and how it is organized over time and space, this is a superb contribution. However, as a work seeking to situate Jewish community life in the context of American political life as a whole, it is far less successful. But we have every right to anticipate, on the basis of Elazar's achievement, further research that will help resolve the current Jewish dialectic of survivalism as an ideology and triumphalism as an organized style.

From *Contemporary Sociology*, vol. 6, no. 3 (1977), pp. 287–89.

42

Bodies and Souls*

Fein, Helen

This is not an easy book to review. *Accounting for Genocide* is fraught with the ambiguity of its ubiquity. It moves from innovation to recitation, from elegance to banality, from sociological imagination to methodological pedantry. The subject matter alone—the destruction of European Jewry in Nazi concentration camps—makes reviewing the book sufficiently taxing to enable one to appreciate the awesome undertaking such a work represented for the author.

This work clearly emanates from the depth of human concern with how a state takes lives. Helen Fein attempts to provide an analytical measurement of the Holocaust. Herein lies the major problem: the book takes an area subject to intense emotions and reduces it to a coolly analytical framework. Ours is, after all, an era capable of transforming the tragic into the technological, of turning moral questions into engineering problems. The author unfortunately can not yet make an integrated study of this subject in cross-cultural or cross-national terms. This is not intended as criticism of this considerable effort. It is to state a fact that must be recognized in any estimation of the book. There is intellectual risk in reducing the Holocaust to strictly sociological proportions. The Holocaust is an issue that has gripped historians, theologians, and every human soul concerned with questions of human survival in an atmosphere of official homicide. If the attempt to render the Holocaust in statistical terms is warranted, its results must perforce be limited.

Holocaust in statistical terms is warranted, its results must perforce be limited.

The title alone indicates the problems inherent in such a work. *Accounting for Genocide* almost seems to reduce collective homicide to a cost-benefit basis, although it is clear that the author intends no such thing. Even the subtitle creates unease. The phrase "National Responses and Jewish Victimization During the Holocaust" is vague enough to confuse the reader as to who are the victims and who are the victimizers. A clearer sense that the book concerns

* Helen Fein, *Accounting for Genocide: National Response and Jewish Victimization During the Holocaust* (New York: Free Press/Macmillan Publishers, 1979), pp. 468.

national responses to *the victimization of Jews* during the Holocaust can be gleaned from the more pungent and hence more elegant subtitle on the dust jacket of the book, *Victims—and Survivors—of the Holocaust.*

If the title alone were a problem, the reviewer might be accused of nit-picking, but the author is capable of the loftiest literary flourishes followed by the dreariest vulgarities. Consider this insightful formulation of the problem of the ends of action, "Max Weber foresaw society's becoming an 'iron cage' in his classic analysis of modernity. But he did not anticipate that the cage could become an elevator, descending mechanically to crush the members excluded from the university of obligation." Somewhat later, she writes on the same subject, "Middle-men minorities are more liable to be ousted because the role they play motivates competitors to improve their own condition by getting rid of them." Similar juxtapositions pervade this effort.

The essential purpose of the book is to explain why and how genocide took place, what were the crucial variables in the task of liquidating the Jewish populations of Europe. This is followed by a second part on the victims' views, which are interesting but irrelevant to the genocidal outcome. This latter section, analyzing the victims' views, is largely derivative and not particularly innovative. Whereas in the first section, we learn that where SS control was most complete and where prewar anti-Semitism was high, scarcely any strategic response by Jews affected outcomes. Even in situations when Jews failed to anticipate or respond appropriately to the full fury of the Holocaust, in nations that had low SS control and where prewar anti-Semitism was minimal, the outlook for Jewish survival was generally favorable. In consequence, the second part of the book is foreordained to be irrelevant to the first. If the victims' response had no notable impact on Nazi genocide policies, then the second part on victims' response is largely beside the point. The reader is left in limbo to decide whether in fact Jewish responses did or did not have any noticeable consequence. This is a vexing problem, but since it is introduced by the author, it should have been fully dealt with.

Fein argues that the more successful the prewar anti-Semitic movements, the greater the number of Jewish victims in the Holocaust. Maps, charts, and data are provided to express how cleavaged relationships in Europe led to a collapse in social solidarity within a nation and finally to Jewish decimation. Many innovative charts show how the success of anti-Semitic movements in pre-World War II Europe had important effects on formulating exact genocidal policies. Even if such anti-Semitic movements were in themselves benign, their capacity to prepare European communities for the Holocaust made the Nazi policy of extermination that much simpler.

Within this macroscopic view, however, serious issues arise. The author claims that prewar anti-Semitism and SS control in 1941 account for virtually all variation in Jewish victimization (86%). But this formulation tends to become largely tautological. The implication that correlates are causes is difficult to sustain. One might equally argue that the size of Jewish communities stimulated movement of the SS toward or away from certain geographical locales, so that the cause in this sense might aptly be the number of Jews concentrated in a given region. Perhaps the enormous investment of personnel and technological power in Poland (rather than, say, Denmark) is simply a function of the number of Jews in an area. Such a concentration may also be related to geopolitical global considerations, (i.e., creating a buffer zone on the Eastern Front).

Prewar anti-Semitism as a measure of susceptibility to the Holocaust does not necessarily enable us to predict wartime outcomes. Countries that were at opposite poles on the anti-Semitism scale, like Denmark and the Netherlands, may have shared in efforts to preserve Jewish communities from total extermination. There is a big gap between anti-Semitism in general and genocidal behavior in particular. The author claims further that when there is low SS control and high anti-Semitism, the number of victims are disproportionately higher than when low anti-Semitism characterizes prewar conditions. Here the question of the relationship between anti-Semitism and genocide is clouded by the role of armed might and the role of Nazi state power, since anti-Semitism is hardly a novelty in many countries of the world. What was new were the technological methods involved in the destruction of a people and the implementation of that capacity on a global scale. Predisposition to a Holocaust may exist just as predisposition to the elimination of blacks may exist in South Africa. But that does not explain the actual implementation of the Holocaust. Anti-Semitism can be considered a constant in Western societies; the variable is the mechanism of state power and state authority.

The author's important insight is to show that there is no mechanical correlation of numbers of Jews with a high number of victims. Small pockets of Jews in low-density areas were also highly victimized; hence, demographic aspects of Jewish settlement do not explain why some nations were more likely to produce victims than others. Helen Fein's work goes far beyond simple demographic explanations of the genocide of World War II. The meat of the book is two early chapters: "The Calculus of Genocide," followed by "The Bonds That Hold, The Bonds That Break." Here the work has a unique importance for sociology. She employs a method for explaining macroscopic materials with microscopic detail. Fein deserves a great deal of credit for her clinical analysis. In "The Calculus of Genocide," the author seeks to show how Jewish communities were systematically disintegrated from the social systems by which they were usually protected, defined, labeled, stripped, isolated, stored, and shipped. She examines three basic theses: the solidarity thesis, the German control thesis, and the value-consensus thesis.

The author sets up tests to measure variables extending from prewar demographic characteristics of Jews, prewar characteristics of national states, German control and time contingencies, native governments' responses to occupation, and facilities and opportunities for genocidal practice. These lead into a crucial chapter on the causes of national differences in Jewish victimization. The charts measure relationships between demographic, sociological, and political factors. She shows that certain factors were not highly correlated, for example, that Jewish dispersal in a nation did not necessarily mean fewer victims. However, high concentration of Jews did tend to encourage high genocidal practices. The author emphasizes discontinuities between the genocidal and pregenocidal period. Disobedience, even if it meant taking risks, was more likely when resistance was universal within a group or community; this in fact was a function of early understanding of what right and whose rules define a political or social situation.

Fein also imaginatively uses the concept of time, namely, the extent to which warning time in the less anti-Semitic stage was adversely related to the stages after 1941. If Jews were in the SS zone in 1941, extermination and deportation began that year. If they were occupied by 1941, but outside the SS zone, Germany initiated deportations in 1942. Deportations began among the less anti-Semitic states in 1943, states that were in the sphere of Nazi influence by 1941 but had resisted or procrastinated longer and were subjected to complete military occupation only by 1943, such as Denmark and Italy. Fein clearly shows that high anti-Semitic states produced almost four times as many victims as did less anti-Semitic states and that when this fact was correlated further with the degree of SS control as World War II reached its crest, the level of victimization climbed considerably and irrevocably. The author further shows that victimization can be understood by first accounting for the level of prewar anti-Semitism but that this in itself does not explain actual genocide, since victims increased sharply during SS control of the state. This occurred only after Nazi occupation. She shows that anti-Semitism is not only the socialism of fools, but the policy of totalitarian rulers as well. Anti-Semitism served as a catharsis not for class conflict but for race conflict. This "ism" substituted Jews as a target for combat with another, usually larger collectivity.

Fein belatedly introduces the idea of a third item involved in the practice of genocide: the absence of any countervailing threat or authority such as the popular response by forces—religious or secular—outside German control. The passive acquiescence in the genocidal system made possible the Final Solution. But curiously this third item is not subjected to the same methodological rigor as the first two (SS control as of 1941 and high anti-Semitic propensities). There is a high level of ex post facto thinking involved in this sort of work. Hindsight about the consequences of the Holocaust encourages one to predict factors significant in the selective destruction of a whole people. The difficulty with this approach, and with the rational model of social change generally, is its assumption of an isomorphism between purpose and policy; Raul Hilberg, in *The Destruction of the European Jews*, long ago exploded this parallelism. Had the war, for example, gone in a different direction, had the

Soviet Union been more vigorous on the Eastern front and occupied Poland at an earlier stage, the level of Jewish extermination would have been much lower. More recently, Bernard Wasserstein, in *Britain and the Jews of Europe*, showed that had the British been willing to trade modest numbers of trucks for equal numbers of Jews, another large chunk of population might have been saved. Not so much rationality, as specific historical forces, had a critical bearing on the extent of the Holocaust.

Curiously, Fein's work does not address larger Jewish issues that bear directly on the question of genocide. There is no treatment of the Zionist tradition, namely, that the absence of a national homeland for Jews made the situation desperate and created a foundation for genocide with impunity. The stateless Jew was key to levels of punishment for the Jewish community. It might well be that this sort of explanation along with others would fail the test of methodological rigor, but the absence of any analysis of Jewish ideologies is serious.

If the second part on the victims' views and resistance seems singularly bereft of the considerations that Fein views as central, it is in part a problem of Judaism itself. Between Zionism and socialism, neither of which dominated Jewish thinking, was the bourgeois vision of an integrated enlightenment that created the foundations for the survival of Jews in liberal states. But the elimination of basic forms of political democracy invited the elimination of Jewish communities. One feels the weakness of a functional analysis divorced from political analysis. The daily struggles of the Jewish communities of Europe were not simply in terms of participation in civil service bureaucracies or in terms of Jewish community life as a relatively vague secular act, but rather they were struggles of Jews with each other. Jews were involved in struggles over socialism, capitalism, and liberalism. In each case, the drastic and dismal failure was in integrating a Jewish interest outlook. This integrating framework was imposed upon them—tragically—in the form of segregation, ultimately in the form of a racial definition of society. This took place at a time when Jewish communities did not have the capacity for national self-defense. The absence of a sense of national liberation ultimately may have been more important than the response of Axis authorities for genocidal policies. That this serious work fails to take up Jewish strategies as part of the process of genocide, seeing them simply as a response, weakens the volume and reduces Fein's work to a series of national reactions to an imposed Nazi order.

The tabular material in the appendixes from page 327 to 357 will be of particular interest to scholars concerned with confirming or verifying the views of the author. This material operationalized along the lines provided by the author almost invariably yields the kind of solutions indicated, but still the zero-order correlation coefficients, such as those with Jewish control organizations or prior segregation, are worked through with skill and imagination. The author converted a highly emotive area into an operational framework that explains how outcomes could possibly have been lessened. On the other hand, one could equally argue that such methodological researches could accentuate a Holocaust the next time around. One could take the Codebook and provide methods of compensation so that such factors as population and satellite rewards and responses could be enhanced. A uniform solution and integrated annihilation would be made possible by pressuring those areas where resistance was strongest or those areas in which anti-Semitism was weak in an early warning period. I realize that this is grotesque rendering of Fein's data, but it is a conceivable end. Ultimately one has to take seriously the role of humans in confounding, even repudiating, this line of analysis, or at least its deterministic implications.

The publisher, while preparing a reasonably edited text throughout, did less well in the appendixes. They are in typewritten form, are in far lighter script than the rest of the work, and are scarcely legible. There are also errors in the placement and location of the maps on pages 39, 46, 59, and 79. The captions are proper, but the maps are not. While these displaced maps do not materially affect Fine's thesis, I hope that in any subsequent printings appropriate changes and corrections will be made so that her argument can be more graphically illustrated.

If my remarks appear severe, it is not for lack of appreciation for the author's accomplishments. Her abilities at statistical reasoning are considerable. Further, there are few better introductions to the social forces that led to genocidal practices. The collection of materials on a nation-by-nation basis is a useful starting point on Jewish resistance to the Holocaust. Still, the absence of any serious linkage between description and explanation or between correlation and causation, repeatedly flaws the results and frustrates the effort. We have a noble book attempting more than is feasible within the self-imposed framework. Even words like genocide and Holocaust are bitterly contested (with claims that the former term may be common to Armenians, Japanese, and Jews, but the latter is a unique phenomenon reserved for the Jewish community). To resolve such issues may require a team of scholars representing many disciplines. Within the limits of a single volume, authored by one person working in splendid isolation from the mainstream of a discipline that has not considered this subject central to its own evolution, Helen Fein has made an important sociological statement, a unique account of a collective murder that haunts our century and stamps us as an age apart from all others.

From *Contemporary Sociology*, vol. 9, no. 4 (1980), pp. 489–519.

43

Ethnicity as Experience[*]

Glazer, Nathan

This volume is one of several riding the crest of the current revival of interest in ethnicity. Given their joint collaboration in the past on a standard work, *Beyond the Melting Pot*, it makes perfectly good sense for Messrs. Glazer and Moynihan to team up again. That the result is a mixed blessing perhaps reflects the present state of ethnic studies as much as any particular weaknesses in the sixteen contributions to this volume. The fact that the volume is based on conference proceedings adds to the reviewer's difficulty. One might say that the parts are greater than the whole. Indeed, it is the whole that I had the greatest difficulty with, in the form of the group of essays entitled "Toward a General Theory." In the field of ethnicity, it is easier to talk of specific linguistic groupings and national minorities than to deal with the conceptual problems of yet another large social stratification variable.

The keynote paper by Glazer and Moynihan is less candid than the brief acknowledgments page, which admits that "we are all too aware that the conference and the book that followed drew heavily from the banks of the Charles River, and that many other persons unrepresented in this book except in footnotes have been working for many years in developing our understanding of ethnicity." Were this recognition of limits carried over to the collection itself, the results might have been better. It is inconceivable that nearly every paper could be written by a Harvard professor or by persons who (with one or two exceptions) have been associated with that citadel of learning as visiting potentates. The assumption that all knowledge about ethnicity can be located at one university is breathtaking, reminiscent of Kipling's concept of the British empire: that only those who speak English can be civilized and all others are heathens. Glazer and Moynihan's choice of representatives is indicative of serious problems in social science research—as if one outpost of the intellectual empire were uniquely endowed to speak on the subject of ethnicity. Fortunately, the welter of materials on ethnicity now pouring forth

[*] Nathan Glazer and Daniel P. Moynihan (editors), *Ethnicity: Theory and Experience* (Cambridge, Mass.: Harvard University Press, 1975), pp. 531.

provides the necessary corrective and positive reprimand to such educational imperialism.

All could be forgiven if the introduction set the tone for what follows. In point of fact, it sticks out like a sore thumb. Unquestionably the least successful paper in the volume, it is conceptually fuzzy: we are promised a theory of why ethnic identity has become more salient and self-assertive over time, only to look in vain for such a theory. Indeed, even the editors do not appear to be certain why ethnic identity has come into its own at this point in time. They resort to a connotational caveat, claiming that they neither celebrate nor dismiss ethnicity. But the problem is that they also neither explain nor analyze it.

They do assert the following. First, ethnicity is strategically efficacious as an organizing principle. But they do not indicate whether the strategy has been evolved by ethnics themselves, by social scientists doing the analysis, or by community organizers in search of new modes of protest. This problem crops up throughout the literature on ethnicity, but it is especially apparent in many of these papers. Second, Glazer and Moynihan propose that the world is not really developing but that we are witnessing the refeudalization of society. While I agree that there is a return to ascribed status as against achievement status in social stratification, why this constitutes feudal behavior is not made clear. It sounds more like an effort to avoid the fact that socialism, specifically in its Leninist approach to the national minority question, has co-opted the rhetoric of nationalism and ethnicity better than either the melting-pot monism or ethnic pluralism of capitalism.

The most astonishing claim is made at the outset: that ethnicity is a new work, or at least has a new usage. Furthermore, the editors assert that there is no possible hope of doing without ethnicity in a society as subgroups assimilate to majority groups. The implication of these remarks, if Glazer and Moynihan are right, is that "a very great deal of radical and even liberal doctrine of the past century and a half is wrong." But what in fact characterizes a good deal of twentieth-century radical and liberal doctrine alike is a competitive effort to appeal to and solve ethnic problems through a differentially interpreted notion of the rights of all peoples to national self-determination. The problem is, as the Soviet Revolution made apparent, is that the right to self-determination is a cultural artifact in its own right—often devoid of actual power to determine anything more than folk costumes trotted out at appropriate times and places.

Even the assumption that their viewpoint is unique, is hyperbolic. Some dictionaries of sociology do not refer to ethnicity or ethnic groups, and one rather impressionistic dictionary of sociology defines only "ethnic groups," not "ethnicity." However, this casts doubt on the merit of dictionaries of sociology, not on researchers. I can hardly believe that a volume produced in 1975 would ignore the monumental contribution of Tamotsu Shibutani and his coworkers in *Ethnic Stratification: A Comparative Approach*, published in 1965. All 626 pages are dedicated to the concept of ethnicity in exactly the sense described in the present volume. Then there is the 1945 work by W. Lloyd Warner and Leo Srole entitled *The Social Systems of American Ethnic Groups*, which also goes far beyond the concept of ethnicity as a subgroup. It seems to me that the view from Harvard is the problem. Were there a view from Chicago—by robert Park, Ernest Burgess, Louis Wirth, or some of their legendary students—it would become apparent that work on ethnicity, as well as the concept itself, is by no means a recent invention.

Glazer and Moynihan miss a perfect opportunity to show that the conservative tradition, linked to German conflict theory, understood ethnicity better than either the liberal or radical tradition. The whole of *Foundations of Sociology*, written by Ludwig Gumplowicz in 1885, uses the concept of ethnicity in precisely its present national, secularized manner. The problem with *Ethnicity: Theory and Experience* is intellectual overkill: Glazer and Moynihan are more interested in establishing the uniqueness of their argument than in probing what is known about ethnicity in the modern period. Ethnicity has emerged as a variable equal to class and race, but the argument that it is new depends ultimately on the contents of this and other books. Curiously enough, the introduction is written as if the rest of the book were a foothill instead of a mountain. In view of the welter of interesting theoretical observations and ethnography, it is unfair to reduce an assessment to one paper or to prejudice a review of the troops because they all came from the same place.

The paper by Harold R. Isaacs is characteristically well written and refreshingly free of jargon. But I am not quite sure that he captures the spirit of the book, for his notion of ethnicity reduces ultimately to tribalism, precisely the older use of the term ethnic groups. Parsons attempts to overcome this shortcoming. His paper has the singular merit of showing that ethnic groups are far more than tribal instincts or impulses, but that ethnicity can at one and the same time be a form of personal identification, national mobilization, and universal myth. In this sense, Parsons serves his systemic scaffold well by integrating the concepts of ethnicity into his own general theory of societal evolution. The paper by Milton M. Gordon supplies an excellent typology relating ethnicity as a dependent variable to class and race, and to independent variables of ideology, power, and the political nature of society as a whole. No indications are given as to how one measures such things as "intermediate trends of power" in an "egalitarian, pluralist society," but the sentiment is certainly noble. The essay by Donald L. Horowitz (no relation) is less a statement on ethnic identity than on comparative ethnic identities. Its main concern is to show that the general effect of nationalist amalgamation was to superimpose identity and that the ethnic problem is a function of societal layers being imperfectly integrated. The notion that international regional integration leads to amalgamation, whereas nationalism drives toward separation is neat and seems testable. However, Horowitz ignores the ways in which ethnicity may function as a transnational cohesive factor. The final paper in the theory section, by Daniel Bell, is provocative. It has the advantage of showing that ethnicity is an aspect of the fusion of status order with the political order, while class is a dimension of the relationship of the economic order to the political order. I am not sure that Bell's case for ethnicity as a kind of primordial desire of those who are *Gemeinde* to create a group defined as *Fremde* can be empirically confirmed. There is a good lesson to be learned in any purely sociologistic account of ethnicity that minimizes the psychological propensities that underwrite many sociological variables. However, the caveat "toward a general theory" does not hold up. It would be more accurate to say that these papers offer five different models in search of a general theory.

The best portion of the book unfortunately draws the least attention from the editors, perhaps because it is the least controversial. The papers by William Peterson, "On the Subnations of Western Europe," and by Andrew Greeley and William McCreedy, "The Transmission of Cultural Heritages: The Case of the Irish and the Italians," are both carefully done. The regional papers by Orlando Patterson, "Context and Choice in Ethnic Allegiance: A Theoretical Framework and Caribbean Case Study," and by François Bourricaud, "Indian, Mestizo, and Cholo as Symbols in the Peruvian System of Stratification," are really fine. I have some reservations about Martin Kilson's paper, "Blacks and Neo-Ethnicity in American Political Life," and John Porter's, "Ethnic Pluralism in Canadian Perspective." Each author in his own way missed the opportunity to talk specifically about ethnic diversity within dominant nationalities. Kilson deals only with the black experience as an aggregate mass serving as role model for newer white ethnics. While blacks do so serve, it is somewhat disappointing that he does not deal with the sort of questions of ethnicity within black life that divide Jamaicans, Indians, East Africans, West Africans, third-generation blacks, and first-generation blacks within the United States, by income and occupation. Porter's paper is dismaying because, as far as I am concerned, it marks a step backward from *The Vertical Mosaic*, his classic book on Canada written in the mid-sixties. One would hope that Porter, having turned his attention to French and English groups, would at least provide explanation of problems of exploitation as he did in the earlier work. What we get is short-run problems and long-run optimism. The overemphasis on linguistic problems at the expense of economic ones means that Porter simply has not taken seriously criticisms of his work by fellow Canadians.

The final section, "The New States," concerning actually the Third World and old empires, again has some excellent papers. Particularly noteworthy is the study by Mazrui of ethnic stratification in Uganda. As he does in so much of his work, Mazrui introduces and infuses his efforts with extremely interesting theories by dropping phrases like "Military-Agrarian Complex." His analysis of ethnicity as it reflects itself in the military makes for refreshing and unusual emphasis in the volume. The brief paper by Richard Pipes is a bit too impressionistic. Written in an ex cathedra manner, it might have benefited by the sort of careful work done by Teresa Rakowska. The paper by Lucian W. Pye on ethnic minorities in China is sound, but it would have been enriched by an analysis of how the Chinese-Communist regime is dealing with precisely the problem of ethnicity and linguistic minorities. He speaks of a growing sense of Chinese anxiety. However, he does not deal with the corresponding efforts of the Chinese government in policymaking at this level. The work of John Lum would be especially important in this connection.

It is hard to summarize this book, and a mistake to dismiss it. There is that irritating cocksureness that pervades much of the writing: a kind of genteel conceit that all is right with the advanced world and slightly less so with the Third World (a phrase, by the way, remarkably absent in this collection). There are only two papers on "the new states." India and China are cast with "the old empires," while the Caribbean and Peru are somewhere in limbo between "the old world and the new." In part, this geographic timidity stems from the fact that so few pieces are written by ethnics themselves. I do not want to get into a metaphysical dispute over *verstehentheorie*, the argument that you have to be one to study one. These debates are irrelevant to the main point: a good deal of the literature is simply blocked out because of ethnic bias. Even a scholar like Porter displays little firsthand knowledge of the French-Canadian literature. Bourricaud takes only perfunctory account of developments since his 1967 book, *Pouvoir et société dans le Pérou contemporain.* The work of Julio Cotler and Anibal Quijamo does not raise even a faint whisper. The same lack of being au courant is evident, but to a lesser degree, in the work of Pye. With such a subject as ethnicity, one would have hoped to elicit the contribution of more of the people involved as participating subjects, no less than objects of analysis. Alas, this is not the case, and, alack, this is the ultimate shortcoming of the book. The view from the Charles River does reveal its limits.

From *American Journal of Sociology*, vol. 82, no. 1 (1976), pp. 221–25.

44

Documenting the Holocaust*

Heartfield, John

There has been a remarkable outpouring of writing on the meaning of photography for society and the individual. Psychologists, sociologists and philosophers have all made serious contributions to the discussion of how photography distinguishes the twentieth century, and perhaps the late nineteenth century as well, from previous eras. Susan Sontag may have best caught the spirit of the new aesthetic when she wrote, "The force of photographic images comes from their being realities in their own right, richly informative deposits left in the wake of whatever emitted them, potent means for turning the tables on reality—for turning it into a shadow."

These two volumes reveal the exact nature of such information deposits, the character of that upside-down reality. Superficially, no two volumes of photographs covering different historical aspects of the same Nazi reality could be more radically different. Heartfield's work is photocollage and photomontage. Grossman's shots of everyday reality in the Lodz ghetto are simply a record in photographs taken at great personal risk, so that a skeptical future would know that these people lived in hope and did not perish in vain. But both Heartfield (formerly Herzfelde, a German Christian and a Communist) and Grossman (a Polish Jew and a Talmudist) had a special vision that the photograph would provide the ultimate record of a desperate period in twentieth century life. They had a sense of photography as an instrument of the struggle against totalitarianism and the historical dimensions of that struggle.

They were consummate craftsmen, photographers with a clinical vision and analytical skill, Heartfield at the macropolitical level and Grossman at the microcommunity level. Heartfield, along with Georg Grosz, was the inventor of photocollage and photomontage, an invention for specifically transartistic purposes. Grossman, in his own special way, produced a homemade Zoomartype lens. He had to develop telescopic lens techniques to photograph from afar events of enormous meaning, such as the deportation of masses of ghetto

---

*John Heartfield, *Photomontages of the Nazi Period* (New York: Universe Books, 1976), pp. 143.

Mendel Grossman, *With a Camera in the Ghetto* (New York: Schocken Books, 1977), pp. 107.

Jews to their final destination. These technical advances were not simply innovations in the technique of photography but responses to cataclysmic events that narrowed the gap between art and tragedy as nothing can, except a holocaust and its genocide.

This is not intended to be some sort of vulgar didactic assertion that form is somehow subordinated to content or that only extraordinary events made extraordinary art possible. Nothing could be further from the truth. I am arguing, along with Ben Shahn, that the shape of content is molded in the crucible of circumstances as well as techniques.

In their very different ways, Heartfield and Grossman do not so much create a reality (although from Heartfield's Dadaist background one would expect that he might) as frame reality. The photograph becomes a morally compelling record of events, a form of evidence that cannot be contravened or contradicted. The photograph cannot be subjected to various, sundry, and endless interpretations by historians or social theorists of all varieties. The photograph in its naked empiricism offers a record of events before which the observer can only stand in awe or, as the case may be, in fear and trembling. The ultimate horrors of Nazism cannot be argued or contravened as can the horrors of Caesarism or Bonapartism.

The image the photographic machine froze was nothing less than history itself—in this case, the history of barbarism. In this very act, the photograph becomes an instrument for cautioning future dictators and future regimes based on repression.

John Heartfield's work characterized an era in which social inequality and organized brutality had become the norm. His technical skill, which came out of the Dada period and rejected mechanistic forms of art, soon developed its own innovative framework that stood *sui generis,* as all great contributions to aesthetics ultimately do. Heartfield's work was also characteristic of a stylized proletarian protest of the 1930s in which the tendentiousness of the photo-artistic message coincided with the political adversary that went under the name of fascism.

As Hitler's era came to a close, Heartfield's work dried up. His kind of photo art did not fare well under the politics of ambiguity. A lifetime in the Communist movement did not equip him to deal with Stalinism or its German equivalent in the same way that he had been able to deal with Hitler. His was a specifically anti-Fascist, not a general anti-totalitarian, message.

Heartfield could not redirect his message to problems of genocide, autocracy, and bureaucratic totalitarianism in general. His unusual peace poster of 1960, *Niemals Wieder* (Never Again!), was simply a repeat of his 1932 poster design. This tragic citizen of the German Democratic Republic, a tutelary state of the USSR, was capable of surviving the Nazi regime only to end up as a charge within an occupying military, despotic Stalinist regime. His only response to tyranny was silence, a silence born not of protest but of confusion.

All who work in mixed media owe a huge debt to Heartfield. His writings for the *Arbeiter-Illustrierte-Zeitung* represented a weekly marvel uniting art, photography, and graphics and delivering a precise and exacting message. There was a passion for detail that is characteristic of all great photographers and artists. He took endless rounds of photographs of a falling house of cards to catch the precise moment to properly describe the myth of the thousand-year Nazi Reich. There was the colossal psychological impact of a Gestapo letter to a German woman informing her what had befallen her husband and loved ones in the concentration camp. Heartfield saw the whole Nazi era as bathed in death.

In Heartfield's work, the Nazi leadership filters through as everyday people attempting to dehumanize the Jewish ghettos, as ordinary lives compressed into a tiny space constantly made tinier by the deportation of the old, the children, and the feeble to their final destination, and constantly made more brutal by being sealed off from the rest of the world.

What is so unbelievable about the Grossman photos—10,000 photographs of 160,000 lives, only a handful of which survived—is that they show that there was resistance, not a Warsaw Ghetto type of resistance, but rather the resistance of human dignity. A postoffice serviced the ghetto alone, since no mail went in or out. Worship was conducted in private homes. Popular street singers sang ballads based on current events. There was a constant effort to find new forms and supplies of foodstuffs. Lodz was also a world of rumors—rumors of destruction, rumors of improvement. It held the horrible ironies of Jews working in basements of the Church of the Holy Virgin, recycling clothing, featherbeds, furs and pelts, the remnants of Jews who had been killed. Grossman also records the Nazis' acceleration of Jewish destruction. He understands the inexorableness of death and the maintenance of life despite all.

The quality of the pictures varies, as expected, but the impact is enormous. Above all, his account reveals incredible dedication and analysis. No attempt is made to achieve special artistic effects, but Grossman displays an innate understanding of photography in motion, the essence of the candid camera. Closeups reveal pain; panoramic shots reveal a deteriorating society. An individual situated in the foreground observes a background of misery. Grossman had a special historical consciousness, and the people with whom he interacted had an identical consciousness.

Ironically, the 10,000 negatives reached Kibbutz Nitzamin in Israel but were lost to the Egyptians during the War of Independence. As a result, there remain only a few of the many hundreds of prints Grossman made, which he had distributed among friends and acquaintances.

The desire to record, to record at all cost, had become part of the consciousness of the inhabitants of the ghetto. All parts of the Jewish community are permeated by this desire, and Mendel with his camera was received with open arms and with full understanding in workshops, hospitals, orphanages, offices, and the streets. People exposed to him their troubles, showed their wounds, opened the doors of their homes. "Let him come in and photograph, let it become known to all those who did not know, to those who would otherwise not believe," one commentator noted.

To compare Heartfield with Grossman is truly to compare apples and oranges. Still, the sociological eye of Grossman rather than the political ideology of Heartfield ultimately provides the strongest images and the most profound and lasting impact. Social life triumphs over design management in the same sense and in the same way that the slaughter of innocents must ultimately prove more potent than the immediate justice meted out to the guilty.

If we question the importance of the photographic endeavor, we need only ponder the importance of the photographs sent back by the Apollo astronauts, to appreciate these volumes on the Nazi era. We have known for 500 years that the shape of the earth is round. Yet the thrill of seeing that very roundness in a series of color prints provided the capstone of what was after all theory. The same is true of our notion of Nazism. It is certainly well recorded, well understood and has been carefully written about by hundreds of scholars. And yet to sec these volumes is to experience a confirmation that this diabolic system actually existed and did everything the historians and sociologists said was done to human beings. Not the Nazi triumph of will, but the Jewish faith in history is ultimately what these pictorial volumes reveal.

From *Present Tense*, vol. 5, no. 1 (1977), pp. 60–61.

45

Eclecticism in Search of an American Theology*

Herberg, Will

As I began marking up and underlining Harry J. Ausmus' intellectual biography of Will Herberg (yes, it is legitimate to "deface" a volume, but a review copy only!), my wife peered over my shoulder and asked, "who are you reviewing this for?" I replied: "for *Congress Monthly* or bi-monthly as the case may be." She then editorialized, "this seems to be a strange book for periodical and reviewer alike." Before the conversation went too much further along this road, I responded somewhat defiantly, "Well Herberg, like Hook [whose autobiography I reviewed in these pages last summer], was a student at the City College of New York. Although unlike Hook, he never made it through the system, a fact that Hook reminded Herberg of on several occasions. Also, both were children of Russian-Jewish immigrants and both made the long trek from radical orthodoxy to anti-Stalinist opposition."

Still, the more I attempted a proper riposte, the clearer it became that similarities and dissimilarities aside, there just weren't too many dodo birds left who could offer commentary on this strange species that has been perhaps too much written about in present times. After all, being archaic is not quite the same as being exotic. More than once as I progressed through this biographical journey, I wondered if this book was needed or if matters could have been left well enough alone with Mr. Ausmus's *Will Herberg: A Bio-Bibliography* issued a year ago. I do not think that I am giving too much away in saying at the outset that I concluded that indeed this book is needed or at least useful, if not always as an exemplar of social research, then as an antimodel of what to avoid in presenting the history and current status of religious ideas. For it should be evident that what typifies a particular period or current in intellectual history is not necessarily the best products, nor for that matter the worst, but some middle point that illumines more by context than by content.

---

* Harry J. Ausmus, *Will Herberg: From Right to Right* (Chapel Hill: The University of North Carolina Press, 1987), pp. 275.

It is no sign of disrespect for Herberg or his biographer to note that the flap copy only partially summarizes the text with any exactitude. For Herberg did *not* "shape theological or sociological theory from the 1930s to the 1970s." To be sure, for the current generation of scholars in both areas, Herberg seems to be a figure only dimly recollected and not always with certitude as to the message he left behind. In theology he was the first to acknowledge his derivativeness, and in sociology he so thoroughly reflected the work of others as to hardly qualify as a figure of any note.

Herberg was, in fact, a first rate popularizer. He was cut from a different ideological mold than say, a Vance Packard or a William Whyte, but the effort to summarize the extant literature and give the findings a new twist and an urgent tug are common to these three individuals. To be sure, the absence of any sense of social milieu is one of the weaker aspects of this biography, particularly the later years. For unlike Herberg's earlier years in the Communist and Socialist movements, which are well documented, the later years are charted as a movement from book to book, idea to idea.

This is a book worth reading in large measure because of the very ordinariness of Herberg's thought and the now equally commonplace odyssey he underwent from communism to conservatism. What is not so ordinary and what Ausmus makes clear is Herberg's use of history to fashion a commitment to the major tenets and themes of the Judeo-Christian tradition. If in our time, the hyphen is exactly where the theological action is, for Herberg the hyphen was little more than a function of longevity and accident. He saw equivalencies between Judaism and Christianity at every turn, and believed that for these two faiths to properly understand themselves meant to understand the other. Ausmus tells this aspect of Herberg very well: "The major differences between Judaism and Christianity lay in differences of mediation, vocation, and orientation. In terms of the first, one's relationship was mediated through the People of Israel, but, in Christianity it was through Christ. The Jew was consequently oriented toward Israel and the Christian toward Christ, with the former focusing on the Sinai-event and the latter on the Christ-event."

It is not without paradox that a figure of the 1950s and so close to Judaism should be so far from the Jewish condition in the post-Holocaust era. Nazism and fascism become simply lapses into paganism or part of the "scandal of particularity." The Jewish experience with its ultimate tragedy and despotism is described by Ausmus in near parodic terms "The conflict between the German National Socialists and the Jews was in effect a conflict between two groups, each claiming uniqueness." Apparently, the fact that the Nazi "group" murdered and the Jewish "group" was murdered in mass counts for little in the "common scandal of particularity." This weird piling up of existential premises led Herberg to declare that justice cannot be attained in history because love, the source of justice fails. But this unlifelike love—disembodied, unsensuous, and needing no metaphysical justification beyond itself, is precisely the source of Herberg's Christianized vision of the American Way as the proper escha-tology for our time. In this fashion, the attempt to establish a hyphenated American religion sadly deteriorates into apologetics that can only, and then with kindness, be called banal.

Soviet communism becomes a substitute for impoverished religion, while American capitalism as surrogate for the American Way of Life serves a similar purpose. The difference is that the Soviets lapsed into tyranny, and the Americans did not. In part, this is a result of the mutual fertilization of Protestantism, Catholicism, and Judaism into the American mainstream, in contrast to the Soviet denial of any sort of plural sources of authority or legitimacy. But this by now commonplace explanation does not explain why Jews were uniquely subject to intimidation, while Christians, whether devout or pagan, were spared decimation or destruction by totalitarian regimes. To have done so would have, as a matter of course, lengthened the hyphen and changed the study of the struggle, between Athens and Jerusalem to show that Athens bequeathed to the American founders a theory of democracy no less than a practice of paganism.

Even if the reader restricts his vision to postwar America proper, the problem of the hyphenated religions does not quite result in the celebration of pluralism. The idea that the center is somehow the gathering place of the political and religious processes alike is not always easy to prove. Herberg's description of the Nixon-Humphrey election of 1968 as good for America because both parties nominated candidates who were "slightly right of center" and would thus "guarantee stability and continuity—essential conservatism— in our political life, and this is a blessing mighty rare in the modern world." Such shabby analysis ignores several vital inputs and outputs of that time: among the former were the assassinations of Robert F. Kennedy, who would surely have gotten the Democratic Party nomination, and Martin Luther King, whose death gave the cause of black equity a special extra-legal dimension. And dare one recollect that the Watergate scandal was undertaken with the support and approval of Richard Nixon, something unthinkable with a Humphrey, in part because he advocated the very Judeo-Christian convictions Herberg so admired.

The root of the dilemma in Herberg's eclecticism is that its parts moved in different, often contradictory directions. The smooth flow of Judaism and Christianity, of Democrats and Republicans, of existentialists and historicists, simply reflected a special time in American history: the 1950s. The Henry Luce notion of a pax Americana seemed to be in perfect keeping with the spirit of the times. It was an age of consensus, and the theological vision of Herberg served to promote that consensus by showing the roots in the immigrant experience of Catholics and Jews and the sources of pluralistic experience of Protestants of many if not all persuasions. Everything seems quite main line in the work of Herberg. The rise of Protestant fundamentalism, the breakup of the political hegemony of the Catholic church, and the strong resistance of nearly all branches of Judaism to becoming Christianized are either not anticipated or, where schisms are recognized, given short shrift.

But of course, this characterizes a minor figure: unable to anticipate events or chart courses of actions. It is also what makes Herberg the quintessential figure of his day and age, one in which every community had a proper group to smooth out differences in understanding between Jews and Christians and one in which building bridges (too often of a one way sort) became the religious order of the day. In this, Herberg was as much a reflection as an analyst of a powerful strain toward consensus through pluralism in American thought and action. And if Herberg's politics is a world without Israel, his theology is a world without Moslems. Like so many before him who invoked the laws and mystique of metaphysics, history—real history—simply went unaccounted for—not unlike Hegel's world history in which Asia and Africa are reduced to paragraphs in the march of Europe toward its inevitable destiny of world conquest through world thought.

Given Herberg's upbringing in the radical Left movement when the Marxian dogma about religion as the opiate of the masses was the sum and substance of its thinking on the subject of theology, one has to credit Herberg with breaking through this shallow shell into a deeper sense of social and personal tradition alike. His ability to utilize Marxian categories of class, ethnicity, and history to understand the place of Judaism and Christianity in American society may be his most innovative contribution, not so much to either theology or sociology but rather to the dry rot of Marxist analysis. The influence of V.F. Calverton, the Marxist anthropologist, was substantial. Still, this in no way detracts from the special contribution of Herberg to the Left-rather than the Right.

Judaism and Modern Man in 1951 and *Protestant-Catholic-Jew* in 1955 are the two pillars of Herberg's thought. But they have quite different characteristics. The earlier book sees the Jewish faith as central to the notion of society over the state, and further, that the individual is more than the society. The uniqueness of the person in Jewish theology is the greatest bulwark against the totalitarian temptation. The uniqueness of the Jewish faith is affirmed in both historical and theological revelation. And if the popular rhetoric of the mid-1950s, existentialism, prevails at the conclusion of this work, it is an existential position rooted more in Buber than in Sartre. Still, one senses that this existential predicament, when generalized, provided an intellectual opportunity for Herberg to run a series of personal parallels in the history of Jewish and Christian tradition and thought.

By the time of the later work, Herberg moved from an essential Jewish position to one in which Judaism and Christianity are said to represent one religious reality. The notion of the Covenant of the Jews with God is transformed to one that "is opened to all mankind through Christ." By becoming a Christian, by worshiping the body of Christ, the Gentile becomes an Israelite.

The massive retreat from a view of Judaism as anything more than a bridge to the present of Christendom, a retreat from his own commitments to Judaism, is dealt with in a far too cursory manner by Mr. Ausmus. Indeed, by seeking to give weight to the subtitle, "From Right to Right," attention is deflected away from the extent to which a more appropriate subtitle might have been called from Judaism to Christianity. For in truth the "three religion America" described by Herberg is upon inspection a Protestant world, with strong Jewish and Catholic components serving to enrich the cultural experience of an American society infected with the Athenian experience of democracy.

Herberg can be said to have been knowledgeable in Judaism, appreciative of Protestantism, and in love with Catholicism. The existential sources of his thought derived from Buber, the pluralistic sources derived from Niebuhr, and the Catholic impulses were more diffuse, but largely derived from the conservative forces that gathered around William Buckley's *National Review* in its formative years. It is a testimonial to how fundamental shifts have occurred within the Jewish intelligentsia that in the 1950s the search for a conservative option invariably led to Christian organizational life.

This search for a conservative option only deepened Herberg's eclecticism. For compounding the faith in American religion of Protestantism-Catholicism-Judaism was a faith in an American ideology of conservatism, pluralism, and historicism. Ausmus makes a valiant effort to interpret this mish-mash as a person in an honest life-search in which the dialectic of the search was more important than the answers. Sadly, a more handy explanation is of a decent auto-didact in love with the world of ideas but not quite sure how to assemble that world in a synthetically unique or an analytically meaningful way. At the outset, I said that this is a book worth reading. But it should be emphasized that this is worthwhile because the human capacity to learn from the errors of the past may be no less than to learn from the truths of today. If this is the case, then Herberg makes a strangely appropriate guide.

From *Congress Monthly*, vol. 55, no.1 (1988), pp. 17–19.

46

The Politics of Genocide*

Kuper, Leo

Leo Kuper is professor emeritus at the University of California at Los Angeles, born and banned in South Africa, and the author of several excellent monographs in social stratification and race relations in African contexts. He is a good man writing on an awful subject and has produced, unfortunately, a mediocre book. This may seem to be a severe judgment about an effort undertaken with deep commitment and intellectual integrity, but his American publisher, who insisted on counting *Genocide* as "the first systematic treatment of the subject," which it is clearly not, must be held partially accountable. The author himself (like the original British publisher) is far more modest describing his work as a series of case studies in domestic genocides, that is, those internal to a society. But the fault is, I am afraid, not only that of overly enthusiastic advertising copy. The author manages to skirt just about every major issue that has arisen in this field of investigation: the relationship between the Holocaust and genocides in general, the relationship between civil conflict and state destruction, and the reasons for the ineffectiveness of international peace-keeping agencies in reducing genocide. The last omission is particularly glaring since Professor Kuper sets this as an essential task.

On a different level, however, it is an excellent basic text, especially for individuals who are not familiar with the subject of genocide. Definitions are invariably fairminded and essentially sound; the appendices, especially on United Nations resolutions and backsliding, such as its attitude toward the Turkish genocide against Armenians, are particularly revealing. The role of the United Nations, or better, its lack thereof, has often been talked about but little understood. At such descriptive levels, the book provides a welcome contribution. The cases selected are for the most part helpful and show a keen sense of the magnitude of the problems of genocide. When we talk in terms of roughly 800,000 Armenians, 6,000,000 Jews, and 3,000,000 Bangladeshis, we have clearcut examples of an enormous portion of a national population

---

* Leo Kuper, *Genocide: Its Political Use in the Twentieth Century* (New Haven, Yale University Press, 1982), pp. 255.

decimated by the authorities, giving us a sober reminder that our century hovers dangerously between creativity and destruction.

The book's problems are less those of sentiment than of method. Equating such phenomena as civil strife between Catholics and Protestants in Northern Ireland with the destruction of German Jewry or the destruction of urban Cambodia just does not work. Even the author acknowledges that in Northern Ireland, victims have been numbered in the hundreds over a long stretch of time, whereas in most clearcut cases of genocide the numbers destroyed are in the millions. Then there is the too simplistic equation of civil war and genocide. Equating the Nigerian Civil War, or even the struggle against Apartheid in South Africa, with cases of undisputed genocide blurs and confuses rather than clarifies what genocide is about, namely the vast, nearly total destruction of large numbers of noncombatants innocent of any specific crime. Further, burdening the United Nations as the source of the failure to control genocide is unconvincing since, as the author is at pains to explain, this organization is primarily a composite of nations and not in itself a sovereign power. Underneath the demand to strengthen the United Nations is an implicit assumption that nationalism should be weakened, something that clearly has not, nor is likely, to take place, and certainly not under the aegis of the United Nations.

In the balance of the review, let me take up some of the thornier issues. The problem of genocide is not a new one, and the need for a literature to move beyond horror and into analysis becomes increasingly critical. It is risky to equate genocide with arbitrary death. Two examples that Leo Kuper has given illustrate a problem rather than indicate a solution.

He raises, for example, the case of India during the partition, in which Hindus and Moslems constituted majorities in different parts of the country, each with the capacity to engage freely in what he calls reciprocal genocidal massacre. However terrible and tragic that mutual destruction was, to speak of it as genocidal in a context of religious competition and conflict risks diluting the notion of genocide and equating it with any conflict between national, religious, or racial groups. This error also appears in his analysis of Northern Ireland, where Protestants and Catholics engage in the meanest and most dangerous kinds of assaults on one another. If one were to tally the numbers of deaths since 1920, they would hardly be above 10,000, surely a terrible human loss and with equal surety an indicator of the risks involved in unresolved conflicts. But it is not genocide. The confusion is evident in Kuper's notion that the removal of the British presence and the withdrawal of the British army before a political solution in Ulster is achieved would invite bloodshed. One might indicate, as many leaders from both the Catholic and Protestant camps have, that the British presence is itself a source of violence and that the removal of the occupying power would overcome a major obstacle to resolution of the civil conflict. Whether this belief is correct or not, we are dealing with the realm of political tactics and international relations but surely not the area of genocide—unless we reduce the term to a fatuous notion of the cultural elimination of certain groups and ideologies.

Kuper also confounds legal identification between Apartheid and genocide in South Africa with the empirical problem: the place and condition of the blacks within South Africa. As the author himself well appreciates, there is a demographic restraint to annihilation. The black African population in South Africa grew from roughly 8,000,000 in 1946 to 19,000,000 in 1980. The Asian population grew from 285,000 to 765,000, and the white population from 2,400,000 to roughly 4,400,000. The demographics alone indicate that genocide simply has not occurred. What may have happened is the fragmentation of the African population and the consequent denial of citizenship rights for most blacks. South Africa is also a classic case of exploitation of the majority by a racial minority in a very specialized context. But it does not service the victims nor anyone else to present South Africa as a case of genocide—which implies the absolute destruction of a people, if not completely then in such large numbers as to affect the future survival potential as well as the present population.

Relativizing the issue of genocide particularly damages efforts to understand the Nazi Holocaust against the Jews. The major problem in such relativizing is that it completely fails to distinguish between the systematic, total, scientific engineering of death and the more random occurrences that are characteristic of other events. If others were to operate under a veil of anonymity such as the Nazis did, they might also attempt a kind of final solution. But whether that is so or not, the notion of the final solution, the treatment of the Holocaust is absent in the work of Professor Kuper. While I myself have argued against celebrating the exclusivity of death, one must take seriously differences between the total decimation of a population, reducing it to a remnant, and the selective, random elimination of political or religious opposition. The very concept of Holocaust fails to appear in Kuper's work and is mentioned only in relation to a book title. It is as if the author were consciously and deliberately attempting to relativize the Jewish case as one of many and was consequently disregarding the specificity and peculiar characteristics involved in the Nazi Holocaust. This undermines not only the moral basis of Professor Kuper's work but also weakens his appreciation of the full meaning of the Turkish assault on the Armenians. The latter was not merely an event that takes place in the Ottoman Empire but is characteristic of the Kemalist democracy that followed. The genocide against Armenians, like the Holocaust against Jews, was special in its totality, in its movement beyond the boundaries of nationalism and rationalism. Both cases are not characteristic of any others—until we get to Kampuchean communism.

Underlying his failure to distinguish between genocide and civil strife on the one hand, and genocide and total destruction such as the Holocaust on the other, is a peculiar inability to distinguish between theory and action, and more specifically, an unwillingness to deal with culture, specifically German and Turkish cultures. Kuper, along with others, has spent a great deal of futile time on problems of ideology.

There is sufficient confusion within Marxism and fascism to make one wary of this line of approach. Perhaps Marxism, in its acceptance of a theory of class polarization, yields to a Manichean vision of a world torn apart, but even a Marxism predicated on guilt by social origin may or may not translate into genocidal behavior. It certainly did in the Gulag Archipelago and the years of Stalinism; it certainly has not in such places as Yugoslavia. Likewise, even with fascism, there seems to be no doubt that the Nazis analogized European Jewry to a cancer that had to be excised and identified Jews with world conspiracy. Fascism in Italy did not have the same genocidal potential. Even within provinces held by Japan during World War II, when Jewish enclaves came under Japanese dominion, the genocidal pattern did not obtain. Any comprehensive analysis of genocide must deal seriously with cultural canons that permit or forbid genocidal behavior. This total absence of analysis of the culture of peoples not given to genocide and those that were, seriously weakens Kuper's book. Ideology rather than culture is held responsible and accountable for genocidal behavior. This is a difficult thesis to prove. The democratic developmentalism of Ataturk in Turkey was absolutely at odds with Imperial notions derived from the Ottoman Empire, yet both democratic and antidemocratic forces within Turkey carried on genocide against the Armenians. The peasant egalitarianism of the Khmer Rouge did not spare us a major genocide. Wherever one seeks an answer based on ideology, the same kind of confusion presents itself, issues that Kuper unfortunately does not address.

Kuper charges the United Nations with doing much less than it should. He argues that its capacities to curtail genocide, much less prevent or punish atrocities, has been blunted. He gives several reasons for this laxity: first, the punitive procedures of the United Nations are weak; second, the United Nations is committed to the sanctity of state sovereignty; and third, the United Nations has established commissions to deal with complaints about human rights violations, that are themselves highly politicized and in the control of a clique of powerful nations whose vested interests are in stilling the voices of opposition. One could hardly argue with Kuper's analysis of the weaknesses of the United Nations, but from an analytical point of view, it is an extremely thin reed on which to hang an analysis of the problem of genocide. The sources of genocide are certainly not in the United Nations. Therefore prospects for solution are likewise not to be found in the United Nations. The limits of the organization are well understood. Kuper might then have analyzed different kinds of national cultures and how punishment and law emerge in various countries.

There is now a burgeoning literature on just these subjects. It might be possible to develop an early warning signal, a concern about problems of law and democratic order, that might limit the possibility of future genocides taking place. But if the genesis of the problem is not in a world organization, then it is hard to believe that the solution will be found there. As Dr. Kuper knows quite well, the United nations is itself the source of so much amoral self-righteousness that its very existence strengthens nationalism and the national ideal.

From a policy viewpoint, the book presents obstacles rather than solutions. The final chapter in the book, "The Non-Genocidal Society," is in fact more nearly a non-chapter. Rather than outlining the features of a non-genocidal society or developing any kind of systematic analysis of democratic order, Kuper recapitulates the main arguments of the book. Kuper argues the continuous need for international public opinion and to limit destructive conflict within plural societies, and to do so through effective peace-keeping mechanisms, but these remain platitudinous, of little analytical value. To be sure, the author himself assumes, and quite correctly, that moral restraints against large-scale massacre are swept away during a crisis.

But does crisis management necessarily require elimination of human constraint and restraint? Once again, precise information about historical responses to specific types of crises is sadly lacking. Perhaps the most evident area of confusion is the murder of nearly 35–40 percent of the Cambodian population by the Khmer Rouge. Kuper proffers the thesis that this was made possible by the United States rather than by the character of the situation within Cambodia and the history of Cambodian culture. For Kuper to say that the government of Kampuchea was justified in its indictment of American imperialism and that this extrinsic factor explains, if not justifies, its genocide is exactly the reverse of the conclusion that one would expect from his theorizing elsewhere that the source of genocide is intrinsic, (i.e., blaming people for their social origins).

When class, race, and religious stigmas are held as ineradicable sins, the potential for genocide and massive murder is enormously increased. The book makes its soundest contribution in tracing guilt not to individual acts but to social background as the explanation for how genocide is rationalized. Were Kuper to have seriously pursued that line of reasoning, were he to have followed his own logic, then he might have made a substantial contribution. As it is, we must be grateful for the summary of the literature and some very interesting insights that may contribute at a later date to the systematic treatment of genocide that this work promises but does not deliver.

Kuper's work illustrates the dilemmas of ideology in confronting genocide. However, the attractiveness of liberal anti-imperialism is less worthy once we witness the sort of regimes that replace the old order. But even this is beside the point. Genocide is a subject of sufficient magnitude and significance to stand in judgment of and apart from *all* ideological posturings. Genocide need not, should not, be enlisted in any ideological crusades. Kuper is entangled in the very web of political statements and ethical norms that his book seeks to overcome. Thus, we are left with what we had at the beginning: a decent man in search of decent answers to an indecent subject matter.

From *Modern Judaism*. vol. 3, no. 2 (1983), pp. 243–47.

47

Jewish History and American Destinies*

Neusner, Jacob

Books on the history of Jews, including the veritable legion of works on American Jews, share a peculiarity: they are informed by a concept of teleology as causality. That is to say, the notion of moral purpose, or in a weaker form, of physical and spiritual survivability, is a theme that haunts such works of purported history. Although profound differences exist in theology and formal analysis, the theme of destiny and history continue to inform works on the Jewish panorama. For all their radical differences, these three books are no exception to the common rule. Whether this makes for richer or poorer analysis is rather beside the point, the capacity for survival and the search for destiny underwrites these analytic efforts. Classical models of historiography developed by Carlyle and Toynbee, rather than the newer scientific, quantitative, or statistical forms prevail.

For Jacob Neusner, the merger of teleology and theology is self evident. It is underwritten by every text of Judaism. For him, the ultimate purpose is simple: "We learn to carry out what we learn, not merely to replicate the teacher. . . . Anything else means merely to go through the motions. Talmud Torah is meant to create greater, more holy human beings, not oxen and dumb asses." Whitfield veers more sharply toward the prophetic rather than the rabbinic mode. He sees Jews as "torn between the personal and the collective, between the particular and the universal, between the singular and the common, between the one and the many."

This position harkens back to the viewpoint worked out earlier by Jacob Talmon. Underwriting the dialectic of Jewish survival is the message of

---

* Jacob Neusner, *Israel In America: A Too Comfortable Exile?* (Boston: Beacon Press, 1985), pp. 203.

Stuart E. Rosenberg, *The New Jewish Identity in America.* (New York: Hippocrene Books, 1985), pp. 290.

Stephen J. Whitfield, *Jews in American Life and Thought: Voices of Jacob, Hands of Esau.* (Hamden, Connecticut: The Shoe String Press / Archon Books, 1984), pp. 322.

morality. The total history of Jews at its best "is inexhaustible in its power to steel believers against both adversity and affluence, inexhaustible in its capacity to help them absorb the torment and void of existence, inexhaustible in its reminders of the precariousness of life even as it cannot fully assuage the pain of loneliness or the burden of toil, or account for the prevalence of want and cruelty and suffering and troubled sleep, even as it cannot truly illuminate the mystery of death." Stuart Rosenberg, while expressing a more conventional series of theological concerns, sees the current revival of interest in Judaism (in the United States at least) as linked to "an awareness that the future of Jewishness was bound up with the meaning of Judaism." And while Rosenberg sees this as part of larger religious trends, he singles out the conversion of Christians (especially women) to Judaism in this period as a personal commitment to "Judaism as a spiritual way of life" and an effort to "discover new insights in its old teachings."

Just as curious as this normative center of historical gravity, which presumably ensures the survival and destiny of the Jewish people, are the sharp differences between writers on Jewish themes in their sense of history itself (i.e., in the causes of such a special, moral purpose). Each of these three writers choose to emphasize quite different aspects of the Jewish tradition. For Neusner, it is the driving ideas of sacral texts; for Whitfield, it is the delicate balance established between civil authority and personal rights; for Rosenberg, it is group identity through spiritual integrity. The locus of moral purpose shifts. The fact of such moral purpose, if one can speak that way, is lasting.

We learn from these books about Jewish beliefs about the future—Jewish worries, concerns, and interests. What worries Rosenberg is less identity than demography. The book is dotted with references to population shifts, numbers of adherents, and conversion processes. As Jews absorbed the general liberal consensus, they saw themselves "losing the assurance that their inner life would continue to mark them out as a unique people." Affluence and liberalism themselves become threatening to Jewish integrity, which is measured in numbers rather than any particular set of beliefs. Neusner is worried about the division of labor in American life that has transformed the role of the rabbi from a traditional Jewish pedagogue into a typically Christian minister. Instead of the holiness that comes from learning, as in past Jewish tradition, learning itself becomes dangerous reduced to a special societal role uniquely embodied by the rabbi. In this way, the teacher and the learner, the essential dialectic of Jewish community life, is displaced by the minster-pontificator. Whitfield sees the commitment to the perpetuation and accommodation of differences, the essence of liberalism, as itself the "expression of Jewish distinctiveness." We are not told what would happen if Jewish conservatism or self-interest were to prevail over the universalistic drives that have characterized so much of twentieth century American history.

What then is the specifically American content about Jews in America, and what remains specifically Jewish in American life? Again, the teleological elements prevail. For Neusner, the philosophical idealist, American Judaism is the "effort of modern men and women to make use of archaic ways and myths in the formation of a religious way of living appropriate to an unreligious time and community." For Whitfield, the culturologist, interested as much in the American themes of theater, films, sports as in the conventional European themes of totalitarianism and the Holocaust, an American Jew is concerned with "how to make adherence to a majestic faith and involvement in a common fate compatible with the comfort that affluence has created and with the liberalism that the public culture has sponsored." And while Rabbi Rosenberg because of his Canadian congregation necessarily adopts a comparative framework, he yet feels keenly that after all is said and done, "Jewish life in Canada seems to be substantially and firmly set upon the same rails and tracks as that of their American cousins." Rosenberg too has an answer about American Jews. He sees it as "the elastic and creative amalgam of ethnicity and religion." This fusion not only serves American Jews but represents "a model for other Americans to emulate."

If I have labored perhaps too assiduously to cite the positions of each author, it is because these books illustrate more than explain diversity in American Jewish life. The mystery remains. One earlier prediction after another has faltered: Jews cannot survive affluence, Jews cannot survive liberalism, Jews cannot survive intermarriage, Jews cannot survive secularization. And yet, each of these books offer partial refutations of these earlier assumptions. They are concerned precisely with the theme of survivability. Indeed, all policy agenda items are seen as elements in a reformation of Jewish life rather than a threat to its survival. To be sure, Neusner is less sure than Whitfield of the positive role of Americanization, whereas Rosenberg is less certain than either of the other two of the demographic consequences of such Americanization.

Well then, as real history stripped of moral judgment (no easy task in the case of these volumes), how do the books shape up? For the proverbial "man from Mars" unlike the "Jew from Minsk" in search of truth no less than meaning still has to make comparative, analytical decisions no less than ethical judgments.

Let it be said that each book has such a different cast of figures or characters as the case may be, that the real issue is what does the reader want? For those who found Irving Howe's *World of Our Fathers* appealing, Stephen J. Whitfield's book *Voices of Jacob, Hands of Esau* will likewise be most rewarding. If one can overlook the irritating confusion of a title page reversing the dust jacket on the order of title and subtitle of this book, one can find here a fine survey of the Jewish impact on a variety of cultural fields. In each field, a key figure—Walter Lippman in journalism, Joseph Heller in literature, Al Jolson in film—is dealt with as a prototype. One might question the centrality of some of these figures, but to place the Jew as culturally central, painted on a broad American canvass, is certainly well worth doing. Whitfield's book points to Jewish survival as a group, as well as Jewish penetration onto the American scene in an acceptable way.

The segment of Whitfield's work "The Jew as Southerner" is certainly fascinating material, but whether this rather rarefied type—small in numbers and ephemeral in Jewishness—actually illumines or beclouds the overall theme of jews in American life and thought remains debatable. Perhaps with the current diaspora of Jews from the Northeast to the rest of America, this sense of regionalism may take on more rather than less value in the period ahead. The least satisfying chapter in the book concerns American Jewish sports fiction. It is weak not because of the analysis of Malamud, Roth, and Harris on baseball, but because Whitfield curiously sustains the myth that "the Jews have left professional competition to the goys of summer." The author may know his Malamud, Roth, and Harris but seems curiously ignorant of Hank Greenberg, Sandy Koufax, or Ken Holzman—just to name a few quite prominent "yids of summer."

Professor Neusner, for his part, lives in a more scripturally explicit world. Codirector of the Program in Judaic Studies at Brown and author of more than one hundred books on Jewish history and theology, the author of this slender volume is engaged in a monologue with himself no less than a dialogue with others. I guess after so many books, one is entitled to talk to oneself rather freely and publicly. It nonetheless is sometimes difficult for a reader, who comes in at the end as it were, to always follow the argument. There is the inevitable taking for granted of a literature that the author knows well, but his readers may not. The appreciation of Abraham Joshua Heschel is a highlighted essay in the book, not the least because of Neusner's shrewd observations on others, like Mordecai Kaplan, whose pragmatism "led to abandoning the effort to think within, and through, the classical literature of Judaic religious experience."

Yet Neusner's work tends to be irritatingly quarrelsome and lacking in compassion. The critique of orthodox Judaism for arrogance despite authenticity, barely escapes from mortifyingly ad hominem premises (i.e., "it would be unfair to invoke the names of Orthodox rabbis who were tried and convicted of exploitation of old and sick people"). The book wanders as well as wonders: chapters on South Africa, Jewish studies at American Universities, casual remarks on blacks and Jews. It is hard to detect an organizing premise in these papers drawn from such diverse organs as *The Brown Review, Moment,* and *Present Tense.* The preface is also not without puffery: "I have included a few notes toward the autobiography I shall never write," quickly followed by "I do not think a scholar should have an autobiography, since a scholar's books and articles form his or her autobiography." The work is simply too personal in style and limited in scope to merit the title *Israel in America. Observations and Asides on Being Jewish in America* might have been more appropriate and telling.

For our Martian readers, perhaps the book by Stuart E. Rosenberg would prove most satisfactory. It does represent a survey of Jewish life that touches all major bases: the Jewish melting pot, American moods, American character, roots of anti-Semitism, Jewishness and Judaism, denominationalism, libertarianism, etc. Still I confess that Charles E. Silberman's new book, *A Certain People*, and the earlier efforts by Nathan Glazer in *American Judaism* and by Sidney Goldstein and Calvin Goldscheider in *Jewish Americans*, provide much more compelling and theoretically unified frameworks than the books under consideration.

A pedestrian quality that hangs over *The New Jewish identity in America* that at times verges on the platitudinous, as when Rabbi Rosenberg holds out the hope that rabbis "may once again become Jewish *scholars*—understood and even respected by their congregants for that *Jewish achievement* alone!" Here, perhaps the author should be referred to Professor Neusner's fears of moral usurpation through role stratification. But it is the demographic determinism that is most disturbing. First, Rosenberg presumes an equation of power with numbers, precisely the reverse of Jewish American history, and second, he also wants to believe that the "resurgent self-awareness" of Jewish life in America will lead to new depth and triumphs. The book gives expression to general hopes and fears but does little to resolve such issues, or to address these in an innovative way.

All of this is said in a spirit of approbation rather than reproach, for these are three decent books by three decent people. The very emergence of choice in American Jewish life, the broad range of options and alternatives—from religious to secular organizational expression, from Jewish individuality to Jewish community—make writing on the history of Jews in the United States a risky proposition. Professor Whitfield captures the dialectic, Professor Neusner the idealism, and Rabbi Rosenberg the tradition involved in Jewish life. But I think that it is safe to say that the sort of comprehensive historiography performed by Salo W. Baron or H. G.Ben Sasson remains a task for future scholars of the American-Jewish condition. For now, works such as these provide in themselves, considerable affirmation and some serious criticism, spiced with an admixture of history and teleology. Such a recipe will not hurt; yet in all likelihood Christians and Jews rather than historians and sociologists will probably turn out to be the prime reading beneficiaries of these books—a fact which should please each author.

From *American Jewish History*, vol. 75, no. 4 (1986), pp. 457–62.

48

The Jews and Modern Communism*

Sombart, Werner

The recent reissuance of Werner Sombart's classic work, *The Jews and Modern Capitalism*, is a welcome event—both in itself and for making available once again this significant effort to understand the relationships between religion and the economy. But rather than simply recreate the past, one should evaluate the present. Specifically, we should reconsider, against the background of Sombart's understanding, the global problem of Jews and their place in a variety of social systems, particularly in the light of the rise of modern communism as a major political and economic force of our age. But before getting directly to our topic, it is worthwhile to briefly summarizew just what the Sombart thesis actually states. For like the so-called Weber thesis concerning the relationship of Protestantism and the emergence of modern capitalism, the actual writings of Sombart are more often discussed than digested.

Sombart employs a benign transvaluation of Marx's capitalism as that organization wherein regularly two distinct socio-economic groups cooperate. They are the owners of the means of production and the great body of workers who possess essentially only their labor power. The pursuit of gain is the mainspring of the system; the procedure is rationalism, planning, and efficiency in the means of production. Economic activity is regulated by a cash nexus requiring exact calculations. The structure of cooperation is induced by a common appeal to the marketplace. In this context, the apparent success of the Jews under capitalism is attributed by Sombart to four factors: their dispersion over a wide area, their treatment as perennial strangers, their semicitizenship, and their liquid wealth. But these objective circumstances are important only in the context of special Jewish characteristics. Religious values are taught to the humblest and the mightiest alike; their loss of a land and hope for return transformed them into a cultural brotherhood, and rationalism is the dominant ideology of Judaism as it is of capitalism.

---

* Werner Sombart, *The Jews and Modern Capitalism*. Edited with an introduction by Samuel Z. Klausner (New Brunswick and Oxford: Transaction Publishers, 1982), pp. 475.

These are, of course, only the bare bones of Sombart's appraisal. Our concern however is to examine the hypothesis in conditions of communism, a system in which the state transcends class forces in the management and planning of the economy. The communist system fuses material and moral incentives to increase productivity and higher living standards through the elimination of presumably antagonistic social and economic forces and classes. One might argue, as do Mosca and Pareto (two of the more eminent contemporaries of Sombart) that antagonisms are not so much eliminated, as transformed from the economic plane of classes to the political plane of bureaucracies or interest groups. It might also be claimed that the enormous increase in centralized authority creates a ruling class out of the administrative elite. Whatever exact empirical status of communism in the Soviet Union or capitalism in the United States, it is clear that vast differences do exist in the organization of production for the purposes of planning social goods for human ends.

The aim here is less the formal properties of the major systems in the world or a quick recitation of competing frameworks of East-West relations, than the condition of Jews under modern communism. Beyond that, it is important to find out how the actual situation of Jews under communism helps us better understand Jews under capitalism, and in this regard, the extent to which the views articulated eighty years ago by Sombart are a help or a hindrance in furthering that appreciation.

Seen in systematic terms, the issue of Jewish survival and modernity concerns not so much Jewish conditions under late capitalism as under late socialism. Living in 1984 rather than in 1904 poses certain analytical as well as empirical responsibilities in evaluating the doctrines of Werner Sombart. What requires delineation is to review the problem of Jews, not historically in relation to the origins of modern capitalism, but comparatively in light of the experience of modern communism. We need to know whether modern capitalism is as decisive a variable in the explanation of Jewish commercial propensities as has been presupposed. Better yet, we should ask whether a political *economy* of Judaism must not finally yield to a political sociology of Judaism, that is, a more broad-based consideration of state power, social stratification, and Jewish participation in both.

Initially, the question of Jews in modern capitalism must be critically examined from a comparative point of view, that is to say how they fare with respect to Jews living under modern communism. Any serious reconsideration of Sombart's work on Jewish emancipation under economic capitalism must begin from new conditions created by 63 years of Soviet history, 25 years of East European history, 30 years of East European communism, the experiences of Jews in Cuba since 1950, their experiences since 1979 in Nicaragua, and their unique position in Chile between 1970 and 1973—the Allende period and its cultural aftermath. Only in this way can one treat seriously the considerations of Weber and Sombart on the relationships between religion and capitalism generally, and the Jewish people and industrialism concretely. Capitalism as a unified world system clearly has been and is being tested by communism as a world system.

Without providing a detailed accounting, readily available in the contemporary scholarly literature, it is clear that Jewry under communism moves from a state of expectation, to atrophy, to one of utter, albeit slow and painful, extinction. In the Soviet Union, the number of those identifying themselves as Jews in census data has decreased since the 1917 Revolution—either through assimilation, immigration, or sheer silence. In Eastern Europe, with the lonely but important exception of Rumania, the condition of Jewish life can best be described as a series of secondary activities in the hands of the elderly and at times in the hands of curators of Jewish artifacts shown on request to visitors. Cuba, a thriving community in 1959 at the time of the revolution, has been reduced to a cluster numbered in the hundreds. Reports on Jewish life in Nicaragua have likewise described an overlay of hostility for Israel as that nation which continued to supply Somoza with weapons long after most other nations ceased doing so. The three-year period of Allende rule saw a sharp polarization, in which "economic" Jews fled, while "political" Jews became central advisors to the socialist Chilean regime.

The exploration of theoretical questions cannot proceed in a historical vacuum. Theories are neither revised nor overthrown by other theories; they are modified and reexamined in the light of experience. In this regard, the overwhelming fact that could not possibly be anticipated by either Weber or Sombart was a situation in which Jews would live under an economic system defined as socialist rather than capitalist. For if Jews have certain innate phylogenetic or historical propensities that transcend those of ordinary mortals, or certain drives that tend to underscore the normal workings of capitalism, these characterological deficiencies (or for that matter superiorities) should reveal themselves in socialism as well. However, the actual course of events in the Soviet Communist bloc disconfirms such atrocious notions of inferiority and superiority based on innate psychic characteristics or mystical theological properties. It therefore behooves us to examine classical doctrines of German sociology not simply for their generosity of spirit toward the Jews, pleasant though that may be, but also in terms of how such doctrinal positions fare in the light of a century of totalitarian social systems.

Stereotypes notwithstanding, Jews have never been entirely united in their preference for a single social system, in sharp contrast to Sombart's broad assumption of a unified procapitalist vision within Jewish life. Throughout German history, there was the struggle between religion and secularism; and in Russia, between Orthodox-Zionist and socialist-Bundist factions. Both indicate how limited was Sombart's knowledge of political preferences within Jewish life. Even after the formation of the State of Israel, such political-systemic differences remained; indeed, some might say they have even sharpened. Those who believed in a strong public sector economy and socialism characterized by the Kibbutz and the Moshav movements were in the majority, but they were opposed by those for whom Israel offered a sanctuary of free enterprise no less than the free exchange of ideas. The difference between the throbbing Jewelry Exchange on the one hand and hundreds of Kibbutzim on the other, demonstrates that Israeli people and society are not exactly unified with respect to economic goals or social systems. In short, the Jews themselves historically never made a collective decision on behalf of a single economic system, not in Israel and even less so in Europe. At most they were accidental benefactors, not conscious agents of the rise of capitalism in Western Europe and not the creators of the agrarian limitations placed upon early settlements in Palestine.

In the same connection—a point that Sombart could readily have observed but did not—a weakness of German Jews trying to ascend is that they were unable to create any unified economic position. The Jewish proletariat was extremely active in the labor movement and in the Spartacist-Socialist movement. But there was also a Jewish bourgeoisie of considerable size and prominence—a powerful, if small, minority exercising influence throughout the period of rising industrialization. What Jewish life in Europe, especially in Germany, did lack was access to state power. It was the great caveat of the fascists that the Jewish element lacked a sense of higher purpose or dedication to the nation. In their economic pursuits, either of proletarian communism or bourgeois instinctual behavior, they were presumed to lack a sense of transcendent national ends. In short, those who excluded Jews from ascending to power within the national context turned the facts about, by claiming that Jews voluntarily surrendered participation in and commitment to a national will and destiny to which they were never allowed admittance.

By the start of the twentieth century, the Jewish question was not particularly an economic question any longer. Both Weber and Sombart failed to understand the political character of anti-Semitism on the one hand and Jewish aspirations on the other. There is a great void in the classics of German sociological literature on the Jewish drive for political emancipation, because so much attention was focused upon the Jew as a purely economic creature or at times, his opposite caricature: the Jew as a radicalizing economic agent. The Dreyfus experience in France was simply not incorporated into German scholarship on the Jewish question.

As a result, it was left to Jewish classical historians to note that the character of repression within most European societies was best identified by either Jewish advancement or Jewish emancipation. In the immediate aftermath of the Bolshevik revolution, Jews were able to advance. Between 1917 and 1929, Jews were found in disproportionately high number in a wide variety of political and cultural fields. Thus, Jewish support for revolutionary causes remained correspondingly high during this period. Even with the first disturbing signs of anti-Semitism under Stalinism between 1929 and 1941, the contrast of the Jewish condition in Russia, when compared with Hitler's Germany, left little room for doubt about the marginal superiority of system.

One may infer that the economics of socialism per se did not hold back Jewish advances. Jews taught at the universities and defined the cultural apparatus during the first twelve to fourteen years of the Soviet experience. It was only with the post-World War II growth of Stalinism as an ideology of anti-Semitism that by political fiat, Jewish support for socialism was sharply curtailed. At that time, there began a concerted effort to prevent Jewish access to upward social mobility through education, such as it was within the framework of life in the USSR. Such curtailments have also taken place throughout the history of capitalism, but in a far less systematic way. One cannot simply point to an automatic mechanical correlation between the rise of capitalism or the rise of industrialism and the successful adaptation of Jews to modernity, but it can be asserted that mechanisms of repression differ under various circumstances.

What begins to be apparent is that the rise of Stalinism, its conscious purge of Jews from state power, was the political root of a new stage of anti-Semitism. This was also true in Germany under Nazism, where Hitler still had a nominally capitalist system. The private sector was highly mobilized toward statist ends, but the private sector was not suppressed, simply controlled. The Jews were suppressed through this quasi-planning mechanism. This indicates the absence of any automatic correlation or fusion of a high level of market economy with a high degree of Jewish emancipation. If that were the case, it would not have been possible to anticipate the kind of negative outcomes in both Communist and capitalist regimes as were witnessed either in Stalinist Russia or in Hitlerite Germany. Thus, one must turn to the political system, at least in part, as an explanation of and escape from the conundrum in which a pretheory of the economic Jew places the analyst.

The mechanistic tendency of classical scholars like Sombart is to speak about the Jews solely as an economic creature. More recently, others have spoken of Jews solely as political creatures, ignoring the rise of twentieth-century bureaucracy—specifically the exclusion of Jews from administrative processes in Germany and their being purged from this process in Russia. A certain flowering of Jewish culture occurred during an earlier prebureaucratic period prior to dictatorial consolidation. However, though there is no automatic correlation between a rise of socialism and a decline of Judaism, or for that matter, a rise of Judaism and a decline of socialism, to the extent that socialism—national or international—bureaucratizes social life, Jews are punished.

By virtue of their marginal social position, their collective morality, and their history (or whatever attribution one wishes to assign), Jews do not easily accept or comply with totalitarian requisites. They are nervous in the face of political or ideological extremism; they are weakened under any condition in which explanations are made based on unicausal considerations of race, religion, or class. In any social order where collective guilt is an accepted mode of reasoning, the Jews as a persecuted group fare poorly. Thus, individualism becomes a Jewish mode of survival far beyond anything envisaged by the Yankee pioneers of individual redemption.

Whether the troubles in the twentieth century come from the Left or the Right, from totalitarian temptations based on biological explanations under Hitlerism or historicist explanations under Stalinism, they leave the Jew vulnerable. Such doctrines confer an outsider or pariah status on Jews (i.e., outside the evolutionary tree or outside the railroad of history). The existence of extremism as exemplified by unlimited state power itself becomes the issue. The problem of totalitarianism, whatever its ideological derivative, becomes the problem to be examined. The charge that Jews are rootless cosmopolitans came from all directions—from Left to Right—from groups to which the concepts of pluralist beliefs and voluntary associations alike were intolerable. Wherever there is a denial of multiple allegiances and denial of voluntary associations, there is apt to follow the seeds of Jewish troubles, troubles that are aggravated by the near uniform exclusion of Jews from the administrative apparatus of a government seeking uniform allegiance.

The growth of Jewish radicalism in Europe and America was part of political integration as well as emancipation. Socialist and radical politics permitted Jewish participation in the political process outside the channels of government and administration. What distinguished German and Austrian Jews from their compatriots in England and the United States was not so much differences among Jewish ideologists but rather the permeability of Western democratic systems in England and the United States and their relative impermeability in Germany and Austria. One might argue that the United States in particular had the capacity to coopt no less than incorporate dissenting elements within Jewish life into the political mainstream, but this in itself is a definition and a statement of the structure of political democracy in one context and its absence in the older European contexts. Thus radical and socialist politics contributed to the expansion of democracy itself in the United States and to a lesser extent in France and England. To the contrary, in Germany national socialism crushed all other forms of socialism, and in Russia a national bolshevism crushed all other forms of socialism. But once again, the essence of the Jewish question increasingly shifts from economic to political forces as the twentieth century wears on. (Scholars like Sombart have remained impervious to this shift in the center of gravity within Western societies.) Thus, although the history of capitalism does not automatically bestow or enhance Jewish emancipation, Jewish existence and emancipation has contributed in many ways to the forms of capitalist development. The Jewish people persevered throughout all kinds of social systems, but their flowering has been less a function of the economics of the marketplace than of political emancipation.

Western democratic cultures, whatever their proclivities to support or criticize the Jews, presume that belief patterns such as religion and culture are part of the private realm, and hence protected against public or political assault. In other words, Jews flourish where a notion of a private culture standing alongside the civic culture is not only permissible but encouraged. Where body and soul equally belong either to the state or to its religious arm, (i.e., a state religion), Jewish existence once again becomes problematic. The Jewish question is not only related to the right of organization but to the voluntary character of organization. To engage in sectarian or private organizational activity of a religious, cultural, or ethnic sort involves a presumption within the dominant culture that pluralism or separation of church and state is a permissible posture. By contrast, the unbridled totalitarian state is decisive in determining the contour and context of the Jewish question, because such distinctions are disallowed.

Political phenomena make the Jewish question theoretically complex, since analysis becomes multivariate on its face. Jewish life is decimated when the creative opposition of the sacred and the secular, or the church and the state, are seen as having to yield to a higher set of integrated political values. Jews suffer, their numbers diminish, and immigration becomes a survival solution where the state demands integration into a national mainstream, a religious universal defined by a state religion, or a near-state religion.

Jews fare well where there is no state religion. Protestant cultures are healthier because religious pluralism inhibits the state from taking unlimited control. It is not that Protestants are more or less prejudiced than Catholics. Indeed not a few studies have established the reverse proposition. Rather, it is simply more difficult to establish a national religion in a Protestant context. The modern Jew serves the function less of Sombart's "last Calvinists" than of born-again pluralists. They are the "last Protestant" group to gain admittance to civil society. Interestingly, in nations (even those undergoing revolutionary upheavals like France) where such religious pluralism was negated or frustrated, Jewish community life suffered. The Jew in turn dramatically pluralized each Western political system. High levels of cultural fragmentation coupled with religious options are likely to find relatively benign forms of anti-Semitism coupled with a stable Jewish condition. Presumed Jewish cleverness or brilliance readily emerges under such pluralistic conditions, and such cleverness readily dissolves with equal suddeness under politically monistic or totalitarian conditions.

The Jewish Holocaust took place in Nazi Germany—a nominally capitalist economy, and the next worse fate befalling the Jews in the Soviet Union—a nominally socialist economy. Clearly, the emergence during the postwar environment of a new national state, the State of Israel, posed new problems and new levels of analysis for older Western democratic governments as well as the older totalitarian regimes. Thus, history's lessons are less about Jewish survivability as a function of capitalism, or Jewish survivability as a function of socialism, or even growth and expansion in these terms, but the dangers of state power: the unbridled role that the modern state has performed with respect to the possible free life and association of the Jews.

The unresolved dilemma in the classical sociological literature is a consequence of the absence of any appropriate consideration of the bureaucratic variable. As a result, when the so-called classical positions of eighty or one hundred years back are reexamined, they are unabashedly archaic. They present a simplistic approach to cultural survival by reducing such issues to psychic properties and cultural propensities.

The issues are far weightier than the turgid German sociological literature at the turn of the century described. Both empirical and theoretical parameters have shifted over time. The problem of the Jew has essentially become recognized as political in character and must be addressed unequivocally by future generations of scholars in such terms. The role of state power and bureaucratic authority provides the essential social conditioning of Jewish life, not this group's presumed innate psychic survival properties based on clever economic manipulations. The point is not what is good for the Jews or what is good for the Germans. Zero-sum game formulas miss the point. German citizens took many religious shapes; Jews after all saw themselves as good Germans. It took a herculean, dedicated organizational effort by the German state under Nazism to break down this association, to disengage being Jewish from being German. The role of the Jews in relation to those who controlled and managed this Nazi system became a manufactured issue precisely because Jewish integration into the German economy during the Weimar period became so complete, in contrast to Jewish alienation from the German state.

German Jews were decreasingly unique in custom and manners as the Weimar epoch wore on. They began to take for granted sameness, not difference, with their fellow Germans. Both Weber and Sombart missed this important fact. Jewish success and failure was measured in terms of German values, entrepreneurial achievement, political participation, and cultural innovation. The Nazi resentment was thus not a function of Jewish difference but of the extraordinary degree of Jewish integration into German economic business and labor. For this reason, the destruction of the Jews had to proceed lockstep with the destruction of democracy in Germany and Central Europe generally.

Anti-Semitism has become a special illustration of a rising xenophobic Russian nationalism. This fact is coupled with a belief that any form of pluralism is alien to Soviet national or international ambitions. While nationalism coupled with authoritarianism leads to the dismemberment of the Jewish people as an entity within Soviet life, it remains unlikely that genocide will be practiced upon its Jewish population—not necessarily because of ideological tolerance, but because there is no class or bureaucratic need to do so. The Jews have been effectively disenfranchised by more than sixty years of Communist rule.

They have been removed from the sources of power, military and bureaucratic as well as political. Therefore the function of Soviet anti-Semitism, while not dissimilar to German nationalism in its claims, does not necessarily have the same dire genocidal consequences. This may be small comfort to those who began with high expectations for Soviet life and the Jewish role therein. But for those who have come to measure events in terms of survival and not progress, the distinction between national communism and national socialism is important. Mistakes at this level are dangerous and not just intellectually frivolous, since the gulf between harassment and even incarceration on the one side and outright genocide on the other is as wide as the distinction between life and death.

The Soviet system did not have as its prime aim the elimination of Jewish values so much as the destruction of the democratic potential for socialism as a whole. As a result, Jewish hopes for emancipation and national liberation were swept away as a byproduct of Soviet policies. The Jewish curse was naiveté, a belief in the legitimacy of the symbols of socialist power. That curse reached its apex under Stalinism, which in turn took seriously only the actualities of state power. When ideologists of the Nazi Third Reich were locating German ills in the Jewish Question, in a quite parallel fashion, the Bolshevik Right came to locate Russian ills in cosmopolitanism (read "The Jewish Question"), while the Bolshevik Left was busily arguing mythic problems of class deviation represented by anti-Semitism.

The question of Jewish survivability, Jewish growth, or Jewish inputs within a given culture can no longer be put in terms of the maturation of the larger economic system, as it was at he start of the century. It is not that economic history somehow is irrelevant, but rather that the economy itself has to be situated in a political network in which Jewish lives, faith, and thoughts come to be determined by the struggle for elementary democracy itself. We possess and have been bequeathed an economic literature but a political anomaly. Therefore, without minimizing just how brilliantly the remarks of Weber and Sombart were formulated, the dismissal of political context led to a misunderstanding or misexplanation of real world events. That is why Sombart in particular fell into disrepute. His analysis did not explain the political inspiration for German anti-Semitism nor its blockage of Jews to the political process.

If we are going to resurrect an analytical framework locating the Jewish Question only in the development of modern capitalism, such a framework will fail in terms of its explanatory purpose. The core issue is Jewish survivability in the development of postindustrial societies. To reify discourse in terms of modern capitalism versus a more modern communism is wasteful and a dangerous form of abstract polarization over the Jewish Question. Such a view presupposes the world of the marketplace as the only world in which Jews can possibly survive—a prima facie false presupposition. Its converse, the assumption of communism triumphant, leads to a critique of the free market instead of a rejection of clever, intellectualized forms of anti-Semitism. What is required is a reconsideration of the Jewish Question as a function of political democracy and state power. Only then will the reductionistic myth of the clever, self-serving economic Jew, a myth which helped fuel the Holocaust, finally be put to a well-deserved and eternal rest.

From *Modern Judaism*, vol. 6, no. 1 (1986), pp. 13–25.

49

Jewish Soul on Ice*

Timerman, Jacobo

Let me start with an admission: I am not enamored of the species of writing known as prison literature. The genre has, to be sure, produced some remarkable documents. Nonetheless, such essays tend to be exceedingly self-serving and self-aggrandizing. Too often, reality is ensconced rather than enhanced. Even the best prison literature, moreover, is Manichean: certain of goods and evils, lights and darks.

I would be less than candid if I suggested that *Prisoner Without a Name, Cell Without a Number* entirely escapes these vices. For example, it is dangerous hyperbole to claim that Argentina is in a condition of barbarism akin to the worst days of Hitlerism and Stalinism. Jacobo Timerman's repeated assertions to this effect blur the distinction between genocidal totalitarian systems and the considerably different bureaucratic-authoritarian system that exists in Argentina. The cacophony of political movements and ideologies, not to mention confusion of goals and policies (well documented by Timerman), only highlights the dissimilarities between contemporary Argentina and Europe's archetypical twentieth-century dictatorships. Indeed, the fact that whatever the outrages perpetuated against his mind and body under incarceration, Timerman at least had the right to personal suffering, marks him as a man who fortunately did not experience the kind of impersonal mayhem committed against millions in Germany between 1933–1945 and in Russia between 1929–1952.

Having registered this caveat, let me hasten to say that his book is, as Arthur Miller has noted, "a lyrical outcry, riveting to read and chilling to contemplate." Timerman is no ordinary political prisoner, but one for whom the pen has always been mightier than the sword. A lifelong journalist, editor and publisher of the newspaper *La Opinion* and founder of two magazines, the author is a writer who was imprisoned, not a prisoner who discovered the power of language. Nor is his book written to enlist others in a cause or

---

* Jacobo Timerman, *Prisoner Without a Name, Cell Without a Number* (New York: Alfred A. Knopf, 1981), pp. 164.

Jacobo Timerman, *The Longest War: Israel in Lebanon* (New York: Alfred A. Knopf, 1982), pp. 167.

to influence policy. It is throughout a description of a man's ordeal that at the same time is an accurate representation of a political catastrophe: the failure of Argentina, God's country, to evolve according to the great expectations with which it began this century. In telling his own story, Timerman documents Argentina's persistent revolutions of falling expectations. He has a sharp eye for detail, plus an unflinching capacity to name the names of his tormentors; he speaks with a frankness that helps illumine a national calamity no less than a personal tragedy.

Since the subject of this volume is also its object, the work has to be seen as an autobiography. Argentina has been able to absorb every kind of political ideology save one: liberalism. It was Timerman's great misfortune to be an old-fashioned liberal. As a result, he writes in an uncompromising way about a militarized state where the factions can only be described in terms of fascism of the Left and fascism of the Right. His captors and occasionally the captive himself seem somewhat confused by this acknowledged Zionist persisting in his support for Left causes in the hemisphere and throughout the world. His interrogators want everything about Timerman to make perfect sense. "Which branch of the Jewish conspiracy did I belong to—the Israeli, Russian, or North American? A true dilemma, since I was born in Russia, had traveled to Israel, and was extremely friendly with the U.S.Embassy."

For Timerman, the problem in Argentina is less one of Left or Right forms of terrorism than of the near-complete displacement of civility by barbarism. Indeed, his final assessment is that Argentina cannot be viewed in political terms because it remains fixated in a prepolitical stage of barbarism. In a curious way, Timerman owes much to the tradition of Ortega Gasset and Jorge Luis Borges. Underlying the autobiographical is a liberal irreverence for quasi-populist politics. There is an unyielding contempt for a society that cannot distinguish between the democratic and the authoritarian or the civil and the barbaric. At this level, the book raises issues far beyond its capacity to resolve.

Timerman himself is deeply troubled by the behavior of the Jewish community of Argentina. He repeatedly alludes to the fact that its leaders preferred to negotiate in silence, through low-profile diplomacy, rather than make the issue of anti-Semitism a public debate. While Timerman's concerns are correct, the quiescence of the Buenos Aires Jewish community stems precisely from the conditions he himself describes as characterizing the nation as a whole. It is difficult to image anti-Semitism becoming part of the public discourse, particularly when the actual history of the Jews in Argentina is Liken into account. Their participation has been largely restricted to the economic realm; they have been denied effective entry into the political realm (according to Timerman, virtually nonexistent) or the military (the preserve of Spanish and Italian ethnic groupings). The relative ease with which Timerman's newspaper empire was dismantled is indicative of this isolation.

It is not only, as Timerman would have us believe, that the sole point of reference for Argentinean Jewish leaders was the Holocaust, but that the community had been nurtured to accept its political impotence along with all Argentines. Argentina is a nation whose political processes are constantly being subverted by an unsteady and unresponsive ruling elite. When the Jew is "a man under total suspicion" in a society characterized by aggressive militarism and state terrorism, asserting democratic debate and human rights becomes problematic. The Jewish community would have required a positive assessment of social and political forces to place anti-Semitism on the public agenda; in a nation without allies there was not much more that could be done. After all, it was simple for Timerman to support Castro. Had Castro supported Timerman, that would have been news. Alas, even those whom Timerman chose to back had nothing but anti-Semitic diatribes of their own to register.

If there is a surprising element in Timerman's memoir, it is the intensity of his Jewish conscience. This did not come about simply in response to his police tormentors and their constant emphasis on Christian nationhood. It was inspired by the centrality of anti-Semitism in mobilizing Right and Left alike. Perhaps nothing better illustrates Timerman's predicament that the recent statement of Adolfo Perez Esquivel, winner of the 1980 Nobel Peace Prize, on the occasion of one of the largest human rights demonstrations held in Argentina since the military assumed direct political power. On April 30, 1981 the Mothers of Plaza de Mayo were told by Esquivel, "We are here in solidarity to find a just solution to this problem [of accounting for anywhere from 6,000–15,000 missing people]. This is a march for Christian peace."

It is hard to imagine Timerman in like circumstances claiming the event to be a march for Jewish peace. Even Jewish martyrs for Argentine democracy, and they are a disproportionately high number of the missing victims, must be draped in Christian imagery. No wonder Timerman, more in despair than expectation, takes Argentine democrats (like Maximo Gainza, the editor of *La Prensa*) to task. It is their silences and sufferances that make the Jew "a man under total suspicion."

There are some strange anomalies in *Prisoner Without a Name*—starting with Timerman, who has an entirely Enlightenment notion of *civitas*, being forced into a captivity where all sense of such civilities had to be suspended for survival. When an agreement for his release was reached between hard-line military and legalistic government factions, the agreement provided that he be stripped of his Argentine citizenship and sent abroad. At the moment of his expulsion, he was placed under the supervision of Israeli security officers who knew no Spanish. He knew no Hebrew then. It took a translator to explain to Timerman the "conspirator" that he was going "home."

Most of all, though, this book demonstrates the triumph of human will over tremendous adversity. It contains so many beautiful passages of transcendent clarity that one almost feels it is unfair to offer just a few examples. On dictatorship: "The chief obsession of the totalitarian mind lies in its need for the world to be clear cut and orderly. Any subtlety, contradiction, or complexity upsets and confuses this notion and becomes intolerable." On action: "Being is more important than remembering. I believe that the reminder of Jewish tragedies, punctiliously invoked by the Jewish community against its adversaries, has been futile in overcoming the paralysis and panic than envelopes it." On politics: "It is a struggle between civilization and barbarism within a country. This barbarism—whether it be private or governmental, civil or military—must obviously be eradicated before it is possible to enter civilization."

It is a measure of Timerman's continuing loyalties that despite the humiliation and denigration he suffered, despite every effort to deprive him of an Argentine identity in a ceaseless attempt to demonstrate that being a Jew is antithetical to national allegiances, his closing remarks reveal him to be an Argentine patriot:

> I know that the Argentine nation will not cease to weep for its dead, because throughout its often brutal history, it has remained loyal to its tragedies. I know that it will succeed in overcoming the paranoids of every extreme, the cowards of every sector. And it will learn how to be happy.

That this conclusion emerges from a figure systematically tormented and tortured itself demonstrates the extraordinary absurdity of the charges that he is an enemy of the state, a conspirator, an antichrist, Marxist, Zionist. Such charges are a litmus test of the paranoid style. Timerman, stripped of his citizenship, finally turns out to be a dedicated son. Perhaps God does still live in Argentina—albeit incognito.

Jacobo Timerman's first book haunts his new one. *The Longest War: Israel in Lebanon* exhibits the same passions and the same furies that motivated *Prisoner Without a Name, Cell Without a Number.* Sorely lacking, though, is the same knowledge.

Whatever one's feelings about Timerman's memoir of personal repression, it was unmistakably a deep response to a lifetime spent on the firing line of Argentine society. This is not true of his reaction to Israeli society. He concedes that the opinions of students, intellectuals, and immigrants, as well as newspaper articles, must be translated or explained to him. Consequently, the bearing of witness that was so compellingly rendered when he related his experiences as a prisoner of the Argentine military, emerges in his last book as strident and derivative.

Timerman's slim volume—two-thirds of which appeared originally in the *New Yorker*—is less an analysis of the assault on Lebanon launched last June than its title suggests, and more one man's searching critique of that war and of an Israel he has barely digested. He addresses the Israeli public in the grand tradition of a politician seeking approbation rather than as a journalist or analyst of current national policy. Characteristically, he treats academics largely with disdain yet is not above hobnobbing with them or gratuitously invoking their authority when the occasion demands, "We cut pathetic and ridiculous figures, Michael Walzer and I."

Although the book is divided into chapters, the rationale for them is difficult to assess. At the start, each chapter corresponds to one week of the war effort, but any sense of chronology gradually disappears in a paroxysm of stream of consciousness writing. Chapter four, the fifth week of the campaign, is dominated by ruminations on the Nazis. In chapter five, week six, Timerman is moved by weary, disillusioned troops returning from the battle front. Chapter six, the seventh week of conflict, plumbs "images of fascism" and the loss of Israel's innocence, not to mention its democratic values.

Timerman's imagination roams unbridled through the remainder of the book—chapters seven through ten plus epilogues entitled "Rage and Hope" and "The Massacre." Several random insights make one realize what he is capable of when exercising self-control. His observations on Likud economic policies that substitute financial speculation for productive investment, on politically-influenced hiring in Israel's bureaucracy and state controlled industries, and on the collapse of civility that he sees spreading throughout the society would all certainly be worth pursuing. His appreciation of the risks inherent in the sort of reactionary partisanship that has underwritten Prime Minister Menachem Begin's government is also provocative, even if already noted by many other commentators.

The book's highlight is its description of the anguish engendered by the bombing of West Beirut and the massacres at Sabra and Shatila, its portrayal of the disastrous impact those events had on the ordinary Israeli's sense of Jewishness. As he did in his earlier work, Timerman exhibits a remarkable ability to capture whole the soul of a nation, or at any rate the psychology that informs its polity. For this alone, *The Longest War* deserves consideration—particularly since the country in question is one where the national psyche counts far so much. The Israeli citizen, in defining his place on the map, must regularly ask himself whether he continues to play a role in history.

Unfortunately, psychological discernment is undermined by sociological vacuity. Timerman writes as if he invented Israel, or really not even Israel, but a new land that did not exist prior to his arrival close to three years ago. He conveys no sense of either the long history of the Jews or the short chronicle of their modern state. He ignores previous Arab-Israeli wars and earlier attempts at forging a binational arrangement between Israelis and Palestinians. The reporting here is no more than crude empiricism that sometimes degenerates into downright conceit. Timerman offers a vision of "we"—meaning Israel—and the Palestinians rebuilding Lebanon. He is unable to grasp that Lebanon can only be rebuilt by the Lebanese, who soon may be free to do so in the absence of a massive Palestine Liberation Organization (PLO) presence, a dominant

Syrian Army, and Israeli meddling. His reductionism erases the multiplicity of issues and interested parties extant, leaving simply Israeli "we"s and Palestinian "they"s, synthesized—with a look toward the brighter future—by "us."

Timerman's extended essay is mired in highly personalistic judgments, too. The fighting in Lebanon is always Sharon's War. Like the Scarlet Pimpernel, "Sharon is everywhere." While Israel's defense minister of course favored the invasion, it certainly was not some personal vendetta. Sharon's interview with Oriana Fallaci made that much clear. From Timerman's depiction, one might think that Sharon is another Juan Peron, an analogy that is ludicrous on its face. The author's overwhelming anger blinds him to what might be a more salient line of criticism.

The ample tragedy of the Lebanon war is less a moral than a military matter. For the first time, the Israel Defense Forces (IDF) proved incapable of successfully executing a surgical strike, of invading Lebanese territory, and routing the PLO without dire consequences for the local population. Until last June, such Israeli military operations had always avoided the agony of civilian casualties and protracted occupation, with pinpoint attacks on enemy forces and strategic targets. An account that focused on this breakdown of military professionalism, it seems to me, would be at once a moving and reasonable protest. But Timerman is so absorbed in self-serving posturing that all complexity must be smothered beneath a landslide of unsubstantiated denunciation. Early in the book, he himself remarks that Israel is a country of great verbal violence—then he proceeds to further the tradition mightily, using a self-righteous mace in the place of analytical argument.

Ultimately, the work is consumed by its egoism. People, places, and occurrences are aggrandized, internalized, made part of Timerman's experience. The marginal nature of his involvement in important events is masked by every device from name-dropping ("I was talking to the writer, Amos Oz,") to converting weaknesses into strengths ("My ignorance of Hebrew is no problem.")

Timerman discovers the truth driving around, picking up "representative hitchhikers," and within a few days comprehends the views of all factions of Israeli public opinion. His prose is harsh, acerbic, first person. In one four-page stretch, nearly every paragraph is an opinionated outburst: "It is a shame that... We are choking here. . . . As you drive along. . . I don't exactly converse. . . I think. . . I believe. . . I am convinced." This deadening style compels one to wonder whether a similar extended diatribe by a less celebrated author would be serialized in the *New Yorker* or be described as "A major, urgent addition to the Knopf fall list."

Beyond all this, no volume of shrillness can disguise a certain loss of nerve from *Prisoner Without a Name* to *The Longest War*. Timerman is "courageous" enough to compare Israel to Argentina and, inevitably, to recondemn the Vietnam War as the unmitigated abomination of our generation. But he cannot respond to his own son, who as a member of the IDF expresses his reluctance to return to the front for a second tour of duty. Timerman is resigned to leaving the young man "in the hands of the . . . Israeli Army," (which sentenced him to 28 days in prison when he decided not to go back).

Timerman ends his book with an appeal to world Jewry:

> Only the world's Jewish people. . . can now do something for us. The Diaspora Jews who have maintained the values of our moral and cultural traditions—those values now trampled on here by intolerance and by Israeli nationalism—should establish a Jewish tribunal to pass judgment on Begin, Sharon, Eytan and the entire general staff of the Israeli Armed Forces. This alone could be the means of working free of the sickness that is destroying Israel, and, perhaps, of preserving Israel's future.

Although this makes a neat Wagnerian exit, the reality is that Israelis have devoted a great deal more energy to the moral, legal, and intellectual implications of Lebanon than have the Diaspora Jews. In a country of some 4 million, a rally of 400,000 demanded the investigation of their government's complicity in a war atrocity—surely an extraordinary political outpouring. It is doubtful that a reasonable fraction of that number could be similarly mobilized among, say, American Jews. This does not necessarily dispute the appropriateness of a peace-now stance; it simply questions the assumption of Israeli immorality.

The sorrow and frustration Timerman succumbs to are valid reactions, shared by many who saw the war in Lebanon as an action affording limited military gains and involving unexamined political risks. Nonetheless, a fair treatment would not consider Lebanon in a vacuum. Direct effects of the invasion have included the removal of a chronic mortal danger to citizens in northern Israel, a critical weakening of Syrian influence, and a significant softening of Jordan's position concerning the West Bank and the recognition of Israel. Indirectly, the war was related to Jerusalem's commitment to the Camp David accords—already dramatically demonstrated by the return of Sinai to Egypt. None of these elements are even remotely factored into Timerman's equation.

Being Jewish may impose special moral requirements upon those who, like Timerman, proffer advice. It does not, however, relieve political leaders of the responsibility to prevent degradation from within and destruction from without. Israel under Begin has confronted external threats more effectively than internal ones, and Timerman might even be right to declare that the process of bolstering the frontiers has led to a certain debasement at home. But by raising this contradiction and leaving it unresolved, Timerman merely underlines the fact that it is not he who has to make the difficult decisions.

The Longest War could have survived Timerman's personality. It is doomed by his impulse to saddle policy options with unrealistic ethical imperatives. Far from pointing Israel toward peace and tranquility, his wartime diary can only exacerbate the tensions that so distress him. New York *Times* columnist Anthony Lewis noted of the *New Yorker* pieces: "Timerman writes with the authority of a survivor." Although that statement would be eminently true of *Prisoner Without a Name*, it would be more accurate to say that *The Longest War* is written with the authority of an ideologue and the fanaticism of an isolate.

Timerman is, after all, an accidental hero. His is the self-image of the radical reformer and secularist par excellence. But to his captors and his opponents he is primarily a dangerous Jew. Timerman intuits this strange dichotomy, but he cannot give voice to this disjunction between self-image and social punishment. Thus, he is held hostage by a Judaism scarcely known, while seeking to fuse it to a secular enlightenment vision that Jews are in the habit of finding demeaning of their interests. The screams and shouts that emanate from these pages are thus better seen as psychic cries in the night rather than social demands for justice at high noon.

From *The New Leader*, vol. 64, no. 11 (1981), pp. 16–17; and from *The New Leader*, vol. 66, no. 2 (1983), pp. 15–17.

50

Anti-Semitic Linchpins*

Yanov, Alexander

One of the strange truths about the Soviet Union is that, despite its strong ideological commitment to the unity of theory and practice, its system has developed in a pure theoretical void. Theorizing is apparently something one does about the West and in the West. Still, the loud silence about the general purpose and pattern of Soviet life remains a puzzlement for its adversaries and a predicament for its supporters.

We now know that, though it may be possible to study or examine the U.S.S.R. from a Marxist perspective, the costs in intellectual terms are too high and the results too clumsy. It thus becomes far simpler to build up a general theory from inductively available information. The first big step in that direction was taken more than twenty years ago by Milovan Djilas, that authentic genius of socialist and nationalist life in Eastern Europe, who appreciated the degree to which the political elites organized around the Communist party to form a distinct exploitative economic class and social sector. But his ideas, resting on a rather modest concept of the concentration of political power, did not dispel the myth of Marxism as an explanation of all things Soviet. Indeed, given Djilas' longstanding background in official Communist party politics in Yugoslavia, it is small wonder that he managed to so thoroughly break the shackles of dogmatism and provide the first major class analysis of socialism as a stratification system.

It is only with the maturation of postwar Soviet life, the evolution of the society along all two familiar lines-external aggressivity and internal satisfaction of consumer wants-that the actual parameters of Soviet society are revealed. It becomes clear that the binding ingredients in Soviet society are national rather than class in character. Indeed, class contradictions are as apparent and as sharp as in Western societies, hence the need for a return to the nationalist pivot.

---

* Alexander Yanov, *The Russian New Right: Right-Wing Ideologies in the Contemporary U.S.S.R.* (Berkeley: Institute of International Studies/University of California, 1978), pp. 185.

Emmanuel Todd, The Final *Fall: An Essay on the Decomposition of the Soviet Sphere* (New York: Karz Publishers, 1979), pp. 236.

Meanwhile, Western images of Soviet life have changed dramatically. The older tolerances dissolve as the newer tyrannies become apparent. Even a veritable mandarin of American Marxism, Paul Sweezy, is now moved to say:

> They have not eliminated classes except in a purely verbal sense. The state has not disappeared—no one could expect it to, except in a still distant future—but on the contrary has become more and more the central and dominant institution of society. Each nation interprets proletarian internationalism to mean support of its own interests and policies as interpreted by itself. They go to war not only in self-defense but to impose their will on other countries. All of this, I think, is now fairly obvious, and of course it is no exaggeration to say that by now the anomalies have become so massive and egregious that the result has been a deep crisis in Marxian theory.

The merit of each of the books under review is that their authors set out, writing at different times and under difficult circumstances, and addressing themselves to specific topics. *The Russian New Right* is at once brilliant and exasperating in its style, which can generously be labeled pre-social scientific. The mixture of analysis, introspection, and retrospection in every paragraph, coupled with anecdotal material at times relevant while at other times random, makes this difficult reading. This said, one must also candidly note that the work could hardly have been written in any other way, given the author and the subject—for Alexander Yanov is one of a growing number of Soviet Jewish political exiles to the West. And just as scholars like Herzen found a home in Paris or London in the last century, the current crop have settled mostly in New York, Berkeley, or Tel Aviv. Yanov wrote this while attached to the Institute of International Studies at The University of California at Berkeley.

His essential thesis, which has created a considerable stir in the international community, is simply this: Marxism has been replaced by nationalism as the fundamental analytic and emotional tool of Soviet ideology. Yanov leaves no doubt in the reader's mind that this "new Right" thinking represents a fundamental impulse in Russian life. What characterizes it is not so much its emphasis on nationalism—which is part and parcel of the dominant tendency of Russian history—but the belief that the Soviet Union is not yet prepared, if it ever will be, for democratic life. So the new Right emphasizes a union of nationalism and religiosity that harks back to a long Russian tradition of Pan-Slavism. The rightists claim the dissident movement outlived its usefulness because it lacked the "affirmative" and "positive" conception of a Russian nationalism that could only be supplied by the "grandeur" of a "new Christian world" in which the Russian nation becomes the "instrument of God." Yanov appropriately points out that "no special Russian alternative to democracy has been known in history; the search goes on with a vengeance."

Yanov has put his finger on the soft underbelly of Soviet ideology, compelling its patterns of development to be increasingly inspired by nationalist ideals, governments and wars. The reasons he gives are succinct: the intellectual collapse of Marxism (or at least the alienation of Soviet opinion from Marxism), its inability to mobilize masses into any form of action, and the corruption of Westernism in Russian life (i.e., the reduction of the Marxist notion of abundance to a vulgar consumptive impulse that overwhelmed traditional values). This transformation of Marxism into multinationalism helps to explain the renaissance of Russian nationalism, a phenomenon not unlike the rise of nationalism in the West, but more profound given the special character of Soviet power. As Solzhenitsyn recently remarked, "we had learnt in a hard school, under the dragon's yoke not to give in—whereas in the West, the dragon has only breathed at them from a distance."

The difficulty is not so much in Yanov's analysis but in his depiction of the new Right. He does not tell us who represents the Left; presumably the center is the bureaucratic apparatus itself with its continued allegiance to the canons of Marxism-Leninism. But since even this technical stratum has adopted many positions of the presumed new Right, including national and political exclusivism coupled with a fierce anti-Semitism, the real problem lies not so much in the juxtaposition of Marxist internationalism with Russian nationalism, but the lack of possibilities within the Soviet Union for an alternative posture, in short, whether the rhetoric of Right, center, and Left has any specific meaning in a Soviet context.

The facts Yanov presents tend to confirm that the entire society has swung toward a xenophobic nationalism. The problems of the Soviet Union are not much different from those of any other country, though the forms may be different—internationalism versus nationalism, involvement in world affairs versus isolation, secular-social trends versus religious-mystical trends. Yanov is describing not only the special crisis of Russian history but the general crisis of world empires in the twentieth century.

Though *The Russian New Right* may fall short in its analytic value, it is a vigorous and essential analysis of contemporary ideological tendencies inside the USSR, far above most Western commentaries in quality. It is highly recommended as a bracing introduction to the inside of Soviet cultural life.

The Final Fall: An Essay on the Decomposition of the Soviet Sphere illustrates the problems of working within Marxist categories to explain the coming demise of the Soviet dictatorship. The resort to the language of crisis and contradiction leads one to expect an impending doom and Armageddon that makes me doubt the decomposition of the USSR is actually at hand. Still, the book is a serious and worthwhile effort to create a general theory of Soviet and East Europe societies. Also, in terms of understanding the enduring character of Stalinism as part of a new Russian nationalism, Todd's effort complements

Yanov's quite well. For example, the distinction Todd draws between the Russian core and the East European periphery is an extremely useful device to explain the Stalinist impulse behind Russian nationalism.

Todd works within the curious presumption that the problem is to crack the Communist system of non-information and that this involves high access to intelligence sources. But we have more information on the Soviet Union, more hard and soft data, than on any other nation on earth. Information is not at all the center of the problem. That Todd sees it as such relates to his belief in a strange sort of demographic determinism, in which the Soviet crisis is somehow made self-evident by a slight rise in infant mortality only in a three-year frame between 1970 and 1973. Apparently he considers it more revealing than a thousand political agendas, yet he uses a three-year time frame and a percentile rise that is only a fraction of one percent. He emphasizes this isolated demographic factor in both the text and the Afterward. But since population change may not correlate with other variables, such as rates of economic development, one must seriously doubt this line of reasoning on methodological grounds.

The slowdown in the rate of Soviet industrial production is common to advanced societies the world over and not necessarily indicative of an irreconcilable contradiction. As societies become more advanced, rates of growth decline even though the G.N.P. remains high. A nation at takeoff point will show much higher rates of growth than mature economies. As a result, it is extremely dangerous to infer the collapse of a society from a lowering rate of investment or industrial growth over a short period of time. Marxology has repeatedly failed to explain the crisis of Western colonialism, and there is little evidence that a similar Marxist analysis will be more valuable in explaining the crisis of the Soviet empire. Thus, the prediction of imminent Soviet collapse is dangerous wish-fulfillment in the guise of social science.

Yanov and Todd agree that anti-Semitism is the crucial linchpin of the ideology of Soviet nationalism. But while Yanov regards China as the USSR's chief enemy, Todd thinks Germany occupies that place. It might have been better if both had recognized the immensity of the Soviet Union and its fear of nations that historically have been its enemies and have occupied either a border land position or a presence on Soviet soil. As in the case of most Western societies, Marxist analysis such as Todd's tends to dismiss the claims put forth by Soviet authorities as a basic explanation for the policy-making framework adopted. It does little good to simply claim, as Todd does, that torpor and nonchalance overwhelm administrative structure, and that the Communist state does not wither away, but rots. This kind of exaggerated reaction to Soviet society—which has been characteristic of vulgar Marxism—may be more emotionally satisfying when applied to the

Soviet Union than the United States, but intellectually it leads to the same cul-de-sac: the same inability to take seriously the potential for survival and the adaptive quality of imperfect societies and to exaggerate the apocalyptic vision of collapse and despair.

One might argue that big-power nationalism is ideologically satisfying because industrial societies generally are successful in fulfilling the wishes and ambitions of its citizens. When nationalism provides a vested interest—as it has for a long time in the United States and as it is now doing on a more modest level in the Soviet Union—only then does a sense of vestedness lead to rapid nationalism and hyperpatriotism. In part, nationalism emerges as a dominant concept not to recapture what was once lost in combat but to preserve what has been gained in industrial development. Neither Yanov nor Todd appreciates the sense in which nationalism is linked not so much to integrating mechanisms based on backwardness but to mobilizing mechanisms linked to progress and growth. That is why the fusion of nationalism to a new Right is so easily shifted to a new orthodoxy—based on the maintenance rather than the overthrow of Soviet power.

One dangerous inference that has recently been drawn is that the end of Marxism-Leninism, the theoretical underpinning of Soviet internationalism in a declining, Western, imperial context, has been replaced by anti-Semitism as the official ideology of the Soviet system. This is not confirmed by any of these books. Rather, anti-Semitism becomes a special illustration of a rising xenophobic Russian nationalism, a belief that any form of pluralism is alien to Russian national goals.

While nationalism coupled with authoritarianism leads to the dismemberment of the Jewish people as an entity within Soviet life, it is unlikely that genocide will be practiced upon its Jewish population—not necessarily because of ideological tolerance but because there is no class or bureaucratic need to do so. The Jews have effectively been disenfranchised by more than sixty years of socialism. They have been removed from sources of power, military and bureaucratic as well as political. Therefore the function of Soviet anti-Semitism, while not dissimilar to German nationalism in its claims, does not necessarily have the same dire genocidal consequences. This may be small comfort to those who began with high expectations for Soviet life and the Jewish role therein. But for those who have come to measure events in terms of survival and not progress, it is important to make the distinction between national communism and national socialism; mistakes at this level are dangerous and not just intellectually frivolous, since the gulf between harassment and even incarceration on one side and outright genocide on the other is as wide as the distinction between life and death.

These works explain well the limits and character of the Soviet authoritarian model. They do not make for pleasant reading. After sixty years of Communist silence on the Russian Question, they attempt to generate a workable and plausible theory of Soviet practice and thus should be deeply appreciated within the context of radical Western thought. There is other, similar work going on. But one could do a lot worse than employ Yanov's and Todd's books as a starting point in developing a general theory of the rise and fall of the Soviet empire; at least in its pure totalitarian form.

From *Present Tense*, vol. 7, no. 1 (1979), pp. 60–62.

Part IV

Social Research as Ideology and Utopia

51

Sociological Pragmatism*

Becker, Howard S.

Fame can, and usually does, have strange effects on sociologists: it leads either to a relaxation of personal and professional drives, in which case the sociological enterprise is done with noticeable sophistication, or it can so heighten the thirst for accolades and acknowledgements that the tasks and even the tools of sociology become a burden to further effort, in which case sociology is subverted in the name of higher realms or abandoned altogether. These papers, conveying as they do two decades of work, reveal a man who is increasingly at case with himself and his materials. Even the choice of title indicates the sense of proportion and balance that has characterized Becker's efforts of recent years.

The papers from the earlier years, particularly those done with James Carper in the mid-1950s, in their very self-consciousness of being novel, are also the least interesting. The three papers coauthored on the elements and development of identification with an occupation (chapters 12, 13, and 14) summarize problems of adjustment of engineers, physiologists, and philosophers so briefly and ineptly that substantive issues in career choice can simply not be explained. Instead, the materials are summarized by noting "that conflict does not necessarily occur in assuming an occupational identity; when conflict does occur, it centers around disparities between parental and occupational expectations." Unfortunately, such an abstract explanation does not readily come to terms with specific problems of adjustments to the materials that await the would-be engineers, physiologists, or philosophers—or even the question of why parents react differently to particular occupational choices. The problem is not conventional occupational expectations, but hardheaded commercial expectations, a choice more likely cherished by parents than by students. Hence, what may present itself as a family dispute is more nearly a differential response to the ideal of economic security. The discounting of economic factors in social decisions permeates these earlier papers—a weakness

---

* Howard S. Becker, *Sociological Work: Method and Substance*, (Chicago, Ill.: Aldine Publishing, 1970), pp. 358.

that is less noticeable as Becker moves along to research in deviance, where economic considerations loom so large.

I mention problems in his early papers not to prove my objectivity by being hypercritical. There is no need to do so. Becker is a close personal friend, and he would remain so, even if he were not among those very few sociologists of this century who are leaving an indelible stamp on the discipline as a whole. What is intriguing is to chart the path from talent to brilliance—from sociology as a style of engagement. By 1965, Becker was working on noncollege youth and specifically on conflicts that are not so much a function of familial or professional tensions a reflection of social class and organization.

> Perhaps because he is interested in the subject matter and not in more abstract goals, the trade-school student may have a problem not characteristically faced by college students. He may have to be concerned because he is interested mainly in the utility of the knowledge he is getting, the maximum amount of knowledge out of his teacher. When we consider that trade schools are profit-making organizations, it seems a possibility that teachers tend to string out the presentation of substantive material so as to spread it over a longer period of time and get more tuition.

As early as 1952, in discussing teacher-pupil relations, Becker appreciated the fact that all institutions have established assumptions about the character of society and the persons with whom they deal. By 1965, he managed to get at these assumptions and make them available to that public interested in problems of education. Indeed, one might read the volume as a treatise in the sociology of education, particularly if one considers learning as the essential core of education.

The first section of the book, "Problems of Sociological Methods," presents the most satisfying writing in the volume. Becker is one of the foremost ethnographers in the profession. Therefore, these papers, some of them prepared specifically for this volume and others that have appeared in relatively inaccessible places, should interest those who wish to follow his career line. At the least, sociologists will proceed with caution when describing survey research and questionnaire data as hard, and field study and life history techniques as soft. Becker is much more apt to turn this around. For essentially he says that the type of analysis is not uniquely determined by level of precision. Beyond that, there are few forms of analysis available to the sociologist that are harder or tougher to refute than field work gleaned in interaction between investigators and investigated.

The phrase sociological method may be a rubric that covers more than it can possibly sustain. Chapters 3, 4, and 5, respectively on field work evidence, life history, and the scientific mosaic and social observation could be classified just as easily as theory and perhaps as part of the sociology of knowledge. Articles

6, 7, and 8, on the nature of a profession, problems in the publication of field studies, and the famous "Whose Side are We On?" all have at least as much to do with ethics as with methods; in fact, perhaps a good deal more so. Even the first two papers, entitled "On Methodology" and "Problems of Inference and Proof in Participant Observation," contribute to fundamental sociological theory; particularly in their examination of how frameworks are chosen, the kind of hidden assumptions sociologists make in their work, the process of developing hypotheses, the credibility of informants, and the construction of social systems. Nonetheless, Becker's strategic decision in calling these papers methodological should be understood in a strategic context. For if one man's ethic is another man's nonsense, the same is not true when it comes to method. Perhaps it should be. Nonetheless, since we have made a fetish of methodology, Becker is quite proper in saying that his own approach should be considered on methodological grounds rather than on ethical grounds—in which case, the word method simply comes to stand for what is objectively true.

All the noisy assaults upon "Whose Side Are We On?" have reflected a seeming incapacity to recognize that behind the assertion of the need for partisanship is not a reductionistic or tendentious desire for the advancement of a political ideology but rather an attempt to get beyond partisanship. The aim is to reestablish an equilibrium in the evaluation of those who are ruled and those who do the ruling. The identification with the poor and with those labeled as deviant or marginals is often intended to redress a one-hundred-year imbalance in the history of Western sociology, which assumes a one-to-one relationship between those who have authority and those who have truth—or at least those who have respectability with those who need problems solved. Beyond that, this major statement offers a theoretical approach concerning the hierarchy of credibility, which in effect signifies that sociologists should not make the assumption that the "men at the top know best." On an operational level, Becker points out how social deviance is often more punished than political marginality, because there are simply no mechanisms of legitimation for deviants as they are for the third, fourth, and fifth political party advocates or even devotees of political violence. That means, too, that there are no juridical safeguards for such people. In this sense, Becker's work is not only eminently political but frankly humanitarian. That one could seriously read this paper as an argument for everything from welfarism to relativism is a tribute to a much lower order of partisanship than Becker is willing to entertain.

This book is also an important theoretical contribution to sociology in its distinction between sociological work and social work. Becker provides a feeling as well as a framework for starting with social facts that have to be understood before being corrected. His volitional model carries with it the further assumption that oftentimes the problem is precisely the fanatic dedication to removing a social problem, instead of a calm acceptance of the fact that there are pluralistic life styles that do not require removal or resolution.

While the emphasis on this theme is more fully developed in Becker's *Outsiders*, it also appears quite noticeably in the third part of the volume, entitled "The Professions of Personal Change." A characteristic example is in chapter 19 on personal change in adult life, where he points out that:

> One way of looking at the process of becoming an adult is to view it as a process of gradually acquiring, through the operation of all these mechanisms, a variety of commitments which constrain one to follow a consistent pattern of behavior in many areas of life. . . . The process of commitment accounts for the well-known fact that juvenile delinquents seldom become adult criminals, but rather turn into respectable, conventional, law-abiding lower-class citizens. It may be that the erratic behavior of the juvenile delinquent is erratic precisely because the boy has not yet taken any actions which commit him more or less permanently to a given line of endeavor."

In other words, perhaps we should put less emphasis on removing juvenile delinquents from society and more emphasis on speeding the process of growing up. This kind of sociological imagination infuses the entire third section of the volume and is the core of Becker's scientific posture.

An unusual aspect of this collection is that sociologism of the type exhibited by Becker, far from leading impersonalizing or dehumanizing people as objects, leads to opposite consequences. There is an almost inordinate emphasis on personal choice and individual change. The concept of socialization is subtly transformed into a modest statement of career lines and patterned transactions that somehow mediate the claims of institutions as structures on one side, and careers of individuals on the other. Then there is the concept of commitment, which figures largely in Becker's work. It is not that all commitments are made consciously or deliberately; nonetheless, he does speak of commitments in terms of valuables with which bets can be made. Just how volitional and deterministic elements intersect, remains largely unexamined. Likewise, in discussing personal changes in adult life, Becker describes commitments as side bets. Social structure, creating the conditions for change and stability in social life, strangely seem to be more permissive in the hands of Becker than for functionalists. It would seem that in adult socialization there is greater emphasis on self-actualization than on any inhibitors to change. The theory of social and symbolic interaction in Becker has an interesting dimension that, though present in the world of his Chicago mentors, was not quite as developed—namely, the role of adult socialization as stretching the capacities of men to become something else. It is a most effective assault on the limits of psychoanalytic theory and its emphasis on child socialization. Growing up is something that goes on all the time. That is why we need a sociology to explain psychoanalytic theory.

For someone who has for so long been identified with the Chicago school and in general with the use of sociologism no less than sociology, Becker's heavy emphasis on personality and human choice is refreshing. Nonetheless, a certain problem arises that is typical of Chicago-school types, old and new, from Park through Becker. That is the exaggerated tendency to see volition and individual behavior as identical and in turn to minimize or slight the role of ideological, organizational, and determinist elements in behavior.

In Becker's world, people are always making side bets, decisions and choices as to presentation and behavior. One cannot help but wonder whether such free choice is first of all structured in the situation or simply in the eye of the actor. Further, the amount of mechanical activity and behavioral response to organizational pressures and institutional constraints is either left out or reinterpreted into terms more amenable to personality (i.e., familial problems, etc). In short, the philosophical bias of the volume in favor of voluntarism may create a more wide open and hence more exotic (albeit deviant) universe, than the one people live in every day.

Sociological Work is a rich resource. It requires no defense and warrants no assaults—at least not from me. It needs only to be read and understood. Becker offers a way of doing sociology and of being a sociologist. In his own quiet way he has given to sociology a mode of integration—of being part of the society the discipline aims to study—that few others can match. It remains to be seen whether such personal talents, albeit extraordinary, can be translated into a school of research for others less gifted by nature.

From *American Sociological Review*, vol. 36, no. 3 (1971), pp. 524–527.

52

Behavioral Science as Ideology*

Berelson, Bernard

This collection of papers prepared from a series of radio broadcasts represents yet another attempt at securing the framework and organizing the content of a school of thought. In sociology alone, we have had quite a number of such efforts within the last several years (Gittler, Merton-Broom-Cottrell, Lipset-Smelser, Becker-Boskoff). The *Lebenswelt* of the social sciences has increasingly come to revolve around styles of professional work rather than individual performance. Perhaps this in itself represents a triumph of the behaviorist position, with its distinctive emphasis on hard data over soft theory. The individual as a hero-type has given way, in the social sciences at least, to the school of thought as an organizational type—*sans heroisme.*

This condition can lead us to either one of two conclusions: first, that various members of various social sciences do in fact see the day of separate departmental disciplines coming to an end; or second, that the concept of behavior (in contrast to the social) is simply generically more inclusive and has fewer major transdisciplinary obstacles. Interestingly, the contributors to this symposium do not entertain this issue. Indeed, with the exceptions of the papers by Donald Young and Robert Merton, basic implications of the behavior approach remain unexamined. Instead we are presented with behavior*ism* as a fait accompli.

The sop to the social scientific conscience is that one may not like the fait accompli, but there it stands, in its robust glory, ready to take on the historic complaints and wails of the antiscientists. But whether the picture is quite so rosy, whether indeed the behavioral sciences really offer the uniformity they are herein assigned, remains the skeleton in the closet. It is not the antiscientists who will be disturbed by such a lack of self-consciousness, but precisely those scientists who believe that the unification of the human sciences may more readily be achieved by the integration of the social and behavioral sciences and not by their isolation.

---

* Bernard Berelson, The *Behavioral Sciences Today* (New York: Basic Books, Inc., 1963), pp. 278.

Any reader finds it difficult to evaluate the good and the useful from the poor and the useless. The level of heuristic employment alone can settle this for each potential reader. Strangely enough, given the behaviorist self-image of specificity, the heuristic and practical is what is least in evidence. The papers have an oratorical quality that is not improved by cold print or old age. For the most part, the essays do not tell us what the behavioral sciences are doing so much over other styles. After all, what would be a *compleat* science be doing with alternative methodological and systematic approaches?

This volume leaves me with the impression that, inadvertently, the behavioral sciences have been reduced to behaviorism as an ideology. The psychological orientation of the volume is more indicative of the ism than of behavior. The papers on the evolution of behaviorism, on neuro-psychology, animal study, cognition and learning, and even that on political behavior and public opinion, all have an extreme reductionist appeal. The behavioral sciences are conceptualized, not so much at a collective and macroscopic level, but in terms of individual performance patterns. The arena of behavior may be society, but society itself tends to be atomized, no less than groupized.

This underscores a dogmatic appeal to take behaviorism as a known entity rather than as one of several available strategies for studying social interaction. Berelson's view, that "there is an inherent distinction" between the behavioral sciences, which are "typically more devoted to the collection of original data," and the social sciences which are "aggregative, indirect, and documentary" is a definition of method that does not allude to the content of the human sciences. He thus leaves intact the very dualism which behaviorism supposedly transcends. Similarly, the distinction drawn between amateurs and professionals is an argumentum ad hominem which explains nothing as to why the behavioral sciences ought to be viewed as something radically distinct from the social sciences. And in the one attempt at stating the content of the behavioral view, Berelson refers to the behavior of individuals or small groups. But this definition in terms of a low range is contradicted by Homans' excellent paper in this same volume, on the grounds that "small groups are not *what* we study, but *where* we often study it." Clearly, the editor paid little attention to this fine distinction.

Berelson insists that the conduct of the behavioral sciences must be "technical and quantitative, segmentalized and particularized, specialized and institutionalized, 'modernized' and 'groupized'—in short Americanized." He next goes on to tell us that behavioral science is part of science, not scholarship. Are we then to assume that not to be a behaviorist is to subvert the conduct of the human science? This is an extremely dangerous linkage. Any association of science with a national style carries with it serious implications of an extrascientific variety. As a matter of fact, it is manifestly clear why these essays form the nucleus of a Voice of America series. Too many of these pages are filled with patriotic phraseology—which speaks well of the Americanism of the contributors but not necessarily of their scientific views.

This collection suffers from a towering confusion between description and prescription—a sin of large dimensions for the empiricist tradition in sociology. Statements to the effect that studies of crowd behavior have become rare because riots and spontaneous events in America have "practically faded" (Lazarsfeld); or "only in America could it be written that "all men are created equal" (Lipset); or "sociological demography has so far had its main impetus in America" (Davis) do a disservice to the American scene. In the first place, the study of crowd behavior is not rare in or out of sociology, (e.g., the work of Edwards, Blumer, Hopper, and most recently, Kurt and Gladys Lang). In the second place, the French Enlightenment formed the essential intellectual background to Jeffersonism—whatever our sociological counterpart to Harry Golden might say to the contrary. And in the third place, the sociological study of demography is neither an American invention nor have we provided the main impetus. The English have at least the same right to claims of priority. (Although, in fairness to Davis, he at least offers his claims with some calm and reserve, and with a sense of European accomplishments.)

The continual references to American anthropology, American psychology, and American sociology—instead of to anthropology, psychology, and sociology in the United States—is more than a linguistic convention or confusion. It reflects a parochial standpoint that can only hinder the cause of the behavioral sciences and feed the European stereotype that American behaviorism is simply *le neo-paternalisme Americain.* To the credit of Alpert, Pribram, and Merton, their sensitivities and avoidance of ethnocentric traps is not an accidental property of the superiority of their papers. In short, if this volume does not tell us too much about the conduct of the behavioral sciences today, it does reveal a great deal about the conduct of some behavioral scientists. And the conceits therein revealed can end up doing the cause of social research more harm than good.

From *The Sociological Quarterly*, vol. 5, no. 2 (1964), pp. 163–65.

53

Social Contexts of
Thought*

Coser, Lewis A.

The publication of Lewis Coser's *Men of Ideas* has to be ranked as a welcome event. The book is written in the *Wissenssoziologie* tradition and might well have been titled *The Social Context and Institutions of Men of Ideas*. Admittedly, this would have been a clumsy title. Yet, it would have removed a number of possible lines of objection to the book, since in fact the work is more concerned with contextual sources and institutional grids than with ideas as such.

The main innovative feature of Coser's book is to show how ideas and ideologies that are employed in the battle for social change oftentimes end up in the unwitting service of bureaucratic management. In effect, he shows that a dialectic of ideology and organization takes the form of high innovation in prerevolutionary phases or in active periods of social change, and the form of high integration in postrevolutionary or nonrevolutionary periods—from France of Napoleon Bonaparte, the brain-trust founded in the New Deal period, and finally to the bureaucratic concentration of ideology in the tumultuous Gomulka period in Poland. Each illustrates this dialectic of ideology and organization. Similar lines of analyses might be performed on such regimes as Sekou Touré's in Guinea, and Fidel Castro's in Cuba. Thus, dynamics of intellectual role performance described by Coser is restricted to the examples adduced.

The book is comprised of a series of short (sometimes too short) essays on selective themes in the institutional networks that intellectuals find themselves in. The various essays are divided into three large sections: (1) "Settings for Intellectual Life," (2) "Intellectuals in the House of Power," and (3) "The Intellectual in Contemporary America." Although the essay form is obviously Coser's natural métier, it clearly imposes certain methodological restrictions, so that the connections among the twenty-six chapters often remain tenuous.

---

* Lewis A. Coser, *Men of Ideas: A Sociologist's View* (New York: Free Press/Macmillan Publishers, 1965), pp. 374.

For the most part, few connections are made directly. Only inferentially are systematic relationships provided.

The first section provides some fine vignettes of the French salon, the English coffee houses, the rise of the Royal Society in England, the professionalization of literary production in England, and the movement among writers from dilettantism to commercialization. But just as we settle into England and France of past centuries we are quickly moved into twentieth-century United States and life in the literary bohemia of Greenwich Village. Interesting opportunities for comparison of Berkeley in the sixties with Greenwich Village in the twenties are not taken advantage of. But since Coser makes no pretense at being definitive, these gaps can easily be filled in by the intelligent reader.

The second section, "Intellectuals in the House of Power," is partially a celebration of men of ideas, as well as a warning that they do not fuse the world of ideas with the house of power. It is Coser's view that though the two often intersect they do so at great risk to both science and policy. A forthright discussion of the concept of policy-science is, however, more implied than stated. As the reader is led to examinations of the Fabians, the Brain Trust, the Abolitionists, the Dreyfusards, and others, there emerges a large-scale critique of the notion of applied social science. Throughout this section, is an implicit warning that men of ideas do not generate the careful exercise of power. However, Coser does not show that non-intellectuals or anti-intellectuals use power and authority more wisely. Issues now confronting men of ideas perhaps require a somewhat different statement. The dichotomy is decreasingly between pure and applied social research, as it is among different forms of application. In other words, the value problem, rather than diminishing in the present period of rising scientific expectations, has become increasingly significant—but not quite in the same way that emerges in Coser's book.

The third section, "The Intellectual in Contemporary America," will be of unquestionable interest to all social scientists concerned with relations between social science and public policy. This section has the merit of taking up materials that are often neglected by sociologists. Here Coser provides a framework, not just for the sociology of knowledge, but more significantly a point of departure for handling problems in the sociology of sociology. The examination of such phenomena as unattached intellectuals, academic intellectuals, scientific intellectuals, and policy-related intellectuals, as well as those involved in the production of mass culture, enables us to piece together a model for studying the intellectual in comparative terms.

Perhaps the major problem with the book is Coser's definition of intellectuals, while meritorious and based very much on the kind of position I personally would like to see more widespread, it can by no means be considered universal. Weber's distinction between men who live off of politics and men who live for politics is used as a takeoff point. Coser's notion of intellectuals is one of people who live for, rather than off of, ideas. But this leads to an extremely narrow appraisal of what intellectual activity is about. It is based on a notion of immortal perfection which can hardly be operationally sustained as characteristic of intellectuals across either time or space. A more generic and less priestly definition of intellectual might have stood Coser in good stead.

In all fairness, it must be pointed out that he provides essentially six (not one) criteria for intellectual behavior: (1) men who live for, rather than off of, ideas; (2) men who go beyond the immediate and the concrete to a more general realm of meaning and values; (3) men with a pronounced concern with core social values; (4) men concerned with style and taste; (5) men exempt from the ordinary run of mundane slogans and norms and, at the same time, exempt from everyday life styles; and finally (6) men who have a need to exercise a play of the mind for its own sake. However, ever if we add all of these criteria together there remains a self-congratulatory note that is not entirely warranted by examining the sometimes strange and other times sordid career lines of many intellectuals.

It is not clear whether those who exercise the play of the mind for its own sake are necessarily free of base power interests. As Coser well knows, having spent his early years in Western Europe, it is quite possible to be concerned with the play of ideas and to relinquish a concern for the core values of society. Not a few men who work in the area of political policy have a high regard for the life of the mind and the play of ideas, but whether they have the same concern for core values or whether they define themselves as men living for, rather than off of, ideas is another matter. Even if Coser's propositions defining the intellectual are necessary elements, they are by no means sufficient for a meaningful definition, nor are they free of the kind of rationalistic bias that casts suspicion on traditional sociological definitions of intellectuals. Especially surprising is how little attention Coser has given to egotistically based, even crudely monetary, sources of intellectual creativity. In this sense, perhaps intellectuals are similar in their career strivings and status ambitions to other social sectors. In short, getting beyond Znaniecki and into a deeper penetration of the stratification system of intellectuals would have been warranted.

The book is less than clear in its treatment of the structural differences between the behavior of natural scientists and that of social scientists. Also, there does not seem to be much sense of the relationships of social scientific activity to the unique circumstances of time and place. An extreme premium is placed on historical analogies as the only form of evidence for the points made. The areas and periods selected for examination, while they lend themselves to the kinds of analogies Coser offers, do not prove whether a more precise historical accounting would either confirm or disconfirm his hypotheses about intellectual behavior in general. Along the same lines, the Hobbesian bias that the union of policy makers and intellectuals tends to be nasty, brutish, and short may be true in a consensus society where there is a normal strain between the intellectual community and the policy-making community, but in societies of a Platonic or more frankly totalitarian variety, it is not so much that the intellectual relationship to policy is nasty, brutish, and short, but rather that the intellectual as such becomes nasty, brutish, and short-tempered-whether he is policy oriented or policy disoriented.

While Coser has, with genuine modesty, pointed to areas of omission, one cannot help but raise the question why there is an absence of any systematic consideration of the phenomenology of intellectual activity. Even if the book is confined to contextual analysis, it would seem that the work of men such as Raymond Aron, César Graña, and Thomas Molnar, among others, might have enhanced the framework within which Coser views his theme. Greater attention to others who have been grappling with these problems, at a more general theoretical level, as well as those who, like Richard Westfall in history and Warren Hagstrom in sociology, have been working on these problems at a more systematic and empirical level, might have provided great aid in finally piecing together a book on *men of ideas*. As it is, we have to be content with a volume that is fragmentary when it is brilliant, and brilliant despite its fragmentary qualities.

Never in any previous period of intellectual activity have academic personnel had so much policy potential or actual scientific control over their data; and, at the same time, never has there been such an unabashed cynicism about the life of ideas. Perhaps the rise of professionalism is less a response to outside pressures than an attempt to handle this problem by allowing people to function exclusively in terms of expertise, thereby entirely alleviating them of ideological and moral dilemmas. These anomalies Coser well appreciates and expresses. On the basis of his sensibilities and sensitivities, this book deserves the attention of "men of ideas."

From *The American Journal of Sociology*, vol. 72, no. 4 (1967), pp. 419–21.

54

The Rise and Fall of Practically Everything*

Crozier, Michel

America has been fortunate in its choice of past critics. In macroexamination of the New World, people like André Siegfried (*America at Mid-Century*), Simone de Beauvoir (*America Day by Day*), and, much earlier, Harriet Martineau (*Society in America*) provided peerless insights. Analysis of whole societies requires of the observer a deep compassion and, above all, a sensitivity to the decency of the peoples and places described. But unlike Alexis de Tocqueville's empathic observations in the early nineteenth century, Michel Crozier's analysis of today's America is critical in intent.

The Trouble with America is divided into two parts ("America's Happy Days" and "The Trouble with America") and eight chapters. But the rationale for this division is elusive, since the themes recur throughout the text. To some extent the analysis is chronological, it begins with an effort to examine labor and intellect in America, based on experiences during Crozier's first visit. Like the rest of the work, this analysis is impressionistic: Crozier exhibits little familiarity with data on labor, organized or otherwise. It is clear that he has spent the bulk of his time in America (and I daresay in France) in universities and think tanks. From such a perch, Crozier addresses America's Constitution, its schools, and public optimism, which he condemns as popular narcissism. Despite his self-description as an independent Marxist, his line of analysis is remarkably like that of preindustrial traditionalists, but the implicit demand for community order inherent in his view leads Crozier to a dilemma of choice. The drive for order does not have the same social roots as the quest for community. Consequently, the premises of Crozier's thinking remain obscure through what is, in effect, an extended essay.

Crazier sees America as a land of instant action and immediate gratification, of unilateral individualism, without regard to community or providence. He

---

* Michel Crozier, *The Trouble with America: Why the System is Breaking Down.* (Berkeley and Los Angeles: University of California Press, 1985), pp. 156.

sees America's malaise as prototypical of Western democracies in general, but as a special case because of American world power. Crozier leaves out of the reckoning his own sense of available options. We never learn what constitutes normal or healthy growth or just what are the new frontiers of the mind he alludes to at the end of his essay. And if Americans do pioneer in new technological frontiers that are beyond the political, why then should they be pilloried for being politically unconcerned or naive? Crozier refers, blandly and in passing, to the "Japanese miracle," but he attempts no analysis of Japan nor does he say how the United States might simulate Japanese industrial values.

An intense psychologism leads Crozier to convert America's economic success into psychic cost. This intellectual tactic was more prevalent in the sociology of the 1950s than it is today, and it worked better with David Riesman and *The Lonely Crowd* (Riesman, not incidentally, provides a nostalgic introduction to this book). In part, this is because Americans are acutely aware of the trade-offs involved in a market society, and economic achievement does not carry with it automatic acceptance of the societal status quo. Crozier asserts that "Americans do not care enough" about the world of others, but it is not clear just what he means. In fact, his work is curiously archaic—as if America had ceased to exist with Watergate, Vietnam, and Kent State. References to specific events of the last ten years are virtually nonexistent. Statements about the recent past are abstract and impressionistic, without regard for evidence. Had Crozier written in a frankly critical spirit rather than from a stance of pained friendship for American ideals, perhaps his criticism would be easier to absorb.

In many respects Robert Bellah shares Crozier's world view. In *Habits of the Heart: Individualism and Commitment in American Life*, Bellah and his associates argue that the American quest for individualism cannot be characterized as narcissism or hedonism but is rather a search for autonomy. Bellah pointedly notes that "however much American extol the autonomy and self-reliance of the individual, they do not imagine that a good life can be lived alone." And in a finely textured postscript Bellah adds that "those we interviewed would almost all agree that connectedness to others in work, love, and community is essential to happiness, self-esteem, and moral worth." Crozier's difficulties in arguing that everything is falling apart become transparent.

Crozier's perception that Americans are an optimistic people is correct, but his belief that Americans have a psychic propensity for naive beliefs and behavior does not explain it. An easier, more ready-to-hand explanation lies in the long-run economic trends that have catapulted the United States to a leading position in every major indicator, from levels of production to amounts of consumption. Crozier does not offer a shred of evidence that the Vietnam War had a severe or long-term negative impact on the American economy. America's pattern of postwar economic growth had little correlation with its political-military decisions. Crozier puts the cart before the horse: it is not that the goal of happiness and an attendant infatuation with goods characterizes this period. Rather, the goal of growth, once accomplished, brought about contentment in its aftermath. Seen in such a light, the American people cannot seriously be characterized as either psychically numbed or morally obtuse.

Watergate and Nixon's resignation contributed to a deep and genuine national learning process. Americans learned that a nation is not its leadership, that system legitimacy can be reaffirmed in the crucible of political turmoil and executive malfeasance, that cleansing a regime is possible without destroying constitutional government. The act of removing a president for cause made the American system more like the premierships of Western Europe. Imperial presidencies became suspect. The centralization that characterized the period from Roosevelt to Nixon ended abruptly with Watergate. Ford, Carter, and Reagan were wise or simply clever enough to realize that the resolution of Watergate required a more modest view of the presidency and a more elevated role for the legislative and judicial branches of government. In that sense, the deep sentiments of a people echoed by its leadership. Although Crozier neither recognizes nor acknowledges these changes, there has been no return to what he refers to as a business-as-usual model. On the contrary, the American system has matured; it has adapted, however imperfectly, to a world in which military defeat and political sin do not shake the democratic convictions of the citizenry.

Crozier's notion that "everything of course begins and ends with the Vietnam War" denies the very historicism he proclaims. He speaks of the war as a strategic error, but does not acknowledge that strategic blunders can be readily overcome. Beyond errors of this humble sort are large-scale, principled mistakes. Writing in the mid-1980s, Crozier nevertheless fails to mention Soviet intervention in Afghanistan, Solidarity in Poland, the rape of Cambodia by Soviet-backed Vietnam forces, the betrayal of the Sandinista Revolution, an Ethiopian Communist regime that has given its people unparalleled starvation and corruption, Libyan aid to terrorists aimed at the destruction of the United States and its allies (including France), and a desperate Soviet response to the Pope that has used the weapons of assassination and state-sponsored terror. Such "post-Vietnam" events have led people throughout the world—not only seasoned sociological travelers like Crozier but desperately poor immigrants—to seek refuge and respite in the United States. This process did not cease with Watergate and Vietnam. These immigrants remain Crozier's private troubles. For the rest of us, the trauma is the globalization of struggle, the need is to evolve some way to preserve the democracies (all eighteen of them), and to extend their power and influence while maintaining the peace—not to retract that power in cynical obeisance to Crozier's forces of maturation or, better stated, darkness.

Crozier moves from disdain for Americans' boundless optimism to distaste for their sense of the immediate. Americans are counselled to forget dreams and become humble. After Vietnam and Watergate, Americans are presumed to require eternal penitence. Crozier is deeply offended by the sense of happiness he detects in Americans, as if the task of analysis were to dictate moral and cultural taste instead of to explain why and how a people express certain moods. Crozier is doubtless, as he claims, a seasoned traveler. But this extended essay also reveals him to be a biased ideologue, whose capacity for theoretical overkill is boundless: America has been cursed with a "megalomaniac sense of abundance. . . collective delusion. . . arrogance. . . lapse of intelligence." His judgments cover everything from the Marshal Plan to the Vietnam War. Do Americans merit a more generous appraisal in the wake of defeat in Vietnam? Hardly. Crozier's charges simply become more fashionable and less formidable. America is narrow and technocratic, revealing a lack of perspective, and finally, a lack of realism. Such unqualified judgments are rendered repeatedly.

Especially frustrating in this caricature of the United States is the absence of any contextual framework. Crozier does not recognize that a global context for American ambitions does exist (stimulated by both Vietnam and Watergate, but especially the former) or that Americans now know that automatic victory is not guaranteed and that virtue does not always triumph. Vietnam has given Americans a new awareness of Soviet power, an awareness that the outcomes of guerrilla victories need not be democratic. Vietnam created not just a mood of isolationism; it also made for deep suspicion of fatuous claims that guerrilla movements are autonomous. The struggles of the United States in Central America may result in a mix of defeats and victories, but at least they will no longer be accompanied by the painful naivete of the antiwar movements of earlier generations. The growing maturity of the American mind helps to explain why the Vietnam past is a prologue. There is not any wish simply to forget the past, as Crozier implies.

The temptation is great to cite data or note other analyses that might correct Crozier. But all the data in the world and all its notables would not shake this author loose from intellectual moorings that require him to see American successes as the source of American sins. His analysis seems to welcome the vision of a permanent downward spiral of the West. Certainly he hopes at least that the West can cut its losses by avoiding the military defeats and political imbroglios that accompany imperial aims. But he fails to recognize that healthy societies absorb crises and survive and grow. Sick societies cave in. Crozier wants his vision both ways: American success is a symbol of its decadence; whilst American failure is also a symbol of its decadence. This is, of course, the essence of the anti-American vision and not of the sociological imagination.

Americans do not lack a self-critical tradition. The extraordinary body of writings on America by Europeans betokens the reverse vice: a too-ready acquiescence to criticism from other shores. America's willingness to be self-critical operates within parameters that do not disregard the context of programs or the purposes of policies. The moral aims of America, however, clumsily executed, continue to be understood as just that: moral in purpose. They are aided by rationalistic and utilitarian traditions derived from France, constitutional and tolerant traditions from England, and romantic literary and philosophical traditions from Germany. What binds the West as a cultural unity more closely than do national systems, is far more important than the supposed grand illusions of Charles de Gaulle or Ronald Reagan.

The intellectual and cultural fabric that gives the West its unified historical character and its sense of moral purpose is precisely what one seeks in vain in Crozier's book. In the final analysis, Crozier's banalities, issued with funereal gloom, tell us less about America's problems than about the ideological troubles of a deracinated Frenchman.

From *Social Forces*, vol. 64, no. 3 (1986), pp. 799–801.

55

Law, Order and the Liberal State*

Dahrendorf, Ralf

When an outstanding talent and a beacon for social science writes a new book or, as is here the case, delivers a series of lectures (the Hamlyn Lectures, to "further among the Common People of Great Britain and Northern Ireland the knowledge of Comparative Jurisprudence and Ethnology") and that series is magically transformed into a book, it behooves the scholarly community to sit up and take notice. This is doubly so because the volume entitled *Law and Order* is written by a self-declared "unreconstructed eighteenth-century liberal." But such self-definition is only partially accurate. For, in fact, Ralf Dahrendorf—sociologist, educator, and politician—is very much a child of his age, an epoch which spans much of twentieth-century Europe.

It is fascinating that, for this eighteenth-century liberal, the figures who loom largest in his discussion of law and order are not Diderot or even Montesquieu but Rousseau and Hobbes, respectively the counter-Enlightenment figure of the eighteenth century and the quintessential figure of the seventeenth-century secularization of politics Dahrendorf's reading of Rousseau as a democrat may surprise those who sometimes juxtapose Rousseau and the Enlightenment. But in emphasizing the ideas of "natural" goodness and "social" deformation, Rousseau's belief in increasing life chances, liberty, and the freedom to choose, as well as in determining what is chosen, Dahrendorf makes a strong case for a figure who not only combined law with order but appreciated the human capacity to move sideways as adeptly as forward.

If Rousseau provides the motif of liberty, Hobbes offers the leitmotiv of order. He does so by indirection, in Dahrendorf's consideration of the Hobbesian Behemoth as a condition of lawlessness, chaos, and rebellion. Ultimately, the Anarch brings about the need for Leviathan. Dahrendorf's concern is not with the history of ideas alone but with a "new wave of totalitarianism" that could "sweep the world," a world in which the delicate balance of law and order tips

* Ralf Dahrendorf, *Law and Order*. (London: Steven & Sons; and Boulder, Co.: Westview Press, 1986), pp. 179.

dramatically and fatefully toward the latter, that is, toward Hobbes's rather merciless state. The author of the finest work yet on Germany—whose knowledge of National Socialism is firsthand—points out, in true Hobbesian fashion it might be added, that "under totalitarian rule there are only two clear views: compliance or opposition. Everything else is at best self-delusion and at worst actual support for terror combined with irrelevant mental reservations." The answer is not to let things get to such a stage. Here, Rousseau's (and now Dahrendorf's) "institutional liberalism" in which law and order rather than norms and sanctions hold sway, comes to define this delicate balance of two abstractions.

Dahrendorf's work is surprising in that the political-science tenets of democracy and citizenship are seen as central to any reconstruction of society, in contrast to the conventional sociological reliance upon norms and conventions. But in fact Dahrendorf's work cuts more deeply yet, since its premise lies in a series of tasks for those who want liberty above everything else—a sharp contrast to the view of economic equality as an overarching goal. Dahrendorf's is on admittedly shaky ground in his personal choice.

As a man of the "wobbly center", self-identified with William Butler Yeats's center that cannot hold, Dahrendorf appreciates the dilemmas of Left and Right. The Right at least pays lip service to enabling law to survive, but, in disenchanting the masses, the Right arranges for a total grip on society. The Left, for its part, arrives at its total grip on society by a negation of liberty, of differences, in the name of equity considerations. Further, in the Left's view of history as unilateral as well as predetermined, the very masses to whom the Left consecrates revolutions are subverted by elites once more.

There is a sense in which Dahrendorf's little book disposes of both the German tradition of Hegel's supreme state and Marx's supreme society. The "dialectic" of abstractions led to a series of concrete decisions in Germany and in Russia in which German political theory, with its *Homo sociologus syndrome*," fostered authoritarianism and lacked even the imagination or the courage to consider deviance as a necessary form of innovation. Even if ensconced in the twentieth-century rhetoric of a Nozick, the critique is of a nineteenth-century legacy to the twentieth-century totalitarian state. The earlier, organicist authoritarianism may be dead, Dahrendorf tells us, but it yields less to democracy than to a historicist totalitarianism.

Dahrendorf is perhaps too modest in disclaiming any desire to offer a program of radical liberalism. For, in fact, the book is a plea for a program—one based on the affirmation of youth, another on the values of work as a form of identity, and ultimately on the translation of concerns for law and order into responsive "institution-building" networks. If it is hard to argue with Dahrendorf, so too is it hard to get a handle on immediate next steps. His work is classically eighteenth-century in a bad sense: it displays thorough disregard and, dare one say it, ignorance of (late twentieth-century) science and technology.

As a result, the resolutions offered seemed forced, stilted, shoved into a Habernas-like mold of traditional categories that just do not fit. The reformulation of questions of law and order in terms of supersonic weaponry and superfast computers finds no place in this volume. The "mechanistic" world of Hobbes, the "dialectical" world of Rousseau can carry one only so far. Beyond such inherited sensibilities of political philosophy are the current extraordinary transformations. While they do not make obsolete the moral concerns expressed by Dahrendorf, they do require a new form. If the Baconian element had been added, this would have been a more powerful intellectual argument. And this is not an idle "if". Dahrendorf has the knowledge of British thought to make it come alive in a new synthesis. That he chose to ignore such possibilities could only have been deliberate in nature. But we are not privy to this level of Dahrendorf's intellectual decision making.

This said, *Law and Order* is a set of serious lectures. It is a classical reformulation of the liberal European option—without the usual sentimental blather with which these reformulations are sometimes presented and with a serious, measured tone. Dahrendorf is a rare bird: a hard-boiled utopian whose belief in the future is strengthened by the catastrophes of the recent past. Out of the ashes of European extremism, fanaticism, and separatism comes this man of decent sensibility, a solid social analyst who understands the legal functions of moral order. This is a solid contribution to the liberal imagination, at a moment in time when one might have begun to despair of the relevance or potential for such a great instauration coming from such an intellectual and political source.

From *American Journal of Sociology*, vol. 92, no. 5 (1987), pp. 1264–66.

56

Is There an American
Power Elite?*

Dye, Thomas

Thomas R. Dye has written a decent book. He adequately summarizes the literature on power theory and adds a needed dimension of analysis: the institutional framework in which power decisions are made. The volume is simultaneously a monograph that grew out of a graduate seminar at Florida State University, where the biographical data for over 5000 institutional elites were studied, a text intended to provide supplementary material in courses on American politics, and a general overview of the literature on power elites.

One of the nicer features is the empirical data which analyzes institutional leadership in a manner that rivals for concreteness the annual issues of *Business Week, Forbes*, and *Fortune*. Also, the book names corporations, civic establishments, governing circles, and individuals who hold power. Though the author appreciates the fact that rotation of power occurs, he provides enough flesh and bone to the statistical data to interest a general audience. Dye also makes a contribution to the theory of power by working through an operational separation of corporate, government, and public interests that is clearly more sophisticated than earlier triads of military, political, and economic interests. In general, we have here a worthwhile study done with a measure of dispassion and notable for its calm in this overheated area of political research.

But upon closer inspection of Dye's work, one notices a strange duality between the sentiments that inspire the volume and the claims it actually makes for power elite theory. The thin line between asserting that power elites do exist and that power elites have a unified agenda is subtly and illicitly crossed constantly.

The work is written within a tradition that assumes the power variable in American society can be conceptually isolated for research and can serve as a basic tool for identifying the nation's institutional elite. The sections that describe the concentration of power in industry, finance, insurance,

* Thomas R. Dye, *Who's Running America? Institutional Leadership in the United States* (Englewood Cliffs, N.J.: Prentice-Hall, 1976), pp. 222.

government, foundations, the law, civic and cultural organizations, and universities, also seek to provide a profile of the people who occupy top institutional leadership. The final section attempts to perform a systematic investigation of institutional elites: how they interlock; why they specialize; who elites represent; their patterns of recruitment, background variables, race, sex, and religion; and in general, the attitudes and opinions that go into the making of institutional elites. The rhetoric is typical of the power elite school, but as one actually explores the contents of each chapter, one encounters serious counterfactualizing. In one area after another, the objections adduced by the pluralist school are registered, begrudgingly, but nonetheless devastatingly. The results show that far more confusion exists at the top of the heap in fact than in theory.

For example, Dye tells the reader that in education the twelve top colleges and universities control 50 percent of the private endowment funds, but they do not control any significant proportion of all higher education resources in the nation. While some corporate leaders gain business power through inheritance, others are of humble origin and come up through the ranks of corporate management. Dye acknowledges that a surprising percentage of top corporate leaders achieved their power by bureaucratic progression rather than by inheriting wealth. Similarly, politicians like Nelson Rockefeller and Charles Percy are directly linked to inherited wealth; but others, like Richard M. Nixon and Gerald R. Ford have no link to power through family background. The same is true for policy and decision makers: some achieve fame through the proverbial silver spoon and purple sash, while others may be immigrant Jews or Italians, like Kissinger and Sisco, who come to power through intellect. Even in that much vaunted bastion of WASP power, the judiciary, the upper-class portrait of previous members of the Supreme Court stands in marked contrast to the middle-class social origins of its current membership.

Dye and his youthful coworkers should be credited for not forcing the data; they do not try to falsify cohesion or consensus where none exists. They admit to the high degree of specialization that clearly limits the theory of interlocking directorates, "it should be remembered that most of the universe of 4000 top position-holders were 'specialists.'" Dye acknowledges that if corporate government and military elites, come together, it clearly does not appear to be through an interlocking directorate, or for that matter, the character of elite recruitment. Moreover, if interlocked positions are outnumbered by specialized roles, as Dye's cross-tabulations suggest, one must assume that as one descends from apex to base in the occupational hierarchy, such specializing tendencies would increase even more.

The characterization of who rules America in terms of social stratification variables is more consistent than in terms of political decision-making functions. On the whole, those at the top are better educated, older, urban, Anglo-Saxon Protestant, while males; very few are blacks, women, or drawn from special ethnic or religious minorities. The real problem is to get from the stratification sample, which indicates strong differences from the general population, to political differentials of equal factoral strength. At this point, the power concentration framework breaks apart since there is disagreement among the power elite about a wide variety of items. Furthermore, the link between social stratification and political decision making is exactly the missing lynchpin in Dye's volume.

One of two propositions would have to be adduced were this link to be established. First, were there a larger number of blacks, women, and other minority groups, decision making would be different, or conversely the absence of these groups makes for a conservative outcome. In fact, the author indicates that there tends to be, especially within the intellectual elite and certain sectors of the political and economic elites, a far more liberal, even radical attitude toward change than appears among the rest of the American population. In short, social origin and recruitment patterns are indeed highly stratified in terms of race, class, sex, and education. It is the jump from the societal to the political that has been the central stumbling block for those who advocate elitist theory. Further, when we examine women in power, like Katherine Graham, Catherine B. Cleary, or Patricia Roberts Harris, one notes that their political behavior is quite similar to that of men with similar class and occupational backgrounds. Such information tends to weaken the argument that there is an exact relationship between the behavior and beliefs of those with social standing and those with political position.

The argument about the political cohesion of wealth is no better than the argument about the political cohesion of the poor. The assumption that an isomorphism exists between social position and political orientation is perhaps the greatest mythological bequeathal of Marxism. Oddly enough, the rise of mass-based movements like fascism, nazism, falangism, peronism, among others have simply not shaken the social science community loose from such a potent myth. The reason is clear enough: the hope, the longing, that the rich shall stumble and fall, while the poor shall cohere and rise is basic to Western culture. From the Old Testament to the Communist Manifesto such correlations have been postulated. And even the best of social scientists like Thomas Dye have a hard time confronting this long tradition—even as the evidence which they marshall tells them to do just that.

From *Political Science Quarterly*, vol. 92, no. 1 (1977), pp. 111–13.

57

Bureaucratic Illusions*

Ellul, Jacques

Early in Jacques Ellul's work he warns the reader that "this is typically French book, that is, the situation it describes pertains to the evolution of French institutions." Unfortunately, the author is unwilling to be confined by his own advice. For we are later notified that France, for better or perhaps for worse, is in the vanguard. In effect, the entire world is astonishingly now going through the current French political experience.

Any reviewer is honor bound to point out that, judged as a work on contemporary French politics, this is an instructive and insightful volume, perhaps overstaffed—Uberbesetz as the Germans might say—but nonetheless worthwhile. However as a compendium of world politics, or even as a guide to the perplexed, Ellul's book is for the most part cloudy, clumsy, and confusing. Indeed, judged from the viewpoint of the American political scene, M. Ellul's book will seem remote, even quixotic, to even his most ardent admirers. For if the major problem in France seems to be that "everything is politicized," the problem in the United States is that everything is depoliticized.

Ellul's message can be stated simply enough: the essential political illusions are first, that the people control the operations of the State: second, that people at least participate in the operations of the State; and third, that political solutions are available to all social problems. While rejecting any populist model of politics, Ellul also tends to dismiss the pluralist model of politics as a conflict of interests generated by differing value commitments. Thus, Ellul is left with an elite model of the modern state, and more profoundly, with the problem of what ordinary men can do about this Leviathan. His answer is that to "dissipate the political illusion," we must "develop and multiply tensions." This conflict model is to be stimulated by a juxtaposition of "private life" versus "political life." But just how this will dissolve illusions is hard to appreciate, since one can cultivate the private life and multiply tensions without vitally affecting the operations of the state. Indeed this very polarization of "personal

* Jacques Ellul, *The Political Illusion*, (New York: Alfred A. Knopf, 1967), pp. 258.

development" and "unitary society" may itself represent a supreme illusion—one fostered by the pessimistic vision of M. Ellul.

The book can be read as a sophisticated critique of de Gaulle's Fifth Republic, or if one prefers, as an elliptical support of that regime. At the secular level the book becomes cloudy. Ellul writes that "the problem is that the conflicts we know today are exclusively of a *political* order." Ellul bemoans this by noting that "in France there are no longer any other tensions because all the rest has been reduced to and assimilated into a monolithic whole." But just as one gets ready for a critique, Ellul undercuts his own point by insisting that "the real problems cannot be resolved by political means." Yet, although political life is "illusory," we are not given any option, since "it would be illusory to go against the trend of the times." But the present is a monster, since "what will be left will be an organization of objects run by objects." It is hard to say whether Ellul is counselling resistance to bureaucracy and dehumanization or acceptance of the inevitable, working to break political illusions by political methods or by abandoning politics for the private life.

Ellul must have been painfully aware of the dilemmas he sets up, since in a special preface to the English translation, he seeks to clarify his position. Indeed, I found this opening section the most useful part of the book. For in it he deals with two characteristics of the French state that seem to have been widely diffused: centralized authority and decision making, and an intense rationalism in setting up political, judicial, and administrative functions. The essential conservatism of Ellul is that he sees the French historical experience as a "mandate for planning," and a "warning" for those committed to the "practice of true democracy." Here the dangers of reification are self-evident, since it must surely come as a surprise to the founding fathers of Western society that the archetypical model, eighteenth century France, is but a prelude to bureaucratic planning and a postscript to mass democracy. I rather suspect that those taking a more measured view of the French Enlightenment and Revolution are closer to the mark than those who perceive the French polity as a Jacobin nightmare that unleashed the bureaucratic state on all mankind.

The translator's introduction is most laudable and clearly presented. However, Mr. Kellen's translation suffers from an exactitude bordering on the pietistic. A slight amount of editing, particularly of the futile introductory clauses to each paragraph, would have helped immensely. But of course, the work is that of Ellul, and the very precision of the translation helps throw the ambiguities of the book in sharp relief. In sum, for the reader interested in current French political debates on the relationships of bureaucracy to democracy, this book will prove most rewarding (although it would serve the reader well to examine Michel Crozier's *The Bureaucratic Phenomenon*—which Ellul warns against—as an antidote). And for those readers interested in a more analytic account, a work of relevance to the American (or for that matter Soviet) political experience, one would still have to look at the work of others: to Europeans who understand America like Raymond Aron, and Americans who understand Europe like Sheldon Wolin.

From *New Politics*, vol. 6, no. 2 (1967), pp. 94–95.

58

American Virtues /
Washington Vices*

Etzioni, Amitai

Amitai Etzioni defines the task of his work *Capital Corruption* as a search for answers to five basic questions: (1) What is the scope of political corruption? (2) Why is corruption particularly debilitating to our political system? (3) Where did the experts go wrong? (4) What does our history teach us about the sources of the problem? (5) How can we marshal a more effective drive to clean up American politics? This is certainly a fit agenda for a sociological work, and indeed, Etzioni's vigor and fearlessness are to be commended by all who would like sociology to play a more active role in public policy. Etzioni succeeds well at some of these self-imposed tasks; less well, however, at others.

I must report at the outset that it is difficult to see how the title is justified, since beyond the obligatory dictionary definition of corruption as evil or wicked behavior, the word itself is casually treated throughout the text. We are left with the argument of the book: corruption is "the use of public office for private advantage" and more specifically perpetrated "by private interests seeking illicit public favors and finding quite willing elected officials." This then is a work on "power profiles"—on how powerful groups, less powerful ones, and the unrepresented form a skyline, "with some overpowering sky-scrapers, some high-rise buildings, and quite a few slums." The dark clouds on this skyline are the PACs.

Etzioni unambiguously declares that "what corrupts American democracy most these days is PAC*ed interest groups*" (author's italics). To be sure, there can be no question that private wealth, or at times institutional wealth (Etzioni is not always clear as to the culprit or the distinction), has increasingly become an influential factor in every aspect of federal politics and is used in actions ranging from buying elections to buying elected officials. It is also the case that

*Amitai Etzioni, *Capital Corruption: The New Attack on American Democracy*, (San Diego & New York: Harcourt Brace Jovanovich, 1984; and New Brunswick and Oxford: Transaction Publishers, 1988), pp. 337.

conservative funds are twice as large as labor-liberal funds (although a substantial portion of such funds are hard to measure on a Left-Right continuum). Beyond that, Etzioni is on perfectly sound ground in noting that contributors to PACs have little, if any, effective control over their contributions. But it is similarly the case that the PAC's themselves also have weak and sometimes contrary impact on the congressional objects of their affections. Further, although a great deal is made of the impact of PACs on legislative behavior, at best a dubious proposition, no claim is made that judicial forces are subject to such pressures—at least not directly. Indeed, Etzioni is himself hard pressed to draw the line between free speech and free spending, because in point of fact PACs are not illegal.

Etzioni must therefore turn to the regulatory aspects of PACs. There are many safeguards for freedom of speech, and special ones attach to members of Congress. Further, the current tax system provides many loopholes and opportunities to use PACs to evade or avoid taxes. Etzioni's critique of corporate tax reductions, subsidies, and loopholes is right on target. But what makes his critique poignant is that the very president whom he castigates most, the incumbent Ronald Reagan, has taken as a personal mission the rationalization and equalization of tax structures. This would indicate that the influence of PACs, while serious in the halls of Congress, has far less impact on governing executive bodies.

Etzioni is strongest as a historian of the political system. His section "Private Power vs. American Democracy" is first-rate populist history. The chapters on the separation of powers in the initial phase of the government, the rise of American democracy through the steady enhancement and expansion of suffrage at the expense of the rule of wealth, the emergence of progressivism in the early part of the present century with its concomitant enlargement of federal safeguards, all serve a useful purpose for those who still believe in a new liberalism in which private rights can be best protected by public authorities.

This section is followed by an essentially fair-minded critique of those who argue that interest groups, though they are not necessarily a defense of the common good, at least supplement democratic views. Etzioni here shows a decent sense of the problem; although the argument that PACs as interest groups "add too much power to destabilizing forces" begs the question, since the notion of too much power implies an unstated normative doctrine of power, and beyond that, a further implication that "community" factors can uniquely limit in a democratic fashion centrifugal forces. Lurking behind Etzioni's view that "special interests are not constituencies" is a rather classical model of constituencies as directly responsible voters, a universe in which those who hold office are fully responsible to those who elect others to office. This town-hall democratic model, rather than any socialist expansion of government, clearly underpins the moral basis of Etzioni's passions.

Etzioni's solutions follow in a strange way from his passions: strengthening public interest groups to act as a counterweight to political action committees, covering the costs of campaigning from public rather than private funds, curbing lobbying. All of these caveats have been registered before. But in some cases at least, the solution could be worse than the problem. It is hardly self-evident that use of "public" rather than "private" funds would ensure greater integrity to the electoral process; it might only lead to a complete breakdown of that process through balkanization, a situation in which everyone becomes a candidate because of the spoils nature of accessing funds. Moreover, would a television-personality parade of candidates really be an improvement on the party system in which candidates must come up through the party ranks?

When Etzioni gets down to it, he reverts to an older view: elitism replaces populism. We are told that "the first step of public mobilization is to place the issue on the agenda of the national town meeting," which in effect, we continually have. This meeting is a function of the media, including middle-brow intellectual publications (such as *The Public Interest, The New Yorker, The New Republic*, and *The New York Review of Books*); newspapers (especially *The New York Times, The Washington Post*, and *The Wall Street Journal* and in particular investigative reporting and an electronic media (led by *60 Minutes* and the network news). The irony in all this is evident—such publications and television news broadcasts are precisely the product of a private sector that is severely castigated elsewhere in the text. Beyond that, what does one do with *The Nation* to the Left and *The National Review* to the Right? Are they excluded from such public mobilization?

There is a dangerous notion that scholarship has no part in these reforms. Etzioni ends the book by noting that critics who chastise "megalogues" like those that Rachel Carson and Michael Harrington conducted, for being scientifically imprecise or relying upon erroneous data, miss the point. Such megalogues "serve to focus attention on a new major issue." But it is, of course, the essence of scholarship to transform megalogues into dialogues, to soften the contours of debate by adding a dash of fact to the flash of concern. Otherwise, I fear that far from reaching the democratic reforms Etzioni seeks, we shall only build bigger and better barricades.

In this equation of political corruption with political action committees, Etzioni fails to distinguish acceptable from unacceptable levels of "corruption." In fact, the historical massification and enlargement of such PACs is an effort to move beyond traditional ward politics. In that sense, the PACs represent a broadening of the political process in America. This is not to deny that elements of corruption have seeped into this process. It is to deny a unique relationship in American history between corruption and political action committees. Indeed, the colorful history and biographies of nineteenth-century urban life, from Boss Tweed to Boss Plunkitt, as outlined in the works of William L. Riordan (1948) and Alexander B. Callow, Jr. (1966), indicate just how much a part of the American democratic grain is corruption in politics.

The implied causal relationship between political corruption and political action committees thus leaves unanswered the ability of the United States to survive its past corruptions. If one may entertain a somewhat different political approach, democracy may be sustained precisely in its ability to distinguish acceptable from unacceptable levels of corruption. That fine distinction, however characterized, is perhaps more central to the present and future of American democracy than demands for a return to town-hall politics.

Recent research on PACs tends to disconfirm Etzioni's fault lines. For example, John P. Frendreis and Richard W. Waterman (1985) have argued that PACs are "neither dominating threats nor insignificant straw men, but simply another of the many factors influencing legislative behavior." Etzioni might well argue that his is a popular rather than a scholarly work and hence not subject to the weight of research findings. But the lengthy list of acknowledgments and the sizable reference bank would indicate that the opinions and views of academics do matter.

Even if we leave aside the moot question of the relationship between corruption and interest groups—except in the metaphorical, almost metaphysical Actonian sense that interest groups, as an extension of power relations in themselves, are forms of corruption—there remains the serious problem of interest group balances. The very emergence of interest groups as a function of congressional paralysis perhaps creates peculiar new forms of what David Riesman long ago referred to as the veto-group effect. The American Civil Liberties Union has as its counterpart the American Legal Foundation; Media Access Project is opposed by Accuracy in Media; the United Church of Christ comes up against the Moral Majority. One can multiply such bipolarity in American voluntary organizations endlessly. The point is not to prove any perfect spread across the political spectrum, but rather that this political spectrum is perhaps served with at least as much dedication and honesty as in the old days when party politics reigned supreme and unchallenged by interest groups.

One might well argue that the problem is not so much corruption as stagnation in American politics. The play of conservative and liberal interest groups has become so neatly balanced that it has led to a virtual political paralysis. The fairness doctrine, for example, which requires a rigorous, even-handed treatment of sensitive issues in the media has led to the reverse; bland treatment and avoidance of critical issues. A powerful communications system, network television, has been reduced to virtual silence on public issues precisely because interest groups are so carefully balanced. This irony of American politics in the mid-1980s is thoroughly overlooked by Etzioni in favor of the obvious. *Capital Corruption* displays a dramaturgical commitment to an equation of interest, powers, and corruptions, and its talented author would rather not spoil his combination of fire and brimstone by undertaking a requisite analysis of options and alternatives.

For the past thirty years, Amitai Etzioni has stood as a moral beacon within sociology against the politics of bureaucratic corruption. And this Weberian sensibility has been all to the good. The problem is that Etzioni has identified virtue with one party and vice with another. And this partisan element is all to the bad. For such a correlation of virtue with liberalism and vice with conservatism simply cannot be sustained by evidence. It is at this level that *Capital Corruption* simply unravels.

From *Contemporary Sociology*, vol. 15, no. 2 (1986), pp. 187–89.

59

Social Psychology in a Dismal Decade*

Gerth, Hans H.

During the early summer of 1960, Mills was working on everything from the classic tradition theme, which was to introduce the *Images of Man* reader, to some initial thoughts on Castro's revolutionary system in Cuba. On one occasion we had for a free floating conversation, talk drifted to *Character and Social Structure*. In discussing the work now and recalling comments made at that time, the matter of priorities, of whether Gerth or Mills was chiefly the architect of the book, can be discarded as irrelevant. At the time of its appearance in 1953, the book had striking and positive attractions for me: a strong dose of creative Marxism, some conventional progressive ideas about the death of liberalism and the insipidities of conservatism, and plenty of good philosophical *weltshmerz*. To be sure, this strange admixture of American pragmatism and European idealism contains some of the best social theorizing produced in the supposedly dismal decade. All of which goes to prove that a reader finds what he wants in a book, especially one as rich in eclecticism as this.

Mills indicated that this was the book he was least satisfied with, the one least likely to succeed, and the book most in need of drastic revision. With characteristic flamboyance and exaggeration, he dismissed the work as intellectual "crap," and blamed his excessive reliance on Max Weber as the cause. I have never spoken with Professor Gerth on this matter, and presumably, he had his own set of responses to the book. Indeed, *Character and Social Structure* is a big book. It has many pages, many themes, many ideas, and—the kicker—many points of view.

The eclecticism is extremely disconcerting. As when we are told that "we have no objection, if the reader prefers, to use the names George H. Mead and Max Weber, although of course they differ from Freud and Marx

---

* Hans Gerth and C. Wright Mills, *Character and Social Structure: The Psychology of Social Institutions* (New York: Harcourt, Brace & World, Inc. 1953), 1964, pp. 490.

in many important ways." In this way the classic tradition was employed to cover a multitude of sins, as if these four names could be plugged into each other without causing the most violent short circuits. But the authors had little choice. They were confronted by a melange of ill-misshaped theories of social psychology, that confronted each other as do the alien traditions of American pragmatism and European sociologism. One can go through the book and pick out those passages and paragraphs that are characteristic of either Gerth or of Mills. What is profoundly more difficult to isolate are the portions by Gerth and Mills.

The learned Gerth could speak of everything from Klatsch to Kant, in discussing symbol spheres. He spoke of social control and command in big international terms of comparative social structures—with Prussian Junkers, Japanese Samurai, and British Gentlemen. Collective behavior, the sociological term meaning uncontrolled or unstructured action, was seen by Gerth in terms of mobs of storm troopers hunting Jews in boulevard cafés or of Klansmen beating up Negroes in race riots. The garrulous and Americanized Mills discussed symbol spheres in such terms as Mead raised, in terms of the motivational functions of language. He spoke of social control and command in terms of the administrative policies of the New Deal, and the organization of a labor bureaucracy in terms of the American Federation of Labor. Collective behavior did not mean much to Mills. Storm troopers and hunger riots were outside his empirical purview. And that which Mills did not experience he rarely appreciated. In addition to this honest-to-God pragmatism of Mills was his emphasis on structure, his fixation with it, so that spontaneous events hardly dented his sociological imagination, as it had Gerth's.

With all of that, there are powerful unifying themes and faiths in *Character and Social Structure.* Gerth and Mills shared a strong propensity to think in terms of conflict models, rather than according to any consensual scheme. As such, problems of social psychology are happily liberated from the ugly clichés of deviance and disorganization—catchall words that have little to do with science and a lot to do with the sociologist's distasteful acceptance of polite definitions of reality. They are also both committed to worldliness, even if they understood that term differently Gerth was cosmopolitan. Mills at this point in his career had not gotten beyond the American shores. But neither of them could be chased into hapless slogans about the "corruptions of power" or the "struggle between democracy and totalitarianism," or "the human impulse to." or such similar tripe. What makes this Gerth's book, are the breathtaking passages about historical epochs, about Caesarism and sultanism, about monarchism and Bonapartism, that are more than simple echoes of the Weberian past. Such references to the past are downright reminders to the future generation of sociologists as to just what we stand to lose in the way of historical insight with the liquidation of big-range sociology. For example, I have seen dozens of essays and studies on Soviet society written by sociologists—who cannot collectivity compare or compete with the plain historicity of an E.H. Carr or an Isaac Deutscher. Thus, despite an incredible eclecticism, the unspent force of a comparative, historical sociology was able to carry the freight of methodological shortcomings.

How does this relic of the filthy fifties shape up against the productions of our decade and the new breed of social psychologists? There seem to be five distinctive trends competing for audience attention in the swinging sixties.

First, there are the experimentalists. This legion of researchers may be found under any technical rubric ranging from the behavioral to the zoological. The key methodological concept is the laboratory. This wing has a hard-nosed belief that replication and control of the experimental situation, followed by a statement of the findings in mathematical or statistical language, is the only real social psychology. Taking B.F. Skinner as typical, the root metaphor is that man is an animal, and hence, the conditions for studying animals in laboratory situations can be simulated in the study of the human animal. In this world of stimulus-response and fields of action, the language of ideology and theology is banished. The peculiar thing, however, is that this experimental social psychology should pursue its own special aims with the zeal and militancy not unbecoming the political dogmatism these gentlemen so roundly condemn. The mortifying aspect of these very modern researchers is their lack of self-consciousness, an inability to detect their own professional marginality. They possess an intellectual narrowness that threatens to engulf them and convert these hard scientists into soft sentimentalists—into crib manufacturers for the rearing of bigger and better juniors.

The form of experimentalism that dominated the fifties was small-group research conducted in natural settings, in which select variables could be controlled. For men like Theodore Newcomb, observations must be so codified as to yield orderliness out of raw behavioral components. By orderliness, the small groupers mean systems of interaction in which "the stronger a given A-to-B positive attraction the lesser the perceived discrepancy on A's part between his own and B's attitudes toward X." Equilibrium and strain, consensus and cooperation, individual and collective systems are all paraded forth as we find out the attraction of Bennington College students or Michigan University dormitory graduates toward each other. The study of social psychology becomes an analysis of attitude variance—attitudes toward making friends, living together, and sleeping together. The outside world shrivels into the life-styles of hothouse students. Lest anyone be deceived into thinking that findings can be generalized, we are continually being warned, in the name of science, that findings may be of local value only. The result is a sterilized, hygienic social psychology. Students "mount tirades," but we never know why. Colleagues are liked and disliked without objective causes. The world of Newcomb's small group is one where a "triple confrontation" (objects, others, and ego) takes place, and we must somehow solve the problem of adaptation.

Just what happens if we don't or worse, don't want to, we are never told. Presumably, violators of the consensus system must be properly dealt with, so that the sociologist may proceed with his search for locating orderliness and tranquility in the human world.

At the other end of the spectrum are the ethnographers who have turned their gaze on the social psychology of symbols, gestures, words, and languages. The leader of this wing, Erving Goffman, occupies a place across the intellectual hall from B.F. Skinner. The books of Goffman, like those of B.F. Skinner, have served to revolutionize the way in which we talk of human interaction—presentation of self, cooling the mark out, total institutions. Goffman built a truly ethnographic system out of the atomic units of personality structure. The jazzed-up language provides the reader with the feeling that these social psychologists really swing. Yet strangely, the experimenters and the ethnographers share a common unconcern for structure. The flux of events, whether under laboratory or field conditions, is unconnected to cognitive definitions. It is an operationalized world, in which the definitions of things—living, dying, singing, or nonswinging—are embedded in the symbols and rituals with which these things are done. The Goffman school is the ultimate in nominalistic orientation. No reality stands behind the event to certify its reality. The world is a performance. People are the performers, and the social psychologist becomes the theater critic turned loose on an unsuspecting universe of role-playing, manipulating, or manipulated actors.

A fourth type of new social psychology attempts to combine in effect the previous two (wherever there is a new style, old synthesizers are sure to follow). The game theorist accepts all the role theory and rule making of the Goffman wing, while insisting that its logic and its methods are not unlike those employed by experimentalists working either in natural or laboratory settings. They inhabit a world of bargains and bargainers, of players who have the goods, and of those who bluff. Every event is made into a psychological sweat, in which parliamentarians and presidents are pictured as playing the game of life with the whole universe, while the little people of the world are seen as playing exactly the same game at lesser levels and with smaller tasks. The social psychologists who have gone into military strategy are legion—in numbers if not in quality. I have yet to learn of civilian casualties in Vietnam—the gap between policy making and physical execution is approximately 10,000 miles, the same distance that this group is from affecting the grand synthesis of everything from children playing monopoly to their daddies playing big business. The social psychological gamesters are distinguished from the experimenters and the ethnographers in that they deal with possibilities but not with people.

A fifth style of work in social psychology has enjoyed a marked success in the sixties. It is the thundering totalism of the alienation school, particularly of the work of Herbert Marcuse and Erich Fromm. Marcuse, a severe critic of Fromm, nonetheless shares with him and with many others from an older generation of European gentlemen, a nostalgic yearning after the lost paradise of the Viennese or Berliner twenties—a snobbish democracy of the educated that never really was. One can never be sure as to when this school is resting on autobiographical honesty or on a system of self-revelations, which like many good revelations from Aesop to La Rochefoucauld tells important truths and genuine observations about the world. More often than not, this is not a school of sociologists so much as a group of avid and good newspaper readers, able to detect world historic trends and frame them in humanistic terms.

The radicalism of this school is slightly soiled by their creation of a world of political devils without political angels. Indeed, it is the latest and the greatest form of *anti-politique* (i.e., pure negativity). Man is alienated, never select portions of the population. Industrialization is the culprit never any specific process in production. Urbanization is horrible, cities stink, never the poor section of the city. Nationalism is evil, never is one nationalism more so than another. The noisiness of this kind of writing casts doubt on the seriousness of macroscopic approaches. It represents, in fact, a step away from the sobriety and seriousness that characterized such great social psychologists as Hull and Koffka, no less than Mead and Freud. If Skinner made the initial incision, and divorced morals from science in an entirely irrevocable way, Marcuse performed the miracle of divorcing science from moral writing in an irresponsible way—so that one either share the morality of the thundering totalists or be cast into the valley of the shadow of death. Each, claiming substance, casts away the other as shadow.

The ultimate question about *Character and Social Structure* is why, since it is such an invigorating text, has it fallen into such nearly total disuse? The answers are complex in the extreme. In the first place, Gerth and Mills employed Freudianism in a more than fashionable sense. It was woven into the fabric of their work as no other American sociologists had dared to use it. However powerful Freudian thought was in a clinical, patient-analyst setting, it never gained respectability either in departments of psychology or sociology. And without such academic respectability, a book that which used Freud in such an extravagant way was doomed to academic oblivion. In the second place, the very employment of Freud by Gerth and Mills pointed up the painful non-therapeutic way in which they used him. In England, in such places as the Tavistock Institute, Freud was used in factory studies, in experimental situations of all sorts. The social psychologists were thus exposed to Freud in a public, practical setting that retained a firm grip in the therapeutic, pragmatic side of psychoanalysis and its offshoots. In the United States, the strictly Germanic impulses prevailed. Even a pragmatist like Mead was an impractical man, caught in the vise of abstract metaphysics. The Freudians became critics instead of constructors. And to the degree to which criticism replaced construction, ideology replaced therapy. In the United States,

Freudianism was cleaved: the analysts simply ignored the critical cutting edge of their master, while the academics simply ignored the therapeutic setting of Freudian analysis. And while there are momentary flashes in *Character and Social Structure* that show some understanding of this issue, the problem could not be tackled straightaway by two authors who already were poles apart methodologically and were moving further away from one another with the passage of time. Thus it is that the career of an intellectually exciting book terminated so abruptly.

With such a cacophony of sound and fury, the re-publication of *Character and Social Structure* must be viewed as a welcome event, if only for the opportunity it provides for looking at the progeny with greater scrutiny than is usually the case. I must say that for me, this is the best book on the subject, written in the English language. Indeed, the clumsy confusion between social roles and institutional rules, the traditionalist, almost Parsonian relegation of social change as a footnote to the "model of social structure," which anchors the book to the least viable part of Weber's *Wirtschaft und Gesellschaft*, clearly dates the book. But my, oh my! What a pair of minds can accomplish even within such a theoretically loose framework. When Gerth and Mills speak of hypocrisy and posing as "the stylization of self-presentations" they clearly anticipate the theoretical innovations of Erving Goffman. When they speak of the status sphere in terms of "the claimant's side and the bestower's side," they go far into subsuming game analogies under their wing. And while they are too enmeshed in the Freudian and Meadian approaches to symbols, language, gesture, and motivation, to make any experimentalist happy, it cannot be said that they are ignorant of the findings made by physiological psychology. And at the macroscopic level of political sociology, Gerth and Mills are eminently more sound on questions of economic development, dictatorship, psychology, or bureaucracy than are the thundering totalists. They see the double process of convergence and competition between East and West as a long-standing one. And if their statements on sea power and land power are obsolete in a thermonuclear epoch, their underlying appreciation of the differences between socialism and capitalism, democracy and totalitarianism, are far more welcome than the denunciations of the modern world that have come to define the limits of radical ideology in the American universities. *Character and Social Structure* is thus more than a book by two outsiders; it is a statement of dissatisfaction with the decade which nonetheless looked forward to a somewhat better future that remained inchoate and inarticulate.

From *The New Frontier*, (1965), pp. 15–17.

60

Political Troubles and Personal Passions*

Gitlin, Todd

Todd Gitlin has written a serious, impassioned, and reasoned book about a decade in American history that has assumed mythological as well as ideological dimensions. The great merit of Gitlin's work is that it is life-sized. Despite the author's centrality to the decade as a former president of Students for a Democratic Society and an organizer of antiwar demonstrations and participant in the Chicago Democratic convention of 1968, he neither minimizes the importance of the period nor enlarges its meaning out of proportion to the rest of the American century. He achieves this by a nice blend of informal social history and autobiographical sensibility. He also makes probing criticisms of the movement of which he was part, avoiding the sort of retrospective God-that-failed ridicule that has become all too commonplace as we head into another *fin de siècle.*

Although this work is written by a sociologist, I suspect that Gitlin would be the first to admit that this is not a sociological work. It is frankly intended as a trade book. The work is intended to secure a large, mass-market audience, and it should be so judged. That *The Sixties* benefits from being written by a sociologist is, however, also a fact. A sense of fairness informs the work. Gitlin sees the 1960s at best as providing an individual with a sense of "unraveling, rethinking, refusing to take for granted—thinking without limits." But he also appreciates that the movement of the 1960s at its worst "came to overvalue the power of sheer will"—finessing rather than resolving the differences between the "strategic and the expressive"—and he observes that the "hip-political synthesis—along with violence—was the siren song of the late Sixties."

I suspect that its very balance, an anguished balance to be sure, will cause Gitlin's book to be more severely critiqued than it deserves to be—perhaps because one of the legacies of the 1960s is the ideological definition of empirical things, in contrast to the empirical analysis of ideological things. As a result,

---

* Todd Gitlin, *The Sixties: Years of Hope, Days of Rage* (New York: Bantam Books, 1987), pp. 513.

this sort of work will, in all likelihood, end up by satisfying few participants in the battles of the decade while winning few compliments from critics of that decade. This is not the first and certainly not the last memoir on a special time in American life. But it is an important milestone in the creation of a social history of the period and should thus be evaluated with the same seriousness with which it was written.

The structure of *The Sixties* is itself a reflection of the eclecticism of the decade. Sometimes with great success and other times with less, Gitlin combines personal narrative of events a sense of larger social history to describe events that he did not personally experience. Such a literary device works well in some chapters, as for example in chapter 14 on the Democratic party convention at Chicago and the ensuing riots between demonstrators and police. Gitlin's "sense of fate and complicity, not a strategy," works well indeed in this strongly experiential chapter. It probably works less well in chapter 7 ("Name The System") which to dissect the rift between radical and liberal strategies and people. In his discussion of ideology, one feels the constraint rather than the advantage of first person narrative.

In the early parts of the book, the great merits of the personal chronicle contribute nicely in describing the fusion of organizations from SNCC to SDS; the formation of an ideology around the *Port Huron Statement*; and the cohesion of issues, from the final assault on Southern desegregation that brought blacks and whites together to a student movement that redressed long-standing and deep grievances in the administration and profession of university life. In this sense, the war in Vietnam served as a capstone to this cohesion of the New Left. It permitted a movement loose and disparate in structure to provide leadership to a disenchanted cluster of minorities, women, students, and deviant types, while utterly confounding political, military, and university authorities who were far better organized but too entranced with their traditional powers to realize the magnitude of the sea of change that the decade betokened.

Perhaps the most refreshing and courageous aspect of the *The Sixties* is the author's awareness of what Paul Hollander called the political pilgrim: a syndrome in which "marijuana-smoking Americans" are feted by "ascetic Asian revolutionaries." Gitlin understands that the "extraordinary impression" made upon visitors to North Vietnam by American radicals was well orchestrated to gain political ends and to hide the social and economic blemishes of a totalitarian regime. In the wave of anti-Americanism that gripped the New Left, "questions that might have emerged in calmer times about the political nature of 'the other side' felt like distractions and were swept into the shadows." To Gitlin's credit, what starts as a murmur of doubt concludes with a clear statement of criticism for a regime that in its despotism snatched a defeat from the jaws of victory. For if the American people as a whole learned a terrible and painful lesson about the limits of political power and military outreach, the American Left as a group learned an equally painful and troubling lesson about the distinction between opposition to a bad war and support for an even worse regime.

The final three chapters are on the implosion on the Left, the fade-out of the decade, and carrying on with the positive residuals of the decade—from egalitarian modes of behavior to self-help communitarian life-styles, reflects an intense disjunction. The author and probably others who lived through these times are torn between a deep feeling of being right about the wrongs of American involvement in Vietnam and, no less, a gnawing sense of being wrong about the rights of America as a decent country with a sound tradition of worthy values.

Gitlin has some understandable trouble with this paradox, reconciling America as a civilization with a specific episode in American history that was less than glorious. This is after all a book on a decade, not a treatise on normative political theory. One hopes that in his future work, Gitlin will turn his attention to just such larger implications of the experiences he describes. Others from Gitlin's period (Tom Kahn, the late Bayard Rustin, Julius Lester, Ronald Radosh, David Horowitz, Peter Collier, James Miller, David Farber, and Harvey Klehr, among others) have begun to make just such a reevaluation—with results that can only be anticipated.

The book has other conceptual problems. For example, if the rise of a women's movement constituted a "revolution in the revolution" (and I think Gitlin makes a decent case for this proposition), the sixties also produced an acceptance of and addiction to the drug culture that effectively constituted a counterrevolution within the revolution. Yet these more unsavory elements of the period, although discussed (for example, the role of LSD on the young radicals) tend to be dismissed, their effects on the countercultural remnants of the 1970s and 1980s is viewed more critically.

Gitlin is thoughtful and serious. But personal narrative and historical analysis do not always fit neatly between the covers of the same book, or the same decade. The movement for sexual equality stretches throughout the century and is not confined to the decade of the sixties; indeed, some feminists have persuasively argued that the 1960s confused liberation with libertinism. Also, premonitions of the drug culture were widely prevalent in the 1950s. And yet it may be this very linkage of narrative and analysis that makes this volume a trade book rather than a scholarly monograph.

If readers of *The Sixties* are in search of a systematic treatise on recent American political behavior or a carefully rendered history of a troubled people in a complex decade, they will be disappointed in this book. But if they are interested in a book that nicely captures in journalistic style the feel, the *verstehen* as it were, of a period, then this should be their cup of tea. Ultimately, the veracity of the work rests on one's estimate of Todd Gitlin as reporter and participant in the events he describes.

The book has what so few books by sociologists include: real people who say all sorts of things foolish and wise, and pass all sorts of resolutions—no less foolish or wise. It describes an era in which history is made up front rather than behind the backs of people. A sea of humanity rather than a set of structures determines events and doctrines. For me, at least, warts and all, this makes Gitlin's book refreshing to read and worthwhile to ponder.

From *Contemporary Sociology,* vol. 17, no. 6 (1988).

61

The Warring Sociologists*

Gouldner, Alvin W.

The war of words between sociological styles is different in content, but hardly less sharp in polemical form, than the ideological battles waged between Hamiltonians and Jeffersonians or Trotskyites and Stalinists. Pure sociologists view applied sociologists as interlopers, surrogates for social workers. Charges abound: Applied types have an investment in social ailments to the point of inventing ills when none obtain. They are considered parasitical in theory and opportunistic in practice. Applied sociologists accuse "grand theorists" of forgetting the human content and context of social science. It is said that if confronted by a man in the act of suicide, the theorist is more concerned with discovering if it is a case of anomic, altruistic, fatalistic, or egotistic suicide than pulling the "subject" off of the bridge.

Examined closely I cannot but feel that the gap between the two groups is largely contrived. The war of words deserves a better underpinning in reality than it has received up to now. But the call to reason is perhaps the least appreciated by those who need social science the most. Which is why the set of papers assembled by the editors on behalf of the Society for the Study of Social Problems has practical importance apart from the merits of the collection as such.

Let us take up the results that this book shows arising from sociological field work. The first immediate finding is the interference effect. This is a sociological counterpart of the Heisenberg effect in physics, in which the role of the experimenter in the natural setting is itself a consideration in defining a problem. While it took a decade to confirm this after Elton Mayo's factory researches, the interference effect is continually reconfirmed in new situations.

Second, there is the marginal effect. The social scientist operating in a practical situation is in some ways necessarily marginal with respect to the people he is dealing with. If he is studying local elites, he is outside the power structure and at best makes salutary recommendations. If he examines delinquency, he

* Alvin W. Gouldner and S.M. Miller (editors), *Applied Sociology: Opportunities and Problems.* (New York: The Free Press/Macmillan Publishers, 1966), pp. 466.

347

risks violating the law by participating in the gang culture. Therefore, in the attempt to remain legal, he is marginal.

Third, we may speak of the reinforcement effect. For example, in a delinquency subculture, researchers may tend to spend much time with the leadership, who may in fact be the most extreme and "antisocial" of the group.

Fourth, we may speak of the *involvement effect*. This generally takes place among industrial sociologists or sociologists in a bureaucratic setting, who are in a position to alter the decision-making process and hence tend to move beyond noting options and their consequences to becoming involved with the decisions the corporation takes. A fifth item is the God-like effect. This is usually found among sociologists working in underdeveloped areas, where the tendency is to view the social scientist as a magician, a seer, and a prophet. This is particularly so when recommendations result in better crops, higher cash payments, a shorter work week, or better living conditions. God help this God-like sociologist if the intended results do not come about!

Finally, there is the investigator-client effect. In any practical setting, it is difficult for the social scientist who is being paid directly by a client to know what the best decision is and not merely the range of decisions possible. The advice given may be tailored to expected norms. This sometimes occurs among industrial sociologists, who in their desire to settle labor-management tensions, raise issues of a peripheral nature, that conform to a management viewpoint. Here then is a whole set of problems raised in the papers of Rodman, Kolodny, Gardner, Jordan, and Miller, among others, which at one time would simply not have been perceived honestly by the sociological brotherhood.

The contributors to *Applied Sociology* illumine a set of applied results arising out of established social theory. A knowledge of David Riesman's concept of veto groups can be employed to arrive at the desegregation of a southern town. Localism, or Toennies's concept of *Gemeinschaft*, may explain an essential link between the individual and the amorphous cosmopolitan center and thus help reduce racial tensions in the South. In criminology, the definition of criminal behavior may be considered a complex pattern of decision making involving discretionary choices by those who administer the law. In the area of community leadership, Merton's notion of influentials may help to describe the actual relationship of power, by indicating levels of influence as a function of monetary position in the community. One study shows that the dominants among the leadership elements are business people, while the sub-dominants are professional people.

The key to the distinction between status groups for these sociologists remains economic wealth. It may also be the case, as is pointed out in another study, that alienation is not the same as marginality, that mediators in small-town life may be so involved in the routine of daily leadership that they become alienated from the larger chores of community life. This lends substance to current sociological views on alienation. Finally, Leon Festinger's theory of compliant behavior can be used to show that the law can act as an educational force in changing people's behavior. Therefore, the passage of civil rights acts is not merely justified in terms of moral necessity but may in fact change the sentiments of those who might otherwise be noncompliers.

In sum, sociological theory indicates that while you may not be able to teach racial equality, you can engender respect for law that aims at racial equality. The papers by Breed, Robbins, Newman, Pittman, Lowry, Greer, and Evan offer this kind of work.

Then there is a special set of papers in which established sociological theory challenges established social welfare notions. One study points out that the continued conceptualization of the aged as a minority group, whatever its political interests, is not justified regarding the aged as a social force. Since the aged lack group identity, they do not perceive of themselves as a social movement and therefore it might be more dangerous than helpful for sociologists in an action framework to conceive of them in this way. In another paper, it is pointed out that the family casework approach often assumes that solutions to family problems automatically improve parent-child relationships, when as a matter of fact, in the so-called normal family, strife between generations may be most manifest. Thus, these two papers by Streib and Sherwood present an interesting view of the role of theory in contradicting applied research and thereby promoting the search for new applied results which challenge old theory.

This brings us to another departure from the expected. Jury behavior, far from being "angry," tends to be extremely judicious. People who in normal circumstances are given to exaggerated responses behave with extreme caution in courtroom situations. Here in the essays by Moore, Feldman, and Simon we have another set of pioneering studies where new applied research negates established theory.

Applied Sociology is a volume not easily ensnared by old paradigms nor does it offer up any new ones. The final portion of the book points to the continuing dialogue, even the continuing agony that sociologists feel about the relationship of social theory and social action. The papers in this section seem not so much to represent a consensus as they do a range of alternative possibilities for viewing the famed "fact-value" dichotomy. One end of the continuum is represented by Ralph Ross. He sees science as a value in itself. As a matter of fact, he declares that the core value which the scientist bears is that of science per se, namely, truth seeking. Somewhat less extreme is the position taken by Robert Bierstedt, who sees the dualism between scientific and public service as everlasting and as equivalent to the distinction between sociology and action. But he also goes on to note the need of the sociologist to be responsive to both his public and his scientific role, even though the twain shall never meet. Occupying the middle ground, Mabel Elliott argues that the solution of this science-action dualism lies in greater cohesion and coming together of sociologists and psychologists. Once they close the gap organizationally, certain problems will fade away.

For Llewellyn Gross, the gap is already closed, since the question consists of how to look at the problem in terms of facts and values rather than resolving the relationships. He notes that a dualism between the two cannot be maintained since the conditions and consequences for both factual and value statements are similar in many essential respects; hence the facts and values used for identifying and resolving social problems may be scientifically defined and prescribed. Alfred McClung Lee takes this line of reasoning to its ultimate by noting that the defenders of the dualism between science and action really have a psychological investment in science as something clean and in action as something dirty. He urges those who want respectability to seek a comfortable cult instead of converting social science into a ritual-ridden secular faith. "Scientific innovation of a fundamental sort has never been legitimate even though it may be later legitimated. It is always unorthodox, agitational, and irreverent."

The final paper in the work, by coeditor S.M. Miller, is a companion piece to Gouldner's opening paper. Gouldner indicates the challenges and responsibilities in developing an applied social science, in achieving the kind of social science in which the rift between policy maker and social scientist can be mended in much the way the clinical treatment of patients resolves the "natural" illness of the patient in the "unnatural" setting of the hospital. Miller, for his part, points out the dangers involved in an applied sociology. He notes how easily the applied sociologist can serve rather than harness power and how readily he can drift into working within the discursive terms set by the interests of his organization. But this is precisely the dilemma that has continued to haunt those who live in the interstices of liberalism and radicalism.

This pioneering effort to introduce the problems of applied social science to a general lay public is subject to many of the strains that afflict the intended clientele. But unlike that clientele and as an instruction to it, the book, its contributors, also its editors shared an appreciation of the self-awareness and current limits of research, as well as a creative potential for designing a future. This makes *Applied Sociology* significant reading for those interested in changing, no less than living in, the world—even if the book only hints at how to change much less live in such a world.

From *Frontier*, vol. 18, no. 3 (1967), pp. 15–16.

62

Culture of Sociology and Sociology of Culture*

Graña, César

César Graña was, by any standard employed, both a complex personality and a dedicated social scientist. The first part of this proposition will be evident to the reader of these essays. It was also readily apparent to those who had the benefit of knowing him, even casually. The second part of this proposition, his profound commitment to social science in general and to sociology in particular, is less easy to detect or describe. Graña was such a brilliant literary stylist, so clearly a writer who took every word of his English seriously, that it is all to easy to overlook that throughout his career his subject matter uniformly remained the stuff of social research: human institutions like museums, urban structures like cities, and political artifacts like ideologies. In short, those elements that distinguish and identify society in contrast to behavior or nature.

The volume of essays before you exemplifies a style of doing work that has become increasingly rare in American academic life: the scholar revises and reconsiders a collection of working papers, some are entirely finished, others are in a penultimate stage, and still others are merely stitched together. In the hands of a lesser intellectual craftsman, many of these papers would long since have been published, and their author honored for so doing. But it is one of the hallmarks of the late Cesar Grana that he was a perfectionist. And if the absence of his name in the annual catalogues of professional production in recent years caused some to question his commitment to play by the rules of the academy, he could scarcely care less. And now that his revisions and reconsiderations are perforce complete, his analytical skills can now be shared with others. Death puts to an end the anguishing search for the better.

Indeed, before his life was cut short in a highway accident in Spain in late 1986, César Graña was not only completing work on many of his briefer works, but was assembling material for a full-scale study of the role of art and aesthetic theory in modern society. In addition, he was developing the working format

---

* César Graña, *Meaning and Authenticity* (New Brunswick and Oxford: Transaction Publishers, 1988).

for a cultural ethnography of Seville—the city in Spain which he most loved and best knew. It might well be that were he still alive, César would consider this publication of his later papers a case of sheer meddling. And while those who knew César will understand that this is a charge that will not readily go quietly into the night, in the final instance we decided that to let these papers languish would have been a far worse decision. Good social research with a human face is too rare a commodity to be squandered or suppressed.

Nonetheless, and in a prima facie sense, sifting the dry bones of another person's literary-sociological remains is certainly a case of meddling. Therefore such a step requires at least a brief explanation. The immense editorial contributions rendered to this project by Marigay Graña, César's life companion and wife, may seem to make such justification superfluous. But I think not. For in the case of these papers, even absent such powerful and indispensable personal support, a case should and deserves to be made for the publication of *Meaning and Authenticity.*

It is hard to say whether Graña had any sort of intellectual master plan. I see scant evidence for this. What he had was the essayist's knack of pursuing a problem in a many-sided way over time. He never quite finished with a problem, since real problems never finish exhausting the moral codebooks that people employ in the conduct of their everyday affairs. So what we have is a lifetime of concern with a series of problems: the relationship of European to American cultural values, social mores and literary manners, the inheritance of aristocratic traditions by the modern intelligentsia, and the place of art in mass society in contrast to the place of people in traditional society. These themes are the raw materials of his trilogy of works: *Modernity and its Discontents; Fact and Symbol;* and now, *Meaning and Authenticity.*

One of Graña's most favored and favorite sociologists was Daniel Bell. I suspect that, apart from his great respect for Bell's efforts to link culture and civilization in its advanced industrial setting, there is the fact that Graña also envisioned himself as a figure interested in the same themes: although he looked backward to find the present rather than looking at the present to find the future, as did Bell.

Another, more elusive element is the parallel respect of both writers for the essay form. As I noted in a review of *The Winding Passage* some years ago, Bell is a premier essayist—as indeed was Graña. Both understood the criteria that Montaigne long ago established for giving substance to the essay form: it must be well written, precise, with a focused theme and it must employ a moral purpose directed to resolving the question: *Que sais-je?* What Graña says of Bell in the opening essay of *Meaning and Authenticity* is no less true of himself, "a thinker, a thought-man, a *penseur*, a muller over things significant. Possibly an uneasy tribute in a profession which has never surrendered its aspiration, at least its ultimate aspiration, to the empirical mastery of the chosen realm." Such is the essence of this posthumous volume.

Coupled with *Fact and Symbol*, this volume is as close as we can get to a culture of sociology no less than to a sociology of culture. This dialectic stamps each essay, which makes some of them hard going for those in search of finite answers. And yet, in the end this dialectic enriches our understanding of both Western societies writ large and the lens of classical sociology through which we observe the big picture. Nowhere is this better illustrated than in the essay "On the Aesthetic Prejudices of the Sociology of Art", in which Graña imaginatively lays bare the emptiness of conventional humanistic assaults on sociology, only to find that sociology has its own uninspected conventions, usually bound up with the presentations of inherited traditions and styles.

Graña's assault on a naive aesthetic realism is no less a critique of sociological dogmatism, techniques of analysis that do little to advance the processes of art to "depict" and not simply "record" the world in its own terms. In this finely grained examination of the connection between individual creativity and the everyday life of collectiv-ivities, one finds the crucial and oft-repeated key message in Graña's own work: art is liberating, and sociology as a bearer of just such a liberating culture is thus part of that larger world of art. This proposition does not obviate the more conventional converse: that art is very much part of the social world. The tensions between individual creativity and social participation are the meeting place of culture and sociology; for Graña it makes possible the love of the former without sacrificing the use of the latter.

Graña has been described at times as a conservative, even by friends. But this is just plainly not the case, unless one means by conservative the exploration and preservation of a sense of tradition. But by such a broad definition, as Graña himself is at pains to explain, Marx no less than de Tocqueville or Taine was conservative. For any sense of the "long tradition," to use Raymond Williams' phrase involves a sense of cultural continuities with the past and within a group. The struggle, if such it be, is in what to keep no less than what to discard, and further, who is to dispose and who is to propose. The sociological task at one level is to explain how people decide to discard some ideas and retain others, while the great majority simply fall into disuse.

"On the Contradictions of Ideas in Marxian Philosophy of History" seeks to understand precisely how defining traditions are retained (i.e., prey on the human mind even under new technological conditions and social relations). But this is also a study of how an ideology like Marxism, which denies the autonomous nature of aesthetic production, is trapped by a set of false alternatives: On the one hand is a determinism that deprives the individual of choice no less than tradition; on the other a voluntarism that makes of Marxian claims to be science a shambles and indeed returns Marxism to the womb of ideology and its own meager inner resources.

This concern with Marxism was no mere abstraction. Graña had a life-long disdain for party politics, none more so than Communist party politics. Several of these essays strongly condemn notions of a Communist party that creates the historical conditions of its ideology and the social conditions for who shall live and who shall die. The earliest piece of "public writing" that César left behind, appeared in *The Dartmouth* of March 24th, 1948. Here we find him commenting on the Henry Wallace presidential campaign thus:

> Liberalism is open inquiry and honest critical answers to honest critical questions. What does Wallace do when confronted with communist infiltration in his party and with criticism of the Soviet State? He answers with countercharges about the imperfections of the American system, a substitute for argument well known to the communist press. . . . Wallace does not understand the nature of dogma. As if the political behavior of the communists were not enough, Soviet scientific pronouncements, literary purges, and artistic dictation have been screaming but one thing: that Stalinism is no longer a part of the Left, but a monolithic dogma, absolute and elusive, which seeks total allegiance and political and intellectual immobility.

These were far from commonplace observations in university life of the late 1940s; in fact, they are still muted sentiments, more grudgingly acknowledged than examined.

What prompts recollection of this extract from an article written forty years ago is that throughout his life Graña held firm to the same principles of artistic openness and cultural freedom that have since become the rallying cry not only of dissidents in Eastern Europe but increasingly of government officials in more enlightened areas from Berlin to Beijing. But even this is less significant than the fact that he made the statement at all. In a cultural climate of near-universal rapture with the Left, Graña asserted the principles of liberalism, certainly not of any doctrinaire sort, but those of the open society as discussed and dissected by people like Popper and Polanyi. Graña's concern with Marxism was thus nothing short of a life-long interest in the conditions that forbid individuals in society to be free.

The totalitarian temptation also compelled Graña to examine how intellectuals as a class, a group that is highly favored in bourgeois society, become the purveyors of ideology and willing accomplices to the betrayal of ideals of free expression. His early essay "On a Sociology of the Intelligentsia" follows closely the analysis of Karl Mannheim in *Ideology and Utopia*. For it is the very appearance of democracy as a modern social movement that separates the intelligentsia from ordinary citizens. The arrogance, the hubris, the readiness to betray its sacred intellectual trust derive from a presumption that democracy needs its elite interpreters to properly "feel the popular pulse." Vanguardism on the Left, and futurism on the Right permit the intellectual to imagine that he is breaking his inherited class isolation. Fault finding is equated with intellectual liberation. Intelligence as a value is betrayed by ideology in search of utopian visions of liberation. Social causes are divested from the very well spring of creativity: private judgment.

Graña's own work rested far more on a sense and sensibility of national structures than of class contradictions. The organization of culture is national, since the language of a society is often national, with regional and local variations to be sure. In this community of culture, social life is organized by a vast array of sentiments and feelings that pass from generation to generation, through family trees that sometimes turn outward and other times turn inward to enrich and protect themselves. This sort of emphasis on self and family was hardly a fashionable position to take. Indeed, sociology has all but abandoned the search for national meanings, despite the obvious fact that being part of a nation continues to fascinate and inform some of the most important writers and writings of the period. Luigi Barzini on Italians, Ralf Dahrendorf on Germans, George Orwell on the English, to name but a few, reveal the sort of shrewd insights that Graña appreciated and utilized in his own ongoing studies of Spain.

Sociologists of the pedestrian had forgotten the obvious: that world wars are fought between nations. In World War I German and French people all became part of the Axis war effort, starting with the working class. And in the United States, England, and other western powers that had similar class systems found the workers forging holy bonds with middle classes to defend the cause of Allied powers. Graña's great strength as a thinker was his love of a people in full-blooded anthropological regalia and not as a mission of a narrow-minded social dogma. His studies of Seville, alas only a fragment of what César had in mind as a long range project for his retirement, show that the title of the volume *Meaning and Authenticity* is especially appropriate. Such abstract terms take place in essentially national contexts, in which the nuance of language no less than the cash nexus define essentially social relationships.

Graña was a dialectical thinker of superb proportions, that are only weakly captured in a book title. For example, "The Bullfight and Spanish National Decadence" can easily be misread. The bullfight is the antitheses of that economic and political decadence through which Spain has labored for so many decades, even centuries. The bullfight provides Spain's "polemical repertory." The folk and popular imagery of the bullfight is the "historical component of the life of the (Spanish) people." God and Bull alike are ever watching, defining the heroic and miraculous, no less than the tawdry and the venal.

Graña's excursion into large-scale systems involves equally large-scale symbols. The victory of the bullfight in Spanish national life coincides with the defeat of Spain's economic preeminence. The panorama of rejoicing are wrapped up with the bullfight, since nationalism itself is so expressed. How is one to give meaning to national integration in an age of decline except through such sentiments? Here then we have a sociology of culture that takes seriously the popular culture and does not diminish it through the shallow notion that poverty, even decadence, can express itself only in revolt, or even worse, in empty formulas about rebellion. In this, Graña had sensed that an authentic sociology, like an authentic movement in any sphere of life, must begin with the sentiments of a people—life as a symbolic fusion of language and art, no less than a grinding material poverty. Like the good anthropologist that he was, Graña appreciated that material poverty and spiritual impover-ishment are radically different concepts. In his commitment to the everyday cultural practices of a people, of a city, of a community, he was probably truer to the original Marxian idea of cultural continuities amidst economic changes than most of the latter-day revolutionary saints. Indeed, he shares this special feeling for the grandeur of ordinary folk with a contemporary, the late Oscar Lewis.

Graña did not so much write about as live problems of national devel-opment. He was a man of three cultures: born in South America, educated in the United States, and dedicated to the culture of Spain, or more exactly, *hispanidad.* These essays provide fascinating points of comparison and con-trast between Mediterranean and Central European traditions, essentially the Germanic style that still prevails in most American departments of sociology. Graña was more the bemused outsider looking in than the presumed insider looking out at the larger world. He took for granted that personal character counts for as much as social standing. And he was less concerned with the cumulative or building block effect of his work than with each piece as a little insight. The size of the study does not uniquely determine the quality of anal-ysis. Perhaps this perspective is part of the aristocratic tradition, in contrast to the bourgeois tradition. But clearly, Graña's method of work shares insights with the reader rather than instructing him in correct thoughts.

In short, César Graña was a fully realized man, a complete person. He pos-sessed a keen sense of the unity of academic practice with intellectual theory. His disdain for simplification and vulgarity, for forcing every issue and every theme into a single variable, led him to take the data of a society as a given. Whether such data were sentiments or habits at the psychological level or class, language or ethnic identification at the stratification level, Graña's con-cern was description as a rich exercise. Narrative held a fascination unto itself. Lessons were derived from the narrative, but by the reader or the observer not by the writer *for* the reader. As a result, César frequently found himself at odds with other members of the department at the University of California, San Diego with which he was long affiliated; for them special concerns or selective variables were more important than the sort of nondirective approach characteristic of his person and temperament.

As gentle and quiet as Graña was in public, in the counsels of departmental affairs, he was fierce and uncompromising. Those who came up for tenure with the support of ethnic caucuses or ideological clusters but without intellectual grounds found in Graña a formidable opponent. One such candidate was rejected by Graña on the grounds of a "disastrous provincialism of outlook and poverty of scholarship. I realize that these are harsh words; but I can find no others." It was the candidate's "wanton reductionism" that ultimately irritated Graña. The grievance of a people should not be allowed to translate into the presumption of being a self-declared spokesperson. Suffering of others does not "justify the abandonment of reasoned and documented analysis, or for the creation of ill-informed, simplistic adversary mythologies." These are not easy utterances to render in an atmosphere of affirmative action.

In one of his many unpublished aphorisms, Graña says that "hypocrisy is the homage that human nature pays to virtue." Graña refused to abide by hypocrisy and did not pay such homage to the mediocre. When a famous figure was urged upon a sociology department in the University of California system, Graña alone opposed the appointment, he did what few of this candidate's defenders did: he read the entire corpus of the candidate's work. He examined and exhumed, book by book and essay by essay, the contents of this scholar's writings. In short, Graña did what the other members took for granted: he evaluated the quality of the scholarship and the character of the scholar that emerges from the work—and only from the work. His conclusions were measured but uncompromising: the candidate's "enterprise is at an end, the product of an exhausted teleological tradition that has no choice but to try to wring out 'new' perspectives by constantly changing the 'dialectical' grounds." Graña was quick to grant that the presence in the department of this candidate would serve as a stimulus: "a force so to speak, who would cause the intellectual life of the department to jump faster." The problem was that this candidate was not especially interested in intellectual coexistence. "And thus I was finally convinced, unlike some of my colleagues, that the risk far outweighed the promise."

These are difficult matters to discuss. The judgment of departmental colleagues upon each other is an intimate matter of preferences, not a science of right and wrong. And in this, Graña's views were certainly no more infallible than those of his colleagues. But the reason for daring to introduce such a discordant note in this introduction is to demonstrate Graña had a certain spine, a dedication to democratic decision making that was isomorphic and parallel to his sociological analysis. His judgments were uniformly cordial and devoid of bile or guile. The judgments he rendered were based on work performed. Even in troubled circumstances, not a shred of paper exists that would show César to be less than fair or on firm intellectual ground.

Graña's concerns are not restricted to the intramural. He was just as willing to challenge university programs (even those he was asked to head) and administrative pretenses. He was asked to direct the The History of Consciousness Program at one of the branches at the University of California. He did not so much resist this appointment as seek clarification. The automaticity, the givenness of a concept like consciousness gave him pause, if not offense. Was the program interested in comparing the constellation of Marxist ideas of class consciousness or James Joyce's stream of consciousness? Of course, Graña full well knew the answer. But he gave the program's administrator a clinic on James, Flaubert, Byron, Dostoevsky, Dewey, Fitzgerald, Mann, and their ideas on consciousness. Graña then went to the ideological heart of the matter, "Consciousness cannot be made comprehensible unless it is defined within some perceivable historical or social circumstance." Whatever consciousness is or turns out to be, it "cannot be regarded simply as a mood, sense, lift, or even structure of perception in itself. It has to be part of a concrete and desirable act of understanding." Graña was willing to head the program, but only if there were truth in packaging: as a program in comparative cultural studies and history.

There was something quixotic in Graña's arguing with a university administrator, attempting to convince the convinced that the equation of the political with the ideological was not healthy for the life of social science or the university in general. But there was nothing dogmatic in his thinking? He nominated Norman Mailer for a visiting professorship, praised Eric Hobsbawm's *Primitive Rebels*, and wrote letters to the San Diego newspapers denouncing Richard Nixon. In this, Graña was a free spirit, practicing the sort of unfettered analysis suggested by these writings. His work offers a sensitizing rather than systematic approach—and in so doing he exemplifies the supple mind and flexible approach that made him special. After all, sensitivities can be refined, whereas systems can just as readily, and with relish, be broken. Graña fought against abstract systems with the weapon of concrete cultures. In so doing, he offered sociology a fresh perspective, one as rare as it was required.

In an unpublished collection of aphorisms and wry commentaries that he called: "A Barroom Napkin Anthology," Graña asks, rhetorically to be sure, "Is sociology a vision of the world or is it a sampling of the world?" Graña does not answer his own query. I would suggest that for Graña it is a vision of the world by the act of sampling. His aphoristic style indicates as much. Graña writes of museums as the "disembodied nature of democratic availability." Which is to say, "anyone can look at the dining hall or swimming pools of the Hearst Castle, but no one eats or swims there." Well, this sample permits a vision, and this characterizes Graña's work in general. Again, I take refuge in another of his aphorisms: "The Liberty Bell, now cracked, rings still. It dies as a concrete object. It is reborn as a cultural object." What is one to make of this? Insight and outlook coalesce, the concrete and abstract fuse in the reader's mind. Observations by the author are internalized as the experience of the reader.

What Graña offers his audience in the final analysis is not only moral lessons embodied in the essay form but the emotional insight embodied in the short story and the intellectual values embraced by the social experience. In this, the second volume of his essays in the sociology of art and literature with which I have been privileged to be involved, I find myself in deep mourning all over again for the loss of this modest, unassuming, and entirely worldly person. He did not publish much in his lifetime, but he thought a good deal. There is little point in bemoaning what Graña did not produce in his years on earth. The aristocratic mode was perhaps too much with him. Thus, it is far wiser to soak up what he did leave us. We become better for the experience, as well as sharper analysts in the process. Graña provides us with no small or commonplace combination of skills in this day and age of ideological polities and utopian sociologies. This rich harvest of mature papers makes it abundantly, nay painfully clear, what a fine figure of a man and a solid citizen of sociology we have lost.

From César Graña, "Introduction" to *Meaning and Authenticity* (New Brunswick and Oxford: Transaction Publishers, 1988).

63

Is the Future an Extension of the Present?*

Heilbroner, Robert L.

The fatal trap for many excellent social scientists—and Heilbroner in ten previous books has proved beyond a shadow of a doubt he is one—is to fall prey to punditry and poor philosophy; and Heilbroner, in *An Inquiry into the Human Prospect*, has done just that. To be sure, any series of reflections on the human future, divided into five quick chapters and collapsed into 150 pages (more like 120 pages if we exclude front matter, blank pages, and overblown acknowledgements) is likely to raise more inquiries than responses. One receives the impression of a potentially decent journal article being expanded to fit the contours of a commercial book, a process not unlike expanding a punchy short story to fit the market needs of a novel-buying audience.

Lest readers of this review think me too critical or unsympathetic, I would like to single out some leading ideas, teasingly stated but underdeveloped, that reveal the high quality of Heilbroner's mind and what indeed might have been the basis for a first-rate journal article instead of a second-rate book.

First and foremost is Heilbroner's introduction of the Hobbesian problem in income distribution—that there is a free-for-all for limited higher income positions. This struggle is compounded by the impossibility of achieving equity in a no-growth, straight-jacketed economy-a situation that imposes intolerable strains upon the democratic institutions of Western society. Beyond that, Heilbroner makes clear that this problem is as profoundly disconcerting to the Eastern socialist as it is for the Western capitalist. Thus, the convergence of industrial systems leads to an emergence of shared ideological dilemmas. In some measure, Heilbroner's thinking is little else than the established notion that industrial societies, whatever the political system, raise similar problems that ultimately triumph over systemic differences. That notwithstanding, he does appreciate capitalist and socialist nations' need for new answers to this shared industrial fate.

---

* Robert L. Heilbroner, *An Inquiry into the Human Prospect* (New York: W.W. Norton & Company), pp. 224.

A rather neat twist on Heilbroner's convergence hypothesis is the absence of social harmony in both the United States and the Soviet Union. Both nations have held out the promise that, with economic transfer from agrarianism to industrialization, real equity would be achieved. Beyond that, the social harmony of classes in the West and sectors in the East never materialized. Quantifiable improvements, yes; qualitative solutions, no. Everything from disintegration of family life; high crime rates; urban disintegration; and, finally, the serious deterioration of environments demonstrate the need for a higher societal analysis based on the imposition of common values on both capitalist and socialist systems, the two chief varieties of the industrializing society. Heilbroner does indicate that this industrial order has its own categorical imperatives: high technological input, extreme emphasis on efficiency, and a faith in the production of large numbers of goods. On the other hand, the transformation from capitalism to socialism either does not materialize or, when it does, takes place under conditions of backwardness that merely replicate rather than overcome the supposed evils of capitalism, and represent two tactical responses to backwardness rather than a rigorous historical determinism. Heilbroner seems to say that the evils are real enough but that the solutions remain as ubiquitous and elusive as ever.

To counterbalance the goodies there are the banalities, which can only be highlighted. For in some strange way, once Heilbroner leaves his area of expertise, he becomes as subject to the fables and foibles of the social sciences as anyone I have raid in recent times. First, there is the business of the population time bomb recited with the same foreboding and loathing most pop literature echoes on this question: monumental increases in human numbers, alarming breakdowns of governmental efficiency, mass starvation, and Malthusian checks that will work only insofar as they are not offset by a large increase in food production. Heilbroner writes as if he is more worried over the solution to starvation than the facts of starvation. This kind of alarmist writing is not only liberal chic, but also largely fictional. The Third World is not all of one piece. True, India has a population problem, but it is equally true that nations like Argentina, Brazil, and even Canada have problems of too few people. Indeed, these countries have worked hard in recent years to stimulate higher populations. Heilbroner has thrown this parallel of underpopulation and underdevelopment largely to the wind, with disastrous effects. It throws him right back into a Malthusian framework in which war, famine, and starvation are almost hoped-for respites from a supposed population explosion.

A second major issue about which one might have wished for greater clarity is the issue of the environment and its natural disruption. Again, one senses that Heilbroner is captive of the common folklore. To speak of "environmental disruption" and "environmental deterioration" in terms of resources that are only wasted, and to further deny the prospect (without investigating what in fact is being achieved) of developing the necessary technology to overcome these environmental problems, is to deny what has hitherto always been the case: the capacity of industrialization to develop solutions and generate appropriate responses to economic imbalances. Quite beyond this, the fact that Heilbroner has for years cogently argued the case for development, practically whatever its costs in human terms, and is now reconsidering the same needs for development because of presumed cost factors in environment terms, indicates an unrealistic form of reasoning, certainly not calculated to inspire confidence in an inquiry into future human prospects.

The most disturbing aspect of Heilbroner's work is his uncritical praise of the neo-Freudian view of authoritarianism, specifically, the notion of a national identification that is equal to the "adult sublimation of childhood obedience." Father fixation, which he refers to as an indispensable precondition for exercise of political action when it is linked to early childhood attitudes about the extended family, is a thoroughly discredited view of nationality. Such a view is reported without criticism of authoritarianism as a political standard. Quite unlike Erich Fromm who postulated in *Escape from Freedom* a similar theory of personal immaturity and political reaction, Heilbroner seems cavalier about authoritarianism. He repeats the theory of infantile regression as a precondition for the politics of nationalism. If this theory were predictive, then there should be a similar set of national outcomes throughout the world or wherever similar child-rearing patterns exist in Western culture. But this is not the case, since similar patterns of childhood development result in such entirely different outcomes as German Nazism, British monarchism, and American republicanism. Most researchers have thus properly called into question this tunnel vision of nationalism, however superficially attractive it may appear to be in the light of Hitler and the Holocaust.

This excessive psychologism indicates a deeper problem in Heilbroner's work, what might be referred to as the metaphysical pathos, a premature surrender to the inevitable. He seems overwhelmed by the need for development and of being pained by the lawful truths of the process of fully developing a society. However, a little less pain might have provided a few more options to these awful preferences. It is one thing to assert the rigor of science, quite another to slip into the dogma that whatever is, must somehow be.

This metaphysical pathos discourages systemic analysis. While there is a discussion of the Capitalist-Socialist axis, the discussion never gets serious enough to warrant reexamining problems that are specific and endemic to this century. The rise of fascism, the power of racism, the redefinition of development as militarism—addressing these isms would have given flesh and blood to the dry bones of this inquiry into the human perspective. Lacking such analysis, what we have are speculations by a brilliant economist looking at reality from the outside, fascinated by events but unwilling to cope with the perversities of the present era. It is almost as if dealing with such issues as European fascism or American racism, Soviet religious and class exclusionism, etc., would have turned this inquiry into a tract for our times. And Heilbroner seems of two minds on how down and dirty he wants to get—whether in fact he wants to convey the human perspective in philosophic or in policy terms.

As a result, the prophetic speculations of the author tend to be insipid rather than inspired. We are told about the end of the giant factory, the termination of huge office complexes, or the end of the urban complex. However, we are not told what will replace these monstrosities or how they are to be replaced and at what cost. Furthermore, we are not informed about efforts which are presently under way in these technical areas to bring to human size this industrial giant. The author seems impatient with what is going on in his search for the outcomes of the century. To end his effort with a plea for the public to take precedence over the private is, it seems to me, not to take seriously what is going on. Disenchantment, disillusionment with the commonweal, the leap into privatization, represents a breakdown in the very public institutions that Heilbroner urges us to adopt anew. The analysis of the future must proceed with a final reflection on why privacy rather than publicity, the individual rather than the collective, has come to occupy so many of our thoughts and practices; why we have been reduced to an individualism that threatens to break out into pure anarchism; and why, in fact, the human prospect is so grim, remaining as mysterious at the end of this volume as at its outset.

It is the task of the social scientist to get beyond the psychic state of feeling either optimistic or pessimistic about the future, and into an appraisal of the human condition that will allow us to live, however lacking in tranquility, in a world made by people in the present. In short, this volume is a disappointing exercise in futurology because it is all too ready to take the present moment in history as the future of actual history itself. In that sense, Heilbroner has fallen victim to the worst fears of his own past writing on economics as equilibrium: a dismal and fatal assumption that whatever is, must be.

From *Business and Society Review*, vol. 4, no. 3 (1974), pp. 101–103.

64

The Banality of Culture*

Henry, Jules

In nineteenth century Europe, there was a tradition of showing respect to the unusual or extraordinary book by writing essays *en hommage* to it. This tradition is long dead. First, most commercial and academic publications have turned to public relations with a vengeance—thinking policy the better part of wisdom trying to review all the books of all the publishers, in neat little one-inch cubicles if possible, in less tidy but equally condensed manner where not possible. Second, not many great books are written any more. If not to publish is to perish, then we can be certain, given man's will to survive, that publications will flow like wine. Quantity has come to displace quality, and worse, to define quality. The concept of book as commodity has seen to that. But there is a third reason why great books are not written often. It is a deep propensity of our age of suspicious cynicism to define someone or some intellectual work as great, only if posterity has made a judgment. In an effort to avoid sentiment, we abjure strong judgment. To compensate for the sickening use of superlatives by public relations factories we avoid firm views. And in an effort to be objective, to uphold the sacred Boy Scout law, we become bland—bringing the object of our attentions down to the same dismal level.

All this comes to mind because I have been confronted by a great book (I mean great, not grim—since the book is filled throughout with charm, wit, and urbanity). I have spent some nights trying to convey this fact within the impossible strictures of the formal book review and the formal shibboleths of praise. I am referring to *Culture Against Man*. It is first of all a great book because it cannot be categorized in conventional social science terms. Professor Henry makes a living by teaching anthropology. But he has been clever enough to forget this accidental fact of personal career, when writing a book. If anyone thinks that the humanistic tradition in the social sciences is dead or passé, let him sample *Culture Against Man*. This is not the petrified organizational humanism manufactured to save academics from a world without Providential Design. It is the humanism of a trained mind—of someone who

---

* Jules Henry, *Culture Against Man* (New York: Random House, 1963), pp. 495.

sees no contradiction between a poet like Keats and a scientist like Benedict, who sees no jarring discontinuities between a playright like Camus and a field worker like Boas. All four of these people are now dead—but their death is redeemed by the living they have nurtured. The incubation period is sometimes long and painful, but the waiting is perhaps a necessary price. Jules Henry has written a book that gives hope to the hopeless and feeling to the embittered. And if the book is not perfect, if it suffers from generalizing without theorizing and from specification without typification, one can only be reminded of the proverb: in the land of the blind, the one-eyed man is king.

Culture Against Man is really two books imperfectly blended to define a unitary picture of how the cultural apparatus of American society has been mobilized in the service of depersonalizing the person, and dehumanizing the human. It is at once an ethnographic report and a theoretical explanation. At the level of ethnographic recording, this is a painful book to confront—not so much because of any starting findings, but because the ordinary, common place speech of high school students, protective middle class parents, and pathetic old men who are declassé, builds up a frightening picture of inhumanity to which we have become callously indifferent. And Henry understands why we have become so indifferent, why the banality of culture can spill over into the banality of evil. It occurs because this is what we are taught to be: by slick ad-men, by innocent magazines for teenagers, by deluded politicians and mistrustful academics. This is not an exposé, since the deluders are themselves deluded, since the cruel are themselves mistreated. The dialectic is that no one escapes unscathed. The cultural machine claims as its victims the myth-makers no less than the mass market. The innocent may be deluded, but the guilty are depraved. The sick and the infirm described in Henry's section on human obsolescence may be narcotized, but the process of dehumanization claims its perpetrators no less than the victimized. This interactionist theory of pathology is the core of Henry's theoretical explanation.

One point which this reviewer found particularly attractive about *Culture Against Man* is the way in which insight functions to create deeper social comprehension. After all, Henry's account of the position of children in middle-class homes is not much different than Arnold Green's examination of this in *The Middle Class Made Child and Neurosis*, nor is his description of old age homes much different than Erving Goffman's description of total institutional life in *Asylums*, nor is his account of the new civilian militarists who design scenarios for World War III much different than my own effort on the *The War Game* (indeed, it is far more cursory and perfunctory). But what it has, that all three lack to one degree or another, is the vision of meanness entailed, the madness involved, in destroying the ability of children to function normally, humiliating the dignity of the aged, and rendering our earth lifeless. He senses and grasps the continuity between the insensitive parent and the senseless policy maker or between the unthinking anticommunism of a high school student and the rhetoric of over-simplified anticommunism that guides public policy. He grasps the elemental fact of the cultural unity of man—the inescapable fusion between the private life of a person and the public careers of people. It is simply not true that the public bastard can be the private saint. This duality of public and private is a myth created by late romantic novelists, a myth created to absolve guilt-to escape through privatizations, into a world where socialization has become a process of seeking self-identity through liquidation of the other. Because Mr. Henry disallows such comforting dualisms of our culture, his book has a cutting edge that devastates the devastators.

Two possible lines of criticism suggest themselves to me. The objections are intended as preliminary and tentative, because I am not sure that I know the answers. Nonetheless, they merit the consideration of those who take seriously a volume such as this. First, the setting of *Culture Against Man* appears parochial when viewed against the global problems discussed. The United States is a region of the world with special problems that both distinguish it from other societies and give it a special connection with other societies. One gets the distinct feeling that for Henry, America is a scaled-off island-acting out its kinship relations in public-relations terms. Thus, the political judgments are rendered in hot-house isolation from larger political considerations.

Clearly, this is not the first nor only anthropologist against whom such a charge can be made. For what is vividly described is not simply cultural forces against human forces, but social forces against human forces. But the concept of society is not clear enough. The phenomenology of this society may be culturally definable, but the history of this society requires some more adequate framework. What is needed is a general concept of the overdeveloped society as a complement to the culturally deprived person. For what Henry is describing is a special kind of starvation—one that comes from having too much of the wrong thing. It is not enough to expose the humiliations of status or of superordination and subordination in specific situations, without evaluating the present nature and kinds of power as a built-in feature of the American economic and political order. Once cast in such a perspective (i.e., some theoretical account of whither we have come and where we are going), the problem of normalizing culture can be connected to the problem of social change. There is a horrible dead end in the particularistic nature of the cultural starvation we are suffering through, an implication of approaching death with little appreciation of rejuvenation and alteration. Henry's final half-hearted attempt at optimism rests on a telos of men being forced into enlightenment "although he (*homo sapiens*) has never accepted it without a bitter fight." However, precisely such a philosophy of history makes enlightenment impossible, since it disallows real development and does not answer which men want what and when.

This brings me to the second point of personal uneasiness. It is the underlying assumption, after the fashion of Rousseau, that things were better in the past, that material culture and civilization are necessarily corrupting by destroying simple unities between man and labor, man and love, man and self. Culture has after all had a civilizing effect: the flagellants are gone (at least in their pristine form), we no longer incarcerate the mentally ill with the petty thief. And whatever the deformities of mass culture, we have made possible for the first time the technological possibilities for a truly integrated form of social life. It is true that the costs of social development in the United States, and no less in other parts of the First World, have been incredibly high; but so too have risen the opportunities, the life-chances, and the capacity for fulfillment. If America is the land of culture against man, it is also the land that has offered a prevision of the future, a land where man has beaten back one natural obstacle after another. I am not advocating an end to the cutting-edge, an end to the need for a radical ideology. Quite the contrary, the need for reconstruction is deeper precisely because the better is the critic of the good. There is no need to become nostalgic, even mildly so, in order to demonstrate the cruelties of a culture turned against itself.

The price of the contractual society, the achieving society, the capitalist society is exacting and high. But were we in a superior position when we had an organic ascriptive and feudal society? It may be my own philosophy of history peeking through, but I suggest that the answer to this is an unequivocal no. Nostalgia which is given a radical gloss can no more pass muster than older varieties of nostalgia given a conservative thrust.

I am not suggesting that Mr. Henry would deny this. I am saying that he may avoid coming to grips with the problem of the past, and more decisively, the problem of the future, because his emphasis is so exclusively on a programmatic description of present realities. He leaves us with the agony. He deposits us in the abyss—a stage which Lord knows we damned well belter comprehend. But out of this muck is fashioned man himself and out of this putrefaction is an ecstatic vision of the tower. Even if we are hoisted up on a Sisyphean dilemma, even if we never scale the heights of egalitarian society or give birth to the culturally meaningful person, the fact remains that like life itself, the attempt is made—haltingly, falteringly, but not completely without success. Out of the madness of Auschwitz and Hiroshima, we may learn to avoid total destruction. We have driven ourselves directly to the edge of time and the ledge of death—is not this confrontation itself novel? Is not this itself a cause for at least a cautious hope?

I choose to think so. Happily, the author shapes such convictions. For the Enlightenment means Voltaire and Diderot no less than Rousseau. The very totality of Henry's criticism gives rise to constructive possibilities. It is the patent absurdity of existence that by going so far down into the bowels of meannesses and madnesses, that we can come away from this book a trifle less mean and a bit less mad. Let it be made perfectly clear: this book is not simply a warning, but in its deepest recesses, a powerful reminder that culture can be used by man no less than against man. The irony is that it takes a book on man's inhumanity to others and self to make it clear that a humanistic vision, when combined with a mind of quality, can still emerge triumphant. The culture of banality must still contend with a Jules Henry, with the culture of civility.

From *The Sociological Quarterly*, vol. 5, no. 2 (1964), pp. 29–31.

65

An American
Rorschach Test*

Janowitz, Morris

Writing about America is a veritable Rorschach test. What an author chooses to write about says much. Selecting the big theme indicates expectations no less than intelligence. In the 1950s, a strong celebrationist mood led commentators like Henry Commager and Max Lerner, among others, to speak of American culture and American civilization as high-water marks in the history of humanity. A sense of impending doom and catasttophe hardly surfaced. In the 1960s and 1970s, after the war in Southeast Asia, racial strife internally, and colossal changes in American popular manners and mores, the mood turned dour and sour. Suddenly books with pessimistic titles (*The Dying of the Light*, and *The Twilight of Capitalism*) began to appear, heralding the impending doom of American society. The more serious writings in this decade have tended to avoid extremes of optimism or pessimism in favor of what might be called an accounting ledger imagery of society. Survival becomes a cost-benefit equation: how much gross national product for how much social tranquility? what valves have to be turned on and off in the political process to create a viable sense of order? Social science writing became equivocal; forecasts of neither eternal progress nor total collapse seemed entirely credible.

This book seriously attempts to perform a middle range social audit of the United States. It neither exaggerates nor minimizes the complexities of the situation. The need for order is seen as consonant with the prospects for democratic community. Unlike most mainline sociological efforts, the book unabashedly discusses the significant issues in a politically alert manner.

This is a book about American society, but it is also a book by a prominent American sociologist. One reason for that prominence is his willingness and capacity to confront social systems as a whole and not just in parts. The field of sociology is in a state of crisis: orientations are fragmented without scientific

* Morris Janowitz, *The Last Half-Century: Societal Change and Politics in America* (Chicago: The University of Chicago Press, 1979), pp. 583.

371

rationale, and declining academic enrollments translate into fewer opportunities for teachers and researchers. Although the public sector has taken up some of the slack, sociology is in trouble by whatever indicators one selects: figures in graduate departments, new faculty appointments, books published, numbers of dissertations in progress, grants approved, etc. Janowitz's book is therefore a welcome event, if only as a reassertion of the sociological claim to provide a special vision of American society as a whole.

Much of the book is taken up with creating an American vertical mosaic: political participation, social stratification, the link between participation and stratification ("a social control point of view"), military participation, or the concept of the citizen soldier. Other areas in this mosaic are bureaucratic institutions, resident communities, mass media and mass persuasion, law and legitimate coercion, and finally, the social consequences of social science analysis. While putting forth the most noble aspects of the discipline as a paragon of reason and common sense in a world where there has been an eclipse of both Janowitz spends much more time distinguishing between fact and value than discussing the actual policy implications of social science in American context.

The Last Half-Century outlines some extremely important trends within American society and does so without the exaggerations common in popular literature and in some current sociology, as well. Janowitz makes it quite clear that political participation in the United States has remained stable and has become even more important in some cases. What has diminished is party loyalty. In a nutshell, what is under question is the moral context of party identification, not the legitimacy of the American system.

The section on social stratification is carefully done, but the study of interest-group politics, which is the key to the expansion of welfare expenditures and reallocation of resources, does not quite address the extent to which interest groups confront political parties to create a new governmental balance. While regional, occupational, racial, and religious differences have declined, the sense that the country is tearing apart has actually grown. Why this should be is not explained.

Janowitz tends to feel that the gap between economic facts and political sentiment partially results from the militarization of American society and the bureaucratization of its political system. This is summarized in a richly textured and carefully reasoned discussion of the transformation of authority from ownership to management and from top-down leadership to middle-range interaction. Janowitz believes the bureaucratic system of industrial relations in the United States emphasizes short-term issues and conforms to a mold of adversarial relations without corresponding norms or institutional arrangements on which to base social control and the ordering of an advanced industrial society.

The themes of the book are however restated rather than resolved. The social control approach reveals its cranky ideological disposition. The seamier side of the country is often discussed in a hygienic way. His first master trend, "there is no evidence for the depolarization of the American citizenry," is not only debatable but concludes with the notion of chronic political stalemate. As a result, Janowitz leaves us unsure whether the system's legitimacy has remained intact or simply results from carefully weighted opponents, while the rest of the society lives in limbo between the interstices of this permanent stalemate.

The second master tendency is the move toward a more complex and differentiated social stratification including a clearer division of labor, as well as ascriptive continuities based on age, sex, region, and primordial attachments. His third master tendency is most dubious: namely, the rise of a deterrence posture requiring a volunteer armed force, increased hardware capabilities, and away from military service based on land war and conscription. Given the current breakdown of the voluntary army notion, and increasing demands for the reinstitution of a draft, this master trend seems to be part of a passing tactic in military history, and not at all a major tendency forging a new American society. The author's own involvement in a policy framework based on hardware and voluntarism may be a well-intentioned effort to civilianize the military, but remains problematic as a master trend of our times.

Even from a social order perspective, his master trends might have been structured more dynamically. The sharp incline of interest and pressure groups causes and not simply parallels the decline in party identification; the sharp increase in hardware is a function of ideological isolationism rather than a firm deterrence posture; the decline of manpower commitments is a function of isolationist tendencies following Vietnam. Other tendencies that deserve mention, go considerably beyond the social order model. For example, the decline of American capitalism and the rise of European and Third World capitalism, the incline of litigation as a basis of decision making based on norms, customs, and morals (i.e., external power rather than internalized authority).

Still, this is a major sociological contribution toward the understanding of American society in the late 1970s. It is seriously reasoned, carefully textured, and tightly argued. If it does not rank priorities or provide the sort of causal explanations or policy options one would have hoped for, it at least poses issues in a profound way and in a style equally amenable to an audience of concerned citizens as to an elite group of political sociologists. This book is destined to become part of the ongoing discussion about the future of American society. If Americans march into the twilight zone it will not be quietly or silently, but with the help of works such as this, they will tread carefully and even reluctantly.

From *Commonweal*, vol. 106, no. 14 (1979), pp. 443–45.

66

A Postscript to a
Sociological Utopian*

Mills, C. Wright

It took me more than two decades to complete this biography of C. Wright Mills. This is in marked contrast to my usual pattern, which is to quickly write essays on social themes, with firm moral judgments that may or may not turn out to be accurate. To spend so much time with a single work is an experience that itself challenges one's sense of personal identity and at times even personal worth.

Let me start with a few words about special problems encountered in producing this work and strategies adopted to overcome them. I am not a historian and have never before written a biography. I have no idea what possessed me to think I could incorporate the historian's craft or, for that matter, the biographer's skills. There were many times during the years when I doubted my ability to complete the work. On such occasions, I was sustained by the belief in this enterprise, by those close to me.

It is difficult to objectify experiences of another person long dead, a person with whom I was sufficiently intimate to be aware of his infidelities and immoralities became part of my awareness, but sufficiently remote that they never become part of my own substance. I had to so acknowledge my own deepest angers and animosities that as a writer I became paralyzed and could not easily carry the task to completion. I reached that point several times in producing this biography. There were years in which I felt that to write even a sentence of this book was too painful an experience to endure.

What ultimately moved me beyond a catatonic state was a feeling shared by those who know the two Rousseaus: the Rousseau of the *Confessions* with all those detailed intimacies of private hatreds and venomous beliefs toward his friends Diderot, Holbach, and d'Alembert, and the Rousseau who wrote the *Discourses on Inequality* with their elegant, formal, clear, rational prose. The

---

* Irving Louis Horowitz, *C. Wright Mills: An American Utopian* (New York: Free Press/Macmillan, and London: Collier/ Macmillan, 1983) pp. 341.

gap between the public and the private, and at times, the real and illusory is so wide in Mills as to be disconcerting. This is not to say that all people of note are necessarily schizophrenic or that people who write about note-worthies have to acquire a pathology to sustain their work. Nonetheless, in writing about people, one is not dealing with a world of virtue and vice but of career and person. Mills had outstanding intellectual talents and equally outstanding personality defects, as these are commonly perceived.

The type of book I wrote, the kind of effort it takes, cannot easily be sustained by a young man. When I started thinking and writing about Mills, more than two decades ago, I was more aware of self than other. I had to reach a point, as Goethe expressed it, where the problem of good and evil was transcended. It is an everyday occurrence to choose between good and evil. The anguishing problem is selecting between good and good, between evil and evil—and harder still, between varying degrees of good and degrees of evil. This Enlightenment sensibility shared by Rousseau and Goethe sustained me during dark moments. Such a view allowed me to reach a point where I could deal with the Millsian legacy in a serious way. Mills's dogged faith in sociology as a twentieth-century form of Enlightenment was a critical factor in my own ability to complete this work.

Let me share with you a few problems that are not discussed in the book. Take Mills's attitudes towards race and sex. Mills was a presumed paragon and precursor of American radical virtue, one of the major forces moving social science toward a democratic horizon. Yet, in memoranda of the mid-1930s from Mills to Wilson Record, Mills refused on principle, the principle of racism, to support progressive programs. Wilson at the time was working in a YMCA education program for Southern sharecropping women in Mississippi and Arkansas. He asked Mills to come and spend a week in the field, especially since the woman who was to become Mills's first wife was working at the Young Women's Christian Association at that time. Mills seemed a natural candidate to become involved in this effort. He refused to do so with rhetorical flourishes that reflected the common, received Southern perspective of the times.

The same was true of Mills's relationships with women a decade later. They were not the best and often exploitative and unfeeling. His attitudes were backward even when judged by the rueful standards of the mid-1940s. While it is facile and unfair to judge others by the standards of the late 1980s, when a kind of liberal rhetoric has become overwhelmingly commonplace on questions of racism and sex, even by the standards of his age, Mills' demeanor and behavior left a great deal to be desired. This foreknowledge by a biographer is extremely discouraging, even demobilizing, for how does one develop an organic picture of the radical as fashionable bigot? Yet this has been a problem, in far more severe form, in the judgments about Ezra Pound.

In C. Wright Mills, I was dealing with a sadly flawed individual, a human being who had biased attitudes on many issues including minorities, Jews, women, and especially blacks. Nevertheless, a figure of omnipresent vision emerges, who struggles with himself on such issues. He provided a professional public with a great sense of what was taking place not only in the discipline of sociology but in the context of American society. He had a remarkable ability to connect his own vision with larger worldly concerns.

* * *

This history of sociology in America illustrates a striking fact of social science in this country as a whole: how few of its significant practitioners crossed over from a purely professional to a larger public frame of reference. In part, this is due to the weakness of the field, its crude empiricisms and ideological vanities. The professional sociologist's attitude toward the public reveals one eye cocked toward self-preservation and the other toward agendas considered imperative for others to carry forth. For many years within sociology, the word journalism carried a largely pejorative connotation. Being called a journalist, a way of being cursed. Public figures, especially those with aspirations to wider recognition, were met with scorn and fear. But Mills employed a journalistic style to move beyond inherited professional dualisms.

Mills's career violated professional totems and taboos. He had an extraordinary ability to cross over from a discipline to larger public concerns. The problem for him late in his career was retaining any sense of the discipline or the profession of social science. He was declared a persona non grata. Wearied of Mills' pamphleteering, leading scholars, like Seymour Martin Lipset and Neil Smelser categorically insisted that he no longer was a member of the American sociological community. This pronouncement was made in the *British Journal of Sociology* just prior to his death in 1962. Being perverse as well as proud, Mills wore this charge as a badge of honor, although I know for a fact that he was hurt and shaken by this allegation.

One of Mills's great strengths and weaknesses was that he would not easily display remorse or sorrow: whatever assaults were heaped upon him were worn proudly. At times, he went further, taking each charge as a personal vindication. Yet he rarely retaliated in kind. Mills avoided public displays of meanness toward others, even bitter foes. Whenever an opponent spoke harsh, vindictive, or recriminatory words, fair or unfair, Mills accepted them. He internalized negative sentiments. Mills even took it upon himself, as part of his growing mythmaking propensities, to embellish and expand upon the charges of others. This absurdist approach eventually cost him professional status. At the time of his death in March 1962, Mills was indeed beyond the professional pale; even assembling a decent quorum of American sociologists who would voice his praises at his funeral was difficult to muster.

* * *

There were reasons for Mills's alienated status, not all of them invalid, many of them quite sensible. My first task as a biographer was professional restoration. How does one restore a scholar as part of the profession of sociology? That is why I edited those early works of Mills, *Power, Politics, and People* (1963), *A New Sociology* (1964), and *On Men and Social Movements* (1965). But how to produce a full-fledged biographical accounting was something else again. The tasks are different, environments are different. I was not helped by the fact that the passions Mills generated had not cooled.

I interviewed a great many people who knew Mills personally. This was a fascinating experience a roll-back of time and space. Those who did not like Mills—and they were many—spoke with enormous, even furious passion about his indiscretions. People in the twilight of their own careers talked to me practically as it they were teenagers, with kind of embittered passion reserved for departed enemies. Those who did like him, and they were few, spoke in such glowing terms that they too exhibited the qualities of unbridled adolescence. Such passion served to confirm for me the importance of Mills as a figure of note. What vouchsafes a person's importance for our time is that they become part of the public dialogue of their time. Mills was important in this special pragmatic sense of ransoming the years for meaning.

Mills's life was part of the American public dialogue in ways that resonated Eisenhower's 1959 farewell presidential address: warning against American rearmament and the military-industrial complex. This was a year after the appearance of Mills's book. *The Causes of World War Three.* In part at least. Mills is important, less because he was an innovating sociologist or even because he was prescient, rather because he realized his fond dream: to become part of the dialogue of his epoch. Mills became identified with those larger issues he viewed as politically central. At this metalevel, there was also a pathology at work. Mills thought of himself much as William James thought about Theodore Roosevelt—a personal truth squad of one. Mills internalized what Norman Mailer once said about himself: he ran for the presidency in his mind. Mills was constantly involved in a mythic and intense dialogue with top presidential leaders. It was an angry dialogue that he conducted, or rather combated one-on-one. There was no political party system, no judiciary or legislative body; it was simply him and them. Eisenhower and Mills. Kennedy and Mills. Egoism and ideology became fused, and even sadly confused.

This combative, largely personalistic mood is reflected in his writings. *Power Elite*, for example, offers no description of a legislative body, only an executive head. Mills had no time for the judiciary. At a time when Edward Shils was writing *Torment of Secrecy* and spending a great deal of time critiquing the FBI, the OSS, and secret organizations, Mills would have none of it. He provided no discussion of the Federal Bureau of Investigation, or the American party system, no admission of political checks and balances of any kind. In Mills we have the quintessential political sociologist as avenging evangelist, avoiding issues mired in complexity and detail. The psychology of the man spilled over into the vision of his world. His was a world of power, not of status; it was a world of head-to-head combat, or make-believe hand-to-hand combat. His was a highly Americanized vision of the way power is structured, a sportive vision—a perennial warfare of cowboys and Indians, even when the latter had been wiped out.

Mills is fascinating because he violated even the myth of why people resonated to him—his presumed radicalism. Andrew Greeley once shrewdly observed that Mills exhibited many behavioral and intellectual traits that were highly conservative. Mills presumably was an outstanding political sociologist. Yet he did not care a farthing about most things that preoccupied this *sub-specie sociologus*: He never voted, he remained studiously ignorant of Congress and Court, he boasted of never having had a political affiliation, and he had contempt for most radical groups. To hear him rant about Communists and Socialists, one would think oneself in the company of his high-school colleague the Reverend Dan Smoot. Then why did radicals pay attention to him, and more importantly, why should any one continue to read this figure? This itself became a major biographical challenge.

*   *   *

Although of Roman Catholic origin, Mills never cast in the mold of St. Francis of Assisi. He was a human figure, the ordinary sort one sees about the Academy. I set about the task of writing a biography of Mills by trying to locate his lynchpin: why he was a peculiarly American type, why he was a Utopian. Does the subtitle work, or is it a simple caveat and device? Clearly, I think it is appropriate to the man at hand.

Mills was American not just because of his Texas birthplace. In fact, he left Texas as a young man and never went back. Mills was the reverse of what Edward Shils intimated in a particularly savage review in the *Encounter.* He was not a Texan on horseback—he never knew how to ride a horse and did not especially like horses. He was an urban figure, entirely part of the development of Dallas as a vigorous and new southwest hub. He had scant knowledge of rural Texas; for the most part he could not care less about farm life. Further, he was an American because wherever else in the world he went, he always returned home. I know of no one who, both personally and intellectually, worked harder at becoming non-American and failed so completely at the task. Though he relished the role of reviling American political policy, he could not wake in the morning and be content without his *New York Times*. When Asa Briggs invited him to come and form a new sociology department at the University of Sussex, in the late 1950s, he responded, "I couldn't do it because you can't get the *New York Times* in Brighton on the day of publication!" This struck me as a quintessential American answer. This is an eccentric reason for not accepting a post, unless one must be in constant touch, if not in tune, with American life.

Mills's Utopianism is a theme I developed the deeper I understood his unfinished works. I was pleased to note in a brief piece in the *International Encyclopedia of Social Science* that Immanual Wallerstein also perceived the Utopian dimension in Mills. His was an Americanism that would connect liberty to history; and in which every individual would count as one, no more and no less, in which individualism was to be rugged enough to allow for collective harmony. His was an America of the nineteenth century, in which government was to be small and communities were to share power. There was a hint of republican virtue and rugged individualism in this kind of commitment. His was an Americanism in which governance was to be self-imposed, an Americanism of Jeffersonian proportions in which the enlightenment principle would prevail and in which the notion of separation of church and state would be perfectly realized. In short, Mills's American never really existed, except as a blueprint. His was a new Atlantis for the first New Nation.

Elements of American eighteenth century society have lingered well into the twentieth century. Mills was deeply attached to these seeming anachronisms. Mills was attached, not to rurality, but to a polity of Jeffersonian dimensions. His early training was in philosophy and his dissertation was on pragmatism and the professionalization of American philosophy. William James, Charles Peirce, and John Dewey were his intellectual frames of reference as a very young man. When he established contact with Europe, it was through the liberal sociology of Karl Mannheim, and later, through other institutional figures like Max Weber. Because of this nativism, he resonated more readily to power analysts like Pareto and Michels, rather than class analysts like Marx and Toennies.

He was a quintessential American in personal forms as well: his ignorance of foreign languages was legion, as Hans H. Gerth took pains to remind all who would listen. It was Gerth who translated the Max Weber materials. Mills appreciated the Weber legacy, but his language was plain English, and Weber's was not-so-plain German. Mills wrote to Mencken's specifications for an American language. The punctuation was sharp, the words taught, and the ideas expressed clearly.

Americanism and utopianism were the legs, underpinnings as it were. But what sort of body does my book have? Once the title and subtitle are resolved, one has to start writing the book. Formal metaphors about bodies, and legs are fine, but beyond the metaphor there must be the work itself, the focusing of vision into an organized framework.

I looked at Mills's high-school and college transcripts and drew some special inferences about the way he viewed the world. For example, in his years at Texas, from 1935 to 1939, he never participated in departmental affairs. He was disinterested in academic politics be they at the philosophy, sociology, or economics department. His academic strategy, largely unconscious at the time, was to take courses with great teachers, in whatever department they were. At Texas this meant economics and philosophy rather than political science and psychology. Only a handful of talented people were in sociology at the time. He pursued the same stratagem at Wisconsin. But it did not work as well because by the time he went to graduate school, professionalism had become much more ensconced. The notion of randomly going from one department to another was frowned upon by senior Wisconsin professors, no less than it is at present. Mills converted this rise of professionalism into the raw materials for his dissertation on the institutionalization of American pragmatism.

The most important aspect about Mills's formative period is that he was saturated in the worth of the intelligentsia as a subclass ideology. He lived in the world of universities his entire life, mocking the source of his strength, his audience, every step of the way. Like a medieval schoolman, he moved from Texas, to Wisconsin, to Maryland, and finally to Columbia, where he spent the greatest part of his short life. He was formed by currents in university life, and had his greatest, some might add exclusive, impact upon such universities. At Columbia, people like Jacques Barzun and Lionel Trilling were at least as important to him, probably more important, than were Paul Lazarsfeld and Robert K. Merton. The university as a whole was Mills' home. The university was Mills' church. He was a secularist with a clerical vision of what the university could do, become at its optimum. I begin each of the first four chapters on the Millsian context with quotations from leading university figures where Mills had taught, because of his great passion for the university as an institution.

Sometimes we mistakenly think that sociology, strictly speaking, is a profession, the overriding assumption bring that what we are or what we do is the field of sociology. It may be for some, but it was not so for Mills. He was marginal and antiprofessional, much closer to Everett C. Hughes's position on occupations than he was toward Talcott Parsons's view of the same subject. He disdained professions, fearing what they did to others, hating what they did for themselves. He distrusted professional training and dismissed graduate training. He only had confidence in the university only as a place of liberal arts with a rational mission. Enlightening the young, not training the careerist, was what Mills believed the university mission to be.

*   *   *

An American Utopian is organized in these university terms. This is perhaps the most fascinating aspect of Mills' life from a biographical point of view.

My task was to situate Mills precisely and accurately. In every instance, this meant situating him at a university. The only location where this approach did not quite work was the University of Maryland. Biographers with whom I have spoken note that they lose a subject for a few years during the research process. Since I lost my subject, I was fascinated to learn (much too late) this apparently widespread phenomenon. For three years from 1942 through 1944, I lost Mills in some black hole. I knew he was at the University of Maryland— at least I knew he was drawing his paychecks there. I knew too that he was writing letters on University of Maryland letterhead. But where exactly was my subject living? Where was the person behind the correspondence? I spoke with many who knew him at Maryland. They could not easily answer this query.

The answer is he was living on the Beltway, halfway between Washington, D.C. and College Park. Mills was in Washington, D.C. most nights of the week and in College Park most days during the week. He did research for the War Administration Board. He was also involved in a variety of researches for the Department of the Navy. He was working in every possible way toward developing contacts within the power elite, intellectual skepticisms notwithstanding. He could not readily he found at Maryland because be was often away from campus. This sounds simple enough in retrospect. Perhaps a humbler biographer would have unscrambled the black hole more adroitly. But not being a biographer, I did not react quickly. It took me several years to find out where he had been. This was an important piece of the biographical puzzle. When the Maryland chapter fell into place, the whole first section took flight. I had solved the most vexing problem of the first segment of the biography. I then felt at case enough to move along to more heady matters.

The second section of the book is on Mills' philosophical and sociological precursors. This is an intellectual history in which I try to show the main lines of influence: Weber, Mannheim, Dewey, and later, the Marxists. The last work he wrote, sadly enough, appeared two days after he died. It was called, appropriately enough, *The Marxists*. The book was half reader, half Mills. It was intended for a broad audience that cared little for didactic debate and even less for inherited ideology. Mills took the tack of a highly pragmatized and pluralized Marxism. His notion of Marxism was a debate between Yugoslavs and Russians. He delighted in Titoism and Maoism, not as doctrines but as options. Indeed, he took pleasure in anything anyone (including Stalin) that made Marxism look like a wide-open public forum. While fully realizing the totalitarian basis of the Soviet power structure, he retained a global vision of socialism that he viewed as the locus of political action. For Mills, Marxism had become a great debate between Tito, Mao, Khrushchev, and various other West European leaders like Togliatti. He loved the idea of a pragmatic Marxism, a personalized Marxism as it were. He welcomed the very debates that Communist authorities in each nation of the East preferred to shelve.

Any indication of how hardened ideological trends have become is that Mills's rather simple, and at time simple-minded, observations about the pluralization of Marxism can barely be whispered in Marxist-Leninist circles without inviting mockery. Mills did not possess a dogmatic or scholastic spirit. He understood the history of socialism, rightly or wrongly from an open-ended, open-hearted, democratic perspective. His was a highly American style of looking at ideological trends. What could be a more down-home American view of Marxism than a wonderful one-on-one struggle between Tito and Stalin and later Mao Tse-tung and Khrushchev. Even late in his life, when a certain hectoring style emerged, he dealt with Marxist systems by attempting to make them sensible, open to reason, subject to the dialogue of the living.

What Mills chose to ignore is that the basis of state power is as national in the East as in the West. The dialogue he saw did not permit his precious ordinary, plain folks the measure of liberty he so desperately craved for them. In pragmatizing Marxism, Mills had to internationalize the context of debate and hence falsify the terms and conditions in which plain people lived throughout the Soviet empire. As Mills painfully came to appreciate, the elite entered the back door once again, as it had in his study of American power, to dominate not as a vanguard of future trends but as the dross of a revolutionary tradition grown cranky, nasty, and brutish.

The third and final segment of my work offered an assessment of Mills's legacy. Here there were many untidy problems to be solved. I did not want to transfer biography into chronology or hagiography, reviewing serially every work Mills had produced year-by-year. Certain decisions had to be made to prioritize his work. For example, I had to determine what to do with *Character and Social Structure.* This work, published a decade after he wrote it with Hans Gerth, was the one that he came close to repudiating in later years. In personal conversations, he made clear his animus for the text. I personally like this book a great deal; the work is a valiant effort at linking social stratification with social psychology. But he himself came near a formal repudiation of that work, first because of his personal break with Gerth and second because of his intellectual abandonment of Weber. I took the position that the book belonged to the time span in which it had been written: the Maryland and Wisconsin period. It thus became part of Mills' historical odyssey rather than intellectual maturity.

A somewhat harder task involved placement of *The Sociological Imagination*, a work that many sociologists have found attractive, but which is a slender work in intellectual terms. I made the decision to put the work in with the Columbia University chapter. It became point/counterpoint to Robert S. Lynd's *Knowledge for What?* In many ways Lynd who, along with Merton, had brought Mills to Columbia, closes out the era of the big picture. It was the last hurrah of a literary tradition that viewed sociology as a fighting credo. If one places Lynd's book next to Mills's the thematic infrastructure and even the psychic tone reveal similarities that suggest a high level of synergy. The pragmatic background of both Lynd and Mills partly explains this isomorphism. There was also a shared antiprofessionalism in Lynd and Mills. They both wrote sociological manifestoes as outsiders—more in the hope of swaying public opinion for sociology than in moving professional opinion away from the field's bad methodological habits.

A third difficult but important decision was to treat *Puerto Rican Journey* as a minor work. Again, this was part of the Columbia research environment. The book was written with Rose Goldsen, Helen Schneider, Ruth Harper, and a number of other outstanding women at Columbia at the time Mills went there in the late 1940s. Mills was a great ethnographer; his intuition about people in dire situations was sharp and clear-eyed. But he was notoriously impatient with research details. And he was not above ignoring, even discarding exact data, if it failed to confirm his intuition With Mills's *Puerto Rican Journey* and other smaller projects of the late 1940s, the data was not permitted to speak for itself—quite the contrary, Mills spoke for the data. He was clearly not always right. The amazing thing was, as Rose Goldsen indicated in her posthumous memoir, how often he was right, given his vigorous massaging of data.

The main decision I next made was to anchor the third section of the book to his work on social stratification—what I called the great stratification trilogy. Early on, I came to the conclusion that if Mills was the quintessential American Utopian I claimed, it would show up in his writings on the American class and power system. In *New Men of Power*, he analyzed the structure of labor, in *White Collar*, he analyzed the structure of the middle class, and in *The Power Elite*, he analyzed the structure of the ruling class. As a trilogy, there are a monumental contribution to the study of stratification. In these three works were to be found the substance beyond the style.

* * *

The irony of Mills's work is that this man, who saw himself remote from sociology and close to politics, contributed little to political analysis and much to sociological analysis. If one accepts stratification as very much within the sociological mainstream, that area was his forte. Stratification was the area of social science where Mills delivered the intellectual goods. Even now, if you read those three books, their freshness and intriguing qualities remain. They are part of the ongoing professional dialogue. It is the one place where the Millsian dialogue is the centerpiece of present academic debates, one cannot examine Robert Dahl on governance without discussing Mills or discuss David Riesman on veto groups without discussing Mills or examine Lloyd Warner on subclass distinctions without discussing Mills. The stratification trilogy was his crowning intellectual achievement.

This was also an important personal discovery. I had three separate interviews with Robert K. Merton. In the final one, he turned when I was about to leave and said: "Isn't Mills really only a matter of sentiment? Is there really any substance to his work?" I confess to being taken aback. Merton's words became the intellectual challenge, equal in importance to the biographical challenge: to see whether there was substance to Mills and if so, what was its nucleus? In the final analysis, if there was no substance, there was no book. Without that third section, I was left with an interesting character rather than a sociological characterization.

From that point on, after 1956 and publication of *Power Elite*, work grew progressively weaker. It became as he himself called it, pamphleteering. His work became intellectually strident in both form and content. There were interesting, but passing insights in *The Causes of World War Three* and in *Listen Yankee!*. But there was an increasingly rasping sound, what Irving Howe calls the bludgeoning approach to the grammar of American politics. Every event had to be hit over the head, every idea had to be painted in black and white. There were no longer intellectual torments, no social shadows, no gray marble. Mills had abandoned the tensions of human interaction for a world of good and evil. He was possessed by a kind of Manichaenism, a poor substitute for pragmatism.

Mills's fascination with Cuba was a good illustration of this Manichaenism tinged with personalism. When he trusted someone, there was nothing he could not see himself doing for that individual. His attitudes toward the Cuban Revolution were shaped by a profound belief that Fidel Castro was the heroic moral athlete of the modern age. Personal acquaintance counted for much with Mills. Early on at Texas, one of his letters of recommendation said Mills was an arrogant young snot, that he talked to his professors as if they were his equals! If one could overcome this aberration Mills could be likeable. From the first, if he saw a professor he liked, he would offer to play handball or share a cup of brew at the local pub. Even now it is unusual for a student to talk over to a professor and invite him out. A professor might suggest doing so to a favorite student, but rarely the other way about. Mills's egalitarianism stemmed from a deep belief that personalities meant a lot and that social structures have to be seen in the context of human interaction. This is what Mills was about; from the day he went to the University of Texas until the day he died, he believed in personalities, and that their good and evil were reflected and refracted in political systems. Such was the extent of his unified theory of history.

Mills's fourth (and last) heart attack occurred the night before a scheduled debate on Communist Cuba with Adolf A. Berle. He wrote, "Now I've done it, now I am going to talk to ten million Americans." What he forgot was that Berle too was talking. Further, that his opponent knew more than he did about Latin America. He also forgot that ten million Americans may watch an NBC show, but they are not necessarily going to be influenced; they may simply view it as another half hour of live entertainment. Mills saw himself as part of the cultural apparatus that he so crushingly examined in his BBC lectures.

Listen Yankee! sold around 460,000 copies. But by that same time Mickey Spillane mysteries sold around 4,600,000. Such transparent incongruities never seemed to enter Mills's thinking. High sales were for him a media event, a magic idea of being the individual heroic type, talking to other heroic types. Like most self-proclaimed American populists, Mills spoke in the name of the people better than he listened to them. He did so from an Olympian height, a stratospheric vision to which he held fast from student days to death.

To his credit at the very end of his life. Mills began to express profound doubts about this pseudo-populist syndrome and started to design an eight-part volume of work on international stratification, of which the *Soviet Journal* (the critical, unpublished narrative of his visit to the USSR in 1960) and Third World issues were to be a part. He once again began to think big thoughts in the structural terms that made him an important stratification theorist. He once more put into place the relationship between the person and the historical, the social and the individual, between liberty and enlightenment. He began to paint on a bigger global canvas. But by this time, he had spent himself emotionally. It was an immense canvas that he could envision, but he could no longer find the patience or perseverance to paint. He could no longer subordinate his person to research tasks. Posturing replaced performance. Social science was finished for him. He left behind an enormous pencil-sketch on the meaning of history and society, but he could not fill in any details. He was no Braudel, Rostovsteff, or Needham. He knew as much. It was time for him to leave this world.

Mills saw America in terms of a tripartite vision of class and a pyramidal commitment to power. He saw labor in terms of both the decency of working people and the corruption of trade unionism and guild capitalism. His vision was different from the kind of reductionist analysis that still pours forth from the Leninist Left. His insights into middle-class life, along with David Riesman's portraits, is probably as touching as any in the sociological literature. His feeling for ordinary people in everyday walks of life remain astonishingly fresh—given his limited empirical contacts. Likewise, his analysis of power, which questions the relationship between holding exercising, concentrating, and deconcentrating power, is impressive and unique.

Whether this adds up to great sociology or a grand tradition is hard to determine. The world has changed sociologically as well as socially in the near quarter century since Mills died—to the point where greatness cannot be measured the way it would in 1951 when *White Collar*, and Talcott *Parson's General Theory of Action* first appeared. To ask which type of sociology will stand the test of time is an empty form of speculation, worse, a presumption.

We have to continually examine where society is going in order to answer the issue of personal or professional immortality. To Mills's everlasting credit, he was wise and decent enough to think about a future by respecting the present, thus avoiding the hubris of declaring what must be, with its implicit conceit about one's own personal fate in the eternal firmament.

This essay reviewing my book on Mills has hitherto not been published. However, versions of it were presented at various universities and associations. I am especially grateful for the fine comments and criticisms offered at Georgetown University, the University of Chicago, Cambridge University in England, and the University of Texas in Austin, of earlier drafts of this statement.

67

Personal Values and Social Class*

Myrdal, Gunnar

Gunnar Myrdal has come to occupy a special place in the conscience of the educated American. It is a position derived in large part from his monumental study of the American Negro, *An American Dilemma*—the closest work a cultivated European has produced comparable to De Tocqueville's *Democracy in America.* But, as so often happens with successive efforts, *Challenge to Affluence* simply fails to come up to this level. Despite the fact that everyone—Right, Left, and Center—seems to feel that this newest effort by Myrdal is worthy of citation and commendation, I must say I found the book intensely disappointing and utterly pedestrian.

The reader is given a "balanced" potpourri of observations, theories, conjectures, and speculations. Much could be forgiven on the basis of the fact that these are lectures intended for oral delivery. But why great men feel their casual remarks to be so sacrosanct that they must be transmitted to cold print exactly as delivered is beyond comprehension. Perhaps because of this oracular quality, the dilemmas of Myrdal as a theorist are more painfully evident than they might have been had the text been spruced up for an academic public. Myrdal parades forth a set of confusions rather than solutions, and convictions rather than proofs. In his effort to be judicious and sensitive to American pride, he often caters to American prejudices (such as his support of the myth of American economic giveaways).

The book is structured in formal economic paradoxes that resolution in a stable equilibrium theory. The underlying theme is that the American economy exhibits relative stagnation, that its record of economic development is highly unsatisfactory given the a continued high and rising level of unemployment, and that a prolonged consumer orientation leaves too little for saving and investment to keep the economy growing quickly. Although Professor Myrdal holds that the American economic crisis is structural in character, he does

---

* Gunnar Myrdal, *Challenge to Affluence* (New York: Pantheon Books, 1963), pp. 172.

not indicate anything in the economy that would need alteration to change present tendencies. The very reverse seems to emerge. A series of political inferences indicate that Myrdal thinks that the American economy is free to act as it wishes, that its higher directorate is volitional in character. Hence, there is a reiterated claim that business should be given a spurt to expand rapidly, which means a revision in the tax structure, which in turn means very little in terms of the structural limits Professor Myrdal alludes to in his work. The further exhortations that we need to have a new educational orientation, a new training and retraining for the age of automation and specialization, and that Americans ought not run the risk of "clamping a class structure upon the nation," are a set of rhetorical statements that seriously weaken Myrdal's claims as an authentic student of American society.

The concept of an underclass itself seems to me a powder-puff notion equivalent to saying, hungry masses or poverty-stricken. It is an emotive rather than scientific term that would, in fact, put the matter of social class in American beyond the pale of structural analysis. There is a strong element of paternalism in Myrdal's suggestions, since he uses the underclass concept not unlike the way the social welfare establishment used the word poor. The United States has a particularly heavy responsibility for these underprivileged. The fact of the matter is that this lack of political articulation is not confined to any underclass but is a general property of the United States social system in an age that has substituted elitist policy making for mass politics.

Everyone will have something to enjoy and quote in this book. Businessmen will be pleased by Myrdal's statements that working-class organization is strong in American and business organizations should emulate this by building up their organizational efficiency. Economists will be happy to hear that while the United States has a heavy dose of short-range planning, it needs much more emphasis on long-range planning. Free trade and low tariff men will find joy in Myrdal's advocacy of the widest possible free trade and tariff aids, rather than tariff barriers, as a means of integrating an international economy. American liberals will be happy to know that American democracy is strong but that the Negro question remains unresolved, and hence American democracy can be made even stronger by an open-ended mobility system. The politicians in Washington will be happy to know that even though they form a tight little policy-making elite with a low level of mass participation, since they are motivated by altruistic responses (as everyone knows), the country has nothing to worry about.

In effect, Myrdal supports every sober economic principles ever held by any sober economic man. He can do this because he is always dealing in terms of benefits and the consequences of affluence and never in terms of the social costs or psychological penalties inflicted by economic development or the social welfare model that underwrites his analysis. No one can really take issue with the *Challenge to Affluence*, since Myrdal is not stating a problem but only a fact: affluence is the essential drive of modern man, and therefore roadblocks to affluence, such as mass poverty, have to be removed. But the roadblock theory always comes upon hard times when it is realized that not everything in life, not even in American life, can be neatly packaged into an equilibrium model and adjudicated through the good sense and good will of good people.

These criticism notwithstanding, there are sound elements in the book. Myrdal's analysis of the lack of participation in public life and his explanation that this derives from a population composed from many national cultures, is well worth further examination. His further point that the lower down on the economic scale one goes, the less member participate in voluntary organizations, is a fundamental social problem no less than an economic fact. Myrdal's comments on specific political matters should be paid full attention, for they represent the position of a European friend of the court. His comments on United States foreign policy in relation to China, the possibility of de jure recognition as a sign of American maturity, his observations on the economic progress of the Soviet Union as potentially good for the United States, and his comments on the reduction of the arms industry all point up the fact that a European centrist appears to a dyed-in-the-wool leftist in an American context.

For all of his erudition, Myrdal seems singularly uninformed on the latest social science findings, either that or he is sufficiently unimpressed to bother with them. Observations on the Negro are taken directly from his own work of 25 years ago. He makes no use of recent statistics that show an increased lag between Negro and white earning and purchasing power. Similarly, Myrdal has a penchant for quoting, citing, or referring to himself to the exclusion of every other scholar. Myrdal comes off not only as a favorite but an exclusive source of quotation.

Gunnar Myrdal's stagnation is nowhere more painfully clear than in his commencement address delivered June 8, 1962, to Howard University graduates. In this article, reprinted as an appendix, he refers to the white reaction to the Negro rights movements as disturbances and as unfortunate incidents. He shows little appreciation of the fact that community solidarity and property rights have become critical rallying points in the mobilization of white, Christian America. On the other hand, he tends to take for granted the progress of Negro-white relationships as something that is proceeding at a natural incline toward full integration. He even points out that the Negroes will cease to be viewed as a special problem or to have a self-definition as a social problem, and will tend to merge their problems into American problems as such. Thus, the matter of slum clearance is held to more important than the specific issue of Negro housing.

It is strange that Myrdal would make such vague formulations and not see that, for Negroes, the slum problem is a color problem and that for him to take a larger-than-life view and argue abstractly for slum clearance adds a self-debilitating and self-limiting note in the conduct of his struggle for human decencies. The sanctimonious tone that Myrdal adopts and that ends with a bizarre statement that the integration of Negroes in American society has proceeded so far that one may say that what is good for America is good for Negroes and what is good for Negroes is good for America, strikes this reader as a concept more observed in the breach than in adherence. That Professor Myrdal would add this commencement address to fill out his volume, slim enough in good pickings without this hortatory lecture, is a sad commentary of what happens to a noble man when he becomes content with his past greatness. In short, *Challenge to Affluence*, far from being a serious response to the position of John Kenneth Galbraith, is at best a volume of pleasant economic vignettes and at worst a set of aimless platitudes.

From *New Politics*, vol. 3, no. 3 (1964), pp. 91–93.

68

The Iconoclastic Imagination*

Nelson, Benjamin

There was a distinct period in American sociological history during which civilizational analysis was not only countenanced but actually considered de rigueur. Between 1909 and 1919, presidential addresses before the American Sociological Society abounded with references to the needs, aims, and future of civilization writ large. It was taken for granted that everyone knew what constitutes a civilization, just as in later years there was a general consensus as to what is a society. But these presidential addresses slowly drifted into pontification, and as they emptied of significant content, the tradition of the big picture itself became suspect. To be sure, macroanalysis has never quite been extinguished; more often than not, large-scale outlooks merely changed labels and became analyses of world systems, developmentalism, modernization, comparative systems study, etc. These sociological analyses carried forth the torch of civilizational analysis, although not with an especially keen sense on the part of the bearers.

These marvelous papers written by Benjamin Nelson over the span of three decades throw into sharp relief the whys and wherefores of the decline and disarray of civilizational analysis. One is deeply appreciative to Toby Huff for bringing these papers together under one intellectual roof. Nelson's unusual gift for a sociological dialectic that combines the basic abstract and the concrete, the universal and the particular, stands out in each essay. In this gift, Nelson is as much an offspring of Hegel as of Weber, although the idealism and formalism of the Hegelian system made it difficult for Nelson to acknowledge this debt. Moreover, he wanted to distance himself from a world-history tradition that failed to take seriously the key element of the modern age—science.

Nelson skillfully links his goal of extending the borders of "comparative historical differential sociology in civilizational perspective" to very concrete settings. He observes that the top of the frontispiece of a 1651 painting contains a "nearly concealed reference at the end of Jehova's fingers to the apocryphal

---

* Benjamin Nelson, *On the Roads to Modernity: Conscience, Science, and Civilization: Selected Writings*, Toby E. Huff (editor) (Totowa, NJ: Rowman & Littlefield, 1981), pp. 316.

Wisdom of Solomon 11:20." He goes on to declare that this reference "is intended to stress the ordered creation of the world and its disposition in number, weight, and measure." It goes back at least to the year 1000 and hence is intended as a pointed response to the Galilean revolution. Nelson's eye for the seemingly trivial detail is important not so much as a parade of scholarship—but as the results of hard-core cross-disciplinary research. Nelson is attempting to establish the common soil of theology and sociology, in contrast to an Enlightenment tradition that emphasizes their dissimilarities. Right or wrong, the constant movement from the most abstract to the most specific sets Nelson's work apart from his imitators.

With an easy but breathtaking insight, Nelson poses a question: "Why did Western Christendom surge forward in the twelfth and thirteenth centuries, while other civilizations such as Islam and Judaism remained essentially stagnant?" For Nelson, the answer to the axial shift is located in the rise of individualism and naturalistic theology, which served to prepare the way for modernization, rationalization, and universalization. There are many subterranean and sometimes not-so-subterranean arguments that Nelson conducts with his peers, from people like the turn-of-the-century Andrew White, who argued the struggle between theology and science, all the way up to a strong dissent from Joseph Needham and his monumental efforts to understand science and civilization in China. In arguing, Nelson is not always fair (for example, his critique of Needham has a niggling quality that clearly has as its byproduct, if not aim, the minimization of Needham's herculean efforts). On the other hand he is always provocative. The effort to push back the origins of modern science by four centuries is not quixotic but rather a concerted attempt to link the rise of modern science with the life of modern society. It is also an attempt to show that the arguments put forth by such great figures as Copernicus and Galileo are not simply adventures in modernity and certainty are not the first flower of scientific analysis, but are rather a tentative break with the medieval consensual system in which science and theology stand together.

Nelson's eye for details is ever present. The struggles of the Jews against their Hellenic and Roman rulers served to preserve rooted solidarities, pieties, and collectivities, he argues, but they also served to inhibit participation in the modernizing quest, except on an ad hoc basis. Then there is Nelson's further idea that Chinese science was too linked to the world of magic to permit a naturalistic unfolding or to permit China to become involved with science as a form of ideological or cultural integration. For Nelson, the idea of civilization is linked to intimate psychological and cultural features that transcend national boundaries. If we can speak of science in the West as transcending provincialism, it would seem equally appropriate to speak of theology as subject to similar societal analyses. Nelson saw his own work, whether on the idea of usury or of reasoning in the medieval world, as a two-front struggle to recast the fundamental rationality of both science and social practice. That such praxis turns out to be religion is perhaps the most debatable and yet provocative of his working hypotheses.

Insofar as any disparate collection of papers can be said to be linked, there are three related theses: (1) Nelson moves the origins of modern science back from the sixteenth to the twelfth century, from Francis Bacon to Roger Bacon in personal terms; (2) he shows that the search for certainly was common to both science and theology and that pragmatic probabilistic theories of science represent a special, later stage in the philosophy of science and have little to do with the origins of science; (3) he explains how the probabilistic tradition was highly important in the experimental phase of science but at the same time was not a unique property of science. To be sure, the argument between church and state was not an issue involving the practice of science so much as implications that had strong, socially radical potential.

Nelson is not so much concerned with the origins of science as with the moral commitments of those who advocated science. The leitmotif of his writing is a critique of all forms of reductionism, forms celebrates of behaviorism or technicism that deny the place of values in the functioning of newly emergent civilizations. Nelson reminds as that at the very point we begin to speak of games of life, they begin to take on the shape of dances of death. In an essay prepared late in his life on the subject of religion and the humanizing of man, Nelson sums up, and far better than this reviewer can the essential dynamics linking worlds that too often are treated as mechanical opposites and as institutional polarities:

> The more closely we study the evidence, the more it becomes apparent that, in the main. Faiths, Sciences, and Machines reinforced one another in the development of Western civilization. Theological traditionalism and mysticism cooperating with a natural science and natural magic helped to produce the new cosmology and technology of the later Middle Ages and the early modern era. The contemporary technocultural cosmos, the fruit of the fusion of science, technology, and organization, occurred in the wake of successive restructurings of rationales of conscience and opinion, and the breakthroughs in the moralities and logics of thought and action since the end of the Middle Ages.

If at times Nelson lapses into a dogmatic tone and a needless pugnacity, he perhaps can be excused, since so many of his papers come at a time when modernization through national science and the polarization of science and values were commonplace shibboleths in the world of academic ideas. Curiously, the book reads better than the individual essays might have at the time of their publication, precisely because we have reached full circle and are more suspicious than ever about the golden calf of science and are much more deeply aware that modernization has its limits. It is to Nelson's credit that he understood long before most sociologists of science that these attacks on modernization and the evil effects of industrialization do not derive as much from conservative theologians as from working men, cultural critics, philosophers, and poets—that is, from the more secular currents of the Renaissance and Reformation. The discontented who have called into question the purely naturalistic and scientific are often not traditionalists but are very often revolutionaries, and hence the ultimate irony and paradox presented by *On the Roads to Modernity* inspires the reader to revolt against modernity not in flat mechanical terms, as in the efforts of theological or scientific mullahs, but in a collective attempt of mankind to resurrect the concept of meaning in science. Nelson draws our attention to science as a search for knowledge and not just information—a distinction that has grown rather than diminished with time.

Toby E. Huff has assembled and arranged these materials not chronologically but philosophically in order better to render meaning to Nelson's work in the history and sociology of science. This is but one area of Nelson's significant contribution. It is to be hoped that in the period ahead Huff will have the opportunity and the support of the publishing community to prepare Nelson's writings on psychology and psychiatry as well as his reflections on more specific aspects of religion and development as both related to the evolution of the social sciences.

One leaves this book feeling that Nelson remains a still undiscovered Jung of sociology, someone whose iconoclastic work on civilizational archetypes provides a potential counterpoint to the conventional functionalist visions of a world of science connected only to its societal parts. Nelson reminds us that behind those societal parts lurk theological and philosophical wholes that remain largely unassimilated but also unassailable.

From *Contemporary Sociology*, vol. 11, no. 5 (1982), pp. 524–26.

69

Malevolence and Beneficence in State Power[*]

Neumann, Franz

These studies in the history and structure of political thought exhibit the precise scholarship common to those who gathered about Max Horkheimer and the Institute of Social Research. The enduring quality of their work is that, irrespective of the correctness or adequacy of a particular analysis, they applied themselves to the major problems of social evolution and individual motivation. It is in this tradition of political sociology that Neumann was nourished.

The strongest side of Neumann's work is his studies in the sociology of law. The essay titled "The Change in the Function of law in Modern Society" is a profound examination of the economic moorings of legal codes and viewpoints. In the nineteenth century, we are told, the impartiality of law, its functioning on the basis of general principles, reflected the nature of a free and competitive economy. In this condition, law in relation to the state power mediated the claims of political forces that were fairly well distributed between several classes rather than concentrated in the hands of a single, highly monopolized class. In twentieth-century conditions of capital concentration, the concept of a general and impartial legal structure either is ideological eyewash or at best serves in the peripheral spheres of society. Neumann contends that in the main, general law has been replaced by direct rule of economically controlling interests. "The apparatus of the authoritarian state realizes the juridical demands of the monopolies." The body of the essay is taken up with a discussion of how ideological changes in legal theory have reflected this changed economic situation. And although Neumann is inclined to use German Nazism as his model, he leaves no doubt that this transformation occurs wherever monopoly replaces the free market.

No less interesting is Neumann's analysis of natural law in terms of historical needs and perspectives. He shares with others the opinion that natural

[*] Franz Neumann, *The Democratic and the Authoritarian State* (Glencoe, Ill.: The Free Press 1957), pp. 327.

law theory is self-contradictory, in that it is compelled to introduce into its conceptual framework nonnormative elements such as power. But he goes beyond this criticism by recognizing that natural law concepts may function for many, even opposite, social ends. It is Neumann's judgment, which this reviewer shares, that the philosophy of law entails some type of natural law matrix. Pragmatic theories that assert the law is nothing but the way it functions in concrete circumstances, in fact deny that one can probe beneath the decision-making layer of law and seek a terminus in the socio-political fabric.

Toward the end of his life, Neumann asserted the Pareto-like premise that political power unqualifiedly dominates economic forces. Since in an authoritarian state, power controls the means of terror, the manipulation of production and consumption, of propaganda and education, he could not envision continued belief in economic determinism. This contrasts with Neumann's earlier thinking, in which law and politics masked the economic foundation. Marcuse, in his preface to this book, asserts that the importance of economics receded in Neumann's later work. In fact, the relation between politics and economics seems to be inverted. The Nazi experience confounded the Marxist theory, and to the credit of Neumann, reality won out.

Another point of inversion is his opinion, formed in the twilight of his career, that the state, that leviathan which he had taken so much pain to reveal as a proctor for defending vested economic interests, could yet function as the representative of universal human interests. It is unfortunate that Neumann, who sought all his life to prove the moral injunctions of political philosophy, should in the end ask the state to assume its "proper task" of restoring a balance between "egotistic interests of private groups." This fundamental shift in theoretical mooring reflected his disillusionment with Left totalitarianism.

Neumann attempted to resolve the dichotomy of his work by searching out a new theoretical basis. Just as Marxism was his leitmotif during 1930–1945, Freudianism assumed a like position in the postwar period. In his earlier phase, the irrationality of fascism could be overcome by the rationality of a planned yet democratic economy. But when it appeared to Neumann that the rational economy itself disguises a propensity towards irrational dictatorial rule, then problems of politics and psychology came to be considered as organically related.

In his last studies on the relation of personal anxiety to political alienation, Neumann goes in for a psycho-political synthesis. The successes of totalitarian systems are viewed as a mass response to the personal pressures created by industrialism. Identification with dictatorial father images, the alleviation of neurosis through ego-renunciation, the conflict between social requirements and individual happiness—these Freudian categories serve to underscore Neumann's larger thesis that neurotic drives lead to an acceptance of totalitarianism (i.e., "the destruction of the line between state and society and the total politicization of society by the device of the monopolistic party"). There is a strong tendency in Neumann's later work to transform psychic and biological factors into basic political laws.

However, even with the shift from Marxism to Freudianism (more specifically a shift from optimism to pessimism), this volume contains the work of a man deeply involved with the big issues of human existence. If it is true that the critical mind is better able than the doctrinaire ideologue to respond to the needs of a changing civilization, then this will serve as Neumann's justification and underline the importance of his intellectual legacy.

From *The American Socialist,* vol. 5, no. 1 (1958), pp. 22–23.

70

Sociological Disinformation*

Parsons, Talcott

William Buxton's book, *Talcott Parsons and the Capitalist Nation-State*, is a curious throw-back, for it reveals the intellectual climate of 1966 far more than that of 1986. The critiques of American sociology and political science hearken to discussions and positions established in the wake of the Vietnam involvement. In itself, this point of view is not necessarily a weakness, but the author's unrelieved lack of self-awareness is an irreparable shortcoming; the crisis he writes about in a breathless mode is indeed in the past tense. As a result, a work composed in the transient blush of a Marxian-oriented Canadian nationalism now reads like a peculiar and pallid anti-American diatribe.

The author's thesis, stated repeatedly and with but slight variations throughout, is that the validation of political sociology is inherently related to the ability of the capitalist nation-state to solve its problems of instrumentation and legitimation. That this may have been one of many consequences of some forms of political sociology and that the validation of a field resides in the interconnection and interpenetration of state systems and class formations are possibilities not entertained. Still, let this ex post facto definition remain. This validation in turn rests upon "liberal Calvinist precepts" held by Talcott Parsons. Thus, the emergence and consolidation of the capitalist nation-state was contingent upon particular patterns of knowledge, produced in part by social scientists (chapters 2 and 8). There is little point to note that Parsons never made such a formulation of his own work. Still, Buxton concludes that such a political sociology is embedded "in the prevailing order [that] is structured in oppressive and inegalitarian ways."

Buxton views his own work as an inventory of such oppressive doctrines and a "radical inversion" of the prescriptive heuristic. Given his constantly reiterated belief that political sociology "was practically linked with and committed to the fortunes of the capitalist nation-state and to the ascendancy of the economic and political elites within it," one can still use this body of

---

* William Buxton, *Talcott Parsons and the Capitalist Nation-State: Political Sociology as a Strategic Vocation* (Toronto: University of Toronto Press, 1985), pp. 331.

knowledge as a "convenient point of departure for elaborating a much more radically disposed social science, equally grounded in political and social life." In other words, a doctrine presumably shot through with alien ideological presumptions can yet be described as a body of knowledge and in turn can be employed by anticapitalists for their own noble "radical rejuvenation." We are assured that "what is needed are 'progressive' versions of such bodies as the Social Science Research Council and the Ford Foundation." Aside from the surprise that these groups, great and small, will evince at being defined as antiprogressive, the author ignores the whereabouts of fiscal sources for such presumed clean funds.

The book ends as it begins: on a strange note of realignment and emancipation. There is not a blessed word of real-world events to intrude upon this scenario. There is no Soviet empire and there is no totalitarian opposition to democracy. There is only a "Cold War America"—an invention of perfect evil, uniting diabolical forces of "elite scientists and big business aiming at the control of ideological deviance." What makes such a vision so terribly disturbing is that in the period of the cold war and in the epoch of McCarthyism, it was social science that stood firm for the "rational management of human interests and affairs." The struggle of Parsons and others for the institutionalization and fiscal support of social science was precisely aimed to serve as a bulwark against fanaticism and irrationality. One might argue that Parsons's critique of McCarthyism did not go far enough, or that his support for equal rights and equal participation of black Americans in public life did not address economic history, or that his ideas about the medical model (professionalization) as a bulwark against the self-interest of the entrepreneurial model did not sufficiently address issues of American stratification. But to convert Parsons's liberalism into a veritable conspiracy against egalitarianism simply cannot be sustained on any other than hostile grounds. Parsons's political pluralism, like his religious open-endedness, was rooted in educational reformism and ideological liberalism. No amount of literary excess by Buxton can alter such simple truths.

Curiously, I found the chapters on Gabriel Almond and Seymour Martin Lipset much more compelling than the remainder of the book, for at least with Almond and Lipset, the issues of political concern are drawn by those critiqued. In both Almond's comparativist perspective and Lipset's analytical political sociology, a sense of the end-of-ideology politics of the 1960s can be gleaned. But here too, the dilemma for Buxton is that resistance to communism on the part of Almond, Sidney Verba, or Lucian Pye is no more reactionary than resistance to McCarthyism on the part of Lipset, Samuel Stouffer, and Edward A. Shils was necessarily revolutionary.

The point of social science, so often missed by bone-rattling critics, is that in its commitments to rationality, research results come upon the hard rock of the ideological sources of totalitarianisms—Left and Right. There was never a cold war consensus (social scientists were in the vanguard against Vietnam involvement), but there was, and to some degree still remains, a democratic consensus. This commitment to an open society is the essential core of social research. This distinction often escapes ideologues.

For those who prefer their Parsons straight, without Buxton's bromides, we have only to look at his own collected papers on political sociology, entitled *Politics and Social Structure* (1969). In fact, Parsons never wrote a specific volume by this title; the closest he came was an essay on polity and society that was largely a restatement of such general categories as double interchange systems, functional equivalence of legitimation, collective effectiveness, the professional complex. When Parsons climbs off his sociological high jargon, we see a true son of Harvard and of such thinkers as Ralph Barton Perry, no less than a sire of Heidelberg and Max Weber. Nazism is critiqued as a fundamentalist revolt against the rationalization of the Western World. Fascism is seen as traditionalist and, hence, as enlisting a mass base that goes beyond and may even betray the power of business and the business of power alike.

In dealing with American society, it is not capitalism but democracy that is seen as central. Parsons's analysis of McCarthyism is described against a backdrop of the globalization of American power and the strains upon democracy that such "enhanced levels of national political responsibility" bring about. Parsons refers to McCarthyism and Birchism as varieties of regressive individualism or institutionalized individualism, designations not at all unlike those he musters in his critique of fascism in Europe. Parsons's critique of Mills's concept of power is serious yet entirely solicitous of the author. Indeed, Mills remarked on several occasions how grateful he was that Parsons, unique among his sociological critics, took him seriously even though criticizing his overwhelming tendency to reduce the concept of power to a notion of power *over* others. Parsons's examination of black enfranchisement ("Full Citizenship for the Negro American") is a tough-minded statement of how nationalism and ethnicity confounded those who abstractly and wrongly assumed that class is central or that blacks would become fodder for the class struggles of others. Indeed, he argues for the positive values of separate identification. The weakest link in the American society, the black community, may turn out to be the most critical rebuke to the Communist diagnosis of the modern world. His distinction between inclusion and assimilation is far from abstract. But it is the democratic system rather than the capitalist system on which the Parsonian world turns.

It is important to appreciate the degree to which critical, pivotal figures in American social research, like Talcott Parsons, remained extraordinarily oblivious to the ideological uses, if not purposes, of their efforts. Buxton is quite right to identify Parsons with the course of American list: the special role of universities in status identification, the professionalization of occupational roles, the organicist components of systemic health and individual well-being, the reconstruction of positivist traditions at the expense of critical elements in social thought—these are themes worth highlighting. The trouble is that Buxton converts these American grains into conspiratorial strains. And even a felicitous literary manner cannot bail out such a futile line of analysis

Buxton's book itself illustrates what it seeks to explicate: the place of political sociology as a strategic vocation. His strategy rejects an entire discipline denying an empirical framework that pits communist nation-states against capitalist nation-states, totalitarian social systems against democratic social systems. This is not to insist on polarities of expression or to deny the interpenetration of big-power interests in the U.S.A. and U.S.S.R.; rather, it is to note how extraordinarily removed from any political reality were the 1960s—a period in which efforts like Buxton's abounded and which ultimately rested on the denial of formal analysis, of political sociology as a discipline of analysis, in favor of political sociology as myth-making. The subversion of social science in the name of political principles has become a 1980s commonplace.

Sadly, in Buxton's animus against all things American and capitalist, he can do no more than accept the strategy he denounces but really only wishes to redirect on behalf of some vague "radical reconstruction." For even Buxton, certain as he is about everything else, does not have the foggiest idea of the correct prescription for the disease of the capitalist nation-state. Needless to say, words like the USSR, Soviet Union, or Russia are neither indexed nor dealt with in this study of political sociology.

From *The New England Quarterly,* vol. 59, no. 4 (1986), pp. 569–574.

71

A Funeral Pyre for America*

Rogow, Arnold A.

Interpreting one's own civilization has always been a touchstone of the success or failure of a particular intellectual vantage point. For the most part, such retrospective analysis either points to a benchmark that *is* (capitalism) or a heavenly choir that *might be* (socialism). Since for these three noteworthy authors capitalism is doomed and bolshevism is soiled, only the socialist future remains to test the adequacies of the present moment.

These three works, each quite distinctive, illustrate this point. These elder (or at least middle) statesmen of the Left, each in his own manner seeks to summarize the American experience through the filter of socialist tradition. For Bell, it is Weber; for Rogow, Freud; and for Harrington, Marx sans Lenin. Each of these typically American intellectuals still resorts to European masters to provide sense and sensibility to their socialist views toward American capitalism. Their efforts seem to tower above others, in part because the generation that followed men like Bell, Harrington, and Rogow failed to make the essential leap from criticism to construction. With the notable exception of such younger scholars as Marcus G. Raskin, Ira Katznelson, and Richard Flacks, the ranks of social scientists (historians have fared better) who have made even a remote effort to comprehend the society they reject with such passion are thin in numbers and even scantier in ideas.

The usual answers are probably accurate: anti-intellectualism, activity isolated from intellect, the very displacement of generational factors that isolated the New Left from even its socialist tradition. But there is one rather elusive property that probably best explains this failure of intellectual nerve. Radical ideology was so centered on self-criticism, inner-oriented critique, and the cult of collectivism generally, that the purification of sociology replaced the examination of society and that domination of a political science association

---

* Daniel Bell, *The Cultural Contradictions of Capitalism* (Basic Books, 1976), pp. 301.

Michael Harrington, *The Twilight of Capitalism* (Simon and Schuster, 1976), pp. 446.

Arnold A. Rogow, *The Dying of the Light: A Searching Look at America Today* (New York: G.P. Putnam's Sons, 1976), pp. 384.

became bigger game than restoration of the American political process. As a result, the analysis of contemporary American society has suffered badly. We must take comfort in the willingness of the remnants of the Old Left, the over-fifty crowd to fill the tragic void in the critical literature. In the world of radical scholarship, youth was indeed wasted on the young. Worse, the idea of radicalism was wasted on new radicals living out old academic conventions within new academic cocoons.

Each of these three books reiterates a familiar theme in the literature of the Left: the crisis and ultimate doom of capitalism. The last chapter of Rogow's *The Dying of the Light* is fittingly enough termed "The Twilight of the Gods." Harrington's sermon is apparent from the title, *The Twilight of Capitalism*; and even Daniel Bell, while showing that the sources of instability are in the "triumph of Weber over Marx," nonetheless describes his penultimate chapter as "Unstable America," with the cumbersome subtitle, "Transitory and Permanent Factors in a National Crisis," restoring Bell's claim to radical credentials. As America celebrates its Bicentennial, the three writers of the Old Left find themselves building a collective funeral pyre. Upon closer inspection, it turns out that only Rogow has dark premonitions for America; Harrington has negative feelings toward capitalism as an economic system for distributing wealth, and Bell's hostility is vented on capitalism as a cultural style for disseminating ideas.

It makes a big difference whether one dislikes America or capitalist culture. For what we have with Harrington and Bell (despite their sharp differences) is a celebration of democracy, of which the United States turns out to be the foremost representative, while Rogow condemns the United States as a "phallic" nation run by "barbarians" and "one-eyed kings." In this sense perhaps Rogow is closer in spirit to the New Left than the Old Left—or at least is making an effort to bridge the gap. What cements these books is a series of dislikes: an economic system that does not provide equity (Harrington); a cultural system that is individualist in temper and bourgeois in appetite (Bell); and a national system that is overfed, overclothed, and overhoused (Rogow). Each author senses that the American problem is not one of goods but of distribution. And each believes that capitalism generates wealth at the expense of equity.

When the variables are parceled out, the sting of criticism is actually offered in modest proportions. For when questions hinge on the reform of the economy, changes in the polity, or an overhaul in the cultural apparatus, America and not Russia is seen as the logical place for such experimentations to occur. This is the frustration suffered by the authors of each of these volumes: their critiques are not suppressed, not condemned, not even paid much heed. Why do these substantial books with their absolute criticisms fail to shake up generations, move policy-makers, or arouse a national debate? Why are they, in fact, lying in the historical dustbin to which they so ruefully assign America and its works generally?

The answers vary from the actual resilience of American society to the insensitivity of the dying system to its own near extermination. Again, I think the answer lurking within each of these quite useful volumes is the absence of alternatives. Each of these people in his own way recognizes that the existing socialist options (i.e., Russia and China) that the United States might emulate are not attractive. For Rogow, socialism is simply a critical label within capitalism. He goes so far as to suggest that the resemblance between European socialism and American liberalism is so marked that both must simply be called varieties of progressivism and reform. Whether this is capitalism's twilight or midnight hour, Harrington can barely get around the problem of his own characterization of the Soviet Union as a bureaucratic collectivist state, and his faith in China and Cuba is barely an existential flicker. Bell, of course, is so renowned as a critic of totalitarian varieties of socialism that he can leave this point in the closet. However, in his effort to base solutions on the "public household" rather than bourgeois individualism or bureaucratic collectivism, the skeleton peeks out of the closet at crucial moments.

These authors describe a crisis without offering us alternatives. Worse, the options available turn out to be even less satisfying than the American society under scrutiny. For Hegel the belter is the critic of the good; here the worse is the only world picture offered as an alternative to the good. Under such a confining situation, these are simply books of economic and cultural doomsday that cannot be taken seriously as models of rebellion, because these present no alternative real-world options. The idea of socialism has been irrevocably tarnished by systems of socialism. The misanthropic nature of the U.S.S.R. makes the miscreant nature of the U.S.A. entirely bearable, even joyously deviant. The myopic inability of these fine scholars to take seriously the cultural contradictions of bolshevism, the dying of light in the Soviet orbit, or the twilight of socialism deprives each book of its natural dialectic. The field of international relations is left untapped as a way to measure contemporary American society and its failings.

A terrible tentativeness haunts these critics of capitalism. Harrington has no doubt that "human life will be radically transformed" because "that future has already begun." What is in doubt is "the most crucial of issues: Whether this collectivist society which is emerging even now will repress or liberate men and women." Thus, at the very end, Harrington can "conclude then with an 'if.'" The spirit of Marx is urged upon us as a comrade in struggle, despite the dual outcome of Marxism so eloquently described by Harrington.

Bell provides us with the virtues of defeat. The early Founding Fathers' sense of destiny was replaced by a "virulent Americanism," and colonialism and hedonism took over. "Today that manifest destiny is shattered; the Americanism has worn thin, and only the hedonism remains. It is a poor recipe for national unity and purpose." To confront defeat, Bell advises "the reaffirmation of our past" followed by "recognition of the limits of resources and the priority of needs, individual and social, over unlimited appetite and wants, and agreement upon a conception of equity which gives all persons a sense of fairness and inclusion in the society. . . ." Harrington's socialist redemption is for Bell part and parcel of the "hubris of classical liberalism." But Bell ends with the conservative plea: a recognition that the "knowledge of power must coexist with the knowledge of its limits." The cultural contradictions of capitalism are presumably to be resolved by a neo-Aristotelian balance wheel.

Rogow, too, is not about to surrender bourgeois virtues, his frontal assaults on the system notwithstanding. The right to privacy must be protected; economic opportunities extended by future totalitarian societies are unacceptable because they are not "free." Benevolence is not liberty. Rogow ends with a conservative plea for liberties as a protection against benevolent fascism and its "loss of equities." We are reminded of "de Tocqueville's wisdom" that equality can lead people to servitude or freedom, knowledge or barbarism.

In the end is the beginning. It turns out that the radical critics of American society do not have any answers; worse, they may not be asking the right questions. But first let us attend to what is worthwhile in these works.

The current crop of writings on Marx and Marxism are so spongy, metaphysical, and oracular that one might well imagine that Marx was a hell-bent-for-leather theologian providing a new vision of heaven and hell. Harrington's enormous strength is his appreciation of Marx as an economist and a social scientist. Through a series of brilliant literary devices ("e.g., bourgeois socialism" paralleling Marx's "feudal socialism," the "spiritual materialist" paralleling Engels's "mechanical materialist," etc.), Harrington attempts to show the contemporary relevance of Marx, even the superiority of Marxian analysis over its revisionist critics. Arguing against ideas such as Bell's postindustrial society, Moynihan's policy making for an unplanned society, and the welfare state as a fundamental change in the composition of capitalism, Harrington does very well, saying that corporate priorities remain essential to the conduct of politics of policies alike. Similarly, his analysis of the spiritual materialists, those who argue the case of Marxism as populism, is filled with rich insight. The "spiritual humanism" of a Castro ends up as a new bureaucracy carrying out the modernization of Cuba under Soviet aegis.

For someone who believes that a "Marxist 'economics' does not, and cannot exist," Harrington does an incredible job resurrecting the dead. In the chapter, "The Anti-Economist" in particular, one finds a basic lesson in Marxian economics: the nature of money and capital, the labor theory of value, the wage form of labor, capital as a relationship; labor as a substance or measure of value. These complex issues are dealt with in felicitous prose, with full knowledge of the sources and a sense of social science as a whole rather than as a parceled-out series of administratively defined disciplines. The six appendices contain a great deal of inner Marxian polemics conducted with sense and decency. His notes on Althusser, Habermas, Popper, Ollman,

Godelier, Colletti, Poulantzas, etc. indicate a writer who takes seriously the entire range of present-day literature on Marx and embody the sort of discussion that should be particularly appealing to those already versed in the arguments presented in the main portion of the text. In short, the analysis is cogent, and the clinical uses of Marxism are convincing, even if the master thesis of the book, summarized by its title, remains strangely obscure and even profoundly dubious.

The methodological base of Rogow's work is the use of personal anecdote in the narrative. In this, he is far removed from the austere economism of Harrington's dialectics. He can move within one paragraph from a description of Maya Angelou in a film she made several years ago to a discussion of black/white sex mores. Personal statements, newspaper items, and policy reports vie with each other for attention. Each chapter contains Rogow's own proximate solutions: city blues can be alleviated by pedestrian malls, pocket parks, decorating subway stations on a neighborhood basis, moving merchandise at night to avoid auto congestion, and so forth.

The chapter on political economy is spiced by many illustrations of competing drives toward opulence and equality, but it ends on the inconclusive note that, while a democratic society always moves toward equality, those who dislike equity will always find ways to establish social distance. This central chapter is more concerned with how social distance is established through snobbery than with mechanisms for reducing social inequality or injustice. The foibles of the rich, whether they are servants of the state or of God, are amply illustrated by newspaper accounts of the way the Rockefellers, Billy Graham, and Norman Vincent Peale live. But whether newspaper accounts of wealth and poverty are an adequate basis on which to decide about the qualifications of political leaders is moot. After all, it might be argued that political corruption is easier to institutionalize among those of impoverished background than those coming from bastions of economic privilege. It takes a very poor boy indeed to risk a Vice Presidency for a $10,000 bribe. In short, Rogow's recitation of anecdotal materials, far from adding up to a self-evident condemnation of American society, serves rather to illustrate the fables and foibles of a "vertical mosaic" of facts and figures of societal imperfection which can be mustered for any society (except, of course, when the gathering of data is politically impermissible).

What evidence is there for Rogow's vision of the dying light of American society? The anecdotal style has a basic shortcoming: he has the unfortunate habit of confusing levels of discourse. His intuitive critique of suburbia, apart from being in direct contradiction to the best evidence we have on the subject (that suburban residents are very much like urban Americans, and then some), includes all sorts of data that characterize American society as a whole. Aggregate data on divorce rates and suicide rates are not broken out by suburban versus urban or rural America; hence we are left with a large-scale non sequitur. Many of his observations, such as "Keep Off the Grass" signs or the character of shopping centers, are at least as true of big-city life as suburban living. Likewise, the mind of the moralist that lurks behind many Freudians is expressed in Rogow's critique of America as a "phallic culture." Despite the egalitarian nature of the American sexual revolution, the phallic culture is said to give rise to "pornographic imperialisms." But if, "in the end, happiness, which includes sexual satisfaction, remains a personal problem and perhaps will be forever elusive," how does the search for sexual happiness come to be characterized in such harsh, even American, terms, since the same tendencies are prevalent worldwide, in the Soviet Union no less than the United States?

The cement that holds this book together is Rogow's vision of America as a dying society, one drawn to thanatos more than eros. It is a society capable of practicing genocide, cultural self-destruction, and colonialist economic practices without knowing it. Rogow is no more willing than the other authors to accept totalitarian solutions for America. Hence the sorts of dictatorial regimes that dot the earth in the name of socialism cannot be honestly considered in his book. Even where he expresses his harshest criticisms in relation to the treatment of blacks as a "final solution," he must also acknowledge that "one can discern in America, if not the faint tracings of an interracial society, at the least, the outlines of a society in which there is more tolerance and mutual respect." So much for genocide in America.

The problems with this sort of analysis are multiple. First, he presents or suggests no real options to the death of America: second, he allows no real counterinformation to filter into the analysis to forestall this sense of waiting for the end, and finally, he submits no evidence that we are witnessing a national malaise unique to this country rather than general processes characteristic of industrial societies in flux. For all of that, the book stands as a useful reminder that the combined power of psychoanalytic and historical criticisms can serve as useful guides in national analysis. We have so many books combining the insights of Freud and Marx at metaphysical levels that it is good to have one employing them in a clinical evaluation of American society.

What is strange about Daniel Bell's book, *The Cultural Contradictions of Capitalism*, is the assumption that, of all ongoing societies, America uniquely has the capacity to resolve these contradictions within the framework of present-day economic, social, and political relations. In an odd way, labeling the book the cultural contradictions permits discussion of the American problem in terms of Protestant ethics, middle-class life-styles, hedonism, and the like. The word style dominates the key chapter of the book on the cultural contradictions, and hence discussions of substance are minimized. We are told that the characteristic style of industrialism is efficiency in costs, maximization, optimization, and functional rationality. This style is contrasted to the anticognitive and antirational modes that lead to apocalyptic moods and anti-intellectual behavior.

Bell sees this disjunction as the historical-cultural crisis of all Western societies. Curiously, we are not told what aspects of either the economy or the polity account for this disjunction, or would permit their removal. One wonders whether societies such as the Soviet Union cannot also be characterized as emphasizing functional rationality, technocratic decision, and meritocratic awards, on the one hand, and apocalyptic moods and antirational modes of behavior on the other. Bell does identify the absence of a central ideological spine in American culture; but he doe not appreciate that this fragmentation is characteristic of industrialism as a whole.

The volume itself is overloaded with the very gadgets which presumably characterize American society. While Bell promises a discussion of deeper and more difficult questions of social legitimation, we are in face given a huge number of issues translated from the economic to the cultural realm. On any given page one may have a discussion of Jean-Luc Godard, Charles Reich, Theodore Roszak. Philip Rahv, and a host of others. As a result, we receive a remarkable feeling of the range of American culture, but in an issue-oriented and individuated way that does not permit resolution of the contradictions Bell raises. The remarkable concluding essay, the "Public Household" derives, intellectually at least, from Schumpeter's work on fiscal sociology. It goes a long way to discuss the basic issues of economics but leaves culture far behind. Curiously, this final essay, which in my opinion makes a genuine contribution to political economy, is largely out of kilter with a great deal of the book. The key issues are stated in a forthright manner—the rise of an issue-oriented society without any overriding sense of purpose; the emergence of a political dominance, characteristic of capitalist and socialist societies alike, that places the state rather than the economy at the center of system maintenance; and the utilization of economic growth as a secular religion and organizing principle of all industrial societies.

The central dilemma that emerges in the Bell volume is that crises and alarms do not really offer much relief from the contradictions set forth. The volume ends with a crisis of belief that perhaps reflects more realistically the crisis of Bell's belief system than that of American society as a whole. To conclude with a reaffirmation of liberalism after having argued for the calamitous outcomes of liberalism, and after having portrayed the tensions between the public and the private, the altruistic and hedonistic, is neither intellectually appropriate nor emotionally satisfying. The double theme of self-conscious maturity and the restoration of the idea of purpose reduces itself to a teleological, even theological, framework. It argues the need for greatness, apart from enunciating the empirical properties of greatness.

The volume ends on a far more indecisive and confused note than might have been the case had Bell dealt directly with the economic contradictions of capitalism as something apart from the long term fall of capitalism. Of course, he could rightly argue that he had dealt with contraction in his earlier volume

The Coming of Post-Industrial Society. In his preface, he sees his new volume as having a dialectical relationship to that earlier work. The problem is that using the language of contradiction, rather than the language of conflict or consensus, obliges one to indicate how such contradictions may be resolved. Since, such contradictions such as Bell's can be resolved within the framework of the present social order (whatever sop he throws the postindustrial society), one is left with a study of cultural conflict rather than of social contradiction. In this sense, the rhetoric of socialism overwhelms Bell's better sense of the requirements of sociology. A less strident rhetoric would have been appropriate to match what is, in the end, a series of modest proposals for a new liberalism.

In their own way, each of these books exemplifies the emergence of a new and critical vision of American society, that moves beyond the celebrations of the fifties and the condemnations of the sixties. They are better books for having done so. Underlining that new intellectual mood is the American revolution of falling expectations: a much deeper and more profound sense that not only has the world shrunk but that the United States role in that world has also been diminished. What prevents these socialist writers from frenetically celebrating this fact is the absence of real alternatives. Neither Harrington, Rogow, or Bell would seriously consider the Soviet option as superior or viable. They might consider West European welfare systems as better in some respects, but even so, that would be more in the nature of personal preference. In short, what starts with fire and brimstone ends with pablum-like calls for welfare liberalism.

These volumes are sober, without the characteristic euphoria of earlier socialist writings. For if the American century has been defeated as an ideological system, so has the Soviet International. As a result, each of these writers is telling us what was, rather than what is to become. The Old Left provides a kind of new pessimism in articulating the *Götterdämmerung* of American society, but it is already obsolete in providing a sense of growth and birth.

One has the terrible feeling that these writers are so locked into nineteenth century categories of capitalism and socialism that they have not properly understood that American society has not stood still, that its problems, much less its practices, can no longer be described solely within the framework of Marxism. As a result, while these three august nd distinguished representatives of the Old Left far outshadow and outweigh their colleagues on the New Left, the problem of what constitutes the Left remains unexamined. Those who set out to change the world might well start by changing the categories with which they perceive that world. Bell gleans this. Harrington is unnerved by this. And Rogow is angered by this. Fortunately, there is intellectual light at the end of the old Left tunnel.

From *Worldview,* vol. 19, no. 11 (1976), pp. 45–48.

72

Political Pluralism and Democratic Power*

Rose, Arnold M.

For more than twenty-five years, Arnold Rose has fused the liberal ethos with the sociological imagination. An intellectual adventure that began in 1940 with his major role in *An American Dilemma* has now reached its intellectual culmination with *The Power Structure.* It might be added that, distinctly unlike most sociologists, Rose's knowledge of the civil culture and the political arena is authentic—an authenticity certified by his service as a representative in the Minnesota legislature and by his relentless defense of civil and academic freedoms in the courtroom and the classroom.

This aspect of Arnold Rose's career is not accidentally related to the book before you—since like all good social scientists, Rose has transformed both personal profile and political commitment into scientific sociology. One may take issue with many of the hypotheses and conclusions he has drawn, but one may not easily contest either the sobriety of his intellectual viewpoint or the worth of the man behind it.

One genuine problem might well be that Professor Rose's involvement in politics at the local level tends to reinforce a populist image of government, which, while in fact present in American society, does not necessarily reflect the structural dilemmas of the society at the national, or even more note-worthy, at the international level. Thus, it may be that the degree of civilian control over the military appears greater from the shores of Lake Superior in Minnesota than from the Bay of Guanabara in Brazil. I doubt that the average American, infused as he is with populist values and oblivious as he often is of overseas commitments, has the same perception of an American military or diplomatic presence as do those peoples who live in the midst of revolutions or counter-revolutions, successful or otherwise, depending on the attitudes

---

* Arnold M. Rose, *The Power Structure: Political Process in American Society* (New York and London: Oxford University Press, 1967), pp. 508.

of the United States military mission and the financial appraisals of United States trade groups, and civilian ambassadorial staff.

The attempt of Arnold Rose is clear enough: to effect a reconciliation of power theories by employing the political analyses of the pluralists, from Arthur Bentley to V.O. Key, and the sociological methods of the elitist school, particularly the contemporary work of Mills and Hunter. That neither of the contrasting schools of macro-political conflict theory will be much satisfied by Rose's analysis is a foregone conclusion and is clearly appreciated by the author himself. One must welcome Rose's calm and dispassionate examination of the available empirical information and his willingness to speculate on the outcome of each theory in the light of the current discussion between pluralists and elitists. Without work such as his, the discussion could well become part of general ideology rather than part of systematic sociology.

In this connection, one of the most telling virtues of Rose's presentation is his appreciation of the generalized state of false consciousness in American society. Rarely does American society truly appreciate the nature of power, neither the trade unionists nor the proletarian class, the business sectors, the political communities, or the intermediary classes that constantly examine their own power in evaluating their influence on social events.

I would not take issue with Arnold Rose on his shrewd observations concerning the generalized misconceptions about power, but rather I would emphasize more the actual disparity between the perception of power and the exercise of power. It might be true to say that big business's understanding of power is as fragile and limited as is that of the big unions. However, from the point of view of social forces and not just social interactions, the actual dominion of power given over to business is considerably more than that given over to labor. This distinction between the perception and the execution of power is precisely what distinguishes pluralists from elitists, the latter being far more concerned with its exercise and the former far more concerned with its perception than is healthy for either. In this sense, I view Professor Rose's book as an attempt to get each major theory of power to confront the other with its particular variety of false consciousness.

There is an ever-present confusion in political sociology between statements of fact (such as the existence of diverse and multichanneled expressions of power in the United States) and judgments about the moral order (such as "the best way to study power in the United States is by examining perceptions or life chances"). It is important to realize that power may be erroneously perceived not only in terms of underestimation but also in terms of exaggeration. Unionists may exaggerate their power. Militarists may overemphasize their war-making potential. In these circumstances, perceptions may stimulate elitist sentiments rather than contribute to the pluralistic framework. Professor Rose's work does a great deal to clarify or at least to catalogue the present confusion between influence and power, between what is perceived and what is actual.

It might well be that there is a qualitative distinction to be made between voluntary community organizations and a bureaucratic national system. From a community point of view, voluntary organizations seem effective and powerful, but from the national perspective, these same kinds of organizations often appear impotent. The nature of power, or at least the perception of power, shifts as the levels of analysis alter. Thus, the power structure in the United States may require one kind of examination when viewed in terms of voluntary community organization, whereas the United States as a power may exhibit different features when considered internationally. Although even at the community level, I venture to say that the degree of interlocking political-economic control is impressive.

One serendipitous finding made by Arnold Rose is the degree to which empirical research demonstrates the existence of a gap between civics and politics, between perceptions of influence and basic political issues within the nation. It is clear that the United States suffers not so much from power concentrations as from a breakdown in political dialogue, resulting partly from a celebration of civil activities. The civic culture may not only vary from actual political behavior but often represents an antithetical frame of reference. Civics often dulls the political sensibilities of the American public. This fact is clearly evident in Rose's work; and is part and parcel of his deep belief in the liberal imagination.

One of the most impressive facets of Professor Rose's book is its revelation of his intimacy with the conduct of power. The last sections, on Minnesota, Texas, the Kennedy presidential campaign, and the Medicare legislation, represent four case studies in political sociology. The case study method is often talked about but too rarely used. In Rose's hands, political sociology is not reduced to cross-tabulating electoral results. He does not suffer from the fallacy of electoral determinism, of assuming that important political events are necessarily linked to electoral behavior. Quite the contrary. There is a strong undertone to Rose's remarks that which clearly places him, no matter how dissatisfied he is Mills's results on the side of the classical tradition, precisely because political sociology comes to represent the study of social interaction among political men and not the study of electoral victories among nonpolitical men.

In this sense, the significance of *The Power Structure* is as much heuristic as theoretical. Chapter 14 may well be considered a guide for the perplexed liberal and the confused sociologist. Written in the optative mood, it forms a basis for social and political action. Perhaps it is necessary to constantly refer to democratic values in order to make good on the various propositions politicians proclaim to be fact. If the hopeful mood generated by Professor Rose's book produces a self-fulfilling prophesy based on liberal values, well and good.

But if this same mood produces a smug acceptance of the American political system, both internally and in its effects on the rest of the world, then I would find this self-fulfilling prophesy more in the nature of a self-destructive fantasy.

Arnold Rose is a shrewd man. He appreciates and understands these various dilemmas. That is why his book manages to remain within the frame of a multi-influence approach without indulging in the kind of flatulent, self-congratulatory conclusions so often recorded in the work of those scholars adhering to pluralism.

This is a serious book deserving of attention and argument. If a political-economic elite theory of American society is to regain favor among students of the social sciences, the empirical and theoretical formulations of the pluralistic, multi-influence school as put forward so cogently by Professor Rose will have to be examined squarely. Just as Rose engages in a symbolic dialogue with men like Mills and Hunter, so too will the future writers on political sociology have to address in an equally serious dialogue Arnold Rose's newest effort to construct a bridge between society and polity—or more to the point* between an empirical sociology and political analysis.

From the "Foreword" to *The Power Structure: Political Process in American Society*, (New York and London: Oxford University Press, 1967), pp. vii–xi.

73

Sociology for Sale*

Zetterberg, Hans L.

The breakup of a scientific system proceeds in two ways: first, superior results from a competing system and method create dramatic rifts; second, discontent and disaffiliation develop from within. The work of Mans Zetterberg offers a remarkable example of the second type of disintegrative process. Mr. Zetterberg is a sociologist long associated with the methodological empiricist wing of sociology. His work is an expression of discontent with the results obtained by most contemporary social studies, and even more, a disaffiliation from the concepts that dominate sociological research agencies. Thus, if by virtue of Zetterberg's insider position alone, one must treat his work with utmost seriousness.

What exactly is Zetterberg's uneasiness with the course of sociological professionalization in America? His answer is framed in terms of five shortcomings in social practitioners and three fallacies in their theoretical armor. To paraphrase these basic flaws: (1) The theory of group work is normative; it serves to give a social or moral legitimization of professional practice, not a scientific legitimization. (2) The practitioners' use of the case study method is capricious and lacks the reliability associated with science. (3) What passes for accumulated knowledge is often accumulated ignorance and malpractice organizationally enshrined. (4) A collection of descriptive facts and trends does not result in specific advice on what action to take. (5) Often practitioners give advice without either conducting original research or drawing upon available scientific laws. As for the fallacies, they are the belief, that social science practice is the same as popularizing its content; second, that the content of knowledge to be applied must match the content of the problem faced by the practitioner, and that the number of social problems is nearly infinite, and by implication, unmanageable.

At the outset, it should be noted that criticisms such as these, though quite severe, have been made before and often by sociologists not enamored with

---

* Hans L. Zetterberg, *Social Theory and Social Practice* (New York. The Bedminster Press. 1962), pp. 190.

the purity of empiricism, and even more sharply by philosophers of science hardly taken with sociology at all. But what is important is that such a powerful broadside is for the first time launched from within the sociological establishment. Zetterberg reflects the anguish of a man who experiences disintegration, rather than one who understands it through ratiocination. That is why his critical remarks have a fresh and authentic ring to them, despite the fact that their content is by now well understood among many professional and practicing sociologists.

Zetterberg is reacting to grand theory the way William James reacted to Hegelian idealism at the turn of the century. Sociology must be practical. It must understand the difference between tough-minded scholarship and tender-hearted sentiment. It must offer useful consultations to useful businessmen. It must make recommendations to policy makers and it must provide a service to industry worth the cost. The notion of impersonal and abstract research must give way to, or at least share the wealth with, the scholarly "confrontation" which of course is personal and highly concrete. However distasteful it must sound to the author of *Social Theory and Social Practice*, Zetterberg presents us with a manifesto, a prophesy of the shape of sociology tomorrow and a warning of what can happen if the prophesy is ignored.

We come now to the heart of the matter: How well does Zetterberg's manifesto succeed? Is he offering a revolutionary boost to sociological theory and practice, or a nostalgic glance back to a time when social science was keenly related to worldly affairs? In short, is this really a worthwhile track to ride along or a smashing dead end?

Perhaps the strangest aspect of Zetterberg's volume, given his justified reputation as a methodologist, is the logical problems posed by his work. The error of looking at the social world in terms of mechanical polarities, or as it is sometimes called by philosophers of science, the problem of reification, is everywhere present. Human action is divided into executive and emotive types. Peoples are divided as tough-minded and tender-hearted, pioneers and protectors. Pattern variables are set up in terms of contingent and impersonal forces. And then there are a number of triadic relations: realms, values and stratifications; descriptions, evaluations and prescriptions. To be sure, although this serves to formulate typologies for the way men behave or the way institutions function, this approach involves a prima facie reductionism, since the dye is cast strictly in terms of black and while, positive and negative variables. The advantages of this sort of reductionism are that social laws can be framed with relative ease. But there is an overriding disadvantage. The laws so framed tend to be highly general phase statements with a very low level and narrow range of predictability.

What Zetterberg leaves us with, then, are not really laws so much as experienced invariant occurrences or simple logical tautologies. Illustrative of the first kind is the following: "The more a person deviates from a prescription given by his associates, the more unfavorable evaluations the latter tend to give him." One might just as well say that "The more a dog disobeys his master's order, the more unfavorable evaluations the latter tends to give him." But this does not explain the mechanisms of disobedience or the reasons for negative feelings, nor does it form the basis of predictions, since Zetterberg's "law" is only a "tend." And counter-factual conditions can be shown in which deviation from norms brings rewards and favorable evaluations. Or take the kind of law statement that says that "the greater variety of offerings in a market call, the greater the response." This is a simplistic truism. It is like saying more people go to Macy's than to the local dress shop because a department store has a greater variety of goods. But this "law," while implying an invariant relationship between numbers of people and numbers of offerings, does not account for a host of intervening factors. A law of diminishing returns may be operative if there are already a large number of department stores in one neighborhood. A specialty store might make more money with a smaller financial investment in such a situation. The costs of providing a saturation range of goods might diminish and not increase profits, etc. Yet a third kind of "law" Zetterberg adduces is that: "The more visible control of an institutional value a person has, the more favorable evaluations he receives from his associates." This is plainly debatable. Such psychological phenomena as resentment, envy, jealousy, are simply not accounted for. No one has ever demonstrated a direct relationship between power and favorable evaluations. Empirically, the opposite is more nearly everywhere the case. If not, rulers would have no need for recourse to coercion, and those without control, visible or otherwise, would have no need to insist on social changes. In this context, Zetterberg's law generalizes the reaction of small numbers of people whose activity is related in simple organization. There can be little relevance for problems connected to complex organization. The possessor of visible control impresses immediate associates or only those in a position to strive for or be affected by it. It cannot extend itself to the larger social realm where the invisible hand governs.

In general, it must be said that Zetterberg's laws suffer from a variety of principle defects. They are framed to exclude changes in the relationship between variables; they are often simple phase rules and not applicable to a wide range of social phenomena; they tend to assume that since the form of law-statements must be logical, that the content of law-statements is nothing but the formal mode as such; above all, the laws offered have no ability either to explain past behavior or calculate future responses. The reification of social events is thus a handicap and not an advantage to investigation. Zetterberg's laws are too easy. They are not wrested from social forces in painstaking effort but flow with suspicious case and simplicity from faith in a bivariant logic.

A large scale problem which Mr. Zetterberg seems not to understand, or at least not willing at this point to confront, is that the analogy of the sociological consultant and the psychiatric consultant is not quite of the same order of magnitude. In a patient-analyst relationship, it is clear that the relation is one in which the paying customer (patient) is in a subordinate position, while the paid consultant (analyst) is in a superordinate position. Now in a policy maker (patient) sociologist (analyst) relation, it is not clear that the former needs clarification. He may simply require rationalization of his behavior, or need guidance in manipulation of the actions of others. Thus the paying customer (policy maker) in this case is in a superordinate position, while the paid consultant (sociologist) is in a subordinate position. This role reversal is of decisive importance, of absolutely critical importance, for those who might like to draw the fee as well as the analogy of the psychiatric consultant. The structure of the particular relations is so different that one must assume not the likelihood of the sociologist performing critical consultation services but rather the improbability of this happening. The organizational advisor seeks to arrange and order his hired human machinery for such ends as perpetuation, efficiency, competition, or advancement of special interest, and not necessarily for socially useful purposes and not always with the consultant's knowing consent; this manipulation leads only to reinforcement of already established function. The inadequate neurotic acquires greater powers of self direction to alter his relation to the social milieu. The former seeks to engineer unknowing consent. The latter acquires the powers of knowing voluntary assent. The sociologist-consultant reinforces an ongoing process. The psychiatrist-consultant (discounting instances of incompetence) restores balance and the power of change to his needy patient.

One cannot help marveling at the ingenuous and naive aspects of Mr. Zetterberg's thought. He discovers the "motivational basis for class struggles" in the "lower class" taking over the "methods of measuring worth that prevail in the higher strata." Clearly, the "motivation" of poor nations desirous of becoming rich nations are the models derived from the latter. But just as clearly, class struggle has an apocalyptic dimension. The root of class struggle is not necessarily to adopt upper-class values but often to negate them and replace them with an utterly different set of values.

Underlying Zetterberg's sociology is a simplistic hedonism, in which motivation is equated and reduced with the desire to have what others already possess. Religious history no less than political history teaches that motivations may be altruistic no less than egotistic, messianic no less than opportunistic. Building sociological "laws" on a reductionistic psychology is not likely to generate many new clients.

Because of this hedonistic psychology, Zetterberg can never really derive a set of workable social laws, beyond the level of personality factors, since he flatly denies that things social really change: "history shows no exception to the rule that class struggles succeed only in modifying existing stratification or in replacing one form of division by another. In no society, ever, has stratification been abolished or equal control of institutional values achieved by all."

420

Here Zetterberg simply misses the point—and the point is that what counts in sociology is the direction of events, the tendencies toward mobility and away from fixity. The replacement of social divisions may entail, and in the revolutionary process usually does entail, not simply a redivision of power but very often an enlargement and expansion of the policy-making and policy-involved sector of society. It is presumptuous nonsense to declare that all history is simply a change in who rules, without acknowledging the fact that history also records the expansions and retrenchments of *how many* rule. Naturally, if one eliminates social change from social structure, the formulation of "laws" is a simple undertaking. But such a negation has only the merit of simplicity, not of truth. Why is it more lawful to say with Durkheim that the history of class society is a history of the redivision of labor, than to say with Marx that the history of class society is a history of the progressive emancipation of humanity? This subject is not a matter of law but a matter of empirical research and further studies. Despite Zetterberg's constant warning to be concrete and to avoid the abstract, his work has precious little concreteness. His exploration of social theories is an exhortation on behalf of antitheory. The actual content of social history is nowhere to be found. Motivations are transplanted from history to hedonism, thus enshrining the metaphysical pathos of "inevitable" differences between types of men.

With all of these criticisms, one can yet be grateful to Zetterberg for his provocative reappraisal, not only of the relation of recommendations to research but for a general estimate of the stakes of sociology in the modern world. Unfortunately, there is an overriding difficulty, namely that Zetterberg has been carrying around the baggage of empiricism for so long that even though he has opened it to find that it was stuffed with much confederate paper rather than with solid gold nuggets, he has really lost sight of the gold nuggets as well. Everything comes as a surprise and a discovery to Zetterberg. It is as if he has imbibed rather than digested the classical tradition in sociological theory. If an inadvertent byproduct of Zetterberg's work is a greater attention to sociological tradition, the fact that it is inadvertent is disconcerting in itself. It would probably surprise Zetterberg to know that a deceased colleague of his, C. Wright Mills, said as far back as the mid-forties: "It is one thing to talk about general problems on a national level, and quite another to tell an individual what to do. Most 'experts' dodge that question. I do not want to."

If I understand Zetterberg correctly, he does not want to dodge this question either. But what distinguishes empiricism as an ideology from an empirical sociology of real content, from a big-range sociology, is that he *does* want to dodge the responsibility for decisions taken at the sociologist's recommendation. What would the colleagues of a surgeon say if the surgeon undertook to make a prognosis or a diagnosis of an illness and then washed his hands off the case—as if the diagnostic process were completely cut off from the operative process. To kill a company by improper diagnosis is logically no different than killing a person by improper medical diagnosis. In either case it is patently absurd to limit the "scholarly confrontation" to analysis *en vacuo*, in isolation from the results obtained. If Zetterberg really wishes to adopt a hard-nosed pragmatic line, he must see the means-ends continuum as extending no less to the sociological diagnostician, and that would mean sharing in the agony as well as in the ecstasy. Pious words to the effect that the sociologist makes "consultations," while decision makers must still suffer "agony and anguish," can only deepen the rift between policy and sociology. It increases the suspicion that the sociologist is not so much performing a role as society's doctor, as he is the role of the quack selling spiked rum as mother's milk and then running to the next town before the truth gets out.

Given a more rationally coordinated social order, Zetterberg's kind of approach would prove most helpful and salutary. But in an irrational set of social orders, the rationalization of the crackpot does not lead to more reason in relations between men, but only to more dangerous varieties of social madness. So that one's respect for Zetterberg's impulse to practical theory must be seriously tempered by the fear that his approach would smooth the ruffled feelings of the businessman or museum curator, but do little to really connect theory and practice in a socially as well as clinically meaningful fashion.

It was inevitable once empiricism in sociology made it canon law to view sociology as an academic commodity rather than an intellectual pursuit, that someone would come along and put the commodity in a fancy package and hang a for sale sign on it. With all the ingenuity of a lop flight sales executive, Hans Zetterberg has written a book, free of jargon, free of complications, but above all, free of anything even remotely embarrassing to the potential buyer of the specialized services of the sociologist. Here we inhabit the happy world of consultants and clients, where tough-minded professors give advice to tender-hearted curators. Why, there are untold numbers of human resources the narrow therapist never dreamed of. Leave the neurotics to the psychoanalyst; Zetterberg's sociologist will claim the even bigger market of the normals. The game goes to the quick. Who, after all, but an empiricist in sociology would have the nerve to display the wares of nothingness and think it only fair to get something in return.

This is not to say that Zetterberg's sociology for sale has not met with stiff opposition. The men in the academy are not unaware that it is one thing to busy oneself with patchy little research projects that don't really harm anyone (they don't really help anyone either of course), but quite another thing for an enthusiast to get so caught up in the commodity values of empiricism as to go out into the world and tell people he's got a salable package. What makes this enthusiasm awkward and dangerous is that people will pay for "right" recommendations, but they will howl like mad at "wrong" or unsuccessful recommendations. The physician who makes a wrong diagnosis has the advantage of polishing off the patient. The sociologist who makes a wrong recommendation has only a lifelong, embittered opponent. Perhaps this is why Zetterberg's researches have not had the kind of enthusiastic support from like-minded colleagues that he might expect as his due.

Zetterberg points out that the sociologist in relation to a businessman may function as an "anxiety-reducing ritual." He then offers as an analogous situation the wedding ceremony, "The minister asks if the man wants this woman for better or worse. The man's answer to this anxiety-provoking question has always been decided. However, it is not a useless ritual. After the ritual the man and the woman do the same things they did before, but they feel more comfortable about it." There is no use embarrassing our Victorian sociologist about what the sly "it" is. However, it must be pointed out that the analogy is utterly fallacious. The "anxiety-ridden" couple may end up in a divorce suit, but they hardly blame the minister for the shortcomings of their marriage! And of course, the very purpose of hiring a sociologist to sanctify a decision is the very reverse. For as Zetterberg himself notes on the next page, "the research or consultation ritual establishes a scapegoat should the decision prove to be disastrous." Too many such disastrous decisions, and the sociologist-turned-cynical-money-grubber-turned-guilt-alleviator may arrive at the beginning of the end of Establishment sociology. Little wonder that Mr. Zetterberg's own professional family in The Bureau of Applied Social Research at Columbia University "did not want to house consultations based on these premises." Businessmen are not stupid feudal emperors. If they do not see the fine garments, they will loudly shout that the sociological kings go naked. And this just won't do. The "market" and the "consultation room" are not fit places for naked kings. The files of The Bureau must remain locked—the enthusiasm of enthusiasts notwithstanding!

From *Studies on the Left* vol. 3, no. 3 (1963), pp. 109–15.

Part V

The Ethical Foundations of Political Life

74

Open Societies and
Free Minds*

Arendt, Hannah

The Life of the Mind represents a culminating philosophic effort, alas not quite complete, but something less than one-third to be guessed at. Even stating the obvious is bound to create some misunderstanding, since Arendt disclaims being a philosopher or "professional thinker." Indeed, publication of a large part of the first volume on *Thinking* in *The New Yorker* magazine, not to mention that the two volumes were issued by a widely respected but thoroughly commercial publisher, might lend some weight to such a disclaimer. But in fact, the work is thoroughly philosophical in the German classical tradition of Kant, Hegel, Nietzsche, and Heidegger. It is a measure of Hannah Arendt's justifiable fame as the author of such works as *The Origins of Totalitarianism, The Human Condition, On Revolution, Eichmann in Jerusalem,* among others, that a work so demanding, so requiring intimacy with major figures of philosophical history, would receive wide hearing. Under the circumstances, one might well have anticipated commercial drivel from editor (Mary McCarthy) or publisher (William Jovanovich). It is to their lasting credit that no such posthumous exploitation is attempted. McCarthy's postface is entirely professional and pellucid. Everyone connected with this project exhibited at least one central element of good judgment ("judging" was to have constituted the final volume of this trilogy). That element is good taste.

The Life of the Mind picks up on themes first expressed two decades earlier in *The Human Condition.* The first two parts of the new work, offered as the Gifford Lectures for 1973 and 1974 respectively, seem to express polar opposites. The earlier work emphasized the active life—comprised of what we

* Hannah Arendt. *The Life of the Mind. Volume One: Thinking,* edited with a Postface by Mary McCarthy (New York: Harcourt Brace Jovanovich, 1978), pp. 258.

Hannah Arendt, *The Life of the Mind, Volume Two: Willing,* edited with a Postface by Mary McCarthy (New York: Harcourt Brace Jovanovich, 1978), pp. 277.

Hannah Arendt, *On Revolution,* (New York: Viking Press, 1963), pp. 343.

are doing: labor, work, action. The new work involves the contemplative life: thinking, willing and judging. But this triad is only superficially antithetical to the earlier one. labor, work, and action are interconnected as biosocial activities, whereas thinking, willing, and judging occupy far more autonomous realms in the contemplative life. The triads remain, the polarities remain. But the special nature of philosophical activities is in asking unanswerable questions and hence establishing human beings as question-asking beings. In this way Arendt sought to get beyond the atomism that afflicts the social sciences in particular—the search for the magical key word: *society* for sociology, *culture* for anthropology, *polity* for political science, *money* for economics, and *personality* for psychology. The magic key is less in the artifact, as stated in *The Human Condition*, than in the demystification of all artifacts, as in *The Life of the Mind*.

The temptation to review this work as if it is flawed by virtue of being incomplete is not simple to resist. But there are so many broad hints, fragments from lectures, and outright statements on judgment, that the work can be examined as a complete effort. The relationships between thinking, willing, and judging are set forth early in the first volume. And like a profoundly risky move in chess, the disallowance of any intertranslatability between the three categories drastically weakens the work. For instead of searching out areas of analytic linkages (i.e., ways in which the act of thinking involves willing and judging), instead of considering each of these as aspects of a naturalistic theory of mind—perhaps along the lines of H.G. Mead or Y.H. Krikorian—we are required to see each aspect as a windowless monad. It is curious that this should be so, since Arendt was so familiar with Aristotle and the remarkable way a sense of emergence created linkages—biological issues into social, social into political, and political into ethical. Indeed, these basic categories have survived 2000 years, and if the contents of modern science are no longer Aristotelian, the twentieth century impulse toward the unity of science remains inspired by the Greeks. This major dilemma notwithstanding, Arendt's work is such a thorough examination into basic concepts that it transcends its own checkmate. She can at least claim a draw between the idealistic and naturalistic traditions that propel her work.

These volumes consecrate Hannah Arendt's life's work, even if they do not effect a synthesis of epistemology and ontology. For the essential statement in *Thinking*, made many times over as variation on the theme of mind, is the quintessential point about twentieth century existence: that it is not the struggle between theory and action that is central but the struggle between theory and theory. Thinking is the hallmark of a free person living in a free society. To reduce action to behavior and then interpret behavior as if it were thought, is for Arendt the shared fallacy of dialectical materialism and behavioral psychology. Whether in the language of revolutionary act or operant conditioning, the pure activist fails to understand that reducing thinking to doing is the end of the process of thought and the beginning of thought control or behavior modification.

In place of the casual slogan about theory and its issuance into practice, Arendt early on poses the question: "What are we 'doing' when we do nothing but think?" For the totalitarian temptation is to assume that those not engaged in the collective will, in the process of bringing about progress, are doing nothing. This is the metaphysical equivalent of the theological fear that idle hands make for idle minds. The reduction of metaphysics to a form of poetry by the positivist tradition is in fact a call for the repudiation of speculation as a human activity in itself. Arendt shrewdly notes that the crisis in philosophy, ontology, theology, social theory, etc., comes into being as a result of pronouncements by the intelligentsia itself. But what makes such premature deaths of disciplines so risky is that what begins as a disputation among intellectual elites, concludes with popular disbelief in the worthiness of thinking as such:

> These modern "deaths"—of God, metaphysics, philosophy, and, by implication, positivism-have become events of considerable historical consequence, since, with the beginning of our century, they have ceased to be the exclusive concern of an intellectual elite and instead are not so much the concern as the common unexamined assumption of nearly everybody. With this political aspect of the matter we are not concerned here. In our context, it may even be better to leave the issue, which actually is one of political authority, outside our considerations, and to insist, rather, on the simple fact that, however seriously our ways of thinking may be involved in this crisis, our *ability* to think is not at stake; we are what man has always been-thinking beings. . . men have an inclination, perhaps a need, to think beyond the limitations of knowledge, to do more with this ability than use it as an instrument for knowing and doing.

Bridling the will is no small matter. Its subjugation to reason is more than an indication that in the hierarchy of thinking, willing, and judging, willing comes in a distant third. That this portion of *The Life of the Mind* was completed before only fragments of the portion on judging were done, should not suggest that the will somehow mediates the claims of thought and taste. Arendt is the political philosopher par excellence; and unlike Kant, her sense of philosophic categories was filtered through twentieth-century awareness of totalitarianisms. She sees will as a constant clash with thinking. In her words, "the will always wills to *do* something and thus implicitly holds in contempt sheer thinking" (II:37). But more, this impulse to will translates itself into the constant search for the *novus ordo seclorum.* The will remains the final resting place of "men of action." Such activists demand forever new foundations, constantly destroying what was and is, in the name of the new and the yet to be.

Perhaps in this Arendt's strong conservatism emerges, certainly her critique of the men of action would so vouchsafe:

> There is something puzzling in the fact that men of action, whose sole intent and purpose was to change the whole structure of the future world and create a *novus ordo seclorum*, should have to go to that distant past of antiquity, for they did not deliberately [reverse] the time-axis and [bid] the young "walk back into the pure radiance of the past" . . . . They looked for a paradigm for a new form of government in their own "enlightened" age and were hardly aware of the fact that they were looking backward. More puzzling, I think, than their actual ransacking of the archives of antiquity is that they did not rebel against antiquity when they discovered that the final and certainly profoundly Roman answer of "ancient prudence" was that salvation always comes from the past, that the ancestors were *majors*, the "greater ones" by definition.

But I suspect that more than conservatism is at stake. For theorists of the act, of freedom, always had a way of terminating their freedom with their own visions of society. Since for Arendt the capacity of beginning is rooted in the human capacity for renewal, it requires no end point. Terminus is not freedom but death. In this sense, freedom as system is a doomsday called utopia. That is why judgment becomes so important for her. For judgment makes transcendence of will possible without a denial of reason. The aesthetic sense is not an accoutrement but a necessary faculty that tells people that what is perfect to one person or one ruler may be imperfect to another person or ruler and downright ugly to yet a third person and a third ruler. She locates the source of democratic survival in the pluralism of judgment.

What has consistently infuriated neo-Platonists and Marxists alike about the Kantian view of aesthetic judgment is its distinction between beauty or taste on one hand and applicability and moral purpose on the other. Arendt states the Kantian argument quite bluntly:

> If you say, What a beautiful rose! you don't arrive at this judgment by first saying, all roses are beautiful, this flower is a rose, hence it is beautiful. The other kind, dealt with in *the second part*, is the impossibility to derive any particular product of nature from general causes. . . . Mechanical in Kant's terminology means natural causes; its opposite is "technical" by which he means artificial.

Judgment thus is concerned with that "enlargement of mind" that derives from evaluating "something fabricated with a purpose." But far from supporting an elitist vision of aesthetics or culture, Arendt draws precisely the opposite, namely a populist, conclusion. Taste is a community sense (*gemeinschaftlicher Sinn*), and hence while not all people are geniuses, all people are capable of rendering judgment. What is so terribly important about this populist vision of judgment as both autonomous from thinking and willing, is that it provides the solution to the problem of democracy and also that basis of unity amongst the *polis*.

But Arendt still leaves us with a problem: the contradiction between the idea of progress as the law of the human species and the idea of human dignity as an inalienable aspect of individual human beings. This presumably would have formed the nexus of the third volume on Judgment, *The Life of the Mind*. For those to whom limitations on knowledge is a fact to be overcome rather than celebrated, the problem bequeathed by Kant and now by Arendt is a challenge of no small magnitude or light consequence.

Arendt suffered a dialectical passion, or at least a commitment to the reality of reification: the warfare between thought and common sense, the Greek question and the Roman answer, the gap between the past and the future, thinking and doing, the active life and the contemplative life, the impotence of the will versus the omnipotence of the will. This gives her writings a tremendous tension, a dramaturgical sensibility that has virtually disappeared in the empirical tradition. Perhaps that is why she can so readily and categorically dismiss Hume's dictum on reason being the slave of the passions as "simple minded," while Locke does only a trifle better as a believer in "the old tacit assumption of an identity of soul and mind." Indeed, the British empiricists fare less well at Arendt's hands than by her master, Kant.

It is to Kant that the work is really consecrated. For her divisions of thinking, willing, and judging derive in great measure from Kant's great works: *Critique of Practical Reason, Foundations of the Metaphysics of Morals*, and *Critique of Judgment*. From the transcendental dialectic of the *Critique of Pure Reason* she drew the cardinal lesson: the insolubility of the nature of providence, freedom, and immortality by speculative thought. But what Arendt does, what is so unusual about her work, is to infuse Kant's deadly logical prose with the excitement of Hegel's dialectical scaffold. Whether by intent or accident—and to know Hannah Arendt and her work, is to know that scarcely a word, much less a concept, happens randomly—Kant is given the ultimate victory in the classical philosophic struggle. This is no cheap victory, but a victory over titans like Plato and Hegel. For Arendt, it is Kant who gives us conscience as a realm of freedom unto itself; it is Kant who understands that judgment is something that can be practiced but not taught, and it is Kant who sat astride the will, uniquely understanding it as neither freedom of choice nor sheer spontaneity of activity. Kant's will becomes Arendt's will, "delegated by reason to be its executive organ in all matters of conduct." Karl Popper's proponents of the closed society (Plato and Hegel) now meet their match in Arendt's proponent of the open society (Kant).

Arendt points to a great divide in modern scientific quests: on the one hand is the positivist quest for truth, and on the other is the rationalist quest for meaning. For her, it is a basic fallacy to confound the two, a fallacy to which even such figures like Heidegger fall prey. The distinction between the urgent need to think and the desire to know, is an operational way of distinguishing thinking from doing. And here, although the Greeks are called upon to bear witness to this distinction, I daresay it is Arendt's Jewishness that provides the missing link. For it is the historical role of the Jews to search and not find redemption and the redeemer, in contrast to the truth announced by Christianity of redemption through the son of God, that really distinguishes Arendt's claims for thinking as the ultimate act.

Here one must confess to a strange myopia in Arendt, an all-too-conventional vision of the history of philosophy as a movement from the Greeks to the Romans to the Christians to the Medieval Schoolmen, and finally to the Germans. But such a mechanical rendition of the history of philosophy fails to explain why Heidegger the existentialist falls prey to the same error as Carnap the positivist. Why does the metaphysical impulse to certainly take precedence over epistemological distinctions? Is not the answer at least in part located in a shared scientific vision of the age in which the quest for meaning is seen as less urgent than the delivery of truth, even the imposition of truth on non-believers, infidels, and heathens? Perhaps in the third volume on judgment such matters would have been addressed. I suspect otherwise. Having rejected the philosophic dialogue written by opponents of the open society, she was powerless to cope with the betrayal of that life in its post-Kantian phase. The elementary forms of democratic expression are described as in mortal combat with the evolutionary Nazi and historical Bolshevik forms of antidemocracy. The allies of the demos are left disarmed so to speak, wrecked by intellectuals announcing the death of intellect.

There was a point in time when one would have had to shuffle in embarrassment for reviewing a metaphysical work in a sociological journal. But these are not such times. With figures such as Marx, Mead, and Husserl anchoring major tendencies in current sociology, no apologetics for reading such a masterful treatise is required, nor need it be hidden under sociological pillows. To be sure, those who represent phenomenological, symbolic interactionist, and humanistic varieties of sociology will probably be far more attracted to these pair of volumes than advocates of behavioral, functional, or physicalist sociologies. But to disentangle a potential audience for such an undertaking is aptly evocative of what Professor Arendt understands as the topsy-turvy world of action and theory:

> The Marxian and existentialist notions, which play such a great role in twentieth-century thought and pretend that man is his own producer and maker, rest on these experiences, even though it is clear

that nobody has "made" himself or "produced" his existence; this, I think, is the last of the metaphysical fallacies, corresponding to the modern age's emphasis on willing as a substitute for thinking. . . . And this is of some relevance to a whole set of problems by which modern thought is haunted, especially to the problem of theory and practice and to all attempts to arrive at a halfway plausible theory of ethics. Since Hegel and Marx, these questions have been treated in the perspective of History and on the assumption that there is such a thing as Progress of the human race. Finally we shall be left with the only alternative there is in these matters—we either can say with Hegel: *Die Weltgeschichte ist das Weltgericht*, leaving the ultimate judgment to Success, or we can maintain with Kant the autonomy of the minds of men and their possible independence of things as they are or as they have come into being.

As long as thinking, willing, and judging are viewed as three basic mental activities that "cannot be derived from each other" and that "cannot be reduced to a common denominator," the very edifice Arendt attempts is subject to the same criticism as any other absolutism. In twentieth-century terms, her work consecrates the collapse of acceptable paradigms in social science and philosophy. Hence the trinitarianism of thinking, willing, and judging can do no more than confront each other in field after field, discipline after discipline. But if Arendt did not effect the grand synthesis (nor does she claim at any point to be after such a holy grail), she sheds a great light on what is ailing our social and behavior disciplines. We at least know what the sources of division are with a precision and a clarity that makes possible new creativity. And that is ultimately what the life of the free mind is all about.

It is ironic that the author of *Eichmann in Jerusalem* should also be a supreme devotee of German high culture. For there can be no mistaking that in philosophy, law, and politics, Hannah Arendt was a complete product of the German *Aufklärung*. The century has been rolled back with these volumes: as if Hitler and nazism had not happened, as if German liberal thought were an unbroken chain of continuities. But this is not the case. And Arendt in her towering works has been a prime mover in enabling us to understand the essence of the totalitarian persuasion. But at the last, she remained true to the tradition of German liberalism. The French language, which she loved, counted for little more than a Cartesian footnote; the English constitutional tradition, which surely nourished her faith in compassionate justice over and against impassioned (nonrational) vengeance, counted for little. Russian democratic thought from Herzen to Solzhenitsyn scarcely existed for her. And perhaps most shattering to those who saw her primarily as a Jewish writer, the Hebrew tradition was reduced to several hyphenated footnotes to Christian theology. In the end, in the long pull, this remarkable woman, scholar, critic, exile, teacher turned out to be not an avenging angel remorselessly pursuing her totalitarian quarry but the last loving product of German Enlightenment: the keeper of a flame she herself had helped resurrect from the charnelhouse of postwar Europe. The dialectical process is indeed mysterious and insoluble as Kant insisted. It brought forth, fifty years late in a foreign language by an exile from Nazi repression, the last hurrah of the Weimar Republic.

* * *

When confronted by intuitive brilliance, one is tempted to review the personality rather than the performance. *On Resolution* is a continuation of discussions first broached in *The Human Condition* and in *The Origins of Totalitarianism.* Since this work is something less than social science and something more than mere speculation, perhaps a prosaic ordering of Miss Arendt's materials is not only forgivable but necessary. Overlooking her contempt for the "modern debunking 'sciences' psychology and sociology," I shall state her position in proposition form and offer possible lines of disagreement and further inquiry.

War and revolution have violence as their common denominator. Conflict derives from fratricidal instincts, and political organization has its roots in crime. Crucial to revolution in the modern age is the concurrence of the idea of freedom and the experience of new social beginnings, of apocalypse.

Revolution gains a new significance as war, its partner in violence, becomes an implausible way to effect social change. Total annihilation has transformed the character of the military from protector of *civitas*, into a futile avenger. Even prior to the nuclear age, wars had become politically, though not yet physically, a matter of national survival because of the widespread fear that the vanquished power will suffer the subjugation of its political organization. Nontechnological factors in warfare have been eliminated so that the results of war may be calculated in advance with perfect precision. Foreknowledge of victory and defeat may well end a war that need never explode into reality. If we are to survive, this cannot become a century of warfare, but it most certainly will become a century of total revolutions. The universal goal of war is revolution. But even without the possibility of limited agreements, revolution will come to define the character of the modern uses of violence and the present impulse toward freedom and liberty.

Revolution in the modern age has been concerned with two distinct drives: liberation (absence of restraint and increase in social mobility) and freedom (political level of life). While liberation is consonant with various forms of government, freedom is possible only through a republican form of government, which explains why the American, French, and Russian revolutions all adopted this form of rule.

The two fundamental models of revolution are the American and French revolutions—though only the French Revolution became the basic model for Marxism. The American Revolution adhered to the original purpose of revolution—realizing freedom—while the French Revolution abdicated freedom in the name of historical necessity. The American Revolution was at one and the same time profoundly political and antihistorical and no less, antipolitical and quite historical.

The French revolutionary model, the model adopted by Marxism and which penetrated the ideological and organizational aspects of the Russian Revolution, was concerned with the social question—with problems of exploitation, mass alienation, and poverty. It was inspired by the idea of compassion but ended in a mindless passion. The American revolutionary model was concerned with the political question, with problems of politics and the predicaments that flowed from an elitist theory of mass human nature. Its revolutionary passion was mediated by norms and hence ended in compassion, or at least a sense of the worth of the process whatever the success of the policy.

The weaknesses of the classic French model are revealed in the abortive aspects of the major revolutions of the modern era—the Paris Commune, the Russian Revolution, and the Hungarian uprising. In each ease there was the rise of two distinctive forces: the party, acting in the name of the people, and the voluntary associations (workers' councils, soviets, communes,) or the people as a collective. In the betrayal of the revolution, the force of power over the people came through the consecration of political parties, whereas the council system, because it failed to realize itself as a new form of government (as in the American Revolution) tended to be shortlived. It is this fact that accounts for the perfidy of modern revolutionary movements—the breakdown of voluntary association and its replacement by a swollen bureaucracy.

These propositions indicate Arendt's morphology of revolution. Although it is not possible to argue this book's thesis in terms of right and wrong, a number of questions arise. The key problem is the relative absence of evidence. How does one evaluate such speculations? The abundant confidence with which *On Revolution* is written is far from persuasive. The unsystematic prose style, which keeps the reader hopping about looking for the continuing threads, does not enhance a ready acceptance of her perspectives, even as one is drawn to her sentiments.

Arendt reveals little knowledge of modern warfare, that is, little about the ambiguities of modern conflict—counterinsurgency, paramilitary struggle, police action, guerrilla action—that would show that war is becoming obsolete. It might be correct to note that thermonuclear warfare would make total international conflict obsolete—since it is like a gun with two barrels pointing in opposite directions. But the absence of any distinction between war and annihilation throws all of the weight of her discussion on revolution into the questionable assumption that war is obsolete by reason of self-interest. The absence of knowledge about problems of contemporary warfare is excusable—war and peace studies are dismal—but conceit is no reply. And when the author states that "the only discussion of the war question I know which dares to face the horrors of nuclear weapons and the threat of totalitarianism, and is therefore entirely free of mental reservation, is Karl Jaspers' *The Future of Mankind,*" she is only revealing her ignorance of a widespread and valuable empirical literature that has just this relationship as its central concern. Nor is the definition of revolution particularly enlightening. To see revolution as having everywhere a violent quality is to fail to distinguish between change in social structure and strategies sometimes used in such changes. Even if we generously assume that Arendt is speaking exclusively in terms of political revolution, violence is not a necessary or sufficient component.

Contradictory statements blemish her presentation: "The part of the professional revolutionists usually consists not in making a revolution but is rising to power after it has broken out, and their great advantage in this power struggle lies less in their theories and mental or organizational preparation than in the simple fact that their names are the only ones which are publicly known." But elsewhere she says that "without Lenin's slogan 'All power to the Soviets' there would never have been an October Revolution in Russia." Which cliche should be believed? Miss Arendt's repeated assertion that the consequence of revolution is always less freedom and liberty than previously existed is belied by an appreciation of the positive outcome of the American Revolution. Indeed, it is precisely her dislike for revolutionary process that causes her to search out special features in the American Revolution not found in Europe.

Arendt belongs in the unusual category of a revolutionary conservative. For although she is bent on demonstrating the negative aspects of Thermidor and Robespierre and the positive aspects of the *Federalist* papers and the founders of the American Republic, she nevertheless is seeking at the deepest level for a way to make revolutionary movements responsible to revolutionary men. Thus it is that councils of workers, soviets, and so forth are held to be useful models of voluntary control. The revolutionists constitute a "new aristocracy" that would properly spell the end of general suffrage. As Arendt puts it: "only those who as voluntary members of an 'elementary republic' have demonstrated that they care for more than their private happiness and are concerned about the state of the world would have the right to be heard in the conduct of the business of the republic." The revolutionary elite would be guardian of the nation. How this differs from the betrayal of revolutions by political parties and how this guardianship could avoid becoming a political party, is not discussed.

Arendt respects the "spirit of revolution" but scores its failures to find an "appropriate institution." She has located such an institution in the voluntary councils that accompany revolutions, but what is amazing is her unwillingness to support her theory with evidence: for example, there is no discussion of the actual strengths or shortcomings of the Yugoslav worker councils or of the Israeli *Kibbutzim.* This is a result of her reticence to address the political revolution of freedom in relation to the economic revolution of abundance. Her comments in this direction reveal an awareness of the potential antagonism between economic development and political freedom, but not a consistent understanding of how and where they intersect.

The big unanswered question of revolution is precisely the mix between economic rationalization and political reason. Polarization of these may make a stimulating treatise, but it cannot define the experimental character of most contemporary revolutions. For Arendt, French and American revolutions were creative opposites. For peoples of revolutionary lands, both stand as selective options in searching for the new. If massive revolution defines the century, it might be wiser to reach for new combinations of policy and publics rather than to look with nostalgia upon the Greek city-states and their prudent elitism, for solutions to modern problems of caste and class. This question the critic must pose for Hannah Arendt, since she has presented many worthwhile issues for this reviewer to contemplate.

From *Contemporary Sociology*, vol. 8, no. 1 (1979), pp. 15–19; and from *The American Journal of Sociology*, vol. 69, no. 4 (1964), pp. 419–21.

75

Tribune of the Intelligentsia*

Aron, Raymond

Raymond Aron. Certainly, no other social scientist has been so universally honored in his lifetime. At the time of death in October 1983, he had received as many emoluments and awards as he had book titles to his credit—no easy feat even in this age of easy academic celebration. Yet, even for those who admired him, questions remain as to the lasting nature of his intellectual achievement and whether it is equal to his political acumen or moral probity.

History, Truth, Liberty is the second collection of Raymond Aron's essays to appear recently. The first, *Politics & History*, was published several years earlier. A third collection of essays, promised for 1988, is to be called *Sociologists, Power and Modernity.* Doubtless, still others will follow, given the indefatigable spirit of his heirs and assigns. Indeed, a solid broad cross-section of his journalistic or editorial writings would help give us a clearer picture of his day-to-day activities.

The reason for this posthumous outpouring, I would argue, apart from his towering importance as a scholar, is Aron's qualities as an essayist. For in truth, Aron is as much a child of Montaigne in stylistic terms as of Tocqueville in substantive terms. Despite his exhortations to the strictly rational, Aron wrote the classically brief essay that contains a moral lesson more than an empirical datum. In this respect, he is markedly distant from the contemporary socio-logical article. Each of the twelve essays in this volume, for example, contain more or less well-defined examples of pitfalls to be avoided if not always paths to be followed.

So much was Aron the essayist, even the journalist in the best sense of that word, that a large-scale effort, such as *Peace and War: A Theory of International Relations*, was less than successful. Details drawn from the current events of the late 1950s and early 1960s kept getting in the way of Aron's

---

* Franciszek Draus (editor), *History, Truth, Liberty: Selected Writings of Raymond Aron* (Chicago and London: The University of Chicago Press, 1985), pp. 384.

Raymond Aron, *The Industrial Society: Three Essays on Ideology and Development* (New York: Frederick A. Praeger, 1967), pp. 183.

Clausewitz-like effort at synthesis. In part at least, this is due to an innate liberalism in Aron that was far deeper than any imputed conservatism. In any context other than France, this would have readily been recognized. But in an ideological environment often defined by the polarities of an abstracted Marxism and a crude if concrete Gaullism, Aron's essentially prudent and mediating efforts seemed an alien and intrusive force in French politics. But liberalism entered into the sinews of Aron's analysis, as when he notes in his essay "On the Morality of Prudence" that "we have tried to make the analysis of international relations independent of moral judgments and metaphysical concepts"—in other words, apart from the very linkage that is the shank of all conservative ideology.

It is important to have these selections from Aron's work if for no other reason than to rescue him from the iconographic tradition to which he is increasingly subject. Essays and introductions on Aron's thought tell us a great deal about his dedication to French national interests, the Judaic tradition, his indomitable will in the face of personal misfortune, public obloquy, his pessimiste jovial or his optimiste triste. But in this display of necrophilia, it is all too easy to lose sight of the actual themes to which Aron repeatedly returned, the strengths that made him such a powerful moral voice and, alas, the weaknesses that made him more widely renowned as commentator than as synthesizer.

The core of *History, Truth, Liberty* is less concept-oriented than people-saturated. Individual greats uniquely embody important concepts. Thus, in the paper on Tocqueville and Marx we are given the brilliant insight that a "purely political revolution, one that does not modify the social infrastructure, does not allow man to realize himself because it confuses the genuine man with the worker locked into his particularity and because man is in conformity with his essence." Aron comes down on the side of democratic liberalism; the trinitarianism of bourgeois citizenship, technological efficiency, and the right of every individual to personal choice. The struggle between liberal democracy and socialist construction is seen as a historical dialogue between Tocqueville and Marx. But, of course, this is a contemporary French reading of the past. In England, the same struggle was locked in the bosom of John Stuart Mill, who embodied both liberal and socialist principles. In Russia, different varieties and strains of socialist politics embodied this struggle over the goals of democracy, with well-known disastrous consequences. In the United States liberal and conservative struggles were conducted as if socialism were an exotic European import. This is not to say that Aron was wrong in his judgments. It is to say that his formulations were all too often limited as well as informed by a continental elitism.

In the analysis of the West and the East, the chapters of this book that take up the penultimate and largest segment demonstrate well the strengths and weaknesses of Aron's continentalism. For in his understanding of the ideological roots of the problem of conflict, the Soviet empire's insistence on historical triumphalism and hence liquidation of the democratic West, the sources of tactics and strategies must be worked through. For as long as this commitment to the inevitable destruction of the West remains the basic agenda as well as telos of Marxism Leninism, then all notions of accommodation must be tempered by a dual realism: the dangers of nuclear conflict (which require appropriate technical responses) and the threats to Western survival (which require appropriate ideological responses). But it remains problematic that "the day the Soviets have the same right to read, write criticize and travel as Western nationals, the competition will have become truly peaceful." Even given such rights, and the movement is currently in such a direction, the likelihood of peace breaking out is slender. For different interests often preempt similar ideologies. And on this does Aron's attempt at synthesis come to a screeching halt.

But this is to draw attention to the weakest aspect of Aron's legacy. His enormous strength is as a political moralist par excellence. It is simple exhilarating to read Aron on the distinction between a philosophy of history and a theology of history in "Three Forms of Historical Intelligibility"; the role of the conduct of warfare in and of itself apart from the origins of a conflict or the diplomacy of a peace treaty in producing the most far-reaching social consequences as in "The Intelligibility of History"; and the plurality of meanings and motives in real history in contrast to the monism of meaning in fanaticism disguised as the inevitable future, as in the great essay on "On False Historical consciousness." If one may be forgiven an illiberal mandate on a liberal spirit: no student should be permitted to enter the field of historical studies without reading and knowing Aron's probing essays on history and its enemies, the sociological messianists.

Even the essays on presumably sociological themes gathered in the fourth and sixth segments are more an extension of Aron's historical concerns than with the actual conduct of empirical research. Thus, in "Science and Consciousness of Society," Aron makes clear the distinction between fairness and objectivity, criticism and dogmatism, individual heroism and collective suicide. And throughout, the examples of Soviet history and Marxist historiography are the foils upon which truth is lanced. Likewise, in the chapter "Social Class, Political Class, Ruling Class," Aron instructs us with scalpel-like precision, and quite properly on the ambiguity of categories and the pluralities of meanings in real world contexts. And in the final segment, "Max Weber and Modern Social Science," we are instructed in the relativity of benefits and injuries, the richness of total history in contrast to the poverty of national chauvinism, the need for rationality in a universe dominated by irrational impulses. It is to Aron's credit that he sees the weaknesses in Weber's relativism, without claiming to have answered such questions as are raised in the Weberian corpus, without sitting on the "shoulders of a giant" as would a gnat in the hair of another man. Aron's modesty was as genuine as his achievement: to see the problem, to state the problem, and to do so even if no answers were presently forthcoming. For it is the essence of rationality, of his rationality at least, to see the struggles of our time as a problem that needs the best efforts of rational people—even if that rationality should come up short in its struggle with the beasts who would be angels.

In reviewing this selection of Aron's essays (indeed other essays as well), one is repeatedly confronted with the European conscience wrestling with problems of democratic liberalism. But it seems to me that Aron did so with an arsenal of ideas that was only half-full. Tocqueville and Weber are set upon to do battle with Marx and Lenin. But in some strange way, it was the Anglo-American tradition, of which Aron was acutely aware (but more on practical than on theoretical terms), that gave the answer to totalitarian regimes and systems. Whether or not Jefferson or Mill, Lincoln or Churchill, or more recent examples of the Anglo-American or constitutional tradition, confronted the evils of Soviet totalitarianism as ideology, they did expose those evils in economical and political practice. In short, Aron's West had two components: the continental and the constitutional, if you will. The former he knew best, the latter applied his teachings best. On this anomaly does Aron's work come to rest. Aron was a paragon of virtue and a beacon of lights—for those Cartesian anti-theorists so highly prized and praised by Tocqueville in *Democracy in America* and an irritant and mystery for those European theorists who could not accept the realities of democracy without a metaphysical shroud. Aron's great strength, and unique contribution, was to live comfortably in a world striving for democracy while lacking adequate theories, rather than to opt for pure theories that yield so little in the way of practical liberties. In this, Aron was the true child of the French Enlightenment and the perfect critic of a German romanticism that promised so much and yielded the free spirit so little.

The three essays comprising *The Industrial Society* are linked more by M. Aron's remarkable person than by any systematic presentation of ideas. Thus, however one may wish to resist the temptation to indulge in the sociology of political knowledge, to examine such a volume otherwise is simply not to take seriously perhaps the most important singular factor in the book as such: Aron's aesthetic vision. The three papers are also connected by a systematic attack on the Left. The first paper is a critique of the thesis that unites the underdevelopment phenomenon with the fully developed nations. The second paper is a strong assault on evolutionary theory, or at least those forms of evolutionary theory which feed the flames of historicism. The third paper is an assault on the convergence hypothesis, which maintains that capitalism and socialism are beginning to approximate one another.

However limited much of the writing is and although Aron remains a prisoner of the ideological parameters he so detests, important coordinates are raised. While Aron's book is not the first effort to attack the idea that socialism is necessary to initiate the developmental process in the Third World, it is one of the few attempting to relate problems of development to those of international peace and order.

In his first paper, Aron shows how developmental theory raises a series of causal issues that continue to plague the field. He centers on what is perhaps the major problem, whether underdevelopment is caused by or necessarily responsive to the fully developed and advanced nations. While he takes issue with those who would deny that every nation, like every man, is responsible for the consequences of his own behavior, he does not really show how national behavior is autonomous. For example, he fails to explain why nations that were not impoverished in previous epochs, nonetheless remain backward. Nor does he explain how the widespread monopoly of research and development gives advanced nations leverage over the underdeveloped nations despite intensive efforts on their part. And while Aron realizes that the single crop economy is a weak point in underdeveloped economics, he does not indicate why these single crop economics seem to persist. As in so many of his works, there is emphasis on ideology at the expense of economies rather than as a consequence of economies. Too often Aron tends to see the problem of underdeveloped areas in terms of administrative strategy rather than as a matter of social structure.

The second study in the volume, ostensibly a response to Morris Ginsberg's tenets that the evolutionary or rationalistic interpretation of development has lost ground, permits Aron a statement of his own faith and reason. He makes some shrewd observations about what he terms the "schedule of development." He notes that whether one starts from a Marxian or Rostovian premise, development seems to imply a range of choices and decisions. The volitional character of development thus means that the quality of existence is differential no less than the goals sought.

Aron's position is that rational choice should not be equated with a plan for social life to proceed through inexorable stages of history or development, but rather as a chance to live in the modern world without having to confront "development" and force it upon the political processes. Unfortunately, Aron, while describing the schedule of development, does not take note of when and how this developmental process is to be realized. Since developmental theory no longer accepts any historical explanation, it remains more rooted than ever in teleology. In hunting for the future by arguing with the past, Aron's volume must be seen as a justification for the continuation of a middle class growth pattern. While the basis of a reliable schedule of growth remains the touchstone of developmental strategy, Aron would prefer to think that the cultural artifacts produced in the West that remain the essential model to be employed by the underdeveloped world. However, Aron does draw our attention to the problem of determining just what can be measured in the developmental process. As an extreme rationalist, he is unwilling to accept that forces outside human volition determine the outcomes of the developmental process. Too often he allows his own detestation of determinism to drift off into dramaturgy. Just as God seems to lurk behind the rationalist philosopher of the eighteenth century, so too Culture seems to lurk behind the idealist social thought of Aron.

As readers of Aron well appreciate, if his critical acumen can at times rise to oracular brilliance, his constructive skills remain pedestrian and at times even absurd. In his criticism of Anglo-American theorists such as Aiken, Lichtheim, and Rostow, Aron exhibits both of these elements. When he criticizes these men, we have some sterling writing; but when constructive alternatives should be posited, he gives us nothing. The conclusion to the book is a series of such dreary banalities as: "the breakdown of ideological syntheses does not lead to insipid pragmatism or lessen the value of intellectual controversy. On the contrary, it encourages a recurrence of rational discussion of problems which, in any case, must be solved pragmatically." Then, in a rather astonishing denial of the premises upon which his book is built, he notes that, "We are more fortunate than previous generations in that we are not forced to make a choice between conservatism and fanaticism." Presumably what will save us is that "we know that modern methods, scientific and technological progress, and the rational organization of labor enable us to achieve the objectives to which liberals and socialists of previous centuries aspired." And finally, as if his palliatives were insufficient, we are given a set of prognostications that have the predictive force of Chinese fortune cookies. "History from now to the end of the century will be dominated by two facts: the hydrogen bomb and the population explosion." And on the very last page we are told that "on a political level, human liberties will never be guaranteed by prosperity. The single party system and the indoctrination of the masses are and will remain threats or temptations." All of Aron's longings and musings get wrapped up into a gnarled bundle of twine that he seems too impatient to bother unraveling.

The book is more a study of developmentalists or at least some developmentalists than it is of development. This would not be so bad had Aron acknowledged this to begin with; however his failure to appreciate the limits of the text inclines one to ponder the depth of his analysis. To appreciate how thoroughly out of tune Aron is with recent developmental literature, one has to keep in mind that his notion of Western developmentalists does not extend beyond Walt Rostow and James Burnham, neither of whom can be considered as recent, and Henry Aiken and Herbert Marcuse, neither of whom can be considered developmentalists. The work of modern developmentalists, the books by people such as Adelman, Apter, Pye, Moore, Verba, and on the Soviet side, Liberman and Kurakov, simply don't exist for Aron. The tragedy is that so many conflicts that are real for him no longer exist in the political world. Although Aron's book can be read either for fun or for profit, it is not likely that contemporary American social scientists will turn to it as an example of how to deal with the relationships between modern industrial processes and developmental policies.

From *Partisan Review*, vol. 55, no. 1 (1988); and from *The American Political Science Review.* vol. 62, no. 4 (1968).

76

Privacy, Ethics and Social Science Research*

Barnes, J.A.

J.A. Barnes's *Who Should Know What?* is an entirely literate, engaging essay in the sociology of sociology. Written in the broad tradition of Robert S. Lynd's *Knowledge for What* and C. Wright Mills's *The Sociological Imagination*, the work makes up in fair-minded decency what it lacks in literary bombast. For a senior honors or first-year graduate course in the ethical foundations of social research, one could hardly choose a better text. Such an overview seems to be Barnes's intent, and his book is clearly successful when evaluated on its own terms. This is not to suggest that the volume successfully resolves the major problems which it poses—it most certainly does not—but it does present the proper issues in a fair-minded way. As a consequence, this work is accessible to those with a minimum of philosophical training.

The slim volume has a certain datedness. It reflects the concerns manifested by social science during the Vietnam era and its Watergate aftermath, rather than those of the current period in which the West is faced by a series of challenges from a Soviet-dominated East and an OPEC-dominated South. Indeed, this very Change in circumstances illustrates one of Barnes's major themes: the difficulty in presuming an axiomatic equation between any social or economic group and the nature of research itself. While he is clearly empathic to the many peoples and situations studied by social science and less than pleased with the linkages between researchers and the powerful, he is supple and imaginative enough to appreciate the degree to which changing circumstances alter images of commitment no less than paradigms.

The book is divided into three parts, nine chapters in all. In an opening chapter, Barnes describes his task as a practical attempt to resolve ethical issues in social inquiry by taking into account the distribution of power among scientists, citizens, sponsors, and gatekeepers. There follow three

---

* J.A. Barnes, *Who Should Know What? Social Science, Privacy, and Ethics* (Cambridge and New York: Cambridge University Press, 1980), pp. 323.

chapters on the historical development of social inquiry, emphasizing the natural science paradigm within which social research on large issues evolved; the institutionalization of social inquiry, by which the author simply means the role of powerful agencies and bureaucracies in manipulating research to certain predetermined ends; and the challenge to universalism, which refers to the powerful reminders, often from radical and Third World sources, of the partisan and hence particularistic characteristics of any authentic social science in a world divided in systems and outlooks.

The second and most innovative part of Barnes's text concerns the process of inquiry: why people want to make or prevent social inquiries and the ways in which information is made public. Here the emphasis is on the differential interests of researchers and the investigated and on the complementary processes of collecting data and communicating results. Barnes shows how these themes directly link up to new computer data-gathering techniques and lead to a much more accelerated notion of professionalization, in the very process of discussing safeguarding and gatekeeping. The third and final part deals with social science as a specialized activity that has significant relations to and impact on the wider society. Here the emphasis is on such issues as professionalism, commitment, privacy, and the nature of pluralistic, democratic societies as sources of continuing growth no less than serving to focus new issues for the social sciences.

That Barnes is himself caught in the dilemmas he poses should come as no surprise. He appreciates that giving full attention to the rights and interests of all parties to an inquiry may cause empirical research to become innocuous and trivial. He also recognizes the need to provide some protection for subjects of investigation, especially those least able to defend their own interests. While this formulation has the full weight of contemporary rhetoric behind it, it may be time to leave such polarizations to the intellectual dust bins. The need of the moment is more to examine how researchers are themselves managed and manipulated than to observe how they serve as managers and manipulators. Barnes gives too little weight to Third Worlders and First Worlders alike as special interest elements. He tends to underestimate the emotive as well as substantive powers of the "powerless," who in fact may command sizable chunks of political turf in advanced no less than in backward societies.

Curiously, Barnes perceives the threat of social science to be great because he exaggerates its potency. The unstated premise of his text is that measures to ensure safety and privacy are needed because of the impact of social research. It might well be that the actual power of social science is less than he suggests and that the actual consensus about values is also less as a result. The concern with privacy may really reflect an implicit belief in an omniscient social science (which Barnes does not really possess any more than I do). The other side of this coin, which is only barely hinted at near the end of the work, is the issue of publicity: social science is and must remain a public act. Efforts to curb publication of findings and results, in the name of higher truths, special interests, or perceived dangers to the downtrodden, all entail the serious danger of censorship—worse, of self-censorship in the name of principle. For that reason, publicity and the right to know are no less part of the framework of pluralist democracy than privacy and the right to deny access to persons. Democracy is a system in tension. It would be foolhardy to deny that social research is also a system in tension, albeit one of lesser proportions and fewer consequences. Barnes presents these tensions well, but his attempt to resolve them is less successful.

For the most part, Barnes navigates perilous waters with admirable clarity and fairness. He is profoundly aware of manifold critiques of the social sciences, especially of sociology and anthropology, as agents serving the powerful while studying the powerless. He is also acutely sensitive to the intrinsic requirements of scientific analysis as such, but he knows that the desire for universalistic criteria reflects the influence of natural scientific models that do not allow for the confusion and contradiction of interests that social research is required to examine. It might have been wiser for the author to appreciate the fact that social science confronts a wider array of ethical issues than of power issues. For example, there are matters of choice among topics that have wide or narrow applications, and there are decisions to emphasize constructive or critical themes. It might have been worthwhile in a volume of this sort to dedicate at least a few pages to the state of the social sciences in the Socialist bloc nations of Eastern Europe. But one can forgive the selective nature of the work, which is after all intended to be intensive rather than extensive.

Less forgivable is the myopia that leads the author to assert with self-righteous indignation that "pirating is a breach of national or international law on copyright" (p. 155) in the context of a U.S. Department of Commerce English-language translation (not for publication) of a French anthropologist's essay on a Montagnard village in Vietnam. While this appropriation may well have been a breach of etiquette, the unwary reader should know that the term pirating refers to acts engaged in for commercial ends by many Third World countries to avoid obtaining legitimate publishing rights and paying royalties to Western publishers of record. It is a problem of great concern to publishers. The example Barnes provides scarcely fits the term.

The biggest disagreement I have with *Who Should Know What?* occurs in the same context. Barnes criticizes the author of this 1957 report for his failure to disguise identity, for in this way the ends of " American aggression" could have been thwarted and the subjects of his analysis "would have suffered during the war no more than other groups did. Had he known how much use was to be made of ethnographic intelligence by the United States forces, he might have taken the precaution of using disguises." The problem here is simply that Barnes is falling victim to the very concerns he raises elsewhere: blaming social research for problems of social life. While he does not urge that the masses should shoot the messenger, he is urging the messenger to dilute, even falsify, the message—which after all is what disguising names, sources, addresses, and places is ultimately about. The reasons that this older style of disguise has fallen out of scientific favor are that it does not work (clever individuals can always detect such things) and that it lessens the worth of ethnography by making it more difficult to determine its truth or falsity. Finally, it moves social science back to a prejournalistic phase in which the obligations of in-depth reporting are subordinated to some presumably higher commitment to set of political ideologies or social values. To adopt this posture is to answer the question, Who should know what? in terms of political ideology not social reality—the very antithesis of what Barnes seeks. This again points out that no final answer can be given to the questions raised, but a higher level of sensitivity and creativity can be sought. We need to carve out a set of values serviceable to social scientists as an interest and a professional group of no more—but certainly no less—social worth than other interest groups in society.

In the concluding passage of the work, Barnes notes that "we need not only empirical social science but also an awareness of the ethical issues that form an intrinsic part of its praxis." This is fine as far as it goes, but it is more important for us to move ahead with the task of showing how ethical issues are themselves subject to social scientific analysis, that is, to move beyond a sociology of knowledge into a sociology of values. I fear that we have become so enamored of problems in the ethical status of social science that we have tended to dampen any corresponding sense of the empirical correlates of ethical propositions. If social science is to be subject to or guided by, a set of ethical postulates, it behooves us to examine in concrete historical and empirical settings the scientific status of these ethical guidelines. The earlier work of Richard Brandt, Ralph Barton Perry, and Abraham Edel in this connection is especially important. The ghostly fact-value formula not only haunts *Who Should Know What?* but plagues much theorizing about the ethical status of social research. We can view moral propositions in one of two ways: as stationary targets at which we take aim with our bow and arrow or as moving targets subject to a wide variety of interpretations. I daresay that before social research gets too uncomfortably close to moral majoritarian fervor, we should recall the shifting nature of ethical propositions and their differential uses. In this sense, the work of Barnes may help us locate the moral framework, but it may also have a dampening effect on social science once the moral beast is ensconced.

From *American Journal of Sociology*, vol. 87, no. 4 (1981), pp. 1006–1009.

77

From Ideological Ends to Moral Beginnings*

Bell, Daniel

Montaigne long ago established the criteria for style and substance in the essay form. It must be well written, precise, with a focused theme and moral purpose directed to the question: *Que sais-je?* These essays by Daniel Bell, written from 1960 to 1980, live up to the highest standards of the essay. Bell brings to his task not only the twenty years of sociology herein covered but a previous twenty years of journalism that obviously contribute to the pungent, targeted nature of his enterprise. His deeply reflective preface itself is well worth the price of the book. I initially thought of excerpting some choice passages, only to decide that there are too many eloquent and piquant ones to choose only a few. Anyhow, Bell is entitled to state for himself how these seventeen essays came to be written and included in this volume.

This book represents not simply the work of a highly civilized, urbane *freischwebende Intelligenz* in the best sense of that much-abused phrase but the sifted excellence of a sociologist in mid-passage. We should all read these papers not only to be in the presence of a vital intellectual force but also to evaluate what that force stands for in specifically professional terms. I am not certain whether Bell claims too much or too little for his sociology, for its significance is less the relationship between goods and information than between the good and the knowable. This formulation may sound a trifle soft methodologically, but it has the merit of drawing attention to Bell's special skill at infusing social life with deeply philosophical meaning.

We enter Bell's world only when we make a commitment to close encounters of a philosophic kind. I do not mean ideological postures or metaphysical abstractions, but the constancy of asking the Aristotelian question: What are the causes and consequences of bringing about change in the realms of being? And how are those realms carved up in our age along social, economic, and

---

* Daniel Bell, *The Winding Passage: Essays and Sociological Journeys 1960–1980* (Cambridge, MA: Abt Books, 1980), pp. 370.

cultural dimensions? What keeps these large issues in manageable proportion is Bell's unswerving journalistic dedication to the concrete. The play of abstract ideas in concrete operational settings sets this man's work apart from that of his fellow sociologists.

The Winding Passage is divided into five parts and seventeen chapters; each of them represents areas of research in which Bell has become well known. In fact, not a few of the essays are distilled versions or microcosms of those larger works. Many themes in "Prophets of Utopia" were taken up in the *End of Ideology.* "Techne and Themis" *extends* positions mapped out in *The Coming of Post-Industrial Society.* And the final section, "Culture and Beliefs," echoes many of the sentiments expressed in *The Cultural Contradictions of Capitalism.* This is not to suggest that these essays are somehow less valuable or valid for having antecedents or descendants; quite the contrary, a knowledge of Bell's larger works will make reading these essays a double treat: first, they illumine his sociological sense of the world; and second, they amplify the larger works by Bell on similar subjects.

I have no quarrel at all with the first section on technology. Indeed, these two essays contain some of the best thinking by a sociologist on the relationship of technology to society, since Ernest Burgess in the 1930s and Fred Cottrell in the 1950s. But I am somewhat less certain that he has resolved the problem of the relationship of the new technology to the social system any better than have his sociological forbears. Even if we accept the Greek distinction between a material culture in progress and a moral culture in eternal recurrent cycle, we still cannot seem to understand the monads. That is to say, although modernity bursts the walls of technology in the early essays, it turns out that in the later essays modernity itself seems to be emptied of content. For Bell, the new code word of the age is not so much progress as limits. But then, we might well ask, what is the connection between the technological and the sacral? There are many teasing indicators of new combinations and permutations but slender connective tissue to the dialectic. The monads remain sealed atomic parts, shrouded in the mystery of being transformed into culture.

It may be too burdensome to expect a series of linkages in the retrospective volume. It is better to read each essay as a separate analytic framework with a moral charge behind it. Read in such a way, each essay is breathtaking in the range of information and quality of imagination. The essay, on "The End of American Exceptionalism" is an especially stunning example of Bell's quintessential liberalism and probably his lingering socialism. Starting with the problem of why socialism has not come to American shores, a myriad of prophecies notwithstanding, he emphasizes the qualities of the legal and constitutional system in the New World, rather than emphasizing economic well being, as have earlier explanations by Leon Samson and Seymour Martin Lipset. If Bell is correct that American exceptionalism has passed away, world capitalism has clearly not dissolved. If anything, the weakening of American capitalism, the wider distribution of world resources and wealth, has been strengthened by the addition of new players on the world scene, often at the expense of the American dominion. That the Eurodollar replaces the American dollar or that natural resources replace consumer goods as major commodities of value may reduce American exceptionalism, may increase moral anguish, but neither necessarily impinges on the character of socioeconomic arrangements on a worldwide basis. A peculiar variety of national myopia prevents Bell from developing an appropriate international frame of reference in which to assess the present-day United States.

Naturally, in such a volume each reader engages the author in private dialogue. It is perhaps best to permit each reader to argue with *The Winding Passage* in his or her own way, without excessive intrusion by a reviewer. (In any event, essays by Bell on the character of postindustrial society and on the New Class were published in the pages of *Transaction*/SOCIETY; these seminal statements in particular should be left to the assessment of other readers.) It is, however, important to draw out Bell's essential sociology, for while Bell is frank enough to state that there is no unifying or singular architechtonic to his work, the variety of themes he addresses do add up to a genuine, if not entirely original sociological framework. One of his major points, with which I am in full concurrence, is that we should worry less about the originality of a theory and more about the originality of a mind using theory to interpret and penetrate the social world.

Bell strongly attacks holism, the viewing of the world as a series of parts adding up to a teleologically determined whole. He argues instead that society is best understood as composed of diverse realms, each obedient to and situated within an axis, which in turn becomes the regulatory or normative principle that legitimates action in that field. Bell situates these realms in the economy, within the principle of functional efficiency; in the polity, with its principle of equality before the law; and in the principle of culture, or the enhancement and fulfillment of self. It is a special aspect of Bell's thought that he tends to be committed to personal fulfillment rather than social order. This identification with Marx rather than Durkheim on so fundamental an issue also separates him from the conservative mood with which he has so often, and in my view, so wrongly been identified by his critics. His emphasis on the cultural has another element, a disenchantment with much that passes for main-line sociology, a moving away from problems of the middle range into analysis that connects such issues as crime and deviance to large patterns. It is interesting to note that these essays become longer and more complex as they move from concrete subjects, such as national character or national guilt, to the larger issues of the present period.

The final essays on the exhaustion of modernism might well stand as Bell's statement about the exhaustion of sociology. Bell's present pursuits are characterized by groping for a new vocabulary. This search for new key words and trends, for new ways to gain a sense of the sacral, indicates his dissatisfaction with an earlier trinitarian model of economy, society, and culture. Although Bell does point the way toward an understanding of the problems in each realm, he has yet to explain how a new integration or for that matter a present disintegration of social scientific paradigms provides help in the pursuit of a new vocabulary. The groping and the lurching are brilliantly etched, but if they lead to a new theology rather than a new sociology, then I am not sure that I share the sense of purpose and challenge captured in this intellectual odyssey.

Now for a slightly negative note: I should like to attend to the two essays that I found least satisfactory. Let me observe that fifteen brilliant essays out of seventeen is so unusual a batting average that negative comment on these two essays only emphasizes my respect for the overall achievement.

Bell's attack on Mills in "Vulgar Sociology" is painfully on target. But unlike almost every other essay, it is pugnacious and ungenerous; it seems more a pique with another variety of essayist and moralist than a key statement of his paradigm. In an age of bubbling optimism and touching faith in the American century, Mills articulated a new pluralistic basis for Leftist thought, a pragmatic vision part of the debates on the Left from which the excitement of the 1960s seemed to flow. (How strange it is that the excitement generated by intellectual debate is now taking place on the Right.) Despite Mills's failure to appreciate the heterogeneity of government, military, and business and despite a line of analysis often flawed by amateurish emulators, this does not deprive Mills himself of moral sophistication in the midst of prevailing sociological orthodoxies. In the former he was unique, in the latter, alas, in a large company. Bell would have been better advised to sustain the pitch of grace and elegance captured in these essays rather than remind his readers of an earlier age when bellicosity and anger toward his opponents was more commonplace.

"Reflections on Jewish identity" is the second essay that I had difficulty reconciling with the volume as a whole. Bell reflects the sorts of problems characteristic of many Jews who came from socialist and radical backgrounds; namely an inability to appreciate that Judaism is not simply a religious supplement to an already rich ideological diet, but itself a total perspective and framework for action. An embarrassing autobiographical excess ends up creating problems rather than explaining them, by emphasizing the moral travails of the author rather than actual conflicts within Judaism. We are rhetorically asked if we must accept a Jewish God, a jealous God: "Do I have to accept the sins of my fathers, and my children those of mine? This is not an academic question, for it confronts us everywhere." This is indeed an academic question, nor is it a particularly Jewish question; Jews are not expected to accept the sins of fathers or bequeath their sins to children. Accepted is the culture of the fathers, and bequeathed in the commitment to that culture. There is more of Sombart's Calvin than Sholem's Moses in Bell's sense of the Jewish. The "community [of Jews] woven by the thinning strands of memory" reflects more on Bell's weakening sense of community and his own reliance upon memory than the actual condition of Judaism. Bell missed a golden opportunity to move to a higher ground of synthesis, by failing to explore in his own Judaism an analytic structure rather than a memory trace.

Bell is so widely regarded as a political figure in sociology, if not as a political sociologist, that it is surprising how little of the book treats political themes, either on a national or international scale. His abilities with technological literature are unsurpassed, and his sense of the economic context of culture and the cultural texture of stratification is again flawless. But whether he is discussing utopian or ideological themes, the level of discourse is often twice, sometimes thrice, removed. Even when Bell examines prospects for mobilization of politics in the United States, it is within a context of the dissolution of "insulated space" as represented by "the contemporary revolutions of communication and transportation." Unlike Seymour Martin Lipset or Reinhard Bendix, on whom political science has had a profound impact, Bell has a deep commitment to the sociological paradigm in a pure and older fashion. Even his heroes (Veblen and Fourier) tend to reveal this. Bell is simply not taken with Machiavelli or Hobbes. It is how politics is impacted from the economic and cultural realms, rather than the workings of the political process, that captures his attentions. In this respect he is perhaps a purer variety of sociologist than his detractors have appreciated. Even in discussing the "decline of authority," where political analysis would seem inevitable, categories remain distinctly Weberian: the status system of society, organizational life, institutional life, professional life, and cultural life. The political life as such is simply not much of a factor in this collection.

The strongest difference I have with Bell's essays is with his mood rather than content. The dark picture of a series of unresolved dialectical conflicts may properly suit our epoch and certainly may explain the decline of the secular and the triumphal return of the sacral. Just as assuredly, within sociology few have better captured this sort of imagery. Only the essays of Edward Shils and Robert Nisbet come close. And perhaps this is the proper posture and stance. My own preference is not to overidentify the pessimistic with the profound but to be more concerned with the character of the next synthesis than with the structure of the present contradiction. In an ideal world of social theory, both tasks can and will be performed simultaneously; if a choice of strategies must be made, the search for new combinations, new ways of overcoming old dilemmas, the smashing of dialectical icons seems more appropriate to the tasks of our discipline. However, in the likely event that this optative mood may be little more than intellectual whistling in the dark, one can scarcely be better equipped to appreciate the cultural contradictions of the structures and ideologies that we live with than by reading and digesting these masterful essays.

A special comment on the physical appearance of the book: it is excellent. It has been so long since I have seen a title and chapter page with a colophon and a type color in addition to black, that I thought for a moment of the old A.A. Knopf volumes. The margins are ample, the type face is handsome, and the book has a general feeling or quiet elegance that properly suits it. The one quibble I have is with the subtitle. Surely, it should have been *Sociological Essays and Journeys*, rather than *Essays and Sociological Journeys*. But for its appearance no less than its content, this book is well worth buying and reading.

From *Contemporary Sociology*, vol. 10, no. 4 (1981), pp. 493–516.

78

Is a Science of Ethics Possible?*

Edel, Abraham

This newest publication of the *International Encyclopedia of Unified Science* represents in my judgment a landmark in the development of a scientific study of moral behavior. The basis of this contention is Professor Edel's singular capacity to move beyond oracular controversies of the good and the right in favor of a comparative, analytic, and functional account of how ethical perspectives and practices effect the content of moral discourse. In Edel's view, the structure of ethical behavior is defined by biological, psychological, social, and historical functions or orientations. Hence, a scientific account of ethics is possible since moral norms are themselves products of an existential field often less open to verifiable statements than are other phases of human relations, but nonetheless subject to empirical claims. Edel makes it clear that adopting an empirical perspective on ethical theory does not require prior settlement of the free-will determinism controversy any more than the forging of political science depends for its sustenance upon the settlement of East-West tensions. Yet, most objections thus far registered against Edel's position, as expressed in earlier writings, amount to little more than a mandate ruling ethical conduct off base to the social scientist on either emotivist, religious, or metaphysical grounds. Unfortunately, the logical disjunction between fact and value made earlier in the century by Max Weber and Emile Durkheim in response to intuitionist social theories now slows down attempts at establishing a science of ethics. This logical disjunction has now become calcified into a metaphysical dualism.

Edel's study is divided into four chapters; the first introduces us to the complex nature of the relation of science to ethics. The material here is quite condensed, and it might be advantageous to the reader to refer to Edel's earlier work, *Ethical Judgment*, in which the biological, psychological and

---

* Abraham Edel, *Science and the Structure of Ethics*, (vol. 2, no. 3, *Foundations of the Unity of Science*). (Chicago, The University of Chicago Press, 1961), pp. 101.

social foundations for this sort of analysis are made plain. Chapters two and three, the core of the book, cover the theory of existential perspectives and the methodological basis for a science of ethics. Here we are provided with a brilliant exposition of available (and inherited) ethical alternatives as well as the specific elements entering into ethical deliberation. The author's notion of existential perspectives is itself best understood as consideration of vantage points through which to frame ethical judgments, without becoming needlessly involved in strident defenses or critiques of these bastions. Edel's rich and varied taxonomies and paradigms express his scrupulous efforts to build an edifice only after providing firm foundations. In offering ten specifications for an existential perspective, five requisites for a scientific method applicable to ethics, three groups of moral subject matter, five types of linkage in establishing models for ethical discourse, seventeen forms of deliberation when adopting a course of ethical action, and thirteen meanings attached to the phrase moral obligation, the author recreates an Aristotelian style of philosophizing all but lost in modern thought. The fourth and final section is a plea for openness in discussing ethical beliefs, and no less, an offer of rich rewards for those patient enough to employ the findings of science in settling moral disputes. This, I take it, is what the author means by his policy-making approach to ethics.

This is not to say that the critical reader will find no fault with this work. Within the confines of this brief notice, I should like to indicate what for me seems to be weak links in a firm expository chain. (a) There is an ambiguous note struck in claiming moral philosophy asks the same kind of questions in the same sort of way as does a science of ethics. This is surely not held true by most theorists in the field, nor for that matter is it so for past ages. Is this something the author would *like* to see come about, or something that *must* happen in consequence of science? In any event, an expansion of this point is sorely required. (b) I am not convinced that the notion of existential perspectives gets beyond, as it aims to do, Mannheim's dilemmas in framing a science of politics in a universe of "total ideologies" and a "global relativism." What assurance can be given that there is not indeed a hidden or displaced existential perspective behind the facade of autonomy? And if this is so, how does the author propose to squeeze both objectivity and existential perspectives into the same general statement of theory? (c) There is a sublime contentment with relativism that is hard to share. Even if we separate functional problems from metaphysical issues, do we not require a choice of selection between positions in advance, or even suspension, of the evidence (i.e., on essentially nonlogical grounds, such as the author's own faith in the curative powers of scientific endeavor)? Is the science of ethics to rest on an exhaustive listing of existential perspectives, or is there a synthesizing principle involved? (d) Edel's use of "policy decisions" as virtually synonymous with "virtue constellations" raises as many issues as it resolves. Are policy decisions to use scientific method in themselves free of, or determined by, moral boundaries? Aren't policy deci-sions often made on the basis of manipulative possibilities exclusively, without regard for moral dimensions as such? Would the RAND approach to survival possibilities in a nuclear conflict become "ethical" by using the analytic tools offered in this study? At what point precisely do moral decisions coalesce with (or distinguish themselves from) practical decisions?

Perhaps I have stated my queries more forcefully than the materials really warrant. But these are issues that are bound to arise and that the author would do well to take up more candidly in future studies. As it stands, ethical rela-tivism can too easily become hostage to an ethical rationalism that can more readily be discussed in the classroom than acted upon in everyday social life.

The very asking of these kinds of questions presupposes an empirical attitude to ethics. And in compelling the reader to direct his energies along scientific channels, Edel has succeeded admirably. The groundwork for an empirical study of moral behavior has now been provided. What remains is the actual descriptive and comparative study of ethical considerations entering such phenomena as determination of wages and prices; the fixing of political consensus; the role of customs, habits, and traditions in moral decisions; the basis of moral decisions made by the mentally ill; and a host of attendant considerations that thus far have received but scant attention among philos-ophers and social scientists. Professor Edel's pioneering efforts have brought us to the point where we no longer need talk about integrative levels but can actually begin the task of integrating levels.

From *Philosophy and Phenomenological Research*, vol. 22, no. 2 (1961), pp. 267–69.

79

The Responsibilities of Sociology*

Ginsberg, Morris

This is a decent collection of papers honoring a decent human being. During the lean years of British sociology, when its very legitimacy was in doubt and when academic positions were few and far between, Morris Ginsberg served through his professorship at the London School of Economics to remind the British academic community that sociology existed, that its theoretical contributions were at least equal to those of political science and anthropology, and that its practical potential in the struggle to unite scientific knowledge with a situated, grounded moral concern was unique.

I am beginning to think that it is a special property of those sociologists trained in philosophy to think of social science as a carrier of rationality against the higher irrationality of ideology. Ginsberg was very much in this tradition. In his case, such considerations largely derived from Sidgwick, Hobhouse, and the English pluralists. For some, the same set of concerns derives from James and Dewey; for others, it is Marx and Engels. No matter the derivation. What matters is the acute sense of larger issues, to which Ginsberg gave authentic expression.

Ronald Fletcher's introduction and appreciation offers a nicely balanced account of Ginsberg's intellectual development and provides a sense of what Ginsberg himself perceived to be the main themes of his work. I found it somewhat flawed by a petulance and argumentativeness that seemed inappropriate to a *Festschrift*. All sorts of opponents and protagonists are vaguely alluded to, and the charges range from Ginsberg's being old-fashioned to his being irrelevant to modern needs. But since we are not told the exact context of these charges or, for that matter, who made them, the vigor of Fletcher's defense seems largely beside the point. The editor's comments on Ginsberg's Judaism also seem off-target-a well-intentioned effort to assert

* Ronald Fletcher (editor), *The Science of Society and the Unity of Mankind: A Memorial Volume for Morris Ginsberg* (London: Heinemann, New York: Crane, Russak, 1974), pp. 292.

the compatibility of liberal Judaism with agnostic humanism. But I would say that, on this topic, Ginsberg is sharper and clearer-eyed than his editor. Nonetheless, in elucidating Ginsberg's central themes, the editor's work is sound: the role of reason in ethical judgment and, above all, the relativity of morals in each society and individual and the objectivity and irreducibility of values and obligations for societies and individuals.

The first part of the volume includes a couple of brief appreciations by Sir Sidney Caine and Lord Lionel Robbins. Both are far too brief to situate Ginsberg in his intellectual milieu, and neither attempts to locate him in his social context. The papers by H.B. Acton and H.P. Rickman are worthwhile summaries that manage to elucidate Ginsberg's philosophic positions without artificially constructing a synthetic viewpoint or omitting some real logical inconsistencies in themes of science and progress. Indeed, the next two papers, by Robert Bierstedt and Leslie Sklair are critical, each in its own way, of Ginsberg's use of the idea of progress. I confess to preferring Bierstedt's calmer and more restrained remarks to Sklair's muscular yet youthful exercises on the same theme. Strangely, I find myself closer to Ginsberg than to his critics, on the centrality of the idea of progress. True enough, the twentieth century, in its sophisticated wisdom, has substituted the theme of development for the idea of progress, but I would suggest that the contents of both are quite similar. Because of this, in his own essays in *Sociology and Social Psychology*, Ginsberg had no trouble accounting for the aspirations and requisites of the Third World in the postimperial epoch.

The second part of the book includes a sampling of Ginsberg's papers on the responsibility of sociology. I confess to unease about this practice. A *Festschrift* is after all about a scholar's work, and it presumes some decent acquaintance with the person being honored, by readers as well as writers. But quite beyond a superfluous touch is the fact that Ginsberg was a sociological essayist par excellence, and hence selections can only repeat, in a rather slender way, the themes covered in his own collections of work. Nonetheless, the first and last of these papers, "The Growth of Social Responsibility" and "The Responsibilities of Sociologists," can hardly be read enough. They remain fresh and vivid, illustrating Ginsberg's central concerns with sociological clarity and moral decency.

The third section, on sociology and society, contains a series of brief papers of mixed worth. The first, by Placido Bucolo, is a survey of main themes in modern society, written from a quasi-Frankfurt orientation, but without much point. Jean Floud's paper on "Sociology and the Theory of Responsibility" is a critique of a few older theories of deviant behavior. However, apart from some nice dissections of the concept of commitment, I fear that she has left out of the reckoning more recent American *and* British contributions to the study of criminology and deviance, and so leaves one with the feeling that this is an older paper reflecting earlier, prelabelling, preinteractionist themes seeking to explain the interactions of sociological and political structures in the study of deviant behavior. Paul Halmos provides a quite outstanding and sustained critique of critical sociology and its assumptions about total crisis and total destruction, what Halmos amusingly calls the "venal perspective of the world of ideas." This paper deserves wide attention and commentary. The final paper and I am afraid the weakest is D.W. Harding's contribution, "The Concept of Peace," is so removed and remote from contemporary events that one is left with the uncomfortable feeling that either nothing has taken place since Gandhism or the author has simply failed to take note of present discourses.

The sad truth is that Ginsberg, his nobility of character and seriousness of intellectual purpose notwithstanding, stood in the second rather than first rank of twentieth-century sociologists. He demanded rationality as the admission ticket to the practice of sociology. But once he had gained admission through the gatekeepers' outstretched moral arms, Ginsberg had little to say of a decisive nature on the specifics of stratification, social psychology, criminology, or any of the middle-range aspects of sociology. Further, given his admittedly restricted, or better, anthropological vision of methodology and theory, his contributions to the large range of sociology, while solid, also betrayed a sense of the abstract. Another way of putting this is that Ginsberg's sense of Aristotelian rationality and his passion for equity were not matched by coming to battle, or even to grips, with the force of irrationality he presumed to tackle head-on. We are simply not told how those who rule have power, exercise authority, or deny in practice that universal equity asserted by all in theory.

The book closes with two fine, sensitive, and all too brief recollections by May Eppel and Maurice Freedman. Both understand, perhaps better than the editor, that Ginsberg's was a fusion of Jewish and Western scholarship-or, perhaps to go Ms. Eppel one better-appreciate that the Western tradition was at least as much Jewish as it was Greek. The bibliography by Angela Bullard is quite good and up-to-date. The book is physically well produced and sensitively edited. However, the enormous price tag condemns it to remain a library curiosity, to be read, as perhaps Ginsberg himself might have preferred matters, in the confines of a world of books-that peculiar physical representation of a quiet rationality unique to the Western liberal tradition that now appears so remote in time and space.

From *Social Forces*, vol. 54, no. 2 (1975), pp. 475–77.

80

The Tragedy of Triumphalism*

DeJouvenel, Bertrand

This is the sort of volume that can too readily be overlooked by professionals. It has all the limitations of the genre: it is a collection of papers and not a unified work. It is released by a now defunct publisher, or better, one absorbed by a larger house (Schocken has been absorbed by Pantheon, which in turn is a wholly owned subsidiary of Random House, whose own corporate identity remains dubious.) Finally, as the editors make plain, this is the work of a figure with few disciples, writing in a tradition outside the main driving forces of Anglo-American and Germanic political cultures.

These obligatory caveats raised, one must give an appreciation to the editors of this volume, who along with Wilson McWilliams provide a useful framework for understanding this sadly neglected, badly maligned figure. Indeed, Hale and Landy provide a model opening essay rarely seen these days. The statement on deJouvenel is literate and articulate, offering an appreciation of deJouvenel's work in a firm historical context: from newspaperman to political theorist. Hale and Landy situate deJouvenel in the context of his times and places. This introduction could serve as a useful jumping off point for a full-scale consideration of deJouvenel in the context of twentieth century French politics. While Roy Pierce, Evelyn Pisier, and Carl Slavin in particular have written useful essays on deJouvenel, the need for a full-scale effort is highlighted by this collection.

DeJouvenel offers intriguing crossover points between liberal and conservative thought, nationalist and cosmopolitan sentiment, and rightist and leftist political action. In this sense, deJouvenel is a reflection of the main tendencies of French life and thought between the two world wars (read European wars), and the major movements in French thought after the second world war.

---

* *The Nature of Politics: Selected Essays of Bertrand deJouvenel*, edited with an introduction by Dennis Hale and Marc Landy, and a foreword by Wilson Carey McWilliams (New York: Schocken Books, 1987), pp. 254.

As such deJouvenel reveals the variety of drifts that reflect personal loyalties even more than political sensibilities. He is, for example, tied to Francois Doriot's Parti Populaire Francais, even as that figure drifts from strong linkages to communism and socialism to fascism and nazism. He interviews Adolph Hitler in 1936 and reports back to France Hitler's assurances of a policy of political friendship to France one week prior to the Nazi occupation of the Rhineland.

DeJouvenel's opposition to this move, and urging of Anglo-French action to curb Hitler notwithstanding, the interview itself had a disorientation and demobilizing impact. And the editor's claim that although reading this interview today is an "unnerving experience," deJouvenel was simply "lied to about German intentions." But of course, the puzzlement remains how so sophisticated a figure as deJouvenel could simply accept Hitler at face value and transmit such "lies" as bona fide.

That deJouvenel was a patriot of France and that his mistakes were never made in the spirit of fascist closure are confirmed by the magnificent statement of Raymond Aron, quoted in a moving tribute to Aron carried in a volume of essays entitled *History, Truth, Liberty*. Since it is not included in the volume under consideration, I take the liberty of citing it in some detail. It may help dispel the myth of deJouvenel's anti-Semitism and neo-fascism.

Shils once asked Aron his opinion of deJouvenel's conduct during the first several years of the German occupation. Aron's answer, repeated and embellished upon in a courtroom context at the very end of Aron's life, went as follows:

> The idea of the French army and the subjugation of France by Germany had deeply shaken and disordered the spirits of those who had to live under it. It was easy for me [Aron] because I had to leave France, being a Jew, and so I could maintain my intellectual equilibrium. But for those who remained behind, the situation was very much harder. Furthermore, well before the Germans were driven out of France, Jouvenel had made amends by serving the *resistance*.

Aron is careful to distinguish political treason and intellectual judgment—no small matter in assessing someone like deJouvenel.

Biographical information aside, the postwar deJouvenel, who set himself the task of understanding the fundamental laws and theorems of political science, remains worthy of study. Indeed, as in the case of Carl Schmitt, (a much clearer and more painful case of collaboration with nazism), one has to appreciate the limits of biography and to examine the contribution of someone like deJouvenel for his theoretical merits. The crossover between personal virtue and intellectual skill is at best ubiquitous. In the case of deJouvenel it is best to take the extraordinary paradigms he has bequeathed us in the study of politics and perhaps ignore (note I did not say forget) personal or political indiscretions. To be sure, it might have been best if Hale and Landy had come to terms with their master on his own intellectual ground, rather than seeking the purification of his behavior as a precondition of intellectual understanding. We all want our intellectual heroes to be men and women of personal probity. Alas, this is not always the case, and in fact rarely is. Coming to terms with this is difficult, involving our own sense of maturation and the recognition that people are not always made of whole cloth, but at times of bits and pieces that do not always come together to form a seamless whole. Thus, while deJouvenel may not be a paragon of virtue, he may still be a source of useful theory.

The papers in this volume are nearly all from deJouvenel's previous writings in the English language. And this is a shame, since there are papers in French that deserve to be translated, and that might shed light precisely on the theme of the inside outsider—the French nationalist and French philosophe writing from a perspective beyond that of English constitutional tradition or German organic jurisprudence. His is a tradition in which figures such as deTocqueville, Sorel, Thierry, and Rousseau loom very large indeed. Still, the essays that are herein reprinted are valuable. For deJouvenel is interested in politics in the context of political science, and in how a science of politics is possible, much less potentially significant.

Each social science faced a crisis in confidence after the end of the Second World War, a struggle with the earlier taken-for-grantedness that everyone knew what the major social science taxonomies represented, and in consequence, what a political science meant. The essays "The Nature of Politics", "On The Nature of Political Science," and "Political Science and Prevision" offer a prologemena to the science of politics that should be required reading for all who dare think of the field as a discipline. Why they are not grouped together by the editors is something I frankly cannot understand. Surely, meaningful intellectual configuration deservedly should have preempted sheer chronology—especially in treating a protean figure like deJouvenel.

DeJouvenel introduces a small group concept of the political with an acknowledged indebtedness to the great sociologist, George Homans, "It is a technique for the addition of human energies by the union of wills." When this union of wills becomes a collective assemblage and forms a purposive form of action, we move from technique to action, i.e., "The characteristic activity of pure politics may, therefore, be defined as an activity that builds, consolidates and keeps in being aggregates of men." deJouvenel goes on to say that "with this definition, I have shot my bolt," This expressive American colloquialism notwithstanding, nothing could be further from the truth. Because deJouvenel moves from action to conception, to the ideas that will make durable, binding and consensual the aggregates of people.

When deJouvenel examines the nature of political science, his work takes on the characteristics of the imperial vision so typical of the master builder in search of social scientists. It turns out that nearly all forms of social organization are subsumed under the label political, that "politics consists of nothing other than human behavior." Thus, having finished off the domain of sociology, he moves to do likewise for psychology: "I hold the view that we should regard as political every systematic effort performed at any place in the social field to move other men in pursuit of some design cherished by the mover." The psychic deviant may become the political leader. deJouvenel next moves along to coopt economics, a discipline we are assured is not to be feared. Politics becomes a way to study the moral passion regarding economic behavior. In all fairness to deJouvenel, he recognizes the imperfect fusion of the economic and the political. And beyond that, deJouvenel has the capacity to be sharply critical of the organicism of Hegelian political theory, of the notion of a "healthy political body," which for him leads to decadence, to a pseudorestorationism of a German Holy Roman Empire that moves away from factualism to fanaticism in the study of politics.

In the the the third paper on this important subject, deJouvenel informs us that it is better to speak of political behavior and institutions than of an organic body politics. In this way we are able to deal modestly and sensibly with political institutions as instrumental in value and character, not as transcendental entities that need mindless support. In this, one senses deJouvenel settling of accounts with totalitarianisms of all sorts. For this reason, deJouvenel advocated the English language tradition of distinguishing between politics and policies. The French language tends to blunt this distinction, this separation between the association of groups for common ends, and the constant redefinition of those ends for the common good. Hale and Landy tend to seek in deJouvenel someone neither Left nor Right, neither liberal nor conservative. But while this might be the case, it is also the case that deJouvenel was a fish out of specifically French water. He developed strong proclivities in favor of democracy—a democracy of fairness, freedom, and civility. It is the last that links the political process with the political science calling. Carey McWilliams in his brief foreword gets close to the marrow of this substructure in deJouvenel's work.

There are several other powerful and prescient papers in this collection of the work of deJouvenel. While they do not replace his larger works, many of which are readily available in English, they amplify the fusion that he sought to create between the political and the political scientific. The papers on authority, forms of government, and means of opposition (again, sadly separated in the volume in favor of a mechanical timetable of original publication) present a shrewd social psychological approach to building up a theory of state power. They also serve as constant reminders that the achievement of sound policies derives not from the suppression of extremes of thought, but by the elucidation and elaboration of those "near to median opinions" that permit democratic societies, politics, and polities to survive and thrive. This is the burden of the final paper on the "team against the committee", namely, the fostering of opposing views as a mechanism of governance and legitimacy.

It was deJouvenel's sad fate to be out of sync with nearly every phase of his environment. When he was a democrat, he was surrounded by an aristocratic mien; then when he became a socialist advocate, he found the extremes corroding the center, the democracy he believed in. When he held out hope for a pacific resolution of European affairs, fanaticism broke out throughout Europe; when he advocated resistance, the regime accepted capitulation. And finally, in a post-war France, in which cultural heroes turned increasing to irrational models in the name of existential and total solutions, he returned to a strong commitment to civil culture and a liberal society.

DeJouvenel changed less than the extremities of the societies in which he lived through in the France of the midtwentieth century. In part at least he suffered for being out of phase. In this, the present collection helps redress the bad hand dealt to deJouvenel by his contemporaries. But admitting the neglect of someone who provided a common sense vision of the political culture, the problem remains why this neglect has been so thorough of an individual placed by the editors of this collection in the divine pantheon of "great political thinkers of the twentieth century."

DeJouvenel's triumph in political philosophy was to ask the original question. His tragedy in political practice was a failure to ask how such questions played out in the realm of real authority. As a guide through quotidian events, he proved less than useless. We are left with the same questions in theory as in biography: whether any relationship or connection exists between thinkers and doers. To answer no, to rest content with bifurcated consciousness, does more to weaken deJouvenel's place in contemporary intellectual history than do formal debates on his attitudes in theory to "the Principate" or his attitudes in practice to Napoleon, Hitler, or Stalin. The moral rub is that this new linguistic wine for old totalitarian regimes is selected by deJouvenel because the term is "neutral, equally acceptable to those who approve of such regimes and to those who disapprove of them." This stretches the limit of objectivity in both political theory and practice. Along the way, such fence-hanging toppled deJouvenel from a place among the pantheon of great social scientists.

From *Encounter*, vol. LXXI, no. 3 (1988).

81

The Two Cultures of Policy*

Kelman, Steven

In an operational sense, the notion of policy is divided between foreign and domestic policy. In the interstices of government, it is well understood that one group of people handles the dynamics of criminology, penology, gerontology, child care, family planning, and education (i.e., domestic policy); and another deals with interest groups, foreign relations, trade policies, and military intervention and assistance (i.e., foreign policy). Leavened as it is by fiscal costs and budgetary constraints, policy in fact has an essentially unitary character. Why then does the myth of the two cultures of policy persist? Like social myths, policy myths are after all Durkheimian facts something to be explained not dismissed. Let us attempt to do so by reviewing some recent books on policy.

One of the more surprising aspects of these texts is how readily they adhere to the conventional distinction between domestic and foreign policy: It is as if domestic and foreign policy were sealed monads having only cursory, if that, relationships with each other. In part, this reflects the way people are professionally educated, which in turn is a consequence of how the administrative-governmental apparatus is structured.

But not only differences in the educational parameters or political expectations of different branches of government explains the two cultures of policy.

---

* Thomas L. Brewer, *American Foreign Policy: A Contemporary Introduction* (Englewood Cliffs, NJ.: Prentice-Hall, 1986), pp. 317.

Roger Hilsman, *The Politics of Policy Making in Defense and Foreign Affairs Conceptual Models and Bureaucratic Politics* (Englewood Cliffs, NJ.: Prentice-Hall, 1987), pp. 326.

Steven Kelman, *Making Public Policy: A Hopeful View of American Government* (New York: Basic Books, 1987), pp. 224.

Marc L, Miringoff and Sandra Opdycke, *American Social Welfare Policy: Reassessment and Reform* (Englewood Cliffs, N.J.: Prentice-Hall, 1986), pp. 169.

Michael Morris and John B. Williamson, *Poverty and Public Policy: An Analysis of Federal Intervention Efforts* (Westport and London: Greenwood Press, 1986), pp. 237.

David A. Rochefort, *American Social Welfare Policy: Dynamics of Formulation and Change* (Boulder and London: Westview Press, 1986), pp. 206.

It is something in the very guts of domestic policy vis a vis foreign policy. Those who take care of social policy are, for the most part, trained in sociology, psychology, and social work. Those who are expert in foreign policy are, for the most part, located in political science, international law, and economics.

But this nifty relationship between professional training and bureaucratic administration is itself hostage to what Clifford Geertz might call a thick description, (i.e., a constituency model). For training involves ideology as well as organization. The ideology of social policy is predicated on what can be extracted from the state in the name of a broad series of constituencies who are outside the system and are not beneficiaries of the formal structure, and social welfare is almost synonymous with domestic policy. But those concerned with foreign policy are dedicated precisely to the enhancement if not enlargement of the state, the very agency that social policy personnel view as their protagonist. Thus, at the heart of the cultures are different levels of commitment to the two principal institutions of modern Western policy: state and society. These stand in unhappy, uneasy relationship to each other, much as do those who wear the mantles of domestic and foreign policy experts.

A further problem is that institutes of policy abound, but the actual number of people who are primarily trained or receive degrees in any area of policy remains exceedingly modest. Professional legitimacy is still bestowed through conventional training in a core discipline of the social and behavioral sciences: sociology, psychology, economics, anthropology, or political science. Still, the fascination with policy exists, even expands. Part of the fascination may be due to the job market and the career orientations of the moment. But I submit that the pull of policy is also its ability to affect outcomes, to change the name of the game from historical determinism to pragmatic invention. This attraction also happens to be at the heart and soul of all social science. Hence, it is that policy as a field of professional endeavor grows, with or without social science endorsement. Witness the plethora of journals in the field, and the numerous books with the word policy in their titles.

One witnesses an avocational characteristic of policymaking, a relationship defined by its practice. Anyone can participate, the rules are virtually nonexistent. One has only to be deeply committed to the needs of the underclass, outsiders and minorities, underrepresented majorities; or the reverse, deeply committed to the maintenance of the national government, firmly involved in promulgating the safety and security of the citizens of a free nation. Even such rhetoric reflects the two cultures of policy. For the sociologist, the buzz words are society, welfare, and voters; whereas for the political scientist the buzz words are state, security, and citizen. Thus, rhetoric matches the reality of a policy environment that is profoundly bifurcated in its visions and mutually antagonistic in its positions. Only those blessed few who see policy as metaphysical madness escape the anguish of such polarities.

The books under consideration here have as their major concern domestic and foreign policy. They are marked by a sobriety and common-sensical nature that is refreshing, if partial. They are worthy of examination, even if they are not quite able to resolve the big issues. The old euphoria of the 1960s assumed that every personal problem had a social solution; those days are gone. In their stead is the new realization of the 1980s that individuals and their communities are often in a state of competition and even conflict for scarce resources. This conflict cannot be resolved by bigger public works programs, since what is scarce is not so much money as talent, desires, and resources.

In *American Social Welfare Policy*, David A. Rochefort, assistant professor of political science at Northeastern University, makes a comprehensive effort to understand the politics of this new social welfare environment. In so doing, he recognizes with refreshing frankness that a critical component is "the degree of personal responsibility attributed to the individual who presents the social welfare problem." Rochefort well appreciates the extent to which social images may contribute to definitions of social problems. Thus, in the field of welfare in the early 1960s, for example, casework services under the AFDC program were greatly expanded in order to aid those on welfare to overcome a psychological dependency that some intellectuals were beginning to label the culture of poverty.

Rochefort's notion of social images provides an intriguing if somewhat schematic explanation of how public attitudes towards psychiatry led to the community mental health centers legislation of the early 1960s and likewise how they increasingly affect organizing the elderly by stimulating an ethos of social reform distinctly aimed to satisfy senior citizens. But while Rochefort is able to deal with the period of expanding social policies rather effectively, he is less able to explain the successes and popular support of the cutback period of the 1980s. He rightly notes that early administration cutbacks in Medicaid and AFDC were relatively easy to achieve but that follow-up rounds became increasingly difficult, since vital interests were directly involved. To be sure, social security has become a sacred cow for Republicans no less than Democrats. As a result, the defense budget depends upon program needs, and policy innovation (in either direction) has come to a virtual standstill. While I find myself in general agreement with Rochefort's analysis (i.e., that cutbacks, like new programs, have limits), it is not the whole story, nor even the end of the story. But it is as far as his book goes.

To extend his analysis, I would argue that what has taken place is a wide rebellion against policy as something issued from above in favor of economic invention as something that takes place below. This is not so much a matter of how much is affected, as who calls the tune. This is the essential populist strain in the Reagan presidency that his arch critics and opponents seem unwilling to acknowledge. And why should they, having so long permitted the policy of liberal elites to speak in the name of the people. In the Reagan era, American policy has moved from social welfare to private workfare. Individuals are making decisions about where to be hospitalized, which doctors to use, which schools children should attend, what lawyers to call upon, etc. This privatization of decision making about social welfare has not always been pleasant. The very self-interest against which domestic policy is often aimed surfaces all too readily and all too often at the expense of minorities and people unable to fight back. Yet, so widespread has this swing become that whoever wins a presidential or congressional term and whichever party is in power, the prospects for a return to war-on-poverty social welfare policies seems slim. In this sense, the Reagan revolution has been successful realizing of its special federalist aims.

A second book with the same title, *American Social Welfare Policy*, is authored by Marc L. Miringoff and Sandra Opdycke, who are connected to the Fordham University School of Social Service and the Hudson River Psychiatric Center respectively. They are very painful aware of the massive shifts in public support for policy costly, tax-based initiatives, but they simply do not like these changes. Indeed, they attack straightaway people like Charles Murray whom they see as having provided in *Losing Ground* "the philosophical basis for the Reagan administration in the area of social welfare policy."

This book is substantially more polemical, even defensive, than Rochefort's. The authors take issue with Davis and Moore on social stratification, Moynihan on family assistance and in general relive arguments of the previous decades, steadily favoring liberal pasts over conservative presents. The strength of the volume is policymaking in valuational, technological, and structural contexts. But the disappearance of the poverty programs under the impact of the funding cuts and block grants still annoys and disturbs the authors. A "rational" planning model is held to be superior to the present "incrementalism." There is a begrudging awareness that a private-public sector mix has led to greater fiscal and programmatic accountability, but the authors voice dismay at the absence of coordinating efforts between the two domains.

The Miringoff-Opdycke book clearly wants to get beyond what it sees as a fragmented system and into a coordinated system—in short a return to more federal government centralization. Indeed, they see the present era as a setbacks to the social welfare institution. They envision a reversal of trends by a new coalition of self-aware and assertive "women, blacks, Hispanics, the disabled, the elderly, the young, Vietnam veterans, and others. Beyond policy then is raw politics; a coming together of such groups will add potency and force to the outside process, maximizing the energy that has been generated by individual constituencies." However, the authors do not offer a shred of evidence that divergencies among the imaginary coalitions may dissolve, as they envision. They do not acknowledge that differences, indeed conflicts, between young and old, black and Hispanic, the disabled and others, can characterize participants as Americans rather than as merely members of an interest group.

The volume on *Poverty and Public Policy* by Michael Morris and John B. Williamson, professor of psychology at New Haven University and professor of sociology at Boston College respectively, closely scrutinizes the sort of assumptions that in the past too readily substituted moral fervor for economic reality. Above all, these authors appreciate the fact that real strategic decisions do not imply the need to choose between presumed goods and evils in the political system. "Despite the vast economic resources possessed by our society these [poverty] programs have been unable to eliminate poverty or reduce it too negligible levels." This is the case, the authors are quick to note, whether Democrats or Republicans are in power. The facts are uncomfortable to all except those true believers in the fiction that net poverty has been reduced, or that net poverty is climbing as a result of any one given public policy, as Levitan has argued.

Morris and Williamson focus on direct assistance methods such as welfare programs, indirect strategies such as employment training education, and indirect strategies such as employment training education and social services. The authors postulate that the longer the period between policy initiatives and tangible human benefits, the less likely that benefits will accrue or that it will be supported by the public. In kind programs and policies are examined as examples of the direct assistance approach, and a parallel assessment is made of indirect strategies designed to increase the incomes of the poor through targeted economic development, education, job training, and employment subsidies.

Despite unusual and laudable care for detail, Morris and Williamson conclude a highly contradictory mode. On the one hand they claim "that there is no reason to expect that straightforward redistribution in conjunction with economic growth, can ever be replaced as the primary vehicle through which poverty policy operates." Yet, they quite fairly confess that "American policymakers and the public are unlikely to look favorably upon this conclusion." So we are left in a cul-de-sac, one not restricted to this book or to others concerned with domestic policy. All deny that domestic policy may indeed have limits that cannot be overcome without serious overhauling of the social system.

There is a strange moral disinterestedness in these domestic texts, as if poverty is uniformly caused and policy is uniformly the remedy. Little in these volumes indicates the relationship between domestic policy and moral predicates. It is not even that moral prescriptions are reviled or ridiculed. It is simply that moral concerns in the development of public policy—whether in terms of teenage pregnancy rates or minority unemployment rates—are not permitted to surface.

This kind of moral myopia in the name of social welfare disguises intellectual impoverishment. If pregnancy rates are high, there should be aggressive promotion of condoms and birth control pills; if black teen-aged unemployment is high, then the argument is made for more and better vocational training centers. In this way, domestic policy becomes the axiomatic preserve of the poor. Moral discourse becomes the prerogative of the idle wealthy (in the name of the poor to be sure).

The demand for a public policy that is politically relevant too often disguises animus for the very moral wellsprings of the republic that generated meaningful politics to begin with. Beyond that, a domestic policy that eschews individual responsibility leads to a culture of poverty, not as a function of weaknesses in the economic marketplace but as a consequence of government efforts to overcome market forces and private sector weaknesses. We are offered a plethora of rights in a universe without responsibilities. These issues must be faced by sociologists and other social researchers if social research is not to sink into acrimony and self-serving platitudes that perpetuate rather than overcome past inequities and injustices.

Let us turn now to the political science side of the policy coin. Thomas L. Brewer's text on *American Foreign Policy* (1986) is by design introductory. It should not be expected to come to terms with broad foreign policy issues. What is nonetheless fascinating is the degree of taken-for-grantedness of what the field covers and which interests are involved. For Professor Brewer things are somehow too clear: the line from public candidate preferences to policy choices; the delicately laced system of nongovernmental and governmental agencies effectuates foreign policy; the place of the Congress, the presidency, and the bureaucracy in this overall gestalt. Somehow, even the conflicts are described within a rational-model framework that seems oblivious to the newspaper realities that constantly parade forth mendacity, corruption, deception, and the sort of agency insularity that prevents effective public policy from being carried out. The Defense Department, the Central Intelligence Agency, the Department of State are lined up like ducks in the pond, making policy in an environment of checks and balances that needs little in the way of interorganizational reform.

Once in a while Professor Brewer slips in a policy recommendation, such as the need to separate the CIA into two agencies, one grounded in intelligence gathering and the other dealing with covert paramilitary operations. The author seems reluctant to claim such a decision would actually result in better policy or even avoid such disasters the Bay of Pigs disaster in Cuba. Ultimately, his is less a work on policy than a primer on the political organization of the government that enables politicians to conduct policy. The author uses a pluralist model in place of an elite model to explain government behavior, but he does not consider that neither may prove appropriate.

The best section by far is his discussion of specific foreign policy initiatives undertaken in the area of nuclear weapons: Salt/Start, the ABM Treaty, offensive weapons limitations; SDI; and nuclear proliferation constraints. That arena where policy means negotiating in a bilateral context rather than in agency reform turns out best for the author.

One notes—overseas scenarios notwithstanding—that the sort of policy initiatives possible outside conventional defenses of the national interest are severely limited. Interestingly, one of the shortest chapters in the book is on human rights. This occurs in part because the leverage of the United States in the welfare, health, and safety of foreign nationals is, to put it mildly, quite limited. This further means that any notion of policy as remedial (as is the case with those engaged in domestic policy) invariably yields to the notion that policy is linked to the national interest and to national survival—if indeed not outright victory. Issues of how terrorism became a mode of expression for social change in an environment where major world wars are no longer possible, or even whether the policies toward terrorism are domestic or foreign in policy implications, simply fall outside the purview of this text. And this is no defect of the book, but rather a consequence of a long tradition of foreign policy that is unambiguous as to its essential tasks and goals, but quite ambiguous as to its means and instrumentalities.

Roger Hilsman is a much more senior figure in foreign policy analysis and a person who in his own right has served in the foreign-policy trenches no less than in the academic foreground as a Columbia University professor of international relations. In *The Politics of Policy Making in Defense and Foreign Affairs*, he asserts, "The actors in international politics are like black-boxes." Hence, "the analyst has no need to know what goes on inside them." What is astonishing is his mechanistic presumption that "all black-boxes are the same in terms of motives, goals, and actions. The only differences are in how big the black-boxes are, how strong they are, and whether they are located in a strategic sense." Ah, if only this were the case! Then the analysis of the place of the Congress, the presidency, the bureaucracy and interest groups would follow. But although Hilsman's analysis is somewhat more elevated, the same presumption of strategic rationality infects his book as it does Brewer's work. Quite unlike Hilsman earlier work, in which when he was more connected to the policy process itself, he allows the "conceptual models" to overwhelm his understanding of "bureaucratic politics"—his best intentions notwithstanding.

It is not uninteresting that his concluding chapter is, "Can the American System Cope?" Hilsman is less interested in human rights, at least in terms of policymaking, than in the survivability of the system. Oddly enough, the argument becomes a longing for a past of power concentration. "The diffusion of power among a welter of small groups seems to explain the society's failure to take steps to protect the environment, conserve resources, take bold measures toward peace, and in other ways provide for the future." So curiously enough, foreign policy ends up with domestic policy—as a crie de coeur for bigness, for centrality of administration. Hilsman sees it ironic that power diffused can lead to evil as surely as can power concentrated. But the weight of his analysis is clearly for bigness, while the implicit weight of value judgment is for democracy. This is the big dilemma that links the two cultures of policymaking. Both have a shared commitment to an activist vision of policy, and that means increasing control from the top. They also have a strong commitment to democratic institutions, and that means the sort of diffusions lead to individualism in domestic policy and isolationism in foreign policy.

Steven Kelman's *Making Public Policy* is a different kettle of fish from most books on policy. Professor Kelman of Harvard University might well be described as the Steven Spielberg of policymaking. He views the policy prism as stimulating good performances by good people whose motives are also essentially virtuous. In its whimsical turn away from a strict ego-oriented utilitarianism, the book is refreshingly free of the usual attitudinizing and sermonizing that pervades too many broad-gauge texts in this field. While accomplishing what other texts in the policy area aim to do—providing a comprehensive view of the operations of the political processes in the major institutions of the federal government: Congress, the presidency, the Supreme Court, and the bureaucracy—Kelman manages to pay detailed attention to the processes of implementation and completion of policy. He also emphasizes the personality dimensions of the process of manufacturing American policy.

In describing this emphasis on implementation, Kelman permits himself to be drawn into a double interchange system. He proposes two "standards" that are separate yet related: "one is whether the process tends to produce good public policy. The other is whether the process of government positively affects how we see ourselves, and how we act as human beings." Sometimes, the "we" becomes a trifle cloudy. One is not always certain whether Kelman has in mind we the policy analysts, we the policymakers, or we the active citizens. But essentially, this notion of public spiritedness that Kelman seeks to promulgate, is, in the words of the old Schweppes advertisement, curiously refreshing. "My contention is simple: when people try to achieve good public policy, the result tends to be good public policy." Alas, the tautological characteristics of this statement are not entirely overcome. Since we are not informed as to what poor public policy looks like, we are never quite sure what is meant at an operational level by good public policy. In short, Kelman's optimistic mood tends to be psychologically satisfying, but curiously (there goes that word again) less than compelling sociologically.

In a paraphrase of Winston Churchill's declaration that democracy may not be a perfect political system, but it is the best one available, Kelman argues that the policymaking process in the United States works, and in any event, "this is the only government we've got." But his is not a Candide-like optimism. Kelman is fully aware that most policymaking is only partially implemented, and even so, rarely in the mode anticipated. Policymaking failures are high, successes are rare. He also understands that the political process itself breeds frustration and unhappiness with the policymaking apparatus. Kelman's conclusion is well worth keeping in mind:

> Lack of knowledge about the linkage between the final actions of government and real world outcomes is an important source of the impression that government does not succeed at solving problems. But it is not that government is failing while some hypothetical others are doing better. It is rather that we are all failing.

For all its urbanity, Kelman's text leaves this reader unsatisfied. The issue is not optimistic or pessimistic moods but the limits of systemic modes available to any given society at any given time. And in the absence of a structural analysis of American society, Kelman leaves us with an optimism that is grounded in sands of process that lack either substance or historicity. There is the all too simple dampening of the distinction between politics as a voice of the people and policy as the voice of the expert. The intellectual fallacy in policy analysis is to see the political process not as a corrective to poor policy but as a frustration of popular politics. Rather than overcome the two cultures of domestic policy and foreign policy, this dualism depends on the policymaking network as a human resource system. Still, as a social psychology of policymaking, Kelman's work must be ranked alongside the pioneering efforts of Lasswell, Janowitz, and Dahl and Lindblom. His effort is that good.

What then makes the policy process so anguishing is that those who argue the case for decentralization and federalism (usually the Republicans) also argue the case for increased defense budgets and higher military security. Those arguing for less emphasis on security and foreign involvement (usually Democrats) at the same time want greater centralization of authority to bring about domestic equalities. In short, the policy process is not the preserve of one party or interest group, but specific policies are hostage to partisan concerns. One sees emerging an appreciation that there really is no policy science as Lazarsfeld hoped or Lasswell aimed for. Rather there is a policy art: a series of aesthetic designs that create an effective mosaic in a successful government and an ineffective pattern in a failed government. The line between success and failure is thin, which means the art of policy is a difficult one. Rational models compete for attention with unbridled corruption; special interests compete with a national consensus; economic budgetary balances with increased bureaucratic size, and all of these objective elements take place in a maze of personalities and performers. This is the stuff of sociological consideration.

Far from being cause for alarm, the existence of the two policy cultures is itself part of the pattern of American governance. For the very competition for scarce resources—between welfare and security demands, for example—is itself part of the dialogue that makes present-day democratic rule a far cry from eighteenth-century inheritance. In the past, decisions were modest and the integration of decision making was simpler. The task of sociology in America is thus not to cook up once again a Comtean recipe but to incorporate the study of policy within the larger study of organizational and administrative life.

The halcyon days when sociology viewed policy as a simple exercise in the advocacy of good old welfare causes is simply untenable: a hollow shell that will not be revivified with Democratic party victories or Republican party defeats (or vice versa for that matter). A sociological view must embrace Mannheim's appreciation that public policy and public planning are both embodied in the texture of a single culture, as well as in the context of a pluralist government. In a larger sense, then, one hopes that the reintegration of policy, domestic and foreign alike, into the life cycle of the social sciences will make for better social outcomes and improved social science as well. In this I should like to conclude with the sage comments of Leonard Saxe in a recent piece on technology assessment before Congress. "Social scientific analysis serves an educative function in the development of policy; it does however, influence policy. In a pluralistic society committed to democratic ideals, that is perhaps all that one should expect."

From *The American Sociologist*, vol. 18, no. 2, pp. 195–204.

82

Counterrevolutionary Values or National Interests?*

Lipset, SeymourMartin

The position brilliantly outlined by Seymour Martin Lipset in *Revolution and Counter-Revolution* on the nature of Canadian social structure can be boiled down into four theses, supported by four kinds of data. The following summary is intended to avoid possibility of misunderstanding or misinterpretation of Professor Lipset's entrepreneurial thesis in a Canadian context.

First, the theme of Canadian conservatism is reproduced in which Canadian values, derived from the special relationships to Britain, are said to help perpetuate an old-world conservatism in Canada. One sort of evidence for this is data concerning lower levels of educational enrollment in Canadian universities, indicating that less than 10 percent of the 20–24 age group, compared to 30 percent in the United States, were enrolled in institutions of higher learning in 1960. The assumption is that high mobility is fostered by high educational possibilities. A second piece of information has to do with the much higher number of police in the United States, vis-à-vis Canada—more than ten times as many in actual gross figures. But interestingly enough, if we consider the ratio per 100,000 population, there is only a slightly higher level of police power in the United States than in Canada. Lipset also cites a third kind of data with respect to indictable offenses, indicating that in a whole series of punishable crimes, from homicide to burglary, forgery, fraud and theft, the United States rates average more than three times those of Canada. This too is assumed to be an indicator of Canadian conservatism, since high criminality is supposed to be a function of high developmental impulses, and low criminality a function of conservatism. Just what the isomorphism is between political conservatism and economic developmentalism is not spelled out by Lipset.

The second hypothesis relates to Canadian counter-revolution as a function of the ecclesiastical character of the predominant Canadian religions, which

* Seymour Martin Lipset, *Revolution and Counterrevolution: Change and Persistence in Social Structures* (Garden City, New York: Doubleday/Anchor, 1970). pp. 416.

have presumably inhibited the development of an egalitarian and achievement emphasis characteristic of religious pluralism in the United States. The basic data for this assertion are statistics on divorce, revealing that Canadian divorce rates—at least up until 1960—were less than 20 percent of those in the United States; hence, marriage as a function of conservatism becomes the underlying, causal variable explaining this religious conservatism. As we shall see later, significant liberalization in Canadian divorce legislation has altered this picture considerably. Moreover, there is some doubt whether divorce rates alone, which do not account for abandonment rates and non-legal separation, really can spell out the difference between marital standards in any two countries. It is also possible that the development of fragmentation in Canada's religion, at the very time religion in America is undergoing a period of intense amalgamation, would further modify Lipset's hypothesis.

The third thesis is that Canada ranks high on a scale of civil authority and low on a scale of personal autonomy; whereas the United States ranks high on a scale of frontier autonomy and low on a scale of civil authority. The evidence for this hypothesis has an eerie quality, but is presented cogently: first, that the Royal Canadian Mounted Police were given unlimited authority in the West (although I doubt seriously that they had much more authority than that provided the Texas Rangers somewhat earlier in American frontier history), and that again, conservatism is illustrated by the fact that "there were no vigilantes or massacres of Indians in the Canadian mining frontiers. Presumably vigilantism and massacres are a sign of autonomy and rugged individualism; or at least anticipate the conversion of virgin lands into industrial heartland. The final piece of data which in this case is more qualitative than quantitative, is the assumption that Canadian frontier separatism was perceived as a threat to the integrity of Canada as a whole; whereas American frontier settlements were never viewed as a threat to secession, and therefore never opposed by the central administration.

The fourth thesis is basically the counter-revolutionary hypothesis as such, that in Canada, colonial toryism made its second attempt to erect an English-patterned social structure. Thus, anti-Americanism in Canada, in traditional terms, is linked to Tory conservatism. Lipset claims that continued Canadian allegiance to the British monarchy contributes to a greater sense of legitimacy for hierarchical distinctions in Canada than in the United States. Hence, "Canadian identity is the product of a victorious counter-revolution, and in a sense must justify its raison d'être by emphasizing the virtues of being separate from the United States." The claim is further made that at present the Left wingers rather than the Right wingers are most anti-American and pro-British; although no evidence is adduced for the pro-British sentiment of the Canadian Left. The final aspect of the fourth thesis is that Canadian identity is based on extrinsic reference points to England and the United States; whereas American identify has no such external reference points, but rather sees its Democratic Left ideology as synonymous with the social content of Americanism.

This is, I believe, a fair rendering of the main positions in Lipset's study, all of which are based on the notion that social structure and personal values are interrelated and interactive. In Lipset's analysis, values are on a par with structures; hence, the movement in his analysis from quantitative to qualitative measures, and from judgments about the psychological condition to statements about economic differentials, is uninhibited with respect to causal sequence for determinist frameworks.

The work done by Lipset on Canada has not gone unattended by critics. Although the volume of such criticism has been slim, its quality has been noteworthy. The first critique basically concerns Lipset's earlier effort, *Agrarian Socialism*, on the Cooperative Commonwealth Federation (CCF) in Saskatchewan, which has long been billed as the first socialist regime in North America. A critique made by John W. Bennett and Cynthia Krueger casts grave doubts on the sort of ideological definitions from which Lipset scans prone to generalize. The main propositions of their critique can be summarized as follows:

Saskatchewan socialism can better be understood as agrarian pragmatism, since the mass of farmers were never converted to socialist principles or politics. There was never a threat of nationalization of collectivization. Such prairie socialism is part of a strong cooperativism, which has traditionally been strong in that region (in both Canada and the United States). Such cooperativist movements do not advocate a basic change from capitalism, do accept profits and private entrepreneurship, and merely seek to extend capitalist benefits, such as medical aid, to wider numbers. Lipset mistakenly viewed this CCF force as a leftward drift, when in fact, such support is largely pragmatic. Whether the ideological rhetoric was Left or Right, the farmers' main concern has always been pragmatic. Socialism is basically an industrial ideology; whereas Saskatchewan cooperativism is basically an agrarian ideology. The rural culture tends to be anti-bureaucratic and individualistic. In this sense, the victory of the CCF was basically an expression of these agrarian conservative instincts, but still largely pragmatic. The anti-Lipset framework is supported by the fact that the Liberal government changed little in CCF-instituted policies and programs. There was no sign of drastic legislative reaction, or popular antagonism for socialism. Thus, unlike the "protest movement becalmed" notion of Leo Zakuta, CCF cooperativism merely became institutionalized. But the end of socialism was not the end of ideology in Canada, only the end of a special phase of prairie pragmatism.

A second critique, made by Tom Truman is more directly related to the theme of revolution and counter-revolution, and to Lipset's wider-ranging analysis and characterization. Truman is adroit in what might be called intrinsic analysis—taking as a given (although without any commitment to the given) the Lipset position on the pattern variables and/or value dimensions in locating differences between the United States and Canada. The essence of his critique can be summarized as follows;

If the percentage of national income spent on education rather than crude measures of the attendance in higher educational plans is the basis of comparison, Canada leads rather than follows the United States in the developmental impulse. If so idiosyncratic a measure as the breakdown of political libertarianism is used as a measure of egalitarianism, then it must be said that it is a fallacy to assume that Canada inherited its legal safeguards from the British tradition. Indeed, the fine art of witch-hunting by the post-war governments proved the equal of the Mccarthy phenomenon in the United States. With crime statistics, i.e., homicide and criminality as symptoms of development impulses, Truman accepts Lipset's figures, arguing instead that high crime in the United States is related to the special circumstances of United States history: racism, monetarism, prevalent income gaps between rich and poor, and the conventional wisdom about crime; whereas Canadian society shows higher propensities to organicism and integrity, and less capitalist extremes show in the economic indicators. The differences between Canada and the United States reside in a concept of equality that is narrowly defined. For Truman, the failure of socialism in the United States is not linked to the incorporation of socialism into a democratic ethos, so much as to the passing from a society of agrarian control to one of white-collar control. In such a situation, the proletarian class never was able to form a mass political movement to secure its own ends, as has been the case to a greater extent with the New Democratic Party in Canada and the Labour Parties of England and Australia. A most significant factor noted by Truman, and one I fear too frequently left out of the reckoning in this matter of values, is the role of World War II in democratizing Canadian goals and ambitions. In part, Truman acknowledges an unthinking support of Britain led to unswerving participation in the war. He also notes, quite properly, how the war changed Canadian aspirations from a minority dependent role to one of unity and parity. In other words, extrapolating from Truman's argument, the phenomenon of war had its own leveling tendencies; and one ought not exaggerate the "counter-revolutionary" strains in the British connection.

Canada was never simply British. It exists in a North American context in which a French-speaking enclave is subordinate to English-speaking dominion, which in turn is subordinate to an American economy. Center-hinterland relationships are actually more like a pecking order of power. This pecking order, rather than any abstract dialectic of revolution and counter-revolution, is at the core of major differences between the United States and Canada.

A third, more recent critique seeks to extend Truman's work by dealing with Lipset's theoretical and methodological assumptions, rather than simply calling into doubt the data on which the findings are based Essentially, John Shiry (1973) argues that the indicators Lipset uses do not measure the values of a population, and certainly not those of the Canadian population. While his analysis extends far beyond the work done by Lipset and focuses with equal concern on the "elitist" assumptions of S.D. Clark and, in part, John Porter, he does recognize Lipset as the originator of much of this type of argument. His analysis falls into the following categories:

The idea that educational expenditures can be taken as an indicator of a nation's mass value system is fallacious. It assumes a citizen participation model of politics that is largely fallacious, based on tautological reasoning and circular argument. Mass values range far beyond the limits of proscribed expression, and hence they cannot be measured by the uncritical use of behavioral data. Thus, values cannot be conceived as basic or ultimate, as Lipset does, but as derived from the peculiar opportunity structure available in Canada. Values are not disembodied spirits, but beliefs that attain importance only within a well-defined institutional arrangement. What Lipset fails to realize is that the study of values must extend into a study of the historical sources of inequality, into mechanisms of social control even more than social psychology. It might well be that the direct study of values is of no profit in acquiring knowledge about social structures. Shiry holds that it is a gross error to assume that levels of expenditures on education, police force size, crime rates, divorce rates, or even levels of investment are end products of a particular set of mass values. They are more likely to be responses by elites to a set of institutional demands and constraints.

One serious problem with Shiry's total rejection of value analysis is that it too lends itself to charges to elitism. Shiry asserts that it is unreasonable to study mass socialization to orientations which assume a degree of active political involvement. But if this is the case, then just what is one to make of the interaction of mass and elites? Does Shiry not assume elite domination of all key decisions, irrespective and without response to mass interests as expressed in mass values? It is surely one thing to argue the case for a more intense study of elite management of those institutions which determine industrialization and package mass values; it is quite another to deny the existence of such mass pressures in the form of values. In other words, even if we accept the charge that there is a need for a study of elite behavior, this does not preclude a study of mass behavior. Similarly, elites are not the only ones with institutions. Masses too have institutions, such as political parties and trade unions. Thus, what is needed is greater dialectical analysis rather than simply more attention to elites—which after all have been widely studied by scholars like Porter and Clark among others.

Without diminishing previous efforts to deal with Lipset's position, or adopting the unseemly posture of assuming a need to "go beyond" critiques already cast, there does remain a cluster of considerations that require further examination. The analysis of national character is a treacherous business, and as field anthropologists have learned, one that may tell us more about the analyst than about those being analyzed. Such character analysis is compounded when judgments about entire societies, particularly complex societies, are involved. Lipset is, of course, aware of such difficulties. To minimize their effects, he employs the dichotomous categories called pattern variable analysis devised by Parsons (universal-particular/achievement-ascription/self-orientation-collective-orientation) and adds to this his own polarized category: egalitarianism-elitism.

This is Lipset's most explicit acknowledgement of his debt to the master of American macro-functionalism. But the Parsonian approach rests on the substitution of value analysis for interest analysis; specifically, it tends to emphasize differences about ideals and aspirations as these are translated into educational and social opportunities; and to drastically minimize differences that may occur between economic classes geographical sections, ethnic and linguistic groups, and between provincial and national exercise of power. In a nation such as Canada, where the sharpest sorts of delineations exist in precisely such terms, to proceed with a pattern variable analysis of nationalism and revolution means either the tacit or overt suppression of key pieces of data, or raising the level of discussion to such a high degree of abstraction that random pieces of information legitimate *a priori* certain kinds of theorizing.

Lipset manages to do both: he limits his discussion to English Canada and excludes French Canada (and thus does not actually examine the degrees to which Canadian identity, even value identity, exists as a whole). He also draws broad-scale inferences about comparative levels of achievement orientation from the thinnest sort of data concerning Canadian higher education. Thus he simply assumes that higher education is a function of high economic aspirations—which no longer seems quite so true in the United States, much less in Canada. Thus, we are in the midst of subjective analysis, rather than sociological analysis. The critic of Lipset's work must do two things simultaneously: indicate how reality and ideals differ, and also how even at the level of ideals, or value theory, alternative explanations are not only possible, but even preferable to Lipset's notion of a Canadian reaction to the United States generated by counter-revolution and fidelity to the British Empire is only partially correct. There is another and different vision of this Canadian love/hate relationships, one based on an unresolved paradox between a desire for the cultural unity of the English-speaking world as a whole, in contrast to a desire for full Canadian autonomy and nationality.

John Porter offers yet a different account of Canadian conservatism: as a phenomenon rooted in strong ethnic differentiation which can result only in those continuing dual loyalties which prevent the emergence of a Canadian identity. As a result, not necessarily the Imperial connection but ethnic fragmentation helps explain Canadian self-abnegation. But like so many other things, what was written less than a decade ago already seems obsolete.

The Canadian experience reveals powerful ties of friendship to the United States, at the very time expressions of hostility are greatest. But what Lipset forgets is that Canada, throughout the twentieth century, has found itself in a cohesive relationships to the United States in all military situations. In World War I, in World War II, and even in some of the United States' mini-wars, Canadian support has been vital. One gets the distinct impression from Canadian literature that the impact of the wars has been greater in Canada than in the United States; not only for the temporary cohesiveness brought about to an English-speaking union, but, beyond that, to a sense of participation not in counter-revolutionary activities, but in the international struggle for democracy. In short, one must not exaggerate Canadian animosity for the United States, specifically in the sobering light of twentieth-century history, in which Canada and the United States were allied with England in its major struggles and triumphs.

The data which Lipset adduces for Canadian traditional behavior derives in considerable measure from marriage and divorce statistics. Here several points should be raised: first, whether divorce is a true measure of an open society is dubious, since many divorces end up in remarriage (something approximating roughly three fourths of all first marriages end up in remarriage); and hence the reinforcement of traditional conservative values. At second look, Canadian statistics tend to dampen the numbers of divorces in French Catholic Canada, and at the same time, do not present evidence on abandonment and separation without legal divorce—a practice common in both English and French Canada prior to the divorce laws of 1967–68. Finally, these very divorce laws, coming as they do belatedly but nonetheless nationally, have tended to promote the idea of divorce not just for reasons of infidelity, but for the more liberal reasons now adduced and in practice in a few of the states within the United States. The Royal Commission Report of 1967, which led to the enactment of-the new divorce decrees of 1968, makes it quite plain that Canada as a whole is at least equal to the United States in its liberal attitude toward divorce. The data on numbers and rates of divorce for the pre- and post-divorce legislation dramatically reveal this new-found Canadian private "liberation."

The information reveals, even if we accept Lipset's criteria that high divorce rates promote values of secularization and ultimately of development, a closing of the gap between the United States and Canada with respect to divorce regulations. Here as elsewhere, the data demonstrate that the differences between Canada and the United States, at the level of values, are better framed in terms of cultural lag than in terms of polarized value preferences.

The data on criminality and homicide similarly reveal marked tendencies toward closing the "cultural gap." The crime rates of Canada, while still considerably under those of the United States, can better be explained by the absence of the extremes of wealth and poverty characteristic of the United States, than by the developmental thesis. Both visible poverty and visible opulence are far less in Canada, and the clustering of working or middle classes is far more noticeable. Add to this the absence of large scale racial strife, and much of the crime difference can be explained without reference to Lipset's developmental hypothesis.

It is interesting to note the change over the decade between 1962 and 1972 in both the rates and velocity of crime in Canada. Even if we take the notion of entrepreneurial deviance as a measure of development, the Canadians score quite high on such a measure. Admittedly, there is a certain peculiarity in adducing crime-rate data and its increase as an expression of high development, or as that kind of dislocation which occurs in personal interaction that can promote high development. Still, if we take this as a true measure, the Canadians have every right to expect equity in development in the forthcoming period.

A severe jolt to the Lipset developmental thesis with respect to crime is given by the fact that discrepancy in data between United States and Canada is far greater for crimes of violence (which have nothing to do with developmental innovation) than for non-violent crimes of pecuniary gain. But even violent crime rates have shot up in Canada in recent years. One must add only that it remains highly quixotic, indeed idiosyncratic, to draw upon such indicators to prove that Canada is either developing or democratizing-or both.

When one turns to the data on religion and religious worship, a similar pattern of closing the cultural gap becomes evident. First, on the rough data between Protestants and Catholics, the ratios are not that much different between Canada and the United States. What is different is the extremely high proportion of French ethnics who are Catholic, and white Anglos who are Protestant. In other words, the raw totals of percentages are not that much different so much as the gap between Catholic and Protestant along ethnic as well as religious lines. Even here the similarities between the two nations are quite noticeable. Rates of attendance are parallel, an absence of fanaticism is common to both nations, and above all, both nations have experienced religious pluralism. A new influx of post-World II immigrants brought to Canadian shores many peoples representing the Jewish religion, the Greek Orthodox Church, the religions of India, and so on. In any event, the very notion of mosaic rather than melting pot is an indication of how little pulling power or compulsion exists within church life in Canada, so that raw data itself does not really tell us very much about the difference between Canadian traditionalism and American modernism. Indeed, the fact that approximately 36 percent of marriages in Canada are intermarriages, and that the 64 percent intrafaith marriages are buoyed by the 90 percent intrafaith marriage situation which obtains in the Jewish community, reveals that religious pluralization is considerably higher than Lipset allows for.

The critical data that Lipset analyzes is that of education, in which he attempts to show that the roughly 30 percent of people in higher education in the United States compare most favorably with the 10 percent in Canadian higher educational life. Indeed, if this were the case, it might be possible to adduce this to illustrate the idea of higher achievement and less ascriptive orientation among United States citizens. But here too we can see the loosening of the ties of the Imperial connection and the strengthening of the ties with the American connection. The growth of Canadian university life has been nothing short of phenomenal in the decade from 1962 to 1972. At the accelerated rate now in existence, it is conceivable that educational mobility among Canadians will rival that of the United States by the turn of the century. What makes this such a remarkable achievement is that Canada, in order to accelerate its educational program, has to pour a considerable amount of excess national profits into higher education; and beyond that, it represents a break in the organizational back of the traditional English oriented university. The mushrooming of Canadian universities, trade and technical schools, indicates indeed a high level of development, both as fact and as explanation. So once again it would have to be said that Lipset's thinking is premised on a continuation of pre-World War II tendencies, rather than post-World War II trends.

The sharp increase in higher education in Canada has moved Canada closer to the United States in percentile levels of enrollment. The narrowing of the gap is equally dramatic at secondary levels of education. Even with an expected leveling out in favor of more balanced growth, the opportunity structure in Canadian education remains considerable, as the Economic Council of Canada reports.

Combined elementary and secondary enrollment is expected to decline absolutely after the mid-1970's, reflecting the sharp decline in total births since the early 106-'s and the fact that the increase in secondary school enrollment ratios will moderate as they approach very high levels. On the other hand, both the enrollment ratios and the numbers of young people attending post-secondary educational institutions should continue to rise (but at a decreasing rate). The increases at the non-university level will be particularly rapid. Some further narrowing in the gaps in enrollment ratios between Canada and the United States can be anticipated. Total full-time educational enrollment for 1980–81 is projected at 6.6 million, compared with 5.8 million in 1967–68. Elementary school enrollment is projected to decline from 4.1 million in 1967–68 to 3.9 million in 1975–76 and to 3.8 million in 1980–81. Secondary school enrollment is projected to increase from 1.3 million in 1967–68 to 1.8 million in 1975–76 and then decline to 1.7 million in 1980–81. In contrast, postsecondary enrollment is projected to more than double between 1967–68 and 1975–76 and then increase by almost one-third over the following five years, reaching about 1.1 million in 1980–81. The projected growth rate in postsecondary education between 1975–76 and 1980–81 applies to both universities and other postsecondary institutions. The growth rate of the latter up to 1975–76 is expected to exceed that of universities.

If crude measures concerning educational expenditures are refined one stage further, we find that by the 1970s Canada was actually producing more Ph.D.s in science and engineering pr capita than the United States. Beyond that, it stood third among industrial countries in the number of qualified scientists and engineers employed in research and development. Indeed, the problem has shifted dramatically from "catching up" to the United States, to avoiding a serious glut of post-graduates on the Canadian market. Recent data suggest a ratio of 3:1 and 4:1 in terms of supply over demand for the teaching field; and a similar but less dramatic oversupply for industry.

The vigor of the Canadian developmental impulse can hardly be exaggerated. For most of the twentieth century, Canada has ranked second among industrial nations in terms of real wage living standards. Indicators of real consumption for a similar stretch of time have placed Canada third in this vital category. Canadian increase in per capita output ran at about 3.2 percent annually for the 1960s, less than the European norms, but still a healthy gain in real economic terms. Further, for 1970, in comparable American dollar terms, the Canadian Gross National Product stood at over $80 billion, with its GNP rates rising faster than the United States'; and in 1971 Canada's GNP jumped by 6 percent in real terms, placing Canada among the highest growth nations in the industrial sector. Twenty years earlier, the Canadian GNP was under 20 billion—so that the rate of real growth can be seen as dramatically on an upswing. Under the circumstancse, it is hard to understand how the "counter-revolutionary" thesis is particularly cogent as an explanation of increasing Canadian economic growth.

It is evident that we have not simply a quantitative problem, but a qualitative one as well. Canada has embarked on a welfare state ideology quite similar to what one finds in the United States, even with the Canadian stated objective to combine welfarism with individual rights. Paradoxically, many present tendencies in Canada, while they heighten pressures toward nationalism, even more directly heighten pressures toward isomorphism, toward Canadian and American value experiences as shared items on the agenda of social development.

One must work hard and imaginatively to bifurcate and bipolarize general data on the United States and Canada. In a series of sixteen social indicators, the positive and negative test scores for the two countries run neck and neck. Divorce data, which Lipset counts on so much for his thesis, is the large exception. But as we have seen, with the new divorce liberalization in Canada, this item too is fast approaching United States norms, in which divorce is used as a measure of a "liberal society" rather than as the existence of "social tension."

Canada is in the same relationship to the United States as the agrarian sector of the United States is in connection to its industrial sector, or for that matter, the Canadian "hinterland" is with respect to the Canadian "metropolitan center". Aspirations are roughly analogous and isomorphic across the nations, but structurally, they represent different parameters. This would indicate that the reference Lipset makes to "values" is indeed quite different from any examination of "interest" elements or "institutional" dominations. The philosophical idealism implicit in the Weberian framework thus comes to distort basic distinctions in two ways: by overstating value differences (i.e., revolutionary versus counter-revolutionary frameworks), and understating institutional differences (degrees of economic and/or political control).

Canada ranks first in the geographic distribution of United States direct investments. Remitted incomes to the Canadians continued its upward trend. The characteristics with respect to dollar investment, new capital outflows, and profitabilities between United States investment in Canada and Latin America are roughly isomorphic; indeed, with the shrinking possibilities of new markets in Europe, these similarities are growing over time. National nuances aside, the branch plant phenomenon is as typical in Latin America as it is in Canada. Both areas serve as manufacturing subsidiaries distributing the full line of parent company products. However, there is a greater emphasis on manufacturing companies in Canada and distribution facilities in Latin America. This is due to the higher amount of open competition for the Latin American markets than has thus far been the case for Canada.

Certain similarities of a non-economic sort must also be included in a sketch of American Canadian relations. The linkages of Canadian military activities with those of the United States are quite parallel to those of Latin America and the United States. The basic linkages are through SACLANT (Supreme Commander, Allied Command Atlantic); military support base to NATO (North Atlantic Treaty Organization); and above all, the air defense coordination through NORAD (North American Radar Early Warning System). In addition, defense matter of joint concern to the United States and Canada is considered by the Permanent Joint Board on Defense, which provides liaison with and advice to both governments. The North Atlantic Treaty Organization established the idea of regional rather than unilateral control. NORAD nonetheless placed the United States in the forefront by virtue of its unique command position following the outcome of the Second World War.

Canadian natural and mineral resources are under far more direct national supervision than their Latin American counterparts; beyond that, there is the sheer availability of such mining and mineral wealth in Canada. Latin America, quite unlike Canada, receives considerable foreign aid and developmental loans; whereas Canada, quite unlike Latin America, has considerable direct investments of its own in the United States. This makes for greater parity between Canada and the United States, and for greater dependency of Latin America upon both the United States and Canada. The relatively balanced import-export situation that obtains between the United States and Canada is unique in the hemisphere. It works to integrate the two nations; whereas the constancy of import-export imbalances, invariably to the disadvantage of Latin America, tends to exacerbate relations between the United States and Canada with respect to Latin America.

The basic nineteenth century American sentiment toward Canada was perhaps never more succinctly or accurately summed up than it was by populist Representative Jeremiah Simpson of Kansas, who in 1892 spoke thus about the hemisphere. "We have some very serious problems to face. Our country is filled up. There is no further west to go. We are full. And we will have to acquire Canada, British America, and Mexico, or overflow." Simpson was not calling for military conquest, but for "an enlightened policy or system which would open up friendly relations with foreign countries, which would give us a market for our surplus, and we would say to the Canadian people: 'Come in under the American flag; join us under a common government, and let us be one people.'" There were many Canadians who were quite ready to respond to such a suggestion, based as it was on a common fear and loathing of the economic supremacy at that time of Great Britain. For its part, Canadian sentiment has increasingly shifted against the worth of the Continental connection, as it had in an earlier period against the Imperial connection. Replacing such a sense of connectedness is the idea of separate nation-state status. Ramsay Cook sums up solid middle-range sentiment when he writes "that we should both keep our frontier open and make certain that our fences are in good repair." He sees no contradiction in this. "To close a frontier suggests the construction of a Chinese wall around an inwardly obsessed garrison suite. A fence is what exists between neighbors who are prepared to trade goods, ideas, and gossip, but who understand perfectly well where rights begin and end. To live and develop, Canada needs fences. No nation will exist for long in a world of closed frontiers." This seems much like a paraphrase of James Eayrs's statement on "good fences"; that Americans "could usefully remember that good neighbors make good friends." Behind these and other like homilies is the bitter lesson that nationalism is a mark of political sovereignty and a stage in the development of economic independence.

If it is possible to conceptualize Canadian responses to the American experience as counterrevolutionary as does Lipset, one can, with equal justification and stronger empirical confirmation, perceive in this response an effort at counternationalism. The forging of a national consensus does not necessarily proceed from a revolutionary war situation. True enough, this is most often the pattern in the twentieth century; but what we are dealing with in Canada is the national consciousness of a middle-class civilization, and the transcendental unity of the bourgeoisie, especially in an advanced stage, does not require armed struggle against former colonialists. Indeed, what deeply impresses me is the extent to which the two World Wars of 1914–1918 and 1939–1945 served as a surrogate revolutionary war effort.

Out of these wartime experiences, not only did a new alignment of world economic powers emerge in which the United States displaced England as the main foreign power in the Canadian economy, but just as significantly, these two conflicts permitted Canada to emerge in a condition of political parity with both England and the United States. Indeed, the fusion of a greater English-speaking union of democratic states was a position perhaps more fervently espoused and adhered to in Canada than in either the United States or England. But when the myth of an English-speaking union became apparent, and when the delicate equilibrium of competition between England and America gave way to an American century in the economic sphere, the Canadians had mustered the political wherewithal to withstand political coercion from the south, and finally to declare a high degree of independence and total political autonomy from England at the same time. And so it came about that the political liberation of Canada took place without a revolutionary war; but to deny the authenticity of that liberation of that account alone, as Lipset strongly implies, is woefully mistaken. But as in other such post-liberation situations, the end of colonialism did not signify the start of the age of aquarius.

The closer one inspects Canadian-American relations, the greater do objective factors of national interest loom as the real determinants of differentiation between the two powers. In this connection, Canadian "exemptionalism" is important. Canadian-American relations can be examined as a series of special exemptions to Canadian business in exchange for special branch penetration of Canadian hinterlands by American business. In exchange for independence, special economic privileges permit Canadian business to operate in an atmosphere of no tariffs or low tariffs. This exemption policy from the United States involves few political and economic costs to the United States.

The study of Canadian-American relations in terms of the dynamic of exemptionalism and exceptionalism affords a way beyond the sophisticated dead-end governing value theory; and no less the nonsensical and less sophisticated dependency model, that arbitrarily assigns external, imperial factors a supreme place without paying proper attention to the inner national logic of a country as large and as wealthy as Canada. Two Canadian writers, R.D. Cuff and J.L. Granatstein, put it well when they note that "the Canadian present has been shaped by the Canadian past. In the current atmosphere of nationalism, with its search for a mythical history, there is a danger that the domestic impulse behind Canada's place in the American system will be over-looked." This formulation is encompassing enough to realize that we are dealing with both Canadian and American realities. The problem is the negotiation of both nations in sound policy, rather than apologetics for, or a denunciation of, either nation in clever formulas.

The importance provided by Lipset is that he has opened up the study of Canada to unparalleled levels of theory and research. The debt owed to him is incalculable. However, his work has also bequeathed formulations that seem less convincing as the century wears on. The research agenda for understanding Canada requires a sense of social history no less than social structure.

From: *Queen's Quarterly*, vol. LXXX, no. 3 (1973). This review portion is drawn from an essay entitled "The Hemispheric Connection." The data mentioned are from this larger version.

83

Knowledge for Democracy*

Lynd, Robert S. and Helen Merrell Lynd

Robert Staughton Lynd might be described as the Sinclair Lewis of sociology. His books *Middletown* and *Middletown in Transition* provide the sociological flesh that makes Lewis's satiric classics, *Babbitt* and *Main Street*, comprehensible as studies in the culture and mores of midwestern America.

Lynd was born in New Albany, Indiana, on September 26, 1892. His major research works, undertaken and coauthored with his wife Helen Merrell, were actually performed in Muncie, Indiana, not far from his birthplace. His background was modest, but he graduated from Princeton University in 1914, and from there went on to earn a Bachelor of Divinity degree at Union Theological Seminary in 1923. A doctorate from Columbia University was granted in 1931 after the publication and in recognition of the first Middletown study. Until his retirement in 1965, he was associated with Columbia. He died on November 1,1970.

Lynd's first major job was as managing editor of *Publisher's Weekly*, the trade magazine of the publishing industry. His next position was director of the small city project of the Institute of Social and Religious Research, which directly, albeit modestly, underwrote the Muncie research. *Middletown* may be the first sociological work to be distributed and promoted to the general public as a trade book. According to Helen Lynd, the book was displayed in book store windows alongside the leading novels of the time. The relationship between his sociology and the quality of writing was at least partially due to his vocational background in publishing, then a rare training ground for a sociologist. Recalling him at the time of his death in 1970, Seymour Martin Lipset noted that Lynd not only "devoted an enormous amount of time to his students," but that he was always available to help them rewrite, edit, and even

---

* Robert S. Lynd and Helen Merrell Lynd, *Middletown: A Study in Contemporary American Culture* (New York: Harcourt, Brace and Jovanovich, 1929).

Robert S. Lynd and Helen Merrell Lynds, *Middletown in Transition: A Study in Cultural Conflicts* (New York: Harcourt, Brace and Jovanovich, 1937).

restructure their papers. His publishing experience clearly remained with Lynd as pedagogue and as researcher.

Today, Lynd would probably be described as an anthropologist of complex organizations. Certainly his work defies easy labeling. Not since Alexis de Tocqueville's *Democracy in America* have we had such a careful analysis of the daily life of America, middle America in this case. The book subjects one Indiana community to the same kind of intense scrutiny that de Tocqueville gave the entire United States. *Midletown* illumined, for a generation of social science, the essence of the American way of life. Probably no other single work published between World War I and World War II so precisely and devastatingly delineated what the nation had become. *Middletown* was described by H.L. Mencken as "one of the richest and most valuable documents ever concocted by an American sociologist," and by Stuart Chase as "an unparalleled work: nothing like it has ever been attempted; no such knowledge of how the average American community works and plays has ever been packed within the covers of one book."

Middletown makes little conscious effort to posit the centrality of one variable or factor over another. It is divided into six large sections. The first, on the economy, documents "Getting a Living." The second and third sections are concerned with family life, linking problems of housing, child rearing, food, clothing, and schooling. The fourth and probably the most innovative section is on leisure. This material includes early mass communication research. It analyzes the leisure activities of middle Americans in pictures and periodicals, selecting and viewing, precisely in terms of mass communication. The fifth section concerns religious observance and practices, analyzing varieties of Protestant worship, but also, showing how organizations such as the YMCA link religion to community. The notion of community organizes the final section, showing how community is related to the machinery of government. The very fragmentation of community points out the insignificance of bureaucracy in the social life of Middletown. These last sections clearly owe much to Lynd's activities in the mid-1920s as a missionary preacher in the oil fields of Montana.

The book took several years to produce. Robert Lynd lived in Middletown with his wife Helen for one-and-a-half years; their assistants lived there for an additional half year. Tables imaginatively illustrate the book, and while some of the data provide only a careful reworking of state and national data, other tables examine sources of disagreement between children and their parents, and books borrowed in the adult department of the public library. These show an imaginative concern with intimate detail rare in the annals of sociology up to that time.

What gives added character to *Middletown* is its historical specificity. The Lynds provide a documentary accounting of the life of a town at two selected periods: 1890 and 1924, rather than attempting to do a detailed study of the history of the intervening years. Such cross-sectional analysis provides a sensitive appreciation of the cultural tension between past and present generations. *Middletown* is in retrospect best seen as an analysis of the secularization process in American society: a veritable model of why modernization occurs and how social change takes place in an advanced industrial society.

Middletown in Transition is another pathbreaking effort in a tradition of reevaluating and reanalyzing data. It examines what happened in the decade between 1924 and 1935. The Lynds took seriously critiques of their earlier work. Their follow-up study, while lacking some of the historical possibilities of the earlier effort, builds upon that earlier work and attempts to apply techniques that had evolved in social science in the intervening decade. As John Madge sagaciously noted, "If Middletown had changed it is also necessary to substantiate the claim . . . that there had been a profound development in the thinking of the Lynds."

Not only did the Lynds return to study the same town; doing so they clearly changed their own estimates of what was important. The machinery of government, for example, was no longer subsumed under community activities, nor was religion given a whole section. It was reduced to a chapter. This reflected changing mores of American society: namely, progress in the secularization that the Lynds discussed at the end of *Middletown*, a sense of new problems emerging in the depression of the 1930s. The world of Sinclair Lewis's early novels had broken down. Class bias gave way to class antagonisms, stating the facts yielded to making clear the sources of power. While Middletown's citizenry continued to retain the values by which it lived, the impact of economic chaos at home and fascism and socialism abroad, compelled Middletown to face both ways. Trade unionism became acceptable; reluctant adaptation to the new world became inevitable. If the follow-up study ends on a note of uncertainty, taken together the *Middletown* studies remain a most significant record of this period in American social life. The Lynds's ability to weave ethnography, stratification, and quantitative data into a meaningful whole has rarely been equaled in sociological literature. One might wonder if their open-ended choice of methodologies makes such broad-ranging work currently suspect. There is strong evidence that Lynd himself had serious questions about how generalizable such field researches actually are.

In *Knowledge for What?* (1939), a book subtitled: *The Place of Social Science in American Culture*, Lynd attempted to come to terms, indirectly at least, with a new methodological emphasis in American sociology. He argued that scholars have become technicians who would lecture on navigation while the ship goes down. This book has a bitter tone; it reveals a pessimistic belief that even if the new methodological sociologists should take the wheel, they would not really know how to steer a meaningful course. It is not that Lynd thought social scientists should go in for pretentious soothsaying, still he recognized that a sense of the fragility of the future should not result in the sorts of inhibitions that make broad-ranging social science research unpalatable.

Lynd clearly was a sociological pragmatist, urging a careful middle course between what C. Wright Mills was later to call abstract empiricism and grand theory. This approach was underwritten by a strong Columbia tendency to emphasize culture over society—a tendency that Lynd very much shared. From John Dewey in philosophy to Franz Boas and Ruth Benedict in anthropology, the emphasis was on a cultural framework, subsumed under society, economy, and the polity. In a special way, Lynd was like a swam in a department where he seemed to be increasingly perceived, by some at least, as an ugly duckling. It was his philosophical anthropology, rather than a lack of statistical methodology, that ultimately frustrated Lynd and led him to shift his priorities from intellectual pursuits to departmental matters.

Lynd was involved in bringing the best scholars to the sociology department of Columbia, even when he doubted the efficacy of the methods used. The methodological wing represented by Paul F. Lazarsfeld and the Bureau of Applied Social Research had Lynd's unwavering support. Although they were intellectually on different wave lengths, Lazarsfeld and Lynd remained close personal friends. Lazarsfeld never forgot the role of Lynd in securing him a position at Columbia in 1940, nor the place of the *Middletown* study in his own community research efforts of the 1930s. Lynd, for his part, made frequent reference to Lazarsfeld's study of the Austrian village of Marienthal in *Middletown in Transition*. Lynd also shared with Robert K. Merton a concern for the middle range of social research. He was probably intellectually closer to Merton than to anyone else among the senior staff in the department of Columbia, and they worked closely on decision-making levels in the department. Lynd was also largely instrumental in bringing Mills to Columbia from the University of Maryland. He was central in a postwar crop of social scientists, headed by Lipset, who in many ways continued the dialogue about culture and democracy in new forms and in a postwar crisis period. Lynd, however, broke his silence between 1939 and 1956 long enough to write an extremely provocative, even crucial, critique of Mills's *Power Elite*.

When one takes into account the paucity of Lynd's writings between *Knowledge for What?* in 1939 and his review essay on Mills in *The Nation* in 1956, the importance of the critique becomes self-evident. Lynd had been preoccupied with the development of a theory of power and democracy ever since *Middletown*. For Lynd, power as a social resource was absolutely necessary for the operation of society. Like physical energy, power could be harnessed for human welfare or corrupted by misuse. The development of democratic goals and the enhancement of a pluralistic national culture is, therefore, a responsibility of any sociological critique of power. The Jeffersonian emphasis on democratic life is precisely the most outrageous hypothesis contained in *Knowledge for What?* Lynd shared with Mills a concern for the proper use and applications of power, which he too had found much abused by elite groups. Yet he chides Mills for failing to undertake an analysis of power that extends its meaning for democracy. According to Lynd, the chief task for the observer of power is to develop a theory of power for a given society. But according to Lynd, this was not what Mills aimed at. He was sorely out of sympathy with Mills's lack of commitment to a liberal democratic ethos and consequently finds that his ambiguous "esposé" lacks concreteness with relation to America as well as any sense of meaningful alternatives. Lynd also found elite analysis in social science limited, if not distasteful, because it obscured or ignored the basic characteristics of a given social system. It bred a superficial analysis that amounted to a way out of dealing with capitalism, socialism, and class structure. In this sense, Lipset picked up on this sense of Lynd's frustration, and his *The First New Nation* in some sense proceeded along the lines indicated by Lynd in his critique of Mills.

It would be unfair to think of Lynd's contribution as residing solely in the work of his students. Lynd was close to present-day Marxist analysis of American society; certainly his claims that Mills overlooked important evidence linking present-day American capitalism and the capitalism of the nineteenth century struck that note. Lynd indicates that Mills did not systematically analyze the American economy and that by focusing on great changes. Mills failed to account for property as a power base linking the centuries. For Lynd, social science needed to understand the chief characteristics of the American system and not a given institution within the social order. Finally, Lynd breaks with Mills by assuming that the capitalist character of the United States defines the quality of society in the United States from the outset.

By all reports, Lynd was fair and tough, deeply committed to the idea of graduate education and to sociology itself as a cultural transmission belt. He also had a lifelong commitment to the Columbia style of education as a civilizing process, civilization itself being measured by its advanced education institutions. He was a plebeian comfortable in a world of patricians. To his lasting credit, the values he espoused and lived by remained consistent and consonant. He linked the sociological tradition and the problems of social science with the democratic culture and the larger problems of society.

Helen Merrell Lynd, two years his junior and his co-worker, carved out a career in many disciplines. She was born on St. Patrick's Day in 1894. Her parents were devoutly religious, with that element of social justice characteristic of many midwestern Congregationalists. She graduate from Wellesley College in 1917, where the strongest single influence was Mary S. Case who introduced her to philosophy, particularly Hegel, and according to her colleague at Sarah Lawrence, Bert J. Loewenberg, "gave her an abiding zest for both." She married Lynd in 1921, taught for many years at Sarah Lawrence College and has remained in the New York City area since her retirement in 1965. If the word *polymath*, someone learned in many fields, has any meaning, it certainly applies to her. Not only is she coauthor of the famed *Middletown* series, which alone would make her a figure to contend with in sociology, but she can also claim a place in the disciplines of history, psychology, and philosophy. She was entirely at home with the poetry of Shelley, the plays of Shaw, and the novels of Dostoevsky. She was versed in the technical literature of an amazing variety of fields—from the philosophy of science to experimental psychology. Perhaps this breadth was essential to a work like *Middletown*, which in its very nature transcended many disciplines and many imageries.

After the completion of *Middletown in Transition*, Helen Lynd carved a path of her own, starting with her remarkable book *England in the Eighteen-eighties*, a work in social history done initially as a doctoral thesis under the supervision of the dean of history at Columbia, Carleton J.H. Hayes. The impact of *Middletown* showed in the organization of *England in the Eighteen-eighties.* It is divided into "Material Environment," "Environment of Ideas," "Political Parties," "Organized Labor," "Religious Education," and "Organization for Change." There is the same dialectical tension between the old and the new; the discrepancy between material abundance and satisfaction of human wants on the one hand, and the continued poverty of the masses on the other. Helen Lynd understood England in the 1880s as being involved with problems of social organization compatible with democratic individualism, a problem also true of the United States fifty years later.

Helen Lynd's style is wide-ranging, with a transparent clarity that disguises the seriousness of her efforts. She worked out the essential tension between freedom and authority in a series of discussion of party life: namely, the tension between conservatives and liberals; between organized labor and what might be described as agitators and reformers; between the High Church and Methodist Quakers and other nonconformists; between the crude barbarism of the private schools and the tragedy of lower-class education, what were called the ragged schools for the ragged classes. A strong sense of the social contradictions in British society inform the book through its examination of a decade of unresolved conflicts involving the principal political actors, writers, and playwrights of the time, all of whom illuminated the central themes of freedom and authority.

While this work seems remote from her classic volume a decade later, *On Shame and the Search for Identity* (1958), in a way it reveals the same sense of dialectical tension in concrete settings. Even in discussing such psychological categories as shame and guilt, the nature of language, and clues to identity, she retained a lively sense of the concrete, constantly illustrating her theme with references to the scientific and literary leaders of the time. It remained characteristic of Helen Lynd that she referred to work as wide ranging as that of C.P. Snow, Norbert Wiener, and Alfred Korzybski, all with a gracious weaving of information and ideas that in lesser hands could easily have fallen apart. This book shares with her earlier work a strong democratic impulse. The authority of the earlier work became a search and realization of identity. Helen Lynd distinguishes between guilt, which is a response to standards that have been internalized, and shame, which is a response to criticism or ridicule by others. Guilt, she argues, is centrally a result of a transgression, a crime, a violation of a specific taboo or legal code by a definite voluntary act, whereas shame is linked to uncovering, to exposure, to wounding, to experiences of exposé, and to peculiarly sensitive and vulnerable aspects of the self.

This work is far more than a purely psychological account of pleasure and pain, and reward and punishment. It involves a general theory of personality development, linked to the evolution of historical thought. The work of Georg Simmel and Dorothy Lee plays a large part. Helen Lynd appreciated the extent to which concepts of psychological analysis are linked to mechanisms of social control intended to minimize conflict. But whether such reduction of conflict is good is determined not by personality adjustment but by historical tendencies. This made Lynd's work quite different from conventional neo-Freudian writings of the 1950s. Her approach to questions of: Who am I?; where do I belong? was strongly linked to sociology and history. Showing how such questions are formulated in ancient, medieval, and modern times, she observed that notions such as pride or shame are linked to general theories of religion, theology, and ideology. For Lynd, it is not the sin of pride but the capacity of pride to transcend shame, and therefore, to reach a new level of identity or even lucidity, that is central in raising consciousness. Unfortunately, she provided few clues as to how the guilt axis and the shame axis can be resolved by creating a pride-humility axis. Still, because at the time the social sciences emphasized intense social control and negative reaction to deviance, *On Shame and* the *Search for Identity* is more than a product of a generation in itself. It is also part of Helen Lynd's longstanding commitment to the idea that individual freedom is integrally linked to social democracy.

Critical acclaim for *On Shame and the Search for Identity* was widespread. Psychiatrists felt her work to be of seminal importance. Franz Alexander noted that "Mrs. Lynd's study goes further in depth and in comprehensiveness than any other contemporary writing on the subject. It is a sensitive, highly suggestive discourse on that most human of all faculties—reflection of the self on the self." And Theodor Reik added that "Her perceptiveness and sensitiveness, especially felt in her differentiation of guilt and shame, as well as her intellectual sincerity and the originality of her observation, made her book a remarkable work." He might have added doubly so, since Helen Lynd was trained in history, wrote a pioneering work in sociology, and taught in philosophy. Helen Lynd, like Robert Lynd, revealed that powerful element of free-thinking autodidacticism that was a family trademark.

A number of her important occasional writings were collected in *Toward Discovery*. In his introductory essay, Bert J. Loewenberg properly notes that "Helen Lynd is concerned with the context of discovery; the environment of ideas; education in contemporary society; and the nature of historical objectivities." He also understands that ultimately, for Lynd, discovery is really a way of growth as well as a technique of inquiry, and that to discover in a true sense also involves a diversity of methods. In this collection of papers all of these themes are amply illustrated.

In the 1950s, Helen Merrell Lynd achieved political notoriety by becoming courageously involved in the response to McCarthyism within university life. Her essay "Truth at the University of Washington" took to task university administration and faculty supporters. Various tenured professors were found to be competent scholars, objective teachers without academic fault, but members of the Communist party and hence incapable of objectivity. Such issues deeply divided the academic community. Helen Lynd was always on the side of the victims of McCarthyism; even her occasional papers showed the same tension between freedom and authority, identity and guilt. Her writings went far beyond placid formalism. During a period when nearly any defense of Communist party members was tantamount to inviting disaster, she was able to write:

> Freedom and truth must be sought in the world we live in, not in a vacuum. With the worst that anyone can say about the Communist Party, I cannot discover any reading of this evidence about what has happened at the University of Washington that supports the belief that there can be more dictatorial power over teachers in the United States by the Communist Party than by Boards of Regents; or that the search or truth is more threatened by Communists than by arbitrary action of Boards of Regents and Canwell Committees. I cannot discover any readings of this evidence which supports the belief that purging Communists is in the interests of independent teaching, or of democracy.

If Robert Lynd had a clear impact on his intellectual progeny, Helen Lynd had an equally powerful impact on familial progeny. They had two children, Andrea and Staughton. The latter in particular, as evidence through his own writings in history and social science and his involvement in everything from the anti-Vietnam War movement to legal advocacy of organized labor in the midwest, exhibits a fusion of radical ideas and social action. Helen Lynd's final statement to the graduating class at Sarah Lawrence in 1964 stands a fit epithet to her careers and writing and those of her husband:

> So we cross the bridge into a new country. We go alone. But we take with us some knowledge of what it means to probe deeply into new worlds of learning and to glimpse all that lies beyond and is yet unexplored. And we take with us the gaiety, the delight, the sustenance of having known each other here—a knowing that will continue with us. We go in expectation of what may lie ahead.

From *International Encyclopedia of the Social Sciences*, vol. 18, (New York: The Free Press, Macmillan Publishing Company, 1979), pp. 471–76.

84

Revolution, Retribution and Redemption*

Solzhenitsyn, Aleksandr

The Gulag Archipelago is a classic statement of social reality. It will rank as a foremost contribution to the literature on power and powerlessness long after the biography of the author ceases to be a point of contention or argumentation. A sure measure of a classic is that any one specialist is unable either to encapsulate or for that matter emasculate its contents. From this flows a second measure of high quality: the desire it arouses in every field and specialist to interpret the book's contents from a particular professional vantage point. In a work such as this, ubiquity and grandeur go together.

Since *The Gulag Archipelago* is a work of autobiography as well as of biography, sociology, and history, it is impossible not to comment or Solzhenitsyn, although the efforts to lionize, as well as to dismiss this extraordinary man, are quite independent of and irrelevant to this latest publication. Yet, *The Gulag Archipelago* also stands apart from the personal career of a single individual, even its author. Indeed, the work is more than the sum of the 277 other contributions to the volume, many made by persons Solzhenitsyn has kept anonymous. While it can be considered as all one piece with his other works, specifically, *One Day in the Life of Ivan Denisovich*, and his more recent novels: *The Cancer Ward* and *The First Circle*, this volume is singular. *The Gulag Archipelago* itself is only two-sevenths of a work, only two parts

*Aleksandr Solzhenitsyn, *The Gulag Archipelago 1918–1956; An Experiment in Literary Investigation* (I: The Prison Industry and II: Perpetual Motion), Thomas P. Whitney (translator) (New York and London: Harper & Row, Publishers, 1974), pp. 660.

Aleksandr Solzhenitsyn, *The Gulag Archipelago, 1918–1956: An Experiment in Literary Investigation* (III: The Destructive-Labor Camps and IV: The Soul and Barbed Wire). Thomas P. Whitney (translator) (New York and London: Harper & Row, Publishers, 1975) pp. 712.

Aleksandr Solzhenitsyn, *The Gulag Archipelago. 1918–1956: An Experiment in Literary Investigation* (V: Katorga; VI: Exile and VII: Stalin Is No More). Harry Willetts (translator) (New York and London: Harper & Row, Publishers, 1978), pp. 558.

of what the author intends as an experiment in literary investigation. Thus, those who would argue that the book has exaggerations or mistakes must be cautioned, first because of the incomplete nature of what is contained and second because on the basis of what is herein contained one can hardly doubt that the next five parts, should they ever appear, would prove no less compelling or convincing.

Solzhenitsyn is a writer. It would be a mistake to call him a sociologist, or for that matter, a novelist. He conveys experiences, he recites the truths of an entire society. He captures the essence of civilization in the behavioral degeneration of one individual toward another. On the other hand, in the tradition of literary realism, his individuals typify and represent an archetype within society as a whole. Beyond that, Solzhenitsyn is entirely a product of Soviet society and of the Russian literary tradition. His intellectual vision is fused with a sense of politics characteristic of Soviet-Marxism as a whole and with a capacity for irony characteristic of Russian literature, particularly its nineteenth-century classic period. He knows nothing of formal social science techniques, could probably care less about ethnographic safeguards, and is not interested in characterizing a society from the point of view of a general theory of political systems. Yet, few works have ever told us more about the political system of the Soviet Union, the history of an organization called the Communist party, or the fate of individuals within the penological system known as the USSR. Solzhenitsyn takes for granted that the Soviet Union itself is a total institution, a network of integrated agencies of coercion dedicated to the survival and promulgation of maximum state power over minimum human beings. Few have been privy to write from inside the whale, yet even those who have suffered similar outrages have been unable to create such a compendium of horrors.

The Gulag Archipelago should be viewed as a series of experiences, a set of lessons in fear and courage, in being oppressed and in doing the bidding of the oppressor, in working the system and in being ground down by the system. Whatever polarities come to the human mind appear in *The Gulag Archipelago*. In this sense, Solzhenitsyn has written the great Soviet dialectic, the supreme work of literary and social analysis that finally, after 70 years, has put the Soviet experience into a perspective that can at least be theoretically tested. Vague, didactic Leninist tracts on the withering away of the state, outrageous Stalinist equations of Soviet life with the principle of happiness, the Brezhnev-Kosygin reduction of détente into a series of statements about mutual stagnation—these mythological politics give way, crack apart in this documentary history of Russian suffering before, during, and after the Russian Revolution. We now have an experiential (rather than the experimental) work that can help resolve questions about the nature of Soviet society or at least permit a huge step forward in the development of comparative political theory.

This book brings to mind, with its documentary evidence of the slaying and imprisonment of tens of millions of Russians, comparison with the Japanese experience at Hiroshima and Nagasaki as recited in Robert Jay Lifton's *Death in Life* and the Jewish experience of the holocaust as recounted by Raul Hilberg in *The Destruction of the European Jews.* But the Soviet experience is unique, precisely because terror was self-inflicted, because Russians killed and maimed Russians. In this sense, the banality of evil spoken of by Hannah Arendt is carried one step further, for the terror is not American airplanes over defenseless Japanese cities or the destruction of European Jews at the hands of the Nazi Gestapo. However awful these other holocausts may be, the enemy was external.

The Gulag Archipelago offers a special sort of Dostoevskian nightmare in which Russian spies upon Russian, Communist betrays Communist, Red Army officers destroy other members of the Red Army. All of this national self-immolation, in Solzhenitsyn's words "cauterized the wound so that scar tissue would form more quickly." But as Solzhenitsyn hints, there is more involved; the Marxist principle of criticism and self-criticism is raised to a pathological new high, in which ideological purification is a consequence of purgation, in which inner-party struggle replaces in principle all party democracy, in which the notion of scientific evidence is overwhelmed by the notion of organization-inspired rumor. For these reasons, *The Gulag Archipelago* has a fascination and a horror beyond even the literature of concentration camps. To die at the hands of a foreign tormentor or of a powerful adversary may be awful, but at least it is understandable. To suffer the same fate at the hands of one's own is a form of barbarism that permits Solzhenitsyn to consider Soviet bolshevism as almost in a class with German nazism. This point has thoroughly outraged Soviet commentators on the book who have grown up with the belief that the Fascist hordes were history's worst example of cruelty. Solzhenitsyn's comparison of the Soviet system to fascism must itself be ranked an act of extraordinary criticism and condemnation. He has stepped over a psychological threshold of commentary few others have dared cross.

The essence of *The Gulag Archipelago* is the equation of Soviet political sociology with criminology and penology: that is, Soviet-Marxist praxis turns out to be the theory and practice of penology, of imprisonment. In Solzhenitsyn's paradigm of imprisonment, every aspect of the Soviet system is converted into a science. There is a science of arrest, involving a structured system of questioning according to various criteria: at nighttime and daytime, at home and at work, for initial arrests and recidivists, independent versus group arrests. Then there is the science of searches: how to conduct body searches, how to check out houses, even urinals; in short, how to flush out people. Then there is the science of purge: how to isolate the victim from his own party apparatus, which Solzhenitsyn calls a grandiose game of solitaire with rules that are entirely incomprehensible to its players. The enormous impact on

Communist cadres does not derive from their presumed vanguard position, but the other way around: from their unique ignorance of the real nature of Soviet society. The ordinary Russian peasant, spared the patina of Marxism-Leninism, was better prepared for the terror than the Party cadre who bought the package labelled "dictatorship of the proletariat." All of these various and sundry facts of the twentieth-century history of the Soviet science of the destruction of personality had very little to do with the lofty claims of Lenin or Stalin. It is as if Archipelago is a nation apart, as if the Archipelago alone had the right, ironically, to experience social science as social engineering while the rest of the society paraded forth under the mythical banner of Marxism.

We have the amazing experience of social science emerging in the Soviet Union as a function of the rise of a prison system involving tens of millions of people. Pavlovian behaviorism, stripped of its humane ambitions, found its fulfillment in the Soviet state. This transition from Marxism to Pavlovianism was made possible because the Gulag Archipelago was more than a geographic sector. The prison system of the Soviet Union was far flung but it was connected psychologically, as Solzhenitsyn said, fused into a context and almost invisibly, imperceptibly, carried forward as a nation of the damned.

In this sense, Solzhenitsyn's *Gulag Archipelago*, while reminiscent of the writings of Raul Hilberg and Robert Lifton, also makes one think of the writings of Erving Goffman in *Asylumns*. He combines both macro and micro analysis. It is a study in working within a system, surviving it and operating so as to make the system collapse under a weight of its self-imposed lunacy and limitless bureaucracy. A great deal of the book's social psychology has to do with the counter-science of prisoner life, the grim humor of survival in which a mistake means a life, and hence a science that has to be equal or better than the various sciences of arrest, search and seizure, and imprisonment inflicted by the state.

One of Solzhenitsyn's major contributions is to note how terrorism functions as a structural feature of Soviet society, rather than as an episodic moment in Russian time. That is to say, Solzhenitsyn does not simply speak about the Stalin era or special quixotic moments in that era where terror was high, but of the entire period of 1918–1956. The Gulag Archipelago existed because the need for terror replaced the practice of liberty within Russian life. Indeed, there was not very much liberty to begin with, since the Czarist era was hardly concerned with the distribution of justice. However, the revolution of mass democracy never took place, at least for Solzhenitsyn, and terrorism immediately became institutionalized. Within this structural framework, there were special eras, for example, 1929–1930, when 15 million peasants were either slaughtered, uprooted or imprisoned; 1937–1938, when party personnel and intellectuals and cadres of the military were entirely wiped out; and again in 1944–1946, when armed forces personnel, prisoners of war, and all persons having contact with the West were similarly destroyed or disposed. Only the purges of 1937–1938 were remembered because intellectuals and Party personnel were able to articulate their mortification. Millions perished in this Yagoda epoch, but still more perished in the other two high-purge periods. Solzhenitsyn indicates that a fourth huge round of purges was being prepared in 1952–1953, this time against Jews and other national minorities. However, the costs were considered so high that even the other members of the Stalin-appointed Politburo withdrew in horror at the thought of another round. Solzhenitsyn does not clarify matters by confusing waves of terror with Soviet military acquisitions after World War II. The occupation of the Baltic countries was ruthless, but it cannot be placed in the same category as mass waves of terror. One would have to offer the same cautionary note with respect to the Civil War period between 1918–1922. By minimizing the gap between peaks and troughs in the exercise of terror, the state thus lessened the need for analysis.

The most fundamental issue of social theory raised by *The Gulag Archipelago* is whether terror is intrinsic to the Soviet system or is confined to the Stalinist epoch covered by the book. Solzhenitsyn's viewpoint is that terrorism is endemic to the Leninist definition, not to mention the early history of Bolshevism, and continues to plague the Soviet landscape. The viewpoint of a rather wide-ranging group of Soviet scholars and observers is that terrorism was a special technique of Stalinism employed to stimulate development and industrialization in a uniquely backward set of social and cultural circumstances. The problem with Solzhenitsyn's position is twofold. Terrorism was a technique employed by the Czarist secret police with equally telling (but limited) effects. Hence it is not solely endemic to the OGPU under bolshevism but is part of the history of modern Russia as such. Beyond that, a second line criticism must be made: that the terror of wartime conditions is finite and determined by military considerations rather than party idiosyncracies. This might better serve to distinguish the exercise of violence in the Leninist phase from the resort to terror characteristic of the post-1929 Stalinist consolidation. It might also help us understand the turn away from terrorism (and toward benign authoritarian rule) in the post-1956 Khruschev era.

While Lenin in practice preferred norms of "socialist legality," nothing in the Leninist corpus would or could limit terrorism as a strategy and tactic of development. Stalinism is thus a direct theoretical consequence of Leninism, not its diabolical corruption. On June 16, 1974, the very day that a *The New York Times* reviewer cautioned against reading *The Gulag Archipelago* as more than a Stalinist happening, the same *Times* carried a news item on the resurrection of the Stalin cult. Ivan Sladnyuk, unquestionably the figure in the Soviet Writers Union responsible for the expulsion of Solzhenitsyn, has just published an assessment of Stalin as a man who adapted rapidly to the Nazi attack and pulled Soviet war efforts together in contrast to Khruschev's characterization of him as a man "paralyzed by his fear of Hitler like a rabbit in front of a boa constrictor."

My own view is that Soviet society has been transformed from totalitarian to authoritarian modalities. The rise of middle sectors, bureaucrats, teachers, party officials, technicians, skilled craftsmen, and so on has created the seeds of a consumer society without a conflict society, a mass society without mass democracy. This authoritarianism permits the continuation of Bolshevik legends and myths but does not permit the reinstitutionalization of the kind of terrorism that existed under Stalin. History, at least Soviet history, moves in a peculiar way: not one step backward to generate two steps forward, as Lenin suggested; but rather, nineteen steps backward to permit twenty steps forward, as Max Nomad has suggested. Thinking in purely Communist terms, empirically at least, has meant a betraying the ideals of mass democracy in favor of a codebook of party elites. The connection between the freedom of individuals and the necessity of development is not an easy issue to resolve, especially in the light of foreign assaults upon the Soviet Union. Rather than speak the unspeakable about the limits of democracy, it is simpler for Solzhenitsyn to retreat into religious self-actualization. But the foreknowledge that history rarely moves lock step with justice may help us better appreciate the Soviet horror without that collapse of moral nerve always entailed in a categorical denial that the future contains the possibility of improving upon the present.

At the theoretical level, Solzhenitsyn is saying that Russia was not ready for socialism, indeed was unfit for it because of its backward economy and political and social conditions. The Leninists attempted to speed up, even defy history, flying in the face of the Marxian assumptions that each social system must run its full course before there can be a normal transformation of capitalism into socialism. But the very backwardness of Russian society overwhelmed the Bolshevik Revolution, and instead of breaking the back of feudalism, the Bolsheviks wound up breaking the backs of their own followers and supporters. The very attempt to speed up the historical process of economic development in the face of lethargy and backwardness boomeranged, and lethargy and backwardness became the hallmark of Soviet development.

Along with others, I would argue that coercion is a necessary component of development, that the sacrifice needed for high development would be impossible without a mythic sense of purpose. In point of fact, the Soviet state constantly spilled over, failing to distinguish coercion from terrorism, failing to distinguish the forms of state self-protection from the rights of citizens. Within such a system the Soviet Union achieved a level of development that, even today, is lower than that of its capitalist adversaries. The outcome was not simply political betrayal, but economic stagnation and a dangerous kind of frustration, not so much within the Gulag Archipelago but among those who might point to the Archipelago as a possible source, indeed a major source, of the central problem of Soviet life—the problem of legitimacy.

Another central theme in Solzhenitsyn's work is the differential forms of punishment meted out to common criminals vis-a-vis political prisoners. The constant denial of the existence of political prisoners by Soviets (and one would have to add, Americans) becomes a charade to mask the criminal nature of the state itself. Thus, legislation is created to distinguish forms of criminality. "For him [the thief] to have a knife was mere misbehavior, tradition, he didn't know any better. But for you [the political prisoner] to have one was 'terrorism.'" Thus, we have the master dialectic between crime and punishment, the individual and the state, the rights of the person and the limits of authority—and perhaps more painfully—the obligations of the citizen and the rights of the state. *The Gulag Archipelago* is compelling not simply as an exposé of Soviet Party history or its penal system but as an introduction to the entire gamut of normative issues that have plagued Western civilization since its inception. Of course, Marx and Engels recognized these issues and dealt with them by fiat, declaring in principle that socialism would witness the withering away of the state. But in Stalinist practice such a diminution of authority never occurred: circumstances always blocked the path of true historical necessity and in the vise of this cruel hoax, tens of millions of Russians were squeezed to death.

In some sense, Solzhenitsyn's volume suffers the defects of its virtues. Like the American prison literature of Malcolm X or George Jackson, it has a searing intimacy that at times disguises a paucity of theory. No large-scale explanation of the Soviet experience, no cost-benefit analysis is forthcoming. One is left the feeling that no meaningful mass involvement in Soviet society was registered in the past 55 years, a point of view which is clearly unrealistic, first given the Soviet Civil War experience, and above all, the large-scale popular support for the state generated during the war against fascism. It may very well be that the Russian people were fighting for the enduring features of Russian civilization rather than the Bolshevik system. Exactly such a Pan-Slavic appeal was made by the Nazis (with mixed results as the archives of Smolensk indicate), an appeal which seems to have left, at least in small measure, a mark on Solzhenitsyn himself. One must wonder whether the Slavophile in Solzhenitsyn explains why little is said of repression and terror under Czarism and why he offers so little in the study of continuities in Russian terrorism.

Ironically, the theory offered to explain Soviet terrorism comes close to a conspiratorial view of history, as if a supreme being were masterminding the takeover of the Soviet world by the devil and the expulsion of God:

> It was essential to clean out, conscientiously, socialists of every other stripe from Moscow, Petrograd, the ports, the industrial centers, and later on, the outlying provinces as well. This was a grandiose silent game of solitaire, whose rules were totally incomprehensible to its contemporaries, and whose outlines we can appreciate only now. Someone's far-seeing mind, someone's neat hands, planned it all, without letting one wasted minute go by.

This is not to deny that real conspiracy existed. Wherever democracy is absent, the potential for conspiracy is present. But to explain such a gigantic event as the death and imprisonment of tens of millions of people as a conspiracy, it seems to me, falls badly short of what is required at the macro level of explanation. The answer is right at hand: the fundamental impulse of both Stalinism and Leninism was rapid development. Industrial development can sacrifice consumer modernization along with the people it involves in the developmental process. One might argue that the amount of terror was not commensurate with the tasks at hand, that less terror and more benign forms of coercion might have achieved the same results, but the denial of the results is what weakens Solzhenitsyn's analysis. His myopia concerning Soviet achievements also denies him the possibility of a real theory explaining Soviet terrorism and returns him to a primitive Christian view of good and evil that later even Christianity abandoned. Goethe once explained that the trouble with Christianity was its impulse to cast problems in terms of good and evil when, in fact, the real ethical problems people face are choices between good and good. This choice of goods, or perhaps of evils, breathes real-life tension into social systems. And it is the absence of this awareness of the struggle between developmentalism and terrorism, between the creative life-giving forces no less than the death-making forces, that makes Solzhenitsyn's work an unrelieved horror, or better, a series of horrors relieved by the author's personal genius as a writer.

The Gulag Archipelago has given us what few believed would ever be possible: a case history of the Communist party of the USSR, not a series of party visions and revisions, not a series of myths and illusions consecrated to the initial holders of power, but a study in state authority untrammeled and unfettered by popular will. The history of the Communist party of the Soviet Union is ultimately the history of crime and punishment in the Soviet Union: the ultimate fusion of politics and deviance.

As a result, it really matters little that this is not a balanced or fairminded work, that it fails to recite properly and fairly the heroic events of Soviet development and of the Soviet people in the face of all sorts of foreign military adversity. Were this a work balancing the worth of the Soviet system on a cost-benefit scale, we would simply have a volume in economic theory or, even worse, a bookkeeping, double-entry system that fails to measure in qualitative terms the monumental architectonics that made possible the Gulag Archipelago. What is so awful about this book is that one realizes that no one remained untouched by the Gulag Archipelago, that, in fact the dirty little secret of the society as a whole was that the Soviet Union *is* the Gulag Archipelago, and that a description of prison life *is* a description of Soviet life. It serves little use to recite the joys of industrial achievement in the face of this awful truth. The Soviet Union became, at least between 1918 and 1956, a total institution. What has happened since then to change the parameters of the game, to limit and curb the prison-house atmosphere of the USSR? Solzhenitsyn does not tell us whether the Archipelago ended in 1956 or whether he simply stopped his story at a point beyond which he had no first-hand evidence. We are left not so much with a conclusion as with a giant ambiguity. Perhaps the issues will be resolved in the next five parts of *The Gulag Archipelago*. Or perhaps there will be no other parts and we will have to reexamine, in the light of this work, the nature of state power, the workings of an economic system, and the consequences, as well as benefits of making a revolution.

The leitmotif of this book is the painful and shameful absence of mass resistance. "Today those who have continued to live in comfort scold those who suffered." Solzhenitsyn adds rhetorically: "Yes, resistance should have begun right there, at the moment of the arrest itself." This sense of moral turpitude, not unknown to a generation of Israelis reflecting on the European holocaust, is all pervasive, not the least because Solzhenitsyn survived his own shame of silence. But he learned his lesson well. *The Gulag Archipelago* can be viewed as a lesson in courage, a statement of personal survival through conditions of imprisonment, intimidation, and indignities. In the fusion of biography with history, this masterpiece comes to fruition, and the dedication "to all those who did not live to tell it" is redeemed.

"I am finishing it (*The Gulag Archipelago*) in the year of a double anniversary (and the two anniversaries are connected): it is fifty years since the revolution which created Gulag, and a hundred since the invention of barbed wire (1867). This second anniversary will no doubt pass unnoticed." In this way a herculean project began as a testament in 1958 and completed in 1967 came into the world. But now that an additional decade has passed it is quite evident that, although pageantry of the fiftieth anniversary of the Soviet Revolution has long passed and the invention of barbed wire did indeed pass unheralded, we have been given as a gift of suffering, a twentieth-century masterwork.

The Gulag is classic because it makes plain the essence of the century, not simply because it was written in our times. The dialectic of the century emerges on countless pages and in endless details. In the guise of socialism we receive bureaucracy, in the place of popular control we are provided with elite management, instead of the liquidation of state power there emerges an augmentation of such power, in place of abundance through industrial development we get deprivation as the price of such development. And ultimately, in place of justice we get the law. If before Solzhenitsyn we were able to recite conventional platitudes about this century being the best of times and the worst of times, we are forced to the grim realization that these have become simply the worst of times. Even in comparison to other troublesome ages such as the fourteenth century, one must recognize as a redeeming virtue the unconscious force of nature wreaking havoc with humanity. The conscious force of repression (sometimes called racial destiny and other times historical necessity) destroys so many people that the concept of humanity itself assumes a tenuous dimension.

It shall come to pass that the literate population of the future, if there is to be a future, will be divided between those who have read and understood

511

the lessons of the Gulag, and those who have not read—or even worse, read and not understood—the broad implications of this "experiment in literary investigation." Already, the cloudy voices of cynicism, fused with the fatuous voices of childlike optimism, have begun to assert the exaggerated political manners of Solzhenitsyn. Using as a pretext his Harvard commencement address, "The Exhausted West" (it is far simpler to make statements and render judgments on excerpts from a speech than work through the experience of three volumes of *The Gulag*), intellectual scribblers and political hags are assuring one and all that Solzhenitsyn not only does not understand American society but has already lost touch with Soviet realities. In the meanwhile, like a phoenix the Gulag remains: beyond contest, beyond dispute, and as is that rare characteristic of a masterwork: beyond good and evil—doomed to repetition in Democratic Kampuchea (Cambodia) and only God knows where else.

The major accusation launched against Solzhenitsyn is his emotivism and presumed mysticism. Underlying this charge is the more serious charge that he lacks adequate analytic categories; hence that his critique is one sided, that it fails to take into consideration the positive achievements of Soviet industrialization. While it is doubtlessly correct that emotional language is used, it is simply nonsense to claim that mysticism is preached. Irony makes the sufferings described and the outrages committed bearable. The catalogue of evils presented never—not on a single page in three volumes—involves any mystical commitment to blind faith or self-destructive acts. To be sure, in so far as any act of heroism, courage, and self-sacrifice involves a transcendent belief in the human condition, Solzhenitsyn stands accused; but to the extent that mysticism is adaptation or surrender to antihuman behavior or acceptance of "man's fate," he is entirely innocent. This is, after all, a special variety of prison literature, and prisoners who write books seek freedom not immolation. Indeed, the burden of the final volume is a testimony to rebellion, resistance, and retaliation. It is an effort to answer the question: "Can a man's urge to stop being a slave and an animal ever be reactionary?" (III:97).

Solzhenitsyn's *Gulag* has an implicit analytic scheme that deserves to be dealt with seriously, even profoundly. For in this towering statement of prison life in Soviet society there are lessons about twentieth-century social systems as a whole. The political sociology of Soviet society illumines the contours of a future that indeed "works." Herein lies its terrors for us all. And if that political sociology spills over into a political theology, it is nothing less than a consequence of universal ideologies confronting each other in mortal, perhaps eternal, combat. And if this creates an aura of Manicheanism, of the substitution of good for right and evil for wrongs, reification in itself must be viewed as a consequence of political systems, of state power reaching out for an ultimate domination of individual life. The "evils" of capitalism that spawned its "goods" was an impersonal dialectical necessity for Marx in the nineteenth century; but the "goods" of communism that spawned its "evils" is a draconian choice made by Bolsheviks old and new and then advertised as a necessity.

Stalin enjoyed posing issues in a pseudo-Jesuitical manner. Every phenomenon became a rhetorical question. "Is such the case? Yes (or no) such is (or is not) the case." Hence, he gave us the political question, the national question, the women question, etc., ad infinitum. Solzhenitsyn's *Gulag* can be read as a parody of Stalinism. He takes these macroscopic "questions" and shows how they work in microscopic concentration camp circumstances. The marriage of Marxist theory and Russian realities was stress laden from the outset. The bitter rivalries and factions within the revolutionary movement attests to this strain. Stalin's great achievement was to have consolidated the Leninist pivot and created a new orthodoxy. But to do so meant an end to rivalries, factions, and debate itself. The doctrine was saved while the intelligentsia was wasted.

The depoliticization of Soviet society is an underlying reality every dissident and deviant must contend with. The ordinary Soviet citizen goes about his business not unlike the ordinary Nazi citizen: learnedly ignorant of events and myopically closed to the human consequences of the Gulag. Rebellion is such an unusual event that its recording by Solzhenitsyn becomes a major aspect of the third volume. While not quite reaching the epic proportions of the Warsaw Ghetto uprising, the record of resistance from Kengir to Novocherkask—personal and political—forms the essential core of the third volume. But such uprisings remain sporadic and isolated. They are handled bureaucratically, involving scant potential for resistance. It is therefore not the character of rebellion that becomes startling, but the simple fact that resistance is even possible. Leviathan emerges as a total way of life, cut off from popular limits.

The Stalinist decision to emphasize economic development and industrialization muted any efforts at personal liberty. Only when work norms were not met or when political confusion arose from a series of crises of succession were any displays of resistance tolerated. What Solzhenitsyn depicts is the first society in which economics is completely sundered from politics, or better, in which bureaucratic systems management becomes the norm. The USSR becomes a country without a polity, and without a people who determine the nature of justice, there can be no morality. Only political participants acting in complete freedom can determine the nature of goodness. The USSR is not only the antithesis of the Aristotelian paradigm; it doesn't even measure up to Platonic communism—since the dialectic of the best and the brightest is reduced to the dynamics of the mediocre and the mindless.

The Christian persuasion notwithstanding, Solzhenitsyn, quite like other exiles who preceded him, continues to be the conscience of a socialism gone awry. Like every Russian of the modern age, he grew up with a belief in the national question as resolved by the socialist system. Lenin and Stalin, in their wisdom, appreciated the fact that no revolution could be successful only in class terms. The ethnic and national viable was the crucial lynchpin to the successful conclusion of the revolutionary phase.

> Only when the twentieth century—on which all civilized mankind had put its hopes—arrived, only when the National Question had reached the summit of its development thanks to the One and Only True Doctrine, could the supreme authority on that Question patent the wholesale extirpation of peoples by banishment within forty-eight hours, within twenty-four hours, or even within an hour and a half.

In fact, the nations of Russia that did not fit plans for unification were extirpated singly and collectively: Chechens, Ingush, Karachai, Balkars, Kalmyks, Kurds, Tatars, Caucasian Greeks, Germans, Balls, Estonians, Karelo-Finns; and, as Solzhenitsyn reminds us, the Jews were being readied when Stalin came to his end in 1953. The numbers of peoples totally liquidated read like an anthropological Who's Who of European peoples. When one asks who inhabited the Gulag, it becomes evident that these millions of minority people were declared the chosen ones.

> Neatness and uniformity! That is the advantage of exiling whole nations at once! No special cases! No exceptions, no individual protests! They all go quietly, because . . . they are all in it together. All ages and both sexes go, and that still leaves something to be said. Those still in the womb go, too, and are exiled unborn, by the same decree.

One might argue that this is the necessary price of national unification. But if that be the situation, it was a price extracted with a gigantic political myth, with the promissory note of the rights of all peoples and nations to self-determination. Ideology and reality were never further apart. What the West did with a melting pot the Soviets did with melting people—a system of hard labor, penal servitude, exile, and death. This has become the style of Soviet substance. Perhaps the end of ethnic groups is an anthropological and historical fact, but the end of people as individuals is a political and military policy. And the Bolshevik authorities saw fit to make no fine, hair-splitting distinctions.

Solzhenitsyn offers a traditional romantic vision of women. If they are not elevated in their nature, they are at least deserving of very special concern. But instead of this being an irritant, one realizes that this is not only a sincere sentiment frankly expressed but a shrewd antithesis to the Marxian equation of women's liberation with socialism. Indeed, the special pains Solzhenitsyn takes with their camp treatment, the abuse they endure as women, would indicate that the Soviet Revolution has transformed society into a whole cloth: with the treatment of women no better or worse than the treatment of peasants, intellectuals, and ethnic minorities. But what does make matters worse is the special vulnerability of women: the unique torments of an unwanted pregnancy, gang rapes by violent criminals as a reward for their abuse of political prisoners, types of work that are brutal and serve as a special form of demoralization for women.

> The body becomes becomes worn out at that kind of work, and everything that is feminine in a woman, whether it be constant or whether it be monthly, ceases to be. If she manages to last to the next "commissioning," the person who undresses before the physicians will be not at all like the one whom the trustees smacked their lips over in the bath corridor: she has become ageless; her shoulders stick out at sharp angles, her breasts hang down in little dried-out sacs; superfluous folds of skin form wrinkles on her flat buttocks; there is so little flesh above her knees that a big enough gap has opened up for a sheep's head to slick through or even a soccer ball; her voice has become hoarse and rough and her face is tanned by pellagra.

But the women came to the Gulag sharing with the men the same illusions, and later, slow emergence of consciousness. Among the early women prisoners were those hauled off into the Gulag driven naked between formations of jailers singing to their tormentors: "I know no other country where a person breathes so freely." But by the fifties, these same women became the ferocious defenders of their fellow inmates, fused into solidarity by long sentences and desperate lives.

> Events outstripped the casual contempt which the thieves feel for *females*. When shots rang out in the service yard, those who had broken into the women's camp ceased to be greedy predators and became comrades in misfortune. The women hid them. Unarmed soldiers came in to catch them, then others with guns. The women got in the way of the searchers, and resisted attempts to move them. The soldiers punched the women and struck them with their gun butts, dragged some of them off to jail (thanks to someone's foresight, there was a jailhouse in the women's camp area), and shot at some of the men.

When the prisoners rebelled at one penal colony and won 40 days of self-determination, this represented the first real breath of freedom these women had known.

> The runaway escapes to enjoy just one day of freedom! In just the same way, these eight thousand men had not so much raised a rebellion as *escaped to freedom*, though not for long! Eight thousand men, from being slaves, had suddenly become free, and now was their change to … live! Faces usually grim softened into kind smiles. Women looked at men, and men took them by the hand. Some who had corresponded by ingenious secret ways, without even seeing each other, met at last!

Lithuanian girls whose weddings had been solemnized by priests on the other side of the wall now saw their lawful wedded husbands for the first time—the Lord had sent down to earth the marriages made in heaven! For the first time in their lives, no one tried to prevent the sectarians and believers from meeting for prayer. Foreigners, scattered about the Camp Divisions, now found each other and talked about this strange Asiatic revolution in their own languages. The camp's food supply was in the hands of the prisoners. No one drove them out to work line-up and an eleven-hour working day.

For the Gulag does not offer a confrontation of traditionalism with modernity, but convention against barbarism. And in the Gulag everyone knew barbarism would win out in the end. Hence "newlyweds . . . observed each day as their last, and retribution delayed was a gift from heaven each morning." Irony of ironies: prisoners knew a freedom denied to citizens of Soviet society as a whole.

The tension of the first two volumes of the Gulag largely derived from the loggerheads at which "criminals" were juxtaposed over and against "politicals." Repeatedly, Solzhenitsyn shows how the regime utilizes criminals to intimidate and even assassinate political prisoners. The lumpen proletariat of Marx is deproletarianized under Stalin, but it performs the same tasks on behalf of the state: from strike breaking to organized mayhem. The cynicism of this is displayed by the offerings of women to the criminals, and moving women into camps where political trouble is brewing. Solzhenitsyn rises above the cheap clap-trap of jail house lawyers who try to interpret every act of imprisonment as a political torment. He uses language exactly and precisely, in short, scientifically.

Their commune, more precisely their world, was a separate world within our world, and the strict laws which for centuries had existed in it for strengthening that world did not in any degree depend on our "suckers" legislation or even on the Party Congresses. They had their own laws of seniority, by which their ringleaders were not elected at all, yet when they entered a cell or a camp compound already wore their crown of power and were immediately recognized as chiefs. These ringleaders might have strong intellectual capacities, and always had a clear comprehension of the thieves' philosophy, as well as a sufficient number of murders and robberies behind them. And what did their word "frayersky"—"of the suckers"—mean? It meant what was universally human, what pertained to all normal people. And it was precisely this universally human world, *our* world, with its morals, customs, and mutual relationships, which was most hateful to the thieves, most subject to their ridicule, juxtaposed most sharply to their own antisocial, anti-public *kubla*—or clan.

Hence, for two volumes these miserable, incarcerated creatures play out a living class struggle while the Soviet authorities offer metastases about the achievements of the Gulag, "a collective organism, living, working, eating, sleeping, and suffering together in pitiless and forced symbiosis."

The tension in the third volume shifts. Prisoners who are ordinary criminals learn, albeit slowly and painfully, the manipulative nature, essence of the regime, while the abused politicals learn to adopt the cut-throat ethic of the criminals—in a kind of Darwinian trade-off. But it is one that worked for a short time at least.

> By 1954, so we are told, it was noticeable in transit prisons that *the thieves came to respect the politicals.* If this is so—what prevented us from gaining their respect earlier? All through the twenties, thirties, and forties, we blinkered philistines, preoccupied as we were with our own importance to the world, with the contents of our duffel bags, with the shoes or trousers we had been allowed to retain, had conducted ourselves in the eyes of the thieves like characters on the comic stage: when they plundered our neighbors, intellectuals of world importance like ourselves, we shyly looked the other way and huddled together in our comers; and when the submen crossed the room to give us the treatment, we expected, of course, no help from neighbors, but obligingly surrendered all we had to these ugly customers in case they bit our heads off.

It turns out that a third category of prisoner exists in Soviet labor camps, distinct and distinctive: the religious prisoner. This well-represented group was extremely important. They bore witness to tragedy, but they did so in a way which confronted the vacuum of Soviet ideology with the force of some higher belief. In their nonviolent commitments, they were the touchstone of conditions for all prisoners. When religious prisoners were tormented, maimed, or shot, that became a cue that all hope was lost. Resistance was the only recourse—futile and folly-laden though it might appear.

The Jews are represented in all three categories. Solzhenitsyn doesn't make much of it; he doesn't have to. The surnames of Gulag residents reveal this fact. Hence, Jews suffer a sort of triple risk: if they engage in entrepreneurial acts they are reviled as bourgeois remnants; if they engage in human rights activities they are condemned as Zionist plotters; and if they assert their religious commitment to Judaism they are obscurantists and fossils substituting ancient dogma to the "science" of Marxism-Leninism. This threefold persecution makes the Jewish condition especially poignant and dangerous. The liquidation of the Jewish population of the Soviet Union just as much an agenda item as their liquidation by Nazi Germany. The Nazis were cruel: they wanted dead bodies as well as dead souls. The Soviet authorities are willingly ready to settle for dead souls only—hoping, like the Inquisition, that the living bodies will convert to communism, becoming in the process productive workers of the state.

One perplexing, even haunting, question that remains is why Solzhenitsyn's *Gulag* can shock and disturb its readers. Surely it is not for lack of a literature on the subject of Soviet state terror. The archives are filled with scholarly treatises and personal testaments alike. And such early efforts as Vladimir Tchernavin's *I Speak for the Silent*, Pitirim Sorokin's *Leaves From a Russian Diary*, and Ivan Solonevich's *Russia in Chains* have the capacity to evoke similar powerful moods and sentiments. To be sure, Solzhenitsyn exhibits an exactitude as well as a collective judgment rarely before assembled in such force. And there can be no question that his fame as a great writer, not to mention the circumstances of his exile from the Soviet Union, also played a part in making the *Gulag* special.

But I think another element is present, one with ominous consequences. Our analysis of Soviet society is, like our analysis of nuclear conflict, too easily based on a spurious exchange theory, on a trade-off between industrial growth or postwar survival and the number of deaths involved. Hence, we are inclined to accept certain levels of death or even mass annihilation if the ends in view can be achieved. Thus if it takes 30 million lives to create a Soviet beatitude, then so be it. But which 30 million? And why one number and not another? Could the same results be achieved with fewer deaths or less suffering? What in past centuries was a sense of historical cost, even necessary cost, for social change and economic expansion, in our century has become a willing and even an enthusiastic endorsement of the idea of costs to achieve not infrequently spurious benefits. I submit that the special nature of Solzhenitsyn's impact derives from his keen awareness of the substitution of engineering for ethical criteria in evaluating the human soul. He does not speak against development but rather for those countless millions who paid the price for development. And in compelling a fresh review of the actual costs paid and the dubious benefits received, he has restored the balance between political realities and moral possibilities.

Even a masterpiece may have flaws. Indeed, Solzhenitsyn's single mindedness would make that inevitable. The major problem in *The Gulag Archipelago* is the rather weak empirics of concentration camp life between 1957 and the present. The transition from totalitarianism to authoritarianism in Soviet life is left unexamined in favor of a vaguely stated premise that only a total overhaul in the Soviet system, indeed a counterrevolution, would change the internal dynamics of Russian life. And yet, even Solzhenitsyn despairs about a present generation of Russian youth who walk about with their portable radios and shaggy girls under their arms and who couldn't care less about the Gulag system.

The Gulag lives. And we have every reason to believe this to be the case. Predetermined prison sentences of dissidents continues unabated. Persecution of the politicals has few rivals in the world. The identical dried-out Leninist rhetoric continues unrivaled. Still, there does seem to be growth in the middle sector and the concomitant demands for observing legal norms that did not formerly obtain. The sheer reduction in numbers within Gulag requires some sort of explanation that Solzhenitsyn is seemingly unable to provide. In this sense, the depolitalization of Soviet society has been so thoroughgoing that the need for an immense Gulag has been reduced to manageable proportions. Perhaps this is more frightening than the Gulag itself, implying as it does a society that has itself become a willing penal colony where good people are given time off for good behavior as long as they strictly observe one rule: thou shall not question the political regime and its processes.

By the time this extraordinary work was completed, a work the author never once saw in its entirety prior to publication, Solzhenitsyn realized its literary imperfections: repetition and jerkiness. What he calls the mark of a persecuted literature. But such repetitions far from being superfluous are essential. The apostles each repeated the story of Christ's cruxifiction and redemption. The magnitude of human suffering is no easy lesson absorbed at one sitting. The afterward offered by Solzhenitsyn is one of those rare moments when the hyphen between the Judeo-Christian heritage is breached, and the Father of historical redemption fuses with the Son, who bears special witness to human suffering. "I want to cry aloud: When the time and opportunity come, gather together, all you friends who have survived and know the story well, write your own commentaries to go with my book, correct and add to it where necessary. Only then will the book be definitive. God bless the work!" When the *Gulag* is published in Russian, in one of those huge editions Soviet publishing has become famous for trumpeting, then we shall have an operational test of Soviet freedom. Until that blessed event, this towering set of volumes will stand between us and going gently into the totalitarian temptation.

From Transaction/*SOCIETY*, vol. 11, no. 5 (1974), pp. 22–26; and from Transaction/*SOCIETY*, vol. 14, no. 6 (1978), pp. 64–68.

85

Social Theory as Revolutionary Virtue*

Sorel, Georges

At first blush, the wonder is that Sorel is remembered at all, much less remains a paramount figure in *fin the siècle* thought. Treatises written on him far outweigh, in bulk at least, the work done on such contemporary luminaries as Michels, Pareto, DeMan, LeBon, Péguy, to name only a few *fin de siècle* and early twentieth-century figures who were equal (or greater) in intellectual stature to Sorel. By fits and starts, Sorel is consistently inconsistent, self-contradictory, monumentally tendentious, fixed in his dislikes, and even more fanatic in his beliefs, no matter how many times they change throughout his career. Despite all that, he has been the subject of at least five dissertations and an equal number of serious postdissertation monographs in English alone. Add to this the preoccupation with Sorel of such elder statesmen of European scholarship as Isaiah Berlin, Leszek Kolokowski, Max Ascoli, and Jacob L. Talmon, and we have a figure to be reckoned with.

How to explain this phenomenon called Sorel, who, anti-system builder though he was, has been able to command and charm contemporaries and present-day scholars alike? The answer is ensnarled in the big ball of intellectual twine of Sorel's writings. He was a veritable litmus test of beliefs and attitudes toward fascism and communism; statism and anarchism; classicism and romanticism; moralism and realpolitics. Sorel anticipated the post-Marxian revolt against reason, not as some abstract formula but as a rebellion against the straightjacket of social history as deterministic. His social world admitted of religion and science, pragmatism and transcendentalism. He was able

---

*Arthur L. Greil, *Georges Sorel and the Sociology of Virtue*, (Washington, D.C.: University Press of America, 1981), pp. 249.

John Stanley, *The Sociology of Virtue: The Political and Social Theories of Georges Sorel*, (Berkeley: University of California Press, 1981), pp. 387.

John L. Stanley (editor). *From Georges Sorel: Essays in Socialism and Philosophy*, translated by John and Charlotte Stanley. (New York: Oxford University Press, 1976), pp. 388.

to reveal the weaknesses of many nineteenth-century system builders, while avoiding the worst sins of eclecticism by remaining a firm adherent to utopian modalities of thought. The *fin the siècle* sense of struggle and betrayal that linked the political to the psychological in French social thought was nowhere better expressed than in Sorel's writings. He was not particularly adept at political economy, and he was an even less well groomed political sociologist. However, he was the premier political psychologist and political philosopher of pre-World War I. With the ongoing expression of concern over how the process of rule is touched by the structure of minds (balanced and unbalanced), he remains a foremost figure from whom social scientists continue to learn.

While it is accidental that both the Stanley and Greil volumes on Sorel use the phrase "sociology of virtue" in their titles, it is not accidental that both emphasize the ethical and moral doctrines promulgated by Sorel. Just as an earlier generation of analysts moved from "later" political Marx to an "earlier" moral Marx, so too the same phenomenon seems to have overtaken Sorelian studies. Between the 1930s and 1950s, with the work of Michael Freund, Fernand Rossignol, James H. Meisel, and Michael Curtis, the political foundations of Sorel's thought—the relationships between violent tactics and revolutionary goals, trade union reform and radical change, human participation and determinist presumptions about historical determinism—were made paramount. Sorel became the paradigmatic figure in explaining the anarchist option to socialist orthodoxy.

In the current climate of normative theory, with the emphasis on firm moral options to the present relativism and with the desperate search for a socialism in which ethics is an essential ingredient rather than a strategic operation, Sorel has been reconsidered. One cannot say rediscovered, since work on him has been continuous since the 1920s. Stylistic crudities and infelicities notwithstanding, he has joined the pantheon of French thinkers to whom it is obligatory to pay homage, even if actually reading him has become less than commonplace. In this reconsideration, there has been a much closer scrutiny of the pre-1908 trilogy, of Sorel's great essay on *Decomposition of Marxism*, *The Illusions of Progress*, and *Reflections on Violence*. Fortunately, each of these works is now available in good English-language translations. Whether the works written before the 1908 trilogy constitute a sociology of virtue, and whether they are of the same intellectual caliber as the later and more overtly political work, is what these two books, at least by indirections, try to address.

When the chances for revolutionary success are high, scholars look to past analysts for antecedents to present-day practice. When changes for revolutionary success are lean, scholars look to past analysts for prospects in achieving a new morality. In this age of conservative preeminence, Sorel looms as a perfect foil since he too wrote his moral treatises in a time of postsocialist psychic depression. The expected socialist revolutions did not come about. Instead, 1848 and 1871 were followed by restoration: nationalist wars, reform in the labor movement, and reaction in the economy. As Stanley somewhat reluctantly points out, when political radicalism heated up after World War I, and Mussolini in Italy and Lenin in Russia took charge, Sorel shed much of his historical pessimism and moral quests in favor of the coarse rhetoric of revolutionaries of the day. Stanley concludes his study by noting that "in this criticism of intellectuals and the exposure of the moral bankruptcy of the Jacobinism that Sorel employs to justify the Bolshevik revolution: Lenin's attempt to force history by creating an ideology for the new proletarian state that will never perish in the hands of revolutionaries who have proved their disinterested and intrepid devotion to the interests of the people and to liberty and truth. Marat and Robespierre could not have expressed this viewpoint better. Once again, the effort to create a consistent Sorel is a myth that collapses on the shoals of the real Sorel.

I feel some unease regarding the phrase the sociology of virtue. Given the fact that, as Stanley accurately notes, Sorel rejected the only sociologist he took seriously and had respect for, Emile Durkheim, and refused to accept empirical theory that "assumes that some sort of order in history allows the movement of peoples to be considered natural and predictable"—the only meaning that can attach to the word sociology in Sorel's use is the modern positivist skepticism about laws governing human history. But such positivism is a far cry from the systematic study of society. Greil is even more frank in noting that "Sorel's own sociology of virtue loses a great deal of its analytical force because of Sorel's inability to sort out the descriptive from the prescriptive." He adds that there is no intrinsic reason that the kinds of questions Sorel asked could not be posed in different form.

> For Sorel, to study a historical period was to read a book about it. Sorel's 'studies' of the socialist movement were based on unsystematic perusal of newspaper accounts of socialist activities, speeches made by parliamentary socialists and conversations with socialists and socialist leaders. One may be permitted to wonder why an admirer of LePlay would not see fit to study workers themselves before writing about the role of syndicates and the practice of strikes in generating new juridical principles.

The statement by Greil is blunt, but worth noting against undue claims of systemic unit of thought. The phrase *social philosophy of virtue* might have been less attractive as a title, but just as clearly more accurate.

John Stanley's book—despite its irritating of all Sorel's commentators and critics as being of equal merit and all of Sorel's own writings as deserving of accommodation—is nonetheless the best book to have yet been produced on Sorel. Stanley is comprehensive, knowledgeable, and fair minded on the implications of Sorelian thought; no less than close to textual analysis. He has worked for a solid decade and then some on Sorelian materials. He writes with loving care, perhaps too much so, as with his excuse of Sorel's anti-Semitic writings as misguided—something to be "dismissed as caused by the passions of that moment"—when in fact they are part and parcel of a double French tradition of Enlightenment anti-Semitism from the Left and Restorationist anti-Semitism from the Right Sorel's anti-Semitism may not have been original, but it was surely not accidental. He was too much a litmus test of his milieu and probably too unable to transcend it to merit a casual dismissal of that special feature that made him attractive to many of his early followers and supporters.

On the whole, these are small blunders on a great intellectual canvas painted by Stanley. The blemishes in Sorel, his vagueness and contradictions, are there to see; but the tremendous achievement, his ability to telescope the philosophic style (i.e., synthetic rather than analytic, developments in the philosophy of science, mass psychology, French literature, American pragmatism, European socialism, and a moral critique of the shibboleths of nineteenth-century thought) make him unique. No other book equals Stanley's in recapturing the collective wisdom—and exaggerations—of Sorel's age. The work is prodigious in scope and clear in its statement.

The Greil volume must be judged by much more modest criteria. It is alter all only a slightly augmented dissertation and betrays its origins throughout. Too much of this slim volume represents a basic primer of Sorelian positions on Western socialism, historical materialism, class struggles, and violent actions. But when the book gets going (with chapter 4) and warms to the task of creating a clear and concise view of Sorel's ethics—as it relates to the legal and moral basis of moral action, political and economic consideration of moral beliefs, and the fragile social networking of intimacy and institutions in the creation of a moral posture—it becomes eminently worthwhile. Greil's focus on the role of institutions in the genesis of moral qualities is valuable and helps give credence to Sorel's sociology of virtue in this context of institutionalization. The theme is important and contemporary enough to merit a much broader canvas than that provided by Sorel. Greil himself was led to the same conclusion. We can only hope that he is capable of taking that next big step in the study of social institutions and how they are molded by individual passions, developing this central theme of the century on its own terms.

There is a useful lesson in this continual work on Sorel: that immortality is by no means assured to those who are consistent, orderly system builders. Contradictory, often confused myth breakers who labor in the vineyards of everyday life may have a sense of the whole and a command of ordinary events that system builders often search for but rarely locate. These two books are welcome additions to Sorelian wisdom and to our literature on political sociology as a whole.

In an age of both academic and linguistic insularity, the fame and fortune of scholars often follows rather than precedes translation efforts, although with our cosmopolitan pretensions we would like to assume the contrary.

Without the pioneering efforts of George Simpson and Joseph Swain on behalf of Durkheim, Talcott Parsons's and Frank Knight's work on Weber and T.E. Hulme's translation of Sorel, I seriously doubt that these giants of European thought would be accorded the fame that later properly accrued to them in the Anglo-American world of letters. Once the floodgates of criticism and adulation are unleashed, more translations follow. But those first pioneering efforts can hardly be minimized as crucial links in the transmission of ideas. Lest we bemoan the loss of scholarship in the present age, it is only fair to add that with the supreme efforts of William W. Holdheim (on Scheler), Gunther Roth (on Weber), H.S. Harris (on Gentile), Rodney Livingston (on Marx), Everett K. Wilson (on Durkheim), among others, the younger generation has more than kept faith with the needs of translating social science classics. Indeed, it has done so in a far more systematic and capable manner than past researchers dared imagine.

A special niche is occupied by John L. Stanley, who along with his wife Charlotte, have not only been involved in the critical analysis of the work of Georges Sorel but also previously translated *Les illusions du progrès.* When one thinks that Sorel's entire reputation in English rested almost exclusively on the translation of *Réfections sur la violence,* the impact of that great French scholar can be properly gauged. Other than my own translation of *La décomposition due marxisme,* I do not know of any other major work by Sorel up to the time of the work of the Stanleys, that has been made available in English. Thus, one must applaud their nobility of effort as well as their real achievement in this unprepossessing area of scholarship.

A certain note of appreciation should be made in the direction of Oxford University Press and its imaginative editorial staff for developing a most unusual "greats" series. Starting with *From Max Weber* and extending through *From Karl Mannheim,* they have now added *From Georges Sorel.* Precisely because the company is select, the idea is sound. One can only hope that Oxford will continue to produce a series that will both rival and supplement the University of Chicago's outstanding Heritage of Sociology Series led by Professor Morris Janowitz. What this adds up to is that the history of political ideas, along with the sociology of knowledge is healthy.

The translations themselves, albeit of selected fragments, are competently done, or so it would seem from my own recollection of working with Sorel documents. But I do feel that Mr. Stanley's literalist interpretations of key words may impede rather than enhance the reader's sense of context as well as contents. Three title headings illustrations will suffice. *L'avenir socialiste des syndicats* is translated as "The Socialist Future of the Syndicates." My own understanding of the contents would lead me to translate this as "The Future of Trade Unions Under Socialism." *Matériaux d'une théorie du prolétariat* is rendered as "Materials for a Theory of the Proletariat," when in fact something like "Elements of" or "Essays toward" a Theory of the Proletariat seems less ambiguous. Finally, *De l'utilité du pragmatism* would be better understood as "The Uses of Pragmatism," since in English, utility and pragmatism are somewhat tautological or at least kindred concepts. But these are minor matters of preference. And when translations are done by team effort, as these were, then the tendency to stick to the literal becomes overpowering and quite understandable.

A somewhat disappointing aspect of this collection is the paucity of materials indicating the extraordinary range of Sorel's mind, from the development of modern physics to the origins of religious systems. He is one of the few peripatetic figures we have had and was probably unequated in imagination and intellectual power until Harold Lasswell arrived on the American scene. Regrettably, there are no selections from the very late as well as very early periods of Sorel's thought. One selection from the 1919–1922 period, when Sorel came to grips with the mortality of his self and the immortality of the souls of others, might have usefully rounded out the Introduction. There is too little of Sorel as an analyst of other theorists. Especially appealing might have been some of his earlier essays from *Le Devenir Social* on Renan, Durkheim, James, Vico, Peguy, and Bergson, among others. As Stanley's introduction makes plain, Sorel was at his best as critic. He was more penetrating as an analyst of the foibles and fables of others than he was a systematic theorist. The tendency in any anthropology of compendium is to assume that selections somehow are drawn from a systematic body, when in fact Sorel was a consummate essayist.

Stanley's own introductory essay and bibliographic appendix is a model of sound scholarship. The analysis is carefully drawn, clear and correct in its details and general outline. It is written in an entirely appealing graceful style well suited to the general audience this book hopes to reach. Stanley knows Sorel's work; he knows the literature on Sorel, and he avoids the usual academic pitfall of ignoring one at the expense of the other. If the events in France that moved Sorel from Marxism to fascism to communism are cloudy, that is because the European intellectual's sense of how they differ did not have the benefit of historical hindsight.

Because of the limited amount of material available on Sorel, one would have hoped that this might have been a more extensive set of papers. But failing that, it might have been wise to simply indicate the availability of *Les illusions du progrès* and *Réflexions sur la violence* in other places and hence exclude selections from these works already easily available, while concentrating on other essays less easily available. On the other hand, the need to offer a balanced, complete picture made Professor Stanley's decision entirely understandable. One can only hope that these translated essays are but a prelude to a larger effort by Stanley to give us a translation, in systematic fashion, of the corpus of Sorel's works. There is a great need for translations of his basic writings in full. An excellent reason for having Professor Stanley serve as translator, or at least chief supervisor of this project, is his fluent knowledge of the Sorelian literature, his sense of both the historical and intellectual setting of this great thinker. It is high irony that as we move toward the close of the twentieth century and hence another *fin de siècle*, once again we witness the cry of linking socialism and Christianity, class and nation, political action and moral virtue, new linkages of social action to political theory. In this resurrection of normative themes, we can hardly do better than to encourage the long overdue exacting effort at translating the works of Sorel. For he was after all a classicist in outlook as well as part of the classical tradition. In the meanwhile, *From Georges Sorel* is an excellent starting point for those not acquainted with this extraordinary thinker.

From *Contemporary Sociology*, vol. 12, no. 4 (1983), pp. 374–76; and from *The American Political Science Review*, vol. 72, no. 1 (1978), pp. 233–34.

86

Visions of Revolution and Values of Europe*

Talmon, Jacob L.

A special group of Central European Jewish intellectuals has helped define the nature of twentieth-century social and political life, giving shape to destructive potentials of our age only dimly understood by those who worshiped at the altar of absolute progress. Central neither to class enthusiasms below nor national hubris above, these people—actually outsiders—possessed a keen insight into the driving fores of the times—notably the unitary character of the totalitarian threat, the tragic gap between promise and performance in the revolutionary process, and the failure of internationalist rhetoric to resolve national realities.

These emigres from Berlin, Vienna, Warsaw, Budapest and their environs were, for the most part, not speaking and writing from a conservative bias or defending constitutional tradition; there was little to defend in the world of crumbling empires in Central Europe. They were not concerned with restitution or restoration of an old order, for they knew old orders to be a threat to their own survival as Jews, intellectuals, and cosmopolitans.

They often discussed socialism and left-wing democracy. They were motivated by a passion for economic justice and elementary forms of democratic rule. Their involvement with the Socialist dream, minus the maddening character of Socialist practice, gave these people a special rhetoric.

Among this group were such persons as Hannah Arendt, Hans J. Morgenthau, Hans Kohn, Franz Neumann, George Lichtheim, Walter Laqueur, Henry Pachter—and Jacob L. Talmon. Jacob Talmon (who died in 1981) was the author of many works. *The Myth of the Nation and the Vision of Revolution* is a key one because it is the final volume of a trilogy on 200 years of modern political life, begun a quarter of a century ago with *The Origins of Totalitarian Democracy* and followed a decade later with *Political Messianism*. This, in my judgment, is the best of the three volumes. In fact, it is nothing less than a masterpiece.

---

* J.L. Talmon, *The Myth of the Nation and The Vision of Revolution: The Origins of Ideological Polarization in the Twentieth Century* (Berkeley: University of California Press. 1982), pp. 632.

Here, Talmon brings us to the twentieth century and ideological polarization as its central feature. In its eclecticism, it seems less a thesis book than the previous volumes, less concerned with establishing a tension based on dialectical opposites not quite as polarized as Talmon imagined—such as democracy and totalitarianism, or empirical politics and messianic relations. The complex nature of the political fabric sometimes got lost in earlier volumes of the trilogy. In *The Myth of the Nation* Talmon displays a much greater sensitivity to the wide disparities within the same thinkers, the same nations, and the same classes.

Talmon did not write history in any conventional sense; strictly speaking, he transcended dynastic history and social history. His was a special kind of intellectual history, history as written by political ideologists who were either politicians or close enough to the political marrow to inform practicing politicians. *The Origins of Totalitarian Democracy* was peopled with figures of the Enlightenment such as Rousseau, Helvetius, and Diderot and with great political actors—Robespierre, Danton, and Saint-Just. *Political Messianism* ranged from technocrats to theocrats, from Saint-Simon to Blanqui, who were in and of themselves both political actors and intellectual leaders. *The Myth of the Nation* continues in this tradition; major figures include Marx and Engels, Lenin and Trotsky-and, in Western Europe, Mussolini and Hitler and their intellectual progenitors. Talmon weaves a tight interchange among social, political, and intellectual events, breaking down conventional distinctions that usually impede rather than enhance a sense of history.

Few genuinely heroic figures appear in Talmon's work, and those who continually announce a utopian future are dealt with severely. That is true for Marx, Engels, and Lenin in the current volume no less than in the previous volumes for Saint-Simon, Babeuf, and Fourier. But there does emerge in *The Myth of the Nation* a sense of the political leader as intellectual but not ideologist—and this offers insight into Talmon and his notion of who constitute the political prophets of peace no less than war.

In the figure of Jean Jaurès, the nineteenth-century French socialist, one can sense Talmon's archetype. He describes Jaurès as having had a passion or fairness, an extraordinary poetic capacity for empathy, a marvelous quickness of sympathy and imaginative insight, combined with an unmatched gift for words. Talmon had those qualities. Those who knew him realized that his concerns were those of Jaurès: a life of intellect and politics tempered by a survivalist attitude toward society. Talmon also read into Jaurès what was true of himself: that these very characteristics made him yield easily to inferior men with narrower horizons or limited understanding but greater self-assurance. Fanaticism and dogmatism and not just democratic dogma were the true enemies of both Jaurès and Talmon.

The Myth of the Nation is divided into nine parts, which I shall summarize briefly here. The work begins with the growing dichotomization of class or nation that took place after the revolutions of 1848. Talmon gives particular emphasis to the dilemmas involved in postutopian Socialist thinking on the role of the nation in the development of a revolutionary strategy based on pure class assumptions. The work then moves dramatically to the world of Germany under Wilhelm I in the late nineteenth century, in which the question of the emancipation of the proletariat is dwarfed by the issue of national destiny.

Europe between 1848 and 1914 was driven by national cohesion more than class emancipation. Whether in Germany or Russia, Talmon saw revolutionary internationalism as a tenuous thread in the face of an overpowering demand for national separatism and survival.

The third section of the book, which discusses Austria, is another case study of the issue of class or nation. The Austrian experience, while limited in global terms, was in fact prototypical with respect to what took place in Europe in the rest of the twentieth century.

The fourth part takes up the special role of the Jewish dimension. Talmon tells us that, while the Jewish role in European history was hardly new, Jews did become dramatically significant during the early part of the 20th century. And, he says, the encounter between Jew and gentile—even more the encounter of the gentile with the Jew-was first as a bourgeois adversary and second as a communist enemy. The Jew appeared as the *extremis*, as an unstable element in the nationalist equation. The inability of large portions of European society to handle situations in which the Jew became a spokesman for both the forces contesting each other led to a breakdown of Enlightenment and Romantic rhetoric.

As Jews became archetypes, animosities against them crystallized from both the left and the right. Consequently, they became the enemy for national and class ideologies and interests, a source of tension rather than resolution. And, as extremism became the order of the day, Jewish centrism—along with gentile liberalism—became identified as the main foe.

The fifth and sixth parts analyze how the dilemma between class and national was finally resolved in pre- and post-revolutionary Russian practice. The seventh deals with how the general will of the proletariat was translated by Lenin and Stalin into a particular Russian national will.

The last two sections point to the alternative fascist-Nazi resolution of class and nation, which emphasized the national question beyond that of class. The Fascists spotted the weakness in classical Marxism, its denial and denigration of nationalism, and their ideologists proved pivotal in developing a theory of socialism basal on ultra-nationalist considerations.

Nationalism, according to Talmon, permitted and even encouraged alliances between communists and fascists. It was also the factor which made the clash within Europe inevitable.

Finally, Talmon takes up the hard questions of the nature of post-World War II problems in a spirit of tentativeness. But the themes of Third World development and modernization are clearly beyond the ken of his worldview. He asks: What is the role of Western democratic forms with respect to Third World demands for political equality? What is the place of the Soviet Union as midwife to national liberation movements and new totalitarian systems? What military formations are taking place in the Third World? What are the inner tensions within energy-rich and food-poor developing areas? The strictly European context of his thought offered few clues, much less firm answers.

Talmon's last work projects a feeling that a new world is unfolding, a world unfamiliar to him and his European colleagues. In that sense, *The Myth of the Nation and the Vision of Revolution*, his final book, is a fitting conclusion not only to a personal career of outstanding brilliance but also to the end of a social epoch-one in which the European sensibility could still impose cultural order upon social chaos.

Talmon understood that his epoch began with the demands of the French Revolution for both a revolutionary process and democratic goals implemented from above. In his world, Europe became a center of political, social and economic experimentation. A rising tide of new social classes tested Europe's commitment to transnational economic involvements in contrast to strictly national political goals. Finally, in Talmon's own century, nations destroyed all visions of class solidarity, much less of human brotherhood, and in so doing deprived Europe of the opportunity to fulfill its highest and noblest dreams.

Talmon's work deserves careful scrutiny. Whatever one thinks about his treatment of particular themes, he provides remarkable insight into an era of European preeminence that no longer exists, and that can no longer determine the fate of worlds. Yet, though the old conflicts may not have much bite, there may still be lessons to be learned in the development of a strange and bland pan-Europeanism: lessons about the value of pluralism and survival in the face of struggles that seem insuperable and unending.

That the price of the pacification of Europe proved so terribly high, taking a toll in so many millions of lives, can only be reflected upon with a deep sense of tragedy. Still, a sense of triumph emerges from under the rubble. Talmon's trilogy informs us of the high risks of all forms of fanaticism. Perhaps the non-European world will profit by these lessons—but the chances of this happening, as Talmon himself makes perfectly clear, seem slim given the imperviousness of new nations to the history of older nations.

It is on a note of sorrow that the present volume (and the trilogy) is concluded. The passing of a great man, and I must add, a good friend, is heralded by the passing of an entire historical era.

From *Present Tense*, vol. 10, no. 2 (1983), pp. 55–57.

87

Knowledge and Its Values*

Weizenbaum, Joseph

One of the great unquestioned myths about the new technology is that the area is free of ideological presuppositions. Indeed, for some, it is a pure escape from the dirty world of politics, while for others it is the higher learning itself, offering the ultimate critique of ideological politics. In this sense, the ideology of the new technology differs little from the old engineering ideology. The difficulty with such suppositions is that they are simply untrue. It is more nearly the case that the politics of the new technologists are extraordinarily naive, even primitive, precisely because political and ideological concerns remain so deeply buried under the surface of platitudes that presume the hygienic status of data. This platitudinous style rivals in form the utopianism of earlier rationalist models: they come packaged with a faith in progress, rivaling any nineteenth century romantic notions of evolution or eighteenth century concepts of revolution.

It is therefore not unexpected, or it should not be unexpected, that there is a rebellion within the ranks of practitioners against the new technology. It is a counter-utopianism that rivals the efforts of Aldous Huxley and George Orwell to debunk and anticipate the sort of dilemmas found amongst earlier advocates of industrialization and urbanization. A long-range view establishes clearly enough that the new technology does not so much resolve as enlarge classical problems of power and its distribution, wealth and its concentration, or society and its stratification. The people one meets in this world of new technology have been met before: planners, programmers, and forecasters for whom activities outside or beyond the system represent calamities not distinctions. At the other end of the spectrum are those for whom the new technology is little else than a device to carry on exploitative relations.

---

* Joseph Weizenbaum, *Computer Power and Human Reason: From Judgment to Calculation* (London: Penguin Books, 1984).

Desmond Fisher and L.S. Harms (editors.), *The Right to Communication: A New Human Right* (Dublin, Ireland: Book Press, 1983).

Judy Erola and Francis Fox, *From Gutenberg to Telidon* (Ottawa: Canadian Department of Communications, 1984).

That opposition to the new technology would come from old humanists is to be expected, if not entirely welcome. But more intriguing is the disenchantment increasingly felt by a segment of inventors and discoverers in the world of computer hardware and software who expected a brave new world and who see classical culture narrowing down myopically. For these individuals, the new technology has been reduced to Radio Shack merchandising; the personal computer has become one more artifact to grace the homes of the middle classes in Western societies. Far from being the liberating tool, it has been reduced to a libidinal toy. The very totality of the critique allows one to easily dismiss these disgruntled "fathers" of a new technology. But to do so is to miss an opportunity to expand our common understanding of the problems of, no less than prospects for, this new technology.

If Joseph Weizenbaum did not exist, his likeness would have to be invented. He is at once an early pioneer in the logic of electronic computers, a theorist of their utilization and a philosophical critic of their unbridled expansion. In this sense, his philosophical effort *Computer Power and Human Reason* should be simultaneously understood at three levels: instrumental, theoretical, and ethical. The trouble, however, is that the worth of Weizenbaum's position must be differentially measured at each level. One problem that "fathers" have is an inability to appreciate the world of "sons." And in computer technology, this form of denial can prove fatal. Weizenbaum, in his stridency and failure to appreciate the immense changes in this area does little to enhance the reputation of the founder of computer language. The fear that home computers primarily equip the child with a "psychic numbing" that further undermines "whatever little moral authority the schools may have left" only extends the earlier arguments of Weizenbaum without deepening or changing his line of reasoning.

The early chapters of *Computer Power and Human Reason* remain unrivaled in the popular literature on explaining the heuristic properties of the computer, the logical foundations of computer power, how computers actually work, and the designing of universes through computer programming. Anyone starting out in the world of computers would be advised to start with Weizenbaum. There have been many works covering technical concepts of computers in a popular way, but few with the genuine graciousness and modesty that characterize the early chapters of this work. Weizenbaum's distinctions, following as they do the earlier work of Norbert Wiener, are simply marvelous: the passion for certainty in science, philosophy, and religion in contrast to the operational quest for control in technology; rules of languages in contradistinction to ways of knowing; and theories as texts versus models as performances. In an area where mechanistic thinking abounds, Weizenbaum's dialectical explanations provide an impressive guide to those in search of larger meaning in the computer age.

Weizenbaum's work on computer models in psychology, natural language, and artificial intelligence are frequently polemical. Weizenbaum takes on such giants as B.F. Skinner, Jay Forrester, and Herbert Simon with relish. He is frequently on target. The metaphorical rather than empirical definitions of such concepts as artificial intelligence within a general theory of information processing as a whole; the presumption that information processing is identical to the "whole man;" the conversion of machine logic into political and social inevitabilities—each of these and many more examples support of Weizenbaum's assault against the "imperialisms of instrumental reason." The corruption of the computer revolution by an "artificial intelligentsia" and the mystification of behavior modifiers and systems engineers are well taken. In this Weizenbaum is a kind of Dostoevsky-like prototype, an underground man puncturing the myths of those who, by faith rather than research, view the computer age as a relief from uncertainty and then turn around the mock all traditional models of certitude.

Where the position of Weizenbaum and other interior critics collapses is in its own ideological proclivities. The critique of excess becomes a critique of power. The uses of computers by members of the armed forces or by practitioners of psychotherapy are declared "simply obscene." Computer science programmers are declared intellectually bankrupt, comparable to people learned in a foreign language but with nothing to say. These interior critics do not claim that specialized uses are technically infeasible, only that they are in their judgment immoral. The question of whether all uses by the military of computer simulation is immoral or solely the work dedicated to certain fields or tasks, is not resolved. Nor are we ever told what constitutes the "inherent message" of things and events. In an era of computer-guided satellite missiles (ASATs) Weizenbaum's concerns are both entirely justified and yet sadly misplaced.

The offer of pacifism with a computerized face is attractive but neglectful of an environment in which one side does not retain a monopoly on actual power, not to mention real weapons that are computer directed. Thus, the interior critics are subject to the same sorts of criticism as are earlier advocates of unilateralism. For what is involved is less an analysis of the efficacy of the uses of the new technology for military ends than a statement about the immorality of such uses. In such circumstances, the authority of the computer scientists who argue against further expansion of the military options (i.e., Star Wars scenarios) is neither greater nor more compelling than that of those arguing opposite premises.

The "arrogance" of the computer scientist is contrasted to the ambiguous but honest quest by humanists (unarmed) for an (unreachable) moral world. Nothing is said about the failure of humanists to resolve such issues through conventional methods in the past. Indeed, humanism in this ideological milieu is simply equated with pacifism.

The destructive, counterutopian picture of the world of new technology is not especially unexpected or even innovative. Such a view fails rather thoroughly to show how the human race is worse off with a new technology than with the old one; it defines neither the mechanisms for realizing a better social environment when arbitrary curbs are placed on technology nor the options for achieving economic growth, social stability, and military parity in a world that retreats from computer power. Blaming the machine, like blaming the victim, offers little promise. The technologist turned pacifist, like the Luddite, gives birth to an entity that exceeds expectations and moves in uncontrolled, unanticipated ways. But there are superior mechanisms of coping rather than standing still or going backward. In short, the better product is still the ultimate critic of the good expectation.

There is another wing to the assault on the new technology—that generated by users rather than inventors and concerned primarily with the dissemination of the product rather than placing curbs on its usages. The UNESCO contributors to *The Right To Communicate* typify this wing of the disenchanted. But unlike the inventors, the users' forum is far more interesting for what they collectively and cacophonously imply than for what these actually say. For what we have is a rather conventional UNESCO-type document in which puffery far outweighs substance. Many of the contributions to *The Right To Communicate* emanate from "working groups" established under the auspices of the International Institute of Communications and encouraged by Unesco, presumably in response to its medium-term plans for a "new human right—the right to communicate."

In some curious way, the users even more than the inventors strike discordant, counterutopian themes. The trial balloon has burst, so to speak, on "the right to communicate" thesis even before it emerged from its UNESCO closet. No sooner did Scan MacBride, the unique recipient of the Nobel and Lenin Peace prizes, summarize "the history of the world as consisting in the history of the ebb and flow of the tide in the incessant endeavors to secure the protections of liberty," than all sorts of hell broke loose. MacBride himself cautiously argued that "governments of socialist and other one-party states should recognize that the right to communicate is a fundamental human right which cannot be denied to their own public without weakening confidence in their own system of government." However, the Soviet contributor to this symposium threw cold water on such a naive approach by noting, and not without telling effect, that the notion of freedom of information as a human right "finds no objective reflection in international law. The right to inform is counterbalanced by specific obligations, which mean that freedom of information cannot be recognized as a principle of public international law." This did not prevent Kolossov of the Soviet Ministry of Foreign Affairs from urging juridical recognition of "a new international order," with what ominous consequences for a free press the innocent victim is left to guess.

Instead of exploring the opportunity provided by such diverse readings of the right to communicate, the users' groups invariably are reduced to a series of statements, platitudes, quasi-resolutions of mixed levels of quality, and views on the subject theses from a variety of professional perspectives and national prejudices. Every special plan—from making Esperanto a language of equality (it might be added, argued forcefully in English—the language of discrimination, domination, and oppression) to making the distinction between "honest information" and "illegal propaganda" central in this brave new world—is argued with a sincerity that in the past was reserved by clerical devotees not information scientists.

This users' group is able to offer, in UNESCO-like fashion, optimistic readings on the "democratization of communication," but in its remarkable inability to note any sort of contradictions in the variety or bundle of rights ranging from the right to be informed to the right of privacy, the entire project ultimately becomes an exercise in futility. The counterutopians soften the very arguments on which a democratic culture is based. And in so doing, they serve only to accommodate Communist ideological requirements and nationalist developmental efforts to exclude free inquiry, in the name of greater parity in information dissemination between the First and Third Worlds.

Underlying much of these right to communicate theses is a philosophical failure of nerve in the communications field. The right of every person to a decent meal does not deny the right of the farmer who grows food to be paid for his labors. By extension, communication rights involve obligations, apparently a dirty word except when employed as a defense of Socialist legality, that do not so much limit the human race from accessing information as they ensure the donors (presumably also human) from being paid or otherwise rewarded differentially for their labors, based on the quality and worth of their communications. Amazing as it seems, scarcely a single line in the bundle of UNESCO proclamations offered pays any attention to the costs involved and hence reimbursement necessary for scholarly or popular communication to have meaning.

This comes about through the denial, by Communist nations and Third World followers alike, of the autonomous nature of culture as a fact of life. Indeed, to speak of the autonomy of culture smacks of the very Kantian belief art for art's sake, that is anathema to such individuals and nations. Here again, we see how in the guise of discussions on scholarly communication and the new technology, a recourse to a very old neo-Platonic and certainly neo-Marxian argument on the need to place culture at the service of class, or less pleasantly, to make art equivalent to propaganda and to define the latter (and by extension the former) by the needs of the ruling hierarchy of the state. Such rights to communicate offer barren fruit, since what is to be communicated is nothing other than the proclamations of the totalitarian state.

The contradictory character of the information environment is sharpened by the political demands for making data a free or public resource, or in other words, a public right like air and water. The commercial utilization of information has become a central force in advanced societies and as a result a radical view has come to claim that a "silent struggle is being waged between those who wish to appropriate the country's information resources for private gain and those who favor the fullest availability." Needless to say, matters of copyright infringement simply do not appear on the horizons of this perspective. Instead dire warnings of "information commercialization" are sounded; with a fear that "proprietary interests take precedence over free scholarly exchanges." The essence of the argument is that corporations are erecting a "wall" between discoveries and discussions, and as a result, ideas are being diverted and even perverted (for military ends) rather than being given disclosure. In this view, arguments about the number of radio stations or newspapers in operation are meaningless, since monopolization creates a standardized package, and the trend toward conglomerate ownership further inhibits the free flow of information. In this way, the robust character of democracy is itself destroyed, along with social accountability and public dissemination.

In this nether world, the only admissible allies of democracy are librarians who unabashedly argue the case for free access to information. Behind such pleasantries is the denial that knowledge is a hard-earned value with costs attached to its promulgation no less than its disbursement. The hidden predicate in this line of argument is that information was once "free" and is becoming less so in the information society. To note that such a presumption of original freedom is as groundless as the notion of original goodness does little to disabuse critics of free-market societies. Nonetheless, it is important to establish ground rules to overcome this current dichotomization between those who insist that every piece of data be paid for and those who argue the free use and disbursement of hard-earned information. Obviously, stretched to their respective limits, both positions represent dangerous exaggerations. The struggle for the control of information is multifaceted. The place of government as a disburser of information is being touted by critics of the open society as a desperate effort to open up the system. But this argument takes no heed of the prospects that solutions advocated may be worse than the problem of information distribution. Government as a single source of "free information" is hardly an improvement over competing networks, agencies, and institutions searching for viable information outlets and markets.

While it may be the case that the costs of generating useful information increase along with the complexity of demands and as the needs of professionals become more exacting, it is also the case that sheer quantity of data outlets or numbers of computer programs in service do not resolve the issue of democratic choice or governmental responsibility. The government serves as a balance wheel between private sector ownership and citizen rights rather than as advocate of either the private or public sector. In this approach, the metaphysical assumption that the free operations of the market are a unique path are no more advantaged than those who argue that only government control of the market is viable. An inventory of relative costs, rather than an ideology of abstracted rights or responsibilities, is an urgent order of business for those concerned with communicating ideas.

Thus, we are once more back to the land of reality, a spiritual land to be sure but one in which obligations co-exist with rights and in which questions of a modest sort, such as copyright protection, become part of the warp and woof of author protection. The recent work by Judy Erola and Francis Fox indicate that bureaucratic and administrative reports need not be turgid, tendentious recitations of official party positions. More important, such emphasis on legal frameworks and normative contexts provides the strongest response to empty slogans and generalizations about national rights.

Every nation has the responsibility to rewrite its copyright legislation in light of the new technology: from the revolution in reprography (happily avoiding the more commonly used phrase Xerography) to the efforts to protect new forms of intellectual property such as computer programs. This act is itself a statement of the ideology of authors and publishers. To the credit of the Canadian approach, it does not seek to limit the communication of information and opinion. However, this Canadian document does seek to define the intricate network of costs and benefits that result from the explosion in communication media (press, radio, television, computers, cable, satellites, recordings, film, theater, home entertainment units, etc.) in a way that will not diminish the very plethora and pluralism of information that characterizes democratic societies.

From Gutenberg to Telidon marks an advance in copyright reform in the United States by recognizing explicitly the moral as well as legal claims attached to the ownership of idea. It does so without weakening the need for dissemination of information. This clear distinction is an essential element of the Canadian approach. It provides a bundle of rights addressing claims of authorship, integrity of product, and length of proprietary interest. The Canadian position also develops a clear-headed set of legal guidelines to remedy infringement. The authors of this document urge relief from violations on both civil and criminal grounds, and in so doing provide a potential basis for implementing at national and international levels infringements involving privacy of information no less than more shadowy issue of piracy.

If I have one significant criticism of the Canadian approach, it is with its acceptance of the American fair-use doctrine, which, as I will outline later in the book, has created such mischief in Western copyright law and traditional copyright in general. The thrust of the Canadian approach, in contrast to the UNESCO approach, is to recognize and secure creators' rights in a communication era and to ensure compensation without needlessly limited the efficient dissemination of information and ideas. Hence the all-too-bland acceptance of a fair-use doctrine, with its vague, easily violated limits, runs counter to the thrust of this report.

It suffices to say that in my estimate the Canadian report offers an excellent counterweight for nations seeking a model to alter existing copyright legislation. This is no mean-spirited, tight-lipped effort to limit information flows but rather a sophisticated attempt to provide the foundations for a postindustrial legal framework that seeks to balance the rights of a society to knowledge, with the obligations of that same society to protect the well-springs of its creative talent who produce such knowledge. The presumption of this report is the protection by copyright of creative work and the payment to creators for providing communication. By extension, the creators of such works are entitled to the same rewards and payments as any other individuals providing goods and services. The Canadian approach strikes a balance between hand work and head work that is too often observed in the breach.

Human rights begin with creative rights. Creations are the work of real individuals, not fictive collectivities. We sometimes, perhaps too easily, forget that governments govern, publishers publish, but only individuals create. The protection of copyright is thus a quite new human right, as these artifacts are measured in the scale of evolution. It guarantees, or at least seeks to guarantee, to the creator of information or ideas a place in the world of bureaucratic demands for order and orthodoxy. Moreover, it does so without eroding the distinction between ideas and powers. The Canadian view is of significance in helping us to move from the anarchical puffing of property as theft, to the careful study of the theft of property. Of course, all reports and recommendations rest upon a social structure in which the marketplace freely determines not only protection of information but differential rewards for such information or ideas. In the topsy-turvy world of *The Right To Communicate*, there are few issues of scholarly communication, since the government personally pays communication agents a going, protected wage to provide delivery of what the evangelists used to call the good news. This sort of criticism is less with the work at hand, than an indication of scientific and legal tasks yet to be addressed: specifically, the relationships of communication to property in a gradation of social environments extending from free-market systems to command/control systems. A *White Paper* of this sort can at least move us ahead to a consideration of such vexing themes.

In each of these three perspectives, what is new is the sense in which the new technology, with its emphasis on communication rather than production and operations in place of ownership, represents fundamental challenges to the inherited ordering of things and people. Yet, in each instance, powerful ideological postures are at stake: the policy uses to which advanced technology is put, the sort of information that is public and how such data become verified, and finally how one can cope with a changing technology without sacrificing democratic principles of dissemination or free market principles of supply and demand.

Surely, one could just as readily locate three other archetypical examples of these ideological tendencies. But the key point is simple enough: the new technological-informational environment does not automatically resolve major dilemmas of our epoch. Indeed, in the very acceleration of data and speed of transmitting and communicating data, many "classical" themes are exacerbated. And if this serendipitous finding is not exactly what people are seeking, then at least it provides a bridge between technologism and humanism—a common core of issues that require and deserve cross-fertilization. The crisis in scholarly communication is not in any particular sense a new discovery. Nonetheless, the breakneck speed of technology in contrast to the snail's-pace changes in the moral order and human behavior points up a fundamental dilemma that has characterized western civilization for two thousand years.

From *Information Age*, vol. 8, no. 3 (1984), pp. 186–187; and from *Journal of Information Science*, vol.6, no. 3 (1984).

About the Author

Irving Louis Horowitz (1929–2012) was Hannah Arendt distinguished professor of sociology and political science at Rutgers University, where he had been located since 1969. Professor Horowitz was editor-in-chief of *Society*, the periodical of record in the social sciences. During the 1960s he was professor of sociology at Washington University in St. Louis, where Transaction Publishers, of which he was president, was founded.

He held major visiting professorships at Stanford, Wisconsin, California, Rochester, and Princeton University's Woodrow Wilson School of Public and International Affairs. He also held overseas appointments at the London School of Economics, the National University of Mexico, the University of Tokyo, Queens University in Canada, and the Hebrew University in Jerusalem where he was distinguished lecturer in the American Civilization program. He served as visiting professor at the University of Buenos Aires three times in the late 1950s.

Among Professor Horowitz's earlier writings are *The Idea of War and Peace in Contemporary Social and Philosophical Theory* (1957), *Radicalism and the Revolt against Reason* (1961), *Three Worlds of Development* (1965), *Foundations of Political Sociology* (1972), *Ideology and Utopia in the United States* (1978), *Beyond Empire and Revolution* (1982), *C. Wright Mills: An American Utopian* (1983); and *Communicating Ideas: The Crisis of Publishing in a Post-Industrial Society* (1986).

Index

545